The Heyday of

American Communism

THE HEYDAY
OF
AMERICAN
COMMUNISM

The Depression Decade

HARVEY KLEHR

Basic Books, Inc., Publishers

Library of Congress Cataloging in Publication Data

Klehr, Harvey.
  The heyday of American communism.

  Includes bibliographical references and index.
    1. Communism—United States—History—20th century.
2. Communist Party of the United States of America—
History—20th century.   3. United States—Economic
conditions—1918–1945.   4. United States—Politics and
government—1919–1933.   5. United States—Politics and
government—1933–1945.   I. Title.
HX83.K55   1984   335.43'0973   83–70762
ISBN 0–465–02945–0

For Elizabeth, Benjamin, and Gabriel

CONTENTS

PREFACE

FOR a marginal political movement, American Communism has attracted an enormous amount of attention. Oddly enough, however, the most important era of Party history has received very little scrutiny and has been widely misunderstood and misperceived. The 1930s marked the height of Communist influence in America. This was an era in which the Party emerged from the fringes of national life and managed to play a supporting role in some of the greatest dramas of the day—the fight for unemployment insurance, industrial unionism, collective security against fascism, and others.

During the 1950s the Fund for the Republic sponsored a valuable project to study the impact of Communism on American life. Besides spawning a variety of specialized studies, the project resulted in Theodore Draper's two-volume history of the Party in the 1920s and David Shannon's examination of the post–World War II years. Draper began, but never completed, a work on the 1930s. Since then, Joseph Starobin's *American Communism in Crisis, 1943–1957* and Maurice Isserman's *Which Side Were You On?: The American Communist Party During the Second World War* have further documented Party affairs. The only serious account of the Party to include the 1930s, Irving Howe and Lewis Coser's *The American Communist Party: A Critical History*, relied entirely on the published record and is now seriously dated. The Party's activities in the

1930s remain largely neglected; the present book is an effort to remedy that gap in the literature.

The main questions I will seek to answer are: What did the Communist party accomplish during this era? Who made its decisions and how? How much influence did the Party have on American life and institutions? Who were its members, and what were they like? In addition to answering such descriptive questions, I hope to explain why the Party acted as it did and what accounted for its successes and failures.

The Communist party did not enter the decade of the 1930s with a tabula rasa. Neither did the end of the period neatly close an era of Party history. While the 1930s are a convenient historical era for analysis, it is necessary to go both backward and forward in time to make the period fully comprehensible. Accordingly, the book opens with a summary of the Party's first decade and some of its most instructive lessons and ends with a brief summary of the World War II years, which culminated in the removal of Earl Browder, the Party leader, from the position of power he had held for most of the 1930s.

The material on the 1930s falls into several broad categories. Chapters 2 through 9 chronicle the Party's activities during its revolutionary era. Chapters 10 and 11 detail the Party's efforts to change its course, while Chapters 12 through 19 deal with the era of the Popular Front. Chapter 20 is devoted to the Nazi-Soviet Pact and its consequences. Two organizational decisions deserve special mention. I have discussed Party policy toward farmers in the early chapters because it was during the first half of the decade that Communists were most active in rural America. Chapters dealing with blacks and youth are in the section on the Popular Front.

No one can chronicle every Communist-sponsored demonstration or organization or discuss the Party's views on every issue without taxing his sanity and his reader's patience. Many Communist activities were either innocuous or of transient interest to all but the handful of people involved in them. I have focused on the most crucial issues and events in the Party's life, treating in some detail the evolution of Communist policy with regard to the trade union movement, the unemployed, intellectuals, and other political parties and movements. Party policy in other areas either receives more glancing treatment or has been omitted. Some areas I have dealt with in cursory fashion, such as Party activities in Hollywood or the Abraham Lincoln Battalion in Spain, have been exhaustively treated elsewhere.

One faces many problems in writing about American Communism, and these vary with the particular period on which one focuses. Until reaching 1935, discussing the Party means describing a small, distinct sect always conscious of its distance from other groups. Even when negotiating or cooperating with non-Communists, the Party maintained its own persona, unwilling or unable to hide what set it apart from other political groups. Party activities were frequently covered only in obscure publications, and the researcher often has only sketchy, conflicting, or biased accounts as sources.

After years in the political wilderness, Communists won respectability after 1935 by blending into the liberal mainstream. They were found in every sector of American life, including, most prominently, such institutions as the CIO, the American Youth Congress, the American Labor party, and the Minnesota Farmer-Labor party. Prior to this time, the story of American Communism can be told via the story of Communist groups or auxiliaries. A thorough evaluation of the Party during the Popular Front is made more difficult because of the Party's greater scope and penetration of American society; it is also complicated by Party members' more ambiguous self-definitions. Once upon a time, only those suspicious and simplistic ideologues who equated unorthodox ideas with Bolshevism could mistake liberals for Communists. The Party itself drew an absolutely clear line between itself and adherents of any other group. Besides a small handful of self-described fellow travelers, only Communists were to be found nesting in Party organizations or auxiliaries. They were hardly bashful about their political beliefs or the discipline under which they labored. After 1935 Communists became harder to differentiate. Not only did they try to look and sound like liberals, but many deliberately concealed their true affiliations.

As a result, someone seeking to chronicle the Party's history faces some major constraints. Aside from a handful of dramatic and well-publicized events, the study of Party history in the early 1930s involves recovering data pertaining to poorly reported and all-but-forgotten episodes. The Party's proclivity to print candid discussions and analyses in its own press helps, but the researcher must still sift and glean the material. After 1935, as noted above, the Party was far less open about its activities. There is not only the puzzle of exactly who was a Party member, although that is hard enough to solve in many instances. Additionally, a scholar must write about the Party without taking full account of all the organizations in which Communists were influential, lest he write an impossibly long account.

In all periods of Party history, the ultimate source of Party policy was the Soviet Union. Even when the Party's tracks are clear and seemingly autonomous, one must search for their Soviet sources. The Soviet

Union, needless to say, has no Freedom of Information Act and has a long, sorry record of altering history to fit the political imperatives of the moment and expunge embarrassing facts.

In dealing with these problems, I have been reluctant to accept claims on faith or on the word of one person. Where discrepancies exist, I have tried to indicate what they are, often including an account contrary to my interpretation in a reference note. If the only evidence for an individual's Party membership is testimony or charges by another individual, I have tried to make that clear. Many of the Communists and ex-Communists who have testified, written, or been interviewed about their experiences over the years have exaggerated, distorted facts, or simply misled their audiences. In writing about American Communism, a prudent researcher must attempt to check written records to confirm individual recollections.

The written record is voluminous, but still not as complete as one might hope. The most valuable source was the Party's own publications. A careful reading, with sensitivity to all the nuances, can teach one a great deal even when the Party was reluctant to dissect its past; at times the Party was quite open about how its decisions were made and carried out. Those readers who might assume that material appearing in the Party press expressed only the views of its author or were private musings can rest assured that the articles were far more authoritative. J. Peters told the Central Committee that "the editorials and articles in *The Daily Worker* are the editorials and articles of the Central Committee. If Comrade Amter writes an article about the C.W.A., this is not Comrade Amter's article, it is the PolBuro's article. If Comrade Hathaway writes an article, it is not Comrade Hathaway's personal article, it is an article expressing the opinion of the PolBuro, and giving the leadership of the PolBuro to the Party."[1]

An invaluable source, without which this book could not have been written, is the archive compiled by Theodore Draper that is now at Emory University. It includes numerous internal Party documents, many given to Draper by Earl Browder, among them some Political Committee minutes, and interviews with a number of former Communist party leaders. Philip Jaffe's archive, also at Emory, contains a number of valuable Political Committee minutes. Scattered at libraries around the country are other internal Party documents; I have used as many as I could find. The most substantial cache of Party material is in the files of the FBI. Acting under the Freedom of Information Act, I obtained more than 30,000

[1] *Party Organizer*, February 1934, p. 21.

pages of material on various groups and individuals. Much of it was useless, but here and there were nuggets of information. There is no doubt that informers and wiretaps enabled the FBI to obtain mountains of information that would illuminate Party history. Unfortunately, the Bureau's filing system makes recovery of all this information virtually impossible and prohibitively expensive. Therefore, I obtained those files which appeared most potentially productive.

The list of those to whom I am indebted is long. It begins with Theodore Draper, whose scholarship in this area has set standards no one has matched. He not only urged me to undertake this study, but also made his superb collection available to Emory University. Mr. Draper also allowed me to examine some of his unpublished writings on the CPUSA in the early 1930s. With his permission, my first three chapters follow his interpretation and general outline. He is not, of course, responsible for any errors. Any merits of this book are owed to him.

Deans Charles Lester and John Palms and Professor Dan Carter were instrumental in bringing the Draper Collection to Emory. Ted Johnson, director of the Emory library, strongly supported this endeavor. The library staff members were extraordinarily helpful in meeting my constant requests and locating materials. In particular, I would like to thank Linda Matthews of the Special Collections Department and Elizabeth McBride in Government Documents. Henry Black made available a treasure trove of Party publications that facilitated my research.

A number of colleagues around the country responded to questions or read portions of the manuscript, including Ken Waltzer, Lowell Dyson, Dave Garrow, Charles Martin, John Haynes, Sidney Hook, Bob Zieger, and Dan Leab. Several people at Emory, including Tom Remington, Tom Walker, and Dennis Ippolito, patiently at first, and undoubtedly with increasing irritation thereafter, listened to this book develop and change over the last five years. Max Gordon, Carl Ross, Harry Haywood, Sam Darcy, and Henry Puro were among the ex-Communists whom I interviewed or corresponded with. To all those Communists and ex-Communists whom I never met but whose interviews with others I used, I also owe thanks. Linda Boyte has typed so much material about American Communism that she no doubt is even happier to see this project reach completion than I am; it would have taken considerably longer without her help.

This project has been supported by grants from the Earhart Foundation, the Institute for Educational Affairs, and Emory University. No individuals at these organizations have tried to influence the project or dictate its conclusions. The project would not have been possible without

Leslie Lenkowsky's assistance. Midge Decter was a source of constant encouragement. Maureen Bischoff patiently steered me through the editorial process. I am very grateful for everyone's aid. An earlier version of a portion of Chapter 13 appeared in the Summer 1983 issue of *Labor History*.

This book is dedicated to my children, without whom it would have been finished long ago, and to my wife, without whom it still would not be completed.

The Heyday of
American Communism

1

The Lessons of
the First Decade

WHEN the Depression hit the United States in 1929, the American Communist movement was already one decade old. How the Party reacted to the Depression, the manner in which it sought to take advantage of this singular opportunity for growth and influence, was not a spur-of-the-moment decision. American Communists came to 1929 with a great deal of baggage from their first ten years—baggage that left an indelible imprint, coloring their reactions to and creating their leadership for the next two decades.

The American Communist movement was born in anticipation of revolution. The first manifesto of the Communist party of America, issued in September 1919, proclaimed gleefully that "capitalism is in Collapse."[1] For a few short, romantic years, the vision of an imminent socialist uprising sustained American Communists. With the end of World War I, a wave of strikes broke over America, culminating in a great steel strike of more than 350,000 workers. Soviets, or workers' councils, were formed in several American cities.

America was not the only country seemingly ripe for revolution.

Across Europe, numerous leaders felt that their governments were haunted by the specter of Communism. Abortive revolutions took place in Germany, Hungary, and Finland. Unrest spread through Western Europe. Among those who confidently awaited the emergence of Communist regimes were the leaders of the young Soviet Russia. In 1920 Lenin insisted that "in almost all the countries of Europe and America, the class struggle is entering the phase of civil war." The Communist International, or Comintern, was founded in March 1919, before there were even well-organized Communist parties in much of Europe. At its second congress in the summer of 1920, the Comintern baldly stated its purpose: "It is the aim of the Communist International to fight by all available means, including armed struggle, for the overthrow of the international bourgeoisie and for the creation of an international Soviet republic as a transitional stage to the complete abolition of the State."[2]

Many American radicals responded to the lure of this revolution. The young American Communist movement that emerged in 1919 briefly held high hopes for itself. In its early days it claimed a total membership of 50,000–60,000 people. The membership records, however, inflated the number by perhaps as much as one-half. More importantly, the members were overwhelmingly foreign-born, largely Slavic. Dominated by men with little understanding of America and entranced by the Russian model of revolution, American Communism quickly became undone. Within a year of its founding it had gone underground, partly to withstand a series of attacks launched by the Justice Department. Many Communists, however, welcomed the clandestine activities as a chance to emulate the Bolsheviks. As aliases proliferated and party members skulked about the country holding secret meetings, the underground phase of Communist history proved costly. Members dropped out, afraid of association with a shadowy, semi-legal group. Others simply lost contact when the Party disappeared. In 1921, the Workers party was formed as a legal party front, but not until 1923 did the Communist party abolish the underground and become a completely legal organization.

Just as debilitating was the inability of American Communists to stay united. From its inception in 1919, the Communist movement was plagued by internal dissension. Two separate and hostile Communist parties had been formed then, and for several years afterward there was a bewildering number of splits, amalgamations, and further schisms which, combined with the semi-clandestine existence of most of the combatants, make early Communist history murky indeed.[3]

By the time the Communists had been united and had emerged from underground in 1923, the Party had only 15,000 members. Almost immediately there was an opportunity to gain a foothold in a larger political movement. Between 1922 and 1924, a Farmer-Labor movement was struggling for life and success. Members of the underground Communist movement, who regarded elections as frauds and were filled with scorn for nonrevolutionary groups, were not impressed or much interested at first. The Party gradually became more interested in the Farmer-Labor movement, and some left-wing forces in the movement became amenable to including Communists in the coalition. The Communists, however, were not content to be junior partners. At the Farmer-Labor convention in July 1923, the Party managed to gain organizational control through delegates from dozens of tiny societies and groups formed by Communists and pushed through its own programs and proposals. Its former allies pulled out of the convention in disgust. By 1924 it was the Progressive party, not the Farmer-Labor party, that ran Senator Robert LaFollette for President. The Progressives explicitly repudiated Communist support, and the Communists responded in kind with biting attacks on LaFollette. The end result of the whole episode was the breaking of whatever tenuous holds existed between the Communists and the American progressive and labor movements.

The Party was unable to escape its isolation for the rest of the decade. Membership plummeted from 15,000 in 1923 to 7,200 in 1925, partly because of a reorganization. By March 1929 the number had climbed back up to 9,300, but this was still fewer than when the Party had gone underground in 1920. Jack Stachel, the organizational secretary, noted that the membership had slowly grown since 1925 and that in addition to the 9,300 dues-payers, 2,700–4,700 others were listed as members but paid no dues. Eighty percent of the members were workers, but most were not in the basic industries such as steel, mining, or chemicals. One quarter were in the needle and building trades. Only 46 percent were trade union members. In other respects, the social composition of the Party was even less satisfactory. There were only 150–200 Negroes. There were few farmers and few working women. Most glaringly, there were too few native-born Americans. Two-thirds of the party members were "registered in the various languages"; only 5,000 spoke English. Although 225,000 people read the Party's foreign-language newspapers, less than one-tenth of that number read *The Daily Worker*, the English-language organ. The Comintern addressed an open letter to the American party in 1929 complaining that it "has been for many years an organization of foreign workers not much connected with the political life of the country."[4]

The structure of the Communist party was also set in the 1920s. For some years after its founding, apart from the underground period, the party structure was quite similar to that of the Socialist party, out of which it had sprung. Lower party units were based on election districts, and there were a number of quasi-independent language federations. One party leader complained that the federations formed "eighteen parties within one party." Their members were isolated from direct contact not only with the American working class but with the Party leadership. In 1925 the Comintern ordered a Bolshevization campaign, designed to reorganize the Party on a more centralized basis. The Party was ordered to organize members into either shop or street nuclei. A shop nucleus was a group of members working in the same factory; a street nucleus was an otherwise unattached group living in a particular neighborhood. Groupings broader than nuclei were subsections and then sections. Large cities might be divided into several sections. Districts, the highest-level groupings, comprised several states—with the exception of New York, which was divided into two districts. The ranking functionary at this level was the district organizer.[5]

Within the national office, the Central Committee—or Central Executive Committee (CEC), as it was known in the 1920s—was the Party's top leadership; a smaller Politburo determined general policies between Committee meetings; and an even smaller Secretariat was responsible for day-to-day activities. A general secretary took overall charge. There were several departments within the national office, ranging from Agitprop, Organizational, Research, and Trade Union to Women's Work, Agrarian, Negro, and Sports.[6]

The organization of the Communist party extended beyond its own confines. Party members who belonged to non-Party organizations such as trade unions or clubs of any sort were required to form Party fractions "for the purpose of increasing the influence of the Party in applying its policy." This included electing officials to office. Fractions were present even in such auxiliary organizations as the International Labor Defense (ILD). These groups, sometimes called mass organizations, were designed to gain the support of those not willing to join the Party but agreeable to working under Party leadership. Detractors labeled them "fronts." They were formed for specific purposes, such as defense of political prisoners or relief of starvation in Russia, and were carefully controlled by the Party.[7]

Its structure gave the Party the theoretical ability to wield an influence far larger than its membership. The Party was supposed to be centralized, easily mobilized, and based on the factory, the heart of capitalist society. Party members were supposed to create effective caucuses wherever they were to extend Party influence beyond its present domain. Auxiliary organizations were to be the bridge between the Party and potential allies. In fact, of course, this was more dream than reality, especially in the 1920s. The Communists were so few that even this structure could not provide nearly the leverage they needed.

Although membership statistics were important, the key figures in a Communist party were not the rank-and-file members. One of Lenin's most important organizational principles was that a revolution required a corps of professional revolutionaries. What was to separate the Bolsheviks from all their rivals was the creation of cadres—dedicated full-time revolutionaries who gave to the party "the whole of their lives." Although the Bolsheviks rather quickly created a mass party after the Revolution, and although they encouraged other Communist parties to do the same, the key element in those parties always remained the cadres. They were a party within the party. While rank-and-file members came and went with depressing frequency, the cadres largely remained. And while the rank and file frequently had only a hazy grasp of theoretical principles, the cadre was trained and tested. It was the cadre which gave the Party its élan, its maneuverability, and an influence out of proportion to its size. And, in this respect, the American Communists were in better shape than the membership figures alone indicated.[8]

The Party was able to develop a considerable cadre during the 1920s. With a few exceptions, the top and even the regional leaders of the Party well into the 1950s could trace their Party careers back to the 1920s. There were, of course, casualties among the cadres. In the first few years there was a shakedown. Some early leaders dropped out, some died, and a few returned to Russia. More importantly, there were schisms. In 1928 James Cannon returned from the Sixth World Congress of the Communist International as an admirer of Leon Trotsky. Cannon quietly began converting members of his faction within the Party— which was itself allied with William Foster in a coalition opposing the Party's leader, Jay Lovestone. Found out, Cannon and his cohorts were promptly tried and drummed out of the Communist movement. The Trotskyists numbered fewer than a hundred but included several well-known Party leaders such as Max Shachtman, Martin Abern, Arne Swabeck, and Vincent Dunne.

The following year it was Jay Lovestone, the Party leader who had engineered the Trotskyists' expulsion, who fell afoul of the Comintern. Lovestone had become Party secretary upon Charles Ruthenberg's death in 1927. He was widely regarded as an unscrupulous schemer and skillful factionalist. His loyalty to the Comintern was unquestioned. In fact, in

7

1925 the Comintern had specifically required the Foster faction, then in control of the Party machinery, to keep Lovestone on the Central Executive Committee. Nevertheless, he began to run into trouble in 1928. He was identified with the policies of Nicolai Bukharin, head of the Comintern, and a man whose political career was about to end. Lovestone's sensitive antennae were temporarily inoperative, and his professions of loyalty to Bukharin continued long after they were prudent. By the time he discovered his mistake and demanded that Bukharin be removed from the Comintern, his action was too late to appease Stalin.[9]

Lovestone's second problem was more complex. In early 1925 the Executive Committee of the Communist International (ECCI) decided that in America alone was capitalism still on the upgrade. Shortly afterward, American Communists, led by Lovestone and his co-factionalists, began to explain the peculiar resiliency of American capitalism. The Lovestoneites argued that as a young imperialist power, America was expanding its economic resources at the expense of Europe. Thus, while European capitalism might be stagnant, or even declining, American capitalism was still growing. Dialectically, however, capitalists could take little comfort, since "the very strength of American imperialism becomes the source of its weakness." American exceptionalism simply meant there would be a temporary time lag in the development of the radicalization of the working class.[10]

Lovestone's enemies in America pounced on such talk as heresy. Once the Comintern in 1928 proclaimed the advent of the Third Period, an era of capitalist decay and revolutionary ferment, Lovestone's problems became acute. Could the American economy be advancing while world capitalism was declining? Could the American Party evaluate the American economy independently of the general line of the Comintern without transforming the Comintern into a loose congeries of independent parties like the Socialist Second International?

In March 1929 the American Communists voted for delegates to their sixth convention. Lovestone, already feeling pressure from Moscow, received an overwhelming mandate—90 percent of the vote. Nonetheless, two Comintern delegates to the convention, Philip Dengel of Germany and Harry Pollit of England, brought instructions for handing the Party leadership to William Foster. The convention defied the Comintern and elected a pro-Lovestone Central Committee. All of the principals then rushed off to Moscow to settle the matter.

A special American commission was appointed by the Comintern to hear the dispute. It met for a month in the spring of 1929. Eight of its twelve members were Russians, including Stalin. Toward the end of the deliberations, Stalin made three speeches that set forth more clearly than ever before or since the relationship between the Comintern and its constituent sections. First, the policy of a Communist party could not be based on the peculiarities of that party's country:

> It would be wrong to ignore the specific peculiarities of American capitalism. The Communist Party in its work must take them into account. But it would be still more wrong to base the activities of the Communist Party on these specific features, since the foundation of the activities of every Communist Party, including the American Communist Party, on which it must base itself, must be the general features of capitalism, which are the same for all countries, and not its specific features in any given country. . . . Specific features are only supplementary to the general features.[11]

Since the Comintern knew far better than any individual party the general features of world capitalism, this formula was a prescription for Comintern control of policy.

Stalin's second point was even more blunt. The claim by the Lovestone group that it had the support of virtually the entire American Communist party was of no account:

> That is untrue, comrades of the American delegation, absolutely untrue. You had a majority because the American Communist Party until now regarded you as the determined supporters of the Communist International. And it was only because the Party regarded you as the friends of the Comintern that you had a majority in the ranks of the American Communist Party. But what will happen if the American workers learn that you intend to break the unity of the ranks of the Comintern and are thinking of conducting a fight against its executive bodies— that is the question, dear comrades? Do you think that the American workers will follow your lead against the Comintern, that they will prefer the interests of your factional group to the interests of the Comintern? . . . At present you still have a formal majority. But tomorrow you will have no majority and you will find yourselves completely isolated if you attempt to start a fight against the decisions of the Presidium of the Executive Committee of the Comintern. You may be certain of that dear comrades.[12]

Stalin was far more perceptive about the loyalties of American Communists than his American antagonists. Lovestone's majority vanished overnight. Not that the American Communists were unscarred by Lovestone's heresy and expulsion. In 1929, Party membership had been 9,300 with several thousand more non-dues-payers; in 1930, despite recruitment of 6,000 new members, the number fell to 7,545. Moreover, the Party cadre was seriously depleted. One Lovestone factional document claimed that seven Central Committee members, six Politburo members, three Central Executive Committee candidates, five leaders of the youth movement, and one member of the Central Control Commission had been expelled. The Party's crisis was still not fully resolved when the Depression began. As late as October 1929, high-ranking Communists were still being expelled. Those unlucky or unwise enough to have associated with Lovestone or anyone else suspected of his heresy were denouncing their pasts.[13]

The Comintern had interfered with the American Communists before but never so blatantly. It would interfere with them again, but it would never have to be as heavy-handed. Those who did not repent were unceremoniously booted out. Those who did repent would never forget the lesson. It was this relationship to the Comintern that set the American Communists apart from any other American party. There were none who were so dependent on the actions of a foreign organization nor subjected themselves to its supervision so voluntarily.

The relationship between the Comintern and national parties was inherent in the statutes of the Comintern. The constituent parties were instructed that they were only sections of the Comintern and that decisions of the ECCI "are obligatory." The ECCI was also given "the right to expel from the Communist International, entire Sections, groups and individual members." The Comintern inevitably was dominated by the Russians. Theirs was the only successful socialist revolution. Behind them stood a host of resources denied to most other Communist parties—money, manpower, and technical aid. Comintern headquarters was in Moscow, and all the key officials were Russians.[14]

The relationship between the CPUSA and the Comintern was no secret. The Communists were not ashamed of it; on the contrary, they were proud. William Foster, appearing before a congressional committee investigating Communism in 1930, was asked a question to which Communists in later years would take the Fifth Amendment or respond in vague platitudes about their commitment to America. "Now, if I understand you," a congressman questioned him, "the workers in this country look upon the Soviet Union as their country; is that right?" Foster answered: "The more advanced workers do." The Soviet Union was the spiritual homeland of American Communists.[15]

There were other reasons for bowing to the will of the Comintern. For ten years, American Communists had used more energy fighting among themselves than fighting against capitalism. The factionalism had been debilitating: the Comintern alone had the authority to end it. The Party had been a failure; could the Comintern do worse? Finally, just a few months after Lovestone's expulsion, the Comintern's vision of the collapse of capitalist stabilization seemed to be coming true. The Great

Depression began. If there was ever an experiment designed to test the Communist party, this was it. All of the objective factors that might spark a revolution were present. Given this unparalleled opportunity, how well did the Communist party do?

To understand Communist actions in America, it is not enough to study the CPUSA. Indeed, simply by focusing on national events, one cannot comprehend why the Communists acted as they did during any era. It was abroad, in Moscow, that the decisive formulations were made which the Americans labored to apply to American conditions. Communist policies and language are incomprehensible unless one recognizes that they were largely responses to Comintern directions.

Communist language frequently was esoteric and specialized, falling uncomfortably on American ears. There were several reasons, but one, certainly, was that the Comintern often developed its formulations in response to European problems and politics. So it was with the theory of the Third Period. The particular definition of a "period" was much more than an exercise in linguistics or Talmudic hair-splitting. The nature of capitalism in a given era was related to a particular inventory of Communist tactics. If capitalism was on the upswing, that dictated a more cautious, reformist Communist stance. If capitalism was decaying, then militancy was the order of the day. The Comintern had defined the first period as one of revolutionary upsurge and the Second Period—from 1923 to 1928—as an era of capitalist stabilization. At the Comintern's Sixth World Congress in 1928, a Third Period was announced during which capitalist stabilization was "still more precarious."[16]

The Comintern's Tenth Plenum redefined the Third Period in more cataclysmic terms. It was "a period of the increasing growth of the general crisis of capitalism and of the accelerated accentuation of the fundamental external and internal contradictions of imperialism leading inevitably to imperialist wars, to great anti-imperialist revolutions in colonial countries." The Eleventh Plenum suggested that as a result of the economic crisis the workers were faced "with the decisive alternatives; either dictatorship of the bourgeoisie or—the dictatorship of the proletariat; either economic and political slavery or—to put an end to capitalist exploitation and oppression." At the Twelfth Plenum, in September 1932, Otto Kuusinen reported that "there is no purely economic way out of this crisis" for capitalists and that "the general crisis of capitalism is rising to a new plane, is entering a new cycle of revolutions and wars." Communist parties now had to prepare. At this plenum it was stated: "We are approaching revolutionary crisis at a whirlwind pace, we are approaching the revolution—the preparation of the proletariat, for the impending struggle for power, is at stake." An official resolution declared that the main task of Communist parties was to ready the workers "for the impending fight for power, for the dictatorship of the proletariat."[17]

Other Comintern formulations were even more important during the Depression, because of their practical implications. One of those was the theory of "social-fascism." For most of the 1920s the Comintern believed that fascism was merely the naked form of the dictatorship of the bourgeoisie, while "bourgeois democracy" was its masked form. The responsibility for the rise of fascism was placed on the socialists, who were regarded as the Communists' worst enemies. In 1924 Stalin noted, "Social Democracy is objectively the moderate wing of fascism." And, he went on, "They are not antipodes, they are twins." At the Comintern's Tenth Plenum in July 1929, Otto Kuusinen charged that fascism and social-fascism were converging and that the struggle against the latter was more important. Other speakers attacked the German socialists as covert allies of fascism.[18]

Comintern spokesmen did not hesitate to speak frankly about the relative dangers of fascism and social-fascism. In 1932, S. Gusev argued that the Communists in Germany should not direct their major efforts against fascism. "This is not correct. It is not correct, firstly, because Fascism is not our chief enemy in the workers' movement, but Social-Fascism is our chief enemy there . . . it is necessary to direct the chief blows against Social-Fascism." One refinement of the theory of social-fascism provided for "left" social-fascists. These were the left wing of socialist parties or any professed revolutionary groups outside of the Communist party. According to the Comintern, these groups, often very insignificant little sects, were even more dangerous than social-fascism, which in turn was even more dangerous than fascism.[19]

The premise of another slogan, "Class Against Class," was that the Communist party alone was a working-class party. All other parties pretending to be so—in particular, the Socialists—were in fact class enemies. The phrase implied that there could not be any alliances with other groups. V. Molotov frankly noted that it "consists in renouncing any kind of agreement with social-democracy." All of this followed logically from the premises of the Third Period. Capitalism was in collapse. Those groups which stood between the Communists and the working class were actually serving the interests of the enemy by deceiving the workers. They had to be fought and smashed. Once their rivals on the left were vanquished, the Communists would be able to deal with the fascists, by then stripped of all their most valuable allies and unable any longer to hide the true nature of their policies.[20]

The final key formulation with regard to the Third Period was the united front from below. In 1920 Lenin had specifically advised the British Communists to offer to cooperate with the Labor party, candidly admitting that their support would be "in the same way as the rope supports a hanged man." The united front, or cooperation with non-Communists, was not designed to advance the interests of both parties. The Communists were to use the coalition to increase their own influence and weaken that of their partners. In 1924 the Fifth Comintern Congress identified three different types of united front. One, the united front from above, made by Communist leaders with leaders of other organizations, was "categorically rejected." A second, "unity from below and at the same time negotiations with leaders," was acceptable only where Communists were weak and social democracy strong. The only type to receive unqualified endorsement was the united front from below. This meant a united front with the rank and file of socialist or labor parties or unions, without—or over the heads of—their leaders. As Dimitri Manuilsky put it in 1929, "The united front tactic is the most unreconcilable struggle against the reformist and Social-Democratic organizations for the working masses." The "United Front from Below" slogan, then, was not precisely what it seemed. The objective of this tactic was for social-democratic workers to repudiate their own leaders and submit to Communist leadership.[21]

The Comintern's formulations were transported to the United States. That they did less damage here than in Europe was due less to the ways in which they were applied than to the relative insignificance of the American Communists compared to the Germans. Even so, the policies served to isolate American Communists, destroy a promising alliance with segments of the non-Communist left, and lead the Party into some futile rhetorical crusades.

The application of the Third Period concept to America was slower and more cautious than its adoption elsewhere, largely because Lovestone, the advocate of "American exceptionalism," survived in power after 1928. The expulsion of the Lovestoneites enabled the Tenth Party Plenum, meeting in early October 1929, to assert that American capitalism was part and parcel of "the crisis of world capitalism and in the specific form of this crisis in the third period." Still, only weeks before the Wall Street crash, those attending the plenum were convinced that the immediate expression of the crisis would be in the South.[22]

When the stock market collapsed on October 24, the Communists, for all their expectant talk about a crisis, were slow to react. *The Daily Worker* waited until October 26 to put a tiny note on page 2, which was filled with rather unimportant news. The front page was preoccupied with the conviction of the Gastonia defendants, Communist labor organizers who were on trial in North Carolina. On October 28, a front-page editorial took note of the crash and calmly stated that "the business boom . . . is coming to a close and the beginnings of an economic crisis are at hand." The economic crisis was not the lead editorial, however. That was reserved for an attack on "Norman Thomas, Candidate of the 3rd Capitalist Party." Thomas was the Socialist candidate for mayor of New York, and denouncing him took precedence over the stock market crash. That editorial did note that the crash made it even more important to free the workers "from the crippling influence of the social reformists." *The Daily Worker* became more enthusiastic as the week went on, exulting in a prominent front-page editorial that "It can't happen now in America —but it did!" The market collapse was a signal, it was pointed out, of a larger economic collapse. News stories on Wall Street finally reached the front page, even if a reception for Soviet aviators in Detroit got a larger play.[23]

In early January the Politburo issued a lengthy statement on the crisis that affirmed its seriousness and warned that the collapse "is as yet only in its first stages." From this point on, the Party was quick to interject the Third Period into its discussions. The vogue for the Third Period even led one Party organization to organize a "Third Period Dance," for which it was censured for commercialization and vulgarization.[24]

The "Class Against Class" and "United Front from Below" slogans arrived in the guise of a trade union policy while Lovestone still held sway. The Communist instrument for working in the union movement was the Trade Union Educational League (TUEL), which William Foster had founded in 1920. The TUEL concentrated on "boring from within" the A.F. of L., building left-wing opposition movements within existing unions. In February 1928, Solomon Lozovsky, head of the Profintern, or Communist Trade Union International, attacked this policy and soon afterward ordered the Americans to organize new trade unions in a variety of industries. Although the Americans resisted, in September 1929 the TUEL was converted into the Trade Union Unity League (TUUL), a full-fledged dual union movement.[25]

The TUUL's program was explicit: "The Trade Union Unity League bases itself upon the principles of the class struggle. Its slogan is 'class against class.' " In the last half of the 1920s the Communists had formed what looked suspiciously like a united front from above in the United Mine Workers (UMW). In fact, when Lozovsky and the Profintern ordered dual unions, the Americans were in the midst of a struggle against

John L. Lewis. They were allied with John Brophy, a Progressive, in a "Save the Union" movement that was preparing a major mine strike. At that very moment, Lozovsky's strictures arrived, warning that this alliance was a sign of their "overevaluation of the importance of the Fascist A.F. of L."[26]

The Communists pulled out of the alliance and resumed the struggle against Lewis shortly afterward in a new union whose goal was not to save the UMW but to supplant it. The premise of Party policy was that in the Third Period, the "fascist" A.F. of L. was incapable of aiding the workers. Therefore a new dual union movement was needed. The Communists could not form alliances with "progressives." The only possible alliance was a united front from below. Foster dutifully defined the united front from below in the trade union field as "united fronts with the rank and file progressive elements against the fake progressive leaders of the A. F. of L."[27]

The American Communists were still faced with other problems of identification. To obey the international Communist line, they had to identify fascism as well as social-fascism in the United States. The chief candidate for the former label was Herbert Hoover. Just after the Wall Street crash, an editorial linked him with the dictator of Hungary: "Horthy and Hoover—Fascists." A Politburo resolution indicated some second thoughts, however. In January 1930 it denied that the Hoover regime represented "fully developed Fascism"; it was only a "big step in the direction of the fascization of the American bourgeois state." Max Bedacht, the Party's acting secretary in 1930, claimed that "the government of the United States is in a process of rapid fascization." He noted: "In America, fascism does not develop even formally as a challenge against the capitalist government of the democratic republic. Here it appears rather as the logical development of American capitalist democracy." Fascization was so difficult to recognize because the change was not dramatic: "The major reason why this transformation is not universally recognized is primarily its gradualness. The fascization of the American capitalist government is a process. But it manifests itself everywhere." In 1930, it manifested itself so pervasively that one Communist leader saw it embodied in the Boy Scouts because that organization had just formed a junior affiliate—the Cub Scouts.[28]

The Party had a somewhat firmer image of social-fascism because it involved old enemies, the Socialists and reformers. Nevertheless, even here there were some delicate problems. Was the A.F. of L. fascist or social-fascist? Who were the "left" social-fascists? One of the more troublesome groups to classify was the "Musteites," or the Conference for

Progressive Labor Action (CPLA), headed by A. J. Muste. A minister who had become a labor organizer, Muste had founded the CPLA in 1929 to agitate for a labor party and militant trade unionism.

The first extended analysis of social-fascism came at the Tenth Plenum in October 1929. The Socialist party was "exhibiting features of social fascism," and the A.F. of L. was a full-fledged social-fascist organization in "close alliance with the openly fascist organizations, with thugs and gangsters and with the police." The Musteites, however, were "the greatest danger to the working class" since they were a " 'left' social reformist group carrying on the policy of the A.F. of L. under the cover of progressive phrases." And the plenum warned: "Any proposals of united fronts with these elements [Musteites] must be mercilessly combatted."[29]

At this point, the Comintern intervened, at the invitation of the American Communists. The new Party leadership, installed after Lovestone's ouster, was preparing for the Seventh Party Convention, the first since the upheaval, in June 1930. On February 15, 1930, the Anglo-American Secretariat of the Comintern sent the American leadership instructions on the forthcoming gathering, including advice about which topics required special attention. Within two weeks the Americans had drafted a lengthy document containing an analysis of American developments and including the characterization of the A.F. of L. as social-fascist and the CPLA as left social-fascist.[30]

The new leadership, hesitant and unsure about precisely how to apply the general dictates of the Third Period to America, decided to consult with the experts. Max Bedacht was dispatched to Moscow with the draft "in order to have it discussed and criticized." He arrived on March 12 and four days later began sending cables back to New York with reports and corrections. A March 23 cable included one brief alteration concerning social-fascism: "AFL PLAINLY FASCIST MUSTE SOCIAL FASCIST NOT SOCIAL AND LEFT SOCIAL FASCIST RESPECTIVELY." Without a hint of the inspiration for the change, Earl Browder soon explained that:

> ... in the first draft of the thesis that we sent out we have continued the mistake we have been making for sometime, in classifying the A.F. of L. and the Muste group together under the designation of "social fascist." It is quite clear and we ourselves have recognized it in all our propaganda, that the A.F. of L. is plainly fascist. It camouflages itself not at all under the phrases of social fascism. We must make the distinction between the openly fascist A.F. of L. and the social-fascist Muste group.

The error was corrected at the Party's Eleventh Plenum.[31]

The Socialists, of course, were repeatedly castigated as social-fascists. Norman Thomas was considered the leading social-fascist. Because the Socialists were influential within the garment unions, the International Ladies' Garment Workers' Union was characterized as "a highly developed social-fascist organization." Occasionally, the Socialists were simply termed fascists. Morris Hillquit, James Oneal, and Algernon Lee were denounced in 1932 as "open fascists"; Sidney Hillman was called a "fascist gangster leader."[32]

"Fascist" and "social-fascist" were handy epithets and were hung on a variety of people. John Dewey and Oswald Garrison Villard were among "the more high-browed social fascists." W. E. B. Dubois' *The Crisis*, the organ of the National Association for the Advancement of Colored People, was called "a Social Fascist journal." The Party often had trouble keeping the labels straight. Although, following Bedacht's journey, an editorial dutifully was entitled "The Fascist American Federation of Labor," the A.F. of L. was occasionally put back in the social-fascist category.[33]

The Gang of Four

The capitalist crisis inaugurated by the collapse of Wall Street coincided with the crisis within the Communist party. Still in the process of sorting out the debris left by Lovestone's fall, the Party was suddenly confronted with an economic depression. The Party's first priority, however, was to install a new leadership. Lovestone had not gone down alone; dozens of important, high-ranking cadres either had left the movement or were politically suspect. Positions had to be filled, none of them more crucial than the post of Party secretary.

Everyone looked to Moscow for some expert guidance. It was clear from Lovestone's debacle that no one who was unacceptable to the Comintern had a chance. Logically, the clear-cut favorite was Lovestone's arch-factional enemy, William Z. Foster. He was the Party's outstanding personality, well-known throughout the United States and within the Party itself. He had been a contender for leadership for nearly a decade, having been in opposition to the now-disgraced Lovestone for the last four years.

The Comintern had once seemed to prefer Foster. At the Sixth Convention of the American Party, in March 1929, it had sent two representatives with confidential "organizational proposals." One of these proposals advised the convention to replace Lovestone with Foster as general secretary. The convention, however, had revolted against Comintern control and, under Lovestone's direction, had chosen a three-man Secretariat that thwarted Foster. Benjamin Gitlow, Lovestone's chief aide, was secretary; Max Bedacht was put in charge of Agitprop; and Foster was made trade union secretary. In removing Lovestone, moreover, Stalin had not spared Foster, denouncing him for factional conniving. Who, then, did the Comintern want?[34]

Boris Mikhailov, a Comintern agent known here as G. Williams, was sent to New York to help reorganize the Party. Officially assigned to the Tass news agency as a correspondent, he found time to write for *The Daily Worker*, attend sessions of the Politburo, and even speak at the Seventh Convention in 1930.[35] Mikhailov also helped to install a new Secretariat composed of Bedacht, Robert Minor, William Weinstone, and Foster, and named Bedacht acting secretary.[36] The new Secretariat ran the Party until an October plenum offered an opportunity for the Americans to sort out the leadership question. The Fosterites must have been galled; three of the four Secretariat members were ex-Lovestoneites. It was crystal clear, however, that the Secretariat was only a temporary measure to see the Party through its immediate crisis. Its four members were being given opportunities to demonstrate their ability and prepare for leadership. Each one had strengths but serious flaws and weaknesses as well.

Max Bedacht had been given the preeminent formal position of acting secretary. An unprepossessing man of forty-six in 1929, Bedacht had been born in Munich. His schooling had ended when he was thirteen. Trained as a barber, he eventually rose to leadership of his union i- Switzerland. He immigrated to America in 1908 and served as editor of German-language socialist newspapers in both Detroit and San Francisco. The split within the Socialist party found Bedacht in California, where he sided with the Communists and quickly lept into Party prominence. His appointment to the Secretariat was a reward for his betrayal of Lovestone in Moscow. Bedacht had held out against Stalin and the Comintern until the very end. Then, tormented by the consequences of defying them, he had publicly capitulated. Bedacht's chief virtue was his blandness. Well liked, he had not been a leading factionalist and had no real enemies. Unfortunately, he had few leadership qualities either. He was neither an organizer nor a theoretician but, as he himself admitted, primarily an old-fashioned agitator. In short, Bedacht was a perfect choice as an interim leader—acceptable to almost everyone but a threat to no one.[37]

Robert Minor was one of the best-known Communists in America. Born in 1884 in San Antonio, he could boast of several famous forebears, including Sam Houston. His father, however, had been an unsuccessful lawyer. Young Minor wandered around the country for several years before obtaining a job as a newspaper cartoonist when he was twenty. Within a few years he was reputedly the highest-paid cartoonist in America, and his economic future seemed assured. Minor had joined the Socialists in 1907. By 1917 he was an anarchist. After his first trip to Russia in 1918, he returned home to denounce the Bolsheviks for centralizing power and imposing an iron discipline on the country. In 1920, however, Minor underwent a dramatic conversion. His about-face led him into the Communist party, to which he now devoted his life and talent. Minor too had been a Lovestoneite, serving as editor of *The Daily Worker* since 1928. When Lovestone went to Moscow, he was so certain of Minor's loyalty that he made him acting secretary and entrusted him and Jack Stachel with a code that would enable them to seize the Party's assets if trouble developed in Russia. The two trusted minions had betrayed Lovestone by revealing the plot, thus earning the gratitude of the Comintern. Despite these assets and an impressive physical appearance, Minor was a political lightweight, at his best serving other men and doing their bidding. So pompous that he "spent much of his honeymoon reading to [his wife] the works of Lenin," he lacked the intelligence, decisiveness, and ability for the top position.[38]

William Weinstone was a more serious contender for power. Only thirty-two in 1929, he already had a full decade of experience in the top Party echelons behind him. Weinstone had been born in Vilna, Lithuania, was brought to America as an infant, became active in Socialist circles while still a student at the City College of New York, and had catapulted into a leading position in the newly formed Communist party in 1919. By 1921 he was heading the New York District, a position he retained until nearly the end of the 1920s. When Party leader Charles Ruthenberg died in 1927, Weinstone made his first bid for leadership, breaking with Lovestone and joining Foster and Jim Cannon in a marriage of convenience. When this *ménage à trois* lost out, Weinstone adroitly made his peace with Lovestone and managed to retain his post as New York leader. Although Weinstone had the advantage of not having been closely connected to either faction, that was counterbalanced by his having angered both of them by his political flip-flops. Indeed, he was derisively nicknamed "Wobbly" for his indecisiveness.[39]

Bill Foster was by far the best-known Communist in America in 1929. Twice during the decade he had carried the Party's standard in the

Presidential campaign. He was well known and respected within the labor movement. And, he probably knew more about and understood the American worker better than anyone else in the Party. Yet, he was not the favorite of either his fellow Party leaders or the Comintern. No one had more of a past to live down.

Foster had been born in 1881 in Taunton, Massachusetts, to Irish immigrant parents who had twenty-three children. He was brought up in a Philadelphia slum and first went to work at age ten. At nineteen he left home and for the next dozen years worked and traveled all across America, trying his hand as a homesteader, sailor, and railroad worker, among other endeavors. He joined the Socialist party in 1901 but, in 1909, abandoned it as not radical enough. The next year he joined the Industrial Workers of the World (IWW). However, in 1912 he formed the Syndicalist League of North America, devoted to "boring from within" the A.F. of L. to capture it for revolution, rather than building a dual union, the approach that the IWW was then taking. Foster's conviction that radicals should work within the established union movement led him to become active in the A.F. of L. Using Chicago as his base, Foster organized packinghouse workers and then, in 1919, led 365,000 steel workers in a strike.[40]

The strike's defeat left Foster casting about for a role. After a trip to Russia he secretly joined the Communist party in 1921, bringing with him a new organization he had just created to work inside the A.F. of L.—the Trade Union Educational League. Foster was given charge of trade union work, while Charles Ruthenberg, the Party leader at that time, directed political activities. However, the disastrous split with the Farmer-Labor movement in 1923 had wiped out the TUEL's minimal influence within American labor. Foster learned one very important lesson from the debacle: in the Communist movement, political leadership would decide trade union policy. He formed a factional alliance with Jim Cannon to oppose Ruthenberg and spent the rest of the decade fighting for control of the Communist party.

Foster was an unlucky factionalist. It sometimes seemed as if everything about his Communist career was jinxed, so that the leadership he so desperately craved would forever elude him. In 1925 a Comintern emissary had taken away the Foster-Cannon triumph at the Party's Fourth Convention on the grounds that the Ruthenberg group was more loyal to the Comintern. Three years later Foster's ally, Cannon, became the founder of American Trotskyism, a sin Stalin did not let Foster forget. Appalled by the Profintern's adoption of the dual union policy in 1928, Foster remained briefly faithful to boring from within the A.F. of L. In addition to having to live down these political errors, Foster had to overcome his own role in the Party during the 1920s. He had been coopted into the leadership as a trade union specialist, and the old-timers in the cadre never let him forget he was a gauche newcomer to the esoteric field of Marxist theory.[41]

To survive in the rough-and-ready factional wars of the 1920s, Foster had become an arch-factionalist, determined to best his opponents at their own game. The new Secretariat was designed to hold the Party together, not to provide leadership. The old factions themselves were tired of the constant sniping and guerrilla warfare. A decade of internal conflict had produced few successes but numerous petty hatreds and grudges. The Comintern itself was fed up with the quarrelsome Americans and their predilection for fighting each other instead of capitalism. Foster was too much a symbol of the past, too scarred by its vicious infighting, to serve as a unifying force.

The Dark Horse

Few people in the Party would have bet on Earl Russell Browder emerging as the leader. He was a drab, colorless figure without a personal following. Although Browder had been a member of all of the Central Committees in the 1920s, he had never been a top-ranking leader and had spent three years abroad, so that he was certainly more of a mystery to the rank and file than the other contenders.

Earl Browder was the product of a native, Midwestern radicalism. The Browder family, of Welsh origin, first settled in Virginia in the 1600s. Earl's father, William, moved to Kansas after the Civil War, trying a variety of occupations and failing at most of them. Earl, the eighth of ten children, was born in Wichita in 1891. Forced to go to work at an early age, he struggled his way up from errand boy to accountant and credit manager for a local drug company by the age of seventeen. In 1912 he moved to Kansas City and, after a brief fling as an entrepreneur, held several accounting positions. Raised in the Populist-Socialist tradition of the Midwest, young Earl joined the Wichita branch of the Socialist party in 1907 at age sixteen. He dropped out of the Party sometime in 1912 to protest its expulsion of William "Big Bill" Haywood for advocating violence and soon came under the influence of William Foster's syndicalist theories. In accordance with the latter's injunction to bore from within the A.F. of L., Browder joined a Bookkeepers, Stenographers, and Accountants local, becoming its president in 1914. He was also active in the Workers Educational League, a local radical group that staged lectures and debates, where he met and worked with Jim Cannon.

Around this time, Browder first met Foster when the latter spoke to his union local. Their relationship was severed, however, by the issue of World War I. Foster had founded the International Trade Union Educational League in 1915. Its 1916 convention took place in Kansas City, and Foster and Browder crossed swords for the first time. Foster believed that the union movement should stick to union issues, ignoring the question of war. (However, he himself would go on to support American involvement in the conflict.) Browder strongly opposed the war and demanded that unionists fight American entry. After Foster's view prevailed, Browder left his local presidency to organize full-time against the war. He and two of his brothers were arrested for conspiracy to violate the draft law and refusal to register. Convicted on one count, Earl spent a year in jail. Out of prison, Browder promptly rejoined the Socialists, a partisan of their pro-Bolshevik left wing. In the spring of 1919, Browder and Cannon began publishing a weekly paper, *The Worker's World*. This sojourn in the Socialist left did not last long; Browder was tried and convicted on the second count of the old indictment for refusing to register for the draft and was sent to Leavenworth Penitentiary for sixteen months. Cannon succeeded him as editor, but he was soon jailed and the paper folded up after nine months.

After leaving prison in November 1920, Browder moved to New York and a job as head bookkeeper for an export-import firm. He lasted only ten weeks. Jim Cannon was by now a leading figure in the Communist movement. He had a problem that led him to think of his old Kansas City co-worker, now conveniently in New York. In Russia, the Communists were in the process of setting up a Red Trade Union International, to be known as the Profintern. They were eager to obtain a strong American delegation to the founding congress, but the American Communists were having trouble coming up with anyone from outside New York. Cannon called on Browder, who promptly quit his job, joined the Communist party, and set off to gather a delegation for the trip. In Chicago, Browder persuaded William Foster, the most famous radical unionist in America, to make the journey. With Browder as its head, a delegation of seven representatives and one "observer," Foster, attended the July 1921 congress. Since Foster's decision to become a Communist remained a secret for two more years, Browder became the liaison between him and the Party leadership. Starting in March 1922, he also was managing editor of *The Labor Herald*, the TUEL's monthly publication. To those in the Party, Browder was regarded as Foster's chief lieutenant and a key figure in Foster's faction.[42]

Browder had no troops behind him. Determined to build alliances to seize party control, Foster cultivated ties with Cannon, who had a power base, and with Alexander Bittelman, who became his tutor in Communist theory. Browder was given the rather insignificant task of being editor of *Workers Monthly* at the end of 1924. His Party career was adrift by the end of 1925. He was then a second-rank leader, not terribly important to Foster and relegated to insignificant jobs. Once again, a summons to Moscow changed his life. In January 1926, Foster sent a message ordering him to Moscow. The Comintern had created an American commission to investigate the party dispute, and Browder was needed. He arrived in time for the last session. Joseph Stalin was present at the hearing; it was the first time Browder had ever seen him. Late in the evening Stalin suddenly addressed him, asking for his observations. Despite Foster's urgings, Browder declined to say anything. This implied declaration of Browder's independence enraged Foster. The visit to Moscow also marked Browder's fealty to a new master. "From that evening," he later wrote, "I became a pupil of Stalin."[43]

Browder spent the next year as American representative to the Profintern. His return to America was unexpectedly postponed by events in China. Chiang Kai-shek, then an ally of the Soviet Union, had requested a visit from an international workers' delegation. When the trip was postponed, the designated American delegate had left for home. The visit was suddenly rescheduled in early 1927, and Browder was added at the last minute. A Pan-Pacific Trade Union Conference was held in Hankow, and the group entered the city beneath a banner proclaiming "Welcome to the Earl of Browder"; the Chinese believed the American delegate to be an English nobleman. The conference created a permanent Pan-Pacific Trade Union Secretariat and named Browder the general secretary. After a brief trip to America to pack up, Browder returned to China for most of 1927 and 1928.[44]

A new Earl Browder soon emerged, publicly challenging Foster for the first time. Although it was obstensibly a political dispute that led to the break, Browder's personal animosity toward Foster played a large role. Foster was cold and contemptuous toward subordinates. Cannon recalled: "One of Foster's traits which I especially detested, after I got to know him well was his different manner and attitude in dealing with different people. To those whom he thought he needed, such as Bittelman and myself, he was always careful and at times even a bit deferential. To those who needed him, such as Browder and [Jack] Johnstone, he was brusque and dictatorial. They must have stored up many resentments against that." They had, and the rancor boiled over when Foster hesitated about accepting the need for dual unions. On February 11, 1929, Browder was one of eleven co-factionalists who criticized Foster in *The Daily Worker* and called for new dual unions. Foster's capitulation only seemed to fuel Browder's enthusiasms; the latter was, in those early months of 1929, a vociferous advocate of the new Comintern line and a stern critic of the Lovestoneites.[45]

Browder had to leave the United States to attend the final congress of the Pan-Pacific Secretariat, held in August 1929 in Vladivostock. He returned in September, ready to devote himself exclusively to American Party affairs, and found the caretaker regime of Bedacht, Minor, Weinstone, and Foster overseeing the Party. His chances for advancement were not particularly bright. Despite his reputation as a trade union specialist, he had scant experience in the field, had never led a strike, and had not edited a union paper for almost five years. He was physically unprepossessing. One colleague remembered him as "mousy"; another referred to him as a "Uriah Heap."[46]

Browder's strongest suit was undoubtedly his Comintern support. Alex Bittelman remembered Lozovsky, the Profintern director, telling him that "the best man for your Secretary would be Browder." At the October 1929 Party plenum, Mikhailov, the Comintern representative, pushed Browder to become secretary of the CPUSA. Browder, however, was above all cautious. He recognized his own limitations and was unwilling to be put in an exposed position before he was ready. He refused Mikhailov's offer. The plenum did, however, mark Browder's emergence into the leadership. Weinstone was taken out of the running temporarily by being sent to Moscow as the Party's Comintern representative. Browder was then added to the Secretariat and placed in charge of Agitation and Propaganda. Bedacht remained administrative secretary, and Minor continued to edit *The Daily Worker*. Although Foster was also dropped from the Secretariat, he was confirmed as the undisputed trade union leader.[47]

Browder was rather unobtrusive in his new post. His appointment was not mentioned in *The Daily Worker* until August 1930, when he was identified as a member of the "National Secretariat." But for those accustomed to reading between the lines, Browder's stock was clearly on the rise. He, not Bedacht, delivered the main report at the Eleventh Plenum in the spring of 1930 and authored the summary appearing in *The Communist*. The Seventh Convention in June finally marked Browder's rise and Bedacht's fall. Yet, again, even the careful reader of the Party press would have had difficulty deciphering events. Although Bedacht and Browder delivered the two major reports, *The Daily Worker* gave virtually exclusive attention to the former and ignored the latter.[48]

Although it was not reported until much later, at the convention a new Secretariat was chosen. It had taken only about one year for everyone to realize that Bedacht was not the answer to the Party's leadership problem. Browder later recalled that "everybody was sick of the secretaryship of Bedacht by then." The Comintern was unhappy with the American Party's performance and even more concerned that Party membership was nearly stagnant. Browder and Bedacht changed jobs, the Kansan becoming administrative secretary and the latter moving to Agitprop while being dropped from the Secretariat. The Secretariat's other two members were Foster, trade union secretary, and Weinstone, organizational secretary. Weinstone, however, remained in Russia for another year. Foster was also unavailable for Party work, serving a prison term for his part in the massive March 6, 1930, New York unemployment demonstration. For several months, then, Browder was given a chance to run the party without sniping or interference. The new leadership may not have been made public precisely because no one was sure how long it would last and there would be less embarrassment at having to alter it.[49]

Lovestone's departure had created vacancies throughout the Communist movement, and the year-long uncertainty at the top produced a considerable shuffling of personnel. Virtually all the members of Browder's leadership team were veteran Communists because new recruits were scarce in the early 1930s. But the members of the new regime emerged from different places, and their odysseys reveal something of the mobility in the Party and the human material available for leadership.

Veterans of the Party's foreign-language groups were enlisted to fill some of the vacancies in the Communist bureaucracy. The Finnish-language leader, Henry Puro, became organizational secretary in 1929 and then took charge of agricultural work in 1930. Boleslaw (Bill) Gebert, the Polish-language leader, an ex-miner, became district organizer in Chicago. The Hungarian leader, a shadowy man going by the name of Josef Peters, was less publicly visible but oversaw the Party's underground apparatus. Mario Alpi, a refugee from Fascist Italy, was editing the Italian-language Communist newspaper until Browder brought him into the national office to run the organization department under the name of F. Brown.[50]

Another important source of new talent was the Young Communist League (YCL). Although it was a small organization at the end of the 1920s, the YCL graduated such important party figures as Harry Gannes, Harry Haywood, John Steuben, Pat Toohey, Leon Platt, Phil Frankfeld, John Williamson, and Carl Winter. One who quickly moved into key posts was Samuel Adams Darcy. Born Samuel Dardeck in the Ukraine, he came to America at the age of two. An early convert to socialism, joining the Bronx Young People's Socialist League in 1917, Darcy was a founder of the Young Workers' League, predecessor of the YCL, and led it in 1925. Darcy spent twenty months, during 1927-1929, in Moscow on the Executive Committee of the Young Communist International and undertaking a brief Comintern mission to the Philippines. Back in New York he served briefly as *The Daily Worker* editor, as educational director of the New York District, and, in 1930, as head of the International Labor Defense. Only twenty-five in 1930, he was a veteran Communist functionary with a wide range of experience.[51]

Most of the leadership was a carry-over from the 1920s. Some of the most promising Communists of that decade were never able to fulfill early expectations and were gradually shunted aside. Others quickly attached themselves to Browder and continued to hold responsible posts or were promoted. Old factional ties had little to do with advancement; Browder was willing to overlook past errors and put the 1920s behind. Ex-Lovestoneites were not excluded from the new leadership. Jack Stachel, a ferret-like intriguer, had been Lovestone's Lovestone—a political schemer and factionalist par excellence. After a brief tour to Detroit as district organizer, he returned to New York to run the TUUL in Foster's absence and then became Browder's Lovestone, in charge of the Organizational Department.

Clarence Hathaway was a St. Paul, Minnesota, native who had been a second-string leader in the Foster caucus throughout the 1920s. Born in 1894, half-English and half-Swedish, Hathaway was a skilled tool- and die-maker with close contacts to the Minnesota labor movement. His party roots went back to 1919, but after the Farmer-Labor debacle of 1923, he had marked time in the organization, spending some time in Moscow. In early 1929 he became editor of the TUUL publication, *Labor Unity*, and later was put on the Politburo. By the end of 1929 he was district organizer in Chicago; he soon filled the same position in New York and was then made editor of *The Daily Worker*. Hathaway was an outgoing, friendly man, a former semi-pro baseball player not averse to having several drinks. He quickly became part of Browder's circle and moved up the Party ladder.[52]

All in all, it was neither a distinguished nor a well-stocked leadership. Party leaders were shuffled around like chess pieces, moved from one city to another, from one job to another. A good Bolshevik was supposed to be capable of adapting to new situations; a professional revolutionary could fit in anywhere. The juggling guaranteed that the top cadres were exposed to numerous facets of party life and a wide range of experiences. It also dramatized how thin the Party was stretched in the early 1930s. Capable leaders were scarce, and they were rushed around the country to fill particularly gaping holes, often leaving equally large vacancies to be filled by someone else.

2

To the Streets
and Shops

IF the only evidence for the Third Period had been Comintern resolutions and unemployment statistics, Party leaders might have had difficulty persuading themselves and their followers that the revolutionary millennium was at hand. However, after nearly a decade of largely futile efforts to gain friends and influence people, the Communists suddenly found the most unlikely workers in the most unlikely places showing no compunctions about allowing themselves to be led by "Reds."

The first such discovery took place even before the Wall Street crash. Gastonia, North Carolina, did not, on the surface, look like an inviting place for Communism. Situated thirty miles west of Charlotte, Gastonia was a mill town whose workers were mostly native-born white Southerners from the hills. They were deeply religious, held to a literal interpretation of the Bible, and regarded outsiders with reserve and suspicion. Conditions in the mills, though, were hideous. In 1929 the Southern textile industry was afflicted by a series of strikes, but only in Gastonia were the Communists able to accomplish anything. In mid-March, Fred Beal, an organizer for the National Textile Workers Union (NTWU), arrived in Gastonia to organize the Loray Mill, a large factory in which yarn was made and automobile tire fabric woven. Of Yankee descent, Beal had gone into the Lawrence mills as a young boy, participated in the famous IWW strike in 1912, and became a Wobbly. After the war he had joined first the Socialist party and then One Big Union, a syndicalist group. In 1928 he joined the NTWU, one of the earliest of the Communists' dual unions, and was active in the New Bedford textile strike that year. Beal organized a union in Gastonia, and on April 1 the workers voted to strike.[1]

Gaston County reacted to the strike with barely controlled hysteria: advertisements in the local paper warned citizens that "Red Russianism Lifts Its Gory Hands Right Here in Gastonia" and advised that the strike did not have economic goals. "It was started simply for the purpose of overthrowing this Government, to destroy property and to KILL, KILL, KILL. The time is at hand for every American to do his duty." By April 4, two hundred National Guardsmen had been mobilized. Their presence did not prevent vigilantes from sacking union headquarters and demolishing a strikers' commissary on April 18.

When the governor withdrew the troops on April 20, the mill organized patrols of newly deputized men to keep "order." Despite an infusion of Communist reinforcements, including Albert Weisbord, national secretary of the union and a leading Communist, the strikers remained on the defensive. Picket lines were broken up by sheriff's deputies. Relief efforts faltered. On May 6, strikers were evicted from company housing. Weisbord advocated the theory of a "rolling wave of strikes," which meant spreading the strike from mill to mill. Although several nearby mills were briefly closed, the tactic of encouraging further strikes merely diluted the union's resources. To compound their problems, local organizers were ordered by Weisbord to make "absolutely no compromise" on the Negro question. In Loray Mills, the advice was hardly practical since, as one organizer noted, "we never saw one [Negro] there."[2]

In a desperate effort to resuscitate the strike, some one hundred women and children marched to Loray Mill on the evening of June 7 to persuade workers to walk out. Before the group got near the mill, police intercepted them and beat up the marchers. They returned to their tent city; soon afterward, an exchange of gunfire broke out. When it ended, Chief of Police Aderholt was dead; two other policemen and several strikers were injured. "The blood of these men cries out to high heaven for vengeance," proclaimed the local paper. "This community has been too lenient with these despicable currs and snakes from the dives of Passaic, Hoboken and New York." Fifteen people, including Communists and local strikers, were charged with first-degree murder. The highlight of their first trial came when the prosecution wheeled in a stretcher. Its cover was removed to reveal an effigy of the deceased police chief in his bloody uniform, an apparition that drove one juryman "stark mad" and caused a mistrial. At a second trial, seven of the defendants were convicted of lesser charges. Some people in Gaston County had still not had their fill of vengeance, however. A mob beat and flogged several Party organizers in early September and wrecked union headquarters in Gastonia and Bessemer City. A week later a truck carrying union members to a rally was stopped, and Ella Mae Wiggins—a strike leader, songwriter, and mother of nine children—was shot and killed.[3]

The aftermath of the strike was hardly more comforting to the Party. The trial revealed splits among the defendants. Beal, on the stand, denied advocating force and violence or the abolition of the Constitution on instructions from the Party. Another defense witness advocated revolution and a Soviet form of government; for good measure, she added that she didn't believe in God. Beal and the other convicted men jumped bail and fled to Russia. Disillusioned by the worker's paradise, Beal returned to America, publicly announced his defection in a 1937 autobiography, and later served five years in a North Carolina jail. The NTWU was driven out of Gaston County and was unable to return even later in the 1930s. Early in July 1929 some 2,100 workers, under United Textile Worker (AFL) leadership, fought a bitter strike in Marion, North Carolina, which ended in mid-September when deputies murdered six strikers. (The NTWU was not involved.) Communist post-mortems found fault with virtually every aspect of the Party's work in Gastonia, from treatment of the race issue to the strike strategy; from duplication of effort among the union, the ILD, and the Workers' International Relief to the Party's esoteric language; from poor use of organizers to poor planning.[4]

The major casualty of Gastonia was Albert Weisbord, a young Harvard Law School graduate from a middle-class Jewish family who had become a Communist in the 1920s and a leader of the Passaic, New Jersey, textile strike in 1926. Weisbord was recalled to New York in June 1929 and dismissed from his position of union leadership. He continued to hope for intervention from the Comintern through the summer, but it was too busy expelling Lovestoneites to come to his aid. Expelled from the Communist party, he rebuffed pleas from Cannon and Lovestone to join their splinter groups and in 1931 formed his own, the Communist League of Struggle. The league took a Trotskyist line but never even achieved the minuscule membership of the other sects.[5]

While the Communist party hardly can be said to have succeeded in

Gastonia, it did receive an important psychological boost. For however brief a moment, the Party had led American-born workers from the South. William Dunne proudly quoted a reporter's observation: "There is not a so-called foreign face among them—not an Italian, Bulgarian or Russian Jew. All bear the kind of countenance that one sees among the valleys and hills of the region, whose people have been free from other admixtures since the early immigration to America." That such people had now joined the class struggle was proof positive that "the inner contradictions of capitalism in the imperialist period bring on economic struggles which speedily take on a political character." *The Daily Worker* noted that "the Gastonia fight is Class Against Class." A party plenum declared: "The struggle in the South symbolized by Gastonia is the best proof of the growing radicalization of the working class in the third period."[6]

Thus, even though it was a small, unsuccessful strike and not even the largest in the textile industry that spring, Gastonia became famous. National attention was riveted on the trial. Not for the last time was the Communist party able to transform a failed strike into a symbolic victory.

While Gastonia quickened Party hearts, it was still located far from the centers of industrial America. Party members could only experience its excitement and heroism vicariously, reading about the exploits of their comrades or attending a rally or speech. And in the heartland of American Communism, New York City, even the stock market collapse did not immediately translate into gains for the Party. William Weinstone, running for mayor, polled only 5,805 votes. That Jimmy Walker, the Tammany candidate, and Fiorello LaGuardia, the Republican, received 500,000 and 375,000, respectively, was less disappointing than Socialist Norman Thomas's 175,697 votes. While the Communist vote had grown by 2,400 in four years, the Socialists' had expanded by 136,000. The lesson was clear to the Party: it had "to strengthen the fight against the Socialist Party, and especially against its so-called 'left wing,' the Muste group."[7]

Elections, however, were hardly the stuff of which the Third Period was made. The Communists put up candidates in only a few cities across the country, and many members resisted electoral activity. The Party decided that talk was cheap; it had to take action. Oddly enough, the Communist party had little previous experience organizing mass demonstrations. The typical Party demonstration had been small and easily organized. "Suddenly a few hundred Party members would appear at noontime, before the White House, National City Bank or some consulate, and picket back and forth." Then they would quickly disperse to avoid the police. The main goal of these demonstrations, a Party leader admitted, was publicity: "We paid more attention to mobilizing the photographers and newspaper reporters than the masses of workers."[8]

The Comintern had more ambitious plans. A directive from the Enlarged Presidium of its Executive Committee in February 1930 called on Communist parties to change the "methods and pace of their work by concentrating their chief attention on the problems of the preparation and the carrying out of mass REVOLUTIONARY ACTIONS OF THE PROLETARIAT—strikes, demonstrations, etc." The Communists had to organize to "fight for the streets." Cadres had to be trained in proletarian self-defense: "As long as our comrades don't go through any training in throwing stones they naturally throw stones more for the moral effect."[9]

In New York the Communists had their first experience in "fighting for the streets" in 1929. A demonstration was called for December 14 to protest American military intervention in Haiti. Efforts were made to mobilize the maximum number of demonstrators: there was no attempt to evade the police. Two thousand demonstrators marched in formation around the Federal Building chanting and singing. Hundreds of police charged the crowd, meeting fierce resistance. The demonstrators marched first to City Hall and then to Union Square for more speeches, as arrests continued. The Communists believed that a corner had been turned. Herbert Benjamin, organizational secretary in New York, exulted that "Broadway had the appearance of a battle ground." Improvements were still needed: "In fact, much of the art and strategy of military organization must be studied and applied in all such struggles." But, "this, the first demonstration of its kind organized under the leadership of the Party in this district, gave undeniable proof of the fighting mood of the masses."[10]

No longer were the Communists to concede the streets to their enemies. In the Third Period, they needed to go on the offensive. A second opportunity quickly arose. In early January a small Party-led union called a strike at Miller's Market on 161st Street and Union Avenue. On January 16, Steve Katovis, a Communist, was picketing in front of the store. During a fight with a policeman Katovis was shot and died eight days later.

Sam Darcy organized the Communists' response. On January 25, a large contingent of Party members marched on City Hall and were set upon by the police. *The Daily Worker* report had the sound of a war dispatch: "Reforming again and again, broken up at one point by charges by 200 foot and mounted police, turning to fight in scores of points against the club and fist-swinging patrolmen, yielding to superior force and retreating, taking their wounded with them as they went—but always returning to the scene—that is the main outstanding feature of the demonstration by 3,000 militant workers of New York, in City Hall Park." Robert Minor was clubbed down; Herbert Benjamin was pulled down stairs and beaten. On the following Tuesday, a crowd estimated at 50,000 by the Communists, packed Union Square for Steve Katovis's funeral. The Katovis demonstration clearly took the Party by surprise. An article in *The Party Organizer* confessed that the turnout had been "underestimated" and insufficient literature prepared to hand out. John Williamson noted that "with the rising tide of militancy amongst the workers we must have confidence in the responsiveness of the masses. The first application of this line, such as the New York Haiti and the Katovis demonstrations, proved the correctness of this change in policy."[11]

The euphoria continued for several more weeks. In fact, the response to the next demonstration was so far beyond expectation that the Communists briefly believed that the transition from a small sect to a mass party had already been made. Once again, the idea came from Moscow. The Comintern had instructed all its sections to hold demonstrations on "International Unemployment Day." After some confusion, the date was finally set for March 6. The Party made very careful and thorough preparations. The Agitprop Department put out an "Outline for Speakers in Unemployed Demonstrations," which largely ignored the immediate problems of the unemployed. In fact, the outline suggested that it was necessary to ready the workers "for the proletarian revolution" and cautioned against "all tendencies of economism and viewing the struggle of the unemployed simply from the economic point of view."[12]

The demonstration surpassed all expectations. The Communist press claimed 110,000 demonstrators, *The New York Times* a somewhat more modest 35,000. The meeting began at 1:00 P.M. as formations of Communists, waving signs and placards, entered Union Square from side streets. After the huge throng had shouted its approval of a series of demands for relief, Sam Darcy, the main organizer, announced the crowd's intention to march to City Hall to present the demands to the mayor. A committee led by William Foster met with Police Commissioner Grover Whalen, and was told that no march would be allowed because a parade permit had not been obtained. Whalen offered, however, to send the committee to City Hall in his own car. Foster responded with inescapable logic: "If this were a meeting of bankers you wouldn't keep them from marching on City Hall." He returned to a speakers' platform, reported on his unsuccessful negotiations, and charged that streets which were handed over to "every monarchist and militarist exploiter of Europe and America" for parades were being denied to the workers. He asked, "Will you take that for an answer?" The crowd howled out a "No," and Foster began leading a march down Broadway to City Hall.

Suddenly what had been "an orderly and at times, bored crowd" was transformed "into a fighting mob." One thousand police charged into the gathering, setting off fifteen minutes of intense, bloody fighting. *The Times* reported: "Hundreds of policemen and detectives, swinging nightsticks, blackjacks and bare fists, rushed into the crowd, hitting out at all with whom they came into contact, chasing many across the street and into adjacent thoroughfares and pushing hundreds off their feet. From all parts of the scene of battle came the screams of women and cries of men with bloody heads and faces." Firemen turned on hoses. The demonstrators responded with denunciations of "Murderous Cossacks" and occasional bricks. Four police and over a hundred civilians were injured, including some bystanders caught by indiscriminate police clubbing.

Thousands of the demonstrators made their way to City Hall Park. *The Times* reported that "armored motorcycles appeared, and a police emergency truck equipped with tear gas, smoke bombs, submachine guns, rifles and riot guns drove into the park." The committee appeared and was promptly arrested on the steps of City Hall. Foster, Minor, and Israel Amter were later sentenced to six months in prison. Thousands milled around the area for hours more, provoking several minor skirmishes. Within two months, Commissioner Whalen, under fire for the police handling of the demonstration, resigned.[13]

Throughout the country, undreamt-of-crowds responded to the Communists' call. *The Daily Worker* claimed more than 100,000 in Detroit, 50,000 in Chicago, the same number in Boston, and 40,000 in Milwaukee. The total estimated to have demonstrated nationwide was 1,250,000, with more than 1,000 arrests. The Party hailed March 6 as "unheard of in the history of the American labor movement in modern times." The demonstrations marked "a historical turning point in the revolutionary development of the American proletariat and signalizes the birth of the mass Communist Party in the United States," according to Will Weinstone. A front-page *Daily Worker* editorial exulted that "where a few tens of thousands had followed the Communist Party, fully a million and a quarter of the American working class now follow its leadership."[14]

Rather quickly, however, the American Communists came back to earth. March 6 was most certainly not the long-awaited breakthrough to the American masses. Demonstrations on May 1 and August 1 were much smaller. The revolutionary masses were proving evanescent. By the end of April there were rueful admissions that the March 6 success was due less to Communist capture of the masses than to the spontaneous outpouring of hundreds of thousands of workers with no other outlet for expressing their feelings. Clarence Hathaway admitted that there was "merely a loose mass of workers, which in many cases we were unable to direct."[15]

The Comintern, too, became more critical. Dimitri Manuilsky reminded everyone that "the revolutionary upsurge presupposes a great systematic work" and "before all we must put an end to the extremely harmful theory of the spontaneity and the elementary movement of our work." Demonstrations left few traces behind. They did little or nothing to build up the Party organization. If the Communist party were to fulfill its responsibilities, it would take more enduring activities than street demonstrations to do so. A Central Committee resolution concerning the May Day demonstrations rebuked the proposals of some Party members "to take Union Square from the fascists and police by force." By the end of the year, Sam Darcy was exiled to far-away California. Herbert Benjamin, the organizational secretary in New York and also identified with the 1930 events, was shipped to Ohio as a district organizer.[16]

The demonstration had come as the Party was preparing for its Seventh Convention, the first since Lovestone's ouster, scheduled for June 1930. In mid-February the Anglo-American Secretariat of the Comintern sent the Americans a letter defining the Party's tasks. The various theses to be produced, and how the pre-convention discussion was to be handled, were specified. By the end of the month the CPUSA had produced a lengthy draft document bristling with Third Period verbiage. The document took "the immediate perspective of mass struggles involving growing hundreds of thousands of workers in direct conflict with the capitalist system and its servants." Was the draft what the Russians wanted? The latter clearly had very specific ideas of what the American Party should say. There was only one way to find out.[17]

Max Bedacht was dispatched to Moscow with the document, arriving on March 12. Four days later the first of several cables went to New York with reports. Bedacht and Weinstone had had "exhaustive interviews" with Ossip Piatnitsky and Sergei Gusev and had secured appointments with Dimitri Manuilsky, S. Losovsky, and Otto Kuusinen. They also expected to meet Molotov. Bedacht and Weinstone then told their anxious comrades: ". . . we are told that no official decision will be made. A letter to the convention will take up the political problems. In today's Polsec [Political Secretariat] meeting Piat remarked that a letter to the convention may not even be necessary, presumably if the theses are satisfactory. An official declaration for the theses, or against, is considered an unduly interference with a political discussion in America. . . ." However, it did appear that some interference was taking place. The cable went on to report that one serious problem was that the theses "are way too long and must be cut at least in half." More significantly, "the 'revolutionary' situation is emphasized too much in our draft." Piatnitsky and Gusev also had organizational suggestions, including how often the Politburo should meet. One week later Bedacht reported several other objections. Only after he and Weinstone had agreed to make the required changes did they wire their comrades that the "POLITSECRETARIAT CONSIDERS CC [Central Committee] LINE CORRECT AND FULLY SUPPORTS CC."[18]

The Americans dutifully revised their theses and published them in a ninety-five-page pamphlet that was re-revised before being adopted by the Seventh Convention in June. This final report came down hard on the need to shift Party work to produce more enduring results: "Our Party is suffering from a decided disproportion between its organized strength and the mass activities which it initiates and leads. The readiness of great masses of workers to follow our Party has led to a most serious underestimation of the value of organization. The reliance on spontaneous response in many instances replaces systematic organization preparations."[19]

Max Bedacht, giving the main political report to a Party convention for the last time, sharply criticized the reliance on spontaneity: "The economic crisis will not automatically bring the workers to building barricades." Therefore, "the Party must definitely abandon past practices of spectacular record action. Such spectacular record action does not create revolutionary life. It merely creates noise for self-deceptive purposes." Bedacht's self-criticism did not save him. Under his temporary stewardship, the Party had made a mark but not one totally to the Comintern's liking. Bedacht himself noted that the Party had yet to turn "from the dominating tendency of a propaganda sect to that of a revolutionary Party of action."[20]

At the convention the Party also reconsidered the nature of its propaganda. Once again, it was Bedacht who sounded the warning: "To elevate the understanding of the working masses to the point of revolutionary action does not and cannot mean to disregard the immediate problems of the workers. It does not and cannot mean to advise the workers on all occasions with the stereotyped phrase: 'You cannot solve your problems except through revolution.'" Not that Bedacht regarded these daily struggles as the be-all and end-all of Communist activity: they were "a method by which alone our revolutionary objective can be realized." His suggestion, however, fit in nicely with the new realism about building the Party. The wild optimism of just months before was being tempered. The road to revolution would not be quite so easy as some had permitted themselves to believe after seeing hundreds of thousands answering the Party's call to demonstrate.[21]

Fighting for the streets and mobilizing large crowds to protest unemployment were not programs and had not enabled the Communists to penetrate the working class. More importantly, by denying that any significant reforms were possible under capitalism, the Communists had offered potential supporters only the options of fighting for a revolution or doing nothing. If they fought for partial demands, the Communists could expose the treachery of the "social-fascists" and thus win converts. Dimitri Manuilsky insisted that it was necessary to connect "the partial demands of the proletariat with the final aim of the proletarian movement." In America, Manuilsky advised, the Party should take the lead in the struggle for social insurance. The Party plenum in November faithfully reemphasized the importance of partial demands. William Foster, in fact, called that rediscovery the plenum's principal achievement. He went on to note: "There has been too much reliance on broad political slogans and too little concentration upon questions of the most immediate interest to the workers." As a consequence, a tendency exists "for our mass work to remain rather in the sphere of general agitation than of actual struggle."[22]

March 6 did have one other important consequence. The day before the demonstration, Representative Hamilton Fish of New York proposed a congressional investigation of Communism. The Fish Committee heard dozens of witnesses and produced sixteen volumes of testimony and documents. William Z. Foster was the star witness. He defiantly told the congressmen that "workers are understanding that the Soviet Union is really their only fatherland" and "the only possible guard for the future security of the working class is the dictatorship of the proletariat and the establishment of a Soviet government." When asked if Communists advocated world revolution, he answered "yes." He further informed the congressmen that "the workers of this country and the workers of every country have only one flag and that is the red flag."[23]

The committee's witnesses ranged from officials of Amtorg, the Soviet trading corporation, to representatives of such patriotic organizations as the Daughters of the American Revolution. Walter Steele, an indefatigable investigator of subversion, generously estimated that there were "slightly over 2,000,000 Communists" in America. Other expert witnesses offered suggestions on how to solve the Communist problem; Grover Whalen, by now ex–police commissioner, thought deporting 500 Communists would do it. Some witnesses described the psychology of radicalism—for example, Lieutenant Make Mills of the Chicago "Red Squad" eruditely pointed out, "The Communist movement is a purely Asiatic movement. The psychology of it is the patriarchs that used to rule their clans." Some expert witnesses discoursed on Communist history; Father Charles Coughlin noted that Communism had its roots in Adam Weishaupt's Order of the Illuminati, founded in 1776. Father Coughlin also revealed that the international labor movement was "headed by Mr. Henry Ford." His testimony duly impressed the committee chairman, who complimented him: "We have had in Washington hearings on this matter, but this is historic." In January 1931, with only one dissent, the committee's report recommended deporting alien Communists and outlawing the Communist party. It was not the last such response to Communist activities.[24]

The Dual Unions

No aspect of Party activity was considered as crucial as trade union work. The Seventh Convention summed up the goal: "The Party can win the working masses for its political leadership only by leading them in their economic struggles; and only on the basis of the Trade Union Unity League will the Party be able to assume the leadership of these economic struggles." The TUUL came into existence in 1929 as a response to Moscow's demand for a revolutionary alternative to the A.F. of L. Despite their misgivings about the new policy, the American Communists had created three new unions by January 1929: the National Miners Union (NMU), the National Textile Workers Industrial Union, and the Needle Trades Workers Industrial Union. All three were formed in industries where the A.F. of L. had its own unions. They were the only full-fledged Communist unions when the Trade Union Unity Conference held its initial convention in Cleveland from August 31 to September 2, 1929, where 690 delegates stated that they represented 50,000 workers.[25]

The TUUL's program was a carbon copy of the Communist Party's. Its analysis of capitalism, the economic crisis, and American imperialism deviated not one whit from the Party line. It contained the same jeremiads against the "fascist A.F. of L." and the "social-fascist Socialists and Musteites." Nor did it make any effort to hide its political connections: "It supports the revolutionary political struggles and the political organization of the working class, the Communist Party." The American Communists were admonished that building the TUUL was of the highest priority. Manuilsky reminded them that "for the Communist Party of America, the strengthening of the new trade unions, which are called upon to play the part of the framework for the whole Communist movement" was the central task. A Party resolution demanded that all members belong to the TUUL, "a lever and the main reserve for the Party."[26]

In fact, the relationship between the CPUSA and the TUUL was so intimate that even the Communists were often unsure about lines of demarcation. Top TUUL leaders like Foster, Jack Johnstone, and Bill Dunne were also Party leaders; cadres were shifted in and out of the unions on Party orders. TUUL decisions were almost always made by Party fractions and subject to review and reversal by Party officials. When union leaders ran afoul of the Party, their union careers came to an end. In accord with Third Period rhetoric, the TUUL's goal in the labor movement was "the united front from below, that is to say, united fronts with the rank and file progressive elements."[27]

The American Federation of Labor had been steadily losing members for almost a decade. Large sectors of industry were almost totally unorganized. The A.F. of L., overwhelmingly an organization of skilled craftsmen, largely white and native-born, seemingly presented no barrier to the TUUL. "The A.F. of L. is in the period of senility," Sam Darcy gloated in 1930, providing "a glorious opportunity for revolutionary trade unionism." The old organization's failure, William Foster explained, left to the TUUL the "organization of the unorganized," particularly in "the key and basic industries" such as steel, auto, and textile.[28]

In theory, at least, there was no inherent conflict between the two labor organizations. If the TUUL spent its energies organizing the unorganized, there might never be a direct challenge. The Party's goal, however, was neither to supplement the work of the A.F. of L. nor to reform it. A Comintern spokesman defined the TUUL's task as "to destroy the American Federation of Labor, the most reliable support of American imperialism." One of Foster's aides emphasized that the purpose of working in the old unions was "to win the members for the class struggle program of the T.U.U.L." and, when the members learn that they "cannot capture the old apparatus," to create new unions. S. Lozovsky, the Profintern's leader, bluntly explained the purpose of working in reformist unions: "There is no need to shout from the housetops 'destroy the unions' as was done in Germany. But that we want to break up the reformist trade unions, that we want to weaken them, that we want to explode their discipline, that we want to wrest them from the workers, that we want to explode the trade union apparatus and to destroy it—of that there cannot be the slightest doubt."[29]

Moreover, the goal of revolutionary unions was light-years away from the more prosaic ends of the A.F. of L. Strikes were not intended to be limited to economic demands but to advance the struggle for power. In 1930 the Profintern placed "as the central objective of the strategy of its forces internationally the development of the mass political strike." The TUUL understood that this meant "imperatively that we broaden our strike struggles, give them more of a class and political character, and direct them against the capitalist state as well as against the individual employers." The Americans were instructed by the Enlarged Presidium of the ECCI "to secure the leadership of the mass actions (strikes, unemployed movements, demonstration, etc.), actions which often break out spontaneously, to lead these actions along the channels of organized political struggles, especially in the form of mass political strikes which will bring the working class toward the task of revolutionary struggle for power." A strike led by a revolutionary union, then, could never be successful if it was limited to economic demands. This meant that Communist-led strikes often took on not only employes but the state and the reformist unions as well. The Communists did not shrink from such confrontations but welcomed them.[30]

The new union movement boasted only three full-fledged revolutionary unions at its founding convention. Its National Executive Board, however, was optimistic about the prospects for success in a number of industries and set up "leagues" as an interim step. By the spring of 1930, eight such leagues had come into existence, six of which were expected to become unions by the end of June. However, by the end of 1930, only the Marine Workers Industrial Union had gotten off the ground. At this time, the TUUL's executive board confessed that its four unions had all suffered "serious declines in membership." The leagues were "only skeletons of what they should be." By September, Lozovsky was warning the Americans against "wholesale" organization of new unions for fear of isolating "the more class-conscious section of the workers from the masses." One Communist dolefully confessed that "without question the weakest sector of our Party work is the trade union field."[31]

Wherever one looked, the situation was dismal. The National Miners Union had called its first strike in Illinois in December 1929 with an "almost complete lack of preparation." Not one strike committee was ever formed, and no advance work had been done. A general strike call for the anthracite areas of Pennsylvania and West Virginia, made by the NMU in April 1930 and scheduled to take effect in September, was not followed up even though spontaneous strikes were taking place throughout the region. In the middle of the year, the NMU leadership was removed and new forces brought in.[32]

The National Textile Workers Industrial Union fared no better. It had already been decimated at the end of 1929 by the purge of its old leadership, including Albert Weisbord. The Marine Workers Industrial Union called a waterfront strike in Philadelphia "completely without the knowledge of the workers in the industry, thus taking the workers by surprise on the morning of the strike." The workers did not respond. The Agricultural Workers Industrial League was smashed by mass arrests in Imperial Valley, California, before it could hold an organizing meeting. The drive to organize metal workers was even less successful. Bill Dunne complained at the Party's Seventh Convention: "I do not think comrades, that we can have mobilized the Party for building the revolutionary unions in the Steel and Metal industry, when we have simply turned Comrade Overgaard [Andrew Overgaard was secretary of the Metal Workers Industrial League] loose among three or four million metal workers. That is what it amounts to."[33]

The TUUL's top leaders were alternately baffled and exasperated by the gap between what they expected and what they had achieved. "The objective conditions were never better for building militant revolutionary unions," Jack Johnstone lamented, "but objective conditions do not create organizations." The most serious problem, it was generally agreed, was the lack of adequate forces. The Party faced a serious disjunction between the role to which it aspired and which the Comintern urged on it and its ability to meet those goals. "The greatest weakness of our Party at present," Bill Dunne explained, "is its lack of capable forces." He singled out the worst weakness as the trade union field, where the absence of trained organizers and leaders was felt the most. Less than half the Party membership of 10,000 worked in basic industries, with virtually none of them in chemical, marine, or railroad work and only small numbers in steel and mining. Despite injunctions from Moscow that all Party members join the TUUL—one cablegram read "COMPULSORY EVERY MEMBER BECOME IMMEDIATELY TUUL MEMBER"—many did not join. In Detroit, for example, only 15 percent of Party members were active in the TUUL.[34]

The Party's shop nuclei were in even worse shape. Despite five years of effort, only 10 percent of the membership belonged to shop nuclei in

1930. Membership ranged from a high of 45 percent in Pittsburgh to a low of 2 percent in New York, the largest district. Half of the nuclei did not even function in the shops; they feared that employers would fire Communists, as Earl Browder admitted in 1931. Many shop nuclei had not recruited a new worker in years. As Browder described their rationale: "The other nuclei then decide to aid the statistics of the district by preserving themselves from discharge through being inactive." Sometimes, one TUUL organizer ruefully admitted, workers were unable to find out who their Communist co-workers were: "In the past we have issued hundreds of leaflets, with demands that the unorganized agree to wholeheartedly, but when the unorganized workers attempt to find the phantom authors of the leaflets, they cannot do so, and the 'struggle' called for in the leaflets remains on paper."[35]

TUUL strikes were not prepared in the shops, largely because the league was trying to organize industries where neither it nor the Party had many members. As a result, most of its strikes were spontaneous. Sparked by intolerable conditions, workers would march off the job and the TUUL would rush in its forces. Jack Johnstone detailed the consequences: "Very little, and generally no preparations for struggle are made, the strikes quite generally [take] place through the spontaneity of the workers and before the Trade Union Unity League gets busy to organize and broaden the strike, it has been broken or [workers go] back to work still unorganized and defeated." Even during strikes, the TUUL itself admitted, broad demands were emphasized and the immediate interests of the strikers ignored: "We have seen local strike demands containing proposals for workers and farmers government, for state unemployment insurance, for the six-hour day, five-day week, etc., while at the same time the most immediate and elementary shop demands of the workers were neglected."[36]

In October 1930 the Executive Committee of the Communist International sharply reminded the Party that it had not fulfilled its job. "Membership in several of the red trade unions has sharply declined," the Americans were told, "very slow progress has been made in the formation of new unions in the decisive industries, [and] the TUUL remains an organization chiefly embracing the Party members and a small circle of sympathizers." The ECCI recommended concentrating on such immediate demands as "wages, hours, speed-up, unemployment, increasing accidents and growing oppression in the factories" and forming grievance committees in the shops. The unions were warned that they had to avoid "abstract politicizing of strikes, and must raise political demands which correspond to the strike struggles." The Party was instructed that its best cadres, including Central Committee members, were to be assigned to work in the TUUL.[37]

Jack Stachel replaced John Schmies as Bill Foster's chief assistant early in 1931, but conditions did not improve. *The Daily Worker* unhappily noted that of the 35 million American workers, 3.5 million belonged to the A.F. of L. and only 15,000 were in revolutionary unions. The Profintern, concerned about the inability of the TUUL to make any headway, chimed in with a resolution that called the situation "extremely serious," suggested that organizing the unemployed was now a more central task than organizing the unorganized, and proposed concentration on key cities and industries rather than a continued scattershot approach. The TUUL dutifully decided to concentrate on the mining, textile, metal, and marine industries.[38]

The TUUL's next big test came in Lawrence, Massachusetts. The United Textile Workers, an A.F. of L. affiliate, was weak there. On February 1, 1931, the NTWU announced plans to lead strikes in Lawrence. The chief organizer was a twenty-six-year-old, Polish-born knitter named Edith Berkman. In July 1930 she was sent to Lawrence and slowly built a small union nucleus in several of the largest mills. When one company was forced to rescind a 10 percent layoff after union pressure, union membership spurted. Employees of the American Woolen Company, angered over a speed up and emboldened by the union's previous success, struck in late February 1931. Within days, all three company mills were shut down and all 10,000 workers were on strike. Very quickly, the owners mobilized their forces and struck back. In less than a week the strike committee was under arrest, and Berkman, William Murdock, and Pat Devine, the NTWU leaders, were held for deportation. The dispirited and disillusioned workers went back to work, claiming a partial victory. For the first time, a TUUL union had organized within factories prior to a strike and struggled to achieve immediate demands. Jack Stachel, though critical of a number of union decisions, was pleased enough to suggest that "the Lawrence strike, if all signs are not misleading, is the turning point in the development of strike struggles."[39]

The euphoria was short-lived. Following the February strike, the union organizers were pulled out of Lawrence and sent to engineer several Rhode Island silk strikes. As a result, a walkout in October 1931 in Lawrence, provoked by a 10 percent wage cut, caught the union unprepared. This new strike was even larger than the first: 23,000 workers shut down every loom in Lawrence. The Communists quickly rushed in organizers but discovered they did not have the field all to themselves. A revived United Textile Workers Union and the Musteites both competed for the workers' affections. Both the NTWU and the UTW had their own strike committees, strike meetings, and even picket lines. After six weeks of struggling against the owners and one another, the workers were routed. They returned to the mills, and the 10 percent wage cut went into effect.[40]

William Weinstone raked the NTWU over the coals for "five weeks of sectarian separation from the masses" caused by "the formal and life-less application of the united front tactics." Instead of taking the lead in pressing for unity and thus demonstrating the A.F. of L.'s treachery, the NTWU had divided the workers. The Comintern and Profintern denounced the Americans for having "isolated themselves by setting up parallel strike organs, isolated from the masses."[41] The debacle finished the National Textile Workers Union. It had begun 1931 confident that it could displace its A.F. of L. rival. By year's end the union was in ruins. Murdock and Devine were deported. Berkman was jailed for seven months and then entered a sanatorium. The last two secretaries of the NTWU, Martin Russak and Ann Burlak, tried to hold the organization together, but by January 1932 there were only 2,000 members.[42]

The other hope of revolutionary unionism was in mining. Preferring a smaller union he could dominate to a larger one with challengers to his throne, John L. Lewis had defeated and expelled many potential usurpers and rambunctious mine locals from the United Mine Workers. The miners were in an explosive mood in 1931. Two insurgent non-Communist groups, in eastern Pennsylvania and West Virginia, led large strikes in 1931. In neither case were the Communists able to gain a foothold. They bitterly denounced the strike leadership as "the most dangerous of all to the workers because it is using militant phrases and pretends to be for a militant platform."[43]

The Communists did, however, lead the largest of the miners' strikes in 1931. After careful and painstaking preparation, 1,000 workers at the Carnegie mines in western Pennsylvania, facing a wage cut, responded to NMU pleas and struck on May 26. Within a week 10,000 miners were out; in three weeks, 27,000; and by the end of June, 40,000. William Foster himself rushed to the mine fields to speak and give "direction to the strike." Alfred Wagenknecht, head of the Party's relief arm, undertook a major campaign to raise money to feed the strikers and their families. Draining its forces in other areas, the Party and the TUUL rushed "about 25 experienced organizers" into the area. An editorial in the TUUL journal called the strike "the most important struggle that has taken place not only in the coal industry but throughout the country since the beginning of the present economic crisis."[44]

True to most TUUL strikes, this one was bitter and bloody. At least two strikers were killed by lawmen. Determined to hold out for a general settlement, the NMU rebuffed efforts by some mine owners to settle the strike. In early July, the Politburo was aware that the strike's advance had "ceased," but the Communists refused for some time to face the consequences. Finally, Arthur Ewart, a German serving as Comintern representative in America, warned that a "strategic retreat" might be necessary. After considerable resistance from Foster and other strike leaders, Ewart's advice prevailed. It was too late to save either the strike or the many miners who faced blacklisting. Late in August, Foster finally called for a "temporary and organized retreat, for the purpose of strengthening the lines generally in preparation for a new advance," a euphonism that signaled the beginning of mine-by-mine efforts to salvage whatever was possible from the ruins of the strike.[45]

The strike was, the Politburo boasted, "the largest strike struggle ever conducted under the leadership of the Party." During its course, 25,000 miners briefly joined the NMU and 1,000 went into the Communist party. While acknowledging the Party's achievements, the Comintern directed a host of criticisms at its handling of the whole affair. The criticisms ran the gamut from inadequate preparatory work to a misunderstanding of how to end the strike. The Comintern firmly reminded the Americans that "the *revolutionization of the striking workers* would be the main object" of the strike but that this goal was impossible unless the Communists exerted "all their energy in the struggle against the employers so as to win the strike" [italics in original]. Years afterward, William Foster admitted that this strike had "dealt the N.M.U. a fatal blow."[46]

The NMU did have one final hurrah in Harlan County, Kentucky, one of the harshest anti-union strongholds in America. In February 1931, local miners began organizing in the UMW. By March 10,000 men were on strike. "Bloody Harlan" lived up to its name; the strike was marked by looting of food stores, beating up of scabs, dynamiting of mines, and gunfire. Outside the small town of Evarts on May 4, deputies and miners engaged in pitched battle. When the shooting had stopped, three deputies and one miner were dead, and thirty-four union members faced murder charges. The strike was broken.

In mid-June, Dan Slinger, the first TUUL organizer, arrived in Harlan County. As the strike in western Pennsylvania dribbled away, organizers representing the TUUL, the Party, the International Labor Defense, and kindred groups poured into the county. By the fall, 3,000 miners belonged to the NMU even though "the state of terror [was] almost incredible." Conditions were deplorable: "The majority of the workers in that region are facing actual starvation," and "will fight, with or without our leadership." Five mines in Bell County, next to Harlan, were closed by an NMU strike that quickly disintegrated. Union organizers, excited by the militancy of the miners, pushed for extending the strike. One of them, Dan Slinger, advanced "the theory that the miners ought to have guns and kill all the thugs and then we would be able to organize them into the union." However, the Party's district organizer in Chattanooga, Harry Wicks temporarily persuaded Earl Browder that an early strike in Harlan would be disastrous.[47]

Although virtually no union organizing took place in late 1931, Frank Borich of the NMU persuaded the Party leadership to sanction a strike. In December a National Miners Union district convention decided to call a strike for January 1, 1932. Eighteen thousand miners were expected to walk out on New Year's Day; only 5,000 did so. By the second day, one organizer was lamenting the lack of picket lines and adequate relief. Within a week the local NMU headquarters had been raided and its organizers arrested. No arrangements had been made to counter the owners' propaganda, which was "having quite an effect upon the miners especially the more backward and religious sections." At the end of the month Borich sent a report to the Politburo admitting that: "It is obvious now that the expectations of the Party in connection with the Kentucky strike were not fulfilled." He confessed a variety of failures. The Party had "concentrated mostly on the blacklisted miners," who had assured organizers that the employed workers would strike. Relief work was inadequate. Preparations for the strike were shoddy. Jack Stachel also admitted that "we were wrong in calling the strike when we did, with the preparations that we had carried through." Stachel traced the error to "yielding to spontaneity." By failing to build Party and union organizations, the Communists left themselves vulnerable to illusions and errors. Referring to the focus on blacklisted miners, Stachel said, "Unemployed miners cannot strike, because they are not inside the mines." By the middle of March the strike had dwindled to ten mines with 795 men. Not until the end of March, however, was it brought to an end.[48]

Although the NMU and the Communists made enough mistakes on their own, they also faced a reign of terror. Unarmed miners were shot down and killed. Reporters were wounded. One miner who gave a copy of *The Daily Worker* to a passer-by was indicted for criminal syndicalism. A local newspaper suggested that "Harlan agitators . . . would be much safer in a pine box six feet under ground." On February 10, 1932, Harry Sims—born Harry Hirsch, an organizer for the NMU and the Young

Communist League—was murdered by one of Sheriff J. H. Blair's deputies.[49]

"Which side are you on?" went the refrain of a song written about Harlan County. For many prominent Americans the question was easily answered. While the Communists were unable to organize a successful strike in Harlan County, they proved masters at focusing national attention on the plight of the miners and the absence of civil liberties in this little corner of Kentucky. The National Committee for the Defense of Political Prisoners, a newly formed Party auxiliary headed by novelist Theodore Dreiser, sent a delegation to investigate the situation. Led by Dreiser and writer John Dos Passos, a committee of eight journeyed to Kentucky in November and helped focus nationwide attention on Harlan County, a process undoubtedly aided by Dreiser's arrest for adultery while in Kentucky. Other committees followed. One, which included the writers Waldo Frank, Edmund Wilson, and Malcolm Cowley, was harassed and driven out of town in February 1932. A student delegation came in March under the auspices of the National Student League, in two chartered buses and several private cars. One bus was stopped at the Cumberland Gap and its passengers hauled into court. When Rob Hall, a young Communist from Alabama by way of Columbia University, refused to give his political affiliation, he and the others were put back on the bus and escorted to Knoxville. The second bus met a similar fate. An American Civil Liberties Union delegation, headed by Arthur Garfield Hays, and a church group, led by Reinhold Niebuhr, came. A Senate subcommittee took testimony.[50]

The National Miners Union, however, never recovered from the Pennsylvania and Harlan strikes. Its old rival, the UMW, made a sudden recovery and led virtually every significant miners' strike in 1932. Frank Borich confessed that the NMU "plays an insignificant role in these life and death struggles of the miners." The NMU "consisted mainly of unemployed and blacklisted miners." The year 1933 was just as bad: while strikes were then endemic in the mines, the NMU led only one, in New Mexico and Utah. Borich was deported in October 1933, and in December a Party conference of mine organizers decided "to work for the unity of the miners into one militant united miners' union." It was a tacit recognition that the NMU had failed. One of the first of the revolutionary unions, it was also one of the earliest to collapse.[51]

The first years of the Depression had not gone well for the TUUL. Its prize unions had failed several critical tests and by 1932 were, for all intents and purposes, moribund. Despite advice from abroad and ritual incantations from its own leading bodies, the Party's trade union work was afflicted with the same tendency to go for the spectacular gesture which had proved so unworkable in the 1930 demonstrations. Despite the A.F. of L's weaknesses, workers did not flock to the Communist alternatives. Even when they did, the TUUL unions proved unequal to the task of keeping them or winning strikes.

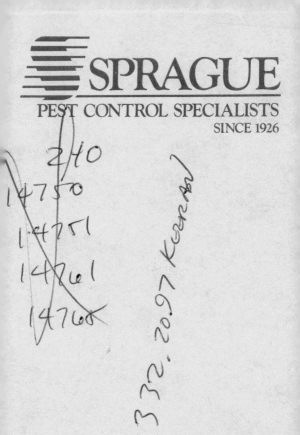

SPRAGUE

PEST CONTROL SPECIALISTS

SINCE 1926

240
14750
14751
14761
14768

332.2097 Kearns

572-6500

3

Organizing the
Unemployed

To THE COMMUNISTS, unemployment was a normal feature of capitalist society. At the end of 1929 Earl Browder noted that the "permanent army of unemployed of five to seven million persons" at the beginning of the year was being augmented daily. "This will be a *black winter* for the working class of the United States," he ominously warned. While arguing that unemployment could only be solved "by the abolition of capitalism," the future general secretary acknowledged that the workers needed "an immediate program of struggle against unemployment, which makes it possible to fight for immediate gains and prevent the bosses from making more vicious attacks, while at the same time strengthen the working class for the bigger battles and finally for the overthrow of capitalism."[1]

In typical Third Period fashion, the Communists' immediate demands ranged from the prosaic to the unobtainable. The first official Communist program for work among the unemployed, issued on December 9, 1930, listed thirteen demands. Predicated on the belief that unity between the employed and unemployed was necessary, they included unemployment insurance equal to full wages, a seven-hour day, emergency relief, worker administration of relief and benefits, and recognition of the Soviet Union. The Party's plan called for the creation of Unemployed Councils. While the TUUL was responsible for their formation, the Central Committee declared that the "Party shall be officially represented" on them. The TUUL, however, was not even capable yet of fulfilling its primary task, organizing the unorganized. In actual practice there was little distinction between it and the Party, so that for some time just who was leading the unemployed was not clear. At the end of January "over 3,000 unemployed workers marched through the streets" of Buffalo, New York, in a demonstration for unemployment relief "under the leadership of the Communist Party." Later, the massive unemployment demonstration of March 6 was called in response to instructions from the Comintern. While the Party and the TUUL jointly sponsored it, Sam Darcy, a Party functionary, was put in charge of its organization.[2]

Nonetheless, Moscow formally assigned the TUUL responsibility for organizing in this field of work: "A broad unemployment movement on a national scale shall be organized, guided and led by the TUUL." The new union center promptly responded, issuing an order that "every local and district League must take immediate initiative in organizing Unemployed Councils. Into these Councils shall be drawn representatives of the revolutionary unions, shop committees and reformist unions, as well as unorganized workers. The Councils shall be definitely affiliated to the respective T.U.U.L. Leagues." The first such council was created in Detroit: in December 1929 it staged a demonstration in the mayor's office. More councils were set up prior to the March 6 demonstration; in several cities they held marches or protest rallies.[3]

Following the enormous turnouts on March 6, a TUUL-called National Unemployment Conference was held in New York on March 29–30. There, 215 delegates from 17 states met to plan for a future, mass unemployment convention in July in Chicago. Pat Devine, formerly the Party's district organizer in Pittsburgh, was chosen national secretary. William Foster and Robert Minor, fresh from their recent arrests, were given ovations. The delegates adopted a program indistinguishable from the TUUL and Party demands, calling for "Work or Wages," unemployment relief at the expense of profits, the seven-hour day, and so on. They also insisted that "the mass political strike is on the order of business for the unemployed," and warned workers "to have no illusions that the government will grant these measures of partial relief." When one delegate, a member of the "hobo brotherhood," rose to speak, he was promptly exposed for deceiving the workers with short-term promises "when what they wanted was 'work or full wages' and a social system like that in the U.S.S.R."[4]

The initial impetus behind the Unemployed Councils soon slackened. By the end of April, Devine was complaining that they were no longer being given enough attention. "There is no stable leadership existing. Most of those who were the [flesh] and blood of the movement before March 6th have picked up their caravans and gone to some other field of activity." By mid-May Devine himself was gone, "called away from the country by personal affairs," and replaced by George Siskind. The Party's Organizational Department lamented "the complete collapse of this movement after March 6th." The July 5 convention of the unemployed in Chicago was similarly a disappointment. Just 1,320 delegates appeared, a far cry from the "mass convention" of 10,000 promised in March. Of these, 468 were either Communists or members of a party youth organization. Another 723 came from the TUUL. After the convention, Bill Dunne complained that few delegates had been elected by Unemployed Councils, which had "made but a bare beginning" in organization. Everything about the convention testified to its total domination by the Party. Dunne and Clarence Hathaway delivered the main speeches. The demands approved were virtually carbon copies of those from the March conference, which had been carbon copies of the TUUL's demands, which had faithfully followed the Party's proposals. After setting up a permanent organization and calling for another national convention in October, the delegates dispersed and the convention was all but ignored in the Party press.[5]

In the September issue of *The Communist*, Hathaway termed the Party's accomplishments in the unemployment field "entirely inadequate." He revealed that from March to the July conference there had been "no organizational activities." Despite a slight spurt after the Chicago meeting, activities had once again halted and "in all districts there had been a distinct decline." Demonstrations were taking place, but "organized unemployed councils are almost non-existent." Bill Gebert complained, "The Unemployed Councils are dying out. Not because there is less unemployment. To the contrary, unemployment is on the increase." He attributed the Party famine in the midst of plentiful opportunities to the focus of unemployment work on demonstrations and mass meetings rather than on organization. Just as was the case in other work, "spontaneity" among the unemployed had not produced desired results.[6]

In August the Party unveiled its solution to the problem: a proposed Workers' Unemployment Insurance Bill. It demanded payments equal to the wages a worker had earned, but at least $25 a week plus $5 for each dependent. The program was to be financed by a tax on incomes and capital. Shortly afterward, however, Earl Browder complained that Communist speakers "emphasized above all else, that to get such unemployment insurance we must overthrow capitalism and establish a Worker's Government." The Party seemed unable to escape its preoccupation with revolution, its scorn for immediate demands, and its inability to organize.[7]

The Comintern was dissatisfied. In October 1930 its Political Secretariat rebuked the Americans for not "organizing and leading the struggle of the unemployed workers" after the March 6 demonstration and charged that "the establishment of unemployed councils has made very little progress and those that have been formed have not conducted sufficient struggle for immediate relief to the unemployed." The American Party was criticized for not applying "sufficient forces to really improve this work." The sloppy preparations for the Chicago conference were a symptom of "the impermissible underestimation" of work needed in relation to unemployment. Even the Workers' Insurance Bill had been launched too slowly. It was, however, to be the key to the Party's future work: "*The fight for full social insurance, especially unemployed insurance, must be placed in the center of the immediate demands of the workers.*" The campaign would require "mass actions, demonstrations, strikes, and the whole struggle directed towards mass political strikes." Detailed instructions about tactics, allies, opponents, and subsidiary demands followed.[8]

By fall the Party was ready for a new offensive. Its first big attack came on October 16 in New York. A demonstration was planned in front of City Hall to demand that the Board of Estimate provide unemployment relief. Demonstrators sang the *Internationale* and chanted "We want work or wages." J. Louis Engdahl, head of the International Labor Defense, was ejected from the boardroom when he interrupted the proceedings. Going outside City Hall, Engdahl attempted to speak. Mounted police pushed into the crowd of between 500 and 1,000, the press of people broke plate glass windows in adjoining business establishments, paper bags filled with water dropped from windows doused the protesters, and a pitched battle with the police ensued.

Meanwhile, inside City Hall, Engdahl's place as tribune of the unemployed had been assumed by Sam Nessin, the twenty-one-year-old secretary of the New York Unemployed Council and a Communist candidate for state senator in the Bronx. Nessin denounced Mayor Jimmy Walker, presiding at the meeting, as "a grafting Tammany politician and a crook." The mayor thereupon lost his temper and shouted: "You dirty

Red! In about two minutes I'll jump down there and smash you in the face." Then, "livid with anger and throwing away his gavel," he started to go after Nessin. At that point police jumped the young Communist and four compatriots, ejected them from the room, threw them down the stairs, and beat them with nightsticks and blackjacks. By the time the one-sided battle ended, "the floor of the rotunda, the stairways, and the fine Colonial panelings were bloodstained." Nessin was hospitalized and charged with inciting to riot. The day after the disruption, the Board of Estimate unexpectedly appropriated one million dollars for unemployment relief for the first time. J. Louis Engdahl was not impressed: he called the expenditure a "crumb" thrown to the unemployed.[9]

The Party's Twelfth Plenum, meeting at the end of November 1930, put forward a six-point campaign to mobilize the unemployed, called for local united front conferences, local hunger marches, mass meetings to elect a delegation to an upcoming Washington conference on the unemployed, and a signature campaign. The program emphasized the concrete. It was necessary, Earl Browder reminded his comrades, to show the workers how the Communists could help them "to solve their immediate problems of bread and butter." The Comintern soon chimed in to tell the Party that the Unemployed Councils "must fight for immediate relief from the state" but should also "set up their own organs to secure housing for unemployed workers . . . to develop mass struggles against the evictions of unemployed workers, and to fight for food for the children of the unemployed." Although the major demand remained unemployment insurance at full wages, the Party was ordered to dispel the impression that it wanted the unemployed to refuse charity relief.[10]

Following this theoretical turn to the practical, a spate of practical activities occurred. Rent strikes, fights against evictions, and hunger marches were suddenly in the news. Alfred Wagenknecht reported marches in seventy-five cities and six states, enlisting 250,000 workers. In St. Paul, Minnesota, a group of unemployed occupied the state legislature for two hours, waving banners demanding "All War Funds to the Unemployed" and "For the Defense of the Soviet Union." Unemployed Councils focused on such daily needs as housing, specializing in moving renters' furniture back into apartments after landlords had put it on the street. Party spokesmen exulted that the Unemployed Councils at last seemed to be gaining a stable organization and leadership. In New York the Down Town Council of the Unemployed held daily meetings of 1,000 or more in front of an employment agency, held regular membership meetings, and collected dues of 1¢ and 2¢ per week. One Communist boasted that "the hunger marches, the demonstrations, the delegations to the city administration" were having a result; they were "forcing some of the cities to appropriate funds and relief for the unemployed, small as they may be."[11]

A new Party auxiliary was also created to lead the Comintern-ordered push for unemployment insurance. On November 11, a number of groups in the Party orbit, including the TUUL, the International Workers' Order (IWO), the Unemployed Councils, and the Party itself held a New York conference to create the National Campaign Committee for Unemployment Insurance and launch a drive for at least 1 million signatures. On February 10, 1931, 140 delegates—led by Alfred Wagenknecht, head of the committee—brought a claimed 1.4 million signatures to the Capitol. Taking no chances, police were out in force. Three delegates were ejected from the Senate gallery for interrupting a debate. The next day the gathering quietly adjourned and went home. Wagenknecht threatened that the next visit would not be as placid: "Next time we will not come with signatures. We will come with organized mass power."[12]

The Communists' visit led to a discussion in the House the following day. Several representatives discussed the desirability of deporting Communists. Fiorello LaGuardia of New York responded that Congress should pass some sort of unemployment relief to trim the radicals' sails. One congressman, at least, took the whole matter much more seriously. Representative Edward Eslick, a Tennessee Democrat fresh from service on the Fish Committee, warned his colleagues that they dared not underestimate the Communists despite their small numbers. He cited Patrick Henry, Mrs. O'Leary's cow, the bubonic plague, and "the man from Galilee" to prove that one match can light a powder keg. And, he warned his colleagues: "The powder keg is out yonder; the match is burning."[13]

The Comintern was less impressed with the modest progress being made in America. At its Eleventh Plenum in March 1931, it made known its displeasure. Ossip Piatnitsky raked several Parties over the coals for shortcomings in unemployed work, but he reserved his sharpest barbs for the American Communists. He first ridiculed their slogans "Work or Wages," saying that "if I were unemployed and in America, I should not have understood this slogan." S. Lozovsky broke in: "And in Moscow you understand it?"—a remark greeted with laughter. Dimitri Manuilsky joined the merriment at the expense of the embarrassed Americans: "Even the R.I.L.U. [Profintern] does not understand this slogan." Piatnitsky was not finished. He also did not like "Don't Starve—Fight" and remarked sarcastically: "I think that few people would wish to starve, even in America." Still another slogan, "Fight for the Seven-Hour Day and the Five-Day Week," was acceptable as far as it went, but by not adding "no reduction in wages" the Americans had failed to differentiate themselves from reformists or those proposing spreading the available work among more workers. Finally, Piatnitsky was not pleased with the Party's "abstract slogans" which suggested that partial reforms were impossible under capitalism.[14]

Piatnitsky came back to the Americans a little later by presenting them as a case study of bad work among the unemployed. It was clear to him that "the unemployed were without leadership. No work was carried on among them." He was also unhappy that in the spring of 1930 a Party plenum had rejected the idea that the Workers' International Relief (WIR) should set up soup kitchens. Louis Gibarti, international representative of the WIR, quickly fired off a letter to the Secretariat of the American Party urging their immediate creation of soup kitchens to feed large unemployed families, the long-term unemployed, and pregnant women. Soon after, Wagenknecht, who headed the WIR and was now directing unemployed work as well, dutifully demanded that the Unemployed Councils "give aid to starving families to the extent possible" while continuing to agitate for unemployment insurance as the major objective.[15]

All of these criticisms were mild in comparison to what came next. Moscow had previously directed that unemployed work was to be under the TUUL's auspices. Now, with the full implication that this idea had come from the Americans, Piatnitsky said: "It seems to me that this is what killed the unemployed movement, because there are few Red trade unions there. They have very few members." Piatnitsky thought that the unemployment movement "must be non-party, not attached to any party, nor to any kind of trade union" because otherwise non-Communist workers would shy away from it. He hastened to add that "the leadership must be strongly in the hands of the Trade Union Opposition or the Red trade unions, even more strongly than it has been up to the present, and, of course, in the hands of the Party. For this purpose no label or title is needed, but efficient energetic work in the spirit I have shown here."[16]

The Americans had begun to emphasize practical work among the unemployed even before this Comintern plenum. A major problem, however, continued to bedevil them. Even the most concrete successes left behind few organizational traces. Wagenknecht complained in May 1931 that six months of fighting evictions had meant that "thousands of unemployed workers' homes were kept intact," but the Unemployed Councils remained puny. However grateful they were for assistance, the recipients did not join the organization. The councils themselves were unable to expand much beyond the Party's own sphere of influence. Toward the end of 1931, Earl Browder sadly reported that the Unemployed Councils "remain narrow cadre organizations which do not have intimate day-by-day contact with the masses." He confessed that "with the removal of two or three comrades assigned by the Party, these organizations would actually collapse."[17]

Things were, however, about to pick up. In August 1931, representatives of eleven European Communist parties met in Prague to develop a new unemployment program in line with the Comintern plenum's views. Their draft recommended that the Unemployed Councils, in order to become "real united front organs," should no longer be subordinate to the Red trade unions. The Communists would retain their control by means of fractions within the councils. The Americans were, of course, amenable. At the CPUSA's August 1931 plenum, Jack Stachel denied that "formal affiliations" with the TUUL were required. In fact, he thought the councils should be organized on a neighborhood basis, not through the revolutionary unions. The Central Committee soon issued a new, ten-point program for unemployed work that called for an immediate grant of $150 to every out-of-work American plus $50 for every dependent; an immediate end to all evictions; free milk to children of the unemployed; and "full wages to all workers unemployed from any cause whatsoever." The new plan also included a National Hunger March on Washington.[18]

A. W. Mills, formerly district organizer in Buffalo, was assigned to take charge of the preparations as organizer of the National Hunger March Committee of the Unemployed Councils. Although the call for the march came from the Unemployed Councils, the Party's hand was, as usual, decisive. Not only was Mills a party functionary, but the goal of the exercise was to advance Party interests. The Thirteenth Plenum proclaimed: "We must aim as a result of the hunger march not only to build organizations of the unemployed, but also to recruit members into the T.U.U.L. unions and the Party."[19]

Another Communist active in the preparations was Herbert Benjamin, destined to direct Communist work among the unemployed for most of the decade. Born Benjamin Greffenson in 1900 in Illinois, the fourteenth child of Jewish immigrants from Vilna, Lithuania, he had left school in sixth grade. He had joined the Young People's Socialist League by the time he was fifteen and the IWW before he was twenty. In 1921 he joined the Communist party in Erie, Pennsylvania, the only "American" in the whole branch. Chosen to attend the underground convention in Bridgman, Michigan, in 1922, he adopted a pseudonym, Herbert Benjamin, and answered to it for the rest of his life.

Benjamin got his first paying Party job as organizational secretary in

Ohio in 1925. The following year he was district organizer in Buffalo, and by 1927 he was moved to the larger Philadelphia district. In late 1929 he was brought to New York as the district's organizational secretary. Benjamin was identified with the large, violent clashes in New York in 1930 and was not a favorite of "Williams," the Comintern representative. Exiled to Cleveland by Browder, he was given an easier post in New York in mid-1931 to enable him to recuperate from malnutrition. He was asked to attend the Prague Unemployment Conference as a delegate and, after his return, to take over direction of the unemployed movement. Benjamin accepted. When he got to Berlin, however, he learned that the Prague conference was already over. After six weeks he went to Moscow, where he spent six more weeks working on an unemployment resolution for the United States. He returned in October, was appointed national field representative, and was sent to Washington to prepare for the arrival of the marchers.[20]

When an advance guard of seventeen hunger marchers was arrested in front of the White House on November 27, the capital braced for trouble. A Secret Service report that was leaked to the newspapers described Benjamin as an "agitator of the worst type." Just days before the march, a forged leaflet appeared in Washington, purportedly issued by the Communists, calling on the workers to arm themselves and seize the government. The new Washington police chief, retired Brigadier General Pelham Glassford, shrewdly downplayed the dangers and defused the potential for trouble. He declared he intended to treat the marchers as "just tourists coming to Washington but with a lot of publicity." He met with Benjamin and, discovering that there was no money for accommodations, found cots for the men and persuaded socially prominent women to pay rent to put up the female marchers. On Sunday, December 6, 1,600 delegates arrived outside Washington and were met by the police, who escorted them into the city. They got off their trucks and hiked the final two miles, four abreast. After the Salvation Army fed them beans and coffee, the marchers proceeded to the Washington Auditorium, where they held a meeting and heard speeches by Benjamin, Weinstone, and Foster.[21]

The following day the marchers, led by the Red Front Band, paraded to Capitol Hill. For the first time in history, Benjamin later boasted, "The International was sung at the seat of the nation's government." However, they moved up the steps to find the doors locked and "automatic shot guns and tear gas bombs trained on them." Two delegations were allowed inside the Capitol; they approached the House and Senate chambers, but those doors were also barred. Benjamin refused an offer to hand his petition to the sergeant-at-arms. "We're not handing in a petition," he responded. "We are making demands in the name of 12,000,000 starving unemployed workers. We demand to enter." Unimpressed, the police shoved the delegations out of the building. From the Capitol the hunger marchers struck out for the White House, where the President also refused to see them or receive their demands. Then it was on to A.F. of L. headquarters, where, inexplicably, President William Green agreed to meet with six representatives. Green started to lecture his listeners that they were dupes of the Communists; they interrupted with boos and jeers and walked out on him. By now the hunger marchers were exhausted. Chief Glassford had laid out meandering routes to tire them out, and many were "just shuffling along."[22]

At a meeting later that day, the delegates set up a permanent unemployed organization independent of the TUUL and chose a National Bureau whose four leading figures were all prominent Communists—Benjamin, Foster, Carl Winter, and A. W. Mills. The following day the Washington police, courteous to the last, found gas for the trucks, helped crank their engines, and happily watched the First Hunger March leave the city. Despite the fears expressed prior to the demonstrators' arrival, the event had been noticeably peaceful.[23]

Three months after the hunger marchers left Washington, a much more violent confrontation took place during a local hunger march in Detroit, one of the cities hardest hit by the Depression. There were only about 800 Communists in the Detroit area. The Unemployed Councils had not been very active. The Auto Workers Union, a TUUL affiliate, was not a force to be reckoned with: John Schmies, then the TUUL's district organizer in Michigan, complained in July 1932 that "until recently, the Auto Workers Union, you might well say, did not exist." In late November 1931 a few hundred people under the lead of the Young Communist League (YCL) held a "Briggs Hunger March" in Highland Park. (The Briggs Manufacturing Company produced bodies for Ford cars.) Although it had been small, the march inspired the Ford members of the Auto Workers Union to plan a similar hunger march to the Ford River Rouge plant. At an unemployed conference in late January 1932, Rudy Baker, the Party's Detroit district organizer, called for a Ford hunger march on March 7.[24]

Somewhere between 3,000 and 5,000 people gathered just inside the Detroit city line, about one mile from the Ford plant in Dearborn. Their demands, which they hoped to present to Ford officials, included jobs for all laid-off workers, a slowdown of the assembly line, and a halt to foreclosures on homes of all ex–Ford workers. Al Goetz, a leader of the local Unemployed Council, called for an orderly march but warned: "If we are attacked, we will know how to defend ourselves." As the marchers approached the Dearborn city limits, fifty policemen from the Ford-controlled municipality ordered them to turn back because they had no parade permit. They refused and continued forward, to be met by salvos of tear gas. Enraged, the marchers retaliated with rocks; the outnumbered police retreated toward the plant, pursued by the marchers. Firemen aimed ice-cold water from hoses on the demonstrators, and the police, augmented by members of Ford's Service Department, began firing their revolvers into the crowd. The stunned marchers began to retreat, pulling the wounded with them, when Harry Bennett, head of Ford's private police, suddenly drove out of the plant into the crowd. Hit on the head by a rock, Bennett was pulled from the battle scene. The police then opened up with machine guns, mowing down the terrified marchers. When the firing finally stopped, four demonstrators were dead and more than sixty were injured. Three of the dead were Communists, two of them members of the YCL.[25]

Police in Detroit responded by arresting forty-four Communists and putting out warrants on Foster, Goetz, Schmies, and two others on charges of criminal syndicalism. Party and auxiliary offices were raided. A grand jury was empaneled to investigate Communism: one of its prosecutors established the tenor of the probe by telling a reporter, "I say I wish they'd killed a few more of those damned rioters." The arrested were soon released and the warrants withdrawn, and the grand jury did not return any indictments. The following Saturday the victims' bodies lay in state at Ferry Hall. Above the coffins was a huge red banner with Lenin's picture. After Rudy Baker spoke, a massive funeral procession of 20,000 to 40,000 people marched to the cemetery, where all four were buried in a common grave within view of River Rouge. One observer "had to remind himself that this was not 'Red Berlin,' but American Detroit."[26]

True to form, the Communists were as angry with the liberal Democratic mayor of Detroit, Frank Murphy, as with Henry Ford. Although his city had given the hunger marchers a permit, the Party blamed him for the "reign of terror" that followed and charged that Detroit police had participated in the shooting. The huge funeral throng carried banners urging "Smash the Ford-Murphy Police Terror." Telegrams from Party units, IWO chapters, and TUUL unions poured into city hall denouncing the mayor. One Communist writer explained that "the massacre brought out the function of Mayor Murphy and the Socialists who supported him—to keep the workers unorganized and trusting in them, and when the workers try to help themselves, to shoot them down."[27]

A few months later it was the U.S. army that faced the unemployed in the streets of Washington, D.C. In 1924, under pressure from veterans, Congress had passed the Adjusted Service Compensation Bill, providing a "bonus" to all veterans of World War I that would be payable with interest in 1945. However, as the Depression took its toll on savings and jobs, pressure mounted on Congress to redeem the bonus certificates. The Hoover administration was just as opposed to this form of unemployment aid as to unemployment insurance. In 1930 Congress did permit veterans to borrow 50 percent of the money due them, but Representative Wright Patman of Texas, who introduced a measure for the immediate payment of the bonus, could not get action on his bill.

Although the bonus was a hot political issue, the Communists were relatively slow to seize on it. Their own veterans' group was not originally interested in the bonus at all. The Workers Ex-Servicemen's League (WESL) was set up in May 1930 after the Comintern, evaluating the results of the March 6 demonstration, advised the Americans of the need for some proletarian self-defense in the face of police attacks. Envisioned as a "defense corps" to protect Party meetings, demonstrations, and hunger marches, the WESL soon expanded its horizons and in late January 1931 called for the payment in cash of the full value of the bonus. As the WESL spent more and more time on the bonus issue, its original role became less and less significant.[28]

Payment of the bonus may not have been the Communists' original goal, but a Bonus March was probably their idea. At the National Hunger March in December 1931, more than 400 veterans caucused and agreed to fight for the bonus. In April 1932, James Ford, the Party's candidate for Vice President, and Samuel Stember, both WESL members, testified before the House Ways and Means Committee on the bonus. They denounced Wright Patman and the Veterans of Foreign Wars for trying to foster the "illusion" that veterans could "win their demands by the maneuvers of the Congressional committees and by the use of the ballot without mass pressure." Ford and Stember called on veterans to organize to pass the bonus and suggested planning "for a march of delegates of war veterans on Congress before it adjourned its seventy-second session." The WESL soon created a National Bonus March Provisional Committee, headed by Emmanuel Levin, an ex-Marine who had been the Party's district organizer in Los Angeles and was serving as business manager of *The Daily Worker.*[29]

Organizing the Unemployed

The Communists were not the only ones getting ready to march, however. Some 300 veterans in Portland, Oregon, left town on May 11, led by a former used-car salesman and unemployed cannery worker named W. W. Waters. As Waters' ragtag group moved across country, it not only picked up recruits but inspired thousands more to make their way to the nation's capital. Eventually, some 20,000 men reached Washington. Police Chief Glassford urged the first arrivals to form the Bonus Expeditionary Forces (BEF), maneuvered the election of Waters as leader, and was himself elected secretary-treasurer. Bitterly critical of Waters, whom they accused of being a police agent and fascist, the Communists reminded the veterans that they themselves were their "most reliable friends."[30]

Most of the veterans were of another mind. Shortly after his arrival, Waters promised the Washington police that the BEF would not tolerate Communists: "If we find any red agitators in the group we'll take care of them and take them to the district line. We came here under the same flag for which we fought." Two men were flogged for handing out leaflets printed by the Provisional Bonus Committee. A week later Emmanuel Levin was thrown out of the Anacostia Flats campground by veterans. A march called by the Provisional Bonus March Committee drew only thirty men and was canceled. Waters later insisted that his "chief problem with the Communists was to prevent the men of the BEF, literally, from almost killing any Communist they found among them."[31]

To their chagrin, the Communists discovered they had lost control of the Bonus March. Levin insisted that the Communists had originated the demonstration, the government charged that Communists were leading it, and established veterans groups denounced it as Communist-controlled. *The Daily Worker,* however, admitted that the Bonus March had arisen "spontaneously" and confessed, in a typical understatement, that the "communists are not leading an overwhelming majority of the bonus marchers."[32]

The Patman Bonus Bill passed the House and came before the Senate on June 17. It was badly defeated. Waters pledged to stay until the bonus was paid, and thousands of veterans settled into makeshift tents or cardboard huts. The veterans' mood turned more sullen, and the WESL stepped up its efforts. Led by John Pace, a thirty-four-year-old ex-businessman from Detroit, they began to occupy abandoned government buildings. Born in Centerville, Tennessee, Pace had worked his way up from factory worker to owner of a small contracting business. He lost everything he had owned in the Depression, joined the Communist party in the winter of 1930–1931, and soon was active in unemployed work in

Detroit. In 1932 he became the Michigan organizer of the WESL and led a contingent to Washington. Pace's group was followed by other veterans, and soon a number of buildings scheduled for demolition along Pennsylvania Avenue housed between 500 and 5,000 veterans.[33]

As Congress neared adjournment, the demonstrations grew smaller and more and more veterans began to take advantage of Veterans Administration help to go home. Some, however, had nowhere to go. On July 28 the police began clearing veterans from the abandoned buildings in downtown Washington. Brief scuffles with WESL vets were brought under control, but then two veterans were killed and two police injured. Chief of Staff Douglas MacArthur, assisted by Major Dwight Eisenhower, directed 600 soldiers, using tear gas and bayonets, to clear the downtown area. That night the army drove through the Anacostia campground, chased its residents across the Maryland line, and burned their shacks. Herbert Hoover justified his actions by claiming that "a considerable part of those remaining are not veterans, many are Communists and persons with criminal records." MacArthur claimed that "the country on July 27th was one week before a revolution." To Earl Browder, the Bonus Marchers were "unquestionably merely the shock troop of the unemployed millions" and "the most revolutionary manifestation ever witnessed in America for generations."[34]

There was, however, a serious disagreement within the Party Secretariat over the Bonus March. When William Weinstone returned from Moscow in late 1931, he began planning to dethrone Browder, still not fully established as Party leader. At the April 1932 plenum it was Weinstone, not Browder, who reported on behalf of the Politburo. That summer he challenged Browder for leadership on the Bonus March issue. Weinstone argued that the Communists were compromising themselves by associating with the "right wing elements" who controlled the march. If the Workers Ex-Servicemen's League could not direct the march, he wanted to dissociate the Party from the affair. Browder later recalled: "We referred it to Moscow to get it adjudicated there and he took it to Moscow with him and he got a crushing defeat there. They supported me 100 percent." One Comintern spokesman even criticized the Party for taking "a completely incorrect line from the very start" by isolating the WESL from other veterans. Another spokesman complained about the inconsistent *Daily Worker*, which could not decide whether the marchers were potential allies or enemies.[35]

Even though they had not been able to control the Bonus March, the Communists were given credit for it by government officials eager to justify their own actions by raising the Red menace. The Communists were thus confirmed in their own estimation that they alone were the saviors of the oppressed. When the Party's Central Committee summed up the lessons of the Bonus March, it declared that the march marked "a new stage in the radicalization of the masses and will become a landmark in the history of the class struggle." While admitting that portions of the movement were politically backward, the Party leadership insisted on its "objectively revolutionary character as a mass movement directed against American capitalism." In spite of all its earlier reminders not to get carried away by a large, spectacular demonstration, the Central Committee declared that "the Bonus March revealed an underestimation of the radicalization of the masses, particularly the new upward surge." During the Third Period hope sprang eternal.[36]

Meanwhile, however, the organization of the unemployed remained as difficult and frustrating as before. The Communists knew precisely what the problem was, but they seemed helpless to solve it. The Party's grip on the Unemployed Councils was suffocating. Herbert Benjamin protested: "Party organizations instead of mobilizing the membership for participation in Unemployed Councils and committees, themselves take over the functions of these united front organizations. Where non-Party workers are attracted to our movement in such cases, they find themselves excluded from all participation in the actual work of planning and leading actions." Rudy Baker sadly reported that the Ford Hunger March had left as few traces behind as most other demonstrations. He attributed this to the fact that "after each demonstration and mass meeting, the Party lost contact with these workers." Functionaries never talked to non-Party people and thus remained unaware of workers' attitudes. Baker concluded that the Party was still "for the workers and not of the workers."[37]

There were isolated bright spots in unemployed work. One was St. Louis, where the Unemployed Council organized the city's first hunger march on July 8, 1932. Five thousand demonstrators forced the mayor to order immediate relief to the unemployed. Three days later, more than 10,000 angry demonstrators discovered that he would not meet with their delegation and began to march on City Hall. The police opened fire, wounding four and arresting forty-eight. Bill Gebert, the district organizer, reported that Party membership doubled and the Unemployed Council experienced a surge in block organizations. The singular success of St. Louis to the contrary, one disappointed Communist called unemployed work "our weak point" in August. He complained that since the Hunger March in December, "very little progress can be recorded in this work and in many places we see an actual backward trend." The failure was blamed largely on Party members' misunderstanding of how to organize the unemployed. Instead of helping the jobless to elect organs consisting of the unemployed, the Communists were accused of gathering "simply a meeting of leading and most active comrades, or even non-Party workers, who come together more or less regularly to speak about work among the unemployed."[38]

To worry the Communists further, in 1932 they faced their first real competition in the struggle for the unemployed. The Socialists set up Workers' Unemployed Leagues. More ominously, Father James Cox, a Catholic priest from Pittsburgh, launched his own unemployed movement, leading 12,000 people to Washington in early January. The Communists were plainly worried, charging that Cox's Blue Shirts movement contained "national fascist tendencies lined up with catholic religion." They recognized that his denunciations of big capitalists, demands for work for the jobless, and threats to organize a "jobless party" could be a powerful detriment to their own influence. Throughout the year he was frequently attacked as a major fascist menace.[39]

The Communist response was to step up attacks on "social-fascists" for misleading the unemployed. A Party plenum in September attacked the Unemployed Councils for allowing "spontaneous unemployed movements" in Pittsburgh, Seattle, and Youngstown to fall "into the hands of social-fascist leaders." In Chicago, where a Socialist named Karl Borders had successfully organized a Workers' Committee on Unemployment, the Communists took the bold step of meeting with "social-fascists." The Chicago Unemployed Council heard that Borders' group, which claimed 15,000 members, was about to call for a united front conference to discuss a relief cut ordered by Cook County. The council, with about 10,000 members, issued its own call, sending invitations to the Workers' Committee and the Workers League of America, an unemployment off-shoot of the tiny Proletarian party. At a preliminary meeting attended by fifteen delegates from each group, various disagreements were hashed out. The main conference, held on October 16, 1932, drew 730 delegates from 350 organizations, including such tried and true "social-fascists" as A.F. of L. locals, Socialist party locals, and Farmer-Labor party locals, to say nothing of four representatives of the Khaki Shirts, considered an outright "fascist" group.[40]

For the first time during the Third Period, Communists were attending a united front conference with people whom they had labeled betrayers of the working class. Lest the wrong impression spread, John Williamson, speaking for the Communist party, lit into Borders and the other "social-fascists." He accused the former of "serving the best interests of the bosses" and called for a united front from below. *The Communist* later claimed that "the conference was not mechanically controlled by us. We probably had direct organizational contact with no more than a third of the delegates." Nevertheless, the Party's candidate for chairman of the conference, Joe Weber of the TUUL, decisively defeated Borders by 360 to 94. Further, Borders' own caucus defeated his proposal to withdraw from a hunger march that had been decided on to protest the relief cuts.[41]

The hunger march was peacefully held on October 31, with *The Daily Worker* claiming 50,000 marchers. The authorities, frightened, rescinded the cuts. One group of Communists maintained, however, that they should not have sat down with Borders, "that by doing so we are compromising ourselves." Another group, led by Alfred Verblin, opposed Williamson's speech as needlessly provocative and unrelated to the immediate issues. Verblin feared that the rank-and-file members of "social-fascist" groups might regard the denunciations as "unnecessary and disruptive" and that such criticisms would "alienate them from us rather than attract them to us." Bill Gebert, speaking for the Party leadership, denounced both views. Refusing to meet with Borders, he recognized, would mean creating "a united front with ourselves," a problem that arose elsewhere: "In almost every other locality the movement is so paralyzed by sectarian tendencies that they cannot arrive at the level of struggle to face such problems." As for Verblin's "capitulary theory," Gebert warned that "unity at any price means no unity of the masses, no united struggle, it means neglect of the struggle."[42]

The unfortunate Borders, having learned that the Communists were willing to sit in the same room with him only to denounce him as a social-fascist and undermine his leadership of his own organization, went on to set up a Federation of Unemployed Workers' Leagues of America that claimed a membership of 100,000, more than twice the Unemployed Councils' claim of 40,000. The Communists, meanwhile, felt they were at last surging forward. Browder credited the Unemployed Councils with actions in at least one hundred cities in September and October of 1932. The Party confidently geared up for the Second National Hunger March.[43]

The second march began much like the first. The Communist party, not the Unemployed Councils, first broached the idea. In late September the Party's Fifteenth Plenum, concerned about the growing menace of social-fascism in the unemployed field, decided that the best way to reinvigorate the Communists' effort was another national hunger march. A few nay-sayers were rebuked for "opportunist tailism." The Unemployed Councils met in October and dutifully set the march in motion. Plans were made for "united front conferences" to elect 3,000 delegates, gather food and clothing, and arrange transportation for nine columns of marchers to converge on Washington. The chief demands were to be $50 winter relief to each jobless worker plus $10 for every dependent in addition to the available local relief. The Party was able to mobilize a network of members and sympathizers across the country to provide assistance and perform various chores. An FBI informant provided the most unlikely story of a source of assistance. He claimed that in return for a contribution from the Women's Christian Temperance Union, the marchers adopted as one of their slogans "We Want Bread Not Beer."[44]

Although the leadership of the march remained firmly in Communist hands, the rank and file were recruited elsewhere. Moissaye Olgin, a leading Jewish Communist, observed that the marchers had been "elected haphazardly on bread lines, in pool rooms, in flop houses, in block committees. Most of them were a raw element, just drawn into the movement." Browder claimed, "A vast majority of the marchers are not Communists, but most of them become sympathetic in the course of the march."[45]

This march would probably have not differed much from the first one if the Communists had had their way. They planned to do almost exactly what they had a year before. But the government had changed its policy. The Washington authorities were still skittish about the Bonus March; they were determined that nothing like it would occur again. Chief Glassford, considered too "soft," was forced out and a new police chief, Major Ernest Brown, installed to pursue a much harder line. Wild tales and rumors helped build a climate of violence. Malcolm Cowley reported that one story going around Washington had one of the marchers' trucks filled with machine guns to be distributed to the unemployed and used for an assault on the White House. Enterprising salesmen sold riot insurance. In Wilmington, Delaware, the police superintendent drove his car into a marcher, and the women demonstrators were herded into a nearby church. Police fired tear gas into the sanctuary and then barricaded the women inside for the night. When the male marchers charged to the rescue of their compatriots, a wild night of fighting followed during which four policemen were injured, two the column's leaders—Carl Reeve and Ben Gold—were "badly beaten," and Gold, and women Party leaders Ann Burlak and Rebecca Grecht were among those arrested.[46]

On Sunday, December 4, 1932, 2,500 hunger marchers finally arrived in the capital and were met by police who shepherded them into a cul de sac. The enraged marchers demanded to be let into the city, but the police commissioner threatened to have his men, armed with machine guns and tear gas, open fire. Outmaneuvered, the marchers bedded down for the night in the open. The following day they huddled in their "prison," many obviously suffering from cold and hunger, while the police openly "jeered and hooted" at them, and frantic negotiations took place to end the impasse. Herbert Benjamin met with Vice President Curtis. The latter refused to permit a parade on the Capitol grounds. After the failure of his mission, Benjamin and the other march leaders decided to parade within their own confined domain. Malcolm Cowley graphically detailed what came next:

> The Red Front Band, dressed in Soviet-style plain grey uniforms, struck up a tune and the line moved forward. A shudder of anticipation passed through the ranks of the police. Holsters were patted and gas bombs passed from hand to hand. "Come on you yellow bastards" one of the policemen shouted. The line of marchers came on, step by step, till they almost touched the rope that marked the limits of their prison. The police stirred happily. The movie men behind them got their gas masks out and began cranking their cameras. Reporters, pencil in hand, prepared to describe the slaughter. Above the tooting and tinkling of the band you could hear the scream of police sirens in the city. Suddenly the leader of the marchers gave an order. The column swung left again, retraced its steps. . . . The police slumped back with an air of disappointment. After all, there would be no riot.

Benjamin, boasting that "we are surrounded by the biggest display of armed force the U.S. Government has ever sent against the workers," warned that if violence occurred, it would be on the heads of the police. The by-now worried Police Chief Brown agreed to Benjamin's suggestion that the police turn their backs to the encampment. Shortly afterwards, Brown returned to inform the Communist leader that the hunger marchers could parade to the Capitol the next day.[47]

The hunger marchers finally reached Capitol Hill on December 6, marching six miles under the most rigid police supervision on record in Washington while 75,000 people lined the streets. Police were all about, three planes flew overhead, and 4,000 Regular Army troops were on alert at nearby Fort Myers. Just opposite the Capitol grounds on Pennsylvania Avenue, the marchers were stopped and two delegations of ten members each went on to meet with the Vice President and Speaker of the House. Later that afternoon, Congressman LaGuardia escorted the marchers to the Maryland line to ensure that there would be no further trouble. Within twenty-four hours, all of them were gone. A small contingent from the Workers Ex-Servicemen's League remained to press for payment of the bonus.[48]

A *Daily Worker* editorial called the march "a splendid victory" and "a

striking defeat of the policy of the hunger government at Washington."
The Communists had reason to be pleased. They had garnered national
publicity, forced the government to back down, and avoided violence. If
there was a disappointing aspect to the march, it was its failure to include
enough non-Communists from "social-fascist" organizations. Israel
Amter, who was chosen to replace Benjamin as secretary of the National
Committee of Unemployed Councils, worried that the councils comprised only a small fraction of unemployed workers and that social-
fascist influence among the out-of-work was growing. The workers had
to be taught, he emphasized, "that there is no need of more than one
unemployed movement in this country, and that we are the champions of
unity."[49]

And yet, the Communists' actions belied their own words. Their
domination of the hunger march was complete. Not only was Amter, a
one-time classical musician, sent in by the Communist party to direct
unemployed work, but Bud Reynolds was elected chairman and Benjamin became national organizer. Eight of the ten leaders at the march
campground were prominent Communists. To the Communists, a successful united front was one that included the rank and file of both non-
Communist and Communist groups under Communist leadership. The
tangible accomplishments of such united fronts as the hunger marches
were less important than their propaganda value and the opportunities
they provided for dramatic and heroic gestures. Building stable organizations was far harder.[50]

4

The Intellectuals
Go Left

THE AMERICAN COMMUNIST movement entered the Third Period with little influence among intellectuals and enormous suspicion of them. The Communists watched carefully as intellectuals, startled and dismayed by the Depression, turned leftward. Well aware that many were looking at the Party as a potential home or at least temporary lodging, Communist leaders were far from regarding this newfound opportunity with enthusiasm. Intellectuals were troublesome. Their class origins made them suspect. They had an annoying habit of independent thinking. They were congenitally reluctant to submit to the discipline that a Communist party demanded of its members. While William Foster exulted that the economic crisis meant that "the hotsy-totsy days for the intellectuals are over," he matter-of-factly predicted that most of them would find their way to fascism and social-fascism. Only "a small percent of these intellectuals, especially those with a proletarian background, will become genuinely revolutionary and real Communists."[1]

Earl Browder opened the new decade with a denunciation of Scott Nearing, a Party intellectual, for his unauthorized publication of a work on imperialism. Nearing was a radical young economist whose outspoken political views had earned him the distinction of being fired from both the University of Pennsylvania and Toledo University. He had collaborated with a young Communist intellectual, Joseph Freeman, in 1925 to write *Dollar Diplomacy*, an exposé of American imperialism. The following year, Nearing joined the Party. At the end of the decade he prepared a new book. Submitted to Moscow, the manuscript was found wanting and permission to publish denied. Rather than acquiesce in suppressing his own work, Nearing resigned from the Communist party, while expressing his earnest desire to remain on friendly terms with it. The Party did not recognize his voluntary departure. He was expelled by the Central Committee, which also deposited him "on the scrap heap of the revolution" and told him in no uncertain terms that "to be a friend of the Party is to be a soldier in its lines. Outside the ranks of the Party, the 'friend' ceases to be a positive factor on the side of the working class in the revolutionary struggle and therefore strengthens the enemy of the proletariat."[2]

Max Bedacht was even less sympathetic to the complaints of intellectuals. One of the few prewar radical intellectuals who remained a Communist, Mike Gold, had pilloried the Party's publishing arm, International Publishers, for ignoring "proletarian literature," one of Gold's crusades. It "makes little attempt to influence either the popular mind or our intellectuals," he complained, and called it "as stodgy and unenterprising, in a Communist way, as the Yale University Press." Bedacht responded by belittling "self-styled 'American proletarian writers' " for an inability to understand real workers. Defending International Publishers, he identified numerous examples of proletarian literature it had published, including Lenin's highly technical *Materialism and Empirio-Criticism*.[3]

In an era when political commitments were anathema to most intellectuals, Mike Gold had made his to Communism. Despite a sometimes bumpy path, he never abandoned it. Born Irwin Granich, he emerged from the slums of the Lower East Side of New York which he so devastatingly sketched in his book *Jews Without Money*. By the time he was twelve years old, Gold had quit school and gone to work. His radical allegiance was first kindled in 1914 when he wandered into an unemployment demonstration in Union Square and witnessed a policeman club an old Jewish woman. He bought his first copy of *The Masses* then and soon saw it publish his own first poem, about police clubbings. Over the next six years, Gold tried to combine literary and political pursuits. He wrote plays for Eugene O'Neill's Provincetown Players, reported on a strike for an anarchist newspaper, and then fled to Mexico to escape the draft during World War I. In 1921 he returned to New York to become an editor of *The Liberator*, the successor to *The Masses*, which had been closed down by postal inspectors for opposing the war.[4]

He was joined on the staff by another Jewish radical whose route to Communism had been quite different. Joseph Freeman was born in Russia but grew up in the Williamsburg section of Brooklyn. A product of a Yiddish-Hebrew household, he gradually immersed himself in American culture but retained the socialist convictions of his youth. A precocious student, Freeman was able to attend Columbia University, where his radicalism was nurtured, thanks to his father's increasing prosperity in the real-estate business. After two years as an expatriate in Paris and London, he returned to America in 1921 and began to contribute to *The Liberator*.[5]

Gold and Freeman were rarities. There were many intellectuals who were disgusted with bourgeois society but very few who were willing to take the step of actually becoming Communists. The absence of a literary-political outlet eventually encouraged a disparate group of intellectuals, few of whom were Communists, to scrounge up enough money in May 1926 to begin publishing *The New Masses*. "The mass of editors and contributors were liberals," Joseph Freeman recalled, "far from understanding or sympathizing with Communism." Even many of the radicals believed the "magazine should not be 'political' but 'artistic' and revolutionary." When Mike Gold assumed the editorship in 1928, *The New Masses* began a steady drift into the orbit of the Communist party but remained far more tolerant of political deviation than the official Party press. For more than a year after being denounced and expelled from the Party, Scott Nearing continued to write book reviews. The anarchist Carlo Tresca appeared occasionally in its pages. V. F. Calverton, another apostate previously read out of the revolutionary movement by Party leaders, contributed articles in 1930. Gold even published Upton Sinclair, a prominent Socialist and frequent political candidate of that arch "social-fascist" party. Defending Sinclair from a critic who doubted his work belonged in *The New Masses*, Gold affirmed a standard of literary criticism that both he and his Party were soon to repudiate: "It is a mistake to judge him solely as a member of the Socialist Party. A writer in the last analysis must be judged by his work; not by his private morals or party affiliations. It is almost impossible to approach literature and art in the party spirit."[6]

What Gold hoped more than anything else to encourage was a new kind of writing that told the story of working people. He wanted *The New*

Masses to aid the development of "proletarian-realism" dealing "with the *real conflicts* of men and women." The new literature "must have a social theme," be direct and clear, be a "cinema in words," and, preferably, be written by workers themselves. No more Proust, the "master-masturbator of the bourgeois literature"; from now on, workers would write for other workers. Joseph Kalar, a worker and "proletarian writer" who contributed to the magazine, felt it needed to do even more. He complained that the magazine still paid too much attention to "paid scribblers" when it should be concentrating on appealing to "lumber-jacks, hoboes, miners, clerks, section hands, machinists, harvest hands, waiters," and others who like to "read a good snappy article on their line of work." The choice open to *The New Masses* was between "embryo artists or the people who sweat."[7]

Joseph Freeman confessed in 1930 that "the revolutionary movement has not yet produced a strong and unified literary group" but held out hope that a change was imminent. Both he and Gold were convinced that it was only a matter of time before writers and artists would emerge who were eager to reflect and bestir the new world being born in America. Not only was *The New Masses* actively encouraging proletarian writing, but a new Party auxiliary especially designed for intellectuals was just getting off the ground. Much was expected of it.[8]

Organized in October 1929, the John Reed Clubs was the first auxiliary to attempt to appeal to intellectuals. It was named for one of the founders of American Communism, a Harvard-educated journalist buried in the Kremlin. The auxiliary's New York club began with only fifty members but an ambitious program. As part of its goal to bring culture to the workers, the first priority was to create a "proletarian culture." An art exhibition at the Workers Cooperative Apartments in the Bronx had works by Art Young, Hugo Gellert, Louis Lozowick, William Gropper, Jacob Burck, Morris Pass, Anton Refregier, and Esther Shemitz. Club members offered classes to workers in music, the graphic arts, ballet, and the theater. The Workers Dance Group announced that its "sole purpose is to serve the revolutionary movement by using the dance as a medium to further inspire the worker to greater militancy in the class struggle."[9]

Small as these efforts were, they excited Communist intellectuals. Joe Pass exulted that 150 workers in Brownsville had attended a symposium on art and had fired enthusiastic questions and criticism at the participants. Gold reported that an art exhibition had elicited strong reactions from workers who "razzed the still-lifes, nudes and several other pieces of stale academicism" while preferring "strong modern stuff." The literature club was off to a slower start, but the irrepressible Gold was filled with grandiose hopes for its future. He even proposed that every John Reed Clubs writer go to work in an industry for several years to become an authority on that line of work. Then, in a few years, *The New Masses* could be put on "an industrial basis." Once that task was accomplished, "instead of having a board of contributing editors made up of those vague, rootless people known as writers, we will have a staff of industrial correspondents" speaking in "the tongue of the working class." [10]

Both *The New Masses* and the John Reed Clubs jumped at the opportunity to send representatives to the Second World Plenum of the International Bureau of Revolutionary Literature in Kharkov, Russia, in November 1930. Although John Dos Passos, the most famous radical novelist in America, did not take advantage of his invitation, Mike Gold led the American delegation of artists Fred Ellis and William Gropper, writers Joshua Kunitz and A. B. Magil, and film critic Harry Alan Potamkin. Politics, far more than culture, was the dominant theme of the meeting. The American delegates reported that "the entire work of the Plenum pivoted around the war danger with particular stress on the necessity of organizing the defense of the Soviet Union." The Americans agreed to a variety of organizational proposals. Before they could formally affiliate to the International Bureau, both the magazine and the clubs had to acquiesce to a ten-point program that called for attracting proletarians, "radicalized intellectuals," and blacks to their ranks, organizing "agitprop troupes," securing more translations of Marxist classics, and so on. Point 3 enjoined them to organize "on a national scale a federation of all cultural groups in all languages," and point 6 directed the John Reed Clubs to build branches outside of New York. [11]

The Chicago John Reed Club, with only fifty members, took the initiative in May 1931 of forming the first Workers' Cultural League in conformity with the Kharkov directives. In mid-June the New Yorkers hosted 265 delegates from 130 groups claiming 20,000 members, who formed the Workers' Cultural Federation (WCF). It was designed to be the Communist party's cultural arm. Its Russian parent sent a telegram expressing "HOPE FEDERATION WILL PURSUE CORRECT LINE IN ITS FIGHT AGAINST IMPERIALISM, AGAINST CLASS, NATIONAL, RACIAL OPPRESSION IN STRUGGLE FOR CULTURE NATIONAL IN FORM PROLETARIAN IN SUBSTANCE." The Russians need not have worried. The WCF manifesto faithfully echoed the Party line, even to the touching faith in the TUUL that was then so characteristic, averring that "the revolutionary trade unions must, in fact, become the basis of all the cultural work." [12]

Not everyone present was a Communist. John Dos Passos attended, and Theodore Dreiser and Upton Sinclair joined him on the honorary presidium. The dominant note, though, was the Communist one. Alexander Trachtenberg of International Publishers, A. B. Magil, and Mike Gold were featured speakers. Jack Stachel appealed "for the creation of a fighting proletarian culture that would be an integral part of the working-class struggle." The delegates, from a potpourri of drama, art, literature, music, sports, and even some Esperanto groups, enthusiastically subscribed to the idea that "culture is a weapon" and adopted resolutions supporting the NMU mine strike then in progress, *The Daily Worker*, and the defense of the Soviet Union. One of the new group's organizers reiterated the WCF's role as an adjunct to the Party; its tasks included helping working-class organizations develop a cultural program, bringing American culture to foreign-language groups, aiding new workers' cultural groups, and creating such new organizations as a proletarian anti-religious union. The fledgling Workers' Cultural Federation, however, barely got off the ground. By April 1932 it had "reorganized for active work." Although some of its constituent units continued to thrive, little more was heard of the WCF.[13]

The John Reed Clubs and the Friends of the Soviet Union also co-sponsored a meeting to protest anti-Soviet propaganda. Mike Gold was joined by non-Communists Waldo Frank, Harvey O'Connor, and Roger Baldwin. The gathering drew 3,000 people and produced an appeal defending the "workers' fatherland" signed by eighty-two intellectuals. Intellectuals committed to civil liberties, as well as those sympathetic to the causes advocated by Communists, were also willing to cooperate with Party members. In May 1930 the John Reed Clubs were able to obtain 135 signatures to a protest against the arrests of workers, particularly those picked up on March 6. Many signers were Communists, but they also included Dr. Franz Boas, Carl Van Doren, Max Eastman, Arthur Garfield Hays, H. L. Mencken, David Saposs, Edmund Wilson, Carlo Tresca, and Sherwood Anderson. Mencken's reply to the appeal noted: "I am probably incurably opposed to communism. But I am also incurably opposed to denying Communists their constitutional rights."[14]

Mike Gold, returning from a wonderful time in the atmosphere of revolutionary Kharkov, told *New Masses* readers that "the congress declared it was of vital importance to enlist all friendly intellectuals into the ranks of the revolution. Every door must be opened wide to the fellow-travelers." Shortly before the Kharkov conference, the John Reed Clubs had created an Emergency Committee for Southern Political Prisoners, with Theodore Dreiser as chairman and John Dos Passos, a club member, as treasurer. By late May of 1931, a more permanent group had been

74

created, the National Committee for the Defense of Political Prisoners. Dreiser, Dos Passos, Lincoln Steffens, Malcolm Cowley, Burton Rascoe, Henry Newman, Franz Boas, and Suzanne LaFollette issued a statement in the name of the new group denouncing the conviction of the Scottsboro boys. That summer the committee made its first investigation in the Pennsylvania mine fields. Later in the year it sent a delegation to Harlan County. The Party's prize catch was Theodore Dreiser. Not yet a Party member (he would not join until 1945), he nevertheless denounced capitalism and urged a Communist vote in the 1931 elections: "Without insisting upon my agreement with the larger aims of the Communist Party, I feel that its candidates and program represent the only current political value worth supporting."[15]

There was an unacknowledged contradiction between the directives of the Kharkov conference to attract intellectuals, provide support to the Communist party, and build a proletarian culture. At Kharkov, for example, the great Mexican muralist Diego Rivera had been denounced as a renegade and read out of the community of revolutionary artists. Among other sins, he was flirting with Trotskyism. The New York John Reed Club made the mistake of sponsoring a public lecture by Rivera on New Year's Day 1932. The club quickly admitted its grave error in inviting a fallen Communist and heroically returned a $100 contribution the artist had made. The mea culpa was not sufficient for Bill Dunne. He was upset not only by the Rivera incident but also by what had transpired at a recent debate between Heywood Broun and Mike Gold on "Communism Versus Socialism." Intellectuals, Dunne muttered, were too "tolerant." Broun was a social-fascist who one day would "join with the capitalist class in murderously suppressing revolutionary struggles of the American working class led by the Communist Party." Dunne reminded the Party members among the intellectuals that to forget they were living in the Third Period, as Gold had done, "was nothing short of a political scandal."[16]

Gold's outstretched arms received another buffeting at the first national congress of the John Reed Clubs in Chicago at the end of May 1932. In accordance with the Kharkov conference recommendations, 37 delegates representing 642 club members from ten cities met to give their organization a national identity. There were sharp disagreements on several issues. Gold wanted the clubs to be a "feeder, the contact organization" between middle-class intellectuals and the Communist party. The manifesto that was developed, reported by Joseph Freeman, did call on writers to become fellow travelers. Although the term later became an insult, it was then meant very positively: it was, Freeman explained, "coined in literary criticism to describe artists and writers who are not members of the Communist Party but who sympathize with the revolution and assist in their capacity as artists and writers." Gold approved but criticized the manifesto for using "the technical jargon of the Communist International."

Many of the delegates could not have cared less about bourgeois intellectuals and brushed aside concerns about links with the Communist party. The Chicago club proudly reported that "our stationery with the hammer and sickle" did not scare non-Communists. Conrad Komorowski announced that the Philadelphia club did "regular work demanded by the Party" and required its members to make themselves understood: "Use of high type of terminology is unacceptable." One of his club's literary contributions to the May Day slogans had been "We struggle for the Marxist-Leninist interpretation of culture and go forward under the Lenin front." The Hollywood contingent reported trouble with intellectual members and firmly specified that they were wanted only if "they were willing to toe the line with the rest of the workers and contribute something specific." A few genuinely talented revolutionary artists and writers like Kenneth Rexroth scorned the idea of attracting well-known writers: "We are not an organization to bring in big names." Even Freeman felt that the clubs' first priority was to be a vehicle for developing proletarian culture. Recruiting intellectuals was for others. "The John Reed Clubs," he stated, "should not go into business as a competitor of the Communist Party."

Gold was not reassured. He warned that too many members of this organization for intellectuals feared success, were jealous of those who had attained it, and were therefore reluctant to welcome fellow travelers: "The John Reed Club has a tendency to develop persons who will perhaps never be artists or writers, who are with the movement in a way, but who kind of make a career of being a member of the John Reed Club." Gold's pleas went unheeded: he was left off the new executive committee of the John Reed Clubs. Its new national secretary was Oakley Johnson, a some-time journalist and academic whose long identification with the Communist party went back to 1919.[17]

There were two other early opportunities to draw intellectuals into the Communist orbit prior to the 1932 election. Instead of welcoming the prospects with open arms or even cautiously negotiating with them, the Communist party responded with campaigns of denunciation designed to establish that sympathy for communism or even the Communist party did not confer any special immunity from criticism.

V. F. Calverton was not himself a formidable intellectual, but his connections and magazine made him a central figure in the intellectual world. Born George Goetz in Baltimore in 1906, Calverton had established *The Modern Quarterly* as an ecumenical journal of the left during the 1920s. Some of his early books and articles drew praise from Mike Gold and William Foster. He wrote for both *The Communist* and *The Daily Worker* in that decade, and Bill Dunne invited him to join the Party in 1926. By the end of the 1920s, however, he was persona non grata. He was denounced in *The Daily Worker* as a Trotskyite and in *The Communist* as a "fascist." Calverton, nonetheless, continued to write for *The New Masses* in 1930. After he disappeared from its pages, the editors maintained a discreet silence about him.[18]

Suddenly, Moscow intervened. The International Union of Revolutionary Writers produced a "Resolution on the Work of New Masses for 1931." It was not printed until September 1932. Amidst a number of shortcomings, the Muscovites singled out one particular weakness:

> As regards social-fascism, *The New Masses* has put up a disgracefully poor fight. In this connection *The New Masses* throughout last year showed manifestations of "rotten liberalism," expressed both in the failure to carry out systematic work in exposing social-fascism as a whole, and in keeping silent about the treacherous role of a number of social-fascist ideologues who had formerly been closely connected with the magazine (Max Eastman, V. F. Calverton).

David Ramsey and Alan Calmer soon produced the longest article in the magazine's history to brand Calverton a plagiarist, an "open collaborator of the ruling class," and both "a maturing fascist" and a "radical fascist." His methods "had all the unscrupulous aspects of a real racketeer." Calverton's forbearance finally snapped. He published a vigorous defense of himself and at last began to move his magazine away from the Communist party.[19]

The Party's second early opportunity to enter a constructive dialogue with intellectuals was spurned much more quickly. Its source was one of the pillars of American liberalism, *The New Republic*. Less than a month after the death of Herbert Croly, one of the editors, Edmund Wilson wrote his friend Allen Tate that he was occasionally trying to convert to Communism. Wilson had been traveling throughout the country observing the effects of the Depression, watching the Communists in action, and fretting about the future of liberalism. Early in 1931 his "An Appeal to Progressives" argued that the psychological crisis of liberalism was even more disabling than its economic woes. Liberalism was nearly bankrupt. It had "little to offer beyond a recommendation of the public ownership of water-power and certain other public utilities, a cordial feeling that labor ought to organize in a non-social-revolutionary way and a protest, invariably ineffective, against a few of the more obviously atrocious jailings, beatings-up and murders of the working class by the owners." It was a time for "liberals seriously to reconsider their position." Only one place in the world seemed to have escaped such a dead end. The socialist experiment in Russia impressed Wilson with "the extreme of efficiency and economy combined with the ideal of a herculean feat to be accomplished by common action in an atmosphere of enthusiastic boosting." It was a time for socialism in America, but the small and ineffective Communist party did not appear to have the capacity to bring it about. American radicals and progressives "must take Communism away from the Communists."[20]

Non-Communists reacted with generally favorable comments. The most plaintive response came from Norman Thomas, who reminded everyone that the Socialist party stood for the selfsame collective ownership of the means of production suggested by Wilson. The logic of Wilson's position, the Socialist leader thought, "ought to lead him and others of like mind to come to the help of the Socialist Party. They will be received as comrades." Homeless and confused intellectuals barely favored Thomas with a glance. "Becoming a Socialist right now," John Dos Passos explained in 1932, "would have just about the same effect on anybody as drinking a bottle of near-beer."[21]

Wilson was not entirely unsympathetic to Communism. He had willingly lent his name to Communist-sponsored petitions, and he admired the Party's spunk. However, instead of looking for some common ground, the Party treated him as if he were preparing the way for Adolf Hitler. Avram Landy did not care about Wilson's objective intentions. Whether or not they were benign, Wilson's article had revealed "a liberal talking 'Communism,' but heading straight towards fascism." Landy called Wilson a social-fascist. Later in the year Bill Dunne charged that Wilson's vision of an independent radical movement was "mulched with Musteite manure." However much the Party might denigrate Edmund Wilson, he was a key member of the intellectual world. At the John Reed Clubs national conference in 1932, the absent critic was a constant object of the delegates' discussion. He was precisely the sort of middle-class intellectual whom Mike Gold hoped to enlist. But the Party faithful remained suspicious and surly. Conrad Komorowski grumpily questioned whether Wilson was even a fellow traveler. There was not yet room for so independent a radical in the Party or even near it.[22]

In the face of an unprecedented economic collapse and a consequent loss of faith in American society, other writers and artists were also des-

perately searching for a spiritual shelter. Few of them were as yet prepared to become Communists. However much they admired the Party's
courage in tackling formidable foes, willingness to fight for the deprived,
and eagerness to identify with the oppressed, most intellectuals still shied
away from the Party's discipline, rhetoric, and identification with Russia.
Many, however, were moving to the left. Some had discovered Marxism.
Others had discovered Russia. And a few were just yearning for some
kind of radical change. Despite its inhospitable behavior, the Communist
party was very nearly the only game in town.

Wilson joined with Waldo Frank, Lewis Mumford, Sherwood Anderson, and John Dos Passos to issue a manifesto in the spring of 1932
calling for "a temporary dictatorship of the class-conscious workers."
Mumford confessed that "I cannot help calling myself a communist."
Sidney Hook, an unorthodox Marxist teaching at New York University,
had done pioneering work on Karl Marx's early writings at the Marx-
Engels Institute in Moscow in 1929 before returning to America critical of
such theories as social-fascism but ready to work with the Communists.
His wide circle of friends, which included Lionel Trilling, Herbert Solow,
and Elliot Cohen, stood ready to do the same.[23]

A group of New Englanders began to inch toward the Communist
party at the same time. Unlike many of the New Yorkers, few were
Jewish. Their leader was a former divinity student named Granville
Hicks. Born in 1901, a Harvard graduate, Hicks was a pacifist. When he
decided that the church had not done enough to abolish war, he abandoned the ministry and wound up teaching English at Rensselear Poly-
technic Institute in Troy, New York. Along with his friends Newton Arvin and Robert Gorham Davis, Hicks read and wrote for liberal and
radical journals. His growing allegiance to Marxism notwithstanding,
Hicks found the Communist party forbidding and unfriendly. He and his
friends had heard that intellectuals had to prove their proletarian mettle
by distributing leaflets on the waterfront, and they wanted no part of
such activity. Another group of intellectuals, including Henry Hazlitt, V.
F. Calverton, Ben Stolberg, Carleton Beals, Lewis Gannett, Kyle Crichton,
Louis Hacker, Maxim Lieber, and Walter White, met regularly in 1931 to
discuss a symposium or book evaluating American culture from a Marxist
perspective. Only a few considered themselves Communists; most "had
leftward, pro-collectivist, or economic-planning leanings."[24]

Still another plan was hatched in 1932 by Hicks, Arvin, and Bernard
Smith, a Marxist editor at Alfred Knopf. The three planned a book "to
survey the state of American culture in its principal departments" and
lined up twenty-odd contributors, some "bourgeois intellectuals who are

working their way to a Marxist position" and other committed Communists. Contracts were signed. The ambitious project quickly became snarled, however, in missed deadlines, desertions, and political sniping. Several promised articles were never handed in. Some contributors dropped out. The non-Communists grew increasingly uncomfortable with the Communists. After several postponements, the whole project finally collapsed in March 1933, at about the same time that an even more ambitious attempt to unite Communist and non-Communist intellectuals came to ruin.[25]

The Communists' greatest triumph among intellectuals in this era came during the 1932 Presidential election campaign. Having moved to the left over the past several years, intellectuals by the dozens publicly endorsed the Communist party ticket of William Foster and James Ford. The medium through which they acted, the League of Professional Groups for Foster and Ford, was a new type of Party auxiliary. It was not directed by a Party member and its membership was overwhelmingly non-Communist. Its brief success and almost equally rapid demise tell much about the Party's attractive power during the Third Period and its inevitable isolation.

The league grew out of the National Committee for the Defense of Political Prisoners. By mid-May 1932, the latter had branched out from its Harlan County activities, obtaining 200 signatures to a petition critical of the Japanese invasion of China. Elliott Cohen, the committee's new secretary, announced in June that Dreiser, Gold, Sherwood Anderson, Waldo Frank, Lincoln Steffens, Lewis Mumford, Malcolm Cowley, Elmer Rice, and Edna St. Vincent Millay had denounced a congressional bill proposed by Martin Dies to deport alien Communists. Mike Gold was so heartened by all the developments that he boasted at the Communist party's nominating convention that "the best known writers in America, the cream of the American intellectual world, is oriented today toward the Revolution and toward the Soviet Union." By the summer of 1932, Matthew Josephson, an adherent of Dadaism in his expatriate days, and James Rorty drafted a manifesto, with Sidney Hook and Lewis Corey doing some of the early writing. Party watchdogs added a heavy-handed preamble. The manifesto was signed by many of the writers who had been wrestling with Marxism, from Hicks, Arvin, Hook, Cohen, and Solow to Wilson and Cowley. Such leading lights of American literature as John Dos Passos, Sherwood Anderson, Theodore Dreiser, Lincoln Steffens, and Matthew Josephson were included. So too were Negro writers Countee Cullen, Langston Hughes, and Eugene Gordon. Fifty-three people originally signed up as members of the League of Professional Groups for Foster and Ford.[26]

James Rorty, the secretary of the league, later stated that only four to six of its members were Communists. Aside from Joseph Freeman and Mike Gold, he identified only Isador Schneider, Joe Pass, and David Ramsey. Nor was everyone who signed entranced by the Communist party. Hook had severe disagreements with the Communists. Lewis Mumford, although impressed by the Party's discipline and élan, was not enchanted by its hypnosis by Russia: "Like the Chinese potters in the eighteenth century, copying an English plate, they would even imitate the cracks and the flaws as well as the original design," he wrote. The league's pamphlet, *Culture and the Crisis*, however, repeated the standard litany of Third Period charges. Some of the harshest language was directed at the Socialists, the "third Party of capitalism." Norman Thomas's "own party is indirectly helping Fascism," the manifesto declared, "by its insistence on democracy, evading the issue of militant organization and struggle." The Communist party alone could "now wring genuine concessions from the ruling class." The signers were convinced that intellectuals and workers were partners: "As responsible intellectual workers, we have aligned ourselves with the frankly revolutionary Communist Party." They added that even those "brain workers" unable to support a revolution should vote Communist to frighten the capitalists.[27]

The Communist party was delighted. Its Fifteenth Plenum criticized the past "hesitation to accept and organize the support to the Communist Party by the leftward-moving intellectuals." One Communist writer gleefully accused the Socialists of using "leftovers" for its list of intellectual supporters of Norman Thomas: "The front ranks of American literature stand steadfastly for Foster and Ford." The first Socialist list contained only twenty-one names, the most prominent being Henry Hazlitt, Stuart Chase, Heywood Broun, George Kaufman, Morrie Ryskind, and Van Wyck Brooks.[28] Speaking before a large crowd of "professional workers" at a Webster Hall campaign dinner, Earl Browder lauded the "historical gathering" and boasted: "We are very glad to see that in these committees we have the very cream of the intellectual life of this country and we think this of great political significance." Forty thousand copies of the pamphlet *Culture and the Crisis* were distributed. League members went on to fill thirty speaking engagements. Earl Browder spoke at league rallies chaired by Charles Rumford Walker and Sidney Hook, and several members added an endorsement of William Patterson's Communist candidacy for mayor of New York.[29]

Once the election campaign was over, some of the league members cast about for another role for their organization, convinced that it could continue to function as a bridge between the Communist party and the intellectual community. The League of Professional Groups for Foster and Ford was dissolved on November 21 in favor of a new organization called simply the League of Professional Groups. James Rorty remained secretary. The Executive Board contained a healthy dose of committed Communists and close sympathizers, along with a few mainstays of the original nucleus: Freeman, Cowley, William Gropper, Lewis Corey, Maxwell Hyde, Joseph Pass, Corliss Lamont, Bernhard Stern, Felix Morrow, Meyer Schapiro, and Ella Winter, wife of Lincoln Steffens. The new league committed itself "to propagandiz[e] and activize the professions, to engage in communist activity on the cultural front, to provide technical aid to the Communist Party and its mass organizations."[30]

From the very beginning, Party members of the league remained suspicious of its purposes. The dangers of its independence quickly became apparent. The first of a planned series of pamphlets was written by Lewis Corey. Under the name of Louis Fraina, he had been one of the founders of American Communism. In 1922 he had disappeared while on a Comintern mission in Mexico, allegedly with a sum of Moscow gold. After years in obscurity, he had suddenly reemerged in 1931 with a well-received book, *The House of Morgan*, achieved a reputation as a Marxist economist, and become an editor of the Encyclopedia of Social Science. In 1932 Corey was active on the Foster-Ford committee. The Communists regarded his prominence in the new league with barely concealed hostility, and they sabotaged a pamphlet he wrote. Corey then took on another league project, editing a book on "rebel Americans." He insiste on ending the book with a chapter on the IWW leader Bill Haywood, and consigning such Communist demi-gods as John Reed, Charles Ruthenberg, and William Foster to a summary chapter. That proved unacceptable to the Communists. Disgusted by the inability of the league to work free of Party discipline and disheartened with the prospect of working with Communists, Corey sent in his resignation from the League of Professional Groups.[31]

If the Communist party needed additional evidence that the league harbored dangerous enemies, it soon got it. Shortly after Hitler seized power, Sidney Hook, just back from Germany, proposed to turn the group into a genuine united front against fascism and to hold a large protest meeting. Joe Pass and James Rorty met with Clarence Hathaway to discuss the proposal; Hathaway refused to countenance any such activities. Rorty was not hostile to the Communist party. He agreed that joining the league "implied commitment to the support of Communist Party policies and activities." His conception of the league, however, was that it had been created "as an independent organization not as an auxiliary of the Communist Party." It had to be open to all left-wing intellectuals "committed to the revolutionary movement in terms of the class struggle." Even Musteites, Trotskyists, and Lovestoneites had to be welcome. "The party," Rorty explained, "should be given opportunity to exercise the only type of control which is practicable, namely, control by conviction." He resigned as league secretary in June, placing the blame for his departure squarely on the Communist party.[32]

With Rorty's departure, the League of Professional Groups faded into oblivion, a victim of the Party's need to control with an iron fist any organization associated with it. The list of signers for its 1933 endorsement of Communist candidates was thin and less distinguished than the previous year's. Had the league emerged a few years later, its fate might have been different. But in 1932 and early 1933, the Communist party was not ready to accept so dramatic a diminution of its organizational control over a purported auxiliary.[33]

The dissolution of the league signaled the Communists' declaration of war with fellow travelers. In December 1932, Sidney Hook was the first league member castigated as an enemy. Sam Don demanded that the Party's theoretical magazine attack Hook's "scholastic and absolute revisionism." Faithful to orders, *The Communist* inaugurated the new year by choosing V. J. Jerome, at one time Hook's pupil, to label him an enemy of the working class. Jerome acknowledged Hook's role in the Foster-Ford campaign but dialectically warned that "despite his objective position among the intellectuals drifting toward the revolutionary movement, Hook is subjectively a force pulling away from it." The following two issues contained lengthy refutations of Hook's Marxism by none other than Earl Browder. If Lewis Corey was too prominent a Marxist economist for the Party to feel comfortable with him, Hook was too good a Marxist philosopher to be allowed free rein.[34]

When the Party declared someone a renegade, it did not hesitate to employ the most violent, intemperate, and sleazy language it could summon. Charles Yale Harrison had the cheek to criticize the Soviet Union for driving Leon Trotsky's daughter to suicide. For his effrontery he was promptly expelled from the John Reed Clubs, accused of being "one of the star hired men of the yellow Hearst press," and denounced for echoing the same line as Archduke Cyril, Pope Pius, Alexander Kerensky, Hamilton Fish, and the leaders of the Second International. A lead editorial in *The Daily Worker* raked over his past, remembering that he had harassed poor workers before as an insurance salesman, reminding one and all that his wife had been driven to suicide "by his peculiar mental and physical reptilian repulsiveness," and concluding that he was "a journalistic cootie, without principle, ready, willing and able at all times to sell his not too extensive ability to the highest bidder," one of "many procurers to Wall Street imperialism."[35]

Such abuse was the lot of many a renegade. It was partly precipitated by anger but also by rage against an emerging anti-Communist intelligentsia. The League of Professional Groups proved to be a school for anti-Communism. Corey, Solow, Hook, Rorty, Cohen, and others became the most implacable opponents of Communism in America. Not until 1935 was the Party able to organize another large, broadly based cultural auxiliary, the League of American Writers, and even then, only a handful of the 1932 group of intellectuals—notably Cowley, Hicks, and Josephson—could be persuaded to go along. In the interim the Party had to be satisfied with a wildly uneven "proletarian culture" that resulted in a few works of talent and a considerable amount of rubbish.

The heyday of the proletarian novel began in 1932. For the next few years the Communists basked in the belief that the future of American culture was in their hands. Joshua Kunitz listed thirty-six prominent writers in 1934 who were grouped "around the John Reed Clubs, the *New Masses* and other organizations supporting the Communist Party." Along with John Dos Passos, Kenneth Burke, and Langston Hughes were such proletarian novelists as Robert Cantwell, Jack Conroy, Edward Dahlberg, and James Farrell. Even as more established intellectuals deserted the Communist camp in 1933 and 1934, younger recruits replaced them. Joseph Freeman boasted that "many intellectuals, with and without a bohemian background, are not only sympathetic toward the Soviet Union but support the Communist movement in this country as well." Philip Rahv, a young radical literary critic and co-editor of the new John Reed Clubs magazine *Partisan Review*, pointed out that "most of the young novelists who have been hailed as the hope of American literature have taken their stand with Communism." Two of those he had in mind were Erskine Caldwell, author of *Tobacco Road*, who contributed a series of articles to *The Daily Worker*, and William Saroyan, who wrote in *The New Masses* that "the Communist program is, for the most part, the most valid and decent I can think of, and I am wholly in sympathy with it."[36]

Despite this rash of new fellow travelers, the Communist party had willingly refused to deal with an entire corps of intellectuals. Imprisoned by its own dogma, it had squandered a historic opportunity to enlist allies.

5

The Interregnum
of Despair

O NCE their heady revolutionary expectations waned, the Communists recognized the need to devote their energies to the dull, difficult, and onerous tasks of organization. The first years of the Depression had brought few concrete results. Strident calls for revolution had succeeded only in isolating the Party. Despite all the objective conditions any revolutionary could hope for, the Communists had been unable to make a significant dent in American capitalism.

Every Party plenum repeated the same disconcerting message: American capitalism was growing weaker, a revolutionary crisis was coming closer, the Communist party was stuck in the same groove. Each plenum would resolve to change this unacceptable situation. The next plenum would sadly repeat the same litany and report that the decisive turn had not yet been made. The Twelfth Plenum, in late 1930, marked the turning point toward mass revolutionary work, Browder happily told the Party the following year at the Thirteenth Plenum. Will Weinstone observed at the Fourteenth Plenum, "We thought at the 13th Plenum we had made the beginning of the turn." At the Fifteenth Plenum in 1932, it was lamented: "In spite of the much more favorable conditions for the development of revolutionary mass work, the fundamental change in the Party's work called for by the Fourteenth Central Committee Plenum has not yet begun."[1]

The Party had largely eschewed the bold revolutionary gestures of early 1930. It had learned by bitter experience and by Comintern directive that it was not enough to issue calls for destroying capitalism or to demand only revolutionary goals. Its trade union movement had nearly foundered on the shoals of its inability to organize, lead, and conclude strikes over concrete economic issues. Slowly and with frequent backsliding, the Communists began to place more emphasis on immediate demands and practical work. The Twelfth Plenum, held after the optimism of March 6 had faded, heard Browder denounce Communists who believed that "immediate demands, concrete demands of the daily life of the workers, acquire less and less importance." It proved difficult, however, for the Communist party to reconcile immediate, practical demands for improvements in the daily lives of workers with the belief that only the overthrow of capitalism could effect a fundamental improvement. The struggle for immediate demands had to have a revolutionary context. By building mass movements to fight for unemployment insurance, relief, and wage increases, Clarence Hathaway maintained, the Party "took the first step toward a revolutionary way out of the crisis, as the beginning of the revolutionary struggle which has as the objective the overthrow of capitalism in the United States and the establishment of a Workers' and Farmers' Government."[2]

The Party's turn to more practical work received impetus from Moscow. The Comintern's Eleventh Plenum in the spring of 1931 criticized "the abstractness of our agitational slogans, the absence of organization, while those organizations which exist were chiefly occupied with the organization of demonstrations." Ossip Piatnitsky particularly singled out the Americans for their reluctance to raise nonrevolutionary demands. The plenum accused its sections of "lagging behind in the work of mobilizing the masses on the basis of the defence of the everyday needs of the workers; in the inadequate linking of the struggle for these demands with the struggle for the proletarian dictatorship."[3]

The turn to the practical coincided with Earl Browder's consolidation of power in the Party. Browder was not less revolutionary than other Party leaders, but his organizational talents fit the new trend far better than his rivals'. He had looked askance at the street battles of 1930. Reporting to a plenum shortly after being elevated to the Secretariat, he took as his main theme a phrase from Lenin, "Fewer High-Falutin'

Phrases, More Simple Every-Day Deeds" to emphasize the need "to get down to work." His reports to Party conferences emphasized building lower units and sections, increasing financial accountability, and strengthening organizational work. After years of bombast, the cadres reacted happily to the new, businesslike atmosphere brought to the Party center by the former accountant.[4]

One by one, Browder's chief rivals were shunted off to other tasks or effectively neutralized. Max Bedacht was removed from Party work in 1931 and sent to the International Workers' Order, a fraternal group that provided low-cost insurance benefits to its largely foreign-born membership. Will Weinstone made his bid for power in 1932. As befitted someone only recently back from an extended stay in Moscow, he denied, while delivering the report of the Politburo to the Fourteenth Plenum, that there had been any significant improvement in Party work from 1931 to early 1932. That summer, he opposed Party participation in the Bonus March and was rebuked by Moscow. Sent back to Russia, Weinstone languished abroad until early 1934. Browder's most serious rival, William Z. Foster, was jailed and had to bear the onus of the TUUL's failure from 1930 to 1932. However, he reemerged as the leading Party spokesman and was nominated as the Communist candidate for President in 1932. Foster then suffered a serious heart attack in early September. For five months during the following year he lived in Russia "recovering from an acute heart attack and a complete nervous breakdown." His full convalescence took three years.[5]

Foster's illness paved the way for Browder's emergence as undisputed Party leader. Suddenly his name, heretofore absent from *Daily Worker* headlines, began to appear: "Cheers Greet Browder at Vet Confab" read the first. "Browder, Communist Leader, Greets the Victorious Needle Trades Union" went another. He made a major address to the League of Professional Groups for Foster and Ford in mid-October. After the Nineteenth Plenum that fall, he was referred to as "secretary of the Communist Party." Jack Stachel called him the "General Secretary" of the Party in early August 1933, shortly after the Extraordinary Party Conference. By the Party's Eighth Convention, his deification was already in progress. A Party journalist exulted that: "America is producing its Stalins, its Molotovs. Undoubtedly many delegates thought this after Browder reported. . . . His address scintillated with the insight of a master of revolutionary theory and practice. . . . Homely words, brief, monosyllabic, in an argument that rose logically, step by step, to uncontrovertible conclusions." After nearly four years, the quiet, unprepossessing Browder had become the leader of the Communist party of the United States.[6]

He quickly moved to install his team in positions of power. For most of 1932 and 1933 *The Daily Worker* had been edited by his enemies, first William Dunne, then Weinstone, and finally Sam Don. Clarence Hathaway was installed there in July 1933 and also elevated to the Secretariat later that year. Charles Krumbein, an old war-horse from the Foster-Browder faction of the 1920s, became New York district organizer. Jack Stachel, Robert Minor, Gil Green, and Herbert Benjamin were other key members of the new leadership.[7]

Browder's leadership did not result in any immediate policy changes. By now, contests for power did not center around issues but around tactics. The basic line came from Moscow; it was inviolate. Both the Comintern and the American Party, however, were entering a period during which the certainties of the Third Period were to be gradually modified and replaced. The result was confusion and some uncertainty in America as the Party sought to adjust to a new era. The Party uneasily balanced the Comintern's demand for more attention to immediate issues with the strident language of revolution.

Late in 1932 the Party focused its energies on so bourgeois an event as the Presidential election. The Communists took the election far more seriously than they had ever done before. The Party's main demand, for unemployment and social insurance, was quite specific and unrevolutionary. Most of its 5 other demands, a considerable reduction from the 130 of 1928, were equally practical, calling for opposition to wage cuts, farm relief, equal rights and self-determination for Negroes, resistance to "capitalist terror," and defense of the Chinese people and the Soviet Union. A well-organized speaking tour exposed hundreds of thousands of people, many times more than in 1928, to William Foster and James Ford. The crowds were large. The Party expected to do well. Negroes had been galvanized by Ford's presence on the ticket. Many of the country's prominent intellectuals had endorsed the Communists, if not Communism. Clarence Hathaway confidently predicted: "We shall poll one million votes this coming November, and will elect many candidates to office."[8]

When the votes were counted, the Communists briefly continued to gloat. In a post-election statement, standard-bearer Foster scarcely could be bothered noticing the Democratic victory: "The outstanding fact in the election result is the manifold increase in the Communist vote." The Party's vote did more than double, from 48,770 in 1928 to 102,991 in 1932. In some key areas the increase was even more substantial, from 1,000 in Cook County, Illinois, to almost 12,000 and from 9,200 in New York City to 24,000. There were 10,000 Communist votes in Minnesota.

And, undoubtedly, many Party votes were never counted by hostile or busy local officials, on top of the fact that many Party members were not citizens and could not vote. Yet, the Communists must have been more than a mite discouraged. While they had done twice as well in 1932 as in 1928, Norman Thomas had increased his national vote by 300 percent, from 289,000 to 918,000, nine times as large as the Communist vote. Moreover, Thomas got 120,000 votes in New York City, 55,000 less than he had received there in his 1930 gubernatorial contest, well behind Socialist Morris Hillquit's 250,000 votes for mayor. Without the presence of Franklin Roosevelt on the Democratic ticket, the Socialist Presidential candidate would surely have done even better. William Patterson, carrying the Communist mayoral banner, received a paltry 24,101. A few months afterward, Browder glumly told a Party plenum that "the general judgement on this election campaign cannot be very favorable."[9]

Contrary to Hathaway's other prediction, the Communists elected few candidates. One person who did win was Emil Nygard, chosen mayor of the small, largely Finnish village of Crosby, Minnesota. A husky ex–miner, ex–harvest worker, and ex–railroad worker, young Nygard had also spent a year in college before being elected on a "united front ticket" called the Progressive Taxpayers' League. His tenure was remarkably unrevolutionary, although he did try to abolish the police commission and replace it with a workers' volunteer corps—an effort blocked by the city council.[10]

Even campaigning for votes could not deflect the Communists from their task of convincing the masses that elections solved nothing. The 1932 demands were only the "first step toward the establishment of a revolutionary Workers' and Farmers' Government." At an election meeting in St. Paul, Minnesota, Foster noted: "Capitalism will not die of its own acccord—it must be killed." In fact, at least in its propaganda, the Party constantly threatened to disregard the electoral process. "It is necessary now," proclaimed the Eighteenth Plenum in early 1934, "to boldly bring forward the revolutionary way out of the crisis, the proletarian seizure of power, proletarian dictatorship, a Soviet America." But it was left to the Party's best-known spokesman to make the baldest statement of the Communist attitude toward American democracy.[11]

Years later, when the Communist leadership was on trial for violation of the Smith Act and government attorneys lovingly drew excerpts from *Toward Soviet America*, the Party pretended that William Z. Foster's book was only a passing aberration—poorly formulated, badly worded, and quickly discarded when its inadequacies were discovered. Foster himself testified that his book had been rendered "obsolete." Earl Browder later claimed that he had never even looked at the manuscript. However, when it was published in 1932 by a capitalist publisher, *Toward Soviet America* was considered a definitive statement of the Communist party. The head of the Party's publishing house stated that "Comrade Foster speaks for the Communist Party." During the Presidential campaign, *The Daily Worker* printed excerpts from the book. Browder may not have read it, but he did praise it as "another big contribution to the struggle of the American working class." The Central Committee's Literature Division wrote all Party editors that "it contains the party program thoroughly elaborated and presents to the reader a complete picture of what the Communist Party is struggling for and the methods of struggle which it uses." [12]

Foster, from his contrast between capitalist decline and Soviet achievements to his denunciations of social-fascists, preached the gospel of the Third Period. He linked the struggle for immediate demands with the need to educate the workers to "the final solution," the overthrow of capitalism. With typical Third Period verve, he warned that this would require an open struggle: "The working class cannot itself come into power without civil war." In the final chapter Foster let himself dream of the day when an "American Soviet Government will be organized along the broad lines of the Russian Soviets." The capital would be transferred from Washington to an industrial center such as Chicago or Detroit, the courts revamped to war "against the class enemies of the toilers," a Red army built to crush counterrevolution, fraternal groups (such as the Masons, Elks, and Knights of Columbus) abolished, all industry and large farms nationalized, agriculture collectivized on the Soviet model, vast projects for social betterment undertaken, crime eliminated, churches curbed and "organized religious training for minors prohibited," education reoriented "on the basis of Marxian dialectical materialism," all forms of communication controlled by the government, and political parties liquidated, with "the Communist Party functioning alone as the Party of the toiling masses." Whatever immediate improvements William Foster demanded under American capitalism paled in comparison to his longing for its judgment day. [13]

Foster was not alone in using these appeals, nor did they disappear as the Party and the Comintern gradually inched away from the Third Period. Browder's emergence as pre-eminent Party leader in 1933 did not end them. Tentative united front gestures to "social-fascists" were made but were seen as unlikely to have much effect. The Communists considered themselves revolutionaries. Fighting for reforms in capitalism could never be more than a tactic to draw closer to the workers. Talk of violence was not uncommon or limited to Party resolutions or pamphlets. Finishing his speech to the Party's Eighth Convention in 1934, a Kentucky Communist noted that "the Kentucky miners have fought each other for the past 100 years, but I want to say it looks [as if] in Kentucky at this time, if the Communist Party follows the line as laid down by Comrade Stalin, and the Communist International and Comrade Browder, the shooting will be turned in the right direction for the setting up of a Soviet government in the United States." Joe North, a Party journalist, used that explicit threat of violence to conclude his article on the convention. A *Daily Worker* editorial noted: "Negro and white workers must struggle relentlessly for the right to armed self-defense, for the right to organize armed resistance to Fascist violence." This was going too far; the following day, under the heading "A Serious Typographical Error," the paper explained that "mass" should have replaced "armed" in both places.[14]

The disappointing results of the 1932 election, however, were only one more straw in the wind. The Party's rhetoric could not hide its lack of progress. The Communists were facing increasing pressure to produce results commensurate with the objective economic conditions. The most nagging concern was the Party's own size. It had entered the Depression as a tiny organization. Three years of the worst economic collapse in American history had not made it much bigger.

American Communism had spent most of its history losing membership. It had started with somewhere around 40,000 in 1919 and whittled itself down to 7,545 in 1930. Membership had then begun to climb, but slowly. It creeped up to 9,219 in 1931. Piatnitsky pointedly chided the Americans at a Comintern plenum, noting that no matter how many new members had been recruited from 1927 to 1932, the total figure never went much above 9,000. "As if someone has ordered them never to go beyond that figure," he cuttingly remarked. The membership finally broke the 10,000 barrier in 1932, spurting to 14,474 in the first substantial growth since the early 1920s and then jumping to 18,119 immediately after the 1932 election. Poised for a great leap forward, Party leaders uneasily watched as membership once again began to shrink in the first half of 1933. By June it was back down to 14,937. Something was wrong.[15]

Actually the biggest problem was not recruiting. Thousands of people went into the Party every year. Most of them, however, went out almost as quickly. For every person who joined and stayed, many more joined and soon, for whatever reason, left. To grow even modestly, the Communists had to recruit hordes of new members. The dimensions of the problem bothered the Comintern. Piatnitsky reported that 7,178 members joined between December 1929 and July 1930. Added to the 8,800 already in the Party in October 1929, this meant that there should have been 15,978 members; there were only 10,768. For just this eight-month period, 7,178 people had to join in order for the Party to grow by 1,968. In other words, it took seven recruits to get two additional members. In later years, the drop-out rate did not get much better. Browder complained in 1931 that "in order to have a net gain of 25 members for the Party we must recruit 100." That the Communist party should have a greater attracting power than holding power is not surprising. Many desperate people saw it as an alternative during the Depression. Once they had some contact with it, they drifted away.[16]

Because the membership was so unstable, the Party was being re-made in the early 1930s. Only a small proportion of the membership of the 1920s survived into the 1930s. A Party registration in November 1931 revealed that 60 percent of the entire membership had joined in 1930 or later. A later check showed only 3,000 of 14,000 predating 1930. The CPUSA's membership was relatively inexperienced and largely unaware of its past. However few of the old-timers there might be, they continued to dominate the Party. Leadership positions went to the 1920s recruits. At less exalted levels, Party veterans were a problem. Many had picked up bad habits. They were suspicious of new members, regarding them with barely concealed disdain and even hostility. Particularly suspect were American-born workers. The largely foreign-born Communists oft-times could not understand why any American would join the Party unless he were a police agent; they did not rush to welcome the new members. "Their repellant coldness toward new members has driven countless members away from our Party," warned one organizer. Just "because a worker doesn't understand what the 'Third Period' is, he is not to be laughed at."[17]

Too many of the veterans were reluctant to engage in mass work. They preferred to remain within their own ethnic cocoons, where their accents and political beliefs did not leave them vulnerable. In Youngstown, Ohio, South Slavic Communists were too busy rehearsing a play to tend to Party tasks; in Connecticut, foreign-born comrades retreated to fraternal activities. Others actually longed for the more exciting days of yore when factional wars kept life exciting: one writer stated, "Talking about inner-party situations constitutes the sum total of their activities." Earl Browder complained that there was resistance to action:

When we began to organize street demonstrations, we always found some comrades who felt that the masses are not ready. When we began the state hunger marches, the first task was to batter down a veritable wall of lack of faith in the support of the workers and disbelief in our own capacity. In the building of the unemployed councils, the entire work has been choked by a paralyzing lack of faith in the readiness and ability of the workers to build these organizations, not to speak of the general lack of confidence in the creative capacity of the revolutionary masses.

Late in 1932 a Comintern expert on America warned that the Party's "sectarianism" would not be overcome until new cadres, drawn from mass work, replaced the obstructionists. Browder later recalled that the "old cadres of the Party were resisting the development of the Party in its mass work." After discussions in Moscow, the Communist leadership decided it was necessary to initiate "a struggle against the lower cadres."[18]

The crisis within the Party was exacerbated by domestic politics. Franklin Roosevelt gave the Communists far more trouble than they had anticipated. For a long time the Communists reserved a full measure of vitriol for him. The Third Period line forbade distinctions among capitalist politicians, and they all received more or less the same unsympathetic treatment. Browder summed up the prevailing opinion after the Democrats' 1930 victories: "There is not a serious shade of difference in program between the two main capitalist parties, nor between them and the third capitalist party (the socialists)." When Roosevelt was on the verge of becoming the Democratic Presidential candidate in 1932, a front-page editorial in *The Daily Worker* summed up his political role: "The liberal pose which he is assuming is to demoralize the working class in the face of the ceaseless offensive of socialism on all fronts."[19]

Once Roosevelt was nominated, the Communists stepped up their attacks. William Z. Foster maintained that there was no difference between Roosevelt and Hoover:

> First of all, let me say that the policy of Mr. Roosevelt's party is identical in all essentials with that of the Republican Party. The platform of the Republican Party could be adopted by the Democratic Party and they could get along very nicely with it. Or the candidate of the Democratic Party could run on the Republican Party ticket; Mr. Hoover could be a member of Mr. Roosevelt's cabinet or vice versa.

Foster also struck a more ominous note, comparing Roosevelt to Mussolini for sprinkling his speeches with "I's." Roosevelt's election was greeted with a front-page banner headline—"Roosevelt to Carry on the Hoover Hunger Rule." Foster warned that "from Roosevelt the masses can expect nothing better than they did at the hands of Hoover." Why, then, had the Democrats won the election? The Party's explanation focused on "mass confusion and misplaced confidence" and foresaw the inevitable failure of his administration: "The very moment of Roosevelt's victory is therefore the beginning of his defeat!" An editorial soon hazarded a prediction: "Yes, the 'new deal' may well prove to be fascism. This smiling india-rubber 'liberal' in the White House is destined to destroy all remaining American liberties."[20]

The headlines of a single week indicate how the attack continued:

Wall Street—Roosevelt Bill, Passed by House, Robs Tens of Thousands of Vets and Members of Armed Forces

Loot Reaches Seven Billions as Banks Fold Up: Hoover and Roosevelt Shaped Plot Month Ago

The White House Is Still a Wall Street Annex

Roosevelt Farm Bill Is Attack on Both Land and City Workers[21]

When the National Industrial Recovery Act (NIRA) was passed, the Communists introduced a new, more strident note into their denunciations of Roosevelt. Browder noted: "Roosevelt is carrying out more thoroughly and brutally even than Hoover, the capitalist attack against the living standards of the masses at home and the sharpest national chauvinism in foreign relations." The main features of the New Deal were "trustification, inflation, direct subsidies to finance capital, taxation of the masses, the economy program, military and naval preparations, militarization, direct and indirect, of labor." Although Browder did not go so far as to call the New Deal an American variety of fascism, he did say: "It is clear that fascism already finds much of its work done in America, and more of this is being done by Roosevelt." The New Deal stopped short of a "developed fascism" but was well on the road: "In the labor sections of the New Deal program [are] to be seen the clearest examples of the tendencies to fascism. This is the American version of Mussolini's 'corporative state,' special state-controlled labor unions closely tied up with and under the direction of the employers." Browder concluded: "For the working class, the Industrial Recovery Act is truly an industrial slavery act. It is one of the steps towards the militarization of labor. It is a forerunner of American fascism."[22]

The shrill tone of the denunciations could not conceal the Party's concern. Roosevelt had quickly succeeded in altering the public mood. Israel Amter admitted that even the Communist party itself had not been immune to Roosevelt's wiles:

. . . the propaganda of the "New Deal" and of N.R.A. has affected a section of the Party membership. In the beginning even some leading local comrades believed that the provisions of the recovery act were such that we would not be able to oppose it.

Amter was even forced to admit that the illusions had some solid grounding:

Certain workers *temporarily* have had their wages increased, some workers have received jobs. Some comrades have come to the conclusion that capitalism is therefore on the upgrade once more—that unemployment is a back issue. *A new early crash and a rapidly mounting cost of living will follow sharpening the situation as never before.*

At the Seventeenth Plenum in October 1933, Bill Dunne confirmed that the New Deal had badly confused the Party. The Party, he said, was "emerging from the bewilderment" induced by the switch from the "crude methods" of Hoover to Roosevelt's "demagogy and ruthless terror." [23]

Thrown into disarray by the unexpected skill of a Roosevelt, the Communists also uneasily watched international events upset timetested formulas. Hitler came to power in Germany, and the Comintern's conviction that social-fascism and fascism were two peas in the same pod began to seem less likely.

The first half of 1933 was a time of stress for the Communist party. Its response was to call an Extraordinary National Conference in New York from July 7 to July 10 "to rouse all of the resources, all of the forces of the Party to change this situation" and convert the CPUSA "into a revolutionary mass Party." The 200 delegates issued an "Open Letter to All Members of the Communist Party" insisting that paper resolutions were no longer enough. The Party's efforts had been inexcusably lax, particularly in trade union work: "It is idle chatter to speak about the leading role of the Party without establishing contacts with the decisive strata of the workers, mobilizing these workers and winning them over to our side." Party backs were stiffened by clear warnings that the New Deal, while not yet "developed fascism," was tending in that direction with the aid and comfort of social-fascists. The Extraordinary Conference did not mark any departure from past Party policy. It did ratify the new leadership of Earl Browder. Henceforth, the organization would be tightened up. More emphasis would be put on financial accountability, lower Party units, and development of new cadres. [24]

By itself, such a pledge was of little more consequence than any of the dozens of such solemn oaths made in the past. What distinguished this one, however, was the circumstances under which it was made. Every Party member was exhorted to read the Open Letter carefully, and every Party unit, nucleus, and fraction was ordered to discuss and implement it. Over the next several months articles would inundate the Party press discussing the impact of the Open Letter on the Party's organizational work and on bodies ranging from the Young Communist League to the Party's Detroit district. *The Party Organizer* devoted an entire double-issue to the Extraordinary Conference, with nineteen separate articles on how its instructions could be carried out in different fields. Even the Party's arch-enemy, Franklin Roosevelt, provided indirect assistance. The NIRA, the object of so much denunciation, helped to stimulate a wave of unionism that washed over even so stranded a vessel as the TUUL. More important, the Comintern signaled a change in tactics that opened new channels for Party activity.[25]

6

United We Stand

THE PROVING GROUND of the Third Period was in Germany, where the social and economic crisis of the early thirties was most intense and where the Comintern had its strongest section. For this reason, every Party, including the American one, had an enormous stake in what was happening in Germany. The Comintern was unwilling to fashion different policies for different countries. It imposed, instead, a general line on all its sections and permitted differences only within very narrow limits. The failure of the line in America, where the Party was weak anyhow, was unlikely to make a big impression in Moscow, but a debacle in Germany was something else. And if something in Germany was alarming the Russians, the repercussions would be felt in America.

The Comintern had not been terribly alarmed by the rise of the Nazi movement. In accordance with Third Period ideology, Hitler's upsurge after 1930 was thought to be a boon to the revolutionary movement, not a defeat. Hitlerism, the line went, was a sign of the mortal weakness of German capitalism; the stronger Hitler got, the weaker capitalism became and the closer the Communists were to power. When Hitler actually came to power in January 1933, the Comintern refused to be shaken. In fact, both the Comintern and those German Communists fortunate enough to be in exile or hiding continued for some time to hold fast to the illusion that Nazism in power brought the German revolution closer than ever. Hitler, they were sure, was destroying German capitalism from within.[1]

The growing success of fascism did require some tactical adjustments. The most important actually began some months prior to Hitler's victory, although its full expression did not take place until afterward. The Twelfth Comintern Plenum suggested in September 1932 that the united front from below needed refurbishing since it had not resulted in any sustained contact with non-Communist workers. The desire to reach non-Party workers was decidedly *not* related to fear about the growing strength of fascism. On the contrary, it was regarded as a means of finishing off the traitorous social democrats once and for all and preparing for the impending revolutionary crisis of capitalism. Communists were ordered to "establish, extend and strengthen permanent and intimate contacts with the majority of the workers, wherever workers may be found." While the "main blow" should still be directed against social-fascism, it was imperative to maintain a "strict differentiation between social-democratic leaders and workers" in order to implement the united front from below.[2]

Previous appeals to workers to join under Communist leadership had largely gone unheeded. If workers were not ready to break away from their leaders before the united front began, Otto Kuusinen explained, the only way to approach them was to enter their organizations and then expose their leadership. Although Kuusinen carefully hedged the circumstances under which such united fronts were permissible, a "half-turn" in Comintern policy was under way. The goal remained the same: "the highest moment of the united front," one authority explained, "is when the social democratic masses will turn against their leaders."[3]

The jolt of Hitler's triumph forced both Socialists and Communists to make gestures toward each other. The Second International proposed a united front on February 19, 1933. Its Communist rival responded in March with an "Open Letter to Social-Democrats." The letter bristled with hostility toward Socialist leaders and their policies. Nevertheless, the Communists generously were willing to let bygones be bygones. The letter called upon all Communist parties "to make yet another attempt to set up the united front of struggle with the Social-Democratic Parties." The appeal was couched in such harsh terms as to make its rejection certain. The promise of a moratorium on denunciations of Socialists was belied by the repetition of virtually every charge ever hurled at them. They were accused of being responsible for fascism even while being asked to join in combatting it. The objective of the Open Letter was consistent with the previous united front policy—to separate Socialist workers from their leaders. The failure of this initiative opened the way for the Thirteenth Plenum in December 1933 to resume sharp attacks on the Socialists as "the main social prop of the bourgeoisie [even] in the countries of open fascist dictatorship." Communists had to struggle for unity "in spite of and against the will of the treacherous leaders of social-democracy." They had to "win over the social-democratic workers for active revolutionary struggle under the leadership of the Communist Parties."[4]

The American Communists responded in kind when the Comintern shifted gears even slightly. At the end of December 1932, a joint meeting with Socialist Karl Borders was used as an occasion to denounce him and to try to capture his followers. Just before the new year, a National Student Congress Against War brought Communist delegates together with a variety of reformers and radicals. Gil Green, head of the Young Communist League, criticized the youthful comrades for falling into the trap of seeking a united front with student leaders who represented "no one but themselves" instead of trying to win over the rank and file. Two months later the Party issued an open appeal to Socialist workers to join a conference on labor legislation in Albany, New York, which was mostly an attack on the Socialist party leadership.[5]

The Americans reacted to Hitler's triumph no differently than did the Comintern. A *Daily Worker* editorial anticipated an early Communist victory: it proclaimed, the "atmosphere is charged with revolutionary lightning." The same editorial was largely devoted to a denunciation of the Socialist leaders, who would surely "become more and more fascist." A small anti-Hitler demonstration organized by the Party in the predominantly German Yorkville section of New York drew only 1,000 people and did not even rate a page 1 story in *The Daily Worker*. Members of the League of Professional Groups, led by James Rorty, proposed a protest meeting. Clarence Hathaway brushed off the suggestion.[6]

What Hitler in power could not do, the Comintern's Open Letter could and did. Twelve days after publishing the Comintern appeal, *The Daily Worker* carried the Central Committee's statement to the leading bodies of the A.F. of L., the Socialist party, the Conference for Progressive Labor Action, and the Trade Union Unity League. After denouncing William Green of the A.F. of L. and the Socialist party for supporting President Roosevelt, the Communists suggested a joint conference. The Party promised that once common proposals were developed, it would cease attacks on its new partners. The main thrust of the document was the need for a united front against Franklin Delano Roosevelt, not German fascism. Offers of cooperation quickly sprang from Party auxiliaries.

The TUUL explained that it "does not aim to split the A.F.L. or other unions." The Young Communist League proposed united action to the Young People's Socialist League. The Needle Trades Industrial Union sent a similar message to the International Ladies' Garment Workers' Union.[7]

The new approach exacerbated a delicate and difficult ideological question. How was it possible to hold out the hand of the united front to the worst enemies of the working class? Clarence Hathaway had to tell young Communists that a forthright declaration of their intent was unlikely to be productive: "Comrades, you cannot make an approach to the Y.P.S.L. if you go to them and tell them that the purpose of the YCL is to smash their organization." This did not mean that there was any real change in view. Hathaway explained that the Comintern had not made its proposal "with the expectation that these reformist bodies (except of course the lower units) will enter a fighting united front. It makes this proposal in the sense of calling the bluff of the reformist leaders, with the viewpoint of exposing these treacherous mis-leaders as the opponents of united action, as the enemies of the workers." The masses, disillusioned by the true colors of their leaders, would then "be won for Communist policies, and for the Communist Party."[8]

Earl Browder directed the following comment to those slow-witted Communists who might be afraid the new stance meant real cooperation: "Have you forgotten that precisely the reason why we make the united front with them is because we have got to take their followers away from them?" Hathaway, also addressing those comrades who thought the Comintern had initiated a new line on the united front, pointed out their mistake. The Party was following "the road which takes the masses over the political corpses of these leaders." The Communist solution to its ideological problem, then, was to explain away the new united front as just another maneuver. Social-fascists were still social-fascists.[9]

This particular maneuver depended on the cooperation, conscious or unconscious, of the "social-fascists." Their position was unenviable. To refuse united front offers was to bear the onus of being splitters and narrow sectarians. To accept the offers was to open their organizations to the Communists' single-minded goal of subverting members. Few other groups could exert as much discipline over their representatives or delegates to conferences as the Communists. None had so dedicated, committed, and large a body of functionaries or so diverse a group of auxiliary organizations whose ostensibly independent spokesmen could be counted on to uphold the Communist position. Many saw the new united front, with its outstretched hand to the "social-fascists," as a very dangerous development.

They reacted to it differently. The A.F. of L. did not bother to reply. The most bitter division occurred among the Socialists. Julius Gerber, the New York City secretary of the Socialist party, refused to participate in a united May Day parade. The Continental Congress of Workers and Farmers, a Socialist-controlled gathering of 4,000 that met in Washington in May, refused to admit Communist or TUUL delegates. The Socialist party's National Executive Committee voted in mid-April not to negotiate with the Communists until and unless the Comintern and the Second International reached an agreement. One Socialist faction, the "Old Guard"—which was largely Jewish, centered in New York, and led by Morris Hillquit, and had ties to the garment unions—was unalterably opposed to dealing with the Communists.[10]

Another faction, the "Militants"—a group which was younger, more "American," and eager to move the Socialist party to the left—favored negotiations with the Communists. Their most prominent spokesman was Norman Thomas. He was not optimistic about reaching an agreement with the Communists but felt it necessary to try, lest the Socialists be accused of sabotaging a united front and younger, more militant party members become disaffected. His efforts did not win any Communist plaudits. In fact, Thomas and his fellow militants were attacked more savagely and more often than those Socialists who wanted nothing to do with the Communists. "With him," Hathaway scornfully explained, "talk of the united front is only a maneuver to deceive the workers." Thomas's reasoning was, of course, precisely the same as that of the Communists, which was why they distrusted him. He wanted to enter negotiations for a united front because he did not think the Communist party was serious about achieving one and he wanted to expose them. At the same time, Hathaway sanctimoniously denied that his Party had any ulterior motives, saying that the Communist bid for the united front "is not a maneuver."[11]

Several individual Socialists did agree to cooperate with the Communists. J. B. Matthews, executive secretary of the pacifist Fellowship of Reconciliation, accepted an invitation to speak at the first large Communist-sponsored anti-fascist meeting at Madison Square Garden on April 5, 1933. He told 22,000 cheering listeners that "the dictatorship of the proletariat is the only answer to Fascism." The first new united front organization initiated by the Party was a Free Tom Mooney Congress in Chicago scheduled for April 30. Although Norman Thomas favored joining the congress, fear that it would be endorsing a meeting run under the Communists' thumb led the Socialist party to decline a Communist invitation to participate. Reinhold Neibuhr and Heywood Broun endorsed the meeting anyhow. Matthews was quickly brought up on charges before the Socialists' executive committee and reprimanded. (This had little effect: he went on to become a staple of virtually every conceivable auxiliary.) Broun resigned from the party, explaining to readers of his column that "in getting out of the Socialist Party one should leave by the door to the left." George Smelkin, national secretary of the Young People's Socialist League, was ousted for participating in the Mooney Congress and in a united front May Day rally. More expulsions followed in Chicago.[12]

At long last, Communist isolation seemed to be ending. One thousand seventy-three delegates attended the Mooney Congress, including numerous representatives of A.F. of L. locals, the IWW, Musteites, Socialists, and even Lovestoneites and Trotskyists. A National Free Mooney Council that was established soon afterward drew the names of Roger Baldwin, Robert Morss Lovett, James Cannon, A. J. Muste, and J. B. Matthews. Robert Minor happily noted that the Communist party "has broken through the iron wall of division of the ranks of the working class" caused by the Socialists and other reformers. In practical terms the congress accomplished very little. No concrete plan for freeing Mooney emerged. The sponsors wound up losing $2,000. After a brief burst of publicity, even *The Daily Worker* ignored the feeble aftermath of the congress. Within one month Mooney himself broke with his Communist aides and turned his defense back to less partisan advocates.[13]

On the whole, however, the portents were favorable. The Party claimed that 600,000 people marched under its leadership on May Day, the largest turnout in some years. In New York a United Front May Day Committee was composed of the CPUSA, CPLA (Musteites), TUUL, and IWW. Even though these "splinter groups" could mobilize only a few thousand marchers, their presence, Hathaway reminded the Communists, "served to refute effectively the arguments of the Socialist and A.F. of L. leaders that 'a united front with Communists is impossible'." Broun, Muste, and Adam Clayton Powell were added to the National Scottsboro Action Committee. When the Workers International Relief, headquartered in Moscow, called for a united front to aid German refugees, the Party quickly created a National Committee to Aid Victims of German Fascism and was able to induce Muste, Matthews, and George Soule of *The New Republic* to join. "We placed Muste as chairman . . . merely as a 'united front' decoration," Browder later wrote. It was not very successful: Browder had to admit that the committee collected very little relief money. More important than its achievements, however, was what the committee indicated about the Communist party's newfound ability to put together an auxiliary.[14]

One of the first converts to the united front was A. J. Muste and his Conference for Progressive Labor Action. Reviled for years as an arch social-fascist, Muste had quickly responded to the Comintern's new policy, endorsing the Madison Square Garden anti-fascist meeting, supporting the Free Tom Mooney Congress, and joining in a common May Day celebration. Muste himself was soon listed on a variety of new auxiliaries. By the fall of 1933, however, the honeymoon was over and divorce proceedings had begun. Muste's sin was that he had begun agitation for a new Labor party, which the Central Committee described as "an instrument designed to hold back the radicalized masses from the path of revolutionary struggle under the leadership of the C.P.U.S.A." The Central Committee soon denounced the errant Musteites once again as "left social fascists." Not only did Muste's plan challenge potential Communist leadership of the masses, but his organization had not proved amenable to Communist influence. Israel Amter complained that "our united front with Muste had been entirely at the top" and called for a change: "We will be able to build up a united front from below."[15]

The Socialists soon discovered that they could not win either by staying out of united fronts or by getting into them. No matter which tactic they adopted, the Communists seemed able to embarrass them. Karl Borders' Federation of Unemployed Workers League was scheduled to hold its first convention in Chicago on May 13, 1933. The Communist-controlled Unemployed Councils sent a call for unity but was brusquely informed by the organizers that they would not be invited and no delegates they sent would be seated. They showed up anyway. After a bitter debate, the convention voted to seat seven delegates from the Unemployed Councils and also recognized three Communists as fraternal delegates. The disgruntled Borders declined the nomination for President, charging that "with the aid of Lovestoneites, Trotskyites and confused innocents," the Communists had captured the meeting. Borders promptly withdrew his Chicago group from the Federation of Unemployed Workers League. Most of the other unemployed organizations that were allied with him likewise departed. The delighted Communist party called the convention "an important step towards developing a united front of the unemployed to struggle against starvation." Early in June the Socialist party's Executive Committee reaffirmed its earlier decision on united fronts, voting 7–4 to forbid lower party units or individuals from joining with Communists without permission. The committee soon reversed itself, however, to allow Socialist participation in a new kind of united front–one in which the nominal leadership was non-Communist.[16]

The New Fronts

Mass organizations played an important role in Leninist theory. "Intermediary mechanisms" between the Party and the people—"nominally non-communist" but "under the party leadership," in Lenin's words—they were described by Kuusinen as a "solar system of organizations and smaller committees around the Communist Party." Hathaway called them "transmission belts to the broad masses of non-Party workers." In the United States, these organizations were often referred to as "fronts." The first big front was Friends of Soviet Russia, organized in 1921 when the Party itself was still underground. Others followed, including the International Labor Defense and the Trade Union Educational League. With the Third Period, however, the manufacture of fronts was stepped up. Hardly a month went by between 1929 and 1934 without some new organization. They ranged from the Workers' Defense Corps, for "training in defensive and fighting tactics," to the John Reed Clubs. There were the International Workers' Order, Labor Sports Union, Workers' International Relief, Unemployed Councils, National Committee for the Protection of the Foreign Born, League of Struggle for Negro Rights, United Farmers League, Workers Ex-Servicemen's League, and so on. The New York District alone boasted in 1931: "We have in our district over 100 different mass organizations."[17]

The theory behind the mass organizations, Hathaway explained, was that they could "be made to reach many thousands of workers not yet prepared for Party membership. Through these organizations, the Party must necessarily find its best training and recruiting ground." Most were headed by trusted Communists. Within each one, a Communist fraction or organized caucus was supposed to ensure Party control. The fractions had "no power of decision" but were required to obtain "the endorsement of the respective Party bodies." They were a monolithic Communist force. "No Party member," J. Peters wrote, "has the right to speak or act in the union or other mass organization against the decisions of the Fraction." Through the guidance of a mass organization, non-Communists could be gradually drawn into closer communion with the

Party while retaining the illusion that the organization was independently making decisions.[18]

"Mass organizations," however, was actually a misnomer, for few of them through the early 1930s attracted the masses. In theory, they were supposed to have a bigger membership than the Party itself; in fact, with one or two exceptions, they were far smaller. Browder once admitted that "in practice they are merely agencies for collecting money by various means to pay their overhead expenses." Their membership divided into three groups. There were Party members assigned to a particular organization. There were sympathizers who were very close to the Party but, for some reason, preferred not to join it. Finally, there were the "innocents," the only genuine non-Communist element, those lured into the groups without fully realizing their background and control. With the possible exception of the Unemployed Councils, there were certainly more fellow travelers than innocents in most of the early united fronts.[19]

Part of the explanation for their failure was the Party's heavy hand. In theory, the Party was supposed to control them but abstain from mechanical leadership. In practice, the Party crudely manipulated the mass organizations. The Party named and removed top functionaries of the auxiliaries at its pleasure. Amter stated that in the Unemployed Councils "we think we can remove and appoint and do exactly as we please. The organizers that we put in are responsible to the Party but have no responsibility to the masses." While he was still leading the Party, Bedacht complained in a memo for the Secretariat that the practice of shifting cadres from the Party to the auxiliaries left the unfortunate impression that the latter were just other names for the Communist party. The lines between Party and auxiliaries were even further blurred by the acute shortage of organizers in the early 1930s. One distressed functionary explained what happened when "we send out an organizer into a new territory. He becomes the Party organizer, he becomes the T.U.U.L. organizer, the I.L.D. organizer, the W.I.R. organizer, etc. The result is that he is so confused he actually [doesn't] know where he stands."[20]

The auxiliaries' internal life left a great deal to be desired. Party units treated them as extensions of the Party. It was far less trouble to issue orders and directives for the auxiliaries to carry out than to go through the charade of discussion and debate. Since the Party controlled the auxiliary anyway, the result was the same. Herbert Benjamin complained that: "Party organizations instead of mobilizing the membership for participation in Unemployed Councils and committees, themselves take over the functions of these united front organizations. Where non-Party workers are attracted to our movement in such cases, they find themselves excluded from all participation in the *actual* work of *planning* and *leading* actions." One internal memo complained, "The Party's guidance in the Unemployed Councils consists of nothing but one comrade bringing down instructions of the Communist Party to the unemployed workers." Consequently, only those who were willing to accept the Party's control were willing to stay in the fronts for any length of time. Others, according to Bedacht, quickly understood "they are not members of a real organization, but at best a tolerated wall decoration in sham organizations."[21]

Some Party units even treated the auxiliaries as cows to be milked for money. One functionary boasted that his district had "succeeded in making the fraternal organizations pay the Party 10% of the income on affairs. With a little pressure that was used lately in some of the organizations the motion for the 10% for the Party was fully accepted, and now it is unnecessary to send comrades to them. They send their amounts in themselves." Hathaway summoned the secretaries of all the Party's New York mass organizations in June 1933 and appealed to them "to rally their membership in an effort to relieve the New York District of the Communist Party of its present financial difficulties." The organizations promised to try to raise $8,000 within fifteen days to meet the Party's deficit. Later that year, Browder had to caution that the Party could not tax mass organizations but could only approach them for voluntary donations.[22]

The theory and practice of party fronts then were almost exactly opposite. The theory was that the Party could reach out to the masses only through the medium of fronts. In practice, the fronts caused the Party to stew in its own juice because they were more or less lightly camouflaged replicas of the Party itself, more like departments of the Party than true extensions. Although the trouble was correctly diagnosed, the solution was not found until the Party was willing to build a different kind of front.

The Party's sudden success with united fronts in 1933 was a combination of new causes and new organizational techniques. The Comintern's half-turn on the united front made it feasible for the Party at last to approach other groups and their leaders. The old fronts had been handicapped from the beginning by their exclusively Communist leadership: without any resistance, they adopted Party positions on every conceivable issue. As a result, they tended to become Communist instruments for work among blacks, trade unionists, or the unemployed instead of coalitions of Communists and non-Communists. As long as Comintern policy forbade contact with "social-fascists," the fate of every Communist united front was sealed.

The Socialist, radical, and liberal leaders who willingly entered into the united fronts when invited in 1933 did so from the overriding motive of anti-fascism. That Hitler's success owed a great deal to disunity on the left seemed to be a stark warning of the need for cooperation. Even if the Communists were not overly concerned about his victory, plenty of other people were. The non-Communist leaders who agreed to lend their names to the new united front efforts were not, except in rare cases, duped or misled. They knew quite well with whom they were cooperating. No one forced or compelled them to sign manifestos or agree to programs. They did so to advance causes in which they believed. When they acquiesced in a statement that carefully echoed Party policy, it was because they either believed in it or felt that the importance of maintaining unity should override any inclination to make a fuss or disrupt harmonious relations.

The new auxiliaries marked a key departure for the Communists. The early ones like the Mooney Congress and the German Aid Committee were unable to accomplish much. The Party was still feeling its way. Its problems were illustrated by the United States Congress Against War in September 1933. Although its name frequently changed to accommodate the vagaries of Comintern policy, this auxiliary, later known as the American League Against War and Fascism, eventually became the Party's most successful one, claiming millions of adherents and an impressive roster of non-Communist notables. Its origins and early tribulations provide a vivid case study of the new Communist approach to the united front.

The story goes back to the World Congress Against Imperialist War held in Amsterdam in August 1932. That international gathering, in turn, was the product of a long-standing Comintern concern about capitalist encirclement of the Soviet Union. The Comintern's Eleventh Plenum in 1931 listed the "fight against imperialist war and military intervention against the U.S.S.R." as one of the three major tasks of all Communist parties. By the Twelfth Plenum, the main task of all Communist parties was stated to be the organization of campaigns "against the closely approaching intervention."[23]

The Amsterdam conference was planned to rally as broad a spectrum of pro-Communist public opinion as possible to defend Russia. Henri Barbusse, the French Communist writer, was chairman. The Friends of the Soviet Union took the initiative in most countries in choosing delegates and did much of the preparatory work. "About one-third of the total delegates at the congress were members of the F.S.U.," one of its leaders boasted in the Comintern organ. Of the 2,196 delegates, only 830 were avowed Communists but hundreds more represented Party auxiliaries. Behind every detail was the Comintern's master propagandist, Willi Munzenberg, who organized the congress, carefully arranged its details, and financed much of it with Comintern funds.[24]

Although many pacifists and other non-Communists spoke at the congress, the delegates unanimously approved a manifesto that accepted the Communist position. The manifesto defended the "steadfast peace policy" of the Soviet Union and blamed all imperialist nations for the war danger. The only concession to the non-Communist delegates was a certain coyness in expression. Enemies of war, the manifesto suggested, could not compromise "with the prevailing system practiced by certain leaders of working class organizations." It delicately avoided calling that system social-fascism. Among the pledges made by the delegates was one "against armaments, against war preparations, and in consequence, against the governments ruling us." Only the masses organizing "to come to power" could prevent a world conflagration.[25]

The war danger that worried the Comintern did not yet emanate from fascism. In fact, there were only two fleeting references to fascism in the entire manifesto. Although the Amsterdam congress attracted a number of pacifists, it was not concerned with opposition to all war. The manifesto warned that so long as capitalism and imperialism existed, war was inevitable. Only the destruction of the existing social system would make it impossible. The official name of the congress was not, as it was usually referred to by its American affiliate, the World Conference Against War, but the World Conference Against *Imperialist* War, and one of its decisions was to create a Permanent World Committee for the Fight Against Imperialist War. The congress soon merged with another Munzenberg creation—the European Workers' Anti-Fascist Congress. The Comintern's bulletin grouped the resulting organization, as well as similar-minded organizations in other countries, under the name of the International Bureau for the Fight Against Imperialist War and Fascism.[26]

An American delegation of thirty-two, led by Theodore Dreiser, Sherwood Anderson, and H. W. L. Dana, attended the Amsterdam meeting. They had left the United States after a raucous farewell meeting in which participants showed their "contempt for rotten liberalism and pacifism" by hooting Arthur Garfield Hays when he criticized the Soviet Union and suggested that dressing soldiers in underwear would be a more effective way of stopping war than the upcoming conference. When the peacemakers returned home, they announced that the American Committee for the World Congress Against War would strive to carry out the program agreed upon in Amsterdam. Oakley Johnson was chosen secretary, Malcolm Cowley chairman, and Dreiser honorary chairman.[27]

By early 1933 its name had been changed to the American Committee for Struggle Against War. A few months later, J. B. Matthews was induced to chair the organizing committee charged with planning the First United States Congress Against War. His major task was to persuade Socialists and middle-class elements to join the Communists in this united front. The first formal invitation to the Socialist party to participate on the planning committee came in a June 3 letter from Roger Baldwin, Dorothy Detzer of the Women's International League for Peace and Freedom, Malcolm Cowley, J. B. Matthews, and Donald Henderson. Only the latter was a Communist. Although skeptical, the Socialist party agreed to send an observer. At the organizing session of the Arrangements Committee on June 14, Earl Browder and Robert Minor were the only two Communist party representatives. Twelve of the other twenty-three people, however, were delegates from such Party auxiliaries as the John Reed Clubs. Donald Henderson was also present as an officer of the American committee, giving the Communists fifteen of the twenty-five votes.[28]

The Socialist party's National Executive Committee met in early July, and Norman Thomas engineered passage of a motion endorsing Socialist participation in the anti-war congress with four provisos. There were to be no Communist attacks on the Socialists. They would be guaranteed speakers at the congress. The Socialists would be given one-quarter of the seats on the Arrangements Committee. Other non-Communist groups would be included. Within a week the Arrangements Committee had accepted the Socialist proposal, the Communists themselves moved the nomination of eleven Socialists to the expanded planning body, and it appeared that a new day had dawned on the united front. The call for the Congress Against War was signed by both the Communist and Socialist parties.[29]

The Communist party, however, had changed only the form, not the substance, of its united front tactics. The Socialists soon discovered that the Communists had no intention of changing their habits. Not that there was much enthusiasm for the anti-war congress within the older party. But it was their inability to enforce their fourth and final condition—inclusion of non-Communist groups—which frustrated the Socialist representatives on the Arrangements Committee. The Socialists were eager to broaden the congress and secure additional non-Communist support. Convinced that no significant union representation was possible unless the TUUL unions, most of them largely paper organizations, were excluded, they tried to oust them and failed miserably. Of the fifty-two organizations that had affiliated with the anti-war congress, only the Communist party and the Young Communist League were avowedly Communist. Thirty-four others, however, were Party auxiliaries. There were forty-five members of the Arrangements Committee: only eighteen were Communists, but many of the non-Communists, like Matthews and Robert Morss Lovett, were so eager to cooperate with them that they could be counted on to support Party initiatives.[30]

The Socialists' belated realization that the congress would follow the Communist party line was not the only shock in store for them. *The Daily Worker* carried a harsh attack on Socialist policy in the American committee on July 17, the same day it printed the joint call for the congress. The Socialists protested, and Robert Minor assured the Arrangements Committee that it would not happen again. Edward Levinson, in monitoring developments for the Socialists, warned the Communists that another breach of their nonaggression pact would end the united front. Though forewarned, the Party proceeded to launch a fresh barrage. For several years, August 1 had been the occasion for anti-war demonstrations under Party auspices. Discussing the planned 1933 rally, the Central Committee called on Socialist workers to join under Communist leadership on that day. At the same time an editorial charged that the Socialist leaders only "pretend to fight fascism" while actually paving its way. The Socialists had had enough and withdrew from the congress.[31]

The Socialist exodus ended up by playing directly into the Party's hands. Without them, the remaining non-Communists lacked cohesion and direction. The Communist party was able to dominate the congress with relative ease. Earl Browder tried later to claim that his organization was never firmly in control of the American League Against War and Fascism, or its predecessors, but sought to act as a restraining force, holding back the leftist intellectuals who dominated the league's early proceedings and wrote its first manifesto. The story of the first congress, however, was a tale of overt Party control.[32]

At the First United States Congress Against War in late September, 2,600 delegates were present. Two halls had to be used for the opening session. Reinhold Niebuhr and J. B. Matthews chaired the separate meetings. Henri Barbusse, arriving to address the meeting, was briefly detained by immigration officials who had been thunderstruck by his declaration: "I am a member of the Communist Party." Only two events marred the harmony for which the Party had striven. Jay Lovestone was nominated to the Presiding Committee. While the Communists were eager to have non-Communist names prominently displayed, Communist "renegades" who had formed splinter groups were not wanted. The proposal was "drowned in a thunderous roar of disapproval." Later in the day, Roger Baldwin raised the issue a second time on behalf of one-quarter of the Presiding Committee. Once again, indignation swept the hall. Matthews, unable to control the crowd, called on Browder. The latter briskly rejected Lovestone. A fight broke out in one section of the hall and ended only after Baldwin's motion was overwhelmingly defeated.[33]

So blatant a demonstration of the Party's control was distasteful to others who were, like Baldwin, relative apostles of cooperation. That evening Browder was confronted with an ultimatum by the non-Communists on the Presiding Committee: either a Lovestoneite joined their ranks or they walked out of the congress. Charles Zimmerman, a former Communist now allied with Lovestone, was nominated the following day and added as a representative of Local 22 of the International Ladies' Garment Workers' Union. When he appeared on the platform to speak, the crowd, either not yet informed of the bargain or too incensed to care, raised such a ruckus that he was unable to continue. Browder had to come to the microphone to plead with his minions "to maintain perfect order" before Zimmerman, whose 30,000-strong local outnumbered by far the Communist party membership, could complete his speech.[34]

Aside from these two embarrassing displays of Party domination, the congress rolled smoothly along. It elected a national committee divided between Communists and fellow travelers. It approved a change in name to correspond to its European counterpart, becoming the American League Against War and Fascism. It accepted a manifesto denouncing fascism, monopolistic capitalism as the source of the war danger, the Roosevelt administration, American imperialism, the League of Nations, and the "growing fascization of our so-called 'democratic government.'" It applauded the "consistent peace policy" of the Soviet Union.[35]

Browder's modest appraisal of the Communist role at the Congress two decades later was an afterthought. At the time he was far less discreet. "The Congress from the beginning," he told the Comintern, "was led by our Party quite openly but without infringing upon its broad non-Party character." The manifesto and program developed at the congress were "politically satisfactory." The youth delegation, 550 strong and largely non-Communist, "in a special meeting openly accepted the leadership of the Y.C.L. in the Congress." Another Party official boasted: "Nobody can say that the Communist Party was not at the very center of the Anti-War Congress—the outstanding feature of the Congress was the work of the Communist Party." The Party had succeeded in gathering a large group of liberals and Socialists to join with it. It had been less successful in attracting real, functioning non-Communist organizations. The American League Against War and Fascism was largely a coalition of Communist auxiliaries and prominent non-Communists with few troops behind them. The Party was still unwilling to share control with other *organizations,* even if it was willing to do so with non-Communist individuals.[36]

The Communist party soon had another dramatic opportunity to demonstrate what it meant by the united front against fascism. The Communists confirmed the deepest suspicions of their enemies by precipitating a riot in Madison Square Garden on the afternoon of February 16, 1934. Nobody should have been surprised that the Communists would disrupt a meeting. Frequent governmental and vigilante assaults on their own meetings had not instilled in them any devotion to the First Amendment. They had long experience in breaking up meetings and frequently boasted of doing so.

Party Violence

Even before the Communist party had emerged from underground in the early 1920s, some of its younger militants were disrupting an American speaking tour of Raphael Abramovitch, an ardent Menshevik opponent of the Lenin regime. Years later, Sam Darcy recalled organizing bands of young Communists to disrupt Abramovitch's speeches. Max Bedacht wrote to all district organizers in 1930 warning that Abramovitch was embarking on another speaking tour and asking them "to organize a similar reception." That same year Victor Chernov, a Russian Social-Revolutionary party leader, met similar treatment. One district bureau noted: "We proceed with the breaking up of [Chernov's] meeting provided we have a minimum of 15 Russian-speaking comrades in the hall." *The Daily Worker* boasted that California workers gave him "a hot reception," transformed his speeches "into a demonstration for the Soviet Union," and sold Communist literature. The Party's Organizational Department wrote the Los Angeles comrades: "Your line and your actions during the Chernov meeting were splendid." When the Civil Liberties Union protested the "unfair and un-American" treatment of Chernov,

The Daily Worker accused it of uniting with "the advocates and practition-ers of assassination of Soviet leaders" and defended violence "used by the workers against the oppressors." Russian émigrés were not the only victims. When Morris Hillquit and Socialist Mayor Daniel Hoan of Mil-waukee were speaking in San Francisco in 1930, Communists broke up the meeting. *The Daily Worker*'s lead headline trumpeted "Social-Fascist Enemies of Jobless Get Answer." Special efforts were also made to pre-vent Trotskyists from speaking.[37]

As the American Communists prepared for the 1932 election, they frankly acknowledged that one way to reach the workers was to invade rallies of their enemies. For too long the Communists had talked only to themselves and ignored their foes. "This has to be changed," Clarence Hathaway told a Party plenum. "We have to send our comrades into the meetings organized by the Socialists, Republicans and Democrats." The Party would succeed "only to the extent that we are successful in literally tearing the workers away from the bourgeois parties." The plenum de-manded "not a single political meeting without Communists present." Earl Browder acknowledged shortly after the election that a few "very zealous, very energetic comrades" understood the instruction "to mean to go in and break up the meetings of our enemies and they proceeded to carry out their Communist duty as they understood it." His remarks were met by laughter. Browder did criticize these activities as counterproduc-tive but also admitted that the Party leadership had not issued a public correction. Despite their rhetoric, the Communists had avoided interfer-ence with Democratic and Republican rallies, correctly sensing that phys-ical abuse would be the least of their troubles if they did so. In any case, supporters of the two major parties were far less likely to listen to a Communist message, and neither was regarded as so serious an enemy as the "social-fascists."[38]

The Austrian Socialist party was the pride of the Second Internation-al, dominating the left in Austria in a way few other Socialist parties could duplicate. A right-wing party, led by Chancellor Engelbert Doll-fuss, was in the process of consolidating a dictatorship. In early February 1934, Dollfuss moved against the Socialists. For four days a bloody civil war raged in Vienna, ending with the Socialists' defeat. Both Commu-nists and Socialists in America launched protests against the Dollfuss government. The Communists also charged that the Austrian workers had been "betrayed by their Social-Democratic leaders" who, it was al-leged, had been aiding the Austrian march to fascism.[39]

The first radical response against the massacre abroad produced a short-lived united front. The Party called for a demonstration at the Austrian consulate in New York. Representatives of the League for Industrial Democracy, its student affiliate, and the Young People's Socialist League had originally agreed to sponsor the rally but were prevented from doing so by a Socialist official. Nevertheless, a crowd of 4,000–10,000 radicals, including both Communists and Socialists, gathered on February 14 and marched around the block. A delegation led by Robert Minor and James Ford, at first ejected from the building, finally got to see the consul. When Minor tried to report to the crowd on the conversation they had had, the police intervened and some fighting took place.[40]

The following evening the Communists held their own "united front rally" in the Bronx Coliseum. Browder, Ford, and Hathaway spoke, appealing to the audience of 8,000 to "forge one mighty united front of struggle" under Communist leadership. Communists were encouraged to attend a Socialist rally at Madison Square Garden the next day. A banner headline in *The Daily Worker* urged "March in United Ranks to Madison Square Garden," and an article warned that "anyone who splits the ranks of the workers at this time helps the fascists, injures the valiant struggle of our heroic brothers in Austria and is a contemptible enemy of the working class." The Party press meanwhile was busy charging the Socialists with responsibility for their own massacre. On one day alone *The Daily Worker* had headlines such as "Social Democratic Leaders Are Already Coming to Terms with the Dollfuss Government" and "Austria Workers Break Chains of Social-Democratic Betrayal, Take Road of Revolutionary Struggle," as well as an editorial denouncing Socialist party leaders. More ominously, Irving Potash, a leader of the TUUL needleworkers union, demanded that a representative of his group be allowed to speak. On the way to the Garden Potash told another Communist, Melech Epstein: "They are not going to hold that meeting."[41]

The Communists, 5,000 strong, marched to the rally in two large groups behind the Red Front Band and a row of banners. Trouble began almost immediately. The Socialist ushers took away the Communists' musical instruments and confiscated their banners and literature. Some fistfights erupted. The ushers tried to force the Communists upstairs, but some "stormed into the arena downstairs" and occupied about fifty rows. While they waited for the meeting to start they vented their anger at invitations that had been made to the "open fascist" Matthew Woll of the A.F. of L. and Mayor LaGuardia, chanting "We'll hang Matthew Woll to a sour apple tree" and "Down with the fascist LaGuardia." When Algernon Lee, a Socialist leader, opened the meeting, chants and boos interrupted every sentence. One Communist, hoisted to the shoulders of some comrades, tried to urge quiet until Woll arrived, at which point he could

114

be stopped from speaking. His plea went unheeded. Some Communists were tossed from the balcony, "beaten and pummeled by enraged Socialist workers."

Clarence Hathaway appeared at the podium as David Dubinsky was finishing a speech no one could hear. Hathaway later insisted that he hoped "to propose to the chairman that I be permitted to make a one-minute appeal for perfect order in the meeting." The sight of Hathaway making for the microphone was all the livid Socialists could bear. They had been denounced, their dead colleagues in Austria had been defamed, and their meeting, being broadcast over a nationwide radio network, had been turned into a shambles. Now it appeared the Communists were preparing to seize control of the microphone. Several men leaped on the *Daily Worker* editor and "struck him with fists and chairs, rushed him across the platform and threw him over a railing to the floor." Hathaway claimed his "scalp was lacerated by the batterings of chairs wielded with Social-Fascist ferocity." As he left the arena, fistfights broke out, chairs were flung from the balconies, and the police rushed in to restore order. As Algernon Lee tried to read a resolution condemning the Dollfuss government, the Communists screamed "We want Hathaway." The only speaker able to make himself heard, black Socialist Frank Crosswaith, spat out a denunciation of Communists as pigs "who will always remain pigs because it is the nature of Communists to be pigs." Finally, the chairman called for adjournment, the audience rose, and each faction sang its own version of the *Internationale.* The Communists regrouped outside, and Robert Minor, on the shoulders of the crowd, led them back to Union Square.[42]

The Socialists reacted with fury. *The New Leader* called Communists "Ishmaels . . . moral lepers . . . unfit to associate with any civilized human beings . . . ghouls. . . . They are misfits and pathological creatures cast up by an unsocial civilization." Twenty-five prominent intellectuals signed an open letter to the Communist party. For many of those who had been part of the League of Professional Groups for Foster and Ford—including James Rorty, Felix Morrow, Edmund Wilson, and John Dos Passos and for others like Elliott Cohen, Lionel Trilling, and Meyer Schapiro—the signing of the letter marked their first public break with the Communists. They deplored the Party's "disruptive action" which had led to "a disaster of national scope in the struggle for unity against Fascism." While regretting the defection of Dos Passos, *The New Masses* wrote off those "vacillating intellectuals who overnight have become metamorphosed from their academic cocoons into revolutionary butterflies, flit dizzily from Zionism to internationalism, from Lovestoneism to Trotskyism and Musteism. When the crucial moment comes they will no doubt flee in an attempt to save their beautiful multi-colored wings from the fire." The defectors, however, were to become the core of the intellectual opposition to Stalinism in America.[43]

Another casualty of the meeting was the American League Against War and Fascism. Its last three Socialist leaders, J. B. Matthews, Frances Henson, and Mary Fox, resigned. Matthews, the league's national chairman, called its difficulties in building a united front now "insurmountable." Other non-Communist organizations withdrew. The Musteites dropped out of the league because it was not a real united front "but in fact represents only one substantial organized labor group, the Communist Party and its affiliates."[44]

Some people could not be dissuaded by any evidence. Roger Baldwin and Annie Gray, of the Women's Peace Society, joined with Browder to issue a league statement calling for continued unity and "the fullest freedom of all organizations to conduct in their own way their campaigns." The statement refused "the function of passing judgment upon such disputes as that which give rise to the resignation of a few members of its committee," castigated deserters, and urged greater efforts to combat war and fascism. Harry F. Ward, a Methodist minister, professor of Christian ethics at Union Theological Seminary, and chairman of the American Civil Liberties Union, replaced Matthews as chairman, and the league was soon preparing for its Second Congress, held in Chicago in September. No dissidence marred the occasion this time. The league refused to make public the list of organizations sending delegates. The Musteites charged that 70 percent of the delegates were from Party auxiliaries. By the Communists' own admission, "the principal weakness at this Congress remains the representation from the working class, the trade unions."[45]

Years later, Browder stated that the entire affair "was distinctly avoidable" and had set back the united front for a year. He blamed his enemies in the Party, opponents of the united front, for provoking the riot, offering as candidates for the villains' role both Clarence Hathaway and Gerhart Eisler. Neither fit the part. Hathaway was one of Browder's closest colleagues. Eisler, a German Communist who had been a Comintern representative in America since the summer of 1933, was also in Browder's inner circle. Described by another Party insider as a "premature Popular Frontist," Eisler had gotten in trouble with his own German party for united front policies. The February issue of *The Communist*, moreover, had pointed out that a transition to a new stage of "revolutionary crisis" was in progress. Under such circumstances the Madison

Square Garden incident most probably had the sanction of the Communist party leadership and represented no breakdown in discipline.[46]

The Socialist party did begin to unravel. Not all or even most of its serious troubles were Communist-inspired. Its divisions were too serious to patch up. The party's right wing began to desert Socialism for Franklin Roosevelt. Some of its left-wing members yearned to convert it into a revolutionary party that would compete with the Communists to overthrow bourgeois government. A few went so far as to join the Communist party, most prominently Harold Ashe, the former Socialist state secretary in California. As if the disagreements between the social-democratic Old Guard and the Norman Thomas Militants were not disabling enough, a Revolutionary Policy Committee with ties to the Lovestoneites enlisted J. B. Matthews and a number of young militants and launched a campaign to capture the Socialist party. In June 1934 the left-wingers led by Thomas, adopted a platform calling for fighting any capitalist war with mass resistance and suggesting that the Socialists would not hesitate to seize power in an emergency with less than majority support. The social-democratic Old Guard prepared to prevent the Militants from gaining control of such institutions of New York Socialism as *The Jewish Daily Forward, The New Leader,* the Rand School, Camp Tamiment, and the Workmen's Circle. The Revolutionary Policy Committee pooh-poohed the changes and called for a dictatorship of the proletariat and a vanguard party shed of reformist illusions. As the Socialist party tore itself to pieces, the Communists began to supplant their old rival as the largest and most influential force on the American left. The full potential of the new united fronts, however, would have to await further developments in Moscow.[47]

7

Goodbye to the TUUL

NO Party organization had been launched with such great expectations as the Trade Union Unity League. Few proved as disappointing. Very nearly stillborn by its second anniversary, the TUUL was a ghostly presence in most industries, where its organizers demonstrated an eerie talent for losing what strikes they did succeed in calling. The TUUL survived into 1935, even enjoying a modest upsurge in 1934 that pushed its alleged membership over 100,000. Nonetheless, its dismal start could never be overcome. Despite a handful of successful campaigns, it remained an albatross preventing the Party from reaching most American workers. Long before it was formally abandoned, the TUUL had proved so unsuccessful that the Communists, under Comintern prodding, were forced to look back toward the A.F. of L.

The Comintern's half-turn on a united front in early 1933 did not fundamentally alter the way the TUUL did business because a half-turn in trade union policy had already been subtly under way for several months. The TUUL unions were so inept that both the Profintern and Comintern feared that unless the Communists were more cautious about forming new unions they would totally sever whatever tenuous links they had to mass labor unions. Fortunately, there was a face-saving option. The TUUL's charter had not restricted it to organizing the unorganized into new unions. Although intended to be an alternative union movement, the TUUL had also assigned itself another, quite separate task: "It organizes," its program declared, "the revolutionary workers within the reformist unions." The pledge was originally only window-dressing. The TUUL did not have enough organizers to staff its new unions competently, much less remain active within the old unions. The Party's 1930 Convention Resolution had exactly one sentence about building Communist fractions in the A.F. of L. unions and four pages on the TUUL, a fair indicator of the relative importance attached to the two tasks. Jack Stachel later confessed that the Americans had gone as far as "telling the workers you can do nothing" in the A.F. of L. By mid-1931 the Profintern called opposition work in reformist unions "a branch of work which has almost completely disappeared."[1]

The casual dismissal of the supposedly bankrupt A.F. of L. quickly began to haunt the TUUL. No great mass of workers had breathlessly followed them out of the A.F. of L.; no groundswell of the unorganized had occurred. The only option was to recruit within the A.F. of L. In December 1931 the Profintern's Eighth Convention suggested a tactical reorientation. A.F. of L. members, supposedly undergoing a process of radicalization, could be ignored no longer. Communists were ordered to fight "for ideological and organizational influence and leadership in the local branches of the REFORMIST and reactionary unions which have mass membership." Needless to say, the goal was hardly to strengthen these bastions of reaction but to destroy them by creating fifth columns. "Strong groups must be organized inside the reformist and other reactionary trade unions, " the Profintern explained, "and the struggle waged to win to the revolutionary trade union movement the rank and file members." Thus, the TUUL controlled opposition work in the A.F. of L.; the latter "must be in the hands of the corresponding revolutionary trade unions."[2]

The Comintern also quietly increased its emphasis on the old unions. The Twelfth Plenum, held in November 1932, did not make any overt policy change but suggested in several formulations how much more important working in the A.F. of L. had become. Communists were charged with the "extension of *permanent and intimate contacts* with the *majority* of the workers, wherever workers may be found." The Party's weaknesses were attributed to "the impermissable weak revolutionary work carried on *inside the reformist trade unions*." Remaining in these unions merely to denounce their leaders was not enough. Neither was just trying to steal their members. Communist parties had "to insure the *immediate restoration and extension of revolutionary positions in the reformist trade unions*." The Comintern did not suggest abandoning the Red trade unions or even slighting them. The "chief danger" remained the opportunistic error of downgrading their role. Nonetheless, work in the A.F. of L. was no longer just a ploy to detach its most militant members and recruit them for the TUUL.[3]

What were the practical consequences of such a view? Jack Stachel noted that where the Party had revoluntionary unions it would seek to convince workers in reformist unions that the failures of their own organization had made the TUUL necessary. The goal would be the amalgamation of the A.F. of L. affiliates into the TUUL to create one class-struggle union. Where no revolutionary unions existed, such as in the building trades, printing, or the railroads, the Party would confine its work to the reformist unions. Stachel explained that new Red unions would not be formed willy-nilly:

> In the United States our main line is new unions based on the fact that the masses are unorganized and that the unions are controlled by the bureaucrats and more and more it becomes impossible to advance the interest of the workers without forming new unions, but where the reformist unions have a mass character our first step is to work through these unions and build our oppositions, and only then do we form revolutionary unions side by side in the course of the struggle, when the necessity arises and we have mobilized masses for it.

Browder added the reminder that A.F. of L. activity was still to be subordinated to the TUUL, noting that whether workers were organized in Red unions or reformist unions, they were "two phases of one task—the development of the revolutionary trade union movement."[4]

These brave words concealed the disarray of the revolutionary union movement in early 1933. The Party was barely visible within the A.F. of L. It had held a "rank and file conference" at a 1932 A.F. of L. convention composed only of elected A.F. of L. delegates. The gathering was admittedly "small." Stachel lamented that "we are now reaping the fruits of our isolation from these organized workers, from our neglect for a long time to work within these reformist unions." He admitted that the Communists' attitude had "helped the bureaucrats to maintain their hold in these unions and made it difficult for us to play a more important role."[5]

The state of the TUUL was hardly more robust. Communist-led unions directed only a few small strikes in 1932. When Earl Browder discussed the state of the Party's union movement in the Open Letter of July 1933, he could only record a catalogue of woes in the most important industries. The Steel and Metal Workers Industrial Union was pitifully weak: "Most workers have not yet heard about the union." The National Miners Union was in tatters. The National Textile Workers Union had

1,000 members, no more than it had counted in 1929. The Marine Workers Industrial Union "remains a small organization isolated from the largest masses." The Auto Workers Union had receded after a brief strike wave. After years of Communist resolutions about its key role, the railroad industry was still "unexplored territory." Jack Stachel reported to his Party colleagues that in 1932 the "majority of the strikes were by members of the reformist unions" or were "fought under reformist leadership."[6]

There was no shortage of explanations for the Red unions' sorry state. Too often, Stachel admitted, the unions were "duplicates" of the Communist party. At its founding convention the Steel and Metal Workers Industrial Union endorsed the Communist platform and the Foster-Ford Presidential ticket. Every TUUL union was led by an avowed Party member, giving the TUUL so openly Communist a gloss that few independent unionists would have anything to do with it. Before every union meeting, the ECCI Presidium instructed, "the corresponding Party committees must discuss the questions which are to be taken up" and "work out suitable directives for the Communist fractions." Party members in the fractions did not have to offer these proposals in the name of the Party, but "other members of the fraction must vote solidly for these proposals." Even the ECCI admitted that despite instructions to avoid mechanically imposing fraction decisions on their unions, Party members frequently destroyed the unions' internal life and turned them into duplicates of the Party. The TUUL was further discredited by its revolutionary posturing. Its strikes might have been difficult enough for any union to win, but reluctance to call them off at opportune moments usually guaranteed defeat. "We were so happy to have strikes," Stachel admitted, "we didn't want to end them."[7]

One of the few places the TUUL made even modest gains in 1933 was in the automobile industry, but its success there was transitory. In November 1932 the Communist party assigned its own cadres to shop work, concentrating on the Briggs body plant in Detroit. When the company announced a wage cut in January 1933, the plant's machines were stopped and the entire factory walked out. A strike committee was elected and augmented by three Auto Workers Union (AWU) officials, including Phil Raymond, its national secretary, and a representative of the Unemployed Councils. The company, taken by surprise, quickly agreed to negotiations; within two days the wage cut was rescinded, and the workers were back in the plant. A spate of auto strikes followed, involving 50,000 auto workers during the year. Of these, 10,000 were led by the A.F. of L., 17,000 by the Mechanics Educational Society of America (MESA), an independent union of skilled craftsmen; and 18,000 by the AWU. The remaining workers went on strike spontaneously.[8]

The Communists were naturally elated that at long last they had gained a foothold in the auto industry. "The Detroit strikes were led by our Union," noted Browder, who called them "the outstanding example of the great possibilities of big results with even a small measure of correct work." To their dismay, however, their foothold rapidly slipped away and the AWU lost control of its strikes. Jack Stachel pointed to the failure to carry on "the struggle against social fascism" as the biggest error of the TUUL union. The Auto Workers Union never recovered and began to shrivel away. Stachel confessed in March 1934 that the union "is today organizationally very weak." That spring the Central Committee dispatched William Weinstone to Detroit as district organizer, assigned to do something about the auto industry, where the TUUL then did not have a single shop organized.[9]

The Comintern's appeal for a united front against fascism produced few concrete results in the union movement. The TUUL assured its rival that it "does not aim to split the A.F. of L. or other unions. We stand for the policy of working with the masses of A.F. of L. unions." The offer was not dignified by a reply. The Party soon resumed its denunciations. By early June, Clarence Hathaway was once again calling the A.F. of L. "social-fascist." When A.F. of L. leaders endorsed the National Industrial Recovery Act, they were even promoted to full-fledged "fascists."[10]

The one effort to build a united labor front with erstwhile "social-fascist" enemies did not get very far. The last gap of the short-lived Communist-Musteite alliance took place at an August 1933 conference in Cleveland. Only 30 of the 82 signers of the call to the National Trade Union Conference for United Action were identifiable Communists, but when the 507 delegates gathered in Cleveland, 146 represented the Unemployed Councils and another 242 were from TUUL unions. Earl Browder later told the Comintern that "the great body of the conference was composed of our own forces; besides ourselves and close sympathizers, only a small group of Muste leaders came." The Communists wanted the Musteites to throw their small but potent labor forces into the TUUL and merge their Unemployed Leagues with the Party's organization. Browder disclaimed Party dominance of one TUUL union: "It is . . . bunk when they say the SMWIU is controlled by the Communist Party," he stated indignantly. "There are not enough Communists in it. There should be more." Unconvinced, the Musteites refused to commit themselves to support the TUUL. They did agree to a joint struggle against the National Recovery Administration and unification of the Communist and Musteite unemployed organizations. Muste, however, soon concluded that the kind of united front desired by the Communists was one they dominated. None of the Cleveland conference's pledges were carried out. The TUUL had lost its one slim chance to broaden its base beyond the Communist party.[11]

No aspect of the New Deal so enraged the Party as the National Industrial Recovery Act, a measure sanctioning industrial cooperation to regulate prices, wages, and production. From the moment the act was introduced into Congress, the Communist party began denouncing the plan as an example of "slave legislation." Browder charged that its labor sections were "the American version of Mussolini's 'corporative state,' special state-controlled labor unions closely tied up with and under the direction of the employers." To the Party, the NRA was stark evidence of the collusion of government, big business, and social-fascist labor leaders to dampen labor militancy. Section 7A, detailing the right to collective bargaining, was vague enough to encourage employers to set up company unions as an alternative to dealing with real unions. The A.F. of L., while aware of Section 7A's weaknesses, nonetheless regarded the provision as an unparalleled opportunity to organize. The Communists accused the A.F. of L. of selling out the workers. "Green Applauds Industrial Slave Legislation" read one headline denouncing the A.F. of L. president. The purpose of the NRA, the Communists asserted over and over again, was "to smash the revolutionary trade unions," leaving the workers at the mercy of class collaborationists.[12]

With so pessimistic and shrill a view of the NRA, the Communist party was unprepared for the sudden lift it gave to the entire labor movement. After several years in the doldrums, the movement suddenly exploded in 1933. There were three times as many strikers in 1933 as in the year before. Jack Stachel was so discombobulated that, within three sentences, he both affirmed and denied that the NRA was responsible for the ferment. "Naturally the strikes did not arise as a result of the N.R.A. The N.R.A. was legislation attempting to arrest the growing strike movement. Yet it is also true that as a result of the enactment of the N.R.A. the number of strikes has increased." The bewilderment was not limited to a few Party leaders. As much as ideology dictated fierce attacks on the NRA, the experience of field organizers with its benefits caused some slackening in vigilance. One trade union functionary admitted that illusions about the act's effects had penetrated into the Party:

Despite the correct Party analysis of the N.R.A., the poisonous propaganda carried on by the government and the reformists about the N.R.A. as a new charter of labor penetrated the ranks of fractions. . . . It seriously affected the Communist work of the fractions and the decisiveness with which our fractions carried on the struggle against the reformists.[13]

The Party did not openly confess its misjudgment. Grudgingly, however, it began to admit that something had changed in American life, making union organizing far easier than it once had been. "The Roosevelt program," Stachel magnanimously conceded at the 1933 Extraordinary Party Conference, "is not a one-sided question from the point of view of results upon the masses." The TUUL, which was meeting at the same time, stressed that "the TUUL unions are not taking full advantage of the tremendous desire of the workers to organize."[14]

A look at published membership figures alone gave the impression that the TUUL was prospering. At the beginning of the New Deal it had 25,000 members. Within a year, another 100,000 allegedly joined. The Shoe and Leather Workers reported an increase of membership from 1,000 to 9,000. The Needle Trades Workers jumped from 12,000 to 20,000. The Tobacco Workers went from 150 to over 1,000, while the Steel and Metal Workers erupted from 1,500 in July to 15,000 by September. The figures were, however, somewhat suspect. In July 1933, by Browder's own account, the major TUUL unions were pathetically weak. And, a Comintern spokesman reported stagnation in all but the Steel, Agricultural and Marine unions after the NRA went into effect.[15]

The Communists attributed their success, modest though it was, to the reorientation and rededication occasioned by the Open Letter. In fact, however, the TUUL was the lucky recipient of a windfall. Its temporary success had less to do with its own merits than with the Roosevelt administration. The NRA encouraged unionization. The TUUL benefited, not because it was Communist but because it was a union. Other unions benefited far more. The once-moribund A.F. of L. added half a million workers by mid-1934, and a variety of independent unions recruited 250,000 more. The TUUL had been left hopelessly behind.[16]

If the Party doyens harbored any illusions about their affiliate's future, these illusions were dashed in 1934 when a series of violent mass strikes took place on a scale never before witnessed in this country. The TUUL had little to do with any of them. "In 1934," Browder admitted, "the Red Unions definitely passed into the background in the basic industries, and to some extent also in light industry. The main mass of workers had definitely chosen to try and organize and fight through the A.F. of L. organizations."[17]

The first of 1934's dramatic strikes came at the Auto-Lite factory in

Toledo, Ohio. A seven-week strike was marked by mass picketing and violent confrontations with the National Guard. Strikers fought pitched street battles, met tear-gas volleys with barrages of bricks, and suffered two deaths. An effort to promote a general strike proved abortive. In years past those incidents would have been a signal that the Communist party and the TUUL were in the vicinity directing the strike along a revolutionary path. In Toledo, however, an A.F. of L. union led the strike with active Musteite support. The Communist party was barely to be seen. John Williamson confessed that the Party "had no organizational contacts—not to speak of groups—with the strikers" and had been reduced to mobilizing members of the Unemployed Councils to strengthen picket lines.[18]

The next labor explosion was even more embarrassing. Truck drivers in Minneapolis, organized in the Teamsters Union, shut down the entire city in a drive for union recognition. When police and special deputies tried to stop picketing of the central marketplace, two of them were killed and the National Guard was called in. In an ensuing confrontation, police opened fire on an unarmed crowd, killing two and wounding sixty-seven. To the Communists' chagrin, the strikers were led by despised Trotskyists. Browder sadly admitted that the Communists had no organization within the Teamsters Union.[19]

The Communists had more success in the maritime strike in San Francisco that summer, but the TUUL could take little comfort from events since it was barely involved. As late as June 1933, not a single dockworker had become a member of either the Marine Workers Industrial Union (MWIU) or the Party. Bowing to the distaste the longshoremen had shown for the Marine Workers, district organizer Sam Darcy urged a small group of radicals he had helped to organize—known as the Albion Hall Group—to work through the A.F. of L.'s International Longshoremen's Association (ILA). The MWIU's paper, *The Waterfront Worker*, was turned over to Albion Hall. One former member later testified that at least eight of Albion Hall's adherents were Party members. Its second-in-command, John Schomaker, was a self-proclaimed Communist. During and after the maritime strike, the Communist party leadership sometimes spoke as if Albion Hall was a Party fraction in the ILA. Jack Stachel, for example, argued that the maritime strike "proves that it is not only possible for the Communists to organize and lead struggles in the A.F. of L. but that it is possible to win the struggles."[20]

Most of the controversy about the Communist role in Albion Hall centered on Harry Bridges, an Australian who had first arrived on the West Coast in 1920. Twice during that decade he unsuccessfully attempted to organize an ILA local. His third attempt to organize a union had better results. Believing he was a Communist, the government spent more than two decades trying to deport him to his native Australia. All that the government had to prove to expel Bridges was that he had been a member of the Communist party. It never could. No comparable effort has ever been mounted against a single individual in American history. The Immigration Service held two separate hearings on the matter. At the first, in 1939, Dean James Landis of Harvard Law School heard thirty-two government witnesses offer a variety of proofs but found them all either unbelievable or not constituting hard evidence. In a second hearing in 1941, thirty-two entirely different witnesses testified. This time the hearing examiner recommended deportation, was reversed by an Appeals Board, and was then upheld by Attorney General Francis Biddle. The U.S. Supreme Court, in a split decision written by Justice William Douglas, overturned the deportation order.[21]

Following Landis's decision a bill had been introduced in the House of Representatives specifically ordering Bridges' deportation. Despite its obvious violation of the Constitutional prohibition against a bill of attainder, it passed 330 to 42. When the Smith Act was passed in 1940, Representative Sam Hobbs of Alabama assured his colleagues: "It is my joy to announce that this bill will do, in a perfectly legal and constitutional manner, what the bill specifically aimed at the deportation of Harry Bridges seeks to accomplish." When it did not, the Justice Department took its turn. Bridges had become an American citizen in 1945, swearing under oath that he was not a Communist. In 1949 he went on trial for perjury. John Schomaker, his old comrade-in-arms, testified that he and Bridges had attended Party meetings together and that both had met regularly with Sam Darcy during the 1934 strike to receive orders. Although it was not allowed into evidence, even Bridges' ex-wife deposed that she still had his Party card, made out in his mother's maiden name. Once again, Bridges denied membership under oath. Found guilty, Bridges was sentenced to five years in prison. In 1953, however, by a 4 to 3 vote the Supreme Court again saved him. The government was not yet finished. Two years later it filed a civil suit seeking his denaturalization. A judge finally dismissed the case. If Bridges never formally joined the Party, he certainly was a devoted ally and helpmate for many years. If the workers would only elect "hundreds of Bridges" in their unions, Jack Stachel dreamed, then the day of revolution would be drawing nigh. The U.S. Government obviously agreed.[22]

When the rank-and-file militants in San Francisco pressured the ILA into beginning a strike on May 8, 1934, Bridges became chairman of the

San Francisco Strike Committee, and 14,000 longshoremen up and down the West Coast set up picket lines. The key demand was for a union-controlled hiring hall to replace the standard shape-up that permitted companies to reward pliant longshoremen and penalize militants and union men. The Marine Workers Industrial Union was the first to call a sympathy strike. That had little effect. A.F. of L. seamen's unions soon followed suit. On May 14, the strike's success was assured when the powerful Teamsters refused to haul cargo off the docks and the San Francisco waterfront was shut down and shipping "completely paralyzed." Early in July, Governor Frank Merriam ordered the National Guard to duty. Together with the police, the Guard tried to clear the Embarcadero and open the docks. A pitched battle ensued. Strikers retreated up a knoll, Rincon Hill, building barricades and hurling rocks at the pursuing lawmen. By the end of "Blood Thursday," 1,700 Guardsmen were patrolling the waterfront, two strikers were dead (one of them a Communist), and 64 men were hospitalized, 31 with gunshot wounds.[23]

San Francisco's Central Labor Council now approved a general strike. Bridges was defeated in a contest for vice-chairman of the Strike Committee. When the first general strike in American history since Seattle's in 1919 began on July 16, 100,000 workers struck. The union leaders, however, brought it to a close within four days. On July 29, the ILA agreed to return to work. Arbitrators later created jointly-operated union-management hiring halls.

However modest their actual role in the general strike, the Communists were a convenient target for both government and business. Mayor Angelo Rossi of San Francisco had no doubt that "this is a Communist attempt to start a revolution and overturn the government." *The Oakland Tribune* ran a banner headline "Reds Plot Destruction of Rails, Highways Is Warning." Vigilante raids destroyed Party headquarters, *The Western Worker* offices, and other suspicious buildings. Hundreds of people were arrested in a police dragnet. Sam Darcy had to go into hiding to avoid capture. The governor denied that he had encouraged vigilante activities but added: "I feel that people have a right to exercise the spirit that marked the activities of their forefathers and determine these questions for themselves."[24]

The Communists were quite willing to accept the credit for what had been wrought. *The Western Worker* pointedly claimed that "the attack is aimed against the Communists because it is the Communists who initiated the move for a general strike." Earl Browder credited the Communist party with orchestrating and guiding the strike. Sam Darcy proudly noted that "the leadership of the strike in San Francisco by Communist and other militant elements is well-known and accepted." The Central Committee regarded the strike as "truly the greatest revolutionary event in American labor history" and a salutary lesson to the American proletariat. It was a "classical example of the Communist thesis" that even purely economic struggles under capitalism quickly lead to a conflict of "the capitalist class against the working class."[25]

Party leaders in New York were, however, unhappy that the TUUL remained on the strike's sidelines. *The Daily Worker* announced that "the Marine Workers Industrial Union has called on striking longshoremen to resist the strike-breaking efforts of the I.L.A." Roy Hudson, secretary of the MWIU, was sent west on a fruitless mission to build up his union at the expense of the ILA. Browder was critical of Party leaders in San Francisco for their failure to denounce the ILA's national leadership loudly and strongly enough and, in general, for being too solicitous of the A.F. of L. In his own defense, Darcy contrasted the ILA's vigor and success in reaching out to other unions to organize the general strike with the isolation and lethargy of the MWIU.[26]

The last of 1934's mammoth strikes was the largest in a single industry in American history. The Communists had very little to do with it. The National Textile Workers Union had never totally recovered from its debacle in Lawrence, Massachusetts, in 1932. Nonetheless, when the A.F. of L's United Textile Workers inaugurated a strike of 65,000 silk workers in late August 1933, the NTWU had managed to gain the leadership of several thousand silk dye workers in Paterson, New Jersey, and briefly revived. Ann Burlak, the national secretary, and John Ballam, national organizer, personally came to New Jersey to direct the efforts. Neither the UTW nor the government mediator would deal with the TUUL union, however. When the strike ended, there had been "no mass influx of the silk and dye workers into the N.T.W.U." This defeat did not discourage the revolutionary union. John Ballam blamed the failure of the strike on his union's "almost complete neglect of the workers inside the A.F. of L. ranks." In virtually the same breath, however, he drew the "first lesson" of the strike as the need to organize the unorganized into the TUUL union. During the spring of 1934, Jack Stachel muttered that it "remains still a very small organization." That fall the Communists paid the piper for their dependence on the TUUL union.[27]

At the end of August 1934 the UTW called for an industrywide strike. Within days nearly half a million cotton, silk, woolen, and worsted workers from Maine to Georgia left their looms. The governor of Rhode Island, in justifying state repression of strikers, announced, "There is a

Communist uprising and not a textile strike." Governor Eugene Tal-
madge of Georgia declared martial law. Across the nation 40,000 militia
were mobilized. Nearly a score of the strikers were killed, including half
a dozen shot down in one small town alone. Francis Gorman of the UTW
ordered his members back to work within a month, on the basis of assurances by President Roosevelt and the National Recovery Administration.
The promises were not kept, and the textile union never recovered.[28]

Even the woes of an A.F. of L. union could not comfort the Communists. Browder squarely blamed his Party's weakness on its underestimation of the A.F. of L. He angrily denounced the NTWU: "The comrades . . .
talked it over among themselves, decided that these A.F. of L. bureaucrats will never lead a real fight, there won't be any real strike; why then
should we prepare for it?—it is a waste of time and energy and nothing
was done. Exactly nothing." During the strike the handful of NTWU
locals disappeared, their members quietly being absorbed into the A.F. of
L. union. Responding to some critics who, emboldened by the UTW's
subsequent troubles, had asked "Why not keep our union and wait until
they enter [it]," Jack Stachel dryly noted: "We tried this policy and found
it was not very successful." Not that the Communists suddenly were
enamored of the A.F. of L. or Francis Gorman. *The Daily Worker* kept up a
barrage of criticisms of the UTW during the strike. Its defeat, the Communists explained with smug assurance, was precisely what they had
predicted.[29]

Still another nail in the TUUL's coffin was the sudden surge of independent unions not affiliated to any labor federation. By the end of 1933,
a quarter of a million workers had joined independent unions. Although
their membership was only 10 percent of the A.F. of L's they had rapidly
passed the TUUL and enrolled twice as many workers as the Communists had in a much shorter time. Particularly disconcerting to the Communists was the fact that these upstarts were reaping the benefits the
TUUL felt it deserved. In mid-1933, for instance, 50,000 shoe and leather
workers went on strike. Forty thousand ignored the Shoe and Leather
Workers Industrial Union to join three different independent unions,
even though, Stachel complained, "we applied the torch which began the
strike movement." In the auto industry the Mechanics Educational Society of America (MESA) supplanted the Auto Workers Union as the dominant force. The National Miners Union virtually disappeared in the mine
fields, where the independent Progressive Miners of America now carried
the banner of opposition to John L. Lewis.[30]

The Comintern's Thirteenth Plenum at the end of 1933 ordered

Communists to "form and consolidate *independent class trade unions.*" Although the suggestion was directed specifically at the German Communists, the Americans took it as sound advice. Reporting to a Party plenum in January, Browder fretted that the TUUL was in danger of being isolated. "We must take steps," he urged, "to insure against the possible crystallization of these independent unions into a separate central body not only outside the A.F. of L., but also outside of our organized influence." He advocated unifying the TUUL and the independent unions, beginning industry-by-industry and ending with a new "independent federation of labor." Three months later the Eighth Convention ordered Party members to penetrate the new unions, struggle against their Musteite, Lovestoneite, and Trotskyite influences, and "work towards bringing together the independent and revolutionary trade unions into an Independent Federation of Labor."[31]

The first Communist embrace of an independent union was not an altogether happy experience for the Party. Delegates from four shoe unions, including the Shoe Workers Industrial Union, met in Boston in December 1933 to merge their forces. The TUUL extended an offer to the united union to enter its ranks and pledged to cooperate with whatever decision the new United Shoe and Leather Workers Union made. It had to swallow hard. As a price of admission into the merged union, the TUUL group was required to suspend all relations with the TUUL. Although the Communists insisted they had 9,000 members in the new union, they were only given voting credit for 6,000, making them a tiny minority of the 70,000-strong union. The merged union also waited just a few months before firing the ex-TUUL leader, Fred Biedenkapp, who had been appointed national organizer. The Communists could boast of only two victories. They claimed to have prevented Lovestoneites from taking the new union into the A.F. of L. and had "become 9000 militant organizers among the broad masses of the shoe workers."[32]

The growth of the independent unions slowed down in 1934. What had briefly looked like a potential alternative to the A.F. of L. turned out to be only a sideshow. The major strikes that year were A.F. of L. strikes. Summing up the Party's trade union line in early 1935, the Central Committee recommended continued work in independent unions but admitted "it is now inadvisable to put the question of forming an Independent Federation of Labor." The independent unions, however, had thwarted the Party. They demonstrated by their growth that most American workers wanted nothing to do with the TUUL.[33]

No one could now doubt the terminal weakness of the TUUL. All of the major strikes of 1934 had been industrial, not craft, conflicts. Yet the TUUL, created to penetrate the basic industries and organize the unorganized into industrial unions, had played only a minor role even in those strikes where it was present. The supposedly craft-dominated A.F. of L. had demonstrated remarkable resilience. Before the TUUL disappeared, however, one of its most fervent advocates was cast into political purgatory: Joseph Zack was expelled from the Communist party late in 1934. His story tells much about the vicissitudes of American Communism.

When he arrived in New York from Slovakia in 1915, the eighteen-year-old Joseph Zack Kornfeder already considered himself a Socialist. Within a year he had joined the Socialist party. Before the end of the decade he had also flirted with the IWW, but the founding of the Communist party found him a charter member. Non-Jewish Communist unionists in New York did not grow on trees, and he was soon promoted to trade union secretary. Once William Foster joined the movement with his TUEL, Zack became a second-rank trade union specialist within his faction. His hostility to the A.F. of L. was long-standing. In 1927, Zack had prematurely advocated organizing the unorganized outside that venerable institution. Since the Comintern was still committed to boring within the A.F. of L., Zack's punishment was exile in Moscow, where he stayed for two and a half years. A Comintern mission to Venezuela followed, ending badly in 1931 when the U.S. State Department had to extract Zack from prison. Back in the United States later that year, Zack was put in charge of the Trade Union Unity Council, which coordinated TUUL work in New York. Party trade union policy had at last come around to his ultra-left views.[34]

Zack's long-standing dream of supplanting the A.F. of L. with a revolutionary union movement was, however, short-lived. He was transferred to Ohio to direct trade union work. As preparations got under way for the Party's Eighth Convention in 1934, his discontent boiled over. Zack contributed an article to the pre-convention discussion reaffirming his conviction that the Party should not "run our trade union work into the opportunist channels of reforming the A.F. of L." At the convention he cast the only negative vote on the trade union resolution. Shortly afterward he resigned from the Party. In turn, several months later the Party expelled him for persistently refusing "to work in the mass trade unions" and for advocating "Smash the A.F. of L. since it is dead anyway." Zack himself explained his break as a consequence of the Party's "new turn of policy from ultra-left to ultra-right." While he took his faith in dual unions with him out of the Communist party, he was not able to take his family out. Both his wife and his small son had remained in Moscow when Zack had gone on his Comintern mission. Despite repeated entreaties, he was never able to extricate them. In 1938 he finally abandoned hope for them, appeared as a friendly witness before the Dies Committee, and began a new career as a paid government witness.[35]

The TUUL did not long outlast Zack, but neither did it disappear before the Comintern desired its demise. In September 1934 the Central Committee issued a resolution on the recent strike wave. While the Party had "finally to overcome and root out all underestimation of work in the reformist unions," it also had to "strengthen the work and leadership of the TUUL." At preparatory meetings in Moscow for the Seventh Comintern Congress in the summer of 1934, a dispute was raging over the future of dual unions. Georgi Dimitroff, Dimitri Manuilsky, and Otto Kuusinen "declared for amalgamation of the revolutionary trade unions with the reformist unions." S. Lozovsky, who ran the Profintern, was less willing to surrender his forces. He found an ally in Ossip Piatnitsky, who agreed that unless and until reformist unions agreed to allow Communists to work openly in them, the TUUL should not disband. In December 1934 the debate ended. The Presidium of the ECCI recommended that the revolutionary unions join the American Federation of Labor.[36]

The TUUL's surrender came in two stages. In November Jack Stachel gave a disheartening report. The NMU was defunct. The NTWU had been disbanded. The MWIU had flubbed in California. The AWU was in tatters. Stachel ordered both the auto and steel unions to disband and join the A.F. of L. The Party's main policy henceforth, he announced, was to "work inside and [build] the opposition within the A.F. of L. unions." Not every TUUL union was yet to surrender, however. Stachel indicated that those with a mass base in industries where a reformist competitor was lacking or weak would stay in business, unless the A.F. of L. were willing to accept them with their leadership and organizations intact. For the moment that included the metal, marine, fur, food, and furniture unions. "We are not," Stachel explained, "in favor of maintaining unions outside the A.F. of L. on principle. But neither do we propose going into the A.F. of L. at any cost."[37]

These brave words vanished remarkably soon after the ECCI suggested in December that the revolutionary unions be put out of their misery. At the Seventh Congress, Earl Browder confessed that the Americans had not totally comprehended the Comintern's signals about the fate of the dual unions in the last half of 1934. We "did not at once understand the full significance of these changes," he said, "or immediately draw the full lessons. We had to learn from the masses. But we learned, having also the advice and assistance of the E.C.C.I." The Party's Central Committee suddenly discovered how futile the continued existence of the TUUL was. It ordered that "the existing revolutionary trade unions and their locals join the A.F. of L. trade unions or the Red Trade Unions can join the A.F. of L. directly." There was no more talk of concessions: "In those cases when collective joining is not possible, members of the red unions should join the unions of the A.F. of L. individually." Some Red unions did manage to negotiate entry into the federation as a unit, their leaders obtaining union positions or some limited autonomy in return for bringing several thousand dues-payers with them. James Matles negotiated such a deal with the Machinists' Union for his Metal Workers. Ben Gold's Fur Workers, larger than their A.F. of L. rival, did not fare badly. Most of the others, however, faded away.[38]

In mid-March 1935, the final national convention of the Trade Union Unity League declared that it had "no further need of continuing in its present form." It gave way to a Committee for the Unification of the Trade Unions. *Labor Unity* ceased publication. After six years, the Communist party's experiment with a dual union movement was over.[39]

From its very beginning the TUUL had carried the Communist albatross around its neck. No one was ever deceived about who guided its destiny. By itself that burden severely hindered the TUUL's activities, but the TUUL added to its own problems. As the league admitted, labor issues often took second place to loftier goals of revolutionizing the workers. After a string of defeats, workers shied away from so jinxed an organization. Where a trade union vaccum existed—and there were many such places in the early 1930s—a revolutionary union could occasionally step in and lead workers. Invariably, however, it went to pieces afterward. Like the older IWW, the TUUL was not temperamentally suited to long-term organization.

The only improvement in the TUUL's condition was caused by the New Deal's labor policies. When the league experienced a mild upsurge in 1933–1934, its own exertions and qualities were less responsible than those of the NRA. Once the Communists saw how poorly they had fared in comparison with the A.F. of L. and the independent unions, they moved inexorably toward liquidating their creation and did so just as soon as the Comintern gave its approval. The influx into the TUUL, relatively small as it was, did give the Communists something to bargain with as they slunk back into the A.F. of L. If the Communist trade union line had changed in 1932, the TUUL would have disappeared without a trace and the Party's isolation from the union movement been almost complete. When the Communists put their auxiliary to rest in 1935, they had in hand dozens of capable union organizers. These men had trade union experience and some knowledge of America's mass production industries. Their talents would be fully utilized only when John L. Lewis had to find people able to build new industrial unions.

8

Down on the Farm

During the Third Period, the very propriety of the Party's recruiting or even working among farmers was not fully accepted. The 1930 draft program for agriculture contained the warning that the "agrarian revolution is a petty bourgeois revolution inherently." The draft also noted that the only solution for the problems of American agriculture was to convert the land into public property, push for common tillage, and guarantee small farmers the right to continue using their land. The Krestintern, or Red Peasant International, although primarily concerned with European peasant movements, criticized the CPUSA's agricultural work in 1930 for "petty-bourgeois reformism." The Krestintern went on to insist "that all things be revamped to conform with the program for European peasants," a policy calling for land for the landless peasants. A pro-Krestintern faction in America also attacked the Party's own agricultural front, the United Farmers' Educational League (UFEL), for its "bourgeois" program and the class background of its adherents; some wanted the organization liquidated. Sometime after the Seventh CPUSA Convention in 1930, the ECCI finally upheld the American Party's rejection of the Krestintern position. Although not willing to write off farmers, the CPUSA approached them cautiously and with some reluctance, with the goal of forming "an alliance of the proletariat with the poor and middle farmers under the proletarian leadership."[1]

Agriculture was a stepchild in party work. Districts were loath to expand any effort in agricultural work, preferring to husband their limited resources for other tasks. While every program or platform had an obligatory section on farm work, minimal space was usually devoted to it. Whenever the thesis drafters needed an explanation for the failures and disappointments in agricultural work—a fairly frequent occurrence—they could always trot out the charge that there had been a serious underestimation of the work's importance. The Communist party was primarily an urban party. Most of its cadres and members did not understand farmers or their problems and were not very interested. Farm organizing itself was extraordinarily difficult, involving as it did great distances, often harsh weather, and a dispersed population. And yet, this largely urban, largely foreign-born, tiny organization managed to make its mark on American farmers. The Party was, however, unable to transform its inroads into any lasting victories. Occasional brief triumphs were quickly dissipated. In agriculture, as in so many other areas between 1930 and 1935, the Communists set themselves large tasks that they were unable to fulfill.

In spite of the opportunities afforded by the farm depression of the 1920s, the Communists had not done much with this chance. Few farmers were Party members; in 1925 only 568 of 16,000 Communists were identified as "agrarian." During the 1920s an Agricultural District was created that encompassed the Dakotas, almost as if farmers were limited to that area—which, in fact, most Communist farmers were. The South, where most American farmers lived, was virtually ignored. The Party's major figure in agricultural work was Alfred Knutson, a long-time resident of North Dakota. Born in Norway, he had become a charter Communist in 1919, after a sojourn in the Non-Partisan League. In addition to serving as district organizer for the Dakotas, Knutson built the United Farmers' Educational League as the first auxiliary in agriculture and published the first issue of its newspaper, *The United Farmer*, in March 1926. He enjoyed a modest success by attracting 5,000–6,000 farmers into the UFEL. For a brief period, Knutson was able to maneuver the UFEL among larger and more influential farm groups and even to attract several prominent non-Communist radicals. The Lovestoneite purge in 1929 cost Knutson his job, however. Despite his abandonment of his former allies, he was demoted. The UFEL, meanwhile, had gone into decline in 1929.[2]

The 1920s were quickly forgotten. The draft program for the Seventh Convention confessed that "hitherto, we must admit, the Communist Party has wholly neglected the agrarian masses." The ECCI agreed, crediting the CPUSA with making a start in the draft thesis but calling practical work among farmers "non-existent." The draft ordered the UFEL to drop the term "Educational" from its name, sharpen the focus of its paper, shift its work more toward the South, and affiliate with the Krestintern. The newly christened United Farmers League (UFL), struggling to issue *The United Farmer* regularly in early 1930, responded promptly to the suggestions by publishing a list of demands ranging from cancellation of debts and taxes for poor farmers to defense of the Soviet Union. Although several immediate demands were listed, the UFL's fear of contamination by petty-bourgeois farmers kept it at arm's length from most farmers.[3]

The first signs of agrarian discontent caught the UFL unawares. Drought and crop failure in Arkansas brought on the threat of starvation. On January 3, 1931, 500 farmers, 200 of them Negroes, staged a riot in the small town of England, Arkansas, demanding provisions from frightened merchants. The Red Cross hurriedly moved into England to supply flour, cornmeal, lard, and sugar. By the end of the month it was providing aid to 500,000 people in the state. Alfred Knutson, the recently disgraced head of the UFEL, turned up in England and, along with another UFL organizer, was arrested on January 24. Using the pseudonym of Frank Brown, he happily reported that "the demonstration was notable as the instance in which masses of poor farmers have followed the policies of the United Farmers League." He expressed confidence that "a solid UFL organization is certain to be built up in Arkansas." Henry Puro, newly installed as director of the Party's farm work, went even further, claiming that there was a nearby Party unit "where these farmers were mobilizing themselves for action." Nearly two years later a *Daily Worker* writer cast doubt on the earlier stories of radical involvement, lamenting that neither the Party nor the UFL had been present in England to give focus to the demonstration. Knutson had managed to arrive after the main action, and whatever he had been able to organize had long since disappeared.[4]

England's little riot had one unexpected and highly significant consequence. An ex-Communist named Whittaker Chambers saw a brief Associated Press story about the event, and it inspired him to write a short, fictional account about a communist dirt farmer who rallies his friends to struggle for food. *Can You Make Out Their Voices?* was published in *The New Masses* in March 1931, reprinted as a pamphlet, turned into a play, and later performed by the Federal Theatre Project. A Soviet critic rhapsodized: "It gives a revolutionary exposition of the problem of the agricultural crisis and correctly raises the question of the leading role of the Communist Party in the revolutionary farmers' movement." Chambers was soon readmitted to the CPUSA and in July 1931 was appointed an editor of *The New Masses*. He had been there less than a year when he was recruited for secret work and disappeared into the "underground," where he would encounter a number of other Communists who had an interest in agriculture.[5]

The United Farmers League sputtered along, unable to gain much of a foothold outside of the northern Midwest. Even there, 1930 and 1931 were chaotic years. Beginning in 1929 the large Finnish-American Communist movement was rent by a civil war, which ended badly for the Communists. In 1930, George Halonen, a prominent Finnish-language leader, departed from the CPUSA and took most of the cooperative movement (a federation of consumer-owned stores) and large numbers of Party members with him. A Communist co-op organization, the Farmers' and Workers' Cooperative Unity Alliance, was set up, led by Walter Harju. Harju's brother Rudolph was made national secretary of the UFL in October 1930, the same time as its headquarters were shifted from Knutson's bailiwick of North Dakota to the tiny Finnish village of New York Mills in western Minnesota. Another Finn, John Wiita, known in the CPUSA as Henry Puro, was also given a new assignment. Born in Finland in 1888 to a religious family, Puro had come to America in 1905. An early Party member, he spent five years in Canada serving as editor of a Finnish Communist newspaper. By 1925, back in America, he was a Politburo member. He served briefly as the Party's organizational secretary before he was assigned to direct agrarian work in 1930, replacing Harrison George.[6]

The disruption among the Finns was disastrous for the UFL. During 1931 *The United Farmer* appeared irregularly, and by the summer it had ceased publication. A Party plenum in late 1931 complained that "we have not even begun to formulate the partial demands" in agriculture. Walter Harju himself admitted at the end of the year that "generally speaking the organizational results have been weak," placing the blame on a lack of cadres. In mid-1932 only 900 farmers belonged to the Party, but Puro remained more worried by the newest members than by those not joining: "There is a danger that the kulak farmers are coming into the movement."[7]

Those farmers who were in the Party were isolated from their fellow farmers. In late 1931, Iowa farmers protested against a state inspection for tubercular cows that resulted in quarantines and slaughter of livestock. The state militia had to be mobilized: the episode marked the beginnings of the farm revolt that was to engulf the Midwest within a year. Yet, Puro complained that Party units in the affected area "did not know anything about this struggle or at least they did not do anything about it," not even bothering to send a report back to headquarters.[8]

The demise of *The United Farmer* left the UFL voiceless only briefly. Charles Taylor, a long-time Communist and one-time Montana legislator, offered his newspaper, *The Producers News*, to the UFL and the Party. It was published in Plentywood, Montana, a small hamlet in Sheridan County hard by the Canadian border. In 1930, 500 citizens in the county had voted a straight Communist ticket and the Party had controlled the county government from 1924 to 1930. "Red-Flag" Charlie Taylor, weighing over three hundred pounds, stood out even among these nonconformists. He had been born in Wisconsin in 1884 and became a newspaperman at age fourteen. Sent into Sheridan County by the Non-Partisan League in 1918 to organize and to edit its paper, Taylor eventually turned the paper into his personal organ. Taylor had been a covert Communist for several years. In mid-1931, he took the lead in organizing the UFL in Sheridan County, turned *The Producers News* over to the Party, and devoted himself openly to the Communist cause. Erik Bert was sent to Plentywood to become editor, and the paper began to pay less attention to local affairs and more to national and international events as interpreted by the CPUSA.[9]

While the Communists were worrying about contamination from kulaks, Milo Reno, a retired official of the Iowa Farmers Union, organized the Farm Holiday Association (FHA) in May 1932 and began calling on farmers to withhold their products from market. The Farm Holiday began in August. Although Reno urged farmers to strike, he denounced picketing or any effort to interfere with farm shipments, admonitions not always heeded by his followers. The Holiday quickly spread across the Midwest, gaining widespread support from farmers and politicians. The immediate reaction of the Communists was hostile. Erik Bert warned in *The Producers News* that higher prices for farm products would hurt workers. "Dollar wheat," he lectured the farmers of Sheridan County, "would come from the pockets of the millions of unemployed." Within a week Bert stood corrected, having discovered that the Holiday movement in Iowa was a strike against the milk trust and not the working class. In North Dakota, the UFL supported the Holiday but urged farmers to send perishables to market, advice that Harrison George castigated as "scabbing part-time." All in all, George charged, the Party was badly prepared for the unrest, confused over how to respond, and floundering.[10]

The farm revolt did provide an opportunity for another group of Communists interested in agriculture. The FHA had organized a mass demonstration in Sioux City, Iowa, on September 9. Ella Reeve "Mother" Bloor, a long-time party doyenne, was organizing in North Dakota with her third husband, UFL leader Andrew Omholt. She wired her son, Hal Ware, to come to Sioux City to help her organize at the gathering, a decision endorsed by the Central Committee. Ware soon arrived in Iowa and began efforts to retrieve the CPUSA's position.[11]

Born in 1880, Ware had been raised in the utopian community of Arden, Delaware. After studying agriculture for two years at Pennsylvania State University, he became a farmer. An early recruit to Communism, Ware went to Russia in 1922 to set up a demonstration farm. His return to America was prompted by Lenin himself. Unhappy about the absence of agricultural material from American reports, the Soviet leader, who had years earlier written a treatise on American agriculture, acerbically inquired of the Americans: "Have you no farmers in America?" Back in the States in 1923, Ware was placed in charge of the Party's newly organized Agricultural Department and sent on a tour of the country to survey agricultural conditions. His advice, however, was ignored and he returned to the Soviet Union in 1925 for three years. During the winter of 1928–1929 he briefly visited America to interest farm implement companies in sending supplies to Russia. After discussions with Earl Browder, Ware and his chief assistant, Lem Harris, came home for good in the fall of 1930. The following spring they set out on a nationwide tour of rural America. Using the name of George Anstrom, Ware published his findings in a pamphlet, *The American Farmer*. He was not simply ignored this time; instead, he came under sharp attack from Harrison George for minimizing the class struggle in the countryside, a euphemism for downplaying the potentially reactionary role of the "middle farmers" and for advocating merely a moratorium on farm debts and not total cancellation.[12]

Seemingly frozen out of agricultural policy-making, Ware decided to create a Farm Research bureau in Washington, D.C., in 1932 to provide basic studies and data on farm activities. He recruited a handful of bright young men to help. The financial angel was Lem Harris, Ware's assistant in Russia. Harris was the scion of a very wealthy New York investment banker. He had graduated from Harvard in 1926, imbued with Tolstoyan idealism. After three years on a dairy farm he had gone to Russia to work as a farmer. As outgoing as Ware was shy, Harris became a public personality while Ware labored in the background. Rob Hall, an Alabama native who was finishing his degree in agricultural economics at Columbia University, became editor of the *Farm News Letter* put out by the Farm Research bureau. Jerry Ingersoll, an Amherst student whose father later was elected borough president of Brooklyn, was put in charge of a school on wheels, a traveling classroom that toured farm areas.[13]

Ware and his young men were a far cry from the Party's existing agricultural cadres. In fact, two distinct groups of farm cadres were present from 1932 on, and they clashed continuously. On one side were those in official positions of power in the Communist party and the United Farmers League. These individuals were hostile to "reformist" farm organizations, mistrusted broad appeals to all farmers, warned against underestimating the class struggle in the countryside, and favored a straightforward Communist party presence among farmers. Many were Finns, like Henry Puro or the Harjus. They had allies among others in the Party like Harrison George, whose background was in the IWW. George had an instinctive hostility to farmers and believed very strongly that the Party should focus on agricultural laborers. On the other side stood Ware and his supporters, more interested in working with reformers and more "American" but handicapped by the doctrines of the Third Period.[14]

Ware arrived in Sioux City, met with a group of Nebraska Farm Holiday members, and made plans to call a Farmers National Relief Conference (FNRC) in Washington in early December 1932. The 250 delegates to the FNRC passed resolutions calling for federal relief programs for farmers, an end to evictions and foreclosures, and a debt moratorium with eventual cancellation. Delegations of farmers met with congressmen, Vice President Curtis, and President Hoover. The delegates also created a permanent organization, the Farmers National Committee of Action (FNCA), with Lem Harris as executive secretary. A newspaper, *The Farmers' National Weekly*, edited by Rob Hall, soon began to appear. All these actions were an admission that the UFL, dominated by the Finns and so closely tied to the Party, had proved incapable of being a united front and had left the Party unprepared to take advantage of rural unrest.[15]

The only large bloc of non-Communist farmers present at the conference came from Nebraska, where the Farm Holiday movement had been taken over by a militant group from Madison County. On October 6, 1932, the group had held one of the first penny auctions in the country, offering a pittance when a foreclosure sale was held, intimidating potential buyers into remaining silent, and returning the property to its owners. A beleaguered town sheriff sadly told outraged forces of law and order that "I am absolutely powerless in the face of such organized outlawry." Harry Lux, an ex-Wobbly and secret Party member, served as the link between the Nebraskans and Hal Ware, and a member of the Nebraska group was elected permanent chairman of the FNRC. Although

Communists played key roles at the conference, the minutes did not reflect a single mention of the Communist party.[16]

After the national conference, state conferences were held in the Midwest to present demands for relief and to plan for action. Local groups were encouraged to form Committees of Action to fight on specific issues. In the months following the FNRC, the Nebraska Holiday group was particularly active. Some 4,000 angry farmers descended on the capital city, Lincoln, in mid-February 1933. Denounced by state Farmers Union leaders as Communist-controlled, the delegates nonetheless nearly assaulted Lem Harris when he attempted to show a pro-Soviet movie and urged them not to include a pro-inflation plank in their demands. The delegates sat in the legislative galleries and saw the frightened lawmakers consider and pass special legislation establishing a temporary moratorium on foreclosures.[17]

This victory was the high point of the FNCA in Nebraska. As other states passed moratorium bills, farmer militancy began to ebb. Under Party pressure, Ware attempted to purge the Nebraska Holiday officers, but succeeded only in reducing the group's influence. *The Farmers' National Weekly* also intensified its attacks on FHA leader Milo Reno for "selling out" farm strikes and labeled him a social-fascist. Ware, realizing the extent of farmer support for Reno and fearing isolation, wrote a frantic letter from the field back to his colleagues, warning them: "Don't print the next issue until you get my full report. We've got to about face." He was too late. In July, Reno responded in kind, verbally slashing at the FNCA, which he had heretofore largely ignored.[18]

Ware's troubles were not limited to the collapse of his hopes for a united front with portions of the Holiday movement. His activities had once again drawn the wrath of his rivals in the Party. In mid-March 1933, the UFL's organ, *The Producers News*, took the FNCA to task for a statement made by its delegation when it was refused an audience with President Roosevelt, citing the FNCA's stance as a clear case of reformist illusions about bourgeois politicians. In Party meetings the FNRC and its offspring, the FNCA, came under mounting attack. As late as February 1933, the Sixteenth Party Plenum had praised the FNRC and exulted that Party farm work had "passed to the higher plane of active participation and leadership" in mass struggles. The chief danger had been identified as left sectarianism or isolation from the masses. At the Extraordinary Party Conference in July, Henry Puro defended the general accomplishments of the FNRC from critics. He devoted more time, however, to attacking the "right opportunist" errors of the FNRC and the Sixteenth Plenum's overestimation of the organization's success. Its program was too reformist. Even though the FNRC met "under the ideological and partly under the direct leadership of the Party," that role was downplayed. "The face of the Party in the sphere of its agrarian demands was not sufficiently shown." Rather, Party members "were trying to adapt themselves to the backward farmers instead of raising them to the level of the more progressive farmer."[19]

The Extraordinary Conference in 1933 also took steps to rein in the FNCA. Afraid that the committee might degenerate "into a kind of branch of a petty-bourgeois labor party," the resolution sharply reminded the FNCA that its local Committees of Action were temporary bodies that should form for some specific activity, such as preventing a foreclosure, and then disband. Harris obediently explained in August that Committees of Action were only temporary united front bodies that organized for a specific relief purpose, developed leaders, and prepared farmers to join a "more lasting" militant group.[20]

Thus chastened, the FNCA held its second national congress in Chicago at the end of November 1933. This conference had a decidedly more Communist tone. Its National Committee was more heavily loaded with Party members. Spokesmen for both the CPUSA and the Socialist party addressed the delegates; Clarence Hathaway, the Communist, received by far a warmer welcome. *The Farmers' National Weekly* was moved to Chicago, and Erik Bert replaced Lem Harris as editor. Hal Ware wrote a brief article in which he warned that even UFL members were mostly middle-sized farmers and that a turn to the left would cost the UFL "many pseudo-radical individuals." He then dropped out of active organizing in the Midwest, turning his energies to a newsletter, *Facts for Farmers*, and recruiting government employees into the Party and an espionage network. On August 13, 1935, his car collided with a coal truck in the Pennsylvania mountains and at the age of forty-five he was dead.[21]

Another casualty of the lunge to the left was Charlie Taylor. Early in 1934 Taylor was flirting with support for a Farmer-Labor movement and was replaced as UFL leader in March after one year on the job. That summer a number of his old Montana compatriots were expelled from the Party for forming a joint electoral ticket with Farm Holiday forces. Although Taylor disclaimed any connection with this group, by the following spring he had spoken out for a mass labor party and in the summer of 1935 he recaptured his old newspaper, *The Producers News*, from the CPUSA in a bitter battle. The Communists charged that Taylor had formerly used the paper to extort money from businessmen. Taylor blistered them for being "parlor reds, the sons and daughters of rich dads or related to some other angel" who didn't understand working farmers.

When he gained editorial control, Taylor promptly moved into an alliance with Holiday forces, published articles by A. J. Muste and Max Shachtman, a Trotskyist leader, and denounced "Stalinites."[22]

The victorious left-wing faction promptly took steps to revitalize the United Farmers League. Alfred Tiala, a Finn, replaced Charlie Taylor as head of the UFL, and when Tiala was jailed for six months, Henry Puro stepped in. The UFL held its first and only national convention in June 1934, with 175 delegates present. Puro optimistically called for 15,000 dues-payers within six months and shortly upped the target to 25,000. The convention proclaimed the need for a response to "the growing attack of the financial oligarchy under the growing fascist rule of the New Deal." Its proposals, embodied in the Farmers Emergency Relief Bill, included abolition of the Agricultural Adjustment Administration (AAA), a ban on foreclosures and evictions, and a massive relief plan controlled by farmers. The Draft Resolution for the Eighth Party Convention attacked "the opportunist tendencies to hide the face of the Party in the farmers' organizations and struggles."[23]

The UFL's strenuous efforts came to naught, however. In January 1934 Tiala was jailed for a foreclosure protest in Indiana. In March, UFL leaders in Sisseton, South Dakota, were arrested after returning an evicted farmer to his home. Mother Bloor was arrested for supporting a women's chicken-pickers' strike in Loup City, Nebraska. None of these activities stimulated much support. Worse, as Puro admitted in September, "organizationally we still remain very loose and weak." The Communist cooperative movement, run by Walter Harju, also remained largely isolated within the Finnish community.[24]

By the fall of 1934, Communist policy was shifting in the direction of a united front with Socialists and other leftists. And in early January, reporting to the Nineteenth Party Plenum, Earl Browder formally called for a turn in agrarian work to the mass organizations to which farmers belonged. Tiala and Puro obediently signed a letter to the Farm Holiday Association proposing a united front against the policies of the Roosevelt administration: "We are aware that there are questions on which the National Holiday Association and the United Farmers League are not in agreement. This should not, however, prevent us from organizing joint activity on the issues we have suggested which are of immediate concern to all distressed farmers." The letter added that "a divided farm movement must inevitably be weaker in this fight than a united one." Lem Harris and the discredited FNCA began negotiations with John Bosch, head of the Minnesota Holiday Association—one of the few viable state units left in the Holiday movement. A tentative agreement was reached, but Milo Reno was able to prevent its implementation.[25]

Party writers meanwhile bemoaned the low state of both rural Party units and UFL chapters. John Barnett admitted that the isolated rural Communists had never been able to attract either farm workers or poor farmers. "The rural units," he added, "function, organizationally and politically, on a very low level." The UFL was in no better condition. Locals were either "reformist" or carbon copies of the Party unit. UFL leaders, in fact, often assumed responsibility for Party agrarian work: "Our Left-wing farmer locals in the majority of places are small, disconnected from the masses, and are not developing in size or influence in the community." The UFL had never been able to escape the stigma of being the Communist party by another name. After five years it had been unable to expand its influence beyond the small circle of Party loyalists.[26]

The Farmers National Committee of Action had one final hurrah, sponsoring a Farmers National Relief Conference in Sioux Falls, South Dakota, in March 1935 to deal with the terrible drought afflicting the Plains states. Three hundred and forty regular and 118 fraternal delegates attended, a considerable decline from the Chicago conference, and issued a call for unity. This did not placate Milo Reno. When Lem Harris appeared at the Holiday national meeting in Des Moines, Iowa, on April 27 to appeal for unity, Reno refused to allow him to speak, had the unity call tabled, and bitterly assailed Harris as an agent of Moscow and *The Farmers' National Weekly* as "that dirty slimy newspaper."[27]

The Central Committee heard a report on the farm debacle at its May meeting. After reaching a high point at the first Farmers National Relief Conference in 1932, the Party, Clarence Hathaway admitted, had undergone "serious retrogression in our work in this field," and "the broad united front policies" that had proved successful had been rolled back. Hathaway admitted that there had been conflict among the agrarian cadres. In a veiled attack on Puro, Hathaway charged that the increased prominence of the UFL and its substitution for the Party had been disastrous. Reciting a catalogue of errors, he accused the agrarian leaders of organizational shortcomings and such tactical blunders as attacking Roosevelt's farm policies as if they were Hoover's. As a consequence, Party influence was almost nil. He singled out Nebraska, where the "left" had gone from 30,000 members to zero. What could now be done to recoup the losses? The key was to penetrate the ranks of the FHA and the Farmers Union. Hathaway admitted that some Party members favored liquidating the UFL, seeing a parallel with the by-now defunct TUUL, but he warned that it should be retained where the UFL still had a mass base. By late 1935, however, after the Seventh Comintern Congress, UFL leaders signified their willingness to support the Holiday program. On December 7, Julius Walstad and Harry Correll sent a letter to all UFL locals to dissolve and join the FHA and the Farmers Union.[28]

Henry Puro paid the price of failure. Stung by the criticism of his activities, Puro resigned from agrarian work. He was appointed a district organizer in remote upper Michigan, where his Party career continued to go downhill. Party membership declined after his arrival. He eventually returned to Finnish work, becoming an editor on a Finnish-language paper. In 1943, embittered, he quietly dropped out of the Communist party and, shortly afterward, became a small-town realtor.[29]

Milo Reno died on May 5, 1936. His successor as president of the Farm Holiday Association, John Bosch, was more hospitable to the idea of a united front. At the 1936 FHA meeting, Bosch and the former UFL forces allied to defeat those loyal to Milo Reno's legacy. The defeated rump withdrew from the FHA and went on to support William Lemke's Presidential bid in 1936. The long-lost Nebraska Holiday Association (Madison County Plan) finally rejoined Bosch's group. On August 28, 1936, *The Farmers' National Weekly* merged with the FHA paper under a Holiday editor, ending the life of the Farmers National Committee of Action. Close to one-third of the committee members appointed at the 1936 FHA convention were associated with the CPUSA. But the Holiday movement was now but a pale copy of the past. By the end of 1937 it had been reabsorbed into the Farmers Union, from which it had sprung, and several of the party faithful, including Lem Harris, became supporters of the larger organization.[30]

The Communist party got little from its farm activities in the first half of the 1930s. The UFL never amounted to much. On the only occasion when it met—its 1934 conference—there were 1,500 dues-payers, and 10,000 nominal members. In 1935 Hal Ware estimated there were 3,000 members. Of six million American farmers, 1,200 were Communists. *The Farmers' National Weekly*'s circulation hovered around 6,000. About all the Party had to show for years of effort in agriculture was the record of abortive united front efforts led by Ware and Harris. By 1936, Harris alone remained to carry the CPUSA into the Popular Front in agriculture. The Farm Holiday Association was not, however, the A.F. of L.; by the time the Party was able to enter it, Milo Reno's creation was on the decline.[31]

While Party work among farmers was hampered by ideological suspicions, there was no such hesitation about organizing farm *workers*, rural proletarians who supposedly belonged in the Communist party. Throughout the 1930s both the Comintern and CPUSA's leadership stressed the necessity of creating a strong agricultural workers' union and attracting agricultural wage workers to the Party: "The remedy for [reformism] is to turn resolutely to the left, to penetrate the agricultural masses, basing our work's greatest weight on the farm proletariat." The 1933 Extraordinary Conference gave priority to such tasks: "The increased propaganda and agitation among the agricultural proletariat, defence of their interests and the attraction of them to the side of the revolutionary proletarian policy are the fundamental tasks of the work of the Party among the agricultural population." [32]

The Communist party sought to organize farm workers into industrial unions under the aegis of the Trade Union Unity League. Numerous strikes, some of them quite large, took place under Party and TUUL direction. Despite these successes, however, organizing agricultural laborers was an incredibly difficult job and lasting achievements were very meager. Some of the most bitter, violent labor confrontations were fought in the hot, isolated fields of California's farms.

The most forbidding area in California was the Imperial Valley, which was physically isolated from the cities by the desert, the Salton Sea, and the Mexican border; was located in a natural depression almost entirely below sea level; and had been transformed from a barren desert to a lush, profitable agricultural garden by a massive irrigation project. The weather was brutal. In midsummer, temperatures of 125° were not uncommon. In this inhospitable climate the Communists had their first try at organizing farm workers. During the 1920s they had done little in this regard. The only radical group that had had much success in organizing farm workers was the IWW, but by the 1920s, the Wobblies were practically defunct. The A.F. of L. had made several desultory efforts to create unions for the more skilled processing workers in packing sheds, but these had left little trace behind. The way was clear for the Party; there was little competition or even scars from past failures. [33]

Frank Waldron, later to achieve Party leadership under the name of Eugene Dennis, first called attention to a strike of 500 Mexican pea pickers at Castroville in October 1928. The Communist party, he claimed, had sent in organizers to lead the strike and had won a slight victory. He called for an increased Party effort through the TUUL and pointed out that the Mexicans represented a "great potential revolutionary force." The opportunity he was waiting for came early in 1930. On January 6, Mexican and Filipino lettuce workers went on strike in the Imperial Valley. Waldron and three other Party organizers rushed in. Even though the TUUL "was late in coming into the strike field," it was able to gain "the confidence amongst some of the workers and to some extent the leadership of the strike among the Philipinos." The strike, however, soon "was sold out by the misleaders," or non-Communists, and the strikers returned to work around the middle of January at lower wages.[34]

Another strike broke out in February among some 1,000 packing shed workers in the valley. These men were largely native-born, and their strike had some A.F. of L. leadership. It was broken before the TUUL could get to work. Rather than wait for the next strike to erupt, the TUUL affiliate, the Agricultural Workers Industrial Union (AWIU), decided to prepare for one among cantaloupe workers. Preparations for this strike were so slipshod, however, that its date had to be changed several times because the organizers were not sure about the dates of the cantaloupe season. The AWIU had been organized during the January strike, largely among Filipinos, with J. C. Miller as national secretary. On the night of April 14, AWIU meetings being held in El Centro and Brawley to plan for the cantaloupe strike were raided. More than one hundred people were arrested. Six organizers were eventually sentenced to forty-two years each in prison for criminal syndicalism. Frank Waldron evaded the police dragnet, disappearing from another courtroom where he was on trial for his activities during the March 6, 1930, unemployment demonstration in Los Angeles. He slipped out of California and headed for New York. Once there, he was sent on to the Soviet Union, where he worked for the Comintern for several years.[35]

The Imperial Valley strikes of 1930 were small and unsuccessful. Later commentators, perhaps misled by the exaggerated early Party claims, have given the Communists and the TUUL rather too much credit, accepting the idea that they led one or both of the strikes, captured control of them, or had a "potent" organization. In fact, the AWIU gained control of neither strike, and both were lost. The union was never even able to hold its planned April 20 organizational meeting in Brawley. Its first effort to plan a strike was thwarted by the police. Several of its key organizers went into exile. The Party's leaders in District 13, which included California, were removed amid charges that they had abandoned the agricultural struggle. The AWIU led or gained control of several other strikes in California in 1931, changing its name in the process to the Cannery and Agricultural Workers Industrial Union (CAWIU), but either lost all of them or saw any organization quickly vanish. In late 1932, Harrison George sadly admitted: "The Imperial Valley strike has left no trace behind (but some San Quentin prisoners)."[36]

Up to 1933 the Party had little to show for its efforts to organize agricultural workers. Outside of California, the only significant CAWIU activity was a May 1932 strike of 30,000 Colorado sugar beet workers. Inadequate provisions for relief and excessive wage demands by the union resulted in thousands returning to work. Because the CAWIU had refused to accept a partial victory and held out for its original demands, a *Western Worker* writer complained, it had lost the strike. By October, the beet strike was over and not a single trace of the CAWIU was left.[37]

In California, the CAWIU continued to suffer from an inability to prepare strikes. There was, for example, a sudden twenty-four-hour walkout by 1,500 pea pickers in the town of Half Moon Bay in June 1932. Although the CAWIU has been given credit for stimulating the strike, it actually reached the strikers only after they had returned to work. Despite the CAWIU's shortcomings and government and employer violence, the miserable wages and working conditions in the fields stimulated a strike wave in 1933. Peas, lettuce, raspberries, cherries, melons, peaches, grapes, cotton—crop after crop was hit with strikes. At last the CAWIU was able to organize and lead the strikes rather than arriving after they had collapsed. "For the first time," Sam Darcy boasted, "the Party and Union led a majority of the agricultural workers who struck in California." Starting strikes was suddenly easy. The CAWIU continued to have difficulty, however, in running them. Its inexperienced organizers were reluctant to compromise and thus found themselves losing control of strikes. Frustrated Party leaders worried that spectacular opportunities were being wasted.[38]

The worst example came when raspberry pickers in the San Gabriel Valley struck in June for 25¢ an hour and 65¢ per crate. Mike Quin, a Party bard, quickly produced a poem, "Hail! Fighting Berry Pickers!", and the CAWIU took firm control. Facing ruin, the Japanese farmers offered a compromise on the fifth day of the strike—20¢ an hour, 45¢ a crate, and recognition of the union. The intransigent Party fraction in the union rejected the offer and railroaded the refusal through a meeting of the strikers. Having failed to reach an agreement through compromise, the growers stole the strike from the CAWIU. Strike leaders were arrested. The Mexican consul was called in to help form a new union, which went on to settle the dispute. Walter Lambert, state TUUL secretary, unhappily complained later that the union had learned nothing from its earlier mistakes but was busy repeating them.[39]

The first major victory for the CAWIU came at the Tagus Ranch near Tulare. Pat Chambers and Sam Darcy arrived in early August 1933 to prepare for a strike among the peach pickers. Chambers had drifted into the Communist party from the unemployed movement in Los Angeles. A handsome young Irishman, slow-spoken and uneducated, he obtained a job on the ranch and began recruiting his fellow workers. To help him, Darcy persuaded Carolyn Decker to become union secretary. In mid-August, 750 of the 800 peach pickers struck, and within two weeks they won 25¢ an hour and returned to work. Darcy did not, however, insist on a union hiring hall, and the union quickly collapsed once the strike ended.[40]

The festering agricultural war exploded in October. Five thousand cotton pickers in Arizona had struck in September. On October 4 they were joined by 15,000 more in the San Joaquin Valley. Strikers formed mass picket squads to prevent the growers from bringing in scabs. When they were evicted from their camps, the strikers built large tent colonies, one housing 4,000 people. The growers turned to violence and intimidation. More than one hundred workers were arrested. On October 11, two Mexican strikers were shot to death, and dozens were wounded in Pixley in broad daylight with state patrolmen watching. Although the local farmers who did the shooting were later tried, they were acquitted. Pat Chambers, the strike leader, was arrested and charged with criminal syndicalism. Under mounting pressure, the governor of California appointed a fact-finding commission to hear the parties to the dispute and to mediate. After hearing the migrants' tales of misery, the horrified members of the commission recommended pay increases and castigated the growers for violating civil rights.[41]

The CPUSA made no secret of its role in the San Joaquin Valley. In fact, one of the CAWIU's major problems was that no sooner were union locals organized than Party locals were set up and the union was dissolved into the CPUSA: "Local meetings soon became so confused with the Party that the workers who were ready to join our Union and fight for the policies of the Union, but not yet ready for the Party, packed up and walked out."[42]

The union's inability to establish itself resulted in a rapid decline once the strike wave of 1933 subsided. There was one final reprise in the Imperial Valley. Several thousand lettuce workers struck under CAWIU leadership on January 8, 1934. The growers retaliated quickly and effectively. A strike meeting on January 12 was broken up by police and vigilantes firing tear gas into the hall. Two hundred strikers were arrested, picket lines were broken up, and $1,000 rewards were posted for the three strike leaders, Dorothy Ray, Stanley Hancock, and Pat Chambers. Just ten days after it began, the strike was called off because of lack of organization and "extreme intensified terror and being unable to maintain picket lines." Al Wirin, an International Labor Defense attorney, obtained a federal court injunction to prevent interference with an open meeting of the American Civil Liberties Union in the valley. In early February he was kidnapped from a local hotel, threatened with branding and drowning, and taunted about the reach of the federal writ: "Injunctions don't go in this Valley." The three strike leaders were jailed for six months. County authorities banned all picketing and workers' meetings, effectively running the union out of Imperial Valley.[43]

The CAWIU claimed it had 10,000 members in the spring of 1934. Membership declined rapidly thereafter. Fewer agricultural strikes took place that year. Most were small, and many were led by A.F. of L. or independent unions. The union leadership faced a battery of court cases. Pat Chambers managed to beat one criminal syndicalism charge, but he and seventeen other officials were promptly reindicted on the same charge, stemming from their activities in the San Joaquin cotton strike. The defendants, arrested on July 20, 1934, remained in jail through their trials, which did not begin until January 1935 and lasted four months. Eight defendants, including Chambers and Carolyn Decker, were convicted of criminal syndicalism and sentenced to 1–14 years in prison.[44]

The growers also created an employers' association, Associated Farmers, which began a statewide campaign to destroy the CAWIU. The LaFollette Committee held hearings in California at the end of the decade in which officials of the Associated Farmers openly admitted their role in passing anti-picketing laws, requiring farm workers to register before they were allowed to work, and arresting and holding union leaders incommunicado. One witness succinctly expressed the association's sentiment: "There is no justification at all for organized union agricultural labor."[45]

The CAWIU was nearly defunct by the spring of 1935. Tulare farm workers held their first gathering in sixteen months in June; they decided to apply for an A.F. of L. charter. Late in July, Pat Chambers and Carolyn Decker appealed to the remnants of their union from jail, asking them to join the American Federation of Labor. The heroic effort to organize agricultural workers in a revolutionary union had come to an end, a dismal failure. The TUUL union had been able to ride the strike wave, even make a few waves itself, but had not been capable of building any permanent structure. Migrant workers were far more difficult to organize than industrial workers, and the resistance of employers to unionization of any kind, much less Communist-led unionization, was implacable and vicious. The Cannery and Agricultural Workers Industrial Union had distinguished itself chiefly for the pluck and courage of its organizers. In strike after strike it had made mistakes that only added to its other difficulties. Even though the Communist party had made farm workers its chief priority in agriculture, it achieved very little return for its efforts. Jack Stachel's report on Party membership in the middle of 1935 indicated that only twenty-three agricultural workers belonged to the CPUSA.[46]

9

Life of the Party

AFTER a distressingly long period of inertia and floundering, Party membership finally began to grow in 1933. The Open Letter in July reversed a brief decline. By the end of the year membership was back to 18,000, about what it had been a year before. One year later it was approximately 26,000, the largest absolute growth the Party had ever recorded in a single year. Still, the Third Period was also a time of frustration. With so many opportunities, relatively little had been accomplished. After several years of the Depression, 26,000 members, while better than the 7,000 of 1930, was little to boast of. Given the state of the union, Browder chided, the Party should have had between 100,000 and 150,000 members by the end of 1934. Party expectations had far exceeded achievements, not only in membership but also in virtually every phase of activity.[1]

The Communist party actually had gained enough members during these years to have been more than twice as large as it was in 1934. If all of the nearly 50,000 people who became Communists between 1930 and March 1934 had remained Communists, some 57,000 people would have filled the Party's ranks. However, 33,000 of them had ceased to be Party members. Why had they dropped out? What caused the problem of membership fluctuation? One of the simplest explanations was inefficiency and incompetence. Hundreds, perhaps thousands, of people applied to join by signing application cards or even paying initiation fees but never received membership books or never were assigned to a Party unit. In New York alone in 1933, 500 people were lost because of these organizational snafus, and the New York District was regarded as one of the best in assigning members. "Nobody," complained a Comintern article, "knows the actual number of members of the Party."[2]

Aside from this bureaucratic mismanagement, the chief reason for the failure to keep members, as given by the Party chieftains themselves, was the unsatisfactory inner life of the Party, especially in the lower echelons. New members, starting at the bottom of the Party hierarchy, went into the "units." The unit was the basic foundation of the Party organization; it was also the weakest link in the chain. Complaints about unit life were legion. In theory the units were the places where day-to-day activities were planned, executed, and evaluated. Whether street units based on geographic criteria or shop units based on industrial concentration, they were supposed to meet once a week. If a member failed to attend he was supposed to account for his absence. For most ordinary Communists, the unit was their major point of contact with the Party. For many it was the only one. It was, then, a matter of no little concern to the Communists that what took place in the units was so dull and dreary that it taxed the faith of the most devoted revolutionary. The main cause of fluctuation, one organizer declared, "is the life and work of the Party, especially the lower organizations."[3]

The list of problems began even before the meeting started. Or didn't start. "Meetings start half an hour to an hour later than they are called for," complained J. Peters, "because the unit leadership is not there, or else we wait for more comrades to come." New members were hardly made welcome. The average member, it was pointed out, "doesn't know anyone in the unit, and no one in the unit, as usual, pays any attention to him." One functionary pleaded with Communists to "stop embracing the whole working class and instead select an individual member of the working class for their embrace." Once things got under way, the uninitiated Communist was apt to become bewildered. He would need a dictionary "because every third word we utter will be unintelligible to him." The meetings themselves were interminably long and uninteresting. A Party organizer complained in 1930: "Today we still have the situation where the agenda of a unit meeting contains 10 to 15 points and the meeting lasts 3 to 4 hours most of which is spent on details of relatively small importance, each of which should have been finally decided by the unit buro." One disgruntled member described a typical unit meeting: "We argue. We discuss. We get excited and, some of us, disgusted. No results. We leave the question for another meeting . . . . The agit-prop speaks; the secretary speaks; everybody speaks; no one to listen."[4]

That member may have been lucky; apparently discussion was a rarity in many meetings. The organizer would monopolize the floor, handing down "diktats" and announcing assignments. A new member complained that his unit never discussed theoretical matters, meetings were "very dry," and give-and-take was rare. Sometimes, when greater participation occurred, it was destructive. "We have in almost every unit," Peters complained, "one or two comrades who will never miss a chance to take the floor. Their destructive criticism and petty quarrelings disrupts the work of the unit and creates an atmosphere which makes it almost impossible to work." Before a new dues system was initiated in 1930, an inordinate amount of time was devoted to passing the hat. "We are swamped in collections," complained one Communist, noting that at one meeting a member could expect to be dunned for tickets to two or three different auxiliaries' dances, *Daily Worker* collections, rent for Party offices, contributions for section affairs, and miscellaneous expenses. At the Fifteenth Plenum of the Party, with an understatement rare to the higher bodies, it was noted that "there is a tendency to confine Party meetings to routine and organizational details, divorced from the living problems of the class struggle.[5]

Although little enough besides enormous patience and tolerance for petty detail was required to sit through a unit meeting, Party members did have onerous demands placed on them. One organizer wrote that until late 1932, "we demanded that each member give all their 'spare' time, the time outside the factory, to the Party." The slogan "Every Evening to Party Work" finally prompted someone to ask whether a worker had "a chance to remain in the Party if he is not ready to give up his present family life." The units were given so many assignments by higher Party echelons that to fulfill all of them was impossible. One tired Communist complained that he hated to attend Party meetings:

> No matter how much I do, I always hate to show my face because there are things I did not do that I was told to do. Directives, directives, directives. . . . Hell, I could not do one tenth of it. I am getting tired. I am just as much a Communist as ever, but I am not 10 Communists . . . . I can't be everywhere all at once. I must sleep sometimes. I have spent enough energy at inner meetings to over-throw the whole capitalist system. My wife won't stand for it either.[6]

The natural reaction of unit members was to avoid or shuck off as many responsibilities and assignments as possible. Many members "spend as much time looking for excuses as it would require for doing, even mechanically, the work the unit requires." Older, more experienced members were often the worst offenders. They pooh-poohed any effort to invigorate unit life, adopted a "spittoon philosophy" denigrating mass activities, and cynically shifted as many burdens as possible onto the shoulders of enthusiastic and idealistic but inexperienced newer members. A new member was greeted not with outstretched arms but with a schedule seemingly designed to exhaust his vitality. "We immediately shove him into T.U.U.L. work," wrote one observer, "which would not be bad in itself, but then comes the I.L.D., the W.I.F., the L.S.N.R. and a half dozen other activities and we completely neglect to give him a theoretical understanding." Caught up in this whirl of activity, some Party members never fully understood what they were doing. Others got tired and dropped out. If the Party demanded all or nothing, it most frequently received nothing.[7]

Prime responsibility for the weakness at the lower levels was placed on a shortage of capable Party leadership. Each unit was guided by a Unit Buro composed of the organizer, the most politically developed comrade, who directed all the work; an agitprop director in charge of education and contact with the community; a financial secretary overseeing dues collection and expenses; and a literature agent handling distribution of newspapers and pamphlets. Typically, none were paid functionaries. Relatively few were workers in shops or heavy industry. Many were leftovers from the faction-ridden days of the 1920s. Overwhelmingly foreign-born, they were reluctant to reach out beyond the small circle of old comrades with whom they felt at ease or were ill-prepared to meet their responsibilities. The Party, a former Comintern representative warned, needed new unit leaders "from the ranks of workers who have distinguished themselves in the mass struggles.[8]

There was no lack of explanations, then, for the sorry state of the units. Doing something significant to change them was another matter entirely. The Party knew what was wrong, but both its structure and its makeup prevented the kinds of reforms that would have solved the problems. Some problems were a result of the disparity between the Party's size and the tasks set for it by Third Period doctrine. Other problems were endemic to a centralized Communist party. In both cases ameliorative efforts were largely futile.

One would have thought that the easiest complaint to deal with would have been the unintelligibility of Party meetings. Yet, the Party clung tenaciously to the esoteric terminology and abbreviations that made Communist language so opaque. Sam Darcy, for one, thought that these foreign-sounding terms were necessary. Communists had to learn "the method, content and inevitably the phraseology of Marxism-Leninism." A Party journalist reminded readers that "revolution is a science [and] every science requires its terminology" to justify Communist language. Intellectual stagnation in the units was even less susceptible to correction. Everyone urged livelier meetings with more discussion. Yet, the very organization of the Party precluded just that. The CPUSA was committed to "democratic centralism." Full and frank discussion of an issue by the units supposedly led to disciplined obedience after a decision was made. In practice, this approach deadened political life within the Party.[9]

The shadowy J. Peters wrote a text on Party organization in 1935. In addition to laying down rules and regulations for Party units, Peters reminded Communists that once a decision was made, be it by a unit or a leading committee, "discussion must cease and the decision be carried out by every organization and individual member of the Party." Some issues were exempt from any question. "Basic principles and decisions, such as, for example, the Program of the Communist International, cannot be questioned." Once the ECCI, a Party convention, or the Central Committee made a decision or passed a resolution, "we do not question the political correctness" but discuss only how best to apply the directive. Given the Comintern's predilection for interfering in Party affairs, major policies were rarely debated in America before they were adopted. At best, the top echelons of the Party might be consulted prior to an important Comintern decision. Rank-and-file members did not debate the pros and cons of the theory of self-determination for Negroes in the South, the decision to build a dual union movement, the relationship between unemployed and trade union work, or the united front from below, before the Comintern issued its ukases on the subjects. Nor, with few exceptions, did the rank and file debate such decisions afterward. What was left to discuss at the grass roots was how to carry out what others had decided.[10]

Many Communists did not mind these limitations on themselves. Marxism-Leninism was a science: like any science, it had its experts. No one would doubt the superior ability of Einstein to explain the workings of the universe compared to the capacities of an undergraduate physics major. Why not defer to the judgments of revolutionary experts on how to make a revolution? A consequence, however, was that unit life could rarely engage its members. Discussion was superfluous, and many Party members recognized that fact.

The demands placed on Party members were onerous. Solving this problem did not require altering the very nature of the Party itself. But the solution was precisely the source of the problem: there were too few Communists. So long as the Party was expected to do so much and remained so small, its members would feel pressured to do everything at once. What made the situation worse was that a substantial proportion of Party members were "paper members," who did little beyond attending meetings. Lenin had expected Communists to be professional revolutionaries. Most American Communists were not. The preferred solution was to draw more people into Party work or, alternatively, use the Party's mass organizations to shoulder some of the load. In most cases, however, the mass organizations were even smaller than the Party itself. Instead of drawing in different people, one Communist complained, "we often substitute the repeated organization of ourselves into new organizations," creating additional work but few benefits.[11]

The most tractable of the problems, at least in theory, was the sorry state of unit organizers. Theoretically, those who were inadequate could be trained, educated, coached, and even carefully controlled until competent replacements were found. In practice, none of these alternatives was very easy. A constant stream of requests and pleas for assistance poured into New York: "You must send us a Section Organizer and you must send a good one," went one demand. New York accused the other districts of thinking it was a "Mail Order Business" with a stock of "ready-made goods of every quality and quantity" and urged them to develop their own organizers. Browder complained that the districts acted as if "the national office incubator shall hatch out about 20 new Marxist-Leninist organizers for them." Party training courses, ranging in length from one to three months, were set up, but districts were loath to send their best people and often shipped off those most easily spared. "The districts," pleaded one Party educator, "should send comrades who show signs of leadership, willingness to work and sacrifice, even if it is necessary to take the comrade away from important work." A "large number" of those trained disappeared from the Party soon afterward.[12]

Somewhat paradoxically, while boredom within the lower units was a bar to retaining Party members, another problem was that the danger in being a Communist undoubtedly frightened people away. To be publicly identified as a Communist was to risk grave penalties. Thirty-five states had criminal syndicalism laws, and Communists were prime candidates for prosecution. Although it was most often Party leaders who were indicted, ordinary members were not immune from either those laws or less imposing ones. Fifteen-year-old Harry Eisman of the Bronx, arrested for striking a police horse with a club during an anti–Boy Scout rally, was shipped off to a reformatory for his crime. Nineteen-year-old Yetta Stromberg, a leader of the Young Pioneers, was sentenced to ten years in prison for raising a red flag above a workers children's camp in Yucalpa, California. For foreign-born Communists there were even graver risks, since membership was grounds for deportation of aliens and there was evidence that an ordinary rank and filer could get into trouble just as easily as a functionary. Party or TUUL organizers were almost sure to get arrested sooner or later at some strike or demonstration. When Party demonstrations degenerated into fistfights and pitched battles with the authorities, even those merely listening to speeches could end up being hurt or arrested. For many Americans, being a Communist was just asking for trouble.[13]

For some Communists, Party life also imposed greater risks. From its earliest days, American Communism included both a legal and an illegal apparatus, the latter sanctioned and required by the Comintern. One of the famous twenty-one conditions for admission to the Comintern required its constituent parties to create a parallel, illegal "organizational apparatus which, at the decisive moment, can assist the Party to do its duty to the revolution." In 1930 the ECCI warned that "legal forms of activity must be combined with systematic illegal work" in the shops. Two years later the Twelfth Plenum instructed the Comintern's sections that among their chief organizational tasks was "immediately" to proceed to "form strictly secret nuclei in military units and the militarized organizations of the bourgeoisie in munitions factories, on the railroads and in the ports."[14]

During the Third Period it was expected that sooner or later every Party in a bourgeois country would confront intensified repression. At the Sixth World Congress, Communists were warned to heed the lessons of the past; they had to be prepared to go underground or face destruction. Hardly a plenum of the Comintern went by without some reference to underground work. At the ECCI's Eleventh Plenum, Dimitri Manuilsky insisted that it was necessary to combine "legal methods of work with illegal methods." At the Twelfth Plenum, Ossip Piatnitsky assured the comrades that they would all be driven underground in the not-too-distant future when war erupted; he issued instructions on how to prepare for the day of reckoning. Among the decisions of the plenum was an order to its sections "to take measures to insure that the Party can promptly pass to an illegal basis in case of necessity." The Thirteenth Plenum was more urgent, noting that "the whole situation demands that the Communist Parties prepare in good time cadres for underground work, that they seriously tackle the question of combatting provocateurs, that they combine the methods of strict secrecy with securing the best contacts with the masses and avoiding the schematic structure and work of the underground organizations." At the same time, Otto Kuusinen announced that "illegal work has acquired greater significance than ever in the past few years."[15]

Less public Comintern instructions came to the American Communists in a document written by B. Vassiliev, a Comintern functionary transmitting the views of the ECCI in 1930. While Communist parties had to fight to preserve their legal status, Vassiliev noted, they also had to be sure that a parallel illegal apparatus was functioning:

All legal Parties are now under the greater responsibility in respect to the creation and strengthening of an illegal apparatus. All of them must immediately undertake measures to have within the legally existing Party committees an illegal directing core. . . . with regard to the legal Communist Parties it is a question of creating under the cover of a legal Party Committee, legal labels and premises, an illegal apparatus.

Vassiliev suggested a variety of measures to safeguard the Party. From among trusted but not well-known comrades, "cells of illegal directing organs must be created." Pictures of leading Party figures should not be published in newspapers, nor should Communists use real names. Facilities for illegal publishing should be created. Special communications links, codes, and ciphers should be readied for when needed, and safe refuges for hiding Party leaders or holding secret meetings developed.[16]

The American comrades did the best they could to follow instructions. As far back as April 1923 the American Communists pledged to "organize various confidential and secret departments of the Party for ensuring its safety and carrying on the Party's underground work." The Party's Tenth Plenum in 1929 warned that "in view of the increasing terrorism of the bourgeoisie it becomes a most necessary task to prepare the normal function for the Party in the coming inevitable condition of illegality. . . . it shall make all necessary preparations for illegal functioning of the leading organs of the Party." The 1934 Draft Resolution for the Party convention emphasized the need to work openly but noted that "the Party must prepare to go underground."[17]

Party leaders were well aware of the underground's existence. They could not have missed injunctions printed in the Party press. Alexander Trachtenberg and Max Bedacht have been identified as Party figures who "might have selected persons for special work."[18] J. Peters was the man who directed underground work. Born in Cop, Hungary, he first entered the United States in 1924 as Alexander Goldberger. During the late 1920s he was a leader of the Party's Hungarian Bureau, and he briefly served as organizational secretary. In the early 1930s Peters was present at the Lenin School and represented the ECCI in America. He also found time to supervise the Party's underground members in Washington.[19]

Other American Communists performed errands for the Comintern abroad. Some served as Communist International representatives in countries ranging from Mexico to China.[20] The practice of using false passports was so widespread that the State Department prepared a passport conspiracy case that included a score of Party functionaries. Charles Krumbein was jailed in both Great Britain and the United States for falsifying travel documents, and Browder himself went to prison for using a false passport.[21]

A few Communists volunteered for even more dangerous work, spying for Soviet military intelligence. One, Nicholas Dozenberg, orchestrated an effort to dispose of counterfeit Federal Reserve notes that ended disastrously. Arrested in 1939, he turned state's evidence and helped convict Browder for using his passport to travel abroad in the 1920s. Juliet Stuart Poyntz dropped out of open Party activities to undertake secret work, but told friends in 1937 that she was disillusioned and ready to break with Communism. She disappeared amid rumors that she had been killed or abducted by Soviet intelligence.[22]

The Party's Social Composition

Some people endured life in the lower units. Who were they, and from what strata of American society were they drawn? What kind of impact did the Party's composition have on how effectively it carried out its mission?

From 1930 to 1934 the Communist party was largely a party of the unemployed. Over 40 percent of the entire Party membership was unemployed in 1932. At the Eighth Convention in 1934, Browder noted that 60–70 percent did not have jobs. In some districts 80 percent of new recruits between 1930 and 1934 were looking for work, and one Party organ put the figure at 90 percent of the new recruits in 1933. As the Depression began to lift by 1935, the percentage of employed began to rise, although in mid-year 11,633 Communists were employed and 12,441, or 52 percent, were unemployed. The preponderance of unemployed members hampered the Party's activities. It partially explains the weakness of the TUUL, since so few Communists were working in shops and factories. Oddly enough, the large proportion of unemployed members did not help very much in the development of the Unemployed Councils because few of these members actively participated in the councils' activities. The contingent of unemployed members also placed financial pressure on the Party and its auxiliaries, since Party dues were based on income.[23]

Few aspects of the Party's composition were as disappointing as its trade union base. "The Party as a *whole* is divorced from the workers in the shops," declared one authority. No more that 10 percent of the 100,000 TUUL members were ever recruited into the CPUSA. In the New York District, less than 10 percent of Party members were active in trade unions of any kind. Only 15 percent of the membership in Detroit was active in the TUUL unions. The Party's attempt to build shop nuclei never got off the ground. At the time of the Open Letter, only 4 percent of the membership belonged to these nuclei. By the Eighth Convention in 1934, their number had more than doubled, from 140 to 328. But only 2,280 Communists, or 9 percent, were organized by where they worked. The bulk of the Party's recruits did not, therefore, come from the shops but from recruitment by unemployed members of their likewise unemployed friends. The Party's renewed determination to root itself in factories and the easing of the depression did lead to an increase in 1934 and 1935. By 1935, one-third of the Party's membership was in trade unions. In New York, the figure was 55 percent.[24]

From its inception the CPUSA had been a Party of the foreign-born. "We must remember," Browder noted in 1931, "that our Party is a foreign-born Party, that it is largely of foreign composition." That year, a report on Party registration noted that two-thirds had been born abroad. The foreign-born contingent ranged from a low of 4 percent in the tiny District 16 (the Carolinas and Virginia) to 90 percent in District 1 (New England). New York, the largest district, was 84 percent foreign-born; Chicago, the second largest, 53 percent. Jews predominated in New York and San Francisco and were plentiful in Philadelphia, Buffalo, Cleveland, and New Haven; Finns were the largest ethnic group in Boston, Minnesota, the Dakotas, and Seattle; South Slavs in Pittsburgh; and Russians and Ukrainians in Detroit. Chicago was a melange of Jews, Russians, South Slavs, Lithuanians, Hungarians, and Poles. Only one-half of the immigrant members were citizens.[25]

The Communists very much wanted to recruit more native-born Americans. It was not simply that their foreign-born membership isolated them from the working class: this was not entirely the case, as America was a land of immigrants and they were concentrated particularly in the basic industries. Still, many of the Party's foreign-born recruits *were* isolated. Its foreign-language groups, which monopolized many members' time and energy, were insular and inward-looking. In 1933, 5,000 Party members—and in 1934, 7,000—were active in these groups. The Party's foreign-born membership did not parallel the national distribution. Finns, a tiny proportion of America's immigrants, lomed much larger in the CPUSA. In 1931, 500 of the 800 Communists in the Minnesota District were Finns. The most decided disproportion, however, was the Jewish presence in the Party. The New York Young Communist League recruited 117 new members late in 1929. It happily reported the news along with the comment: "The results are also good in national composition, the majority of the new recruits being young Americans and not Jewish." A national registration of the YCL garnered 1,859 names, of which 655 were Jewish and 453 Finnish. There were all of 119 "Anglo-Saxons" and 20 Negroes. A 1931 registration counted at least 19 percent of the Party as Jewish. The Party's largest district, New York, was overwhelmingly Jewish, and foreign-born Jews from Russia and Poland were prominent in nine other Party districts. The Needle Trades Workers Industrial Union was one of the few TUUL unions to sink any roots in factories. Most of its members were Jewish garment workers.[26]

The Jewish impact on the Party was probably even greater than numbers alone indicate. A large proportion of the cadre was Jewish. Between 1921 and 1938, no Central Committee had fewer than a one-third Jewish membership; most were about 40 percent Jewish. Jews were even more numerous among the second-level cadre. Party headquarters and most auxiliaries were centered in New York, the home of most Jewish Communists.[27]

Despite the prominence accorded a few Communist women, the Party had trouble recruiting females. In the 1930–1933 period the percentage of women was under 20 percent. Only 1,600 women were in the entire Party in early 1931, 1,000 of whom were in New York and most of the rest in Chicago. By 1933 the number had doubled, with 3,287 women comprising about 19 percent of the Party. Women Communists numbered over 6,200 in a partial registration in 1935, or slightly less than one-quarter of the Party. Gratifying as the increase was, the Party was not entirely pleased with the composition of its women members.Their chief auxiliary in New York, the United Council of Workingclass Women, was virtually a Jewish monopoly; 97 percent of its 1,000 members were Jewish. Far too many female Communists were housewives, nearly half in both 1932 and 1933. Even when this percentage declined in 1935, it was office workers and teachers, not industrial workers, who joined. Aside from in a few large cities, the Communist party could not attract many women during the Third Period.[28]

One of the most bothersome aspects of the Party's composition was its geographic concentration. New York was top-heavy with Communists. Between 1930 and 1935, approximately one-third of all American Communists lived in that one district. The percentage varied somewhat from year to year, falling to 22 percent in 1933 but rising to 32 percent, or 8,754 members, in 1935. In second place was Chicago. Between 1930 and 1932 it usually had about one-quarter of the Party membership. Cleveland and Detroit each had about 8 percent. Thus, in 1932 a majority of the Party was in two cities and more than three-quarters was concentrated in four. By 1935 the Chicago share had fallen to 11 percent, and San Francisco had shot up to contest it for second place.[29]

Most of the country was terra incognita. National conventions were dominated by delegates from a handful of cities. "National" tours by Party organizers generally ended in Chicago. A disgruntled organizer in California complained that the national office largely ignored the nether reaches of the country beyond Chicago: "It is not healthy," he said, "that we must wait for presidential election years to have a leading comrade come to the Coast." John Williamson complained in 1931 that "in each district, there are tens of good sized industrial cities where our Party hasn't a single member, not to speak of scores of smaller towns." The South remained pretty much of a wasteland, Birmingham being one of the few places where there were more than a handful of members. The largest vacuum, however, was between the Mississippi River and the West Coast. One Party district alone, the tenth, included (until a 1933 reorganization) Missouri, Arkansas, Texas, Oklahoma, Kansas, Iowa, Nebraska, Wyoming, Colorado, New Mexico, and Utah. It covered one-third of the whole United States and was twice as large as France, Germany, England, and Italy combined, yet it had only a tiny membership. As late as 1932 there were only 1,000 Communists in all of District 13, encompassing California, Nevada, and Arizona.[30]

There was more to New York's preponderance in the Party than merely numbers. Throughout the country the cadre was permeated with New Yorkers. In 1932 a Comintern official complained that in not a single district in America was the Party leadership composed of indigenous workers. Instead, it was mostly New York cadres shifted from district to district. There was always such an excess of available cadres there and such a shortage everywhere else that young and ambitious New

Yorkers could make their mark away from home. "They liked," Browder recalled, "to go out in the field where they had no competition and plenty of work to do." This situation was a source of both strength and weakness. On the one hand, the Party desperately needed organizers in places where the local talent was thin or nonexistent. A ready pool of eager Communists willing to go into the country meant that the Party did not have to wait passively for experienced organizers to arise indigenously. On the other hand, within the Party, as Browder noted: "There was always a contrast between New York and the rest of the country." New Yorkers were more "foreign." They were more likely to be Jewish. They were less likely to be industrial workers. By not being representative of the populations they sought to convert, they contributed to the other burdens that the Party carried in trying to expand its influence.[31]

The typical American Communist of the early 1930s was most probably a white, foreign-born male, between the ages of thirty and forty, and unemployed. Even if he had a job, he was unlikely to belong to a trade union. By 1935 more people who were native-born, employed, and trade unionists were joining the Party. But as the Third Period drew to an end, the Communist party remained what it had been for some time, an organization with a decidedly unsatisfactory social composition for a fomenter of revolution. There had been no sudden surge of applicants during the first half of the 1930s. A slow, steady growth had taken place, partly because the Party had managed to reduce its dropout rate. Party members, however, continued to come from the same places and groups. Probably they were people already favorably disposed to Communism who changed their status from sympathizer to member. The Party had not made dramatic inroads among previously ignored groups.

Because of the hardships associated with Party membership, many communists did not become Communists. Toward the end of 1935, Browder claimed that in addition to the 30,000 Party members, there were 50,000 people "immediately surrounding our Party, ready and fit to become Party members," who were kept out only by the "sectarian inner-Party life." He also argued that all who belonged to Communist-affiliated mass organizations were sympathizers and estimated their maximum membership at 300,000 in 1930 and 500,000 in 1934. In notes prepared for the 1934 convention, he listed 450,000 people in mass organizations, "workers organized through the effort of the Party." Fully 375,000 were listed as being in the TUUL (100,000), Unemployed Councils (150,000), and language organizations (125,000). Another 44,000 were credited to the Party itself, the YCL, and the Pioneers, a Communist children's organization. The only other listed group with a mass membership was the International Labor Defense, with 20,000 members. Much of this numbers game was bluff and bluster, however. The Unemployed Councils were nowhere that large; the TUUL, already in the process of dissolution, had not grown because of its Communist affiliation; and much of the influence of the language organizations was due to the International Workers' Order, a Party-led auxiliary that provided low-cost life insurance to its members (62,153 in 1934). And because Party members tended to belong to more than one mass organization, the actual number of workers influenced by the Party is overstated.[32]

By 1934 the Party did control newspapers that published daily or weekly in twenty-one languages. Their circulation ranged from the 22,000 daily readers of the Yiddish *Freiheit* and Finnish *Tyomies* through the 5,000 who read Russian, Greek, Armenian, Swedish, and Yugoslavian papers down to the faithful hundreds who bought Japanese, Estonian, and Lettish publications. The total circulation of foreign-language papers was 131,000. By comparison, *The Daily Worker* did not reach sales of 50,000 until the fall of 1934. Inflated though these figures may be, they indicate that a substantial number of foreign-born Americans were getting at least some of their information and views of the world from the Communist party.[33]

As the Third Period drew to a close, the Communist party had a little to cheer about and much to regret. At long last its stagnation had ended in 1934. The TUUL had grown. The mass organizations claimed larger memberships than ever before. The Party itself had grown to over 25,000 members and the YCL to 6,000. Tens of thousands more clustered on the outskirts of these organizations. On the other hand, measured against the objective conditions in the country, the results were less cheering. Party membership was still less than it had been in 1919. Its social composition was not satisfactory. The TUUL's growth had been so relatively small that it was forced to go out of business. The "masses" in the mass organizations were partly chimerical. Considering the years of depression, and the Communists' goals of provoking a revolutionary crisis, and achieving a Soviet America, the Party had failed badly.

10

Changing the Line

THE TRANSITION from the Third Period to the Popular Front was a long, drawn-out process with much hesitation and caution. The process began in 1934 and continued through the Comintern's Seventh World Congress in the summer of 1935. The initiative for the change came from the Soviets as the meaning of Hitler's triumph sank in. Other democratic and semi-democratic governments began to give way to more and more reactionary regimes. According to the doctrine of social-fascism, communists should have welcomed these events, which were presumably destroying their adversaries on the left and stripping away mass illusions about capitalist society. However, suddenly confronted by the specter of a fascist Europe, the Soviets hesitated.

On February 6, 1934, several right-wing, neo-fascist groups called a massive demonstration in front of the French Chamber of Deputies. Fifteen people were killed and more than 1,600 policemen injured. The Communists spurned a Socialist plea for a defense of the republic. As the chaos spread, both Communists and fascists joined to battle the police on the streets. The Communist leadership continued to minimize the fascist danger and assert that the only way to defeat it was to institute a unified front from below, tearing the Socialist workers away from their leaders. Finally, on June 24 the Comintern sent the Party a telegram ordering unity with the Socialists "at any price" and even sent along a draft unity agreement that included a provision forbidding criticism by either party of the other. Within days, the French Popular Front was under way. The Comintern had recoiled from the possibility that a divided left would permit a fascist or right-wing government in France.[1]

Throughout 1934 there were other portents of change. After several months of flirtation with the once-despised League of Nations, the Soviet Union became a member on September 18. Maxim Litvinof bustled across Europe seeking security pacts. A Socialist-inspired uprising in Asturias, Spain, in October drew Communist support. And on May 28, Georgi Dimitroff of Bulgaria was announced as the main speaker for the long-delayed Seventh Comintern Congress, scheduled for 1935. Dimitroff had been the chief defendant in the 1933 Reichstag Fire trial, where his defiance of the Nazis had transformed him from just another obscure Cominternist to an international hero of the anti-fascist struggle.

Sharp divisions existed within both the Comintern and the Soviet Party. A recent official Soviet account has identified Dimitroff and Dimitri Manuilsky as proponents of a new line in June and July of 1934 and has cited Otto Kuusinen, S. Lozovsky, V. Knorin, and Wang Ming as opponents who "at first defended the obsolete guidelines and only agreed to certain changes in tactics." The latter individuals soon saw the light "in the course of intensive discussions" and "themselves admitted the need" to revise the old doctrines.[2]

At the same time, a move to oust Stalin apparently gained ground within the Soviet Communist party. It came to a head at the Seventeenth Soviet Party Congress in late January and early February of 1934. Sergei Kirov, boss of the Leningrad Party, received a hero's welcome that rivaled Stalin's. While the Party congress was still in session, the "February Days" in France shocked the delegates. In an unprecedented display of concern, work was interrupted for nearly two days to discuss this latest danger. In the balloting for the new Central Committee, Stalin received fewer votes than any other candidate, winning the election only because the number of candidates equaled the number of vacancies. Party documents from the Congress referred to him only as "Secretary" rather than "General Secretary," suggesting that he had been reduced in rank. Stalin soon ended all uncertainty by having Kirov murdered on December 1, 1934. Old Bolsheviks by the thousands went to their deaths for allegedly conspiring in the assassination that Stalin himself had arranged. Even as he settled accounts with his critics, however, Stalin altered the Comintern's policies.[3]

No phrase so succinctly sums up the Third Period as "social-fascist." The Comintern did not retract its charge that social democrats had been social-fascists in the past. At the Seventh Congress, major speeches by Dimitroff and by Wilhelm Pieck of Germany repeatedly pilloried the social democrats for spurning Communist offers of united fronts. The Comintern did, however, admit that it might have been overzealous with the fascist epithet. Wilhelm Pieck confessed that "a mistake equally as grave as the underestimation of the fascist danger was the fact that fascism was discerned even where it did not exist. . . . These mistakes were due to the absolutely false conception that all bourgeois parties are fascist." He announced the belated discovery that democracy, even under socialists, did have its limited uses: "The proletariat has an interest in retaining every scrap of bourgeois democracy and [using] them to prepare the masses for the overthrow of the power of capitalism." There was a qualitative difference between fascist and other governments, Dimitroff argued, even traditional dictatorships. Fascism was not just another bourgeois government but "open terrorist dictatorship."[4]

Late in 1934, Ossip Piatnitsky had pondered the question of whether German social democracy still remained the main prop of the bourgeoisie. Since no mass organization of social democrats was left in Germany, he logically concluded that they could no longer be so characterized. He still clung, however, to some old formulations: *"The united front from below has always been, and still remains, the fundamental form of the united front.* But this in no way means that we exclude the adoption of tactics for a united front from above. In many cases even now it will be possible to get a united front from below, *but there cannot be a united front which comes only from above."*[5]

At the Seventh Congress, Georgi Dimitroff offered to forgo any criticism of groups or parties willing to unite in the fight against fascism. He hoped this would lead to joint activities, including struggles for economic gains, political organization, and self-defense, that would "create the necessary *broad active rank and file of the united front,* the training of hundreds and thousands of non-Party Bolsheviks in the capitalist countries." Dimitroff, who was elected general secretary of the Comintern, becoming the first non-Russian to hold such an exalted rank, added a reminder that the united front required "a single Party of the proletariat in each country." Among other conditions, three essential prerequisites of such unity were the rupture of the social democrats' ties with the bourgeoisie, their acceptance of democratic centralism, and their recognition of "the necessity of the revolutionary overthrow of the rule of the bourgeoisie and the establishment of the dictatorship of the Proletariat in the form of Soviets." The new united front did not involve a change in strategy. The Party's goal remained the same: the swallowing up of its rivals on the left. It had recognized, however, that the strident and provocative behavior of the past had not succeeded and would not succeed.[6]

When it came time to confront the "Class Against Class" slogan, the Comintern rewrote history. At the congress, Wilhelm Pieck said the slogan was "not aimed against the united front of the Communists with the Socialists for the struggle against the bourgeoisie" but, on the contrary, "presupposed" such a united front. The phrase had not meant that Communists could not support Socialist candidates in elections or that they should attack reformist unions or set up their own union movements. "Our Sections in other countries mechanically took over this decision of the German Communist Party," Pieck complained, "ignoring the absolutely different concrete situation existing in their own particular countries." One British delegate forced Pieck to confess that the Comintern leadership might bear some share of responsibility for the dual union movement.[7]

The Third Period itself was unceremoniously laid to rest. At the Seventh Congress, bold predictions of a revolutionary upsurge were coupled with mild disclaimers suggesting that no revolution was contemplated. Pieck boasted that "the forces of the bourgeoisie have grown weaker; the forces of the proletariat have grown stronger." Everything was causing "the idea of storming the citadel of capitalism to mature in the minds of ever larger masses of proletarians." Nonetheless, it was the Communists who had been desperately forced to seek new allies and tactics. And Pieck himself confessed that for the immediate future, "proletarian democracy" was not on the agenda.[8]

The danger of fascism was great enough to induce the congress to consider alliances even with nonproletarian forces. The French had been given permission to go beyond a united front—which meant an alliance with other parties of the proletariat—to a Popular Front that included bourgeois elements like the Radicals. The Communists were ready, Dimitroff proclaimed, "to arrange joint actions between the proletariat and the other toiling classes interested in the fight against fascism." He stated that the establishment of a *"broad people's anti-fascist front* on the *basis of the proletarian* united front is a particularly important task." The Popular Front concept was not an explicit repudiation of the earlier belief that fascism was so slight a danger that the Communists need not fear it and could by themselves counter it. But the idea was as complete a confession of error as the Comintern could muster.[9]

At the very outset of the Comintern's great change, everyone admitted that the new viewpoint—however seemingly far-reaching—was only tactical. Responding to critics who thought that the Moscow decisions indicated a confession of past failure or marked a strategical shift, Earl Browder explained:

> The Seventh World Congress formulated a new tactical line because new conditions have arisen, not because the old line was wrong. The Communists are Marxists, Leninists, Stalinists. We adopt such tactics as best suit the concrete conditions. We will adopt new tactics again when changing conditions will demand it. What Communists do not change, of course, is their strategic aim—the proletarian revolution and Socialism. Naturally, the Seventh World Congress made no change in that at all.[10]

The American transition to the Popular Front was even more hesitant than the Comintern's. "If one is not interested in directives from Moscow," Browder noted in 1934, "that only means that he is not interested in building socialism at all." But what did Moscow want? Until the conflicts within Russia were resolved, the signals sent abroad were unclear. Despite prior indications, however, the American Communists were not prepared for the dramatic changes ordered by the Seventh Congress.[11]

The Madison Square Garden riot and its aftermath, including the collapse of Socialist support for the American League Against War and Fascism, had temporarily frozen any kind of negotiations for a united front with the Socialists. Even the Militants, savoring their victory over the Old Guard at the May 1934 convention, were reluctant to embrace the increasingly insistent Communist calls for a united front. Norman Thomas and Earl Browder soon exchanged a series of letters on the advantages and pitfalls of cooperation. The Socialist leader—responding to a Communist request for a united front on the need for wage increases, unemployment insurance, farm aid, increased rights for blacks, and a struggle against war and fascism—referred the offer to the new National Executive Committee, where he had just obtained a majority. While the Socialists hesitated, the Communists continued to couple appeals to their leadership with reminders that they would never surrender the united front from below. Browder reiterated that his Party should concentrate on winning Socialists "from below to the united front." To further the united front, a *Daily Worker* editorial suggested that Socialists vote Communist rather than for their own party in the 1934 elections. In September the Socialists formally rejected cooperation.[12]

The Socialists had one major disadvantage through all the negotiating and maneuvering about the united front. They were a party in the process of decline. Consumed by inner-party turmoil, they had lost faith in their ability to survive. For the first time in eight years, Socialist party membership declined in 1935. The Communists had passed them in 1934 and continued to forge steadily ahead. In New York City the Communist vote in 1935 was 51,336, a 20 percent increase from the year before. The Socialist vote, 66,143, was down more than 27,000. For the first time since 1919, the Communist vote in Manhattan was larger than that of the Socialists. The Communist party might not have become a mass party, but it was in the process of replacing the Socialists as the preeminent party of the left.[13]

Communists and Socialists did strike agreements on a number of specific issues, particularly after the Seventh Congress. The Socialist-controlled National Unemployed Convention voted for a united front with the Communist Unemployed Councils. A number of Communist candidates in local races withdrew in favor of Socialists. The Communist-controlled National Student League and the Socialist Student League for Industrial Democracy merged to form the American Student Union. But, ironically, as the Communist party responded to Moscow's directives to build a popular front against fascism by marching toward the right, the Socialists meandered in disarray to the left. One party was in the process of abandoning revolutionary rhetoric while the other was adopting it. In a debate with Earl Browder in November 1935, Norman Thomas complained that the new united front tactics were too broad and indiscriminate. "The alternative," he told a packed Madison Square Garden, "is Socialism or Fascism, not democracy or fascism, as would seem to be the case in the new Communist line." Browder touchily denied that his party had lost its revolutionary fervor: "If our Socialist friends are afraid we will not join them in a future taking over of power when the situation is ripe, let them be at peace on this question." Nonetheless, the Socialist Militants, who had vanquished the opponents of cooperation with Communists in their own ranks, hesitated to embrace Communists whose new policy was so catholic as to consider alliances with bourgeois parties.[14]

The Communists read other groups on the left out of any potential united front. As they gradually emerged from isolation, they had less and less use for A. J. Muste, regarding him as a threat to their efforts to establish hegemony on the left. Late in 1934 the Trotskyists, in a dazzling display of radical footwork, engineered unity with Muste, creating the Workers party, which soon attracted a hodgepodge of ex-Communists including Joe Zack and Albert Weisbord, along with radicals like Sidney Hook and Communists-to-be Louis Budenz and Arnold Johnson. The Communists primly warned the Musteites that they were buying pigs in a poke. The Trotskyists were soon to be on their way into the Socialist party, minus Muste, but the Communists looked askance at these hated renegades.[15]

A fortuitous circumstance permitted the Party to launch an all-out attack on the new Workers party. Sergei Kirov was assassinated just about the time of the party's formal unification. His death occupied most of the front page of *The Daily Worker* on December 3, 1934. An uninformed reader might have been forgiven his puzzlement over the amount of space devoted to the leader of the Leningrad Communist party. An impassioned editorial pledged to build a Soviet America and issued a dire warning: "To our enraged class enemies we give the word of the Roman gladiators, 'Tremble, for you have cause to fear.'" The party passionately defended the Soviet terror that followed. Browder linked the assassination with Muste, Jim Cannon, Max Shachtman, and Joe Zack and used it to call for a renewed struggle against the Party's enemies on the left.[16]

"Social-fascism" remained in the Party's arsenal through 1934. The last important left-wing political figure to earn a constant stream of abuse as a concealed fascist was Upton Sinclair, surely one of the most unlikely politicians ever to gain a major political party's nomination for governor, even in California. One of the earliest muckrakers, Sinclair had won lasting fame and helped secure passage of the Pure Food and Drug Act with his exposé of the Chicago stockyards, *The Jungle*, published in 1906. He was fifty-four years old in 1933 and had been a registered Socialist for much of his adult life, as well as a perennial candidate for public office, never coming close to victory. In September 1933, Sinclair altered his registration to become a Democrat and began campaigning for governor of California on a production-for-use platform that promised to End Poverty in California (EPIC).[17]

The California Communists made a few attacks on Sinclair's program, including ones that accused him of using "every demagogic trick of the Nazis"; warned that he was "old and befuddled, but the honey that drips from his political lips is winning over the electorate"; and demanded exposure of "this faker and forthcoming fascist." Nonetheless, the Communists began to negotiate with the Sinclair forces in early 1934 about supporting his candidacy. Sam Darcy later claimed that they had reached an informal agreement: the EPIC movement would not nominate a candidate for controller. The Communists would run Anita Whitney, scion of an old California family, for that post, and not run anyone for governor, allowing their supporters to vote for Sinclair. At the Party convention in early April 1934, Darcy presented his plan to the Politburo. He was rudely rebuffed. Browder instructed him to expose and denounce Sinclair and, in the bargain, to run for governor of California himself. The

Party's national convention adjourned on April 8. The following day *The Western Worker* began a series of articles blistering Sinclair as a deserter from the radical movement. Other stories and headlines characterized the ex-Socialist as "California's most dangerous Social-Fascist" and "Sinclair—Fascist A la Mode." When Sinclair responded by attacking the Communists, he was rewarded with a renewed charge that he was a social-fascist and an editorial rebuke that he was "crawling on his belly" to avoid charges that he had any sympathy for Communism. Early in May the Communists nominated Darcy for governor, a young Negro named Pettis Perry for lieutenant-governor, Pat Chambers for the senate, and Anita Whitney for controller.[18]

To everyone's astonishment, Sinclair won a decisive victory in the Democratic primary. George Creel, his shell-shocked foe, lamented: "When I crossed the Tehachapal into Southern California it was like plunging into darkest Africa without gun bearers." Franklin Roosevelt, confronted with this fresh evidence of the oddity of California politics, gave his general approval to his new Democratic colleague, musing to aides that one of the virtues of federalism was that even if Sinclair won, EPIC would only affect California. The Communists interpreted Sinclair's victory as a triumph of deception. Many people believed "that he does really represent the same things as the Communists do, but that he has a more practical and easier way of achieving [them]." To Sam Darcy, Sinclair was "backed by the bosses" as an alternative to communism: "The Sinclair candidacy and campaign, therefore, constitutes the most immediate and main danger to the interests of the working-class and revolutionary movement. It represents the up to now largely successful efforts of the capitalist class to turn the leftward movement of the masses into safe channels for itself." A front-page editorial in *The Western Worker* warned that Sinclair would discredit real revolutionaries: "Precisely this role which Sinclair is now playing for the fascists in the state of California was played by the socialists in Germany and Austria to make way for Hitler and Stahremberg, and the Syndicalists in Italy, to make way for Mussolini."[19]

That was not good enough for the Party leadership. A *Daily Worker* editorial called Sinclair a better fascist than the President:

Sinclair's specific program of labor camps, isolation of the unemployed on farms, reduction of taxation for the bosses, wholesale inflation, are an extension of the most fascist elements of the New Deal. Sinclair actually, far in advance of the aims of the New Deal, differs from the Roosevelt program only in that he plunges ahead towards its fascist goal with great speed.

Unhappy with Darcy's lukewarm denunciations of Sinclair, the Politburo sent Robert Minor to tour the West Coast in mid-October. A sample of Minor's rhetoric can be gleaned from a front-page story he wrote for *The Western Worker*. Sinclair was making "a special effort to put over the program of the most reactionary, most imperialist and war-mad heads of the big trusts." His program was "strike-breaking, union-smashing, reducing wages, enslaving labor, foreclosure of farms, ranches and homes, robbing the middle class for the benefit of the biggest bankers of California, destroying the political and civil rights of the people and preparing the way for the Second World War." Sinclair was "Hitler-like," his EPIC "has already gone far in transition toward open Fascism," and his platform "has a definite fascist essence."[20]

California conservatives did not agree. Apparently blind to its own interests, the Republican party—fueled by unprecedented contributions from panic-stricken Hollywood moguls, large industrialists, bankers, and corporate farmers—launched an enormous public relations blitz to destroy the Sinclair menace. Robert Minor might have regarded the Democratic candidate as the spear-carrier of finance capital and fascism, but the Republicans were more realistic about him. On election day Sinclair lost badly, getting only 850,000 votes, a quarter-million behind the Republicans' count. Sam Darcy polled only 8,799, far fewer than Anita Whitney, who led the Communist ticket with 80,000 ballots.[21]

Fresh evidence that Sinclair was not the candidate of emerging fascism did not dissuade Minor from cramming the Californian into his preordained pigeonhole. Minor did admit that pro-fascist forces in America had opposed EPIC while Sinclair was supported by "the overwhelming majority of the working class, almost the entire membership of the trade unions," and other "Progressive" forces. Since the classic function of social-fascists was to deceive the workers through glittering but meaningless slogans, why had the captains of industry undercut their champion? They were afraid, Minor calculated, that Sinclair could not control his own followers, and they eventually decided he was not needed to dupe the workers. Still another puzzle to the Party leadership was why the Communists had done so poorly. Minor launched an attack on the California comrades for their failure to press the anti-Sinclair campaign with sufficient venom. They had made "some very grave mistakes," both "of political analyses and tactical policy—[which] contributed heavily to our inability to lead the mass wave that arose largely out of economic struggles led largely by our Party."[22]

Reading these criticisms, Darcy seethed. He had been forced into a campaign that threatened to weaken the Party's gains on the West Coast.

Unhappy with Darcy's performance, the Party had dispatched Minor to ensure that Sinclair was denounced vigorously and coarsely enough. Moreover, Minor's critical article was only the first part of a series. It was "to be continued" in the next month's *Communist*. Darcy demanded that his reply be published, and he threatened to resign at a Party plenum in January 1935. Instead of receiving an expected rebuff, he found Gerhart Eisler as an ally. Eisler effected a compromise. Minor's second article never appeared. Browder "gently chided Minor for having gone 'too far,' " although he had only been carrying out Party policy. A reply that Darcy wrote was supposed to be published but never was. After ignoring entreaties for months, why had the Party leadership suddenly stopped its fierce attack on Sinclair? Darcy's threat alone, even combined with the unhappiness of the California Party, would not have been sufficient to force Eisler and Browder to terminate so abruptly a policy that seemed to have Comintern approval. But before he agreed to Eisler's compromise, Browder had taken a trip to Moscow.[23]

The 1934 election results had not been totally lost on the Communist leadership. Sinclair was one of a number of seemingly left-wing alternatives to Roosevelt who had made a respectable showing. Huey Long in Louisiana, the LaFollettes in Wisconsin, and Floyd Olson in Minnesota had all swept to victory on platforms more radical than the New Deal. At the same time, the Communist vote grew by 80–100 percent between 1932 and 1934. In New York, for example, the Communists' gubernatorial vote increased from under 25,000 in 1932 to more than 41,000. The Socialist vote was still much larger, almost 80,000, but up only 8,000 from the previous election. Still, neither the Socialists nor the Communists had, in the eyes of Earl Browder, "succeeded in engaging in its support the masses who were tending to break away from the two traditional capitalist parties." In an article prepared for publication in November—before his trip to Moscow—but not published until February 1935, Browder pondered the implications of those election results and concluded that 1936 could see the emergence of "a mass party in opposition to and to the Left of Roosevelt." The danger was that it would be an anti-Communist party. Of the four alternatives Browder foresaw, three were unpalatable: a Progressive party based on LaFollette, Sinclair, and similar figures; an essentially similar Farmer-Labor party; and a Labor party "dominated by a section of the trade union bureaucracy assisted by the Socialist Party and excluding the Communists." Such parties, Browder wrote, would all promote "class collaboration and a subordination of the workers' demands to the interests of capital, of profits and private property." The vehicle to which the Communist star had to be hitched was a Labor party of a different kind.[24]

The ECCI Presidium met in early December 1934. Its major preoccupation was the French Popular Front; opponents of the front mounted an attack on the new policy. Otto Kuusinen and Dimitri Manuilsky defended the French policy and, according to the official Soviet interpretation, "stressed the international significance of the French Communist Party's experience." Browder brought his Labor party proposal with him to Moscow. After the presidium repulsed an attack on the Americans for daring to proclaim, at their Eighth Convention, that they were the inheritor of the traditions of the American revolution, (some purists regarded 1776 as a purely bourgeois event), it permitted them to adopt the new policy.[25]

The new Labor party policy merely involved a transfer of the more flexible united front policies to electoral politics. The Communist party was not proposing its own dissolution or surrendering its commitment to the revolution; on the contrary, the Party would "continue more than ever to agitate and propagandize about the necessity of fighting for a Soviet America." Nor was it suggesting a compromise with the New Deal. The Labor party was a response to "the clearly discernible beginnings of a mass disintegration of the old Party system" and the need "to show the class kinship of Roosevelt's policy" with those of other bourgeois opponents. And neither were the Communists offering to cooperate with the various organized left-wing forces already in existence. Such bourgeois reformers as Governor Floyd Olson of the Minnesota Farmer-Labor party had to be exposed and their influence destroyed.[26]

What the Communists wanted was a Labor party in which they exercised a predominant force but had a fig leaf to cover their involvement. The stress was on building a "united front from below" in the political field. "The Communists enter the movement for a Labor Party," the Politburo announced, "only with the purpose of helping the masses to break away from the bourgeois and social-reformist parties and to find the path to the revolutionary class struggle." The Party formula was "a Labor Party built up from below on a trade union basis but in conflict with the bureaucracy, putting forward a program of demands closely connected with mass struggles, strikes, etc., with the leading role played by the militant elements, including the Communists." The Communist party, Browder was realistic enough to admit, "cannot expect, however, that it will be able to bring directly under its own banner, and immediately, the million masses who will be breaking away from the old parties." While it was still premature to build a national political party, a plenum declared that, where local conditions warranted, "the Party then should itself, or through people and organizations close to the C.P., take the initiative in giving organizational form to this movement."[27]

The new Labor party policy did generate controversy within the Communist party, less for its substantive content than for the fact that Browder announced it in a speech at the National Congress for Unemployment Insurance in early January. The congress, which was a large, united front gathering called to inaugurate a campaign to secure passage of a Communist-inspired unemployment insurance bill, was hardly the place where Communists were used to hearing new initiatives from their Party. *The Daily Worker* was caught off guard: it merely printed as an editorial a portion of Browder's speech under the headline: "Communists Are Prepared to Join Labor Party Movement." Responding to a *fait accompli*, the Central Committee met two weeks later and organized a sixty-day discussion on the new line. *The Daily Worker* denied that any violation of Party democracy had occurred. At the Seventh Congress, Browder admitted that the Party's Labor party, which still existed largely only in the minds of its beholders, had not gotten very far. The Communists had wrongly resisted broadening the party to include farmers. They had also erred in limiting its demands to those previously advocated by the Communist party instead of also taking positions on issues ranging from inflation to public works. What had not changed was Browder's firm conviction that the new party would pick up some of the pieces of the discredited Roosevelt administration. Labor party or Farmer-Labor party, it was an alternative to, not an ally of, all existing parties even though it would cooperate with elements of other left-wing groups.[28]

Reconciliation with Socialists was hard enough; it was difficult not to think of them as "social-fascists." Bourgeois politicians, however, were another matter. From the day of his inauguration, Franklin Roosevelt had been pilloried for preparing the way for fascism. The prevailing Party line was that while not himself a fascist, the President gave aid and comfort to those who were and was unwilling to resist them and incapable of doing so. Over and over again *The Daily Worker* and Party leaders warned that the New Deal was a "step in the direction of fascism," that FDR would soon resort "to more and more fascist measures against the workers," and that his program was "a war and fascist program." Roosevelt himself was variously described as "the leading organizer and inspirer of Fascism in this country" and the agent through whom a cabal of bankers and industrialists was "exercising their hidden dictatorship." When Norman Thomas had the temerity to see the fascist danger in private gangs, an editorial rebuked him for ignoring the real source of worry: "It is the White House that is the central headquarters of the advance of fascism." The logic of this position required the Party to minimize attacks made on Roosevelt by such right-wing organizations as the Liberty League. An editorial dismissed the league's polemics as all wind: "Its differences with Roosevelt are not fundamental." After the 1934 election, the Party interpreted the Democratic victory as one that "apparently strengthens the governmental machine for the carrying out of the program of monopolies formulated by the Liberty League."[29]

Amid this orgy of anti-Roosevelt rhetoric, one shockingly discordant note appeared. On July 23, 1934, Stalin gave an interview to the English novelist and socialist H. G. Wells. Not published until October 8, the exchange included both a reiteration of a revolutionary line and praise for Franklin Roosevelt:

> In speaking of the impossibility of realizing the principles of planned economy while preserving the economic basis of capitalism I do not in the least desire to belittle the outstanding personal qualities of Roosevelt, his initiative, courage and determination. Undoubtedly Roosevelt stands out as one of the strongest figures among all the captains of the contemporary capitalist world. That is why I would like once again to emphasize the point that my conviction that planned economy is impossible under the conditions of capitalism does not mean that I have any doubts about the personal abilities, talent and courage of President Roosevelt. But if the circumstances are unfavorable, the most talented captain cannot reach the goal you refer to.[30]

This praise for the man they had been denouncing as the chief instigator of American fascism so startled the Communists that when they reprinted "the only complete text" of the conversation they omitted the entire passage. An editorial, though, referred to Stalin's words, placing a negative and inaccurate interpretation on them: "Stalin does not fear to define the traits of Roosevelt which make him a peculiarly effective agent of the Wall Street capitalists at the present moment, his shrewdness, his ability to maneuvre, his capacity to wield mass influence." Not until New Year's Day, 1935, after Browder's return from Moscow, did *The Daily Worker* admit that "it was incorrectly announced that the full conversation was being published" and print what it had previously left out.[31]

Browder's sojourn in Moscow did not, however, halt the attacks on Roosevelt. Despite Stalin's warm words, the American Communists seemed convinced that he remained a fascist danger. Bill Gebert repeated the charge that he "paves the way for war and fascism." One editorial noted that "the steady trend to fascism inherent in Roosevelt's New Deal finds new confirmation every day." A news exposé linked the President to J. P. Morgan and identified three Cabinet members, including Henry Wallace, as closely associated with fascists.[32]

As the date for the Seventh Congress approached, the attacks on Roosevelt became more frequent. As late as July 5, 1935, the New Deal was being castigated for "advancing fascism." A discussion outline for the congress, prepared by the Agit-Prop Commission, noted of the administration: "This is not fascism yet, but it is *the road* to fascism." F. Brown, the Party's organizational secretary, proclaimed: "The fundamental trend in the United States, it is clear, is the orientation of the American bourgeoisie towards fascism. This is expressed through the Roosevelt administration primarily and by the Longs, Coughlins and other reactionary forces secondly.[33]

During the congress, the American Communists also published a series of pamphlets on the envisioned Soviet America: *Seamen and Longshoremen Under the Red Flag, The Miners' Road to Freedom, The Negroes in Soviet America, The Farmers' Way Out: Life Under a Workers' and Farmers' Government*. At the same time a *Daily Worker* editorial ridiculed reports appearing in *The New York Times* that the Comintern had decided to push the world revolution into the background. The American Communists were in for a very unpleasant surprise when they got to Moscow for the Seventh World Congress.[34]

Georgi Dimitroff made his first major address to the congress on August 2. Very little of it applied specifically to the United States. A fascist victory in America, he noted with understatement, would severely alter the world situation. Preventing it required a broadening of the antifascist movement to include creation of a non-Communist Workers and Farmers party that "would be a specific form of the mass People's Front in America." The Comintern leader gave an oblique criticism of the-CPUSA's policy, arguing that fascism in America appeared in an antifascist guise, trying to cloak itself in the robes of the Constitution and appealing to those disillusioned with the bourgeois parties. He implied that fascism was distinct from the two major parties. Eleven days later, Dimitroff responded to the discussion of his report. He singled out the United States as the prime example of a dangerous misreading of history:

> Even now we still have survivals of a stereotyped approach to the question of fascism. When some comrades assert that Roosevelt's "New Deal" represents an even clearer and more pronounced form of the development of the bourgeoisie toward fascism than the "National Government" in Great Britain, for example, is this not a manifestation of such a stereotyped approach to the question? One must be very partial to hackneyed schemes not to see that the most reaction-

ary circles of American finance capital, which are attacking Roosevelt, are above all the very force which is stimulating and organizing the fascist movement in the United States. Not to see the beginnings of real fascism in the United States behind the hypocritical outpourings of these circles in defense of the democratic rights of the American citizen is tantamount to misleading the working class in the struggle against its worst enemy.[35]

That paragraph was sweet music to Sam Darcy's ears. Added to the American delegation only at the Comintern's insistence, he had complained to both André Marty of France and Dimitri Manuilsky in Moscow about the Upton Sinclair episode. Just before the American delegation met with Dimitroff to hear the sections of his report dealing with their country, Dimitroff asked Darcy if the Party's line was that Roosevelt was leading America toward fascism. Darcy said yes. After summarizing his report, Dimitroff praised Roosevelt's policies and lit into the Party for its sectarian attitude. Everyone sat in stunned silence. Dimitroff asked Darcy if he wanted to say anything. To Darcy this vindication was highly gratifying: "Not only was it wrong to attack Upton Sinclair, the man of the left as a Fascist; it was even wrong to attack Franklin Roosevelt. . . . I shook my head trying not to be too obvious in my delight." Neither Comrade Foster nor Comrade Browder wished to protest. Having made his point, Dimitroff asked if there were any amendments. Hearing none, he softened his language in the published draft.[36]

Browder never acknowledged so unpleasant a confrontation. "The Americans," he wrote, "had no controversial issues with the Congress line." He denied that the American delegation ever met with Dimitroff during the congress and hinted that Dimitroff was not referring to American Communists at all in the critical paragraph but to Russian Communists opposed to the Popular Front. Yet, once Browder returned home, he changed the Communist line on Roosevelt and the New Deal.[37]

At a press conference immediately after returning, Browder suddenly exhibited a change of heart about the respective dangers of Franklin Roosevelt and the Liberty League: "The Roosevelt administration," he said, "has not been an effective fighter for American liberties. . . . But those who are talking most in the newspapers about preserving liberties, the so-called Liberty League, represent forces more reactionary, more antidemocratic, more dangerous to the liberties of the American people than the Roosevelt administration." The new Party line undoubtedly caused confusion. A few days later, the "Questions and Answers" column of *The Daily Worker* asked whether the Party was now supporting Roosevelt as "the lesser evil" and answered emphatically: "No! . . . The development of the New Deal is towards fascism and war." That formulation was somewhat softened a few weeks later. The Roosevelt regime, the same column concluded, "is no barrier to the fascist menace" represented by "the main centers of developing fascism in the United States [which] are the Hearsts, the Coughlins, the Liberty Leaguers, the Chamber of Commerce, the National Association of Manufacturers and other representatives of the most reactionary sections of the capitalist class." Thereafter, the New Deal was attacked because it was no defense against fascism but "on the contrary is clearing the ground" for the fascists or was retreating before the fascist threat.[38]

The Communists took Dimitroff's words in Moscow literally. Now, the only barrier to fascism was seen as a Farmer-Labor party. "The danger of growing fascism in the United States is real," the Central Committee announced. "If the masses are not aroused in time to this danger and if they are not mobilized to meet and check it through a powerful Farmer-Labor Party, 'it can happen here!' ... The continuing reliance of large masses upon Roosevelt as a check against Liberty League reaction and fascism will play into the hands of the reactionaries and fascists." Franklin Roosevelt was not such a fascist threat as were the forces grouped around the Liberty League, but this most emphatically did not mean that he was worth supporting as a lesser evil or that his defeat was not eminently desirable. All the American Communists had done was demote Roosevelt from Public Enemy Number 1 to a secondary role.[39]

The Seventh Congress also marked a watershed in the Comintern's relationships with its constituent parties. For years, American affairs had been openly discussed at plenums and presidiums, Comintern directives openly published, and past Party decisions praised or, more often, castigated. America was not discussed less in the Comintern in 1934 and 1935, but more discreetly. Not only did a more cautious line dictate greater discretion, but the Soviet Union also had cause to be more reticent. As part of the price for obtaining American diplomatic recognition in November 1933, Maxim Litvinov, the Soviet foreign minister, had signed a protocol in which his country agreed "not to permit the formation or residence on its territory of any organization or group ... which has as an aim the overthrow or the preparation for overthrow of, or the bringing about by force of a change in, the political or social order of the whole or any part of the United States, its territories or possessions." The American negotiators were convinced that the clause covered the Comintern. Litvinov, on the other hand, was more coy. In response to a press question he stated: "The Third International is not mentioned in the document. You must not read into it more than was mentioned." And he blandly denied any ties with the American Communists: "The Communist Party of America is not concerned with the Communist Party of Russia and the Communist Party of Russia is not concerned with the Communist Party of America." *The Daily Worker* also rejected any suggestion that the agreement in any way covered the Party's relationship with the Comintern.[40]

The first American ambassador to Russia, William C. Bullitt, had long been sympathetic to the revolution. As a young American diplomat he had headed a fact-finding mission to Russia in 1919 that sought to learn the terms for resuming normal diplomatic relations with Russia. He had impressed Lenin even though his mission failed. Bullitt had been married to John Reed's widow, Louise Bryant. One of his first acts as ambassador was to place a large wreath at Reed's burial place in the Kremlin. His early days in Moscow were filled with cordial meetings and parties at which top Soviet leaders, including Stalin, plied him with promises of cooperation. Very quickly, however, he became disillusioned with the Bolsheviks' unwillingness to keep their promises. One sore spot was the continued Comintern interference in American affairs.[41]

In August 1934, Secretary of State Cordell Hull had Bullitt inform Litvinov of a variety of violations of his pledge, including the Comintern's Thirteenth Plenum in December 1933 and the participation of Americans on the Executive Committees of both the Comintern and the Profintern. The State Department warned, in response to a Russian feeler, that fiery speeches by American Communists at the Seventh Congress would also be viewed seriously. Bullitt even hinted that the upcoming meeting might cause a rupture in diplomatic relations. According to the ambassador, Litvinov, Vorishilov, and V. Molotov were sufficiently worried that they asked Stalin to cancel the congress. The Comintern's sensitivity about jeopardizing American-Soviet relations led Manuilsky to order Gene and Peggy Dennis, preparing to return home after years of work abroad, to leave their five-year-old Russian-speaking son in Russia since his "speaking only Russian during the five days of the ocean voyage, at passport control and in the first months of our return was a liability" that could not be risked.[42]

Although Americans spoke and participated at the congress and the United States was discussed by Dimitroff and Pieck, the subject of communism in America was downplayed. Bullitt reported to Washington that while the United States was "juridically and morally justified" in breaking relations, it should not. The only mitigating factor he saw was that attacks on the United States were less severe than on other countries. A written protest from the State Department was rejected by the Soviet government, but the ensuing Young Communist International Congress received minimal publicity in the Soviet press, and reported references to the United States were scant.[43]

Meanwhile, the practice of sending Comintern representatives to oversee the activities of Communist parties came to an end. In a revealing statement, the official Soviet account proudly states: "The day-to-day management of the parties passed directly into the hands of the parties themselves." The last of the mysterious and powerful plenipotentiaries of the world revolution in the United States was probably Gerhart Eisler, a German who arrived in the summer of 1933. Comintern work had always been an outlet for Communists in disfavor in their own parties, and Eisler, out of sympathy with his German comrades, was dispatched to America. In Moscow he had served on the Anglo-American Secretariat, where he "did a very large part of the writing" of the Open Letter of 1933. Once here, he adopted the pseudonym "E. Edwards," spoke at Party meetings, supervised *The Daily Worker*, and dealt with such dissidents as Joe Zack. He quietly left the country in 1936 for Europe, not to be replaced.[44]

In public the Communist party downplayed its ties to the Comintern. Testifying before the McNaboe Committee, a New York state investigating body, in 1938, Browder bravely insisted that if the Comintern were bold enough to send any orders to him, he would throw them in the wastebasket. The following year, William Foster told the Dies Committee that the Communist party's relationship to the Comintern was actually quite informal and no one paid attention to the international body's statutes. The Comintern had not, however, suddenly cut its sections loose to fend for themselves. American representatives were still stationed in Moscow. Party leaders made frequent treks back and forth across the Atlantic Ocean and Europe to seek advice, direction, and the resolution of differences.[45]

Still another way for Communist parties to be sure that they were not straying from orthodoxy was to observe carefully what other Communist parties were doing. The Americans paid particular attention to the French Communists. Browder told a Party plenum in 1937 that the "Farmer-Labor Party [was] conceived as the American equivalent of the People's Front in France." After the Americans abolished trade union fractions, Jack Stachel told his Politburo colleagues that "we got a big lead from the French Party." When Foster grew unhappy with his Party's People's Front policies, he appealed to the French example for a model of how Communists should act.[46]

The Comintern was not an unmitigated blessing for Soviet foreign policy. While the advantages of having tame political parties and fronts throughout the world were obvious, this could also prove embarrassing or awkward. Communist parties were rarely powerful enough to influence foreign policy, but after 1935, Soviet leaders desperately wanted friendship from bourgeois nations. Toning down Comintern activities had the virtue of making overtures to foreign governments easier and also reduced the difficulties of approaching potential partners in a Popular Front who might have qualms about cooperating with a group too obviously taking directions from abroad.

Prior to 1935 one could count on Comintern plenums to discuss openly what the various sections, including the American one, needed to do. The Party press was not bashful about printing Comintern directives. Henceforth, the Comintern's hand in American affairs was less noticeable and less heavy. Major decisions were no longer announced quite so baldly in the pages of *The Communist International* or *Inprecor*. Plenums at which Comintern leaders delivered stinging rebukes for errant activities were passé. Decisions were now communicated with more circumspection. Party leaders thrashed out policies in private discussions and consultations with Comintern leaders. The first major test of the new method came in 1936. The Communist party had to decide what to do in the Presidential election. As usual, the answer was far too important to be determined in America.

11

Turnabout on FDR

THE most difficult demand of the Popular Front era was the requirement of an alliance with the distinctly nonrevolutionary Democratic party. For four years Earl Browder and company had reserved some of their choicest invective for the New Deal and Franklin Roosevelt. The Party had been admonished by George Dimitroff at the Seventh Congress for persisting overlong in its animus. Even that rebuke, however, had signaled only a slight shift in Party policy from attacking Roosevelt as a crypto-fascist to denouncing him as an ineffectual barrier to fascism. The Party began the election year of 1936 a vocal and adamant opponent of the President. By the November election, things had changed. The Communists found themselves in the same political bed with such unlikely groups as Old Guard Socialists in devoutly wishing to see Franklin Roosevelt reelected. Long scorned as the ultra-leftists of American politics, the Communists were now far more moderate than their one-time *bête noir*, the arch "social-fascist" Norman Thomas. The transformation was not easily effected. In many ways this about-face was far harder for Communists to swallow than any others they had made in the past.

Following the Seventh Congress in 1935, the Communists had looked forward to creating a new Farmer-Labor party that would unite various radical forces for an all-out struggle against Franklin Roosevelt. Reporting to a Party plenum in November, one year before the election,

Browder insisted that "we cannot fight against reaction by supporting Roosevelt," adding that "the masses" had to build their own party. It could not be just another Party auxiliary. Approving the creation of a Farmer-Labor party at the Comintern congress, Dimitroff admitted that it "will be *neither* Socialist *nor* Communist. But it *will have to be* an antifascist party and *not* an anti-Communist party." That was easier said than done. There were pitfalls and problems with nearly every potential Party ally, ranging from the labor movement's newly formed Non-Partisan League, closely tied to such leaders of industrial unions as John L. Lewis and Sidney Hillman, to the Minnesota Farmer-Labor party under the guidance of Governor Floyd Olson; from the Wisconsin Progressives to the California EPIC; from New York's emerging American Labor party to the Washington Commonwealth Federation and the American Commonwealth Federation formed by Charles Beard, John Dewey, and Alfred Bingham.[1]

Neither Browder nor the Party seemed overly concerned that a fullfledged new party might throw the election to the Republicans. On New Year's Day a *Daily Worker* editorial insouciantly brushed off the consequences of Roosevelt's defeat: "A big vote for a Farmer-Labor Party in 1936, even if Roosevelt is defeated, will go a long way toward putting a crimp in the union-busting, liberty-strangling drive of the Wall Street corporations." Late in January, Browder made a Boston speech calling for a Farmer-Labor party in 1936 even at the risk of Roosevelt's defeat. A few days later he did write that only a Farmer-Labor party could stop the country's drift to the right and rally the voters to the left, preventing a Republican party victory. The next day, however, a *Daily Worker* editorial called for a fight against both the trusts and the New Deal. And the following month, making his first speech on a nationwide radio hookup on CBS, Browder himself intimated that Roosevelt was not much different from any Republican: "The New Deal, which aroused such hopes among the people, is in ruins and bankrupted. . . . Tweedledum and Tweedledee are still twins, even when one wears the cold mask of Hoover and the other the professional smile of Roosevelt."[2]

Unfortunately for the Communists, their putative allies had little interest in their scheme. After the Seventh Congress, Governor Floyd Olson of Minnesota, long denounced as a social-fascist, invited Browder to visit him while the Party leader was in Minneapolis. They agreed to consult in the future, but Olson soon made known his support for FDR. In New York, right-wing Socialists and the garment unions were cooperating with reformers like Fiorello LaGuardia to create the American Labor party as a vehicle to back the President.[3]

A Farmer-Labor party, William Foster had noted, "should be based on the trade unions." But John L. Lewis and Sidney Hillman would not countenance any third party that would jeopardize the reelection of the man who had done so much for labor. The Communists were incredulous. "When Roosevelt spit in your faces," Browder complained, "you looked up at the sky and complained that the weather was getting bad." When Labor's Non-Partisan League was formed, a Communist editorial attacked it for sidetracking the Farmer-Labor movement: "To support Roosevelt is, as has been proved time and again by the bitter experiences of the past three years, to strike a blow at the economic struggles of the workers. It is to hogtie them in the battle for higher wages, against company unionism, for the right to organize, for industrial unionism and the other burning needs of the working men and women of this country." By the beginning of 1936 it was very obvious that little labor support would be forthcoming for a Farmer-Labor party. John L. Lewis, the Communists glumly admitted, was supporting Roosevelt "100 percent in the next election." Browder had to confess that it was a serious blow for the Farmer-Labor party: "This decision does not mean that there will be no Farmer-Labor Party this year on a national scale; it only means that John L. Lewis and his closest associates by their decision made the road more difficult and took away some of the immediate potential power of the movement."[4]

Other, less traditional movements were also preparing for the election. Dr. Francis Townsend's plan to pay $200 a month to every American over age sixty had swept the nation by 1936. The weekly newspaper of the Townsend enthusiasts had a circulation of over 300,000, more than three and a half million people belonged to Townsend Clubs, and an unbelievable twenty million people, 20 percent of the nation's adult population, had signed petitions asking Congress to enact the Townsend Plan. Before his assassination in September 1935, Huey Long of Louisiana had been preparing to create a third party based on his own "Share the Wealth" program. One hundred fifty thousand people subscribed to Long's newspaper *The American Progress*. Long's speechwriter and assistant, the Reverend Gerald L. K. Smith, when forced out of the Louisiana political machine after Long's assassination, soon attached himself to Dr. Townsend. Father Charles Coughlin, a Roman Catholic priest at the Shrine of the Little Flower in Royal Oak, Michigan, had set up the National Union for Social Justice in 1934; by 1936 he was denouncing President Roosevelt to his radio audience, which, estimated at thirty million per week, was the largest in the world. He had a greater volume of correspondence than any other American. By 1936 these three unorthodox politicians had joined in an uneasy coalition as the Union party to support the Presidential candidacy of Congressman William Lemke, a North Dakota progressive embittered by Roosevelt's farm policies.[5]

The Communists had no use for either Father Coughlin or the Long movement, considering them the "main centers of developing fascism" along with the Liberty League and William Randolph Hearst, and at various times suggested that Long or Coughlin was a candidate for the job of an American Hitler. The Party also opposed William Lemke's farm reform bills, which were supported by the Farm Holiday movement. Dr. Townsend, on the other hand, was deemed a suitable catch for the new Farmer-Labor party. Alexander Bittelman wrote a sympathetic pamphlet assuring the Townsendites that the Party was "heart and soul" with their demands, disagreeing only with the plan for financing pensions by a sales tax. When Townsend held a friendly interview with Clarence Hathaway in January 1936, the doctor expressed his willingness to cooperate with labor and radical groups to launch a third party. Once Townsend joined with Coughlin's Unionists, however, Alexander Bittelman gave the definitive Communist assessment of the whole crew, denouncing Coughlin as a "fascist," Lemke as a "stooge" for Alf Landon, and Townsend as "hypnotized and bamboozled by Storm Trooper [Gerald] Smith."[6]

The Farmer-Labor party was a failure, not from want of trying but from the attraction of FDR. For the Communists to persist in their attacks was to risk isolating themselves from virtually all prospective Popular Front allies. By the same token, the Comintern took an interest in the Party's decision. If Franklin Roosevelt was not a bona fide Popular Fronter like French Premier Leon Blum, at least he was more friendly to Russia than the Republican party was likely to be.

The initiative, as usual, came from Moscow. Early in 1936, talking to a young New Dealer, Browder was advised to go slow on a Farmer-Labor party because the Communists would find themselves aligned with Roosevelt before the election campaign was over. The Party leader assumed that the information had originated with Soviet Foreign Minister Maxim Litvinov. Meanwhile, Sam Darcy, who had remained in Moscow after the Seventh Congress as the Party's representative to the Comintern and head of its Anglo-American Secretariat, was expressing his fears that a Farmer-Labor party, by splintering the left, would cost Roosevelt the election. Supported by Manuilsky, he spoke to Dimitroff, who concluded that Foster and Browder had to be consulted. While awaiting their arrival, Manuilsky told Darcy that Stalin agreed with him—the Party should support Roosevelt.[7]

Browder and Foster left for Moscow in mid-March 1936. They arrived shortly after the signing of the Franco-Soviet Pact and Germany's audacious coup in reoccupying the Rhineland. Foster picked up a hint of the prevailing winds and supported Darcy in front of Dimitroff. Browder remained reluctant to endorse Roosevelt, feeling that Communist support might give Roosevelt one million votes and cost him five million. The Comintern leadership digested this information for two weeks and then gave Browder the authority to decide how best to aid Roosevelt's reelection. In a private conversation Dimitroff told Browder that he alone could handle such a delicate and convoluted strategy: to run for President while trying to avoid harming the interests of another candidate.[8]

When they returned to America the Party leaders continued to attack Roosevelt. "Profits—His Creed," one editorial proclaimed, while another charged "Union Leader Supporters Silent as Roosevelt Yields to Tories." But Clarence Hathaway dropped a hint that the Party was about to abandon its insistence on a Farmer-Labor opposition to FDR in 1936. He distinguished between a Farmer-Labor party and a Presidential ticket in 1936. The Communists, he indicated, still hoped for the latter but were willing to support building a new party for future elections if they could not achieve it.[9]

The Politburo met on May 9 and 10, augmented by district organizers and leading Party functionaries from around the country. They received the news from Moscow. It was now impossible, Browder told them, to organize a broadly based Farmer-Labor ticket for 1936. Local and state parties might be built, but the most vital issue for the Presidential election was that "the designs of the Republican–Liberty League–Hearst combination must be defeated." The new line was publicly revealed by Browder in Madison Square Garden on May 20, 1936. Roosevelt did not come in for much praise: he occupied, said Browder, "a center position between the demands of the masses and the pressure of those reactionary forces" in the Democratic party. A new and greater danger, however, existed. "The main enemy of the people of America today is the Republican–Liberty League–Hearst combination. We must place as the center of our work in the election campaign the need for combatting this reactionary bloc and defeating its plans in 1936."[10]

The Communists soon had an opportunity to demonstrate their new realism about a Farmer-Labor party. The Minnesota Farmer-Labor movement issued invitations to some eighty-five individuals to meet in Chicago at the end of May to discuss a national Farmer-Labor party. Governor Olson insisted on inviting Browder. The invitation to the Communists was significant. For the first time since the LaFollette debacle in

1923, they had been accepted back into the polite company of reform politics. Olson's gesture cost the conference some of its prominent participants. The Wisconsin Progressives and such allies in the American Commonwealth Federation as Alfred Bingham and Paul Douglass bowed out rather than meet with Communists. Browder, however, was a voice of moderation at the meeting. While he warned that "it is impossible for us to believe that Roosevelt will halt this trend toward reaction and fascism in America" and advocated an "all-inclusive National Farmer-Labor Convention" to establish a new party, he stated that such action would be exclusive of a Presidential ticket. Nor did Browder protest loudly when the meeting accepted a resolution effectively ending the dream of a Farmer-Labor party in 1936.[11]

At the Party's Ninth Convention, held from June 24 through June 28 in New York, Browder and Ford were nominated to carry the Communist banner in the election. The 750 delegates were youthful, largely native-born workers, and the Party took the opportunity to emphasize its new image:

> Across the galleries, flaming red streamers with white letters carried slogans of faith in victory; The unity of labor can crush fascism and prevent war! For a free, happy and prosperous America! Keep America out of war by keeping war out of the world! High in the rear of the auditorium an immense canvas showed the spirit of '76—drummer, fifer, standard bearer—carrying red and American flags intertwined. Out of these emerged the faces of Washington, Jefferson, John Brown, Lincoln, Frederick Douglass; beneath them the slogan: Communism is twentieth-century Americanism.

Robert Minor, making the nominating speech, rhapsodically called the Party leader "an average American," a "new John Brown of Ossawatomie."[12]

In his report to the convention Browder criticized Roosevelt for retreating before reaction and declared that it was an error to depend on him to aid the masses. But Browder also noted: "The Communist Party declares without qualification that the Landon–Hearst–Wall Street ticket is the chief enemy of the liberties, peace and prosperity of the American people. Its victory would carry our country a long way on the road to fascism and war." On that note of optimism the Communists set out to help elect Roosevelt while opposing him. They sought to have their cake—seeming opposition to him—and eat it too—real opposition to Landon, with a consequent united front with pro-Roosevelt forces in the CIO and the Farmer-Labor movement.[13]

To the untutored observer, the Communists' behavior in the 1936 campaign must have bordered on absurdity. In retrospect, knowing how extensive Roosevelt's landslide would be, the elaborate Communist acrobatics appear to be exercises in futility. The fears that a Farmer-Labor party or the Union party or the ultra-left Socialist campaign or even the Communist ticket could draw off enough votes to elect Alf Landon now seem far-fetched. At the time they did not. The Communists were not alone in believing that the Republicans might unseat Roosevelt. This concern was not, however, the only reason for the Party's decision to run its own candidates and seek to defeat the Republicans. The Communist campaign had to preserve its embryonic links to the Farmer-Labor movement, which itself strongly supported Roosevelt. However, it had to avoid tagging Roosevelt as the Communists' candidate, a label that the Party was realistic enough to realize could be exceedingly costly. And the Party could not afford to neglect totally its own ideology and viewpoint.

The first attempt to reconcile these themes was not entirely coherent. A draft resolution on Browder's report to the Ninth Convention noted that the Party was not "indifferent" as to "what kind of government will come into power as a result of the 1936 elections." It was supportive of the unification and "concentration of all forces" of the working class and its allies to defeat the Republican–Liberty League–Hearst combination. But the Party would not depend on Roosevelt because he "has proven to be no barrier to reaction and fascism," and it sharply criticized Labor's Non-Partisan League for its faith in the President. The Party's aims in the election were to crush the reactionaries and prevent "Roosevelt from obstructing the crystallization of a Farmer-Labor Party." By mobilizing the masses for independent political action, the Communists would create "the conditions for [a] higher form of struggle—for the socialist revolution, Soviet power and socialism." By supporting Communist candidates, voters were employing "the best and only way of endorsing and supporting the struggle for the unity of the working class and all toilers against the offensive of capitalist reaction, against the menace of fascism and war, against capitalism and for a Soviet Government and Socialism."[14]

This farrago defied understanding. The Party was for the defeat of Landon but not for the election of Roosevelt. It wanted to use Roosevelt to defeat Landon but to prevent Roosevelt from defeating a Farmer-Labor movement. And, on top of all this, it asked voters to support the Communist ticket in order to endorse a Soviet government and socialism while criticizing Norman Thomas for making the election issue socialism versus capitalism.

As the campaign got into stride, the schizophrenic Communist position became less jarring. More and more the need to prevent a Landon victory took precedence over every other theme. In a press conference before the Party convention began, Browder noted: "The Democratic administration with all its evils will not be so bad as the Republican would be." Accepting his Party's nomination, Browder told a nationwide NBC radio audience that a Republican victory "would be a major misfortune for the American people. We call for their defeat at all costs." Lest anyone jump to the unwarranted conclusion that "at all costs" might mean even at the cost of supporting Roosevelt, Browder added that "we do not support Roosevelt, although we direct the main fire against Landon." In the months ahead, Landon, generally considered a progressive Republican, was accorded the sort of abuse once reserved largely for social-fascists. He was, Browder insisted, only a front, a "figurehead" for the "fascist-minded men of Wall Street." Landon was reviled as a tool of the Hearst–Liberty League–Coughlin forces, cunningly masked by his "bosses" to hide their project for a fascist America. By late summer Browder had less and less to say about Roosevelt's failings and directed his fire more and more at Landon. Opening his campaign at the Denver Municipal Auditorium, he came out for a "critical attitude towards Roosevelt" but told his audience: "We are in full agreement with the progressive unions and the bulk of the Farmer-Labor movement that Landon and Knox are the chief enemy which must be defeated at all costs."[15]

In answer to a question at the National Press Club, Browder gave another rationale for the Party's stand, suggesting that the separate Communist campaign was designed to save Roosevelt from himself, to see to it that he would not give away the election to Landon.

... We have no illusions that a minor candidate will be elected, but we have seen too much in the past of what happens when there is unanimous support from the Left to Roosevelt. What happens then is that Roosevelt begins to try to win over some of the Liberty League following, to blur the issues between reaction and progress, and thereby makes it easier for Landon to be elected. ...

The Communist ticket was not in the field to defeat Roosevelt but to pressure him: "The more support he gets from the left," Browder explained, "the more he goes to the right." The argument was that Roosevelt did not believe in anything. A middle-of-the-roader in the Democratic party, he vacillated between the reactionaries like John Nance Garner, who were virtually indistinguishable from the Republicans, and the progressives. Unless left-wing pressure forced him to resist the reactionary pleas, Roosevelt would capitulate to them. If he surrendered, he would lose the election. To win, he had to move to the left. By forcing him to do so, the Communists, according to their own analysis, were forcing him to win.[16]

The Communists' carefully qualified support for Franklin Roosevelt did not convince very many people. Conservatives and other anti–New Dealers felt there was no doubt about the affinity of Communists and Roosevelt. To its arch-enemies, the New Deal was Communist-inspired no matter what the Communist party said or did. Speaking to a Liberty League banquet in January 1936, Al Smith, no longer the Happy Warrior, denounced his one-time friend and political ally for betraying American principles: "There can be only one capital, Washington or Moscow," he warned. "There can be only one atmosphere of government, the clean, pure fresh air of free America, or the foul breath of communistic Russia." Father Charles Coughlin found the President to be a watered-down version of a hated philosophy: "Roosevelt," he charged, "stands for a poor brand of Russian Communism." And newspaper magnate William Randolph Hearst lambasted the "imported, autocratic, Asiatic Socialist party of Karl Marx and Franklin Delano Roosevelt."[17]

Nothing short of abandoning the New Deal could have endeared Roosevelt to this group. But charges that the Communist party was actually fronting for Roosevelt also cropped up from other sources during the campaign. *The Chicago Tribune* published a Donald Day dispatch from Riga, Latvia, reporting that Moscow had ordered the American Communists to back FDR. Columnist Dorothy Thompson picked up and publicized the charge. Browder waxed indignant, denying the charge but hinting that the Americans had not made their decision in private: "We are an American party," he explained, "making our own decisions and have received no 'instructions from Moscow' à la Hearst; at the same time we are an international party which fully informs the progressive forces of the whole world of what we are doing."[18]

Perhaps the most annoying charge of collusion with the Democrats came from the Socialist party. Norman Thomas was once again running for President. For years the Communists had been urging the Socialists to shuck off their social-democratic Old Guard, swing to the left, and embrace the cause of revolution. Now the Socialists had. The Old Guard had broken away in 1936 to support Franklin Roosevelt. Norman Thomas campaigned on a slogan of "socialism versus capitalism" and insisted that no capitalist politician would make any difference if elected. A Landon victory, he maintained, would not leave the working class any worse off than Roosevelt's reelection. While the Socialists had swung sharply to the left, the Communists had passed them heading to the right.[19]

For a brief while the Communists had hoped that they could persuade the Socialists to agree to a joint Presidential ticket. In June, for instance, Alexander Bittelman suggested that with the end of hopes for a Farmer-Labor ticket, the Party "begin to orientate for the eventuality of a joint Socialist and Communist presidential ticket in 1936." The Socialists rejected a Communist offer of cooperation out of hand. They did not intend to compromise with bourgeois politicians or give covert support to the Democratic party. The Communists looked positively tame by comparison, campaigning on a slogan of "Democracy or Fascism." One Socialist leader gleefully pointed out that the Old Guard, the most fervent opponents of any cooperation with the Communists, had "followed a line akin to the Communists" and both were united in seeking a Roosevelt victory. Norman Thomas charged that the Comintern had ordered the CPUSA to give Roosevelt "indirect support." Browder reacted quickly and angrily. "If correctly quoted," he charged, Thomas's speech "sounds as if it were borrowed from the Hearst editorial pages." He also promptly whipped off a telegram of protest. Technically, Browder was absolutely correct. The Comintern had not ordered the Americans to give "indirect support" to Roosevelt. It had wanted direct support but had left the decision up to Browder, who had worked out the actual policy.[20]

Within the Communist party itself, the new line was quite clear. Not everyone was happy. Party organizers like George Charney, faced with hard and specific questions about how Communists and sympathizers should vote, "found if difficult to counsel a vote for Browder." Charney remembered: "There were many in our party who disapproved. We were straying from the class struggle and the fight for socialism and sowing new illusions among the people." The Party's subterfuge did not persuade James Casey, managing editor of *The Daily Worker*. He had left *The New York Times* in 1934 to spruce up the Communist newspaper. In late August 1936 he resigned, denouncing the Party's election campaign as "hypocritical." It was designed, he charged, "to swing the support of its membership to President Roosevelt."[21]

That the Communist message was received and understood is apparent from the election returns. The Party's Presidential vote actually declined from its 1932 total, but local candidates ran far ahead of the Browder-Ford ticket. The total vote for Browder—79, 211, or 0.17 percent of the nationwide votes—was a sharp decline from Foster's 102,221, or 0.26 percent. In New York City, where Browder got 32,000 votes, Communist candidates for assembly seats amassed 61,000. Two congressional candidates were elected by the entire state in 1936. The Party's candidates, Roy Hudson and Simon Gerson, each polled around 69,000 votes, compared to Browder's 35,000 statewide. The Party leader happily noted that "even by the narrowest standard of measurement, the vote for the Communist ticket, which circumstances this year removed from all direct relation to the scope of our influence, shows considerable growth except on the Presidential ticket, which will probably show a slight decline.[22]

The Socialists meanwhile suffered a crushing blow. Thomas received twice as many votes as Browder, but his 187,000, or 0.41 percent, was a devastating decline from the 884,000, or 2.22 percent, of 1932. Moreover, for the first time, local Communist candidates in New York outpolled their Socialist opponents, dropping the latter into fifth place behind not only the Republicans and Democrats but the American Labor party and the Communists as well. The Socialists' revolutionary posturing cost them dearly within their traditional union strongholds, whose leaders abandoned, in some cases for good, the Socialist party for Franklin Roosevelt. Another Communist goal, to strengthen the Farmer-Labor movement, was "achieved in varying degree in the various parts of the country, with some advance almost everywhere." The American Labor party in New York, the Progressive Federation in Wisconsin, the Farmer-Labor party in Minnesota, and the Commonwealth Federation in Washington all achieved breakthroughs.[23]

More than anything else, the Communists emerged from the election with a new image, in large part because of Earl Browder. Even though his vote total was far from impressive, Browder made his mark as a leader in this campaign. For the first time a Communist candidate spoke before such august bodies as *The New York Herald Tribune*'s Annual Forum, the National Press Club, and the Institute of Public Affairs at the University of Virginia. No Communist had ever received such respectful attention from the press, with numerous news stories, feature articles, cartoons, pictures, editorials, and listings in straw polls. All in all, a Party writer noted, Communists were "getting into the newspapers to a greater and less biased extent than in any previous election campaign." Audiences around the country were large and enthusiastic. When Browder was arrested for vagrancy upon arriving in Terre Haute, Indiana, to speak, the nation's press jumped to his defense with an unprecedented outpouring of concern for the Communist party's right to campaign without hindrance.[24]

The Communists had every reason to be satisfied. They had executed a very difficult and complex maneuver—to make sure that Landon was defeated without openly supporting Roosevelt, and to differ with the CIO and its Farmer-Labor allies without getting estranged from them. Most of the credit went to Browder. This campaign was his graduation card as a Communist leader. He had demonstrated to the Comintern that he was capable as well as reliable. The campaign made him a nationwide figure whose every word was picked up by the press, who was invited to speak by the best people and institutions, and who was the mass leader the Party had been looking for. For years Browder had been regarded as one of the least colorful of the Communist leaders. In 1936 his sober, quiet, somewhat ponderous style suddenly fit the Party's needs. He looked and sounded respectable, no small feat for a Party that now wanted to be respectable. His talents had become apparent. For the next nine years, to the American public, he was American Communism.

Once the 1936 election returns were tabulated, the American Communists had a difficult decision to make. It was one thing to prefer the lesser evil in an election and quite another to support the administration that took shape and form afterward. The New Deal had been nearly four years old before the Communists could grudgingly admit that Franklin Roosevelt might indeed be a barrier to fascism. Even during the campaign, the most the Party could say for the President was that he was not as bad as Alf Landon. Someone who had to depend on the Communist press for all his information might have supposed, in fact, that Landon was running against a phantom, so exclusively did the Party focus on the danger of his election. In a post-election summary, Earl Browder sounded as if no one had voted *for* Roosevelt: "The balloting on November 3 could be called 'the great repudiation.' The large majority of people were first of all voting against Hearst, against the Liberty League, against Wall Street, against Landon, against reaction, fascism and jingoism." Much as they would have preferred to ignore him, however, the Communists had to come to terms with Franklin Roosevelt.[25]

They finally did so, but not without a great deal of anguish. What made the task particularly difficult was that by and large the Party had to jettison its goals and tactics to enlist in the New Deal coalition; Franklin Roosevelt did very little to attract the Communists. Contrary to the fears and alarms of his critics, who believed he had sold out to Communism, Roosevelt gave the Party little incentive to support him. He made no radical domestic gestures. Although Party leaders often cited his attempt to pack the Supreme Court as a welcome sign of his commitment to breaking the grip of conservatism in American politics, it was a lost cause practically from the beginning and hardly revolutionary. In foreign policy, Roosevelt's behavior was neither bold nor entirely to the Party's liking.

One of the more enduring myths used to explain the Communists' about-face on Roosevelt is the undeniable difference between what is called the first and second New Deals. The first three years of the Democratic administration, from the inspiring hundred days to the Supreme

Court's dismantling of the National Recovery Administration and the Agricultural Adjustment Administration, saw the ascendancy of the planners whose solution to America's economic woes was a large-scale regulation of business by government. Beginning in 1935 with such legislation as the Wagner Act and Social Security, the New Deal put in place a welfare state. While it is true that Roosevelt's new policies made it easier for the Communists to snuggle up to the New Deal, these policies were certainly not the decisive factors impelling them to do so. The Party was openly scornful of the Wagner Act when it was first passed and dismissed Social Security as a cruel hoax. No doubt these measures made the Party's attacks on Roosevelt harder to sustain, but the Communists had no trouble vilifying A. J. Muste and Norman Thomas as their worst enemies for years. When the Communist party changed its mind, it did so not because Franklin Roosevelt had changed his policies but because the Comintern had changed its ideas.

To cloak their surrender to the New Deal, the Communists had to dress up in the garments made by the Comintern. Ever since the Seventh Congress, its constituent parties had dutifully pursued a Popular Front with socialists, laborites, and bourgeois groups in the interest of stopping fascism. In Europe, an alliance between socialists and Communists created a significant political bloc. The United States was different. It had no sizable Socialist party. There was no national Farmer-Labor party. The Communists still remained a tiny minority of the working class. The American Popular Front, therefore, had to take a different form than in Europe if it was to be at all successful. Once before the American Communists had tried to fit their experiences into Comintern theory by proclaiming that American exceptionalism required adaptation of tactics different from those used in Europe. The Party had been rebuffed by Stalin in terms so strong that no Communist leader was likely to risk so perilous a journey without strong Comintern support. Between 1937 and 1939 the American Communists, with Comintern endorsement, traveled a long way down the path of "revisionism."

The Communist party's political line after the election, in late 1936, was a mass of contradictions. Still committed to the idea of a Farmer-Labor movement as the American form of the Popular Front, it could not get around the stubborn cleaving of its potential allies to Franklin Roosevelt. The Party's initial reaction, a natural response to past conditioning, was to distance itself from the administration. Reporting to a Party plenum in December 1936, Browder charged that without mass pressure against Roosevelt, the Popular Front would not get built. In fact, Browder stated: "The Democratic Party leaders and Roosevelt want nothing of the kind [a Popular Front]. They want everyone to be quiet and wait for whatever the new Congress will bring them. The Democratic Party wants to restore good relations with its extreme Right wing and with the reactionaries generally and still continue to absorb all Farmer-Labor sentiment and prevent its crystallization."[26]

At the very least the American Popular Front would have to challenge the Roosevelt administration; it might have to oppose it. At this time Browder saw a "growing split of the Democratic Party" and anticipated one portion of it joining the Farmer-Labor movement to create a powerful Popular Front organization:

We must find the way to unite the movements already outside of and independent of the Democratic Party and Progressive Republicans together with those that are still maturing within the old parties, and not yet ready for full independence. This means that we must conceive of the People's Front on a broader scale than merely the existing Farmer-Labor Party organizations.

When the fissure came, the Communists would be able to build a third party. "We want to hasten the formation of a national Farmer-Labor Party as much as possible," Browder explained, because "only the organization and struggle of the masses, independent of capitalist parties and politicians, will realize their demands and expectations, through Congress and outside of Congress, and prepare the way for greater concessions later on." To midwife such a birth would not be easy. The Party would have "many difficult, complicated and dangerous problems to solve."[27]

Roosevelt's behavior after the 1936 election was not calculated to drive the Communist party into his arms. He embargoed arms shipments to Spain, cut Works Progress Administration jobs for the unemployed, and otherwise angered the Party. The embargo was greeted by an editorial entitled "A Blow to World Peace and Democracy." One story attacked "Roosevelt's Crass WPA Double-Cross," and the Party-influenced Workers' Alliance announced nationwide demonstrations to protest the cuts. Editorials blistered the "New Deal budget" as a "challenge to the American people" and denied that farmers could look to Secretary of Agriculture Henry Wallace to represent their interests. Alexander Bittelman took comfort that "uncritical belief in Roosevelt among wider masses is rapidly disappearing."[28]

Communist carping to the contrary, the labor and progressive movements refused to desert Roosevelt. Caught between its theory and reality, the Party wavered. Bittelman spoke up for orthodoxy. Announcing the Communists' full support for President Roosevelt's scheme to pack the

Supreme Court, he insisted, nonetheless, that in order to defeat reaction an "effective independent political organization" had to be built outside the two-party system. At virtually the same time, Clarence Hathaway drew a different lesson from the same event: "We can see now that the People's Front will not immediately and in a pure form express itself as a Farmer-Labor Party. It will develop in the form of every kind of progressive and opposition movement inside and around the Democratic Party." For the first time there was a hint that, absent an imminent split in the Democratic party, the Communists would cooperate with its progressives.[29]

Earl Browder and William Foster visited Moscow in April 1937 to discuss the Party's problem. When they returned, Browder carried with him a seemingly minor but significant change of emphasis in the Party line. Instead of seeking to draw left-wing Democrats out of their Party, the Communists had decided to invite themselves into the Democratic party. The decision was unveiled at a Central Committee meeting held from June 17 to June 20, 1937. Browder confessed to an odd disparity. Sentiment for a People's Front was growing. The Communists were becoming an acceptable ally in all kinds of movements where they had heretofore been shunned, ranging from the labor movement to insurgent state Farmer-Labor parties. Yet, a national Farmer-Labor party remained as unobtainable a goal as ever despite all the Communists' beseeching. None of their allies would file for divorce from Roosevelt. The labor movement, Browder noted, simply would not abandon the President. Progressive groups in a number of states shared the CIO's reluctance. Browder admitted that these groups were getting too much from the New Deal to cut themselves adrift and gamble on an untried third party. He warned that Communists would be unable to convince workers that there was no difference between "a liberal government with labor sympathies and participation" and "an openly reactionary one."[30]

At the December 1936 plenum, Browder had looked forward to a third party emerging from a split within the old parties. He now saw another possibility. The two-party system itself, it seemed, could accommodate the Farmer-Labor movement. It would not grow outside the two main parties but "within the womb of the disintegrating two old parties. It will be born as a national party at the moment when it already replaces in the main one of the old traditional parties, contesting and possibly winning control of the federal government from the hour of its birth." Not even the party's name was crucial: what was important was that the material basis of the old system had disintegrated. In place of the old parties "there emerge the clear outlines of two new parties, carrying over much debris of the old, but representing something new—a political alignment dominated, not by regional differences among the bourgeoisie, but by class stratification among the masses of the population. There is no longer any fixed party structure in our land. Everything is in flux. Everything is changing."[31]

If a new class-based two party system was in formation, an independent third party was no longer needed. Instead of being a coalition of insurgent forces, the People's Front in America would be a combination of those forces with the left wings of both the Republican and, more often, the Democratic parties. Rather than expend energy in difficult struggles to overcome legal and political obstacles to a third party, the Communists had new tasks. In those states where the Farmer-Labor movement was weak and the CIO was the dominant progressive force, the Party was to accept the program of Labor's Non-Partisan League. The objective was to encourage "systematic and organized activity within the Democratic Party (in some places, the Republican Party), making the fullest possible use of the democratic possibilities of the primary election machinery to name decisively anti-fascist and progressive candidates, and formulating a clear program of progressive social and labor legislation." Wherever an acceptable candidate appeared on a Democratic or Republican ticket, the Communist party would support that candidate. Only when and where working through the other parties to nominate acceptable candidates failed would the Communists run their own candidates.[32]

The Central Committee promptly adopted a resolution proclaiming the new wisdom:

> Experience has shown that the People's Front cannot now be limited to the Farmer-Labor Party which is not yet acceptable to the most important forces essential to its success . . . .These forces, which still express themselves politically largely within and around the Democratic Party, are clearly ripe for inclusion in a broad People's Front movement that does not call upon them to split organizationally and to form now a new party.

After two years of heaving and straining for a Farmer-Labor party, the Communists had surrendered it in fact if not yet in theory. They did not choose their course; they were forced into it by the strength of Franklin Roosevelt's mass following. Continuing opposition to Roosevelt might well have endangered the Party's new positions in the CIO and state Farmer-Labor movements. By jumping on the Roosevelt bandwagon, the Communists removed the last element of strain with those groups. He did not capitulate to the Communists; they capitulated to him.[33]

The surrender, however, was not yet complete. The Farmer-Labor idea remained in place although ignored. An important segment of Party leadership clung to the hope that the concept could one day soon be given due homage. At the same plenum which for "now" resolved to work through the Democratic party, William Foster petulantly warned his colleagues not to place too much faith in that party: "We must be especially on guard against tendencies to weaken or discard the Farmer-Labor Party slogan." Alexander Bittelman warned that the Roosevelt administration was hardly "the genuine class representative of labor" and that the Communists' relationship with the Democrats was only an "alliance and coalition for specific purposes and specific aims." Even Browder, the most enthusiastic advocate of the "broadening out" of the Farmer-Labor idea to encompass part of the Democratic party, was cautious about placing his faith in Roosevelt: the Communists were to support Roosevelt's "progressive" policies while criticizing "with full sharpness his retreats before reaction."[34]

It took an issue of foreign policy to turn the Communists into unabashed enthusiasts for Franklin Roosevelt himself. In November 1936, Germany and Japan signed an Anti-Comintern Pact that raised the specter of a two-front war against Russia. A year later Italy joined them, and Hitler mused about adding France as well. A Soviet mutual-assistance pact with France did not seem of much value: when German troops reoccupied the Rhineland in March 1936 in direct violation of treaties, neither France nor Britain acted. While the Western democracies adhered to pledges of non-intervention in the Spanish Civil War in 1937, Germany and Italy encouraged General Franco's rebellion with men and material. On Russia's borders Poland was openly hostile, while the three small Baltic states feared antagonizing either Germany or Russia. Finland and Rumania both held back from any alliance with Russia.

No issue raised as many sticky problems for Communist theory in the Popular Front era as that of support for the war preparations of bourgeois governments. Communist parties had first sprung into existence during World War I in reaction to Socialists' actions—their support for their own governments' war aims, or their refusal to work for the defeat of those governments as a springboard for revolution. To suggest that Communists should support their countries' bourgeoisie had been ideological heresy. Yet, that was precisely the dilemma the Comintern faced. To permit the Comintern's sections to keep up their struggle against rearmament, military conscription, and similar measures might, in direct proportion to the Communists' strength, prevent capitalist nations from creating a credible military force able to deter Germany. A militarily weak France or Britain was no help to the Soviet Union. Shortly after the Franco-Soviet Pact was ratified, Stalin dutifully announced his government's "complete understanding and approval of the policy of national defense pursued by France for maintaining its armed forces at the level corresponding to the needs of its security." Although the French Communists immediately dropped their opposition to an extension of military conscription, this hardly signified a decisive shift in Comintern policy.[35]

The Seventh Congress had not done much to change Communist policy in this area. The *rapporteur* on the international situation, Palmiro Togliatti, asserted that "a new imperialist war for the redivision of the world is not only inevitable, is not only being prepared for in all its details by every imperialist power, but can break out and surprise us at any moment." The "imperialist powers" were warned not to expect any help from Communists in their plans. "During this crisis," Togliatti warned, "we shall fight with all our strength at the head of the masses to convert the imperialist war into a civil war against the bourgeoisie, we shall fight for revolution and the conquest of power." Just because the Soviet Union had signed an agreement with a bourgeois government did not, Togliatti noted, imply that it had committed Communists of any other nation to any particular policy. While Communists would vote for alliances with Russia, they would continue to oppose military budgets, armaments, or any other effort to militarize their nations. The Seventh Congress approved a resolution demanding that the Communist parties of "all capitalist countries must fight against military expenditures." Togliatti patiently explained the error of those comrades who thought "the conclusion of the mutual aid pacts means losing sight of the perspective of revolution in Europe." Those unable to fathom "the profound inner consistency of this position" did not understand "the real dialectics of events and of revolutionary dialectics.[36]

The Seventh Congress did suggest that some capitalist wars of national defense, particularly those undertaken by small nations, were legitimate. But the crucial elements in any collective-security concept were the great powers. If the Communists continued to hamstring the democratic governments' defense preparations even while the fascists busily rearmed, they risked reducing the formers' willingness to stand up against aggression and their future ability to carry out whatever commitments they might have made in mutual security pacts with Russia. However, a contradictory view also existed: the Communist leaders felt that capitalist governments awaited only the right opportunity to turn their destructive power on Russia, and feared helping them to build up that might.[37]

More than approving increased defense spending, however, the Comintern placed its faith in collective security as the way to halt fascism. Only unified action by the democracies in concert with Russia could contain aggressors. On this score, the Soviets had much to worry about. The efficacy of their treaty with France, the only major power to agree to a mutual-assistance pact with Russia, was in doubt. When American foreign policy showed a glimmer of support for collective security, the Soviet Union and the American Communists were delighted.

The Comintern's emphasis on collective security created unique problems for American Communists. The Party had supported abolition of ROTC "as we fight against all moves of American imperialism to build up its war machine." Beginning in 1933 it had carried on a frenzied campaign against the Civilian Conservation Corps (CCC), accusing the administration of creating "forced labor camps" to militarize American youth. The Party made "Against the Roosevelt War Budget" one of its chief slogans for an anti-war demonstration in 1936.[38]

The Communists' attitudes on war did much less to isolate them than did many other vestiges of the Third Period, since a strong strain of isolationism ran through the history of American progressivism. A large proportion of the American League Against War and Fascism was drawn from religious and pacifist circles that were either willing to overlook the Communists' support of some wars or did not realize that the Party opposed only imperialist wars. A substantial proportion of the forces that the Communists hoped to gather in a Farmer-Labor party were generally unsympathetic to fascism but wanted no part of Europe's quarrels. To opt for collective security was to risk jeopardizing those ties. When the Party had been confronted by that risk in 1936 if it continued to oppose Roosevelt, it had chosen to surrender the dream of a third party. When foreign policy intervened, however, the Party did not hesitate to accept the risk.

The Party did not entirely sever its links to the anti-war advocates. In accord with Comintern policy, it continued to denounce all military expenditures well into 1937. "A billion dollars is the budget appropriation for the Army and Navy for 1937. This means a billion dollars for war preparations," explained Alexander Bittelman, advocating the immediate withdrawal of all American forces from overseas. "Not a cent, not a man, for armaments and war!" Four months later he demanded that the struggle against rearmament "must be carried on with redoubled energy."[39]

Opponents of war, however, had not stopped with seeking to contain military expenditures. They had been far more successful in campaigning to keep America from becoming involved in any future European conflagration. The Nye Committee Hearings in 1934 emblazoned on the American psyche the message that "merchants of death" had been responsible for dragging America into a bloody foreign quarrel in 1917. A nearly unanimous Congress passed neutrality legislation in 1935 to prevent America from becoming involved on any side in any future fighting. The Party squirmed but denounced the measure: it "paralyzed this country as a force for peace," Bittelman complained, because it failed to distinguish between aggressors and victims. Browder coined a new slogan for the pliant American League Against War and Fascism in 1936—"Keep America Out of War by Keeping War Out of the World"—to suggest to pacifists that America would not be able to escape involvement in a European conflict. When Congress voted to ban the sale of munitions to either side in Spain early in 1937, only John Bernard, the Communists' closest ally in the House, voted no. "Neutrality itself, in the present world situation, is unneutral," Bittelman futilely exclaimed, pleading with progressive congressmen to combine their anti-war sentiments with an anti-aggressor policy. "Peace," Harrison George lectured them, "is and can only be indivisible. Security is and can only be collective."[40]

When the President spoke out on behalf of collective security, the last vestiges of Communist hesitations about him vanished. Speaking in Chicago on October 5, 1937, Roosevelt warned that America's traditional isolationism would not protect the nation if aggression continued to go unchecked. To avoid war, the United States should join with the "peace-loving" nations of the world to "quarantine" aggressors. Public reaction to his speech was less than overwhelmingly favorable. There were mumbles about impeachment from isolationists, denunciations from congressmen and other public figures, and silence from most of his traditional supporters. Public opinion was not swayed: polls showed around 70 percent of the population in favor of having even stricter neutrality laws bind the President, and nearly three-quarters advocating a national referendum before the United States could go to war.[41]

Prominent among the scattered endorsements of the Quarantine Speech was that of the Communist party. A few days later, Browder visited a Canadian Communist gathering and told it that "all the more clearly, then, because of our past criticism of President Roosevelt's foreign policy, must we of the Communist Party declare our full and complete support to the line laid down in his Chicago speech." The issue was so important that Browder was temporarily prepared to sacrifice many Farmer-Labor allies: "Everyone must line up on one side or the other. Whoever is opposed to collective action for peace is an enemy of peace, an agent of the international bandits."[42]

Roosevelt's speech was the final hurdle in the Party's tortuous race to embrace him. Although his endorsement of action against aggressors was not followed by any action, he now became a full-fledged leader of the Popular Front. In another speech to the Canadian Communists, Browder linked the President for the first time to another Party hero of the moment, John L. Lewis.

> Democracy today is destroyed in much of the capitalist world. It is fighting for its life in the remainder. It can survive under capitalism only to the degree to which there are successfully carried out such programs as those of John L. Lewis and the Committee for Industrial Organization and the economic reforms and the peace program of President Roosevelt.

The Politburo met on November 18–19 and formally adopted Roosevelt's program as the basic program of the Popular Front. The Party had no illusions about why Roosevelt had come out for collective security. He was only reasserting the "traditional objectives" of American foreign policy, objectives dictated by imperialist interests. Nonetheless, "at the present time" those interests required blocking fascist aggression with a collective-security policy. Still, Browder allowed that Roosevelt's pronouncement "when taken together with the more concrete proposals of the C.I.O legislative program developed in Atlantic City on October 11, provided a rounded-out People's Front program of an advanced type. That does not mean to say *we already have* a People's Front to realize that program. No, we have it only in a small, elementary, unstable form. But the program for such a front is here." After years of searching, American Communists had finally located the American Popular Front and given its blessing to Franklin Roosevelt.[43]

12

The Democratic Front

THE "Democratic Front" idea marked the Communist party's full acceptance of what was later to be branded revisionism. The retreat from revolutionary activities and even from the notion of a vanguard Party was justified with words and phrases once derided as the epitome of social-fascism. Between 1937 and 1939, American Communists adopted many of the policies later denounced as "Browderism." They did so with the full approval and support of the Comintern.

The Party leadership trooped off to Moscow in late December 1937 to thrash out disagreements about the Party line. When the leaders returned, the stage was set for an announcement of a new tactical policy that represented a dramatic break with previous Communist positions. The occasion was a combined Central Committee meeting and Party Builders Congress on February 18, 1938, that brought hundreds of leading cadres to New York. In Browder's absence, Clarence Hathaway made the opening report. He informed the Party's elite that the Communists' goal was no longer a Popular or People's Front but a Democratic Front, a coalition "of the forces opposed to the fascists." Gene Dennis later included workers, farmers, and the middle class—the elements of the Popular Front—along with "important sections of the upper middle class and certain liberal sections of the bourgeoisie" as elements of the new coalition. Like the Popular Front, the new line in no way required socialism.

Browder defined the Democratic Front's program as "the minimum of those measures necessary under capitalism to preserve and extend democracy, all those things which have been the heart of the American tradition in the past, ever since the revolutionary foundation of the United States." This goal could best be attained within the Democratic party. The 1936 election, Browder wrote in *Pravda* in April 1938, had been a watershed, marking a great shift of "class forces" and a "great movement of workers and farmers to gather around the Democratic Party" while the upper classes swung to the Republicans.[1]

If that had been all there was to the Democratic Front—an embrace of Roosevelt and his wing of the Democratic party—it would scarcely have been necessary to make so much of the shift in language. Until Browder returned from Moscow in 1938, American Communists were calling the People's Front "the central tactic for checking and crushing fascism." *The Communist* was filled with articles on the relationships of various groups to the People's Front. After the February Party meeting, the People's Front was displaced. Alex Bittelman now exhorted Communists to "organize the democratic front." James Ford quickly made the transition from the People's Front in Harlem to the need to rally Negroes to the Democrat Front. V. J. Jerome faced a dilemma in reviewing Earl Browder's book *The People's Front*, which contained nary a word about the new concept. He solved it by captioning his article "Charting the Course of the Democratic Front." There was only one holdout. As late as April 1938, William Foster continued to implore the Party "to build the People's Front in all countries." He knew that the adoption of the term "Democratic Front" had more than linguistic significance.[2]

The Communist party did not like to advertise what the precise difference between the two fronts actually was. Bittelman cryptically noted that "building the democratic front achieved the policy of the People's Front." Gene Dennis announced that the Democratic Front was "the concrete application of the People's Front policy in the conditions of a rising democratic mass movement." One of the very few frank statements about the implications of the shift came from Clarence Hathaway in his speech inaugurating the Democratic Front. *The Daily Worker* editor explained that the Communist party had, of necessity, decided to accept a junior and somewhat hidden role in the coalitions it was helping to build. The Democratic Front marked "a recognition on our part that at this moment, at this stage of political development, it is not possible for us to realize a full-fledged People's Front such as we have in France or Spain." While Communists should strive for such open alliances, they ought not to be discouraged or deterred or resentful if they were not welcomed with open arms:

> In most cases, however, we will have a different situation where our Party, as a Party, will not be admitted into this progressive force that is brought together for the purpose of the campaign. There also we should support the progressive movement, not demanding the admittance of our Party, not making this a condition for our support of the democratic forces, but showing by our activity in the campaign, by our energetic support for the progressive candidates, that our Party is a constructive force entitled to entrance in the progressive movement, thereby paving the way for entrance at a future time.[3]

By April 1938, as the Communists prepared for the Tenth Convention, the Party line was set. In Minnesota and Wisconsin the Party was to rally all democratic forces behind the dominant Farmer-Labor and Progressive parties; in New York the Communists supported the American Labor party and tried to ally it with progressive forces in both the Democratic and Republican parties; in Washington, Oregon, and California, the Communists were to build the Commonwealth Federation and similar bodies by working in the Democratic primaries; and in most other states they were to support Labor's Non-Partisan League in contesting Democratic primaries. Only in certain districts and where no alternative to reactionaries existed were Communists to run on a Communist ticket. Whether progressive and Democratic political forces wanted them or not, the Communists were determined to be their ally.[4]

As part of their new concern for the Democratic party, the Communists had no kind words when Governor Phillip LaFollette of Wisconsin launched his new third party, the Progressive party of America. News stories and editorials galore pounded home the message that this party threatened the unity of American progressivism around Roosevelt. A Central Committee statement, worried that the Progressive party would "divide rather than unite," charged that the party had "provoked a chorus of jubilation and triumph" among "the camp of reaction of fascism." Instead of succumbing to LaFollette's lure, believers in progress were encouraged to build the Democratic Front around Franklin Roosevelt: "This and this alone is now the path to the progressive Farmer-Labor Party on a national scale."[5]

Nine years earlier, in 1929, Jay Lovestone had been expelled from the Communist party and vilified as an "American exceptionalist" for daring to suggest that since economic development varied from country to country, so too must the pace of the revolutionary movement. Now, quietly and with no fanfare, the American Communists acknowledged that the American working class was less advanced than Europe's. Contrasting France and Spain with America, Alex Bittelman admitted that the People's Front movements abroad were characterized by "working-class unity and by a *great influence* of the working class vanguard upon the class and its allies," while in the United States "we have a lower stage in the process of working class unity" combined with "a relatively smaller and less influential proletarian vanguard." As a result, American Communists had to learn "not to seek to impose upon the forces of the democratic front, mechanically and artificially, such policies and forms of organization as may fit some sectarian pattern and scheme but which will surely check the growth of the democratic front." No other major Communist party adopted the "Democratic Front" line to justify a subservient Communist role to a bourgeois government. Nonetheless, Browder was able to deal with the rise of the Democratic Front in America in *Pravda* with no adverse Comintern reaction.[6]

Integral to the Democratic Front was the theory of the lesser evil. This principle, once scorned as the stock-in-trade of unprincipled politicians, now became a proud part of the Communists' litany. Prior to Roosevelt's embargo speech, Browder justified keeping "the majority organized on a less progressive platform for which they are ready to fight even if it is the middle-of-the-road progressivism of Roosevelt." Even that admission, however, soon gave way to a more positive view of liberalism. "The program of the democratic front," Browder explained to the Party's Tenth Convention, "is not a Socialist program." Nonetheless:

> If we cannot have socialism now, and obviously we can't until the people change their minds, then in our opinion, while the present capitalist system exists, it is a thousand times better to have a liberal and progressive New Deal, with our democratic rights, than to have a new Hoover, who would inevitably take our country onto the black and sorrowful road of fascism and war.[7]

The Communists now presented themselves as the most ardent defenders and heirs of bourgeois democracy. "We openly proclaim," Browder announced, "that we subordinate our own special program for the reorganization of society to the will of the majority of democratic and progressive people." The Party appropriated one of the great theorists of bourgeois democracy—Thomas Jefferson. In his speech to the Tenth Convention, Browder lauded Jefferson's defense of majority control of government, democratic control of the economy, and sufficient state power to repel selfish domestic and foreign interests. Browder cited these conditions as the building blocks of socialism. Only a judicious updating of Jefferson's principles was needed to ensure the "complete amalgamation of Jefferson's teachings with those of Marx, Engels, Lenin and Stalin." James Ford spoke glowingly of "Jeffersonianism as continued and brought to higher levels in Marxism-Leninism."[8]

The Party also discovered that bourgeois democracy was a way station to socialism. Gene Dennis and Gil Green argued that in pursuing the Democratic Front "we will not only help save our class, our people and our country from the horrors of fascist enslavement, but we advance the historic objectives of the working class for achieving the socialist reorganization of society." Earl Browder denied any incompatibility between fighting for mundane, liberal demands and progress toward socialism: "Everything that organizes and activizes the working class and its allies is progress toward socialism; likewise, everything that weakens and discourages the forces of reaction goes in the same direction." By that token, anything from building the CIO to fighting budget cuts in social service programs to helping defeat a right-wing congressman was justified as a step toward a socialist society.[9]

At times some of the Party's leaders went even further. Gene Dennis entertained the idea of downgrading the Communist party, seeing the possibility that the People's Front of the future might be a "political federation, operating, insofar as electoral activity is concerned, chiefly through the Democratic Party primary, as the emerging People's Front and democratic front movement is already doing in a number of states." Browder confessed that a successful reform movement might retard the struggle for Communism but refused to let that danger stop the Democratic Front. "Proletarian dictatorship can become a practical order of the day in America," he wrote, "only if President Roosevelt's promise of a higher standard of living under the present system is defeated or betrayed. We of the Communist Party are prepared to cooperate with everybody who will help to win that higher standard of living for the masses."[10]

Not every Communist liked these kinds of formulations. Alex Bittelman admitted that "there are numerous ways and means to enable people to approach Marxism" but was clearly uncomfortable with its projected marriage to bourgeois democracy. He wrote, "There is only one Marxism—Marxism-Leninism—the teachings of Marx, Engels, Lenin and Stalin. Only one." And William Foster warned in mid-1937 that "we must remember that the Communist Party is not only a Party of progressive immediate demands, but also the Party of the proletarian revolution." Detecting a slackness in the "mass propagation of its revolutionary objectives," he also hinted that he was having serious policy differences with the Party leadership over its new policies.[11]

Just as many of the old policies and familiar epithets were packed up and put aside for the sake of the People's and Democratic Fronts, so too did a number of prominent Party leaders edge into obscurity or lose their influence. Party leadership required different talents in the new era. The same skills that served so well in the Third Period did not necessarily translate to an era of negotiations and compromise. Many Communists, of course, were able to make the transition with ease. Earl Browder was one.

A leftist when the Comintern demanded leftism, Browder had never had quite the same enthusiasm for violent confrontations with authorities that others did, but he had flung the Third Period war cries about with the best of them. Step by step he had nudged some of his reluctant comrades along as the Comintern ordered less militant postures. In the process he had emerged as the Party's undisputed leader and with the credit for its rise from rags to respectability and some success. Browder's apotheosis began in 1936; by 1938 it had become a miniature cult of personality befitting a Bolshevik leader. Other Party leaders paid him frequent and public tribute. When he missed an important Party plenum because of illness, Jack Stachel first reminded the delegates that they lacked "his sharpening of the various questions which only he, in his own way, can do." Even Browder's absence, however, testified to his virtues. He had trained the Party so well that "we have been able to carry on as we have, without his personal guidance and presence." The leader's forty-seventh birthday called forth a signed paean from twenty-one Party leaders saluting him as a "steady unfaltering guide" and attesting that he was "beloved as co-worker, as man, as a sterling Bolshevik comrade." At the Tenth Convention, virtually every speech began with fulsome praise for the man from Kansas. Mike Gold summed up Browder's role: he bore "exactly the same relationship to Communism here that Stalin does in the Soviet Union."[12]

Most of Browder's chief aides were, likewise, veterans of the movement who had demonstrated an ability to accept the new line. Gene Dennis, who moved into the national center in 1938, had first made his mark in 1930 when he was indicted for criminal syndicalism for his role in the earliest Imperial Valley strikes. He had faithfully served the Comintern for most of the decade, once as a "rep" in the Far East and later as the American Party's representative in Moscow. Between those duties, Dennis had been state secretary in Wisconsin. Arriving in 1935 just as the

Party began its honeymoon with the Farmer-Laborites, he oversaw the establishment of relations with the Wisconsin Progressives. Dennis's biggest catch was Meta Berger, widow of the one-time Socialist sachem of Milwaukee. Under Dennis's tutelage, she became a devotee of the Popular Front, her famous name providing the Party respectability and entree to influential Socialists and Progressives in Wisconsin. Dennis had demonstrated that he could smoothly work with non-Communists. He was also a Comintern favorite. In 1938 he returned from Moscow to become the Party's legislative director. In 1933 that post would have required little acumen, since the Party largely contented itself with denouncing what Congress did. Now, the position required tact and finesse as well as political sophistication. Dennis had to negotiate with a variety of independent congressmen and bureaucrats unafraid to listen to Communists. He swiftly became one of Browder's closest aides.[13]

Several other members of the inner circle were old warhorses. Jack Stachel oversaw the Party organization. Gil Green, whose rise in the YCL had almost paralleled Browder's ascent in the Party, served on the Politburo. An ex-seaman, Roy Hudson, was put in charge of trade union work after being frozen out of the new CIO National Maritime Union because its leader, Party ally Joe Curran, disliked and mistrusted him. Loyal to Browder, Hudson obediently followed orders and avoided independent initiatives. Clarence Hathaway, still editor of *The Daily Worker*, continued to be entrusted with sensitive assignments, but his role as Browder's closest political adviser was gradually usurped by Dennis.[14]

The new Party line was far from popular with many others in the Party leadership. The symbol of the resistance to Browder was William Foster. Like an historical relic, he remained in place as Party chairman. In public only Browder was given more deference. In Party councils, however, Foster was increasingly isolated. Foster was hardly an instinctive leftist. During his long Party career he had committed sins of every variety, right as well as left, and his attacks on Browder had come from all directions. More than anything else Foster wanted to run the Party; it galled him no end that Browder did. Foster may not have had a consistent ideological quarrel with Browder, but he did express many of the resentments of other old-timers. He felt uncomfortable subordinating the Communist party to the larger goals of the CIO and the New Deal. He worried that the Party was losing its identity and distinctiveness. And he disliked the way several friends and long-time Communist stalwarts were being treated. Foster, however, was not able to accomplish very much. His frequent appeals to the Comintern got him nothing but criticism. Within the Politburo he received blistering attacks from almost all his comrades when he complained that Browder had failed to utilize his talents.[15]

The first overt disagreement had taken place in early 1936. Reluctant to support a Farmer-Labor party without assurances of labor backing, Foster eagerly endorsed Sam Darcy's idea of direct support for Roosevelt. Within months after the election, however, Foster was carping that Browder was too solicitous of the Democratic party and not enthusiastic enough about a Farmer-Labor party. Foster and Browder took their disagreements to Moscow in April 1937. In 1939 Foster told his Politburo colleagues that Browder had come in for severe criticism there. Yet, within one month of returning home, at a June plenum, Browder was even less enthusiastic about a Farmer-Labor party. For the first time he broached the possibility that a new third party might not be needed, that the Farmer-Labor party might grow within the womb of the Democratic party. The official Soviet history of the Comintern reports that while in Moscow Foster criticized Browder for idealizing Roosevelt and thinking that his forces "would act as one of the main factors of the Popular Front," but reports no Comintern decision—which suggests that Browder was given a go-ahead to proceed with his policies.[16]

At the June 1937 plenum, Foster came very close to avowing openly his break with Browder. He cautioned his fellow Communists not to place too much faith in the Democratic party: "We must be especially on guard against tendencies to weaken or discard the Farmer-Labor Party slogan." More important, he implicitly criticized Browder's understanding of the People's Front concept. Foster did not object to a People's Front, but he insisted that it required a vanguard role for the Communist party: "In the French People's Front the role of the Communist Party as the vanguard stands out sharp and clear, although the official posts are mostly held by other parties." By contrast, in America, the party "does not yet occupy such a definite leading position," particularly in day-to-day struggles. Its work "must be carried on so openly that the masses can clearly see what the Party is actually doing." The Party "must not be simply a helper or auxiliary to the various current mass movements. . . . It is not enough that the Party be active; its activities must also take on a leading character." Foster specifically indicated his displeasure at such right-wing tendencies as the "inadequate criticism of Roosevelt and Lewis."[17]

The Party's reaction to Roosevelt's Quarantine Speech only added to Foster's discomfort. So did the increasing fervor with which the Party clasped John L. Lewis to its bosom in 1937. Realizing that without the Comintern's intervention he was lost, Foster prepared to appeal to Moscow to reverse Browder's heretical policies. Late in December he and Browder once again set out for Russia. On his way to Moscow, Foster attended the French Communist party's congress outside Paris. Once again he lauded their People's Front. Communists had been given governmental responsibilities and clear recognition as partners in a common endeavor. Why, he asked, should not the American Communists demand as much? The Party deserved a leading role *as a party* in any coalition it entered. In a thinly veiled criticism of his own party's caution and modesty, he wrote: "Especially in this basic matter of exercising political leadership, so fundamental to the building of the Communist Party and its influence, the Communist Parties in all the capitalist countries would do well to study the proceedings of the Congress." In Moscow, Browder and Foster joined Gene Dennis for discussions with the Comintern leadership. At stake was the American Communists' relationship with the Democratic party and Franklin Roosevelt.[18]

The existing accounts of this meeting diverge so sharply that it hardly seems possible that everyone was talking of the same event. Like so many episodes in Communist history, the decisions reached later proved highly embarrassing to most of the participants. Since no public record of what went on was known to exist, all were free to re-create events to suit their retrospective political viewpoints. Fortunately for the sake of historical accuracy, it is possible to piece together the Comintern's deliberations. Unfortunately for the official Communist version of the Party's history, the facts reveal the staunch support of the Comintern for what later was called Browder's revisionism. To his chagrin, Foster learned that he had badly miscalculated the Comintern's desires.[19]

In 1939 at a Party Political Committee meeting (the new name for the Politburo), Foster recalled the trip to Moscow. Browder had accused him of "wavering on the main line of the Party." After a heated discussion, Georgi Dimitroff had charged that Foster "represented certain sectarian remnants." Gene Dennis then reminded Foster that in Moscow Browder had presented the position of the Political Committee and the National Committee while Foster had stood alone, maintaining that "the Party was following at the tail of Roosevelt and Lewis." Dennis added that "the position of the Comintern is expressed in the resolutions which were adopted at the 10th Convention which were drafted by [Browder]." The differences were not between Browder and Foster but between Foster and the entire Political Committee. Rather than criticize the Americans for their actions, the Comintern had applauded them. Dimitri Manuilsky had said that no other Party had to make as sharp a break with sectarianism and that the CPUSA had made "the greatest strides in a turn in its mass work." Dennis concluded the committee meeting with a warning that Foster had better learn to follow Browder's lead. Not only was the latter the Party leader, but he also spoke with the authority of the Comintern: "It is important to mention this here because we should understand the position of the comrades of the Comintern."[20]

Foster was not the only old-timer disgruntled by the new regime. Bill Dunne was an incurable leftist who had a hard time adjusting to the new line. Testifying before Congress in 1934 on behalf of the Communist party, Dunne was in his element, denouncing the Wagner Act as a strike-breaking bill. Five years later Browder coolly told the Dies Committee that Dunne had incorrectly stated the Communist position. Moreover, Dunne had orchestrated an embarrassing Communist revolt in the American Newspaper Guild to replace fellow traveler Heywood Broun with a real Communist. Browder intervened, and Dunne bitterly protested that the Party was surrendering its autonomy in the CIO to cement ties to John L. Lewis. Dunne was exiled to his native Montana, where his alcoholism went out of control. By 1938 his usefulness to the Party was over. Another casualty was William Weinstone. Once a contender for Party leadership, he had been shunted aside in 1932. After two years in Moscow, he was assigned to Michigan as a district organizer. For a few years, he produced impressive results as the auto industry became the key battleground of the CIO. By 1938, however, his stewardship was under attack because of growing factionalism in the United Automobile Workers that was caused by the Communist issue. The Party leadership blamed Weinstone for driving union president Homer Martin into the arms of Jay Lovestone. Weinstone, defended only by Foster, was removed from Michigan and relegated to an inconspicuous position in the Party's educational apparatus.[21]

Like Dunne, Sam Darcy had a reputation as a leftist within the Party. Unlike him, Darcy readily adapted to the People's Front. In some ways he had been a premature advocate of cooperation with liberal politicians and the labor movement. Darcy had encouraged Harry Bridges to fight within the A.F. of L. while the TUUL still existed. He had tried to arrange a deal with Upton Sinclair before cooperation with bourgeois political parties was fashionable. He had urged the Comintern to back Roosevelt in 1936. He returned to America in 1937 from his assignment in Moscow. After brief service as national education director, Darcy was assigned in early 1938 as Central Committee representative to the Party's Ninth District, encompassing Minnesota, Wisconsin, and the Dakotas. He quickly became embroiled in a feud with Browder about the Party's covert relations with the Minnesota Farmer-Labor party, and at the Party's Tenth

Convention was demoted to an alternate member of the National Committee. To the bitter Darcy it was clear that the new line was a "plan to transform the Communist Party into a semi-secret society for conniving in other organizations instead of an independent mass party of its own." Soon afterward, he moved to Philadelphia as state organizer and bided his time. His disagreement with Browder had only been postponed, not forgotten.[22]

Most of the crucial positions in the Party continued to be filled by old-timers. Party leaders in key states were mostly veterans of the 1920s. In New York, Israel Amter, Charles Krumbein, and Rose Wortis ran things. Similarly, in Rhode Island (Ann Burlak), Illinois (Morris Childs), Massachusetts (Phil Frankfeld), Alabama (Robert Hall), Washington (Morris Raport), Ohio (John Williamson), California (William Schneiderman), Pennsylvania (Pat Toohey, Martin Young), and Minnesota (Nat Ross), Party leaders could boast of more than a decade of experience.

Just below the top echelons, however, a new generation of Communist leaders was emerging. Party ranks had been thinned out by the large-scale migration of experienced organizers into the CIO in 1936 and 1937. The rapid growth of membership and formation of hundreds of new Party units required an equally rapid expansion in the number of functionaries. Young men and women, many of them Depression-era converts to Communism, were quickly pushed into secondary leadership roles. George Charney gave up a career as a lawyer to become organizational secretary of the Party in New England. Two years later, considerably more experienced, he became "org sec" in the key Harlem district. Since James Ford, the Harlem Party leader, was kept busy at the national level, Charney had even wider responsibilities than his title implied, handling most of the Party's dealings with New York congressman Vito Marcantonio. Young heroes back from Spain like Steve Nelson, John Gates, and Bob Thompson were also groomed for leadership positions.

These younger Communists knew little about the Party's past. Their formative political experiences were the Depression and the rise of fascism. Most had been Communists just long enough to remember the isolation of the early 1930s. To them and many thousands of the new recruits who flocked into the Communist party in the last half of the 1930s, Earl Browder was the leader who had brought the Party out of the wilderness and enabled it to link up with progressive movements of every description. Even had the recruits been fully exposed to the arguments of Foster and his friends about the need for a vanguard role of the Party and greater independence of the New Deal and the CIO, they would not have listened. The Communist party had come a long way since the 1920s. The specter of revolution that had animated the first generation of Communists was less vivid among this one. They still desired a socialist society, but its urgency was no longer the political issue. Fighting fascism and struggling for reforms took precedence.

The Party's newfound enthusiasm for the Roosevelt administration could not have come at a more inopportune time. Beginning in the summer of 1937, economic difficulties mounted further. By the fall, the nation was reeling. The stock market collapsed in an eerie replay of 1929. The index of industrial production, which had painfully climbed back virtually to its 1929 level, plummeted, losing a third of its value by February 1938. Unemployment once again skyrocketed, reaching Depression figures of over 11 million. The President's response was far from bold. At first, resistant to a significant increase in government spending, he bravely talked of a balanced budget to restore business confidence. Not until April 1938 did he launch a massive government spending program.[23]

In years gone by, such dismal economic news would have provided enough ammunition for a hundred Communist denunciations of capitalism. There would have been loud and insistent assaults on the ineffectual nostrums of bourgeois politicians, coupled with calls to put an end to an economic and political system incapable of escaping such cyclical crises. Indeed, the Comintern's economic expert, Eugen Varga, gleefully predicted the onset of a new capitalist crisis. The American Communist party, however, wanted no explanations that cast aspersions on Franklin Roosevelt. He had just been proclaimed an indispensable part of the Democratic Front. How could he be saddled with blame for the economic collapse without the Communists withdrawing their support? But, how could the crisis be explained without reference to the administration in power?[24]

Earl Browder provided the Party's answer at a Politburo meeting in November 1937. He flatly affirmed that "this recession is not a necessary development at this time." The roots of the crisis were political, not economic. "Monopoly capital," he charged, was deliberately prolonging and deepening the recession to combat the progressive movement. Borrowing a phrase much in vogue, Browder accused it of a power play: "Monopoly capital has gone on a sit-down strike. It is trying, by direct action, to cancel the mandate of the people of November, 1936." The Party supported increased government regulation of business, more social spending, public works, and unemployment relief to meet the crisis. Browder very carefully avoided blaming or even criticizing the President.[25]

The idea of a sit-down strike of capital flew in the face of Marxist economic doctrine. Foster, sniffing an opportunity to expose his enemy as a dangerous revisionist, brought the issue up during a January 1938

218

meeting with Comintern leaders. The idea of a sit-down strike of capital was just the sort of theoretical unorthodoxy that resulted from "tailing" after Roosevelt. However, Browder not only won a Comintern endorsement of his pro-Roosevelt foreign policy views; he also was vindicated on the recession issue. Dimitri Manuilsky indicated support of Browder's heterodoxy on pragmatic grounds: whether American capitalists had planned the recession or not, they should be held responsible. Not long afterward, Eugen Varga did an about-face, arguing forcefully that the recession was "largely due to political factors" such as "the deliberate sabotage of the most reactionary sections of the United States bourgeoisie." Browder returned home to boast to the Party's Tenth Convention in May that the Communists had been the first to popularize the phrase "sit-down strike of capital" and to put the blame for the economic woes where it was deserved.[26]

Roosevelt's foreign policy was no more to the Communists' liking. No issue so touched the Party or did more to bolster its influence among liberals as the Spanish Civil War. Like Communists the world over, the American Party did what it could to aid the Spanish Loyalist government. Communists had denounced neutrality legislation that failed to distinguish between aggressor and victim. They created committees which raised large sums of money for humanitarian and technical aid to Spain. And they recruited soldiers to fight in Spain. The first large contingent of one hundred left from New York on Christmas Day, 1936. Three thousand Americans eventually arrived in Spain, forming the Abraham Lincoln, George Washington, and, with Canadians, Mackenzie-Papineau Battalions of the International Brigades. Most were either Communists or sympathetic to the Party: Browder boasted in 1937 that more than 60 percent were Party members.[27]

During their tenure in Spain, the Americans took enormous casualties in battle after battle. More than half never returned home (a handful, between eight and fourteen, were executed for either military insubordination or political unreliability). To most Americans, the Communists' willingness to fight against Franco and his fascist supporters was dramatic evidence of the Party's commitment in the war between democracy and fascism. That the Soviet Union sent aid to the Loyalists only increased the Party's prestige in the West.[28]

Despite President Roosevelt's encouraging words about combatting aggressors, his foreign policy remained an embarrassment. The United States did nothing to aid the Loyalists. Seven months after Roosevelt's Quarantine Speech, Browder complained that in practice nothing had changed. The "everyday practical policy in Washington continues along the reactionary line giving aid and comfort to the bandit governments in their aggressions, and to Chamberlain's policy of surrender to and complicity with them." When the United States recognized the Franco government, Browder called the act an "unforgivably stupid and criminal surrender to the Chamberlain 'non-intervention' policy towards Spain" and added: "Thus did the Roosevelt administration gratuitously smear itself with complicity in the fascist aggression and destruction of democracy in Spain."[29]

On the positive side there were statements from the President himself, expressing his aversion to the fascist dictatorships and aggression. Secretary of the Interior Harold Ickes made some flamboyant anti-fascist speeches that *The Daily Worker* applauded, and he even served as honorary chairman of Spanish Refugee Relief. But, the Party was able to retain its enthusiasm for Roosevelt only by attacking his aides and not him for the government's policies. Secretary of State Cordell Hull was among the least-liked Cabinet members, and Under-Secretary of State Sumner Welles was attacked for connivance with fascism. The latter was denounced as "the open leader of a pro-fascist clique" in the State Department, a "tool of the Tories," and a spokesman for "world fascism." In May 1938, when the Spanish Loyalists desperately needed help, Secretary Hull reaffirmed the policy of noninterference. *The Daily Worker* went after him with a furious front-page editorial that carefully avoided mentioning the President's name, as if Roosevelt were head of some other government and Hull were not his subordinate.[30]

Nothing could now stop the Roosevelt bandwagon in the Communist party. In a radio interview after the mid-term 1938 elections, Browder discerned a new two-party system in which the Communists had been integrated: "We are learning to take our place within the traditional American two-party system, which seems to have much vitality yet, even though the real two parties now cut across all the old party labels, and can be more realistically identified as the New Deal and the anti–New Deal Party." By the end of the year Browder had personalized the party system even more; the Roosevelt party confronted the anti-Roosevelt party. "Franklin D. Roosevelt," he told a December plenum, "is clearly the chief figure in the progressive or liberal camp. . . . the symbol which unites the broadest masses of the progressive majority of the people." In a speech in Mexico City, Browder identified "the Roosevelt Party" as the bearer of everything progressive in American society:

It stands for government work or relief for the unemployed; trade union organization for collective bargaining for the employed workers, with legal minimum wages and maximum hours; social insurance for the unemployed, the sick and old people; governmental regulation of big business and stock markets; governmental development of hydro-electrical power resources; enforcement of the rights of Negroes; protection of all civil rights; support to students; conservation camps for the youth; governmental aid to maintain agricultural income; aid to building houses for the people; condemnation of and resistance to the Rome-Berlin-Tokyo alliance, and the good neighbor policy to Latin America.

After the Munich Pact, the Party abandoned its last quibble about American policy. "We cannot," Browder proclaimed, "adopt a negative position to the question of armaments."[31]

It was only a short step for the Communist party to go from supporting Franklin Roosevelt to denouncing opposition to him as treason. Left-wing enemies of collective security and the Democratic Front, such as the Lovestoneites and Trotskyists, were denounced as "agents of fascism" and accused of "carrying out the policies and desires of the general staff of the Japanese armies and of Hitler and Mussolini." Browder sneered that "for every dirty job the reactionaries and fascists want done among the workers, these vermin will find a high-sounding 'revolutionary' theory and slogan." To ensure that such filth would not infect its membership, the Party's Tenth Convention included a provision in a new constitution that prohibited a "personal or political relationship" with Trotskyists or Lovestoneites, who were "organized agents of international fascism."[32]

The New Deal's enemies on the right were accorded similar treatment. Father Coughlin remained a favorite target: "Treason to America Speaks Through Coughlin" read one headline. Alex Bittelman attacked the "spokesmen of monopoly reaction, the fountain-head of fascism in this country" as "the betrayers of America and Americanism." *The Daily Worker* fulminated against critics of Roosevelt: an editorial entitled "What Treason Lurks Behind the Attacks on Roosevelt's Message?" referred to "a rising hatred of democracy, a growing sympathy for fascist reaction on an international scale." One Communist writer discovered an historical precedent—"Andrew Jackson Democratic Fighter Against National Treason"—who had also struggled against monopolists. This writer pointed out that "the American democratic republic occupied in the eyes of the European upper class somewhat the same position which the Soviet Union holds in the eyes of redbaiters today."[33]

No policy better symbolized the idea of the Democratic Front than the Party's attempted reconciliation with Roman Catholics. During the Third Period *The Daily Worker* had carried out a vociferous anti-Pope campaign. Churches, an editorial explained, were always hostile to workers because they were "personally owned and controlled by the same class of multi-millionaires who own and control American industry." Workers and farmers who were churchgoers could become Communists, but "we do not advance to leading positions those who still follow the Church." As late as June 1935, the Party was still described as "the irreconcilable foe of religion."[34]

As with many Party initiatives, the impetus for a change came from abroad. The French Communists, with the approval of the Comintern, extended an "outstretched hand" to Catholics in 1936. Within a year of Browder's 1937 visit to France, *The Daily Worker* was hailing "progressive" Catholic priests and Mike Quill was explaining to the uninformed that "St. Patrick is a People's saint." Earl Browder extended "the hand of fellowship to our Catholic brothers" to join in a defense of civilization. He told the Party's Tenth Convention that both Communists and Catholics sought the same things—"justice, truth, and fair dealing between man and man"—and both were subject to canards about being agents of a foreign power. Browder happily reported that "a growing number" were joining the Party: nothing stood in the way of a good Catholic becoming a good Communist.[35]

Confidence and self-assurance permeated the Party's Tenth Convention, which opened in New York on May 26, 1938. One thousand five hundred delegates arrived from the length and breadth of America, ranging from old war-horses like Mother Bloor to such exotics as Joe Clark, an American Indian oil worker from Oklahoma. Robert Trout of CBS reported live from jam-packed Madison Square Garden to a nationwide radio audience. William Foster announced that "Communism is 20th Century Americanism," while Earl Browder—speaking before an enormous outline map of America emblazoned in red and white with "Jobs, Peace, Democracy, and Security"—proclaimed the Communists' commitment to the Democratic Front. It was a far cry from the days of the Third Period.[36]

13

Organizing
the Unorganized
Once Again

N
O SOONER had the Communists completed their journey back
into the none-too-enthusiastic arms of the American Federation of Labor
than they had to watch another fissure. The Committee for Industrial
Organization (CIO) was launched late in 1935, less than a year after the
Party had sunk the Trade Union Unity League. Having just abandoned
their own venture in dual unionism, the Communists reacted uneasily to
this new phenomenon. Not until 1937 did they finally accept the necessity
of a separate trade union structure. Once they made up their minds,
however, they threw nearly everything they had into the CIO and were
able to become a major force in the American labor movement. In no
other sector of American life did the Communists gain as much legitimacy
or influence. The Party did not found, run, or dominate the CIO. But
Communists were a major force within its constituent unions and in its

national office, and they built an alliance with the CIO's non-Communist leaders.

The history of American Communism is full of ironies, but the most extraordinary one is the role of John L. Lewis in inviting the Communist party into the CIO. For most of the Party's history prior to 1935, no labor leader was more despised than the dictatorial leader of the United Mine Workers. Throughout the 1920s, the Communists fought Lewis's administration. Jay Lovestone could imagine "no worse gangster in the entire A.F. of L." and "no worse parasite in the labor movement." During the 1930s, pictures of Lewis in *The Daily Worker* bore captions like "The Arch-Betrayer," "The Bosses' Agent," and "Scab-Head." One headline read "Lewis Plans to Trick Miners Once Again with N.R.A.," and the Party denounced him for praising the New Deal and relying on Roosevelt's promises. Even when Lewis introduced a resolution at the 1934 A.F. of L. convention calling for industrial unionism, a Communist editorial scorned the proposal as a product of the "Green-Lewis bureaucracy" running the A.F. of L. On the eve of the climactic 1935 convention of the A.F. of L. in Atlantic City, New Jersey, the Communists remained firm in their hostility to Lewis. William Foster listed the miners' leader as a potential supporter of a fascist or semi-fascist party. Earl Browder did rebuke some Communists for suggesting that the division within the labor movement–the split between Lewis and A.F. of L. president William Green, who was resisting industrial unionism–"has no significance for us, because Lewis is as much of a reactionary as Green." But the Party leader accused Lewis and his supporters of trying "to make use of the deep-going currents among the radicalized masses for their own reactionary needs."[1]

If the Communists despised Lewis, he returned the compliment with interest. John Lewis did not lightly tolerate opposition within the United Mine Workers, and the Communists had been among his most implacable foes. During the early 1920s, Lewis pointed to several Party officials sitting in the balcony at a miners' convention, denounced them, and ordered "that you remove your carcasses without the door." Angry miners promptly beat the Communists senseless. Around the same time, the UMW issued a special report purporting to expose the Trade Union Educational League's role in the disruption of the American labor movement. To Lewis, his Communist enemies within the UMW represented "the first step in the realization of a thoroughly organized program of the agencies and forces behind the Communist International at Moscow for the conquest of the American continent." That these two seemingly irreconcilable foes should end up sharing the same political bed surely ranks as one of the more unexpected developments of labor history. John L. Lewis was the prototype of the American labor leader the Communists hated. He ruled his union as autocratically as any in the country. He had supported Herbert Hoover in 1932. He despised and distrusted Communists and sought to drive them from the union movement.[2]

Two developments were to force these unlikely allies together. The first was Lewis's commitment to organizing the unorganized into industrial unions. The second was the People's Front. Without the second transformation, the first would have meant nothing to the Communists. Before the Comintern met in 1935, Lewis's cautious advocacy of industrial unionism had won him no plaudits. Afterward, the Communists discovered his virtues.

The A.F. of L. met in Atlantic City in October 1935. On the crucial resolution requiring the federation to issue industrial charters in mass production industries, Lewis got only about 38 percent of the votes. No sooner had the convention adjourned than he and a group of union leaders created the Committee for Industrial Organization, designed "to encourage and promote organization of the workers in the mass production and unorganized industries of the nation and affiliation with the American Federation of Labor." By November 23, Lewis had resigned as a vice president of the A.F. of L.[3]

"The Communist Party," William Foster boasted years later, "gave its most active support from the beginning" to the CIO. It did not. The sudden movement by Lewis was profoundly unsettling to the Communist leaders. Barely half a year earlier they had buried the TUUL, convinced after six years that dual unionism was the road to ruin and isolation. As early as 1934 a confidential Party memo claimed that Communists controlled 135 A.F. of L. locals with 50,000 members, two Central Labor Councils, and several districts and had organized opposition groups in 500 locals. By 1936, 15,000 Communists were union members. Sixty sat on the Central Trades and Labor Council of New York. In Chicago, Morris Childs boasted, "we now have scores of Communists occupying leading positions in numerous local unions, district councils, and central labor bodies." The Communist-led Fur Workers had managed to negotiate a return to the A.F. of L. union they had left years before. "Our most prized achievement of the past period," Browder told the Seventh Congress, "is our success in the struggle for trade union unification." Having finally returned to the A.F. of L. and established themselves, could Communists now blithely risk leaving it again and endangering their tenuous ties to the labor movement?[4]

To add to the Party's unease, none of the founding members of the

CIO was known as a particularly close friend of Communism. To the contrary, Lewis, David Dubinsky, Max Zaritsky, and Sidney Hillman were long-standing enemies. The only high-level union official close to the Party in any of the unions that initiated the CIO was Francis Gorman of the Textile Workers, but he played no role in the new grouping. Jack Stachel complained that "on the whole these people, Lewis, Hillman, Dubinsky, etc., were ready to accept an attack on Communism and they even favored this." Moreover, while the Communists were in the midst of their campaign for an anti-Roosevelt Farmer-Labor party, Lewis and Hillman were determined to do everything in their power to reelect him. The Communists took this zeal for the Democratic party as another ill omen of the direction in which the CIO might go.[5]

For all these reasons, the Party was less than exuberant about the CIO's formation. It was greeted by a short, inconspicuous editorial. Instead of hosannas there was an understated announcement that successfully managed to stifle enthusiasm: "The Committee for Industrial Organization formed by eight international A.F. of L. unions should stimulate the organization of the unorganized workers into the A.F. of L." The main skeptic was William Foster, who had just returned to full-time Party work after a three-year recuperation from a heart attack. To Foster's discomfort, the CIO appeared to have the makings of a dual union, and he dreaded the possibility of an open split with the A.F. of L.[6]

As a result, Party pronouncements were cautious and somewhat contradictory. When Lewis resigned as a vice-president of the A.F. of L. he earned a mild rebuke from *The Daily Worker:* "The resignation of John L. Lewis as a vice-president of the American Federation of Labor is not merely a temperamental outburst on the part of Lewis—no matter how ill-advised." And the editorial concluded with a warning that "the workers in the A.F. of L. should be on guard against any tendency to carry these developments toward a split." The following day an editorial called for support of Lewis with no qualifications: "Every worker must give his support to John L. Lewis and to the industrial union bloc which he heads." William Foster, however, emphasized a different theme, repeating over and over again the need to avoid a rupture in the A.F. of L. The CIO's purpose was limited to a campaign "to unify and strengthen the A.F. of L., to organize these unorganized workers in the basic industries into the A.F. of L." The Communist party supported "the struggle of Lewis and all others in their fight to achieve the unity and strengthening of the A.F. of L. unions through elimination of craft barriers."[7]

For the next two years the Communists continued to hope that the fissure in the labor movement would not grow into a split. The Central

Committee blamed the A.F. of L. for the dispute and called for "a united American Federation of Labor upon the basis of industrial unionism and the organization of the unorganized." However, even after the A.F. of L.'s 1936 convention in Tampa endorsed the suspension of the unions in the CIO, the Communist party advised the latter not to give the A.F. of L. a pretext for further widening the conflict. Not until 1937, when the Congress of Industrial Organizations began issuing its own charters to unions, did such Party-dominated unions as the Fur Workers, Harry Bridges' Longshoremen, and the Transport Workers Union leave the A.F. of L. for good. Foster continued to oppose the Political Committee's unequivocal endorsement of the CIO even into 1938, urging that Communists press it to unify with the A.F. of L.[8]

Since the Party was cautious about the CIO, it was also cautious about John L. Lewis. Even a measured tone, however, was enough to shock Communists long habituated to trading insults with him. Bill Dunne seemed stunned when he printed probably the first favorable comments about Lewis in a Party publication. Writing of Lewis's activities at Atlantic City, Dunne made no attempt to hide his surprise: "It sounds strange, and it is strange, to say that John L. Lewis this morning partially paid off a long-standing debt for the Communist Party of the United States and the thousands of militant workers who kept aloft the Crimson Banner of the class struggle when labor officialdom accepted continual retreat as its major policy." That same day, an editorial mixed praise with aspersions about Lewis's past and doubts about his motives: "Whatever may have been the record of John L. Lewis in the past, whatever may be his motives at present and his activities in the future, there can be no doubt that through him there spoke not only the one-half million members of the U.M.W.A. but all that is best, most clear-sighted and progressive in the American trade union movement."[9]

Only one A.F. of L. leader received unreserved Communist praise. Denounced by the Party during the 1934 textile strike, Francis Gorman later endorsed the Communist position on a Farmer-Labor party. Reporting on the 1935 A.F. of L. convention, Jack Stachel noted: "Gorman stands out as the most advanced of the old-time officials who occupy a position of prominence in the trade union movement" and praised him in glowing terms as one who "more than anyone else of the top leadership of the A.F. of L. unions expressed the sentiments of the broadest sections of the organized workers."[10]

Whatever their reservations about the CIO, the Communists were anxious to work with it. And John L. Lewis, that arch-foe of communism, was anxious to have them. Both sides had something to gain. The Communists needed the respectability and legitimacy as labor leaders that were available under the CIO's umbrella. They wanted to establish themselves as an integral part of the labor movement, a goal that had eluded them for fifteen years. For his part, John L. Lewis needed organizational support to build the CIO and was not averse to accepting it from whatever direction it came. The Communists had organizers galore. Lewis was neither tricked nor deceived. He had been fighting the Communists for fifteen years, and they had been fighting him ferociously. If he now made a deal with them, it was because he got something from them, not because he was taken in. Warned that Communists were flocking into the CIO, he supposedly responded, "Who gets the bird, the hunter or the dog?" Lewis was supremely confident that he could use the Communists to achieve his own purposes and run them out when he wanted to.[11]

The exact origins of the CIO–Communist party agreement are shrouded in mystery. It was Lewis who sent out the first signals. After the Atlantic City convention he gave Marguerite Young of *The Daily Worker* an exclusive interview. Early in 1936 he met with Clarence Hathaway and mentioned that old feuds should best be forgotten. Everyone was welcome in the CIO; there would be no discrimination against Communists. The next steps were left to the CIO's director, John Brophy, who had worked with the Communists during the 1920s in the UMW. Like so many other dissidents, Brophy had been driven out of the union and the industry by Lewis, who found a use for him when he prepared to launch his new crusade. After Lewis's meeting with Hathaway, Earl Browder and Brophy rendezvoused at a New York hotel. It was their first meeting since the 1920s. They quickly reached an understanding to work together. "They wanted our cooperation and they wanted our field organizers," Browder recalled. Brophy "agreed that there'd be no discrimination against our people and they'd be treated on the basis of their individual merits and not as a category."[12]

Brophy did more than negotiate with Browder. One of the first people he hired for the CIO's national office as publicity director was an itinerant radical newspaperman named Len DeCaux. A native of Great Britain, DeCaux had rebelled against his upper-class education at Harrow and Oxford and, determined to enlist on the workers' side in the class struggle, had emigrated to America in 1921. He was precisely the type of man John L. Lewis had long battled. Like so many other CIO staffers—including Adolph Germer, Powers Hapgood, and Brophy himself—DeCaux had once been a dissident in the United Mine Workers. He had worked with the Federated Press, a labor news service filled with Communist, anarchist, and radical Socialist reporters. He had worked for a railroad brotherhood head, Albert Coyle, whose support for John Brophy in 1926 had infuriated Lewis. In his autobiography, Brophy denied that he had any "idea that DeCaux worked closely with the communists" when he hired him. DeCaux, however, had joined the Communist party of Great Britain in 1925. In the United States, early in the Depression, he became a member-at-large of the Communist party after a meeting with Clarence Hathaway. When DeCaux discussed his new job with Brophy, he was less than completely candid but made no effort to hide his political leanings: "I told him frankly that I had close sympathies with the communists, had many friends among them, and associated myself with them in a number of ways, though not organizationally." And just in case Brophy missed the point, Jay Lovestone, an old acquaintance of both men, warned him of DeCaux's ties to the Party.[13]

Brophy had nothing to do with hiring the Party's other link to the CIO hierarchy. Lee Pressman was John L. Lewis's idea. Born in New York to immigrant Jewish parents, Pressman had established an enviable record at Cornell University and Harvard Law School. In the spring of 1933, Jerome Frank offered him a job in the Agricultural Adjustment Administration. The AAA was plagued by disputes that abruptly ended with the discharge of its radicals, including Lee Pressman. After a brief stint as a lawyer for another federal agency and then in private practice, Pressman persuaded an old friend, Gardner Jackson, to introduce him to Lewis, who hired him as general counsel for the Steel Workers Organizing Committee (SWOC) and, eventually, the CIO. Pressman was not just another capable lawyer with radical sympathies. Early in 1934, Harold Ware had recruited him into the Communist party. For about a year the young lawyer met with a Party unit of government employees once or twice a month. Among his compatriots, Pressman told the House Un-American Activities Committee years later, were John Abt, a future employee of the National Labor Relations Board (NLRB) and later chief counsel to Sidney Hillman's Amalgamated Clothing Workers; Nathan Witt, future secretary of the NLRB; and Charles Kramer, who held a series of appointments in New Deal agencies before going to work for the LaFollette Committee investigating civil liberties violations. When he left the federal government, Pressman later claimed, he resigned from the Communist party. His break, however, was organizational, not ideological. Pressman's sympathies were no secret within the CIO, but he never told either Lewis or Murray that he had actually been a Party member.[14]

The CIO badly needed organizers. Nowhere was the need so crucial as in the steel industry. When Lewis and Brophy made a deal to obtain Party organizers, it was steel they had in mind. The Communists did not disappoint them. Late in 1935 Browder had told a Party plenum that "especially here [in the steel industry] our Party must enter with all its forces and resources in the campaign of organizing the unorganized." It did. A feeble A.F. of L. shell, the Amalgamated Association of Iron, Steel, and Tin Workers (AA), had long had the nominal right to organize steel-workers into an industrial union. When the TUUL's Steel and Metal Workers Industrial Union had dissolved in 1934, many of its loyalists had joined the AA. The Communists still controlled several lodges. The AA signed an agreement with the CIO in June 1936 to hand over its charter to the new Steel Workers Organizing Committee. Very quickly scores of additional Communists were hired as SWOC organizers. As fast as they were hired, the SWOC asked for more. William Foster boasted that 60 of the 200 full-time SWOC organizers in 1936–1937 were Communists. John Frey told the Dies Committee that almost 50 Communists were on the SWOC payroll and that 59 had been delegates to its first convention in 1938. John Williamson proudly reported that "in Ohio our entire Party and Young Communist League staffs in the steel area were incorporated into the staff of the committee." [15]

One promising Communist who was sent to the SWOC to lend a hand was George Powers. His Party career illustrates the back-and-forth movement of Communists between the Party and the CIO. Born Morris Poberski in Russia in 1905, he entered the United States as Maurice Powers in 1923. Within a year Powers had joined the Communist party in St. Paul, Minnesota. In the late 1920s he was an enthusiastic participant in the factional wars that convulsed the largely Finnish Party in Minnesota. Sent south as a Party organizer, Powers served as a functionary in North Carolina and as a TUUL Textile Workers Union organizer. In 1930 he and five other Communists were arrested in Atlanta for distributing Communist literature and charged with inciting to insurrection, a capital offense. While his case meandered through the courts—it was eventually dropped—Powers finished his stint with the National Textile Workers Union. He worked briefly with the TUUL in Philadelphia and then was assigned to the Steel and Metal Workers Industrial Union in Baltimore, where he tried to organize at Bethlehem Steel's huge Sparrows Point plant. From there he went into the AA in 1935 and was made available to the SWOC in 1936. After two years in the CIO he became secretary of the Communist party's Western Pennsylvania District. The Dies Committee cited him for contempt in 1940. In 1944 Powers once more popped up at Sparrows Point, employed in the shipyard and active in the effort to build the CIO's Political Action Committee. Shortly afterward, he returned to a Party position in Pittsburgh. Powers slowly started drifting away from the Communist party after World War II: by 1952 he abandoned it for good in deference to his union career. When he wrote an account of the steel union in western Pennsylvania, he never mentioned the Communist party.[16]

If George Powers finally opted for the union he had helped to build, another tough young Communist organizer sent into the SWOC made quite a different choice. Arvo Holberg was born to Finnish parents who lived on the Mesabi range in Minnesota. His parents were charter members of the Communist party. Holberg's formal education stopped after the eighth grade, but his Party education continued at the Lenin School in the early 1930s. After returning in 1933, he worked for the Young Communist League in the upper Midwest. Convicted after a demonstration in Minneapolis in 1934, he told the court that "when the time comes" he would fight to overthrow the government. In 1936 Holberg was in Youngstown, Ohio, when he was assigned to the SWOC. During the 1937 Little Steel strike, Holberg, who by now was using the name Gus Hall, was the SWOC organizer in Warren, Ohio. When seven men were arrested, they acknowledged being members of a union dynamite squad that had bombed the homes of nonstrikers and railroad tracks and bridges leading into the plant. Some of the men implicated Hall as the ringleader. When he was tried more than a year after his alleged confederates had been convicted of felonies, Hall pled guilty to a misdemeanor—malicious destruction of property—and was fined $500. The young organizer's notoriety did not endear him to the union leadership, and he soon returned to more prosaic Party tasks, rising to become state chairman of the Ohio Party. After serving in the navy and resuming his role in Ohio, he was brought to New York in 1950 to be groomed for national leadership. Convicted under the Smith Act along with other leading Communists, Hall jumped bail and fled to Mexico. He was captured and returned to America, and did not resume his Party career until 1959, when he deftly engineered the ouster of Gene Dennis as general secretary and replaced him. He was still the Party's leader in 1983, enjoying a longer tenure than any of his predecessors.[17]

Communist assistance to the SWOC went beyond providing such seasoned organizers. Boleslaw (Bill) Gebert was assigned by the Central Committee to work with the fraternal groups of the foreign-born so prominent in the Pittsburgh area. Gebert was a highly regarded Party veteran who had been entrusted with many sensitive assignments ever since the founding of the Communist party. Himself a native of Poland, he had immigrated in 1918 and gone to work as a miner. Gebert had quickly risen to prominence in the Polish Federation of the Socialist party, from whence he had joined the Communist movement in 1919. His Party positions included district organizer in Chicago and Pittsburgh. He had also remained prominent in Polish affairs. In 1930 he led the Polonia Society, a mutual-benefit society for Polish workers that he had founded, into the newly formed Communist auxiliary, the International Workers' Order (IWO). "Practically every steel worker is a member of some sort of fraternal social organization," Gebert noted. He set out, with SWOC approval, to mobilize those organizations to support the union. "There is unlimited opportunity," he explained, "for Communists in fraternal organizations, for the national bureaus of the respective papers, really to play an important role in the American labor movement." Just prior to the 1936 election, Gebert convened a Fraternal Orders Conference in Pittsburgh. Five hundred delegates from fifteen fraternal societies and a hundred fraternal orders gathered at the Slovenian Hall. Max Bedacht, head of the IWO, was also present. John Lewis sent a friendly message. Phil Murray spoke, thanking the delegates for their assistance in building the SWOC among their members and in their communities, and Gebert was chosen to head the Fraternal Orders Committee. The SWOC also hired Benjamin Careathers, a well-known black Communist organizer from Pittsburgh, to enlist Negroes in the union. Careathers was the guiding spirit in a February 1937 conference of 186 Negro delegates from 110 organizations with 100,000 members. The delegates pledged their help to the SWOC.[18]

Perhaps the greatest gift the Communists made to the CIO was their role in the United Auto Workers' sit-down strike in Flint, Michigan, early in 1937. When the strike ended in February with a signed agreement between Lewis and the head of General Motors, no one could be unaware of the CIO, and the United Auto Workers (UAW) was launched as a potent organization. The Communists in the UAW may not have invented the sit-down concept, but they knew a good idea when they saw it. The Flint strike was largely the work of Communists. Wyndham Mortimer, the UAW's vice president, was assigned by the 1936 union convention to direct the fight against GM. When Homer Martin, the UAW president, transferred Mortimer from Flint, Bob Travis was sent in as a replacement to direct the strike. Both Mortimer and Travis were Communists. They relied heavily on the 60–100 Communists in Flint during the organizing days because the local union was so heavily infiltrated by company spies. They were aided by intelligence from Charles Kramer, the LaFollette Committee's chief investigator in Detroit, who provided committee material that helped identify company spies. Kramer too was a Communist. The strike committee chairman, Bud Simons, was a Communist, as were "nearly all of the seven members of the strike committee." One, Walter Moore, was the Party's section organizer in Flint. Henry Kraus, a Communist, edited *The Flint Auto Worker*. Maurice Sugar, the UAW's attorney, was very close to the Party. Lee Pressman supervised legal strategy.[19]

Non-Communists were involved in Flint as organizers, and John L. Lewis himself conducted the crucial negotiations that led to a union contract with the world's largest automaker. Still, it was Communists who formed the backbone of the strike leadership. William Weinstone, the Party's Detroit district organizer, had not been apprised of the strike until it was imminent. He counseled caution but was told that nothing could stop it. During the strike he conferred frequently with Travis. After it was over he linked "the fact that the Communists were active, particularly at the most decisive points of the struggle" to the "success of the whole battle." And Mortimer remembered that "the main strategy of the sitdown strike itself was conducted by the Communists."[20]

The Communists contributed organizers and, frequently, leadership to other CIO unions. Before long, they occupied crucial positions in nearly a dozen new unions.

The United Electrical, Radio and Machine Workers Union (UE) was the largest Communist-dominated union. Beginning with only 19,000 members in 1936, it grew to 137,000 a year later. Its president, James Carey, a callow twenty-six-year-old, was never a Communist. However, the director of organization, James Matles, was a TUUL veteran who had faithfully led his Metal Workers Industrial Union remnant into the A.F. of L. in 1934 and back out again in 1937 in accordance with Party policy. Matles was one of those Communists who found it expedient to hide his past. Although he wrote the Dies Committee denying that he was a Communist, he had been much franker to his comrades in 1934, writing in *The Daily Worker* of "our Party." Secretary-Treasurer Julius Emspak's exact status was more of an enigma. The leader of an independent union at General Electric in his hometown of Schenectady, New York, Emspak denied to the end of his life that he belonged to the Party. Others told of sitting with him at closed Party meetings. Louis Budenz identified him as a participant at National Committee meetings under the pseudonym of Comrade Juniper. Avowed Communists held important positions throughout the UE. William Sentner, president of UE's District 8, was a highly visible Communist leader in St. Louis. James MacLeish, president of District 4, was a Communist. During the 1940s Dave Davis, business agent of Local 155 in Philadelphia, and Nat Cohen, executive board member of Local 475, served on the Party's National Committee. James

Lustig, a full-time UE organizer, had been a Party candidate for public office and a veteran of the Hungarian Bureau. Dozens of other UE organizers and officials had close Party ties.[21]

The Transport Workers Union (TWU) was even more of a Party club. In 1933 the Party's Extraordinary Conference had demanded concentration in basic industries. Charles Krumbein followed up with a suggestion that "we should consider for concentration . . . city transport." The New York District assigned its cadres the task of organizing the city's transit workers, who were "hitherto untouched by our movement." By 1936 a Party district committee boasted of its headway "in Traction, where the Union, built and led by our comrades has grown to the strength of 5,000 members." Communists, claimed Rose Wortis, New York's trade union secretary, "are among the foremost builders of the union."[22]

The first TWU president, Thomas O'Shea, was a Communist. When he was asked to step aside by the Party in late 1935 to make way for the election of Mike Quill, he did so, although, embittered, he was later to turn up as a friendly witness before the Dies Committee. Quill, known in New York as "Red Mike," was the union's president until his death in 1965. A fiery speaker who claimed to have fought with the Irish Republican Army, Quill faithfully served the Communist party until 1948. He never openly admitted Party membership, but several witnesses placed him in Party units, saying that he paid Party dues and recruited union members into the Party. He himself later admitted to attending Party caucuses and fraction meetings at CIO conventions. And he made no secret of who his friends were: "I would rather be called a Red by the rats than a rat by the Reds," he explained to one audience. Austin Hogan, president of the powerful New York local, was identified as a Communist. Douglas MacMahon, a national officer, acknowledged years later that he was a Communist.[23]

The most open Communist in the TWU was John Santo, by 1939 secretary-treasurer of the union. Born in Hungary in 1908, he joined the Communist party within a year after his arrival in America in 1927. For several years Santo worked in Cleveland for *Uj Elore*, the Party's Hungarian-language newspaper. In 1932 he was a Communist candidate for public office. Following the Open Letter of 1933, Santo was transferred to New York and assigned to organize the transit workers. Although the TWU was not publicly a TUUL affiliate, Santo was a member of the Trade Union Unity Council. He ran into trouble with immigration authorities after revelations of his past by the Dies Committee in 1939. Deportation proceedings were begun, were suspended while he served in the army during World War II, and were resumed in 1948. Santo resigned his union position and voluntarily returned to his native Hungary in 1949. After a rocky beginning—he was apparently considered as a possible defendant in the Rajk purge trials—Santo rose to a position of responsibility in the State Meat Trust. Living under a Communist regime, however, even in a privileged position, proved far less enjoyable than he had imagined. In 1956, following the Hungarian revolution, a disillusioned John Santo fled to Austria. Seven years later, through the intervention of Francis Walter, chairman of HUAC, he received a visa to return to America. He told the committee that thirty years of devotion to Communism had come to an end for him.[24]

The Party made inroads among white-collar workers as well. The first two officers of the State, County and Municipal Workers, Abram Flaxer and Henry Wenning, were both Communists. Wenning, the national organizer, had joined the Party in 1934 but was expelled the following year as a Lovestoneite and "economist." He explained to a congressional committee that he soon returned to the Party's orbit, although "I never joined the Party after that again. I never technically became a bookholding member of the Communist Party from 1935 on. At the same time, I must, in all honesty, state I certainly was virtually a member of the Communist Party in every sense of the word, let us say, from 1936." Flaxer's ex-wife testified that in 1935 the union president "told me he was joining, and he told me subsequently that he had joined under the name 'John Brant.'" He never made his affiliation public, "feeling it would hamper his work and interfere with the recruiting in his union." Wenning also identified his ex-colleague as a Communist: "It was always understood between us that we both were members." Confronted with these charges, Flaxer, whose union had been expelled by the CIO and who was now president of the United Public Workers of America, took refuge in the Fifth Amendment. The editor of the union's newspaper, Helen Kay, had gotten her start in journalism as editor of *New Pioneer*, organ of the Young Pioneers, the Party's children's affiliate, in 1933.[25]

The American Newspaper Guild's president, Heywood Broun, was a fellow traveler, as was Executive-Secretary Jonathan Eddy. Garland Ashcraft, elected treasurer in 1935, was a Communist. The United Office and Professional Workers of America (UOPWA) was led by Lewis Merrill. Although he also never openly admitted his Party affiliations, Merrill was a Communist. Eleanor Nelson, secretary-treasurer of the United Federal Workers, was at least a Party sympathizer. Arthur Osman, president of New York District 65, the largest local of the United Retail and Wholesale Employees in New York, was a close Party ally.[26]

One of the smaller CIO affiliates, the Federation of Architects, Engineers, Chemists and Technicians (FAECT), achieved notoriety incommensurate with its size. One of its alumni was convicted atomic spy Julius Rosenberg, who joined the FAECT in 1939 and soon became chairman of the union's Civil Service Commission. The union organizer who recruited him, Vice President Marcel Scherer, was himself charged by witnesses before congressional committees as having been involved in espionage during World War II at the Livermore Radiation Laboratory in California. No charges were ever filed, but the FBI worried about Communist domination of this small—under 10,000-member—union. Lewis Berne, the president, was a Party member. However, Scherer, the founder of the organization, had a Party record that few unionists could match. Born in Rumania in 1899, he came to America as a young child and was brought up in a Socialist household on the Lower East Side. Scherer, a brother, and a sister all became charter members of the Communist party. At City College of New York, where he majored in chemistry, Marcel was known as "the Bolshevik chemist." He attended the Lenin School, was active in the Workers' International Relief, and for a time served as secretary of the Friends of the Soviet Union. His wife, Lena Davis, was herself a long-time Party leader in New Jersey, rising to district organizer in the late 1930s.[27]

More proletarian unions had their share of Communists. Harold Pritchett, president of the International Woodworkers of America, denied his Party affiliations, but William Foster years later admitted that he was a Canadian Communist. When Pritchett faced immigration troubles, Vice President O. M. Orton moved up the union ladder. Several union members testified that Orton had solicited them to join the Party. The largest local in the East, in New York, was led by Sam Nesin, once Mayor Walker's least favorite Communist. Morris Muster of the Furniture Workers was allied with the Party; far closer was his secretary-treasurer, Max Perlow, who had led his TUUL union into the A.F. of L. and then the CIO. Perlow was a Party veteran who had made the error of following Jay Lovestone out of the Communist party in 1929. Suitably chastened by the experience, he pleaded for exoneration and was readmitted in 1933. The Mine, Mill, and Smelter Workers Union had elected Reid Robinson president as an anti-Communist in 1936. Robinson drew steadily closer to the Party, however, until his and the Communists' positions were indistinguishable. Ben Riskin was hired as director of research, while another Communist, Harold Sanderson, became Robinson's secretary. Kenneth Eckert, head of the Unemployed Council in Toledo and a graduate of the Lenin School, moved onto the union's executive board.

Maurice Travis, who became the union's leader in the 1940s, was also a Communist.[28]

The head of the Packinghouse Workers Organizing Committee, Van Bittner, was a Lewis ally, but Henry Johnson, the assistant national director, was close to the Party. In Chicago, the union's heartland, an old TUUL nucleus dominated the union, including Don Harris, organization director, and Herb March, the district director, who had been a Young Communist League organizer. In 1948 the Party's own newspaper identified March as a member of the national committee. Both Grant Oakes and Joe Weber, leaders of the Farm Equipment Organizing Committee, were Party members. In 1937 John L. Lewis gave a CIO charter to organize agricultural workers to Donald Henderson. For at least the previous two years Henderson had been assigned to agricultural work by the Communist party. He became the president of the United Cannery, Agricultural and Packing and Allied Workers of America.[29]

Several maritime unions were led by Communists and fellow travelers. Harry Bridges seceded from the A.F. of L. in 1937 and brought the International Longshoremen's and Warehousemen's Union (ILWU), into the CIO. He was rewarded with appointment as CIO regional director for the West Coast. The American Communications Association, consisting largely of radio telegraphers, was led by Mervyn Rathborne. Originally associated with an anti-Communist faction, Rathborne changed his mind in 1935 and swung to an alliance with the Party and, quite possibly, membership in it. Vice President Joe Selly, who succeeded Rathborne in 1940, had never been a telegraphist: he was recruited from the FAECT. The small Marine Cooks and Stewards union was led by Hugh Bryson, another Party-liner. Joe Jurich, president of the International Union of Fishermen, was another very close Party ally. By far the largest maritime union was the National Maritime Union, which traced its history directly to the TUUL's Marine Workers Industrial Union. Joe Curran, its president, was often accused of Party membership. He vigorously denied it. There was no similar doubt about most of his fellow union officers. Ferdinand Smith, the secretary-treasurer, and Blackie Myers, the vice president, were Communists, the latter sitting on the Party's National Committee.[30]

The Fur Workers were led by Ben Gold, an open member of the Party and its National Committee. The Shoe Workers' leader, Powers Hapgood, had apparently briefly been a secret Party member in the 1920s. His successor, Frank McGrath, had been a member of the TUUL's Shoe Workers Industrial Union. The National Die Casters Association, which later affiliated to the Mine, Mill union, was led by Edward Cheyfitz. One of its regional directors was Alex Balint. Both were identified by several witnesses as Party members.[31]

In addition to these union leaders, Communists and their close associates were found in other CIO positions. For example, at the CIO's first constitutional convention in Pittsburgh in 1938, Emil Costello, Lou Goldblatt, and John Clark represented state industrial councils. Phil "Slim" Connelly, Elmer Fehlhaber, and Harold Christoffel came from city councils. The Party did not stint when it came to sending its cadres into the CIO. By the scores they moved from Party work into trade unions. So many did so, in fact, that a severe shortage of Party organizers resulted. The "main organizational problem before the Party" at its 1936 convention was the "replacement of the leading forces absorbed by the trade union drive and by the activities in the united front movements, with new elements from among the most promising forces in our ranks." Earl Browder was accurate when he told a Central Committee plenum in 1937: "We communists are a small, though important, part of this great mass movement. We are giving all our best forces and mobilizing all our organizations to assist the work of the CIO."[32]

In fact, the Communists' standing in the CIO was so secure by 1937 that, looking to the future, the Party deliberately held back some of its comrades who wanted to leave the A.F. of L. Louis Weinstock led some 15,000 members of the Painters local in the New York area. The Hotel and Restaurant Employees' Union in New York was dominated by two TUUL veterans and Communists, Mike Obermeier and Jay Rubin. The American Federation of Teachers' Local 5 in New York, the union's largest affiliate, was a Party stronghold. Its vice president, Dale Zysman, was a Communist who used the pen name of Jack Hardy. Bella Dodd, a secret Party member, was the union's legislative representative and the real power. Although many of the militant teachers, Communists and non-Communists alike, wanted to leave the A.F. of L. and obtain a CIO charter in 1937 when the labor split became final, the Party ordered its people to stay where they were. Roy Hudson and Rose Wortis were sent to the AFT's 1937 convention and "laid down the law." Bella Dodd remembered later that the Party rationale was that "it had enough power within the CIO whereas in the A.F. of L. the Party's forces were diminishing."[33]

By 1938 the Communist party was a force to be reckoned with at CIO conventions. No less than 40 percent of the international unions were either led by Communists and their close allies or significantly influenced by them. The Communist-led unions were not, for the most part, the CIO's giants. Only the Auto Workers, in which Party influence was significant but not dominant, and the UE were among the CIO's largest affiliates. Both John L. Lewis's UMW and Sidney Hillman's Clothing Workers were free of Party influence. Despite its scores of Communist organizers, Phil Murray's Steel Workers were likewise dominated from above by a non-Communist group. The Textile Workers Organizing Committee, run by Hillman, was also largely free of Communists. Most Party-dominated unions were small. With a handful of exceptions like the Maritime Workers, Fur Workers, and ILWU, the Communists had succeeded only in organizing a small share of each industry. Some claimed memberships far in excess of what they actually had. Other unions often made the same exaggerated claims with regard to members, but even if all the Communists' figures are regarded as accurate, the Party-influenced bloc in 1937 claimed around 650,000 members compared to 600,000 in split unions and 2 million in non-Communist ones.[34]

Many Communists in the CIO were not as eager to proclaim their beliefs as the Party might have hoped. Jack Stachel complained that "a large number" were "known only to small circles as Communists." John Williamson, noting the "important and sometimes decisive role" that Communists were playing in the CIO, lamented that "the covered character of the work of many leading Communists who occupy strategic posts of trade union leadership results in the real contribution of our Party not being made publicly at this time." Roy Hudson warned a Party plenum that "we must show our comrades that after a certain period, concealing our identity deliberately breeds distrust among workers. They cannot understand why we are ashamed; why we hide the fact that we are Communists." The trend was deeply disturbing to William Foster, who feared that the cadres' desire to avoid the limelight created a danger of the Communist party falling "into a sort of trade union economism. This tends to liquidate our Party in the mass trade union movement."[35]

As much as they worried about "hiding the face of the Party," Communist leaders confronted serious dilemmas in overcoming the problem. There were no legal bars to Communists holding positions of union leadership, but the CIO did not have a revolutionary agenda. Aside from adding to the prestige of the Party, union leaders had no incentive to identify themselves as Communists. They could do exactly what the Party wanted them to do as unionists pure and simple. They joined dozens of Party auxiliaries and signed up to support Party causes. They altered their views with shifts in the Party line. But they could maintain the fiction that they were only "progressives." Such a smokescreen avoided unpleasantness with the CIO leadership—which would have been discomfited to acknowledge publicly just how many of its unions were led by Communists. Lewis, Hillman, and Murray knew quite well with whom they were dealing. Lewis in particular played the game with consummate hypocrisy. Well aware that numerous Communists worked for the CIO, he was still capable of dismissing one who impetuously bragged of his Party membership, piously declaiming: "I will not have a Communist employed by us."[36]

Discretion also minimized complaints from union members, few of whom were Communists. In union after union, Party influence was concentrated among the leadership and paid bureaucracy. Success at the top was not, however, matched by large numbers of Communist union members. In January 1938 there were roughly 75,000 Communists. Only 27,000 belonged to trade unions. Not even all of these were in the CIO, which at that time was claiming more than 3 million members. Jack Stachel pointed to one weakness after another in 1938. The Party had "a few thousand miners" but this was not enough. Out of an auto union of 400,000 members, only 1,500 were Communists. It was hardly necessary "to emphasize our weaknesses in the steel industry." Textiles were a disaster area. As Stachel put it, "Here is an industry of way over a million workers. We recruited 206 into the Party. We didn't have very many to start with." As usual the railroad brotherhoods were not a bright spot: "There are railroad workers in every district, state and city. But there are not enough in the Party." Nor did the situation improve significantly before World War II. The high point in steel was just over 2,000 in 1939, 1,300 the same year in the UMW, and 1,100 in the UAW. Reid Robinson estimated that no more than 10 percent of the Mine, Mill membership was either Communist or sympathizers. There were 2,000 Communists in the 85,000-member UOPWA. The TWU's former president estimated that less than 5 percent of its rank and file were Communist. In the National Maritime Union, with more Communists than most unions, the Party was still largely a coterie of officers. No CIO union had a majority or even substantial minority of Communist members. In the larger ones, the Party presence was infinitesimal.[37]

That imbalance was not entirely a debit. For one of the few times in its history, the American Communist party had the opportunity to lead organizations with large numbers of non-Communists. Unlike the auxiliaries of the 1920s and early 1930s, these unions were not filled with the already committed. Unlike some Party organizations, they were not facades behind which stood only mythical masses of members. Communists had to cooperate with non-Communists and lead non-Communist memberships. This new situation called for new relationships between the Party and its trade union members. The days when TUUL leaders were often Party functionaries and simply carried out Party orders would

240

no longer do. From obscure Party wheelhorses, these union leaders were suddenly catapulted to some degree of power and responsibility. The experience was not unsatisfying, and it loosened the leaders' organizational ties to the Party. They had less time to be bothered with the burdens of ordinary Communists. Someone like James Matles, Browder later chuckled, might attend his local unit meeting once a year.[38]

To a large extent Browder was eager to accommodate these men's demands. Only the Party's national leadership had the right to interfere with union leaders, and even it was wary of too blatant an intervention into union affairs. Len DeCaux and Lee Pressmen vehemently denied that they took orders or directions from the Party. Lewis Merrill described Browder's habit of allowing Party unionists wide leeway to do as they wanted within their unions so long as they paid lip service to the Communist movement. Not all unions were treated equally. Those with a delicate factional balance required more Party attention than others. But, the Party was determined not to push its union leaders so hard that they faced irreconcilable conflicts between their union duties and political beliefs. For the moment, it was more concerned with demonstrating just how easy it was to be a Communist union leader. And formal meetings were hardly necessary for Party leaders to communicate with union leaders. Browder later noted that Party unionists only had to read *The Daily Worker* and stay alert to know what Communist policy was.[39]

Those who look only at the benefits the Communists got from the CIO—and those benefits were plentiful—look at only one side of the story. They ignore what the Communists gave in return. They denuded their own organizations, surrendering many of their best cadres, some permanently. They relinquished the rigid control they had traditionally exercised over their trade union cadres. They gave up some long-cherished principles, not the least of them being a refusal to acquiesce in condemnations of their own ideology. And they abandoned the right to criticize John Lewis. No American, not even Franklin Roosevelt, was accorded greater deference.

Once the Communist party had decided to support the CIO wholeheartedly, John L. Lewis became its favorite public figure. With the full flowering of the Democratic Front, John Lewis and Franklin Roosevelt were hailed as the saviors of American society. Democracy, Browder noted in 1937, "can survive under capitalism only to the degree to which there are successfully carried out such programs as those of John L. Lewis and the Committee for Industrial Organization and the economic reforms and the peace program of President Roosevelt." Party theorist Alexander Bittelman hailed "the programmatic declaration of President Roosevelt,

the declarations and statements of policy by John L. Lewis, and the legislative program of the C.I.O." These "already form a basic program of the
People's Front behind which stands the overwhelming majority of the
American people." Lewis's denunciation of fascism at a meeting in Mexico City in September 1938 prompted Browder to say that Lewis
"emerged, with that speech, not merely as the greatest American trade-
union leader, not only as one of the most potent representatives of American democracy, but as a leader of world democracy."[40]

Lewis was not the only ex–labor dictator and "social-fascist" to be
presented laurels, although no one else was treated to such fulsome
praise. An abrupt about-face toward old enemies in the needle trades was
also necessary. International Publishers had the bad luck to publish Jack
Hardy's *The Clothing Workers* at just about the time of the 1935 A.F. of L.
convention. Critical of the "class-collaboration" practiced by David Dubinsky, Hardy was also less than complimentary about Sidney Hillman.
Mild as the criticisms were in comparison to the Third Period insults
leveled against the same men, the rebukes were now intolerable. Hardy's
book was repudiated in *The Daily Worker*: "It is regretful that the book,
written some time ago, appeared at a time when all indications point to
important changes in the approach of our union leaders, without taking
account of these changes, which are destined, if realized in practice, to
transform the complexion of the internal life of the union and make more
effective the struggle for better conditions."[41]

Even the caveat that the Communists expected to see a democratiza-
tion of the union movement did not survive for long. In the CIO's early
days, Party spokesmen cautioned that full internal democracy was necessary to prove the bona fides of such once-suspicious characters as Lewis,
Hillman, and Dubinsky. Earl Browder admitted to a Party plenum that
"some comrades" had raised a question of what guarantees the Communists had that they would not be betrayed yet again by men who had
fought them in the past. All he could offer in reply was a promise that the
Party would not let up in its struggle for democracy within their unions.
Bill Gebert was critical of the autocratic UMW and warned against "the
feeling that there is no need for a clear-cut class program in the miners'
union because Lewis is in favor of industrial unionism." Such sentiments,
however, did not long survive the Communist-CIO alliance. Two years to
the month after he had attacked the UMW's autocracy, Gebert was much
more understanding of why the union's districts did not need the right to
elect their own leadership. He praised the Constitutional provision restricting that right, which left control in the hands of the UMW
leadership.[42]

To keep the peace in the CIO, the Communists were even willing to forgive their union allies' pro forma declarations of hostility toward Communism. In 1935 and 1936 they had been adamant about the need to end all discrimination against Party members. The struggle for industrial unionism, Browder insisted, required trade union unity, "which is totally incompatible with red-baiting." Gebert pledged continuation of a struggle to reverse a United Mine Workers convention denunciation of both fascism and communism. By 1938 Gebert viewed the provision in the UMW constitution prohibiting Communists from belonging to the union with more equanimity, noting that "in recent years this provision has not been enforced." A *Daily Worker* editorial admitted that "we would have welcomed the elimination of this dangerous clause" but added that "Communists did not consider it opportune to raise the question at all at this convention, especially since it already has so little meaning in actual life." The Communists learned to live with the anti-Communist provisions, even after the United Auto Workers, for example, barred them from holding union offices. For the sake of preserving their positions they even went along when the 1940 CIO convention unanimously passed a resolution denouncing "policies emanating from totalitarianism, dictatorships and foreign ideologies such as Nazism, Communism and Fascism." Even more startling, the resolution was introduced by Lee Pressman.[43]

The Party also decided to disband its union fractions and abolish its shop papers. For years, membership in fractions had been required of all Communists in mass organizations. Its new circumstances led the Party to conclude that the fractions were more a hindrance than a help. They might jeopardize the Party's alliance with the CIO leadership by giving the impression that the Party was waiting for the opportunity to challenge those leaders for their jobs. By giving up the fractions, the Communists hoped to reassure their non-Communist allies that they had no intention of seeking control of their unions. At the International Ladies' Garment Workers' convention in May 1937, David Dubinsky urged delegates to prohibit all organized groups in the union. Dubinsky was no friend of the Party; nevertheless, he was then still in the CIO. The Communist delegates enthusiastically agreed with his proposal. Fractions, they argued, might be required in reactionary unions but hardly in democratic, progressive ones like the ILGWU.[44]

In the American Newspaper Guild, meanwhile, Heywood Broun, once the object of constant Party derision but by 1937 a devoted fellow traveler, faced a challenge from Communists for the presidency. Meeting Browder on a train from Washington to New York, Broun bravely offered to quit rather than serve as president if the Party opposed him. Browder later claimed that he was startled to learn, after the discussion with Broun, that Bill Dunne had encouraged the Party's fraction in the ANG to oppose Broun; Browder had the Politburo stamp out the revolt. The episode convinced him that fractions might endanger important alliances. Less than a year later, Jack Stachel happily told a Party plenum that "we are already on the way to abolishing the Party general fractions." Rose Wortis asked: "Can we advance the cause of the workers and our Party by getting together a few hundred Communists in a fraction meeting to discuss union policy, when the main line of the union is a progressive line which we fully support?" Fractions sowed mistrust among non-Communist allies, who resented the closed meetings and the impression of mechanical Party control. The Communists, Wortis insisted, could better achieve their objectives by speaking up at union meetings, where their superior arguments and positions would carry the day democratically. Instead of wasting their time meeting with each other, Communists should be mingling with their non-Communist fellow workers.[45]

Abolition of the fractions scarcely bothered the Party's own union leaders. In fact, it gave them even greater autonomy. At the Ninth Convention in 1936, Party unionists had been instructed that "all Communists must at all times take a position on every question that is in line with the policies of the Party." As Lewis Merrill later explained: "The only difference was that we did not even have to consult the Party members. God pity the party member who voted the wrong way. All we had to do was to give orders, pass the word along." Party unionists, freed from the annoying details of dealing with fractions in their unions, thus had the best of all worlds—a dependable bloc of votes that could safely be taken for granted. A *Daily Worker* writer explained that under the new procedure "the leading comrades in every union consult with one another on problems."[46]

Not all Communists were entranced with the new tactic. Years later, Bill Dunne bitterly denounced Browder for having handed Communist cadres and press over to John L. Lewis by abolishing fractions and shop papers with no corresponding concessions. Some old-timers who nostalgically preferred the old-time religion might have been unhappy, but William Foster was not one of them. In September 1939 he reported with evident satisfaction that "Party members do not now participate in groupings or other organized activities within the unions . . . [the Party] has liquidated its own Communist fractions . . . Communists are the best fighters for democracy and discipline in the trade union movement and are resolutely opposed to all forms of group or clique control."[47]

Foster's enthusiasm had only developed, however, after a long-simmering controversy about the Party's role in the United Auto Workers highlighted its delicate balancing act. No situation so tested the Communists' determination to avoid conflict with non-Communist CIO leaders or so dramatized the potential hazards of failure. The UAW was a battleground for a bewildering array of personalities and factions. Its president, Homer Martin—a former college hop, skip, and jump champion and one-time minister who was called "the leaping parson"—was a compelling speaker but an erratic administrator. His insecurities were fed by the Communists' leadership of the UAW's sit-down strikes, the horde of union officials drooling for his job, and his evident inability to control the unruly membership. Martin had been wary of the Communists as early as the summer of 1936, when he removed Wyndham Mortimer from control of the union's organizing in Flint. Matters escalated during the Chrysler sit-down strike in March 1937. John L. Lewis reached an agreement with Chrysler calling for all sit-down strikers to abandon the plants while the major issues were being negotiated. Many strikers briefly resisted, challenging not only Martin, who toured the plants pleading for ratification, but Lewis, who had signed the agreement. Convinced that the Communists were behind the revolts and were seeking to embarrass him and seize control of the UAW, Martin prepared to purge them from the leadership. To buttress his position, he struck up an alliance with one-time Party leader Jay Lovestone. Suddenly supplied with a corps of sophisticated ideologists and organizers by Lovestone, the UAW president prepared to smite all his foes whether they were Socialists, Communists or merely anti-Martin.[48]

As in other CIO unions, the Party leadership was intent on preserving the peace in the UAW. But William Weinstone, state secretary of the Michigan Communist party, did not explicitly condemn the Chrysler sit-downers' rebellion at first: he noted that "it was natural" for workers to resent the evacuation and pointed out that their "militancy is one of the strong points of the union." Only after *The New York Times* published reports that the Party was behind the rank-and-file revolts did Weinstone issue a firm denial: "The charge attributed to Homer Martin that Communists obstructed the recent evacuation of Chrysler plants is absolutely untrue and unfounded." Just two months later Earl Browder attacked unnamed comrades in Detroit for their behavior during the Chrysler strike. They "rush into snap judgements on big questions of trade union policy, consider that the trade union leaders have been mistaken or have unnecessarily compromised the workers' demands and from this conclusion pass immediately into a head-on collision with those leaders and the workers who follow them." The Party's line was to remain united behind the strategy of the CIO leadership and John L. Lewis: "Some comrades were entirely in error in thinking they saw intolerable compromises and wrong methods in the settlement of the Chrysler strike."[49]

Weinstone's rebellion did receive some support from William Foster, who had not been enthusiastic about the Communist party following John Lewis's lead so uncritically and was in the process of attacking Browder's People's Front policy. Speaking at the same Party plenum where Browder denounced the Detroit errors, Foster first admitted that in the Motor City "Communists have too sharply and also incorrectly criticized the progressive elements and thereby needlessly alienated great masses of workers." He then attacked: the greater error was "making too little criticism of progressively-led movements. This Right tendency is manifested, among other examples, by inadequate criticism of Roosevelt and Lewis, and by a failure to put forward our own program (including our revolutionary slogans) in the mass movements led by these men." The Party had to reassert itself, reestablish its separate, revolutionary identity, and strike out more on its own.[50]

Neither Foster nor Weinstone got much support from the rest of the Party leadership. In July 1937 Bill Gebert, dispatched to Detroit to aid Weinstone, tried flattery to assuage Martin: "No small credit" for the tenfold growth of the UAW, he wrote, "goes to the international officers of this union, headed by Homer Martin." He soon followed with an article indicating that the Communists wanted the dissolution of all factions within the UAW and were supporting Martin for reelection at the 1937 convention. Martin later testified before the Dies Committee that Gebert had offered him complete support if only he would cooperate with the Party. "I was taken up on the mountain, and I was shown the promised land," he related. Even after Martin continued his vendetta against the Communists, Browder wrote him a conciliatory letter, suggesting he had been "misinformed" by Jay Lovestone.[51]

Until the fall of 1937, Walter Reuther had been one of the Party's favorites in the UAW. Allied with the Communists, Reuther was also an opponent of the Socialist party's unification with the Trotskyists. After the 1937 convention *The Daily Worker* had printed a picture of the three Reuther brothers and described them as "champions of the united front within the Socialist Party and opponents of Trotskyism as a counter-revolutionary movement." When Reuther gave covert support to a spontaneous wildcat strike against Pontiac late in 1937, both Weinstone and Wyndham Mortimer also gave encouragement to the strikers. The first *Daily Worker* report was likewise enthusiastic.[52]

The Communist top leadership in New York was outraged by this initiative into sensitive union issues. On December 5, Lawrence Emery of *The Daily Worker* repudiated his earlier jubilation. Jack Stachel was dispatched to Detroit to discuss "a number of mistakes and weaknesses that have arisen in Detroit, reflecting a weakness in the application of our People's Front policy." Stachel ominously reported back to his colleagues: "As to whether some individuals will be able to make the turn, to continue to remain an obstacle only time will tell." Late in December the Politburo harshly condemned the Michigan Communists, denouncing unauthorized strikes as "against the interests of the workers," and warned "we are not going to allow the Socialists to make our line any longer. . . ." The Michigan Communists had still one more blunder to answer for, however. In January 1938 the UAW Executive Board unanimously approved a resolution that called for the removal of all U.S. forces from China and passage of the Ludlow Amendment, which would have required a national referendum before a declaration of war. The Socialist party, opposed to collective security, had strongly endorsed the steps the UAW now approved. So had the Lovestoneites. Since the Party supported collective security, it was horrified that its forces on the board had acquiesced with Martin and the Socialists on this issue: it was a "symbol of the complete confusion and capitulation of all our forces in that Board."[53]

The Communists had meanwhile secretly negotiated an agreement with Richard Frankensteen, a Martin ally, in December. After meeting with Foster, Weinstone, and Mortimer in April 1938, Frankensteen publicly repudiated Homer Martin, prompting the latter to attempt to expel all his enemies from the UAW. When the dust cleared, Martin had been ousted from the UAW. With Frankensteen in their camp, the Communists also broke with their one-time Socialist allies, the Reuthers.[54]

On one of their missions to Moscow, Browder and Foster argued over Weinstone's activities in Detroit. The Comintern refused to sanction Weinstone's jeopardizing the Popular Front. In mid-1938 he was transferred from Michigan; this marked the end of his tenure as a high-ranking Communist. Most of the remainder of his Party career was spent in the field of Party education. At a Political Committee meeting in March 1939, Party leaders took turns recounting how Weinstone's activities had endangered the Communists' delicate alliances within the CIO and pointing out to Foster that his criticisms of John L. Lewis were just as dangerous. Jack Stachel explained that "nobody can dispute that WWW [William Wolf Weinstone] did not carry out the line of the Party and did serious damage to the Party." Gil Green added: "The errors made by WWW, for example, in Detroit, if continued, if developed elsewhere, if

247

not checked, were errors that could have destroyed the entire position of our Party in the eyes of the wide masses." Bill Gebert confessed that Weinstone's "record in the application of the [Political Committee] line in a district was more than unsatisfactory. . . . The mistakes in Detroit and there were numerous mistakes committed by WWW primarily, could not be excused." Even Foster admitted that he "agreed without one word of dissent to [Weinstone's] being demoted" because Weinstone supported "outlaw strikes." Browder reminded everyone that the Party's position in the CIO was quite delicate. "Our greatest problem today," he explained, "is breaking down all suspicions in the minds of people who have no other obstacles to collaboration with us except their suspicions. People suspect us of merely biding our time until we can make a coup and stab them in the back." Weinstone's tactics and Foster's criticisms exacerbated those fears.[55]

Communists had two motives for appeasing CIO leaders. The first was simply to preserve their ties to those labor leaders whom they recognized as their allies. The second motive was more straightforward. Communists were doing so well in the CIO that it hardly seemed worthwhile to cause trouble. There was little need to advertise their presence. So long as anti-Communist provisions had little practical effect, it did not seem worthwhile to precipitate arguments and trouble by opposing them. So long as the Party could achieve its end without using fractions, it seemed senseless to stir up resentment by encouraging them. For by 1938 the CIO's Communist connections were causing it no end of trouble. The spate of sit-down strikes in 1937 prompted an obscure Texas congressman to introduce a resolution calling for a select House committee to investigate the goings-on in the labor movement. Martin Dies lost this vote in March 1937, but one year later he got an opportunity to probe the more general topic of un-American propaganda activities in the United States. During the House debate, Clare Hoffman of Michigan cited the need for an investigation of "the Communist leaders of the C.I.O." His definition was broader than most: "Earl Browder, the American Communist leader, told us what he would do; John L. Lewis and his C.I.O. executed the threat." Hoffman wanted his colleagues to know that behind the CIO stood the specter of the Soviet Union:

The C.I.O. when it left the parent body, carried with it practically all the red radicals who were in that organization, and these elements and those men, who owe allegiance not to America; who believe in the doctrines taught in foreign lands—not in the principles which have made our Nation what it is, are the ones who have caused the trouble in the C.I.O.[56]

The Dies Committee did not limit itself to trying to link the CIO to the Communist party. Like an unguided missile, it swerved all over the landscape spewing forth a combination of fact and fiction. Before it was through the committee had also delved into the WPA, the Federal Theatre Project, the Farmer-Labor party of Minnesota, California agriculture and California Democrats, the president of Howard University, and the Roosevelt administration. Its sallies were providently timed to cause discomfort to Popular Fronters. In the midst of the 1938 election campaign, witnesses appeared to link Governor Elmer Benson and his allies in Minnesota to the Communist party. Benson would go down to defeat at the hands of Harold Stassen. Governor Frank Murphy of Michigan suffered the same fate after the committee came to Detroit to hear witness after witness pillory him for his conduct during the auto strike.

Despite the Dies Committee's concern for a wide range of problems, it spent an inordinate amount of time listening to testimony about the CIO. John Frey, head of the Metal Trades Department of the A.F. of L. and an implacable opponent of industrial unionism, was the first committee witness to get front-page attention in the nation's press. Frey allowed that most CIO members were not Communists but provided the Dies Committee with lists of alleged Communist organizers and leading CIO officials he believed were Communists. One list included 288 people. Another was of 59 alleged Communist delegates to a convention of the Steel Workers Organizing Committee. Still another included Communists in the National Maritime Union. Frey agreed that John L. Lewis was no Communist; he doubted that John Brophy was either, but accused him of collaborating closely with the Party and charged that the Communists had "failed to secure a foothold in an American trade-union movement until the C.I.O. was organized." Joseph Zack, another witness, observed that Sidney Hillman did not collaborate "with the Communist Party. I think the Communist Party collaborates with Sidney Hillman."[57]

As the Dies Committee loosed its broadsides, it was joined by angry American industrialists. Even the pure and simple business unionism of the A.F. of L. had been anathema to large portions of American industry. When business leaders confronted the CIO, they did not see John Lewis or Phil Murray or Sidney Hillman across the barricades, but the grim visage of Joseph Stalin. Tom Girdler of Republic Steel equated the SWOC with the Red Terror. "Must Republic Steel and its men," he asked, "submit to the Communistic dictates and terrorism of the C.I.O.? If America is to remain a free country the answer is no." The National Association of Manufacturers distributed more than 2 million copies of Joe Kamp's *Join the CIO and Help Build a Soviet America.* Even former friends began to attack the CIO's alliance with Communists. After returning to the A.F. of L. David Dubinsky charged that *The Daily Worker* was the CIO's organ. A left-wing journalist, Benjamin Stolberg, wrote a series of articles for Scripps-Howard in early 1938 exposing Party influence and proclaiming that "Stalinism is a danger in the CIO."[58]

In public the CIO leadership refused to retreat. Phil Murray asserted that the SWOC asked for "no political passport from any worker." Allen Haywood, a regional director of the CIO, acknowledged that Communists were in the organization but defended "the right of a man to belong to any organization politically that he chooses. We welcome them all as workers." John L. Lewis dismissed the whole issue by casting aspersions on its authors: "Do those who have hatched this foolish cry of Communism in the CIO fear the increased influence of labor in democracy?" John Brophy denounced "red-baiting" in an interview with the Communist *Midwest Daily Record.* Still another CIO leader, Van Bittner, shuddered and said that "if I were to choose between William Randolph Hearst and Communism, I would choose Communism."[59]

In private, however, the attacks did take a toll. The Party was sufficiently worried by threats to the alliance with the CIO leadership that it did not protest several steps which reduced its influence in 1938 and 1939. John L. Lewis restricted Harry Bridges' writ as CIO West Coast director to California. Allen Haywood replaced John Brophy as national director. Phil Murray eased Communist organizers out of the Steel Workers. And most significantly, Sidney Hillman and Phil Murray, the CIO's representatives to the troubled UAW's 1939 convention, served the Party its hardest pill to swallow. They opposed both Party ally George Addes and Party member Wyndham Mortimer for union president. A Party delegation led by Earl Browder and including Louis Budenz, Bill Gebert, and Roy Hudson ordered the Party members at the convention to support the CIO's choice, R. J. Thomas, an old Martin ally.[60]

The fact that they tried to keep a low profile and accommodated the wishes of the CIO leadership does not mean that the Communists' role in the CIO was unimportant. It was precisely because they got so many benefits from being an integral part of such a large labor organization that they were so careful not to endanger their place. For the first time in its history the Party could claim that it was not only in touch with the union movement, but helping to lead it. There was no need to confront non-Communist labor leaders; the Party's policies were in congruence with theirs. Party leaders consulted with union leaders. Union leaders hired, promoted, and aided fellow Communists, using a patronage system to spread Party influence in the unions they ran. Along with many of their non-Communist brethren they signed appeals and open letters, lending a cachet of labor legitimacy to a variety of Party fronts and causes. They introduced and steered to passage resolutions faithful to the Communist vision of the world and its problems within their unions and, occasionally, within the CIO. No other organization so critical in American society had so strong a Communist influence.

14

States Left

URING the Popular Front, resistance to working with the Party crumbled nearly everywhere on the American left. No better gauge of the Communists' rise from the pariahs of American life is available than the willingness of politicians to cooperate with the Party. To New Deal ideologues committed to reform, the Communists were useful, even welcome allies. To some practical politicians they were disciplined, organized, tireless workers able to mobilize voters and turn them out on election day. Even the Popular Front, however, was not enough to dissipate all the ill will and hostility the Communist party had created in less than twenty years. Significant segments of American society hated and feared Communists, for good reasons and bad. There were risks in accepting Communist support, of which most politicians were quite cognizant. The Party's fortunes varied from state to state, depending not only on the strength of the local Communists but on the political configuration in each area. The comparatively large Illinois Party made hardly a dent in the powerful Democratic machine in Chicago, while the much smaller Washington Communists played a critical role in the wild and woolly politics of the Pacific Northwest. New York State's peculiar electoral system made it easier for the Party to become a crucial factor in Empire State politics. And the open, fluid Party system in maverick Minnesota aided the party in its infiltration of the Farmer-Labor movement.

Washington State

No state proved as congenial to the Popular Front as Washington. One standard quip was that there were "47 states in the Union and the soviet of Washington." In no other state did so many Party members win election to the legislature or wield as much power within the Democratic party. The instrument through which the Communists achieved so much success was the Washington Commonwealth Federation.[1]

Until the Depression, Washington was a securely Republican state. Inspired by the Democrats' 1932 success and Upton Sinclair's capture of the California Democratic party in 1934, members of Technocracy, the Seattle Unemployed Citizens League, and other radical groups founded the Commonwealth Builders, Inc. (CBI), in August 1934. The CBI endorsed production for use, not profit, and set out to capture the Washington Democratic party. Its dominant figure was a Seattle barber named Howard Costigan. Born in Seattle in 1904, Costigan became a radical after witnessing a massacre of Wobblies in Centralia, Washington, in 1919. A fervent supporter of Franklin Roosevelt, he started a regular radio program and quickly become the CBI's most prominent personality. A CBI-endorsed senatorial candidate, Lewis Schwellenbach, won a Senate seat in 1934. Numerous CBI supporters were elected to the state legislature, where, outnumbered and outmaneuvered, they clashed with the regular Democrats led by Governor Clarence Martin.[2]

Nearly all of this activity passed the Communists by. The Washington Party was small and isolated. In 1933 Morris Raport was sent to Seattle to succeed Alex Noral as district organizer. Born I. M. Rappaport, of Russian-Jewish origin, he had once been a Wobbly but had joined the Communist party in Canada in 1920. Until the inauguration of the Popular Front, he had little success. The Party candidate for mayor of Seattle in 1934 got only 1,792 votes. The average number of monthly dues payments for 1934 from District 12—which included Washington, Oregon, and Idaho—was 1,426. Moreover, the Party's hostility to any independent Farmer-Labor movement had led it to denounce the Commonwealth Builders as fascist and following in the footsteps of Hitler and Mussolini. When Earl Browder came out for a Labor party in early 1935, the Washington Communists obediently pressed efforts for unity with the CBI. At its first convention in March 1935, however, the Builders adopted a resolution banning Communists from membership. When the CBI's successor, the Washington Commonwealth Federation (WCF), held its first convention in October 1935, an uninvited Party delegate, there to propose a united front, was refused a seat. Works Progress Administration (WPA) project unions, led by Communists, were denied affiliation or expelled from the WCF in early 1936.[3]

Morris Raport nonetheless told local Communists that their major task was the "building of the Washington Commonwealth Federation." During the 1936 mayoral contest in Seattle, the Party endorsed the WCF candidate. Despite the ban on Communists, some Party members were delegates to the April 1936 WCF convention representing labor or fraternal groups. The convention lifted the prohibition by simply not repassing the exclusionary rule. Soon, Bill Dobbins, a Communist representing the Project Workers' Unions, was on the WCF board, as was E. Harold Eby, a professor at the University of Washington and editor of the last volume of Vernon Parrington's *Main Currents of American Thought* who had secretly joined the Party in 1935. More than anything else, however, it was the conversion of Howard Costigan, executive director of the WCF, to the cause of Communism that gave the Party its entrée.[4]

As the Party reconciled itself to Roosevelt, Costigan saw its virtues. "I didn't join the Communist Party in the true sense of the term," he later told congressional investigators. "The Party joined me." Sometime in 1936 he approached Morris Raport and became a Communist. With Costigan's support, the Party, already active in the WCF, quickly became the single most powerful force in the organization. In the 1936 elections, the Party supported all the WCF candidates, running only a gubernatorial candidate to oppose Governor Martin. Morris Raport gleefully reported that the Party "devoted all its energy to building the Federation and defeating the reactionary forces." While it was not affiliated, the Communist party "is an integral part of the Commonwealth Federation."[5]

Over the next three years the Communist party's influence in the WCF continued to grow. The strongest CIO unions in the state were led by either Communists or fellow travelers. They included the ILWU, the International Woodworkers of America, and the Inland Boatmen's Union. Several A.F. of L. locals, including the American Federation of Teachers at the University of Washington, and the Building Service Employees' Union—whose international vice president was Carl Bradley, the Communist party's 1934 senatorial candidate—had a significant Party presence. The unions were not the only WCF affiliates to supply a Communist influence. The Workers' Alliance, which claimed to have 10,000 members, was led by Harold Brockway, an avowed Party member, and by H. C. Armstrong, who later testified that he had joined the Party in 1936. Moreover, in June 1937 Costigan launched the Old Age Pension

Union (OAPU) to enlist the elderly and lobby and negotiate on their behalf with public agencies. Within a year the OAPU had 20,000 members and it soon grew to 38,000, making it the largest affiliate of the WCF. Its first leaders were not Communists, although one testified that he was so close to the Party that he attended fraction meetings. A year after the OAPU was launched, however, William Pennock was appointed its director.[6]

Bill Pennock was one of the WCF's brightest young men. Recently graduated from the University of Washington, he had been coopted into the leadership of the WCF. Soon, he not only was the organization's treasurer but represented youth on the WCF Executive Board. Although he seemed an unlikely choice to head an organization of old people, Pennock had one important credential. According to his own later testimony, since late 1936 he had been a secret member of the Communist party. Following Pennock's accession, the OAPU was inundated by Communist party members, including its president in 1939, State Senator N. P. Atkinson.[7]

Their control of many of the WCF affiliates and the aid of such Party members as Costigan gave the Communists a commanding position within the federation itself. Not only was Costigan executive secretary, but Communists soon dominated the Executive Board and the staff. Costigan later estimated that by 1937, fifty-six of the seventy-two members of the board were Communists. One Communist who worked on *The Washington New Dealer,* the WCF organ, later guessed that 90 percent of its staff were Party members; both of its editors were Communists.[8]

The Communist leadership exulted over its new status. Raport told readers of *The Communist* that the WCF could boast "more achievements than had ever before been accomplished by any liberal group" during the 1937 legislative session. With one-third of the seats in the House, the WCF bloc had engineered repeal of the state criminal syndicalism law, as well as passage of a graduated income tax amendment, a state employee minimum wage law, a pure food and drug act, and a measure authorizing an increase in relief expenditures. The 1938 elections brought even more good news. Bucking a nationwide conservative trend, the WCF not only gained control of the state Democratic convention but doubled its membership in the state House and tripled it in the Senate. The WCF was now, Raport boasted, "the dominant factor in the Democratic Party" and "the vanguard of the New Deal forces." Between 1936 and 1939, riding on WCF coattails, a host of Communists were elected to the state legislature. Witnesses later identified eleven House members and three senators as secret Communists. Fraction meetings were held under the auspices of the Committee on Dykes, Drains and Ditches, the innocuous committee to which the regular Democrats who controlled the legislature often consigned left-wingers.[9]

The Communist party did not reach these successes unchallenged. Both regular Democrats and Republicans bitterly assailed the WCF as Communist-dominated. During the 1938 elections, the WCF's opponents in the primary labeled the federation a "Trojan Horse for the Communist Party." In the general election, Raport complained, "Stalin and Browder were the most publicized men in the campaign." Despite all its advances, the WCF was never able to control the legislature; even after the 1938 elections it was dominated by a coalition of conservative Democrats and Republicans, and WCF candidates were unable to win the governorship. WCF candidates also went down to defeat in the 1938 elections in Seattle.[10]

The Communist party also had to achieve its successes secretly. Relatively few of the Communists in the Washington Commonwealth Federation, the Old Age Pension Union, the labor movement, or the legislature acknowledged their affiliation. Raport had indiscreetly boasted in *The Communist* in April 1937 that "known Communists have leading positions" in the WCF and that "many of the leaders are Communists." A local newspaper taxed Costigan with these and other assertions of Party influence. Costigan proceeded to deny that *any* avowed Communists were members of the WCF and also asserted that he did not sympathize with Communist aims or "I would be a member of the Communist Party." For his part, Raport called such Communists as Dobbins, Eby, and Pennock "prominent liberals and progressives" and insisted that they "had absolutely no connection with the Communist Party or any of its activities." A year later Costigan added: "I am not a member of the Communist Party and have never been a member of the Communist Party." Kathryn Fogg, a state legislator, testified that she had joined the Party in 1937 as a secret member. H. C. Armstrong had become a Communist in 1936 but never carried a card; it was kept at Party headquarters. Pennock did not openly avow his membership; neither did future congressman Hugh DeLacy, a Communist elected to the Seattle City Council in 1937 who became WCF president.[11]

Actual membership in the Communist party, while it grew appreciably between 1936 and 1939, was always modest. From 1,137 in 1936, membership remained stagnant until early 1937. It reached 1,714 by mid-year and 2,115 by early 1938. By the end of that year there were 1,800 members in King County (Seattle) alone. Membership doubled in 1938 to 5,016 and continued to grow in the first half of 1939. But Washington Communist leaders themselves worried that their advances had been bought at a price. Louis Sass complained that Party building had not kept pace with the advances in mass work. Instead of hiding their allegiances, Party members needed to recruit from among their contacts: "Certainly, we don't want our comrades to become careless [and] recruit indiscriminately but we do expect them to approach those in whom they have complete confidence and trust." And Raport worried that "while individual comrades are accepted as leaders of the non-Party organizations, our Party itself does not appear independently in the day-to-day struggles."[12]

Perhaps nowhere else in the country was the Communist party as successful in building the Democratic Front as in Washington. Without insisting on formal recognition of their role, Communists not only helped to forge organizations committed to support of the New Deal and the CIO but came to dominate them. Washington Communists discovered just how open and permeable American political parties were. "You are a member of whatever you say you are," Terry Pettus recalled, explaining how a relatively small group of activists could win control of a large segment of the Democratic party. One witness before Washington's Canwell Committee told of attending a Democratic precinct meeting where he and his wife were startled to discover they were the only non-Communists present. Combined with their avid support for the New Deal, such tactics enabled the Communists to make startling gains in the state.[13]

Minnesota

Minnesota Communists faced a more difficult and treacherous road in constructing their version of the Popular Front. They had more than a decade of activity to live down. As far back as 1924, Minnesota Farmer-Laborites had learned, to their sorrow, the dangers of coalitions with the Communists. During the Third Period the Party heaped even more scorn on the Farmer-Labor party. Floyd Olson, who was elected governor in 1930, 1932, and 1934, was the Communists' favorite target. Olson was pilloried as a social-fascist, accused of working with Trotskyists, denounced as a strikebreaker, called an "unscrupulous demagogue," and so forth. The Farmer-Labor party itself was variously slandered as fascist, social-fascist, anti-labor, and "bourgeois progressive," depending on the Party line of the moment.[14]

Prior to the Popular Front, the Party somewhat modified its rhetoric and changed its tactics. However, the new line on the Farmer-Labor party that was developed in 1934 and 1935 was hardly calculated to win many friends for the Communists. In accordance with the idea of building a united front from below, they called upon members of the Farmer-Labor party to overthrow their leadership, adopt a militant, revolutionary program, and then join the Communists in building a better world. The Central Committee adopted a resolution in August 1935 that divined a growing split in the FLP between workers and farmers on the one hand, and party leaders, politicians, and union bureaucrats on the other. While conceding that "this class differentiation does not yet express itself in the acceptance by the workers and farmers of the entire program of the Communist Party and the revolutionary way out," the document urged Communists to provide leadership and programs for the masses that were now moving leftward. An accompanying editorial in the Minnesota Communist newspaper advised militant Farmer-Laborites to remain in their party but also to join the Communist party, in order to prepare the ground for the overthrow of capitalism and the inauguration of Soviet power in America.[15]

The same resolution gave marching orders to local Communists to join the Farmer-Labor Association (FLA), the organizational arm of the FLP. It was "advisable for Communists and Communist sympathizers to strive to secure the official nomination on local tickets of the Farmer-Labor Party in the coming municipal elections," and it was also "advisable that the Party should strive to secure the election of Communists and militant workers and farmers as representatives of their organizations to county and local executive committees where the policies and decisions of the Farmer-Labor Party are discussed and formulated."[16]

The Minnesota Communists were not without resources. For years they had been the largest of the Party's state units, and the Finns of northern Minnesota had been the Communists' backbone. Other Party members lived in the Minneapolis–St. Paul area. By 1935 defections had taken a toll, however, and their numbers were not large. Nat Ross, sent to Minnesota as district organizer in July 1935, later estimated that there were 500–700 members in the whole state when he arrived; just under 1,000 Communists registered in January 1936. Ross himself was symbolic of the new American-born Communists who were coming to play a greater role in the Party during the Popular Front days. Born in New

York to Russian Jewish immigrants, he attended Columbia University on a scholarship, graduating Phi Beta Kappa in 1927. A year's stay at Harvard Law School was followed by graduate study for a doctorate at Columbia. There, Ross became active in Communist front organizations such as the International Labor Defense and the Anti-Imperialist League. Leaving Columbia in 1929, he joined the Communist party just before the Wall Street crash. Early in 1930, Browder sent him to southern Illinois as a Party organizer. After one year he was promoted to section organizer in Indianapolis. A year later he was assigned to Birmingham as district organizer for Alabama, Georgia, Tennessee, and Mississippi. It was taxing and dangerous work. Ross and his wife changed residences every few months, accepted no visitors, and carefully hid their real activities. After three years of this regimen he was transferred to Minnesota.[17]

Following the Seventh Congress, the Communists began to make their peace with the Farmer-Labor party. On October 18, 1935, Browder passed through Minneapolis on a speaking tour and held a secret meeting with Governor Olson. They reached an understanding. The Party's Minnesota District Committee adopted a resolution entitled "Build the FLP" early in December. It hailed the Farmer-Labor party as an answer to the failures of the New Deal. With not a trace of humor or shame, the Minnesota Communists charged that "the capitalist parties slander the Farmer-Labor Party and its leaders. By various insidious methods they are trying to disrupt the Farmer-Labor Party from within." The Communists' only concession to their past behavior was to admit "that in relation to the Minnesota Farmer-Labor Party some serious mistakes were made in the past," mistakes that had led the Party to isolate itself. Now "the Communists will support the Farmer-Labor state administration and all those Farmer-Labor public officials who will help to improve the conditions of the toilers."[18]

The bitter attacks on Olson and his programs ceased. In return, Olson and the left wing of the Farmer-Labor Association welcomed the Communist party as a legitimate partner in Minnesota politics. Communist delegates were seated at a Conference for Progressive Social Legislation, held on November 30 and December 1, 1935, to draw up a list of measures to be considered by the legislature. Earl Browder and Clarence Hathaway were invited to the May 30, 1936, meeting in Chicago called by the Minnesota Farmer-Laborites to discuss a national ticket in 1936, despite the fact that their presence led several notable third-party advocates to stay away.[19]

Most importantly, however, Olson let down the bars to Communist membership in the Farmer-Labor Association. Since 1925 a clause in its constitution had denied entry to anyone who advocated the violent overthrow of the government or opposed representative democracy. Since early 1935 the Party had encouraged its members to try to join local FLA clubs. Now the FLA welcomed them. In January 1936, forty-two Finnish Workers Clubs dominated by the Party affiliated themselves with the FLA. Joe Moreland, a Communist organizer in northern Minnesota, boasted that he and four other Communists were delegates to the forthcoming state Farmer-Labor convention. Although Moreland—under his real name of Joe Van Nordstrand he became state CIO secretary-treasurer in 1938—decided not to attend when the Farmer-Labor State Committee pointed to the constitutional bar on Communists, the Party was well represented at the gathering in April. Nat Ross claimed that forty Communists were delegates. Clarence Hathaway returned to his old haunts, conferred with Olson, and guided the Party caucus. The Communists supported Olson, and he helped defeat an effort to expel them. The Party and the left wing of the Farmer-Labor movement had come to an informal agreement and alliance.[20]

There was a brief hitch caused by Olson's support for FDR early in 1936. Clarence Hathaway complained that Olson was moving too close to the Democratic party in return for New Deal endorsement of the FLP and arranged to have Nat Ross file for Congress in the Farmer-Labor primary against Dewey Johnson as a "warning" that the Communists could not be taken for granted. Hathaway also delivered a blistering attack on Minnesota Communists for "right opportunism" and being too apologetic about their past errors. Their slogan, "Build the F-L-P," had to be transformed. He attacked Olson and announced that "our sharp and justified criticisms in the past" were correct. This temporary reversion to the past did not last long; on Browder's advice, Ross withdrew from the congressional contest and the Communists enthusiastically supported the Farmer-Labor candidate.[21]

The Popular Front got greater impetus as a result of the 1936 elections. Just after the Communist party's embrace of the Farmer-Labor party in December 1935, Governor Olson appointed his banking commissioner, a small-town banker and lawyer named Elmer Benson, to a vacant seat in the U.S. Senate. After Olson's death in August 1936, Benson won the governorship. Ernest Lundeen, who had collaborated with the Party on unemployment legislation, was elected to the Senate, and the FLP gained five House seats and improved its standing in the legislature. Following the election, Browder held up the state as a model: "Where our strategy was realized in its most satisfactory form—as in Minnesota—we had no state ticket at all, but were among the most effective campaigners for the Farmer-Labor ticket."[22]

From 1936 until Hubert Humphrey engineered their expulsion in 1948, Communists played a major role in the Farmer-Labor Association and, through it, the Farmer-Labor party. For two short years, from 1936 to 1938, the Party enjoyed a status it had never before attained in any American state. The People's Front in Minnesota did not achieve as large a mass base as in Washington, nor did as many Communists, concealed or open, rise to positions of political influence. Yet, in no other state in the Union did the Communists have so intimate a relationship with the executive branch and the political party that controlled it. The major factor in the Party's success was the friendliness of the Olson and Benson administrations. Both governors gave Nat Ross money for organizing work. Both put Communists on the state payroll. Orville Olson, a secret Communist, was hired as personnel director of the state Highway Department, a major source of patronage, and during the Benson administration he served as the Party's link to the FLA. Both of Benson's closest advisers and confidants, Abe Harris and Roger Rutchick, were Popular Fronters. Rutchick, Benson's executive secretary, was accused of attending a closed fraction meeting in 1936 and had close ties to Nat Ross. Neither Harris nor Rutchick, however, had to manipulate Elmer Benson. He enthusiastically supported Party causes. His picture graced *The Daily Worker* nearly every day in the spring of 1937. That summer he flew to New York to lead a large American League Against War and Fascism rally. He had Communist leaders like Sam Darcy, sent to Minnesota as a Central Committee representative, to dinner at his house.[23]

At the same time, Communists became a significant factor in the Farmer-Labor Association itself. Many clubs were small, and an influx of Party members could easily overwhelm them. Not only were the Communists hard workers, but many were very capable speakers and organizers. Farmer-Laborites frequently welcomed the Communists as militant progressives and anti-fascists. In some cases they knew with whom they were dealing. In others cases, they did not. Many Communists chose to keep their affiliations secret, since no one publicly identified as a Communist could play a role in the state administration or in the higher echelons of the FLP. As a result, an advocate of the Popular Front in the FLA might be either a Popular Front liberal or a Communist.[24]

At least as important in solidifying Communist strength in the FLP was the rise of the CIO. Unions wielded a significant bloc of votes in the

FLA; after 1937, many of them were led by Communists. In northern Minnesota Ilmar Koivunen, a Communist, led the lumberjacks in the International Woodworkers of America. The chief CIO steel organizers on the Mesabi Range were Martin Mackie, a well-known Communist, and Joe Van Nordstrand, who had been a Party organizer. When the two were replaced by Phil Murray in 1938, Van Nordstrand became secretary-treasurer of the state CIO. In the Twin Cities area, the two largest locals in the state, both in the United Electrical Workers, were led by secret Communists—Bill Mauseth and Bob Wishart. Communists dominated the Duluth and Hennepin County CIO councils. Sam K. Davis, the Party's candidate for governor in 1934, edited *Midwest Labor*, the CIO's organ. Even the Minneapolis A.F. of L. had a Communist core. Swan Asserson and Bob Kelley, both Communists, led Local 665 of the Hotel and Restaurant Workers Union. James Flowers of the building trades union and several other representatives of the Central Labor Union (CLU) were also Party members. Others in the CLU occasionally or frequently cooperated with the Party. All in all, it was not hard to see why Gene Dennis insisted that "the most advanced and progressive Farmer-Labor Party movement in the United States" was in Minnesota.[25]

The Minnesota People's Front encountered trouble, however, almost as soon as Benson became governor. Within a few months of his inauguration, assorted political errors by both Popular Fronters and Communists had emboldened anti-Communists in the FLA. Some of the problems were not entirely of the Party's making. The final split between the A.F. of L. and the CIO produced strains in the FLA, since neither Benson nor the Farmer-Laborites made any secret about which unions had their sympathies. As they drew closer to the CIO, such one-time strongholds of the FLA as the St. Paul Federated Trades and Labor Assembly and the Duluth A.F. of L. Council began to withdraw their support. Members of the latter were particularly irritated by Congressman John Bernard, who not only enthusiastically championed the Popular Front but also remained on the Steel Workers Organizing Committee payroll as an organizer during his term in Washington.

Meanwhile, a powerful Trotskyist movement caused further difficulties in the Minneapolis Central Labor Union. Led by the Dunne brothers, Teamsters Local 544 was both hostile to the Popular Front and reluctant to cooperate with the Farmer-Labor party. To these antipathies was added the loathing that Communists and Trotskyists felt for each other. Early in 1937, Farmer-Labor Mayor Thomas Latimer of Minneapolis, a member of the American Committee for the Defense of Leon Trotsky, was denied re-endorsement by the local FLA, which was dominated by Communists and their allies. Instead, it nominated Kenneth Haycraft, a liberal willing to work with the Party. Angry A.F. of L. unions, Trotskyists, and moderate Farmer-Laborites bolted the convention and held their own rump meeting to nominate Latimer. However, the FLA State Committee not only accepted the Haycraft nomination but tabled a resolution of opposition to the Communist party. Haycraft won a very close primary election before losing overwhelmingly to a Republican in the general election.[26]

The Popular Front encountered other problems. Governor Benson himself was a poor politician—stubborn, bellicose, short-tempered, and self-righteous—who hardly seemed to care that he was offending an important segment of his party's support. In remarkably short order, he was frightening Minnesota citizens with the help of the Communist party. After the 1936 elections, Clarence Hathaway had urged a "people's lobby" to push reform legislation through to law. With his own ambitious legislative program stalled, Benson gave his blessing to the idea in early April. The People's Lobby was led by John Bosch of the Farm Holiday Association and drew endorsement from a number of CIO unions and the FLA. On April 4, 2,500 people met in St. Paul. The next day they marched to the state capital and pushed their way into a Senate room, dispersing a few legislators. Some 200 demonstrators, Communists prominent among them, camped in the Senate Chamber for the night. Early the following morning Benson stopped by, told them they had "done a good job," and asked them to leave, which they did. The damage, however, had been done. Angry legislators, indignant newspapers, and even some Farmer-Laborites were outraged. Nat Ross, however, exulted that the action "brought greater sections of the masses into close contact with the known Communist leaders in the mass organizations."[27]

The episode also fueled the growing hostility within the FLA toward both Communists and Benson. Hjalmar Petersen, once Olson's lieutenant governor, orchestrated that hostility in 1938. Starting a campaign to deny Benson renomination, he charged that the governor had welcomed Communists "with open arms." Aware of their vulnerability, the Communists were far less visible in 1938. They toned down their claims of influence. No article dealing with Minnesota appeared in *The Communist* between June 1937 and October 1938. The 1938 FLA platform was positively mild compared to its predecessors. At the state convention, Benson managed to avoid an open discussion of the Communist role in the FLA.[28]

That role was not public. Immediately after the 1936 election, Martin Young had addressed a letter to the Central Committee complaining that "our relations with [the FLP] was not political nor normal." Instead, "it was more or less a relationship with the top, very secretive not only to masses at large, but even to our own membership and sympathizers." Party membership in May 1938 was only 2,100, twice as many as in early 1936 but hardly a force to reckon with. What made the number significant was that four secret members sat in the state House and one in the Senate, others dominated the large CIO unions and several A.F. of L. unions, and still others held high positions in the FLA or were close to the governor.[29]

In the early spring of 1938, Sam Darcy, sent to Minnesota as the Central Committee's representative, attempted to challenge the backdoor relationship between the Party and the Farmer-Laborites. He privately convinced Benson that public criticism of the Farmer-Labor programs by the Party would defuse much of the Communist issue. He wrote Browder asking that Communists withdraw from the FLA and stop running for election as Farmer-Laborites. By making it clear that the Communist party supported the FLP but did not want to dominate it, Darcy hoped to dampen the anti-Communist brushfire that threatened Benson. He received no direct reply. However, a few weeks later, at the Tenth Party Convention, Gil Green and Gene Dennis engineered Darcy's demotion from the Central Committee. Darcy soon transferred to a position in Philadelphia, angry that Browder planned "to transform the Communist Party into a semi-secret society for conniving in other organizations instead of an independent mass party of its own."[30]

Hjalmar Petersen failed to wrest the FLP nomination from Benson, by less than 20,000 votes. In the general election Harold Stassen buried the governor by nearly 300,000 votes out of the 1.1 million cast. Most FLP congressmen went down to defeat with Benson. The rout energized anti-Communists in the FLA. Surviving officeholders wanted to be rid of the Communist albatross before they next faced the electorate. Old allies like Senator Ernest Lundeen, still an isolationist, had no use for the Party's new emphasis on collective security. The FLA state committee ordered enforcement of the constitutional provision barring Communists from membership. Although the Communists and their allies counterattacked, at the February 1939 state convention the anti–Popular Front forces won control, declared Communists and Nazis ineligible for membership, placed restrictions on affiliates designed to eliminate the Workers' Alliance and ethnic-cultural clubs dominated by the Party, and expelled fourteen delegates for having signed Communist petitions in 1936. Yet, the Popular Front was not over in Minnesota. Communists remained powerful within the state CIO, and they and their allies retained control of some FLA centers. The Party's political power, however, had badly waned.[31]

New York

The Party did not have as much success in New York, the heartland of American Communism, where it was dwarfed by well-oiled political machines in many city governments and in the labor unions. Not that the Communists were without influence. They were a potent force in the American Labor party (ALP), which quickly gained the balance of power in state elections. The ALP was created in 1936 as a vehicle to aid the reelection of Franklin Roosevelt. Many of the one-time Socialist leaders of the garment unions were preparing to support the President, who had done so much for labor, but they wanted to endorse Roosevelt without voting for him on a Democratic line traditionally identified with corruption. Many Jews and Italians, long resentful of the Irish dominance of Tammany Hall, resisted identification with the Democratic party. The solution was suggested by New York's unique election laws, which enabled a new political party to obtain a line on the ballot while still nominating the same candidate or candidates as a major party. Since the votes received from two or more parties could be added together, Roosevelt could simultaneously be the Democratic candidate and the ALP candidate. This allowed radicals, municipal reformers, and trade unionists to support him without the pain of pulling a Democratic lever. The real importance of the ALP was its role in state and municipal elections, where its threat not to nominate the Democratic candidate (or, occasionally, a Republican), and thereby to draw off enough votes to throw the race to the opposing party, made the major parties take its wishes into account.

The Communist party faced both personal and institutional roadblocks to establishing close ties to the new party. The ALP's leadership was largely drawn from New York's needle trade unions, traditionally bastions of anti-Communism. One of the groups that had members in the ALP was the Social-Democratic Federation, the "Old Guard" breakaway from the Socialist party. Moreover, as a new political party the ALP did not yet have to answer to its membership; party leaders ran it as they saw fit. There was also an explicit ban on Communist members of the party.[32]

None of these obstacles prevented the Communist party from sending its members into the ALP. The first barrier to fall was the new party's support for Roosevelt's reelection. In May 1936, Alexander Bittelman was critical of both Sidney Hillman and David Dubinsky for their support of the President. By August he noted that the Communist party and the ALP had "one central thing in common"—beating Landon. Early that month, two Party-dominated groups, the Trade Union Committee for a Farmer-Labor Party and the People's Committee for a Farmer-Labor Party, announced their intention to affiliate with the ALP. Shortly after the election, state Party leader Israel Amter indicated that "the building of the American Labor Party is a central task" for the Communists.[33]

Intent on defeating Tammany Hall in 1937, the Communist party even supported the ALP's mayoral candidate, Fiorello LaGuardia. For years the feisty mayor of New York had been subjected to a stream of abuse such as only the Communists could provide. He was, variously, one of many "bourgeois politicians parading as progressives," a master "at the strikebreaking art," "the Bankers' Mayor," and the nearest thing to a fascist in New York. During the spring and summer of 1934, *Daily Worker* readers outside of New York might well have imagined that the White Terror had come to town. A front-page editorial called "For United Action Against LaGuardia's 'Economy'-Fascization Program." One news story was headlined: "LaGuardia Cops Beat Fur Union Leader Unconscious." Another front-page editorial noted, with a bow to history, that "the LaGuardia Administration, in its rapidly advancing attacks on the workers, has now taken as its model police methods of the darkest days of czarist Russia." While the Party offered "unconditional support" to all ALP nominees in 1937, it was restrained about LaGuardia. The best that Israel Amter could find to say about the Little Flower was that his "record certainly is an advance over the reactionary Tammany administration that preceded him." Still, the Party announced the withdrawal of virtually all its own candidates in order to support him and the ALP.[34]

The election returns demonstrated that the Party had become a significant bloc in the American Labor party, which had itself become a potent force in the city. LaGuardia won reelection by some 452,000 votes; he received 482,000 on the ALP line, or 36 percent of his total vote. Twenty-two percent of the entire vote cast was given to the ALP. Four of its nominees were elected to the City Council, including Mike Quill. Although the Party had endorsed the ALP ticket and dropped most of its own candidates, it had kept one council candidate in each borough in the race to test its appeal. It was able to do so without harming the election chances of its ALP allies because of New York's peculiar system of proportional representation for the council, adopted in 1936. The Party called on its supporters to "Vote Labor and Communist" by casting a first-choice ballot for the Party and second- and third-place choices for ALP candidates. Israel Amter got 18,325 first-place votes in Manhattan, Isadore Begun 20,946 in the Bronx, Pete Cacchione 30,235 in Brooklyn, and Paul Crosbie 4,609 in Queens. True to Party pleas, most of this vote went to ALP candidates as the Party members lost. Cacchione missed election to the council by less than 500 votes. The Party's 74,115 first-place votes were more than 15 percent of the ALP's total vote for La-Guardia and 21.9 percent of the total first-place votes for Communist, Socialist, and ALP candidates. Compared with 2.6 percent of the first-place votes in 1936, the Party had gotten 4.6 percent in 1937. "The Communist Party vote," an editorial declared, "was decisive in the Labor Party victory. The ALP leaders should concern themselves with these considerations."[35]

There were other reasons for Communist cheer about the results. The Socialists had hesitated about joining the LaGuardia coalition before belatedly climbing on the ALP bandwagon. Their councilmanic candidates fared poorly, finishing twelfth to the Communist's fifth-place showing in Brooklyn and twenty-fifth to the Party's eleventh in Manhattan. The Socialists had less than half the first-place votes garnered by the Communists. Thomas Dewey, a young Republican lawyer, won election as district attorney in Manhattan. The Communist party did not formally endorse him, but he was, Charles Krumbein noted happily, "a labor-supported nominee." Dewey's Trade Union Committee was headed by Louis Weinstock, a Communist leader in the Painters' Union. Dewey, Browder later recalled, asked for and got Communist support.[36]

Once the election returns had been digested, the Party was more convinced than ever that its decision to cooperate with all progressive forces, including selected Democrats and Republicans, was sound. Shortly after the elections, Stanley Isaacs, President-elect of the Borough of Manhattan and a LaGuardia Republican, appointed Simon Gerson, *The Daily Worker*'s city hall correspondent, as "confidential inspector" and put him in charge of press relations. The twenty-eight-year-old Gerson, an open Communist who served on the Party's State Executive Committee, was a veteran of the YCL. His Party career had included a stint in Gastonia during the textile strike in 1929. Despite protests, Gerson kept his position for three years.[37]

The Party regarded its new status as confirmation of the value of coalition politics. Speaking to a plenum shortly after the election, Browder called the ALP campaign one "approximating that which the Communist Party has been urging for two years—the People's Front Policy." Charles Krumbein saw the election as a "laboratory" in which the new line had been tested. In a speech inaugurating the Democratic Front, Browder was even more effusive, citing the results as "the outstanding example of the possibilities of labor's political action." Enthusiasm for LaGuardia also picked up. One *Daily Worker* correspondent praised the mayor as having been a New Dealer before FDR; by early 1939, Browder was including him in a holy trinity with Roosevelt and Lewis as the stalwarts of the progressive camp.[38]

The Communists brought several valuable assets to the ALP. New York was home to the largest concentration of Communists in America, 30,000 by 1938. Together with Party sympathizers, they constituted a significant and disciplined voting bloc. Most read at least one Party publication every day. They could be quickly mobilized. Since New York served as headquarters not only for the national Party but also for innumerable auxiliaries, the city was filled with functionaries able and willing to devote time to political organizing, literature distribution, and the directing of volunteers. The city CIO was dominated by Party-influenced unions that provided additional manpower—the NMU, TWU, UOPWA, State, County and Municipal Workers and Fur Workers. A number of A.F. of L. unions—the AFT, Painters, and Hotel and Restaurant Workers—fell in the same category. The Party also skillfully played on New York's ethnic loyalties. In Harlem, Adam Clayton Powell was favorably disposed to the Popular Front. Vito Marcantonio, a close Party ally, was a hero to Italians; Mike Quill flaunted his Irish heritage.

None of this would, by itself, have prevented an anti-Communist campaign in the ALP. The needle trades leaders had not hesitated to combat large Communist factions within their own unions. They certainly knew who the Communists and their sympathizers were. Although many of the CIO leaders did not advertise their Party ties, secrecy was not as prevalent as in Washington or Minnesota. What comforted the ALP leadership was how self-effacing the Party was. It made no waves within the ALP. Its members did not challenge Party policy or defy its decisions. Instead, the Communists willingly, cheerfully, and enthusiastically supported the New Deal, both domestically and internationally.

The 1938 election campaign demonstrated just how accommodating the Party could be. The Communists disliked Democratic Governor Herbert Lehman; his public opposition to Roosevelt's court-packing plan demonstrated a serious flaw to them. Charles Krumbein even argued against giving Lehman support. Yet, once the ALP nominated him, Krumbein and the Communists fell in line: "Notwithstanding a few acts that aided the reactionaries," Krumbein explained, "he remains a man of liberal persuasion." Rather than be isolated, the Party was ready to support a politician for whom it had little enthusiasm. Its only complaints were that the ALP had not done more to broaden its appeal beyond Italians, Jews, and CIO members and that it lacked sufficient internal democracy. But, Israel Amter hastened to add, "Our interests do not lie apart from those of the progressives." Even Eugene Lyons, who pleaded with the ALP leaders to oust the Communists, admitted: "It's small consolation that for the most part, at this stage, the Communist strength is not directed against the interests of the ALP." But, he warned, this strength was a "loaded gun" pointed at the heart of the party.[39]

Just how potent the Party had become was demonstrated on election day. In most states, Party candidates had been withdrawn from the ballot. A few had been left on to test public sentiment, among them Israel Amter, who was running for congressman-at-large in New York State. He got 105,681 votes while Lehman received 418,979 on the ALP line. The Party thus represented one-quarter of the ALP vote, as *The Daily Worker* quickly noted, and its votes were, Browder claimed, the key to Lehman's victory over Dewey. Communists and Socialists were moving in opposite directions. In 1936 Amter had gotten some 65,000 votes for president of the Board of Aldermen in New York City; his 1938 vote was 97,000. Harry Laidler had received 47,051 votes for that position in 1936; the better-known Norman Thomas only got 18,000 votes for Congress in 1938.[40]

It was not only the Communists' growing electoral power in the ALP that concerned the Social Democratic Federation (SDF). Worried by the Communists' movement into ALP clubs, Eugene Lyons warned against "Communist Maranos" who "have succeeded in capturing many key district organizations of the American Labor Party." *The New Leader* denounced ALP support for Vito Marcantonio, a "communist stooge," in his bid to return to Congress. By May 1939 the SDF had adopted a public call for the ALP to enforce its constitutional provision against Communists, with Louis Waldman warning that Communists already controlled a majority of Manhattan clubs and many others in Brooklyn and the Bronx. Not until after the Nazi-Soviet Pact, however, would ALP leaders begin truly to fight the Communists. By then, they would discover to their chagrin, the Party was too firmly entrenched to be ousted.[41]

California

California Communists had been premature Popular Fronters, urging the Party to permit them to support Upton Sinclair for governor in 1934. Forced to attack Sinclair, the Communists had dangerously frayed what few ties they had built to progressives. Despite that burden, however, the Party had a number of assets to call on once the Comintern gave its permission for cooperation with non-Communists. The Party had led several years of struggle in the state's agricultural valleys, enabling a corps of young Communist organizers to gain invaluable organizing experience. Still another pre–Popular Front activity redounding to the Party's strength was its base in the International Longshoremen's and Warehousemen's Union (ILWU). The Party's activities on behalf of the imprisoned Tom Mooney had also enabled it to cooperate with a variety of non-Communists.

With only 2,500 members in 1936, the California Party had influence far beyond its numbers. Within just a few years, Communists and their close allies dominated the CIO. Harry Bridges was chosen its West Coast director. Don Healey, state head of Labor's Non-Partisan League—whose wife, Dorothy, held important positions in Party auxiliaries—was also a Party member. CIO state president Phil Connelly publicly denied Party membership but was a secret member. In addition to Bridges' ILWU, several other CIO unions in the state had a heavy Party influence, including the Cannery Workers, white-collar unions like the Newspaper Guild and the State, County and Municipal Workers, and such small maritime unions as the Marine Cooks and Stewards. The UAW's chief organizer in the state, Lew Michener, was close to the Communists; in 1939 he was supplemented by Wyndham Mortimer. An active Communist community in Hollywood, meanwhile, provided money and celebrities to the People's Front. Communists and liberals mingled in organizations like the Hollywood Anti-Nazi League and the Motion Picture Democratic Committee. The statewide Workers' Alliance had a different constituency but more members. By September 1939 its 186 locals had 12,000 dues-payers and claimed a total membership of 42,000, under the leadership of Alex Noral, formerly the Party's district organizer in Washington. Party membership grew during the Popular Front from 2,510 in early 1936 to 3,400 a year later, 5,300 in mid-1937, and 6,000 in 1938.[42]

These assets served the Party well as it built a relationship with liberal Democrats prior to the 1938 election. The Communists refused to nominate their own candidates unless no progressive was in the race. They were active in the Democratic Federation for Political Unity, which labored to elect Culbert Olson as governor. Bill Schneiderman boasted that the Party had become "an important factor and a recognized voice in the labor and progressive movement." Through it all, the Party was a voice for moderation. Although supporting Olson, Schneiderman insisted that "the democratic front cannot be limited only to the most advanced progressive elements" but had to include even moderate Democrats. "We Communists," he explained, "have been carrying on a struggle against a leftist sectarian approach." When civic reform groups undertook a recall campaign against the mayor of Los Angeles, the Party not only lauded the move as "a significant demonstration of the American democratic process at its best" but even endorsed Judge Fletcher Bowron, a conservative Republican who won the election. Schneiderman warned California labor to beware of employer efforts to provoke strikes to discredit the left; by following a policy of moderation, "using the strike weapon only as a last resort, public opinion can be rallied to place the responsibility where it really belongs."[43]

The Party's choice for governor, Culbert Olson, was a Los Angeles attorney whose first taste of state politics had come through the End Poverty in California movement. Elected to the State Senate in 1934, he earned a reputation as a liberal and a supporter of Popular Front causes. He used that reputation to win the Democratic gubernatorial nomination in a crowded field. Olson had few qualms about secretly meeting with Communist leaders to obtain their support. After he had become vociferously anti-Communist following the Nazi-Soviet Pact, Anita Whitney, one of the state's best-known Party members, publicly noted: "I would like to ask Governor Olson: When you met in your own home with the leaders of the Communist Party in 1938, and accepted our assistance and support for your election, you did not think we were anything but good Americans, did you?" Earl Browder, speaking to a meeting of the California Communist Party's Executive Committee in late August 1938, remarked: "The question of endorsing Olson—he doesn't want us to endorse him. Then we should not do it. There's more than one way to skin a cat." Whitney herself, running for state controller on the Communist ticket, received over 100,000 votes.[44]

Others in the Olson administration had a closer relationship to the Party. Several witnesses before state and federal committees testified that Lieutenant Governor Ellis Patterson was a Party member; he filed one libel suit denying the charges. Whether or not he belonged to the Party, Patterson was a devoted adherent of Communist positions. Starting out in politics as a liberal Republican member of the legislature, he had been repudiated by his own party in 1936 but won reelection as a write-in candidate. When he ran for lieutenant governor with the endorsement of Labor's Non-Partisan League, he gained the Democratic nomination in 1938 and swept to victory with the rest of the ticket as California, defying a nationwide turn to the right, elected its first Democratic administration in the twentieth century. Even before his inauguration Patterson was provoking controversy, speaking to Popular Front organizations and picketing ships carrying scrap iron to Japan. His New Deal ardor cooled considerably by 1940 when the Communists broke with the Roosevelt administration. In 1942 Patterson supported an avowed Communist running in the general election for state senator in Los Angeles, an act which did not prevent his own election to Congress in 1944. Carey McWilliams, head of the Division of Immigration and Housing, was accused of being a Party member. He denied the charges but did belong to more than a score of Party auxiliaries. The state's Young Democrats were heavily sprinkled with young Communists and their allies. A number of other political figures were close to the Party, including State Assemblyman Augustus Hawkins, later a congressman. By late 1938, Earl Browder was so pleased that he praised "the great work of our California Party which is better than any thesis in showing us the road to victory."[45]

It was the Communist issue in state government that helped discredit Olson's administration. California conservatives fumed about his pardon of three labor figures associated with the Party who were convicted of murder in 1937. By the time most of the hullabaloo took place, however, Olson no longer was in the Party's good graces. Olson's major headache was the State Relief Administration (SRA), the only large state agency not subject to civil service regulations. The SRA became the focus of a hunt for Communists. Many of its relief clients belonged to the Party-dominated Workers' Alliance. Its staff belonged to the Party-influenced State, County and Municipal Workers. Its administrators, one legislative committee charged, were using the SRA "for the development of the Communist program."[46]

The first investigation of the SRA in 1940 was led by a former Party ally. Sam Yorty had been a left-wing Democrat serving in the state legislature. One ex-Communist had named him as a Party member in 1936 and 1937. However, Yorty was embittered because the Party, despite its respect for this "militant New Deal state assemblyman," threw its support for mayor of Los Angeles in 1938 to a Republican in the interests of building the Democratic Front. He turned on the Communists. After Yorty's committee had finished savaging the SRA, State Senator Jack Tenney won approval for a more permanent "little Dies" committee. Like Yorty, Tenney had previously been accused of Party membership. President of his local musicians' union and composer of *Mexicali Rose*, he had once tried to repeal the state's criminal syndicalism statute and spoken before such groups as the Hollywood Anti-Nazi League. By the fall of 1939, however, a conflict within his local union resulted in his ouster. The embittered Tenney then supported a bill to remove the Communist party from the ballot, which Olson signed. The first Tenney Committee was set up in 1941; for the next two decades it pilloried Communists, radicals, and liberals alike with increasing bitterness and scant regard for the distinctions among them.[47]

The South

Nowhere in America did a People's Front face greater obstacles than in the South. Not only was the Communist party small, isolated, and hard pressed to keep free of Southern justice, but it was a largely Negro organization in a region where only whites held political and economic power. Its goal of self-determination for Negroes terrified most Southern whites, who regarded even the granting of political equality to be a revolutionary step. The Southern districts of the Party remained small and weak. In District 17, Alabama, "the Party is virtually illegal," one member wrote in 1934. District 16, encompassing North and South Carolina and portions of Virginia, only had about one hundred dues-paying members, half of them in Richmond and Norfolk.[48]

With few exceptions, the Party's Southern organizers were more noted for their courage than their talents. Few Southern states were important enough or had large enough memberships to justify the dispatching of leading cadres to supervise their activities. Alabama, with Nat Ross and Rob Hall, was an exception. Elsewhere, less seasoned or skilled Party members were in charge—W. G. Binkley in Louisiana, Jack Strong in Florida, Homer Brooks in Texas, and Ted Wellman in Tennessee. Paul Crouch, district organizer in the Carolinas and Virginia, did achieve notoriety, but not in the Party. A North Carolina native, Crouch was a Socialist when he joined the U.S. army in 1924 and arrived in Hawaii. Within a year he had been court-martialed for Communist activities and sentenced to forty years at hard labor. Released after three years at Alcatraz, he promptly joined the Communist party. He visited Russia, where he was photographed in a Red Army uniform, and directed the Party's anti-militarist work in the late 1920s. So promising a start did not soon lead to major Party appointments. Crouch spent nearly the next decade in Party backwaters, serving as district organizer first in Utah, then in the Carolinas. He moved to Alabama in 1938 to edit *The New South* and oversee the Party's work in the Southern Conference for Human Welfare. Two years as district organizer in Tennessee, from 1939 to 1941, were followed by a job as county organizer in Alameda County, California. After only a year of service there, he dropped out of the Party cadre and gradually moved further and further away from his old beliefs. By the end of the decade he had begun another career as a government informer at numerous hearings, during which his reputation for veracity suffered grievous and permanent damage.[49]

The Party's earliest efforts to escape its isolation were aided by the receptivity of left-wing Socialists to its united front bid. Old Guard Socialists were scarce in the South. Many of the church-trained, Christian Socialists scattered throughout the region were radical and eager to cooperate with Communists. In December 1934, several prominent Southern Socialists signed a united front agreement with Nat Ross. They announced a joint struggle against war and fascism, including the Ku Klux Klan, and pledged support for labor, the unemployed, and the Scottsboro Boys. Around the same time, the Communist-directed Sharecroppers' Union (SCU) made a bid for a united front with the Socialist-led Southern Tenant Farmers' Union (STFU). The two groups soon held a joint meeting in Washington, D.C., and began to cooperate. At an All-Southern Conference for Civil and Trade Union Rights in May 1935, representatives from the SCU, the STFU, the International Labor Defense, Commonwealth College, Highlander Folk School, the National Association for the Advancement of Colored People, the American Civil Liberties Union, and church groups all gathered. Driven from several meeting places in Chattanooga, Tennessee, the representatives finally met in Monteagle and heard pleas for a united front.[50]

It took the Seventh Congress and the transformation of the united front into the People's Front to enable the Communists to move into more fertile fields. The Party's new, more moderate line made it possible to reach out to people and groups it had once shunned. "We cannot cry 'white chauvinism' against every Southern progressive white who still carries with him, despite a generally progressive position, considerable remnants of the old race prejudice," Rob Hall told the Party's Alabama District Committee. Alabama Communists would support political candidates with sympathy for labor and farmers even if they did not fully measure up on the "Negro question." Out-and-out racists were excluded, of course, but the Communists no longer pushed self-determination. And Southern liberals, long scorned for their hesitancy, moderation, and caution in race relations, were now acceptable allies.[51]

It was not just the Communists who had changed. The South, too, was undergoing a transformation. The CIO launched organizing campaigns in 1937, and some Communists got staff jobs, particularly in the steel mills of Birmingham. Court decisions made Communism less risky. Early in 1937 a unanimous Supreme Court struck down the conviction of Oregon Communist Dirk de Jonge, convicted of criminal syndicalism for participating in a peaceful Party protest meeting in 1934. Although refusing to rule on the constitutionality of the syndicalism law, the Court held it inapplicable to peaceful meetings. A *Daily Worker* editorial happily noted that it was the first time the Court had upheld fundamental Constitutional rights in a case involving Communists. A few months later, a divided Court narrowly overturned Negro Communist Angelo Herndon's conviction for possession of Communist literature, ruling that the Georgia insurrection law could not be used to prevent Communists from openly recruiting and proselytizing new members. That same year, four of the Scottsboro Boys were finally released from jail by the state of Alabama.[52]

Emboldened, the Communist party in the South began to emerge from underground. The first All-Southern Communist Party Conference was held in Chattanooga in September 1937, with Earl Browder and James Ford in attendance. One hundred and thirty-three delegates showed up. John Ballam, the Central Committee's Southern representative, reported that nearly half had joined the Party since 1935. Party membership in the South showed gratifying gains. Alabama reported 900 members in the spring of 1938. By mid-1937 there were 274 Communists in the Carolinas, 409 in Texas, 522 in Mississippi and Arkansas, 167 in Kentucky, 123 in Louisiana, 304 in Florida (572 in 1938), 111 in Virginia, 259 in Oklahoma (500 in 1938), and 99 in Tennessee. Three thousand members in all of the South hardly made the Party a mass movement but did represent substantial progress. The South still lagged behind the rest of the Party, Rob Hall told the District Committee, but was catching up.[53]

Southern Communists also gained influence in larger organizations than the Party. One group they dominated from the very beginning was the Southern Negro Youth Congress, which attracted many Negro college students. Among its founders and officers were such future Communist party activists as Ed Strong, Louis Burnham, James Jackson, and

Esther Cooper. In accordance with the new Party line, Communists were encouraged to enter the Democratic party in the South. James Ford explained that the historic ties between Negroes and the Republican party had been sundered: "The Republican Party is not what it used to be. Neither is the Democratic Party the same Party it was ten or even five years ago." Claiming both Abraham Lincoln and Frederick Douglas for the Democratic Front, Ford insisted that "we stand in need of winning the Negroes for the pro–New Deal Democrats."[54]

By far the most controversial Southern organization the Party ever dealt with was the Southern Conference for Human Welfare (SCHW), whose origins lay in Franklin Roosevelt's desire to build the New Deal in the South. During the spring of 1938 he began encouraging Southern liberals to take the lead in focusing attention on Southern problems. That summer a national report issued by the administration dramatically pointed to the South's economic backwardness. Liberals planned a convention of Southerners to respond to the report. Meanwhile, a Southern radical, Joseph Gelders, was attempting to organize a civil liberties conference to dramatize Southern repression. He met with the President in June 1938. The economic and civil liberties themes were soon combined into the Southern Conference for Human Welfare, which gathered more than a thousand delegates in Birmingham that November. Such prominent Southern politicians as Senator Lester Hill and Governor Bibb Graves of Alabama, leading editors and publishers, and distinguished scholars either were present or sent greetings. Eleanor Roosevelt and Aubrey Williams, deputy administrator of the Works Progress Administration, appeared to lend the blessings of the New Deal. Clark Foreman, scion of a distinguished Atlanta family, was elected treasurer; Frank Porter Graham, president of the University of North Carolina, was selected to be chairman.[55]

The announced Communist presence was quite small. Rob Hall proclaimed that five Party members were in attendance as delegates. But other Communists were present, representing Party auxiliaries such as the Workers' Alliance and the American League Against War and Fascism. Eugene Dennis also arrived in town to oversee Party operations. But this tiny group of Party members hardly overwhelmed the hundreds of non-Communists, who included many sophisticated politicians and vociferous anti-Communists. A handful of resolutions such as that calling for freedom for the Scottsboro Boys was by 1938 no more a sign of Communist sympathy than was support for the collective security plans of Franklin Roosevelt. The Party accepted a minor public role and avoided controversy. Rob Hall admitted that "our Party contributed in a modest but constructive manner" to the success of the first conference. His only criticism was that more farmers, A.F. of L. members, and middle-class Southerners should have been present. Overall, however, the Southern Conference was "a brilliant confirmation of the line of the democratic front advanced by Comrade Browder at the Tenth Convention"; Communists should participate with others in coalitions supporting the New Deal. Earl Browder later denied that the Party had initiated the gathering or that he had consulted with Joseph Gelders about it.[56]

The Party's influence in the SCHW was not limited, however, to its public members. Its most prominent asset was Gelders, an organizer of the SCHW who was head of its Civil Rights Committee, which concentrated on abolition of the poll tax, and was the SCHW's only full-time employee from June to October of 1938. Brought up in Alabama in a comfortable Jewish home, Joseph Gelders had begun a conventional career as an assistant professor of physics at the University of Alabama. In August 1935 he had joined the National Committee for the Defense of Political Prisoners, a Party auxiliary. Within two months he was on his way to New York as the organization's secretary. The following August he returned to Birmingham as the committee's Southern representative. One of his first campaigns involved protests over the brutal beating of Jack Barton, a local Communist leader. On the evening of September 23, Gelders was slugged and kidnapped near his home, thrown into a car, and pounded with blackjacks as it drove fifty miles. He was dumped out on a deserted stretch of road, flogged fifteen to twenty times with a leather strap, and left for dead. As with the other beatings meted out by local police and vigilantes, no one was ever prosecuted for the crime, even though Gelders identified two of his assailants. Whether he was already a Communist or made into one by the beating is unknown. Reporting on the All-Southern Communist Party Conference held in September 1937, John Ballam spoke of "the report of Comrade Gelders of Birmingham." Years later, Hosea Hudson identified him as a fellow Communist. Gelders himself always denied he was a Communist, assuring liberals in the SCHW that he did not belong to the Party.[57]

The SCHW's first executive secretary, Howard Lee, was another concealed Communist. A protégé of Claude Williams from Commonwealth College, Lee had been active in the American Youth Congress, where he was closely allied with the Communist faction. He assured Frank Graham that he was not a Communist. Years later he admitted to the FBI that he had been a Party member from 1938 to 1949. Lee's replacement in 1941, Alton Lawrence, who was borrowed from Labor's Non-Partisan League, was nominally a Socialist but had been a secret Communist for some years. Several other alleged Communists held staff jobs after 1941, when a left-wing Christian Socialist, James Dombrowski, became executive secretary. A youth spin-off of the SCHW, the League of Young Southerners, was first led by Howard Lee and then by Reverend Malcolm Cotton Dobbs, who was named by two witnesses as a secret Party member.[58]

During and after its short decade of life, the SCHW was denounced as a Communist front. Conservative newspapers attacked its first meeting in Birmingham in November 1938, and the Alabama Council of Women's Democratic Clubs charged that the gathering was Communist-dominated. A leading delegate from Virginia privately resigned immediately after the first conference on the grounds that Communists were being accepted as delegates. The Dies Committee quizzed Party treasurer William Weiner for confirmation of its belief that Communist party funds had been used to finance the meeting. Paul Crouch wrote a sensational article after his defection from the Party stating that the SCHW was a classical front group that he had helped organize, finance, and run. The House Un-American Activities Committee produced a report on the SCHW in 1947 labeling it "perhaps the most deviously camouflaged Communist-front organization." Senator Eastland's Subcommittee on Internal Security returned to the attack in 1955, years after the SCHW's demise, explaining that it "was conceived, financed and set up by the Communist Party in 1938 as a mass organization to promote communism throughout the Southern States."[59]

Like many liberal organizations during the People's Front era, the SCHW had its share of Communists, some of them pretending to be "progressives." Occupying key administrative positions, they supported liberal measures and cheered the New Deal without any apparent unease. By keeping their affiliations secret, they enabled themselves to play important roles in an organization that would otherwise, for self-protection alone, have had to hold them at arm's length.

The People's Front era marked the Party's entrance into state political life. Communists gained positions of influence in political parties and in insurgent movements that exercised substantial power in state politics. They were important, if often unacknowledged, partners in progressive coalitions or political parties. Some of their secret members even served in positions ranging from Congress to the state legislature.

Washington, Minnesota, New York, and California were not the only states where Communists infiltrated other political parties. Party members in Illinois were encouraged to vote in the Democratic primary in early 1938, even though such an action would prevent them from signing petitions to put the Communist party on the ballot for the next two years. It was more important to build "unity behind those candidates who expressed best the program of the democratic front." In Ohio the state Party, while withdrawing its own candidates, held back from openly endorsing the Democrats. Communists in Wisconsin joined the Farmer-Labor Progressive Federation despite its ban on Party members, withdrew their own candidates to support the FLPF, and proudly noted that "scores of leading Federationists, including a number of its candidates and some of those elected to office, are known Communists."[60]

The Popular Front also had its costs, however. Because neither Communism nor the Communist party was acceptable enough, a politician could rarely afford to espouse either publicly. Even an open acknowledgment of Party support could endanger a political career. The ALP, Minnesota Farmer-Labor party, Washington Commonwealth Federation, and Wisconsin Farmer-Labor Progressive Federation all had clauses in their charters formally barring Communists from membership. Southern liberals by and large looked askance at openly avowed Communists in their ranks. Somewhat bitterly, Earl Browder explained after the Nazi-Soviet Pact that the Party had been an integral part of the progressive New Deal bloc "as long as we did not make too much noise about it" in either Congress or the states. "When these gentlemen thought they could use the support of the Communists, we became almost respectable. Never quite respectable. Almost." Communists were acceptable and tolerated if they were not conspicuous as Communists, an easy enough feat when they appeared to be loyal New Dealers. They provided manpower, organization, and links to such mass organizations as the Workers' Alliance and CIO unions. "They not only needed us to round up the people for these things," Browder observed, "they even needed us often to help them draft their speeches. They didn't know how to do it."[61]

The reticence of many politicians to acknowledge the Communists' role stemmed from fear that an open embrace of the Party would provoke a backlash. Browder noted with some regret that "our Party is as yet not officially recognized and accepted as an organic part of the broad democratic mass movement," but urged his members not to press the point. Communists, he insisted, only aggravated and antagonized their non-Communist allies by emphasizing their importance and value in the Democratic Front. He urged a policy of modesty. Even if Communists were in the forefront, they should "emphasize our minor role in these ordinary everyday aspects of the work" so as not to offend others. While such tactics protected Communists and enabled the Party to expand its influence, they also left the organizations which they joined vulnerable to charges that Communists were manipulating them or using them for their own purposes, fueling the suspicions of Party enemies and opponents of liberalism.[62]

Communists were not Democrats even though they joined the Democratic party in California and Washington. They were not Farmer-Laborites even though they participated in that party in Minnesota, nor were they ALP'ers despite joining it in New York. Neither were they Southern liberals. They were Communists, members of a political party that had its own agenda and requirements. The People's Front did not change the Party's insistence that its members make their allegiance to Communism a priority. Those Party members who held responsible positions in the Farmer-Labor party, Clarence Hathaway conceded, had to carry out their duties loyally. "It becomes still more necessary," he added, "that they maintain the closest relations with Communist Party committees, units and leading comrades." No one could forget "these elementary rules" that Communists in mass movements were, first and foremost, Communists.[63]

Many of them disguised their loyalties in order to function within these other parties. For a brief period, a Communist could do so and avoid any serious conflict of loyalties because the Party's goals and those of other organizations happened to coincide. When they no longer did so, Party members became vulnerable as the Communists set out to alter the direction of these other parties. Increasingly, members and leaders of liberal groups became convinced that Party members did not belong in their organizations.

15

The Unemployed
Meet Congress

W ITH THE ADVENT of the Roosevelt administration, the Communists quickly discovered that the unemployment marches and demonstrations which had raised the hackles of the Republicans no longer had the same effect. In fact, the government effectively disarmed the Party and forced it to turn to other, more conventional political tactics.

The first lesson came during the second Bonus March in May 1933, which had a more decided Communist tinge than its predecessor. It had been called by the Veterans National Liaison Committee, two of whose seven leaders—Emmanuel Levin and Harold Hickerson—were avowed Communists. Leaders of other veterans' groups, including William Waters, denounced the committee's organizers as Communists. The New York contingent, leaving from Union Square, vowed not to start trouble but warned that unlike the old Bonus Expeditionary Force, its ranks were filled with fighters who would not be quite so passive: "No matter how many police are in front of the White House we will walk in," one claimed. Organizers predicted that 50,000 veterans would descend on the city, but only about 2,000 appeared.[1]

Instead of preparing for an invasion, the administration treated the supposedly Communist vets as honored guests. Before they arrived and registered, Louis Howe, Roosevelt's secretary, had organized a bivouac at Fort Hunt, an abandoned army camp ten miles south of Washington. Quartermaster trucks ferried men out to the Virginia countryside; the Veterans Administration supplied buses to transport them to their meetings in the Washington Auditorium. Electric lights were set up, tents erected, blankets and meal kits distributed, and shower baths built, all at government expense. Army cooks served up filling meals—breakfast included eggs, baked potatoes, coffee, bread, and jam—which were described by the men as better than they had gotten while enlisted. White House aides visited the camp and arranged for a concert by the Navy Band. Eleanor Roosevelt paid a visit on May 16, waded through ankle-deep mud, and led the vets in singing "There's a Long, Long Trail." A few days later, Franklin Roosevelt had three veterans in for a half-hour chat while 1,000 of their comrades remained outside. The President swore that his heart ached for them, but he insisted he would still veto the Bonus bill if it passed Congress. It did not seem to matter. One of the petitioners called the President "the most likeable fellow I ever met." When the President offered all the vets Civilian Conservation Corps jobs at $1 a day, 1,000 signed up and the leaders admitted they had been "whipped" and outsmarted. The contrast with the first Bonus March could not have been sharper.[2]

The net effect was disastrous for the Party. The Liaison Committee docilely agreed to be housed at Fort Hunt. The newspapers found the pampered marchers in an expansive mood, eating well and singing old war songs. A small group of vociferously anti-Communist veterans demanded to remain in Washington and provoked several small confrontations with police. When Emmanuel Levin tried to appeal to the 200 or so right-wingers to join their comrades at Fort Hunt, the police had to interpose themselves to prevent them from pummeling him. Levin and Harold Hickerson finally resigned from the Liaison Committee in the interest of harmony. One year later the Communists were able to gather only 1,400 veterans in Washington, under the auspices of the Veterans Rank and File Committee. Once again, Fort Hunt was made available and the Federal Emergency Relief Administration met the $30,000 expenses.[3]

The diminishing returns from demonstrations were not the only cause of the malaise in unemployed work. The Extraordinary Party Conference in 1933, which emphasized increased work in industry, had an unsettling effect as well. Although Party leaders denied that this meant downgrading the importance of unemployed work, they had only limited resources; to shift people to one area usually meant to slight another. Israel Amter, then national chairman of the Unemployed Councils, bemoaned the serious slump in unemployed work that had resulted by October 1933 and repeated his complaint four months later. Comrades blithely assumed that it no longer mattered. Most of the unemployed who had been drawn into the Party's orbit had drifted away. And the Party had failed to respond to the challenge of the New Deal. While the Communists continued to insist that Roosevelt was no better than Herbert Hoover, the new administration was creating the Civil Works Administration and the Public Works Administration. Neither solved the unemployment problem. Still, like Section 7A of the NIRA, which recognized labor's right to organize, the new agencies gave hope to millions that the New Deal was moving to deal with their needs. "The workers were filled with illusions" about the New Deal, Amter wailed. Instead of enlightening them, the Unemployed Councils had remained "passive." Herbert Benjamin later admitted to a string of Party errors in its unemployed work, foremost among which was the failure to recognize the new administration's achievements.[4]

As the Communists watched their unemployed work flounder, they shifted their attention from loud demonstrations and confrontations to the halls of Congress. Washington, D.C., had been a frequent target of protest marches, but the Party's preferred method of lobbying had hardly been calculated to endear its causes to Congress. A Party gathering in Washington could be depended on to loose a flood of angry anti-Communist rhetoric in Congress. The Party now prepared to employ for the first time more traditional techniques of persuasion. Their chosen instrument was a plan known as the Workers' Unemployment Insurance Bill; it would be the focus of Communist efforts for the next four years.

First put forward by the Party in 1930, the proposal had been hoisted at every occasion when the Party-led unemployed demonstrated. However, the Comintern's Twelfth Plenum in September 1932 charged that "insufficient attention has been paid to the organization of the struggle for the partial demands of the unemployed" and ordered Communists to "devote special attention to the wide mobilization and organization of the broad masses of the unemployed for a struggle for their every-day demands and social insurance." The Comintern's advice was taken to heart. Slightly redrafted, the bill became the focus of a new effort in 1933. In contrast to later proposals for unemployment insurance, this one was short, simple, and, to Communist ears, sweet. It insured all workers for the full period of joblessness. They were to be paid full average wages with a minimum of $10 a week and $3 per dependent.

The funds were to be raised by a tax on incomes over $5,000 a year and administered by workers' councils. The entire bill was barely half a page long. No one was left in any suspense about who was responsible for the bill. It was, a *Daily Worker* editorial proudly noted, "proposed by the Communist Party and endorsed by the Unemployed Councils."[5]

The Communists launched a new, vigorous campaign on behalf of their bill in the fall of 1933. Their first priority, oddly enough, was to sell the idea of unemployment insurance to their own members and sympathizers. Many Communists refused to believe that capitalist politicians would enact any reforms; others doubted that Communists had any business promoting ameliorative measures in lieu of revolution. Israel Amter identified the Party's task as overcoming the "open disbelief that Unemployment and Social Insurance can be won" and the corresponding attitude that the demand for unemployment insurance was only an agitational slogan, not to be taken seriously. The Unemployed Councils announced a drive for endorsements for the bill from city councils, labor unions, and fraternal organizations. The International Workers' Order launched a united front of fraternal groups to push its cause. Communists in the A.F. of L. created a Trade Union Committee for Unemployment Insurance and Relief to agitate for a reversal of the labor group's long-standing opposition to government aid. By the time Louis Weinstock, the committee's national secretary, testified before a congressional committee in 1935, he could report that the measure, now known as the Lundeen Bill, had secured the support of more than 3,000 locals, many central labor organizations, six state federations of labor, and five international unions.[6]

Readers of *The Daily Worker* were treated to a barrage of endorsements over the next two years. Hardly a day went by without the announcement of another organization petitioning Congress to pass the Workers' Unemployment Insurance Bill. William Foster proudly claimed that more than 5 million Americans had been recorded as favoring it. Not all the Party's lobbying on the bill's behalf was so traditional, however. A delegation from the Downtown Unemployed Councils in New York invited themselves into the home of Representative Samuel Dickstein to demand his support and protest his special committee's investigation of fascism and Communism, which was then in progress. The police, lying in wait for the intruders, used blackjacks and ejected them. And, the Party's Eighth Convention hardly endeared the program to capitalist politicians, given its insistence that "these things must be won even though it means the destruction of capitalist profits" and would prepare the workers for revolution.[7]

The Party arranged to have the bill introduced in Congress. On February 2, 1934, Representative Ernest Lundeen of Minnesota put the Party's bill, with two minor changes, into the hopper as H.R. 7598. Lundeen had only been elected to the House in 1933 but was far from a political neophyte. First elected to Congress as a Republican in 1917, he had voted against entering World War I and had been the first congressman to defend the young Soviet government. When he was defeated for reelection, Lundeen became a Farmer-Laborite and suffered a series of political defeats during the next decade, before his reelection to Congress. The Communists had long considered him no better or worse than any other reform politician; one typical headline of the Third Period announced: "Ernest Lundeen Exposed as Social Fascist." Nor did his introduction of the bill make Lundeen an instant Communist hero. William Schneiderman, the Minnesota district organizer, wrote that neither Lundeen nor his party supported unemployment insurance. Lundeen had only responded to mass pressure. "We must not forget," Schneiderman thundered, "that the whole record of the Olsons, Lundeens and Bennetts belies every word they say." An editorial the same day endorsed Schneiderman's comments and accused Lundeen of being lukewarm about H.R. 7598. Perhaps coincidentally, Lundeen made little effort to push for action on the measure.[8]

The Party timed the opening of its National Convention Against Unemployment on February 3 to coincide with the introduction of H.R. 7598. Nearly 1,000 delegates implausibly claiming to represent 2 million workers gathered to "fight against the whole hunger program" of the New Deal. There was little pretense about who was in charge. Israel Amter and Herbert Benjamin gave the main reports. Prominent Communists spoke, and the convention sent its greetings to William Foster, "the outstanding leader of the American workers." Besides endorsing H.R. 7598, the delegates changed the Unemployed Councils' name to the National Unemployment Councils of the United States. Delegations were sent to visit both William Green and Harry Hopkins. The A.F. of L. leader was much less friendly. He declined to support unemployment insurance. Hopkins met with seventy-four of the delegates for two hours. While he told them he supported insurance in preference to relief, Hopkins refused to endorse any bill. Told that the Communist party had proposed the Workers' Unemployment Insurance Bill, he responded: "Send it to me, will you. I'd like very much to read it."[9]

One year later the Party repeated its efforts. Before the 1934 election, an arrangements committee issued a call for a National Congress for Unemployment and Social Insurance to be held in Washington in early

January. Many of the signers, like Earl Browder, Max Bedacht, Louis Weinstock, and Roy Hudson were Communists; others, like Malcolm Cowley, Heywood Broun, and Roger Baldwin, were fellow travelers; and a few were liberals willing to cooperate with the Party. Herbert Benjamin served as executive secretary of the National Sponsoring Committee, which declared its support for the Lundeen Bill and denounced all other alternatives for serving "only to deceive and divide those who aspire to a greater measure of social security." Benjamin hoped for a broad united front: "Under no circumstances must this Congress be merely a gathering of the unemployed. Nor must it be a gathering of delegates from only the revolutionary and left wing organizations." The Unemployment Councils, Israel Amter announced, would throw all their resources into preparing for the congress "to get the greatest possible representation at that Congress from all kinds of workers' organizations. The local units of the National Unemployment Councils must be the driving force in every locality in the preparation for this Congress." For weeks prior to the start of the congress, *The Daily Worker* was filled with news of endorsements and demonstrations in support of the Lundeen Bill, denunciations of other plans, elections of delegates, and blaring headlines about growing unemployment. After the congress was over, Amter boasted that it "represented the broadest united front of any character that has been held in the United States in recent years." Two thousand four hundred delegates appeared, and non-Communists were accorded prominent positions of leadership. Still, the congress was as notable for who stayed away. Neither the Musteites nor the Socialists attended.[10]

The Party did try to minimize its control of the proceedings. The National Unemployment Councils waited until January 8, 1935, the day after the congress adjourned, to open their convention. The unemployment congress set up a National Joint Action Committee for Genuine Social Insurance to continue lobbying efforts. Aside from Benjamin and Amter, prominent roles went to such non-Communists as Arnold Hill, Mary Van Kleeck, Elmer Brown of the International Typographical Union, and Harry Ward. Ernest Lundeen appeared to announce that he was reintroducing his bill and pledge that representatives from the National Congress for Unemployment and Social Insurance would get to testify before Congress on its behalf. Communist affairs did, however, intervene. The biggest story that came from the convention was not the drive for unemployment insurance but the revelation by Browder that the Communists now advocated a Labor party.[11]

The Communists had been the first to get an unemployment insurance bill introduced but were not the only ones. Shortly after Lundeen had first proposed H.R. 7598, Senator Robert Wagner of New York put forward what came to be known as the Wagner-Lewis Bill. A new Wagner-Lewis Bill, containing the Roosevelt administration's plans for Social Security and unemployment insurance, was introduced in January 1935 and immediately became the focus of congressional debate. To the Party, the Wagner-Lewis Bill was an abomination; Communists angrily charged that the administration measure was an attempt to head off mass pressure for an effective bill. "If you are for the Wagner-Lewis bill," Benjamin told a House committee, "then, regardless of the reasons you may give for this, you are objectively and actually supporting the effort of the ruling class to defeat our demand for genuine unemployment and social insurance." Although it was the only measure that stood a chance of passage, Benjamin advised a vote against it. Reporting to the Central Committee in January 1935, Browder saw Roosevelt as moving to the right to bridge the gap between himself and the Liberty League; one example was his policy on unemployment insurance. Virtually every feature was distasteful. The policy depended on the states to create unemployment insurance laws. Payments were to be financed by a payroll tax, not from general revenues. The measure did not cover those currently unemployed. Benefits were too low and stopped after only a few months. Agricultural and domestic workers were excluded. Herbert Benjamin had only gotten through two pages of his twenty-one-page denunciation of Wagner-Lewis when the House Ways and Means Committee decided his time had expired and unceremoniously ejected him.[12]

The testimony on the Lundeen Bill held by a subcommittee of the House Labor Committee, chaired by Matthew Dunn of Pennsylvania, became a Communist showplace. Herbert Benjamin later claimed that Lundeen allowed him to plan and direct the sessions. Many of the liberal Democratic representatives, angered that the Wagner-Lewis Bill had first been sent to Ways and Means instead of Labor, missed no chance to express their contempt for it and emphasize the superiority of the Lundeen Bill. Most of the eighty witnesses who appeared in February 1935 were enthusiastic about H.R. 2827 (the new designation for the Lundeen Bill). They should have been. Although Dunn noted that only two witnesses represented Communist organizations, at least forty-two were either avowed Communists or represented Party auxiliaries. They ranged from Browder, Benjamin, Bedacht, and Amter to E. C. Greenfield of the Cleveland Small Home and Land Owners Federation, Andrew Omholt of the United Farmers League, and a slew of delegates from the Unemployment Councils. For nostalgia buffs, there were appearances by Mrs. Edward Bellamy and the utopian novelist's grandson and granddaughter.[13]

The Party had meanwhile enlisted another important ally in its struggle for unemployment insurance. Shortly after the Second Hunger March in 1932, Earl Browder suggested that a professional group supporting unemployment insurance should be formed. In April 1934, Mary Van Kleeck, a prominent social worker, announced the formation of the Inter-Professional Association (IPA), which was careful never to identify itself with the Communist party the way the other auxiliaries did. It did not even rate a mention in Eugene Lyons's exposé of the Red Decade. Very few of its leaders were avowed Communists, but Herbert Benjamin, listed as a cooperating member of the Executive Committee, was the IPA's secretary. The association's stated purpose was to lobby for unemployment insurance—which it did with enthusiasm throughout 1934 and 1935. The IPA provided several benefits for the Party's unemployment bill. Although small, never having more than 1,100 members, it had a distinguished roster that gave the measure respectability from the world of academia. Several of its economists and lawyers testified to the economic soundness and constitutionality of the Lundeen Bill.[14]

Members of the House Subcommittee were credulous enough to accept what the Communist witnesses said. Embarrassing or probing questions were not allowed to mar the occasion. Lew Bentzley of the Farmers National Committee of Action generously claimed to speak for 110,000 members. Manning Johnson of the League of Struggle for Negro Rights outdid that, enrolling 136,000 people. Amter gave the Unemployment Councils a "membership and following" of 500,000. Dunn and Lundeen traded compliments with Ella Bloor, who announced that "I represent the farm women." Lundeen deferred to Bedacht because he was sure the IWO head knew more about the topic than he did. The subcommittee accepted the IPA's figures on the Lundeen Bill's cost. Some of the witnesses did provide the congressmen with vivid pictures of the misery caused by unemployment. Their stories of suffering and privation gave the issue an immediacy that was lost among the welter of statistics being considered by the Ways and Means Committee. Herbert Benjamin praised the Committee's openness: "For the first time in the history of Congress, a Congressional committee opened its doors not only to a few more or less representative leaders of the workers but to the workers themselves."[15]

There was still one more feather to be added to the Party's cap: the House Labor Committee approved H.R. 2827 by a vote of 7 to 6 in late February. Tainted as the vote was—one opponent had to leave before the bill slipped through—it marked the first time a congressional committee had recommended any unemployment insurance plan. Earl Browder later

boasted that the favorable vote "forced Congress to adopt an unemployment insurance scheme," albeit the considerably less satisfactory Wagner-Lewis Bill. Beating the administration's measure out of committee,
however, was the last victory that advocates of the Lundeen Bill could
win. Far from feeling threatened, the House leadership simply crushed
the measure. The Rules Committee refused to send the Lundeen Bill to
the floor, although its proponents were allowed to offer it as a substitute
for the unemployment insurance provisions of the Social Security Bill.
Vito Marcantonio of New York warned that the Wagner-Lewis Bill offered a "new delusion," not a New Deal. It created a "vicious anti-social
system." No one brought up its Communist origins, but the Lundeen Bill
was nonetheless rejected 204 to 52. Not all the votes on its behalf came
from admirers of its radical approach to unemployment. Conservatives
who hoped to make the Social Security Bill unpalatable enough to force
its defeat provided the bulk of the support. Such advocates of H.R. 2827
as Lundeen and Marcantonio then joined with a handful of conservative
Republicans to cast futile votes against the imposition of Social Security.
The final vote was 372 to 33.[16]

Lundeen's ties to the Party became even closer after this defeat. In
one exclusive interview with *The Daily Worker*, he lavished praise on
Lenin. In July 1935 he and Marcantonio walked out of a Farmer-Labor
meeting, called by Thomas Amlie of Wisconsin to discuss a third-party
alternative to Roosevelt, because Communists were excluded. Addressing
a meeting of the Friends of the Soviet Union at Madison Square Garden
late in 1936, then Senator-elect Lundeen began his speech with *Tovaris-
chi*, or "comrades." From an ogre of the Third Period, Ernest Lundeen
became a hero of the Popular Front. Ben Gitlow later charged that Lundeen was actually a "paid under-cover agent of the Communist Party"
from 1926 until his death in a 1940 plane crash. More likely, however,
Lundeen simply calculated that an alliance with the Party on the issue of
unemployment insurance could bring enormous publicity and rescue him
from the obscurity that afflicted most junior congressmen. After only two
terms in the House and with little to his credit besides the introduction of
that legislation, he was elected to the Senate in 1936. His role as a Party
favorite did not last long, however. As Party priorities changed, Lundeen,
unwilling to alter his lifelong isolationism, was denounced as a reactionary by Earl Browder at the height of the Democratic Front period.[17]

Lundeen was but the first of a host of congressmen whom the Party
rushed to embrace after it abandoned its ideological purity. Minnesota
Farmer-Laborites and Wisconsin Progressives, once scorned, became political allies. New Deal Democrats were praised. Congressmen needed no

longer be judged by how ardently they served Communist interests but by how militantly they espoused New Deal positions. The Roosevelt landslide of 1936 brought into office a few dozen devoted liberals and a handful of radicals who, added to a small group elected in 1934, coalesced into a progressive bloc in the House. The Communists saw this new group as the force that might help transform American politics. They were a small minority who fought mostly losing battles: to significantly increase WPA and direct relief appropriations, to pack the Supreme Court, to pass wage and hour standards, and to achieve goals such as tax reform, flood control, and greater farm aid. The Party had pilloried the first New Deal of the NRA and Agricultural Adjustment Administration as a long step toward fascism. It had been unable to abide the second New Deal, ridiculing and sneering at the Wagner Labor Relations Act and Social Security. After denouncing the New Deal for four years, however, the Communist party jumped on board just as it foundered. Instead of being able to contribute to the further expansion of the New Deal, the Party joined a movement already past its better days. His smashing 1936 victory to the contrary, Franklin Roosevelt lost his mastery over Congress. The swollen Democratic majority could not pass crucial legislation. Conservative and regular Democrats looked askance at the President's plan to restructure the judiciary and the executive branch, afraid that too much power had already passed into his hands. Only a few major New Deal measures would pass Congress between 1937 and 1939. Most others withered and died.

The progressive bloc in the House was, nonetheless, a remarkable group. Probably never before or since were so many radicals in Congress. Most of the forty-odd progressives, led by Maury Maverick of Texas, were nothing more than New Deal liberals from all over the country, Lyndon Johnson of Texas among them. There were a few stray Republicans, including Usher Burdick of North Dakota and Charles Tobey of New Hampshire. The radicals were a smaller group. Three Democrats from Washington—Warren Magnuson, John Coffee, and Charles Leavy—has been elected in 1936 with the support of the Communist-dominated Commonwealth Federation. There were seven Progressives from Wisconsin, products of the LaFollette movement, including Thomas Amlie, secretary of the House progressive bloc, and an anti-Communist. His colleague Gerald Boileau, the group's floor leader, was somewhat more friendly. When the Party inaugurated its new *Midwest Daily Record*, Boileau had telegrammed greetings and "heartily endorse[d] this action." Minnesota's five Farmer-Labor congressmen included Henry Teigan, former state secretary of the North Dakota Socialist party. To defeat fascism,

Teigan told *The Daily Worker*, he supported "every intelligent effort to unite the workers, farmers and the common people in general under a program of action similar to the popular front that proved successful in both France and Spain."[18]

By far the most outspoken and unlikely Farmer-Laborite, however, was John Toussaint Bernard, probably the only native-born Corsican ever to sit in Congress. Originally an iron-ore miner on the Mesabi Range, Bernard had been a city fireman in Eveleth, Minnesota, for a decade. He was an active Farmer-Laborite and decided to run for Congress in 1936. Nat Ross, the Communist party's district organizer, later claimed he had convinced Bernard to run. To Bernard's own surprise, he was swept into office in the Democratic landslide, an event that Earl Browder described as "more or less an accident in politics." Bernard never admitted to being a Communist until he announced his decision to join the Party in 1977 at the age of 85, but he faithfully echoed Party policies. "Bernard," Earl Browder later said, "was a good man but a man who let other people completely do his thinking."[19]

Bernard hired known, open Communists to work for him, including Marian Bachrach, later indicted under the Smith Act, as his secretary. He adopted Party positions even when they enraged his Duluth constituents. Minnesota and the Farmer-Labor movement had been traditionally isolationist. Bernard cast the sole vote against the emergency neutrality bill embargoing aid to the Spanish Republic. After returning from a visit to Spain, he not only urged American support for the government but cooperated with the Friends of the Abraham Lincoln Battalion. The congressman also managed to alienate the powerful A.F. of L. unions in his district by his unabashed CIO partisanship, extending to his employment by the Steel Workers Organizing Committee while in Congress. The irrepressible Bernard was also given to displaying his opera-caliber voice by bursting into the *Internationale* in restaurants. After his constituents retired him in 1938, Bernard decorated a host of Party fronts before being hired as an organizer for the United Electrical Workers in 1942. When he next appeared before Congress, it was as an unfriendly witness before the House Un-American Activities Committee in 1952. Bernard was surly, argumentative, and reticent about his past and present activities, pleading the Fifth Amendment. A quarter of a century later, he publicly became a Communist, the only ex-congressman ever to acknowledge Party membership.[20]

With less justification or evidence, several others members of this unruly legislative group were accused of Party membership. One ex-Communist witness, testifying before the Dies Committee in executive session, named Franck Havenner, a progressive from California, as a Communist. Democrat Jerry O'Connell of Montana contributed to *The New Masses,* traveled to Spain with Bernard, and in 1937 wrote *The Daily Worker* that it was "America's outstanding daily labor paper." After losing a reelection bid in 1938, O'Connell—who assisted the International Labor Defense, the American League for Peace and Democracy, and various Party organizations to aid Spain—briefly worked for the IWO. Although at least one ex–Party member, Barbara Hartle, charged he was a Communist, such normally positive government witnesses as Louis Budenz and Manning Johnson carefully noted only that O'Connell helped the Party but they had no knowledge of whether he was a member. O'Connell himself vehemently denied Party membership.[21]

Few of the progressives fully lived up to the Party's hopes. Most kept a careful distance from Communists. Gene Dennis was frequently in Washington as Party secretary for politics and legislative affairs. His wife complained that she and her husband were by and large treated as pariahs:

A few congressmen like Vito Marcantonio of East Harlem, John Bernard of Minnesota, and a couple of mavericks from Wisconsin and Washington state, saw us openly in their offices, often took us to lunch and, as Meta Berger had done in Milwaukee, pointedly introduced us to colleagues along the way. But most of the New Deal legislators, labor leaders and government agency people met Gene cautiously in borrowed apartments under security precautions reminiscent of our years abroad.

Moreover, so disparate a group proved unable to prevent the disintegration of a New Deal majority in the House. Even so crucial a New Deal measure as the President's Executive Reorganization Bill found the progressive bloc in disarray. The measure, fervently backed by the Party, lost by a vote of 204 to 196. A few liberals opposed Roosevelt. So did two Farmer-Laborites from Minnesota. And so did six of the seven Wisconsin Progressives—all except Amlie, who on this issue found himself allied with the Communist party. "The curse of the progressives," Hathaway complained, "is an extreme individualism that does more to aid the reactionaries than could be offset by dozens of progressive deeds or speeches." Few of the progressives who were willing to deal with the Communists survived the 1938 Republican victories. Twenty-two members of the progressive bloc were defeated, four others lost bids to move to the Senate, and three more left the House. The losses were particularly heavy among the radicals. Only two Wisconsin Progressives survived. Four of the five Farmer-Laborites from Minnesota lost. Maverick, Amlie, and Boileau, the progressives' leaders, were all absent from the new House. Contributors to *The New Masses* fared even worse. O'Connell, Bernard, and Bryan Scott of California all lost.[22]

The 1938 elections provided only a bit of solace to the Communist Party—the return of Vito Marcantonio to the House. For the next decade there was no congressman who so eloquently or consistently defended and articulated Communist positions. On issues ranging from foreign policy to unemployment insurance, Marcantonio faithfully expressed the Party line. His devotion to the Party, which did not flag until the late 1940s, earned Marcantonio an unending stream of abuse from colleagues, the press, and anti-Communists. Called everything from "Kremlin-minded" to a Communist stooge, he nonetheless kept winning the endorsement of his constituents. Seven times they sent him to Congress, even though in his last six races he carried the Communist albatross into the campaign.

Vito Marcantonio was born, brought up, and built his political career in East Harlem's Little Italy, a squalid slum that housed more Italians than any other area in the United States. His polyglot congressional district also included Puerto Ricans, Negroes, and Jews. The region's first champion was Fiorello LaGuardia, an unorthodox Republican. Marcantonio headed LaGuardia's political machine in East Harlem for several years and served as a surrogate son. Deposed in the Democratic landslide of 1932, LaGuardia became New York's fusion mayor in 1933. The following year Marcantonio, running as a Republican, unseated James Lanzetta, a Tammany Democrat whose most notable achievement in office had been a speech urging his fellow legislators to think of the poor landlords as they debated housing legislation. Marcantonio's margin of victory was a scant 247 votes. Once in Congress he found himself an anomaly—a Republican to the left of Franklin Roosevelt. Christened the "Pink Pachyderm of Congress," he pleaded for enactment of H. R. 2827 and voted against the Social Security Bill. He introduced the Relief and Work Projects Standards Bill, written by the Unemployment Councils. He withdrew from a Labor party planning conference because Communists were excluded. When Brazilian police tortured and murdered Victor Baron, a Comintern operative and the son of Harrison George, Marcantonio demanded a State Department inquiry on the basis of information furnished by Joseph Brodsky, the Party's attorney.[23]

By 1936 the Communists had no better friend in Congress. That May, Browder told a Party meeting that it "would be very stupid" not to support his reelection. (The Party had opposed him in 1934.) Marcantonio's closeness to the Party, however, cost him dearly. Incensed by his alliance with Communists, American Labor party leaders denied him an endorsement. Marcantonio was relegated to only the Republican line on the ballot and was swept out of office by the FDR tidal wave. He spent the next two years building his ties to the People's Front movement, as a lawyer for the Workers' Alliance, and as president of the International Labor Defense. Upon announcing his candidacy for the House in 1938, he secured the ALP nomination, as well as the Republican nomination through the intercession of Mayor LaGuardia. George Charney, then the Party's organizational secretary in Harlem, emerged from a meeting with Marcantonio "convinced that our future was wrapped up with Marc; if we were the vanguard, we had to allow a place for Marc, for he was a vanguard all by himself." The Party and its auxiliaries flooded the Eighteenth Congressional District with volunteers. New York's left-wing unions threw in their resources: they registered voters, staffed headquarters, turned out the vote, and watched the polls.[24]

Marcantonio's successful 1938 campaign proved to be the model for all his future victories. The abundant resources of New York's Communists and left-wingers provided manpower that none of his rivals could match. New York's multi-party system enabled Marcantonio to win nomination from several political parties—occasionally he was the nominee of Republicans, Democrats, and the ALP—and insulated him from the dangers of isolation on the Republican ticket. Even when he was restricted to the ALP line, the inability of Republicans, Democrats, and Liberals to agree on a single candidate to oppose him enabled the congressman to win reelection with a plurality of the vote. His largely Italian constituency remained loyal to a local boy who had made good, regardless of his politics. And few politicians could galvanize a crowd as Marcantonio could. It was rare to find anywhere else in America the combination of personality, electoral system, constituency, and Party resources that accounted for Marcantonio's success. The Communist party made one effort to recruit Marcantonio just after the 1938 campaign. He had no desire, however, to subject himself to Party discipline. Earl Browder recalled: "We developed closer and closer relations till he was actually our spokesman in Congress." Marcantonio, however, remained an isolated, ineffective congressman whose fidelity to the Party line did little to endear him to his colleagues.[25]

The short-lived surge of the People's Front in the House coincided with the formation of still another Party auxiliary. Like so many other organizations created during the period, the Workers' Alliance was quite different in some ways from the unabashed fronts of the Third Period. Its decidedly nonrevolutionary goals allowed its leaders to mingle easily with New Dealers and cooperate with them. But, like virtually every other auxiliary, the Workers' Alliance was firmly under Communist control.

Ever since non-Communist unemployed organizations had appeared, the Party had agitated for unity. This proved elusive because unity to the Communists during the Third Period meant capturing the members of other groups over the heads of their leaders. Late in 1933 David Lasser, head of the New York Workers Committee on Unemployment, rejected a united front with the Unemployed Councils, prompting Israel Amter to urge his members to desert to the Communist-led group. "Build the united front in spite of your leaders," Amter exhorted. The National Unemployment Councils in mid-1934 issued yet another plea for unity "over the heads of these splitting leaders." When the Communists took the lead in organizing the National Congress for Unemployment and Social Insurance, scheduled to meet in January 1935, only a handful of officials from non-Communist unemployed groups signed the call. Socialists came to the first planning meetings for the Congress but then left. The Musteites stayed away entirely. Amter complained that both groups had refused to accept the councils' help in staging demonstrations late in November 1934, causing them to be "pitifully small."[26]

Three months later the Socialists opted for unity. Their turnabout was a product of both a shift in Communist policy and the inability of Socialist leaders to control their own organization. At the Congress for Social Insurance in January 1935, Earl Browder unveiled the Communists' support for a Labor party. Shortly afterward, the Lundeen Bill made its mark in Congress. The Socialist party finally endorsed H. R. 2827; so did its unemployed organization. The inaugural convention of the Socialist-dominated unemployed organization, the Workers' Alliance of America, took place in early March 1935. Herbert Benjamin's plea for unity drew an ovation. In his speech he denounced red-baiting. *The Daily Worker* suggested that Benjamin had upstaged all other speakers, receiving a warmer reception than Norman Thomas, and ignited a revolt that had nearly toppled David Lasser from the chairmanship. Following Benjamin's speech, a proposal from the Resolutions Committee criticizing the Unemployment Councils as Communist-dominated was withdrawn and the delegates unanimously authorized the National Executive Board to begin negotiations for unity. "We won the Workers Alliance convention without any previous agreement with Lasser," Benjamin recalled.[27]

Unity negotiations among the Workers' Alliance, Unemployment Councils, and Musteite National Unemployed Leagues began in April 1935. Matters went slowly, with the participants haggling constantly.

Not until April 1936 was a merger consummated between the Workers' Alliance and the Unemployment Councils. To achieve it, the Communist-dominated body was forced to give up its name and accept a minority of the seats on the Executive Board of the alliance. Formal control of the Workers' Alliance rested with the non-Communists. Lasser was chosen president and Benjamin organizational secretary. The Executive Board was dominated by old members of the Workers' Alliance; they outnumbered old Unemployment Council members about two to one.[28]

Lasser quickly learned, however, that Communist strength was not all concentrated among its open cadres. Arnold Johnson, national secretary of the Musteite National Unemployed Leagues, announced in March 1936 that he had joined the Communist party: "We stand with the Soviet Union," said the statement issued by Johnson and two fellow defectors. "We, as true Communists, call upon all comrades who believe likewise to forget their self-righteous sectarianism and opportunism and work for the realistic program of the Communist Party of the U.S.A. and of the Communist International." Johnson, a graduate of the Union Theological Seminary, had represented the American Civil Liberties Union in Harlan, Kentucky, in 1931. The following year he moved to Ohio to organize the unemployed. A long-time Muste follower, he persuaded many of his subordinates in the National Unemployed Leagues to follow him into the Workers' Alliance.[29]

Benjamin, who had secretly persuaded Johnson to join the Communist party, had also recruited another leading Musteite, Louis Budenz. Alex Noral headed a small independent unemployed group, the California Federation of the Unemployed. Although not counted as a Communist member of the board, Noral was the Party's former district organizer in Seattle. By October 1936 Herbert Benjamin could detail some remarkable advances to the Politburo. Communists controlled seven of the twelve state organizations of the Workers' Alliance, containing 75 percent of the membership. Beginning with only seven of the twenty-three seats on the executive board, they now held eleven. And, organizational advances were not the only benefits accruing to the Party: "The convention," Benjamin explained, "has brought us contact from sections of the country where we have had no contact for years, in the main American elements, and this gives us an opportunity of really spreading out throughout the country with the program of the Party."[30]

The new opportunity for recruits for the Party's unemployed work was welcome. The massive campaign for the Lundeen Bill to the contrary, the Unemployment Councils had not been prospering. Unemployed work had continued to recede in importance as the trade union struggles consumed more and more attention. Adoption of the Social Security bill dampened the Party's continued struggle for more generous unemployment insurance provisions. At the time of unification, Benjamin noted, "all the unemployed organizations were in a state of decline." If one depended on the numbers tossed around by their leaders, one would never have known it. Between March and December 1934, the Unemployed Councils issued 90,875 membership cards and sold 137,000 dues stamps. Even that was "only a small fraction of actual membership." Israel Amter grandly assured the House Labor subcommittee considering the Lundeen Bill that the 500,000-strong "membership and following" of his organization stood behind the measure. A few months later, Benjamin claimed 300,000 members in 859 locals in 42 states. The Workers' Alliance used even more grandiose figures: in 1936, just prior to unity, it claimed 600,000 members. The figures were only vague approximations. The Party's organization, Browder later noted, "was not a membership organization [but] a cadre organization" and "there was never any basis upon which its following could be even estimated with any degree of accuracy." When the merger took place, Benjamin privately told the Politburo that the Unemployment Councils had all of 8,500 members and the Workers' Alliance between 15,000 and 20,000.[31]

With the united front successfully consummated, the Workers' Alliance grew. No one was precisely sure how much. Because it was a federated body, with locals affiliating to its state organizations, the alliance was never entirely sure of its size. Testifying before a House Committee in early 1939, Benjamin gave its dues-paying membership at 260,000 with approximately another 140,000 in arrears. Much of the alliance's expansion, however, was due to a change in federal relief. The Works Progress Administration (WPA), created in April 1935, quickly became the largest federal relief program in history. The Workers' Alliance prospered along with it. WPA workers were much easier to organize than the unemployed, since they had job grievances that needed correction. And, unlike the unemployed, they could afford minimal dues. Despite Herbert Benjamin's warning, shortly after the unity convention, that the alliance had to guard against becoming merely a trade union for WPA workers, it soon was exactly that. By 1939 some 75 percent of Workers' Alliance members were WPA employees. The unemployed movement functioned, Benjamin admitted, "to a considerable extent as a trade union of WPA workers." It "became lost in details involving grievances of W.P.A. workers, failing to give sufficient attention to the problems of those unemployed who were unable to get on the WPA, although they were the vast majority." As the WPA expanded or contracted, so too did the alliance.

Its fate was inextricably linked to the success of the government agency, making the pressure group a partner of the New Deal agency.[32]

Its initial response to the New Deal had not augured well for the Workers' Alliance's future alliance. When the unity convention took place, the Communist party still regarded Franklin Roosevelt as its enemy. "Unity of All Unemployed Must Be Achieved to Fight Roosevelt's Program," read the headline over one article by Herbert Benjamin. Months after the 1936 election, the Party and the Workers' Alliance remained skeptical about the President: another headline announced, "Alliance Maps Nationwide Demonstration Against Roosevelt's Slash of WPA Jobs." The Workers' Alliance had more difficulty than most Party auxiliaries in executing the shift in attitude toward Roosevelt. It represented those WPA workers whose grievances were directed against the government. Angry confrontations over a host of issues required the alliance to restrain its praise for the WPA. More importantly, however, the WPA was consistently on the defensive after 1936. Congress continually sought to cut WPA appropriations, and the administration was forced periodically to announce massive layoffs.[33]

An amendment proposed by Congressman Clifton Woodrum to the 1938 Appropriation Bill forced the government to announce a cutback of nearly half a million WPA jobs. Herbert Benjamin denounced Roosevelt's miserly $1.5 billion relief request and charged that he "once again showed a disposition to retreat before reactionaries." Benjamin called for a "gigantic, mass 'pink-slip' march to Washington" to protest. A Workers' Alliance convention adopted the march idea. A *Daily Worker* editorial endorsed the plan "to halt the relief cuts decreed by the Roosevelt administration."[34]

Just before Congress adjourned for the summer in 1937, Senator Schwellenbach of Washington and Representative Allen of Pennsylvania, "on the initiative and request of the Workers' Alliance," introduced a resolution to prevent the dismissal from the WPA of anyone unable to find a private job at prevailing wages in the trade for which he was trained and fitted. The National Jobs March soon became focused on forcing passage of the resolution, but Congress adjourned without taking any action before the marchers even reached Washington. Compared to the hunger marches of the early 1930s, the National Jobs March was rather tame. Instead of the "gigantic" masses predicted earlier, only 2,500 people showed up. They camped in a tent city on the banks of the Potomac River near the Lincoln Memorial, in tents supplied by the WPA, and met in the Labor Department's auditorium. Soaked by days of rain, the bedraggled marchers walked quietly to the White House and the Capitol, coming to life to hoot only as they passed the Chamber of Commerce building.[35]

The Communist party plenum which announced that the Popular Front would henceforth be built largely within the Democratic party took place in June, after the march had been called but before it took place. The great mass march that was to launch an assault on the New Dealers instead turned its wrath on congressional reactionaries and went out of its way to praise the President. The leaders of the Workers' Alliance did criticize President Roosevelt—"Congress and the Administration Can Stop the WPA layoffs" was one slogan—and at a meeting with Harry Hopkins, David Lasser complained that Roosevelt "has failed us." But virtually all of the publicity before and during the march was directed at Congress' failure to act. Hopkins promised that there would be no more WPA job cuts in the current fiscal year. Nothing would be done for those already fired, but they would be placed on furlough, eligible to return to the WPA when new appropriations were received.[36]

In years gone by, the Communists would have dismissed such a concession as a meaningless sop. There would have been loud demands that those already fired be rehired. Angry pickets around the White House would have denounced the sellout. Instead, the marchers quietly left town and Herbert Benjamin announced that never before had "an administration given such direct concessions to the unemployed." The honeymoon had begun. The following year Benjamin admitted that unemployment was just as high as in 1932. Yet, the old methods of struggle were no longer appropriate: "Times have changed. The fight of the past eight years has not been in vain. The attitude and policy of the government have changed." Political action and not demonstrations was what was needed: "Responsible leaders of the unemployed are not likely to advise any action which would jeopardize the necessary collaboration with the powerful unions and the influential progressive movements generally." Just in case anyone failed to understand, Benjamin added that in the interests of the People's Front, there could be no demonstrations "against progressive officials supported by organized labor and progressive forces."[37]

The Workers' Alliance became a normal pressure group. Yearly battles over appropriations and deficiency appropriations in Congress brought the alliance and the WPA closer together. Relief was not the most popular government program, so the WPA was grateful to have a loud pressure group reminding Congress that too severe cuts might initiate social disorder. Earl Browder described the scenario often played out: "Whenever the WPA had an appropriation up, Congress would shave it down to half. Then we would put on demonstrations in six cities; Congress would bring it up to two-thirds. We'd put on another series of demonstrations and they'd get their appropriation." The administration was not unappreciative or unaware of what was taking place. According to Browder, Benjamin took him to a meeting with Aubrey Williams, deputy administrator of the WPA. Williams supposedly suggested that it was necessary to stage more demonstrations to pressure Congress, and Browder highmindedly responded that the time had come for the administration to win its appropriations without such tactics. Benjamin met four or five times with Harry Hopkins to discuss the Party's domestic policies. More often he held informal talks with Williams and David Niles of the WPA. In May 1939 the Workers' Alliance sponsored a Right to Work Conference to press for full employment. Before the conference, Lasser and Benjamin spoke to Roosevelt, who indicated that he supported them but that they had to convince "those sons of bitches on the Hill." Following this meeting, the WPA provided campsites, tents, and the use of government buildings for the gathering. According to Benjamin, David Niles even paid some of the bills with money contributed by Eleanor Roosevelt.[38]

The WPA did not cooperate with the Workers' Alliance just for the sake of gaining higher appropriations. In its upper echelons was a group of executives who welcomed the advent of the People's Front. David K. Niles, a veteran of the 1924 LaFollete campaign and active in the futile effort to save Sacco and Vanzetti, was a frequent contact between the administration and radical groups. Jacob Baker, an assistant administrator of the WPA and later president of the CIO's United Federal Workers, was praised in *The Daily Worker* for bringing "many progressives into the WPA administrative staff." Such other people as Hallie Flanagan, director of the Federal Theatre Project, and Henry Alsberg, director of the Federal Writers Project, had long been associated with and sympathetic to left-wing causes. None were Communists, but they were New Dealers. After the Seventh World Congress, Communists represented a potential ally. Before leaving for Moscow in the spring of 1936, Earl Browder had some contacts with "those bright young executives that surrounded Hopkins, very fine men and very capable and very frank and outspoken." They did not want to see a separate Farmer-Labor party to add to what seemed Roosevelt's other barriers to reelection. The Communists fully embraced the Roosevelt administration only when the New Deal began its retreat, buffeted by desertions of Democrats and an inability to pass major programs. Under these circumstances, some New Dealers were happy to have allies, particularly energetic ones, wherever they could be found.[39]

Few government officials so symbolized this dilemma as Harry Hopkins's deputy administrator of the WPA, Aubrey Williams. Born in Alabama to a working-class family, Williams enlisted in the French Foreign Legion and then transferred into the U.S. army to fight in World War I. A one-time student pastor, he finally settled on a social work career. Harry Hopkins put Williams in charge of the Civil Works Administration in 1933 and then brought him into the WPA in 1935. That same year, Franklin Roosevelt appointed Williams executive director of the National Youth Administration. He continued to hold both jobs until resigning from the WPA in 1939. Aubrey Williams was no Communist. Like other New Dealers, he earned the Party's enmity before 1936 and after 1939. A devoted and dedicated liberal, he remained faithful to Franklin Roosevelt when the Communists were castigating the President as a fascist and again when they labeled him an imperialist. Nonetheless, during the People's Front era he did not hesitate to cooperate with Communists. He held at least one meeting with Earl Browder. He frequently met with Herbert Benjamin. A letter from Williams to the Workers' Alliance in 1936 extended it WPA recognition as a collective bargaining agency for its members. Speaking to a Workers' Alliance gathering in 1938, he reminded his listeners: "We've got to stick together. We've got to keep our friends in power." He praised David Lasser and "his sidekick, Benjamin."[40]

Williams' outspokenness brought him denunciations as a Marxist or Communist sympathizer. Right-winger Joe Kamp sputtered that Aubrey Williams was "the most dangerous man in the government." Congressman Hamilton Fish conceded that Williams might not be a Communist, but called him "one of the pinkest of the pink." Williams' past record finally caught up to him in 1945. Nominated by Roosevelt to head the Rural Electrification Administration, he confronted a wall of opposition. The Farm Bureau disliked his association with the Farmers Union, a Popular Front organization. Senator Bilbo of Mississippi was upset by his bold denunciations of racism and his effort to outlaw Jim Crow practices in Capitol buildings. Even Williams' old pastor wrote in a letter that his denial of the divinity of Jesus Christ should disqualify him from government service. None of these issues, however, did him as much damage as the charges of undue sympathy for communism. There were three citations from the Dies Committee, although Williams denied he was ever a member of any of the three organizations identified as Communist fronts. Senator Harlan Bushfield of South Dakota discerned radical sentiments in many of Williams' old speeches. Senator McKellar denounced him as a Communist stooge.[41]

Rather than meet the Communism issue head on, Williams chose to play the role of innocent. Instead of frankly admitting the New Dealers' brief de facto alliance with the Party, he dissembled. Had he praised the Workers' Alliance? At the time, he claimed, it was not yet Communist-controlled. Had he cooperated with the American Youth Congress? At the time it was still independent. Had he praised Herbert Benjamin in April 1938? He did not then know that Benjamin was a Communist. The Senate committee considering his nomination did not believe him. That a politically sophisticated, high-ranking government official could have been so unaware strained credulity. In fact, of course, Williams knew exactly with whom he had been dealing. His reticence only fed suspicions that he had something dishonorable to hide. The Senate rejected his nomination, 52 to 36. Williams returned to Alabama, where he published an iconoclastic farmers' newspaper and briefly headed the Southern Conference Educational Fund, one of the last gasps of the Popular Front in the South. He died shortly after his one-time protégé Lyndon Johnson became President.[42]

The ties of the Workers' Alliance were little secret from anyone who wanted to know. One Party activist from Harlem who served on the National Executive Board, Mrs. Frances Duty, resigned in 1938. She told the Woodrum Commission investigating the WPA that "the Workers' Alliance is the Communist Party." She knew nineteen of the twenty-five board members from 1937 as Communists. Secretary-Treasurer Benjamin was not the only prominent Party member either. Harold Brockway had been the Communist candidate for governor of Washington in 1936; Wallace Talbot had run for the same office in Utah. Arnold Johnson, Sam Wiseman, and Alex Noral were similarly well known. David Lasser remained president, however, enabling the Workers' Alliance to preserve a facade of independence.[43]

Born in Baltimore in 1902, David Lasser might never have rubbed shoulders with the Communists if not for the Depression. He was graduated from M.I.T. in 1924 with a degree in engineering, served in 1929 as president of the American Interplanetary Society, and edited scientific magazines in New York. Lasser voted for Herbert Hoover in 1928. The Depression jolted him out of the scientific world and he became a Socialist. By 1933 he had become active in unemployed work and was soon the executive secretary of the Socialist-dominated New York Workers' Committee on Unemployment. At first he resisted the Communists' overtures for unity. Once convinced that they would accept a minority status, he finally acceded. The Socialist party, then in the process of disintegration, proved a weak reed to support Lasser. At the same time, he became an enthusiast for the People's Front. He visited Russia in 1937 and exulted that the Communist regime had solved the social security problem. The workers had plenty of leisure and job security to boot. "The Soviet citizen," he allowed, "does not fear regimentation of his mind and activities." In 1938 he resigned from the Socialist party. Two witnesses before the Woodrum Committee stopped just short of claiming he was a Communist: Frances Duty testified that Lasser had met with Israel Amter at Party headquarters, while Ralph DeSola, at one time head of the Communist fraction of the New York Writers' Project, claimed he had met Lasser at fraction meetings. Lasser himself swore under oath that he was no Communist. By the late 1930s, however, his organization was dominated by the Party.[44]

The Communist approach to work among the unemployed shifted during the People's Front years, making cooperation with people like Lasser easier. The tragedy of the Workers' Alliance, Frances Piven and Richard Cloward have charged, was that "during the brief and tumultuous period when people were ready to act against the authorities and against the norms that ordinarily bind them," the alliance rejected "pushing turbulence to its outer limits" and instead "set about to build organization and to press for legislation."[45] So facile a charge ignores the problems that the Communists faced once the New Deal came to power. The old, spontaneous eruptions of the unemployed grew smaller and smaller. New Deal programs, however inadequate, stole the Party's thunder. Somewhat to its own surprise, the Unemployment Councils discovered that demonstrations against Congress produced fewer results than lobbying within Congress. The Workers' Alliance likewise found out that the unemployed were very hard to organize; whatever influence it had was as a trade union for WPA workers.

The abandonment of large demonstrations, however, was not a decision made by the Communist leaders in unemployed work. The growing menace of fascism made the People's Front the first priority of all Communist parties. In the United States this required an alliance with the New Deal, and the Party eventually accepted that fact of life. Had it chosen to adopt a policy of confrontation with Roosevelt, its very tentative acceptance within the labor movement and the liberal community would have been endangered. The Communists already knew the penalties of revolutionary purity—their policies of confrontation had left them tiny and isolated through 1934.

Their newfound moderation opened up undreamt-of vistas to the Communists. Congressmen took them seriously—not, for a change, as harbingers of violence, but as a political force to be conciliated and addressed. Administrators solicited their views. Most were still wary of too open contacts, but the Party could take comfort in its growing political muscle. No less than in the labor movement, the People's Front had altered dramatically the Party's standing. If it still had proved unable to affect government policy to any significant degree, it had established a temporary and partial relationship with the New Deal.

16

The Youth

I T IS the young—idealistic, committed, and unfettered by the past—whom Communists have seen as their natural constituency. The leadership that emerged in the early 1930s, however, was largely middle-aged. Browder was forty-one in 1932; Foster, fifty-one; Bedacht, forty-nine; Weinstone, thirty-five; Hathaway, forty; and Minor, forty-six. The rank-and-file membership was not much younger. In 1934, the average age of Party members was thirty-six. Forty percent were between thirty and forty years old, and 35 percent were over forty. The Communists were distressed by their weakness among young workers. Only 2,204 Communists, or 8 percent of the Party, were under twenty-five in 1935. The Party's Eighth Convention sharply condemned "the present underestimation and neglect of daily systematic work among the young workers" as a dangerous "reformist remnant" that hindered the struggle for Soviet power.[1]

The Party sponsored or influenced a variety of organizations for the young. One of the least successful was the Communist counterpart of the Boy Scouts—the Young Pioneers. It had languished through the 1920s, never recording more than 3,000 members and enrolling only about 1,000 by 1930. During the Third Period, its strident propaganda to "Smash the Boy Scouts" was accompanied by appeals to the children of workers to pledge allegiance to a group that fought "Against Bosses'

Wars! Against Child Labor! Against Bad School Conditions!" and, inevitably, "For the Defense of the Soviet Union! For a Workers' and Farmers' Government!" It finally dawned on Party leaders that such was not the road to the hearts of children. Max Bedacht complained in 1931 that there had been a tendency to make the Pioneers "a sort of children's Communist Party" and announced a new policy likely to be more appealing to them: "Play and sport shall no longer be banned from the lives of the Pioneers." The new regime ushered in an era of expansion, so that by 1934 12,000 children were in organizations affiliated to the Central Pioneer Bureau.[2]

The major Party organization to attract young workers was the Young Communist League. Unlike the auxiliaries, the YCL made no pretense of independence from the Communist party. From its name to its platform, it dutifully served as an echo of its parent organization. At its Fifth Convention in 1929, it proudly announced that it "pledges its loyalty to the Communist International." The Executive Committee of the Young Communist International emphasized that all its national sections had to be "the closest assistant of the Communist Party." Gil Green, for many years the leader and symbol of the YCL, called the organization that he led the "closest co-workers" of the Communist party. In his story the cooperation and overlap between the two are manifest.[3]

Born to Russian-Jewish immigrants in Chicago in 1906, Gilbert Greenberg graduated from high school as class valedictorian. Instead of going to college, he joined the Young Communist League in 1924. He held various jobs before becoming district organizer of the YCL in Chicago in 1927. At about the same time, he shortened his name. After a brief stint in New Bedford, Massachusetts, during a textile strike, Green was brought to New York in late 1928 to become a full-time youth functionary. He successively edited *The Young Worker*, served as the New York State organizer of the YCL, and then was made organizational secretary in 1931. The organization in which he worked was undergoing problems in the early 1930s. Following John Williamson's graduation to the adult party in 1929, John Harvey succeeded him as national secretary of the YCL, largely on the basis of an Anglo-Saxon background. After a brief, unsatisfactory tenure, Harvey was replaced by John Steuben, who had to be removed by Browder in 1931 for resisting the Party's orders. Steuben's ouster did not end the squabbling in the YCL. At a 1932 plenum, leaders of the New York chapter were rebuked for their reluctance to deal with non-Communist youth. Still another charge against the YCL was its emphasis on cultural issues rather than economic struggles. Soon afterward, the YCL was entrusted to Green, who directed the Party's youth work for much of the remainder of the decade. Better suited to the more open and relaxed atmosphere of the People's Front, he nonetheless could make the necessary transitions from soft lines to hard lines and back again when necessary. Attending the Seventh World Congress of the Comintern in 1935, Green was chosen to serve on the ECCI as a youth representative and was also named to the Executive Committee and the Secretariat of the Young Communist International.[4]

The organization he took over in 1932 had a host of problems. As befitted a junior Communist party, most of these mirrored the woes of the adult group. The YCL and the Party shared the same difficulties with respect to size, fluctuation, and composition. The Comintern wanted the YCL to be larger than the Communist party. So did the Party. It was necessary, Browder lectured the Party's Eighth Convention, that the league "instead of being less than a fourth the size of the Party, must be expanded in the next period to become larger than the Party." This never occurred. After reaching a low point of 2,300 in mid-1929, YCL membership rose steadily but slowly to 3,000 in 1931, 3,750 in 1932, 6,000 in 1934, and 8,000 in mid-1935. One functionary sarcastically noted that even if the YCL had kept all who joined between 1932 and 1934, it would have been a "thriving" organization of 16,681 members. At its height in 1939, with 22,000 members, the YCL remained only one-quarter the size of its adult partner. By Browder's criteria, it was short more than 300,000 members.[5]

Everyone wanted the YCL to be well stocked with young American workers. It was not. At its 1929 national convention, John Harvey lamented that it was "a very small organization largely isolated from the masses of young workers with an unsatisfactory national and social composition." Well over 50 percent of its tiny membership were New York Jews and Finns from Superior, Wisconsin. There were only 119 Anglo-Saxons and a paltry 20 Negroes. More than half were students, office workers, and petty-bourgeois elements like farmers. Most young workers were from the needle trades and not basic industries. Things did not get better. As the YCL grew in the 1930s, one leader declared in the Comintern organ, it did not improve its composition. In 1933 Gil Green complained that fully 35 percent of the YCL members were students and farmers, about 50 percent were unemployed, and most of the rest worked in small shops, not large factories. Its composition was "extremely poor."[6]

One additional handicap under which the YCL labored was that it was not always taken seriously by adult Communists. The Party, greedy to make use of people who demonstrated capability, had a habit of raiding YCL ranks to seize its most effective organizers. Green complained in 1931 that in some areas the adults were denuding the league: "Instead of the Party helping the Y.C.L. wagon, moving it out of the ditch, we find the Party truck usually pushes the Y.C.L. wagon further into the ditch and grabs all the people that were on this wagon, puts them on the truck and rides away to the destination." The Open Letter in 1933 admonished the Party that "an end be made to the underestimation of youth work." Just one year later, however, Browder noted in despair that the YCL continued to be regarded "as a sort of probationary kindergarten" from which anyone of talent was quickly plucked. A resolution passed by the Eighth Convention in 1934 after Browder's complaint demanded once again that such errors be corrected. "Without winning the youth," it reminded all Communists, "it is impossible, when war starts, to turn it into civil war." And Otto Kuusinen reminded young Communists at the Seventh Comintern Congress that "we want to attack our class enemies in the rear, when they start the war against the Soviet Union. But how can we do so if the majority of the toiling youth follow not us, but, for instance, the Catholic priests or the liberal chameleons?"[7]

The YCL had ambitions to be more than a junior Communist party or a duplicate of the older organization. It should be a school for Communism, one of its leaders explained, "ready to admit those not yet Communists" but "willing to learn to be Communists." In some superficial ways, it was less rigid than its adult counterpart. For example, *The Young Worker* discussed and analyzed the World Series years before *The Daily Worker* deigned to acknowledge capitalist sports. There was even a certain Bohemianism among the young Communists that grated on their elders. "Those Party members who do not do so now (especially youth) should dress like ordinary American workers," pleaded one organizer in 1931. Mike Gold complained in 1933 that Young Communists "never wore hats and never patronized the barber." Not only did their appearance aid the police to single them out at demonstrations, it also diminished their effectiveness. Workers regarded them "as a species, not of revolutionist, but of freak."[8]

In all important respects, however, the YCL was a carbon copy of the CPUSA. As a section of an international body, it sent representatives to Moscow and hosted Young Communist International "reps" in America. The YCI representatives were not just observers. When a portion of the YCL leadership tried to emphasize cultural matters instead of economic struggles in 1932, the offenders were severely rebuked and their errors "corrected with the aid of the Young Communist International." There were the same demands emanating from Moscow to concentrate on specific targets, build cadres, and reduce fluctuation along with similarly lengthy, turgid theses and resolutions flowing back and forth. And the youths engaged in the same bitter factional wars with the same results for unlucky Trotskyists, Lovestoneites, or doubters of the Party line.[9]

Ineffectual as it was, the YCL did provide one important benefit to the Party during the Third Period. Just as the TUUL, a failure at bringing the masses into the Communist union movement, trained a generation of Communist union leaders, so the YCL, in this era a small organization, provided invaluable experience and a route to the Party for a corps of future functionaries. Many others came to the Party from another source—a Communist student movement that laid the basis for one of the most successful Popular Front ventures.

Prior to the early 1930s the Communists had historically paid little attention to college students. Just as the Party regarded intellectuals with suspicion, so too did it denigrate undergraduates as unreliable bourgeoisie. The YCL, itself frequently a stepchild within the Party, long scorned or ignored student work, preferring to concentrate on organizing young workers. Kuusinen sadly reported in 1935 that "formerly, many members of the Young Communist League looked down, for instance, on the student youth." That same year Gil Green admitted that "in many sections of our Young Communist League we still accept student youth into our ranks as something of a necessary evil."[10]

The center of the student Communist movement was New York City. For much of the 1920s, students and administrators at City College had argued over compulsory Reserve Officers Training Classes. For several years young Communists orchestrated a constant stream of protests, many marked by minor violence and disruptions. In the City College administration, led by President Frederick Robinson, once dean of the School of Business, they found an adversary whose response to student anger and militance only encouraged further trouble. Si Gerson, a young Communist, president of the school's Social Problems Club, and the leader of anti-ROTC sentiment, was suspended in 1928. Max Weiss, the sophomore president of the Social Problems Club, was suspended in the spring of 1930 following his arrest for distributing Communist handbills. Readmitted, Weiss was suspended once again in February 1931 for issuing an unauthorized publication, *Frontiers*. Ten other students suffered the same penalty.[11]

In the fall of 1931, young Communist students from around the city formed the New York Student League. It soon changed its name and its scope to the National Student League (NSL) and pretended to be independent of the Communist party. An official publication explained that it "is affiliated to no political party and it is controlled by the membership itself." One of its leaders, Rob Hall, assured the group's first convention that the NSL was not a Communist organization. It was admitted that "a good many members and leaders of the N.S.L. are Communists," although this statement was quickly qualified by a note that they "have been elected purely on merit." The NSL's opponents, however, recognized its loyalties. Joseph Lash of the Socialist Student League for Industrial Democracy noted in 1934 that the NSL "has been and still is the student wing of the Communist movement in this country." Friends of the league were even more indiscreet: Earl Browder told the Party's Eighth Convention that the NSL was "another auxiliary movement of great importance." And the league's own members were sometimes prone to nagging reminders of their ties; Walter Relis instructed young Communists that "only the local Y.C.L. can insure the perpetuation of the N.S.L."[12]

The Party found little that was offensive in the program or activities of the National Student League. The NSL enthusiastically joined in the same kinds of attacks on the Socialist party, which it described as "the best defender of each national bourgeoisie against the spread of revolutionary discontent"; it supported the TUUL against the A.F. of L.; it attacked the NRA as "similar to the fascist institutions in Italy and Germany"; it asserted that "only a change in the very basis of society can offer any permanent solution to our problems"; and it deferred to the working class as leaders of the revolutionary movement. During the 1932 election campaign, the NSL's paper attacked the Democrats, Republicans, and Socialists with the same vigor. Only one party received an unqualified endorsement: "The Party which combines sound revolutionary theory with the day-to-day struggle in the interests of the workers is the Communist Party."[13]

The National Student League's biggest contribution to the Communist party may have been its alumni, many of whom went on to distinguished Party careers. They included Rob Hall, Joseph Clark, Theodore Draper, Joseph Starobin, and Adam Lapin. The NSL also managed to keep New York's colleges in an uproar for several years.[14]

The fledgling National Student League's first venture into national affairs came in March 1932. Its leaders picked a cause that had attracted much media attention and publicity—the repression of civil liberties in Harlan County, Kentucky, scene of the National Miners Union strike. The first contingent of students, under the tutelage of Rob Hall, left Columbia University by bus on March 23. Reaching Knoxville, Tennessee, they wired the governor of Kentucky and asked for protection during the remainder of their journey. They did not get it. An angry mob stopped the bus as it crossed the Cumberland Gap. The Kentucky district attorney, perhaps having delusions of grandeur induced by his war with the Communists, asked for their passports. Getting down to the business at hand, he then warned that "[if you] deliberately stick your head in the fire" it would get burned, arrested the entire bus, and escorted it back across the Tennessee border. Tennessee's governor promptly noted that "we don't want a bunch of Bolsheviks, Communists or anarchists interfering with the peace of Tennessee citizens." While Donald Henderson, one of the NSL's leaders, hustled to Washington to appeal to Congress to protect civil liberties, the college students hurried back to their campuses to organize demonstrations on more congenial grounds.[15]

Henderson shortly thereafter described the student trip to Harlan County as a turning point. For the first time, he exulted, students were "definitely lining themselves up with and under the leadership of the revolutionary working class." Had the NSL continued activities in the same vein, however, it is doubtful if it could have elicited much response. The Harlan trip, in fact, was hardly typical of the NSL's activities over the next few years, for its leaders soon learned that students were far more interested in campus issues than union organizing or civil rights violations in remote corners of America. And there was no lack of complaints emanating from the campus.[16]

The Harlan delegation had barely returned to school before Columbia University students had a chance to protest an injustice closer to home. Reed Harris, editor of *The Spectator*, the student newspaper, had been printing editorials attacking collegiate football, ROTC, and censorship. He had also enthusiastically endorsed the NSL trip to Kentucky and launched a campaign to expose mistreatment of student waiters in the school's cafeterias. With consummate poor timing, the administration suspended Harris as editor and then expelled him from school just a few weeks short of graduation. The Social Problems Club, the campus affiliate of the NSL, called a protest rally in front of Low Library that attracted 4,000 people. Although most of them supported Harris's reinstatement, a contingent of college athletes—acting, according to *The Daily Worker*, "as a fascist group"—also turned up to hurl eggs, bags of water, and small tear gas bombs, allegedly "manufactured in the college laboratory." Following the skirmish, an estimated 75 percent of the undergraduates honored an NSL call for a student strike. The episode had meanwhile attracted the American Civil Liberties Union's attention. After negotiations between the ACLU and the university, Harris was reinstated.[17]

To the young Communists, the Harlan trip and the Harris protest were signs that the campuses were stirring. Max Weiss predicted that "the first large-scale crack has been made in the shell of 'neutral non-class' idiocy within which the student body has been kept for decades." Weiss also, however, reflected the Party's assessment of the importance and priority of the student movement. "The very class nature of the mass of students," he announced, "precludes all possibility of their playing an independent role." As part of the petty-bourgeoisie, students had to put themselves under the leadership of the working class.[18]

One of the student leaders who took that lesson to heart was Donald Henderson, the NSL's executive secretary. Few members of the Columbia faculty spoke up for Reed Harris. The only teacher to identify himself with the students was Henderson, a graduate student in economics who was also on the teaching faculty. He was not destined to remain there for very long. He had begun his political life as a Socialist, even serving on the board of directors of the League for Industrial Democracy (LID). He resigned, however, from the Socialist party in 1931 and announced his affiliation to the Communist party. When the NSL was established, Henderson, its executive secretary, attacked the LID as "a major obstacle to the development of a revolutionary student movement" and invited his old colleagues to defect to the new group. In 1933, during his fifth year as an economics instructor at Columbia, Henderson was suddenly fired. No mention was made of either his NSL activities or his arrest a few months before during a protest over CCNY's termination of another radical, Oakley Johnson. College authorities accused him of incompetence and pointed to his failure to finish his dissertation on the history of the Communist party of the United States.[19]

Angry students attributed the firing to Henderson's radical activities and quickly undertook a campaign on his behalf. Two thousand students massed in front of the college statue of Alma Mater on May 15 as a casket labeled "Academic Freedom" was solemnly borne in. After speeches by William Browder, Earl's brother, and J. B. Matthews, the students destroyed an effigy of university president Nicholas Murray Butler, and 500 of them marched to Butler's house before dispersing. Henderson abandoned academic life for good, becoming secretary of the American Committee Against War. In 1934, he was appointed national agricultural organizer for the TUUL. Three years later he became president of the CIO's United Cannery, Agricultural and Packing and Allied Workers Union, completing the transition demanded by the Party—from radical student to the working class.[20]

Just a few months before Henderson's dismissal, another Communist teacher, Oakley Johnson, renewed the turmoil at City College. An

English instructor in the evening division at CCNY, Johnson had a longer history than most of fraternal relations with the Communist party. He had been a Socialist since 1912, had been an official in the Michigan Socialist party in 1919, and had served as a delegate to the founding conference of the Communist party. He joined the Workers party, as the Communists were then known, during the 1920s. His formal affiliations were not, however, widely known or publicized. During the 1930s Johnson maintained a public facade as a non-Communist fellow traveler. He told a House committee in February 1932 that he was only a Communist sympathizer. Not until many years later would he admit to having been a Communist in the early 1930s. Johnson's troubles at CCNY began when the Liberal Club asked him to become their adviser in January 1932. Despite its name, the group was partial to Communist speakers. Dean Paul Lineham grew more and more perturbed by the club, particularly since its members had been active in protesting plans to impose tuition and increase fees. Before the fall term in 1932, Johnson was notified of his dismissal. This set in motion a series of protests that helped convulse City College for several years.[21]

A mass meeting of 1,000 students, held on October 26, 1932, to protest Johnson's firing, quickly turned unruly. As they marched through the main college building, shouting and disrupting evening classes, some students activated fire alarms. Four people were arrested, including Donald Henderson. They were taken to the courthouse for arraignments, followed by a big crowd; sixteen more were arrested there. President Robinson suspended ten CCNY students who had been convicted of minor offenses. He and Dean Lineham were soon tried by a "court" of 1,400 students in the Central Opera House. Three judges in black robes, all from the Liberal Club, heard prosecutor Joseph Starobin, one of those suspended, present his case, after which the audience found the administrators guilty of persecution and sentenced them to be removed from their offices. Enraged by that affront to his dignity, Robinson soon suspended twenty more students for their participation in the trial. Students responded with a strike on February 25, 1933, after which those previously punished were reinstated. By this time Johnson was all but forgotten. He soon went off to a teaching position as an assistant professor at Moscow's Institute of Foreign Languages. His departure, however, did nothing to calm the fires at CCNY. Before the academic year was over, another issue had thrown the campus into even more turmoil.[22]

From its earliest days the student movement had been concerned with the war issue. Joseph Cohen (Clark) attended the World Anti-War Conference in Amsterdam in August 1932 as an NSL delegate before going on to the International Conference of Revolutionary Students. Henri Barbuse, one of the chief organizers of the Amsterdam conference, asked the NSL to organize a national anti-war student conference in the United States. The ensuing gathering, the National Student Anti-War Conference, held in Chicago in late December 1932, turned out to be one of the earliest united fronts between Communists and non-Communists. Close to 700 delegates appeared, with large blocs from Party-controlled organizations and pacifist groups. Although both the Young People's Socialist League and the LID complained of Communist dominance, some of their members were also present. Communists and pacifists found agreement on a minimum program of struggle against imperialist war. To placate the Socialists, the young Party members agreed to drop a pledge of support to the American Committee for Struggle Against War, which had embodied a denunciation of the second Socialist International in its program. That sort of heresy quickly drew the disapproval of the Communist hierarchy. While praising the meeting, Gil Green criticized the Communist students for their compromises and for failing to conduct a sharp enough struggle against the leadership of other groups. Instead of seeking unity with their rank-and-file members, he charged, the Communists had made united fronts from above.[23]

Despite its premature united frontism, the Communist student movement had launched a successful "peace campaign." On American campuses, moreover, lurked a ready-made villain that symbolized American militarism and the universities' complicity with it: Reserve Officers Training Classes. Nowhere was ROTC as contentious as at CCNY. The first battles against compulsory drill had taken place in 1925 and continued in a desultory fashion for several years until the faculty set up a three-year course in hygiene as an alternative to military drill. May 29 was the date for the annual ROTC exhibition, irreverently dubbed Jingo Day by the radical students. In 1933 the NSL mounted an anti-war demonstration outside of Lewisohn Stadium, site of the ROTC parade. Some 500 students were carrying picket signs and chanting when President Robinson arrived to review the troops. Either provoked by their rudeness to him or temporarily demented by the sight of dissenting students, Robinson suddenly turned on the protesters. Wielding an umbrella, the choleric president flailed away at his tormentors, who did their best to escape his attack. Robinson later insisted that he had been attacked. In any case, he quickly resorted to his favorite tactic when dealing with radical students. Eight people were suspended, including Adam Lapin, secretary of the Student Council, and Walter Relis, president of the Social Problems

Club. Nor was that the end of Robinson's revenge. By the end of the school term a faculty committee had expelled twenty students and suspended eleven others. The charter of the student newspaper, *The Campus*, had been lifted and three student organizations, the Social Problems Club, The Liberal Club, and the Student Forum, had been dissolved by administrative fiat.[24]

The travails of City College were not yet over. President Robinson extended an invitation in the fall of 1934 to a group of Italian fascist students touring America to enjoy the hospitality of City College. When the sixteen Italians arrived at a ceremony to greet them, they were faced by a picket line that had been encouraged by the Student Council. As Robinson rose to speak at the reception, he was greeted with derision—to which he responded that the offending students' behavior was worse than that of "guttersnipes." Greater friction was yet to come. Edwin Alexander, a leader of the CCNY chapter of the NSL, had been selected by the Student Council to speak on its behalf. Administrators pleaded with him not to offend the visitors' sensibilities. He denied any intention to be discourteous but brought "anti-fascist greetings from the student body of City College to the enslaved, tricked student body of Italy." With that, the meeting dissolved in chaos. Theodore Draper reported that "professors and the visiting fascists surrounded [Alexander], the students in their seats rose and massed forward to his defense and the scene became one of bedlam." Five hundred angry students met thereafter to demand Robinson's ouster. Once again suspensions and expulsions began. When the dust had cleared, the faculty had expelled twenty-one students, suspended six others, and put twelve more on probation. The Student Council was suspended and investigations launched into several student publications.[25]

An even more effective and dramatic way to protest against war developed in the 1933–1934 school year. The NSL had dutifully addressed an open letter to the Student League for Industrial Democracy's 1933 convention calling for amalgamation of the two groups. The letter elicited little enthusiasm. Joseph Lash, the SLID's leader, noted that the NSL "has been and still is the student wing of the Communist movement in this country." Given the major disagreements between the Socialists and the Communists, any merger would be doomed to failure. The two groups did manage, however, to join forces for specific events. Late in December 1933, 350 students, mostly delegates to separate but simultaneous SLID and NSL conventions taking place in Washington, marched to the White House to denounce ROTC and the militarization of American society. Presidential secretary Louis Howe met with a small delegation, including Joe Clark and Joe Starobin of the NSL and Joe Lash, who presented him with a petition signed by 5,000 students.[26]

Pleas to authorities were only one part of the new campaign against war launched by the students and not the most important at that. Early in 1933 the Oxford Union in England had adopted a resolution that it would "not fight for King and country in any war." The Oxford Pledge quickly caught the attention of American students and helped stimulate plans for anti-war rallies at which students would affirm their refusal to fight. The first nationwide student strike against war, sponsored by the NSL and SLID, with the aid of the American League Against War and Fascism, took place on April 13, 1934. Organizers claimed that 25,000 students answered their call to boycott classes or otherwise participate. Most of the activity took place in New York, where *The Daily Worker* estimated that 15,000 participated. By the next year the anti-war strike was a major event on American campuses. With the added endorsement of various and sundry church groups, the strike dwarfed the inaugural year. By one estimate, 175,000 students participated, only 30,000 of them in New York. The highlight was mass recitation of a modified form of the Oxford Pledge that only required adherents "not to support the government of the United States in any war it may conduct."[27]

The growing numbers of students willing to take part in anti-war demonstrations and civil liberties protests on college campuses was not matched by a growth in the NSL's organizational prowess. Left to its own resources, in fact, the National Student League might have done no more or better than some other Communist auxiliaries that led dramatic struggles in the early 1930s but stagnated as other reform groups and organizations prospered beginning in 1934. The NSL had never been large. Its first convention in 1932 had attracted forty-five delegates from nineteen schools. The second, held in December 1932 in Chicago, drew 150 who claimed to represent 1,400 members scattered in 200 colleges and high schools. One year later 237 delegates came to the convention at Howard University, but over half of them were from New York. Few Southern schools were ever represented at NSL gatherings, nor were there many Negro members. Except for representation at a handful of large state universities in the Midwest and on the West Coast, a few expensive and elite private liberal arts colleges, and Chicago's Crane Junior College, the NSL was primarily a New York organization. Even at CCNY, where its activities won it more attention than anywhere else, it had only 150 members late in 1933. While the National Student League had been organizing and leading some dramatic protests, it had not succeeded in becoming a mass student organization. When the NSL and SLID finally did merge in 1935, the former contributed only between 600 and 700 members while the latter had between 2,000 and 2,500.[28]

Union with the SLID offered the NSL an escape from its isolation. As in their adult party, the young Socialists were badly split between social democrats and more revolutionary enthusiasts. The advocates of closer cooperation with Communists were stronger among the young. Gil Green explained to the Seventh Congress that the Socialist youth "does not have a bureaucracy in the sense of the one that exists within the Socialist Party." They were, he advised, more militant, more amenable to the united front and possibly even to Communism. For the young Socialists, the Comintern's abandonment of the Third Period and endorsement of the People's Front removed the last barriers to a complete merger. Four hundred delegates from the NSL and SLID met in Columbus, Ohio, in December 1935 to form the American Student Union (ASU). It was the first merger of Communist and Socialist bodies, predating the formation of the Workers' Alliance by four months. Leading positions in the new organization were carefully allocated to the respective groups. From the SLID, George Edwards of Southern Methodist University became national chairman; Joe Lash, national secretary; and Molly Yard of Swarthmore College, treasurer. From the NSL, James Wechsler of Columbia was picked as editor of *The Student Advocate*, Celeste Strack of Berkeley as high school secretary, and Serrill Gerber as field secretary. Wechsler, Strack, and Gerber were all members of the Young Communist League.[29]

The American Student Union was never very large, reaching 20,000 members in 1939. Its members and leaders, however, were among the most articulate and sophisticated student activists. Their influence on their peers was considerable. Despite some acrimonious internal battles, the ASU very quickly became one of the Party's People's Front strongholds. From its very first convention the ASU was the scene of bruising battles between the Communists and their allies, on one side, and young social democrats and Trotskyists on the other. The Communist party's newfound devotion to collective security and abandonment of a revolutionary foreign-policy line prompted most of the disputes. As the Communists moved further to the right on the political spectrum, they struck up an alliance with pro–New Deal forces while being attacked from the left as traitors to revolutionary Marxism.[30]

The focus of ASU debates was the Oxford Pledge. As the Communist party moved from attacks on imperialist wars and American militarism toward support for collective security, the Oxford Pledge became more and more of an embarrassment. Delegates to the first ASU convention had taken the pledge. A group of Socialists, however, introduced a resolution that attempted to flesh it out, specifying that the Oxford Pledge would be applicable whether Japan invaded America, America invaded Japan, or America was allied with progressive nations in a war against fascism. The motion was defeated in favor of an NSL-supported measure opposing any war the government undertook but naming only Germany, Japan, and Italy as threats to world peace.[31]

By 1936, the Young People's Socialist League (YPSL) had been substantially captured by the Trotskyists who had entered the Socialist party. They had no intention of endorsing collective security. Like Lenin in World War I, they insisted that good Bolsheviks could not support their bourgeois governments in war. When Hal Draper, leader of the YPSL contingent in the ASU, needled two young Communists for no longer supporting the Oxford Pledge, they noted defensively that the YCL "was the first advocate of the Oxford Pledge." A YPSL-sponsored resolution at the 1936 ASU convention opposing collective security lost by only thirty-seven votes, and the convention avoided even mentioning the concept in its program. Joe Lash gave an indication, however, that support for the Oxford Pledge was not written in stone. He insisted that, unlike pacifists, ASU members regarded the pledge as a means to an end, not an "ethical absolute."[32]

By the following year the Communists and their allies were able to be rid of the Oxford Pledge once and for all. Meeting in November 1937, the ASU's Administrative Committee voted 6 to 5 to dissociate from the Youth Committee for the Oxford Pledge; four YCL'ers had been joined by Lash and Robert Spivack to make a majority. One month later the ASU's third convention met at Vassar College. Greeted by a message from President Roosevelt, the delegates settled down to a verbal brawl over the Oxford Pledge. By a vote of 282 to 108, the convention endorsed collective security. YPSL members and their allies soon set up their own organizations, the Youth Committee Against War and the Committee for Youth Needs. While they remained formally tied to the ASU, they took little further part in its activities. The Party's victory in the American Student Union had been assured. The consequences were hardly revolutionary, however. At the 1937 ASU convention, President Roosevelt had sent the delegates his greetings. He repeated them in 1938 when the convention "almost unanimously accepted the New Deal and its social goals as the goals of the A.S.U. itself." One year later the ASU convention featured cheerleaders, a band, and the Campus Stomp ("everybody's doing it, ASU'ing it").[33]

It was not covert manipulation that enabled the Party to win over the ASU to its program but an alliance with such people as Joseph Lash. Entering CCNY as a supporter of President Robinson, Lash had become a Socialist in 1929 and grown active in the SLID. He went onto obtain a master's degree from Columbia, but politics, not scholarship, engaged more and more of his time. Lash cooperated with the NSL in the early 1930s. He went to Harlan County in 1932 and sponsored united front anti-war demonstrations in both 1934 and 1935. Prior to the Comintern's Seventh Congress, he had rejected overtures for a merger of his group and the NSL. However, he was impressed by the congress and by the NSL's agreement to allow the merged organization to retain both its SLID name and affiliation to its adult counterpart. Lash magnanimously proposed, at a merger meeting in September 1935, that a totally new group, the American Student Union, be formed. During the next four years Lash moved closer and closer to the Party. A trip to Spain in 1937 completed his conversion from pacifism to advocacy of collective security. Although he had wanted to join the International Brigades, he had to be content with making speeches. Two months after returning he resigned from the Socialist party, criticizing it for standing aside from the Popular Front because of Communist involvement. Lash never did join the Communist party, but he came very close. "I had regarded myself as a non-Party Communist," he later wrote, "participated in a Marxist study circle organized by the Party, was waiting only to leave the A.S.U. to formalize my relationship to the Party, and in fact was discussing going to work for *The Daily Worker* when the Nazi-Soviet pact was announced." After his break, he told the Dies Committee that he had even attended some YCL board meetings as a guest.[34]

The Communists' greatest triumph in youth work was, however, accomplished not by the ASU but by the American Youth Congress. The AYC was a delegate body that claimed to speak for all American youth. The idea for a youth congress had been the brainchild of Viola Ilma. an apolitical young woman impressed by similar organizations in Europe. Early in 1934 she sent out invitations to every variety of youth group, inviting each of them to send representatives to a youth congress in August 1934. Among those invited were the Young Communist League and the National Student League. Not all young Communists jumped at the invitation. Gil Green informed the Seventh Comintern Congress that some of his members "felt a bit uneasy in such strange company" and did not want to attend. With aid from Earl Browder and the Party's Central Committee, however, "we decided to go to the Congress and meet the enemy face-to-face."[35]

Even before the conference began, a coalition made up largely of young Communists and young Socialists was mapping plans to keep Viola Ilma from dominating the event. When the American Youth Congress met at New York University in August 1934, Ilma's high-handed attempt to prevent the delegates from electing their own officers failed. *The Daily Worker* charged that her goal had been to use the AYC "to introduce a widespread system of transient camps, apprenticeship periods with little or no pay for all youth who are graduating from schools and the putting of youth onto barren lands as a substitute for unemployment insurance." John Spivack insinuated in *The New Masses* that Ilma had close ties to the Nazis and was somehow hoping to serve their interests. For her part, Ilma announced that "Communist gangs have perpetrated a plot" and set up her own, rival congress, which soon sank from sight.[36]

There were Communists aplenty at the congress, but they were joined by such non-Communist groups as the Boy Scouts, Girl Scouts, young Zionists, young Socialists, and religious organizations, with there being seventy-nine groups in all. *The Daily Worker* exulted over the breadth of the resultant united front. It presented a "remarkable picture never before seen in the United States. Young Christians, young Socialists and young Communists, pacifists and those who are ready to use arms to overthrow capitalism, gathered together, tossed aside differences" and agreed to a minimum program to combat unemployment, war, and fascism. The Continuations Committee of fifteen, charged with creating a permanent organization, included not only Theodore Draper of the NSL and Gil Green of the YCL but Hal Draper of the SLID, Aaron Levenstein of the YPSL, Alfred Bingham of the Farmer-Labor Federation, Jeanette Krutis and Waldo McNutt of the YMCA, Elizabeth Reed of the National Student Federation, and representatives of a union and Negro groups. The AYC was easily the broadest and largest united front the Party had been able to fashion in years. Unlike such organizations as the American League Against War and Fascism, it had constituents that were primarily bona fide non-Communist groups claiming 1.7 million members. To the Party's delight, several of its proposals received approval, including the Workers' Unemployment Insurance Bill, a denunciation of the Civilian Conservation Corps, and an anti-war resolution similar to the American League Against War and Fascism's program.[37]

Communist spokesmen were not bashful about their role in the AYC. Shortly after the first gathering, Browder boasted that its "political center of gravity is work of the Y.C.L." and that "practically all the basic proposals and policies came from us and from those influenced by us." The Party leader was so impressed that he used the success in youth work to chide the adult Party. "How is it," he complained in May 1935 to the Central Committee, "that the Youth are making greater successes than the Party with one-fourth the strength of the Party? They make twice or three times the advances in the united front that the Party generally does." At the Comintern's Seventh Congress, one of the few aspects of the American Communists' work receiving praise was the youth field. "Our young comrades," Otto Kuusinen gushed, had "achieved a great success" at the first AYC; by the second congress they "already enjoyed a position of authority at it." At the Sixth Young Communist International Congress, Wolf Michael singled out the AYC experience as a model: "This is an example of how to influence the masses of youth instead of commanding them in a bureaucratic way."[38]

The Party owed its success in the AYC to more than the force of its arguments. In addition to the official Communist members of the AYC's leading bodies, there were both secret Communists and fellow travelers who aided the Party's domination. James Wechsler, once a young Communist and a leader of the ASU, charged years later that "the fraud began that summer of 1934 when members of the Communist fraction posed as simple peasants from the hinterlands to obtain top posts" at the congress. He reported seeing the successful candidate for chairman of the AYC, Waldo McNutt, at a YCL fraction meeting the night before his election. McNutt had officially represented not any Communist auxiliary but the Rocky Mountain YMCA. His successor, William Hinckley, was named as a Communist by witnesses before HUAC. Wechsler claimed that Hinckley was a Communist but said he did not know whether Hinckley actually held a Party card. Hinckley denied Party membership to the Dies Committee. The AYC's executive secretary, Joseph Cadden, and its legislative secretary, Abbot Simon, were also identified as Communists by various witnesses.[39]

Other leaders of the AYC were fellow travelers. None better exemplified the breed than Jack McMichael. A native of Quitman, Georgia, and a graduate of Emory University, McMichael was an ordained Methodist minister. When he was chosen chairman of the AYC in 1939, he was chairman of the National Intercollegiate Christian Youth Council, the college division of the YMCA and YWCA, and had just returned from a year in China and India. He resolutely opposed "red-baiting" in the AYC, accusing critics of the Party of hindering the group's work. "Some so-called enemies of Communism from the outside tried to break up the unity of this Congress," he charged in 1939. McMichael—who was often accused of being a Communist, both in the AYC and later when he was executive secretary of the Methodist Federation for Social Action—flatly denied before a congressional committee that he had ever been a member of either the Party or the YCL. He defended his association with Communists in more spiritual terms: "Remember about Jesus and the publicans and the sinners and I considered the Communists sinners and I followed the practice of Jesus."[40]

Communists were not found only at the top of the AYC. The Young Communist League was much quicker than the adult Party to understand the need to work within bourgeois organizations. After the first AYC meeting, some young Communists, as Gil Green put it, wanted "to narrow the movement a bit. We were afraid of the mixed class composition of the united front." Rather than write off bourgeois youth organizations, the YCL decided to "enter these organizations not with the purpose of destroying or weakening them, but of work to transform them from centers of bourgeois influence into centers for united front struggle, of proletarian influence." Green noted that "through pursuing such a policy in the course of less than a year our Young Communist League built 175 units within these mass organizations and through these has begun to anchor the united front down below." These Communist factions in non-Communist youth organizations also worked to elect their own representatives to AYC meetings.[41]

The young Communists' tasks in the AYC were considerably eased by the Party's devotion to the New Deal and collective security. Most of the AYC's efforts were devoted to securing passage of the American Youth Act, which would have provided government training and jobs at $25 a week for unemployed youth. Introduced into Congress several times, the bill never was approved but did stimulate larger appropriations for the National Youth Administration. Periodic pilgrimages to Washington to lobby for their proposal brought AYC leaders government recognition as spokesmen for American youth; the organization was granted a slot on the National Youth Administration advisory committee, and its leaders were consulted by the administration. The Seventh Congress considerably eased foreign-policy problems. Early in 1935, Max Weiss and Charles Wilson had issued a bloodcurdling warning in expressing the Party's view of war: "We Communists are so sincere and so earnest in our fight for peace that we are prepared, and we work to prepare the masses, to carry on the most determined fight for peace, to carry through the most effective measures, up to and including the measures of revolutionary civil war against those who stand in the way of peace." By 1937 the Party had embraced collective security and President Roosevelt. When a coalition of delegates from the YPSL, ILGWU Local 22, the Southern Tenant Farmers' Union, and the Young Poale Zion challenged

322

the support of collective security at the 1936 AYC congress, they were overwhelmingly defeated. At the 1939 congress, the Communist delegates even joined in condemning the Soviet Union. Although Gil Green protested against the phrasing of a resolution opposing both fascists and communist dictatorships, the YCL wound up voting in its favor.[42]

The AYC enjoyed the patronage of Eleanor Roosevelt and support from scores of other distinguished Americans. According to Joseph Lash, Mrs. Roosevelt admired their "earnestness" and idealism. Among the patrons at one AYC dinner in February 1939 were Mickey Rooney, Archibald MacLeish, A. A. Berle, Fiorello LaGuardia, James Farley, Admiral William Byrd, Clare Boothe Luce, Orson Welles, Thomas Watson, Herbert Bayard Swope, Dorothy Canfield Fisher, Ernest Hemingway, Henry Morgenthau, and Mrs. Felix Frankfurter. Possibly the AYC's most glittering moment came in August 1938, when it served as host to the second World Youth Congress at Vassar. Five hundred delegates from fifty-four countries converged on Poughkeepsie, New York, including fifty Americans claiming to represent 15 million young people. The congress was unanimously endorsed by the New York City Council; was sponsored by, among others, Admiral Richard Byrd, John L. Lewis, Senator Gerald Nye, and Dr. Homer Rainey; and was addressed at the opening session by Mrs. Roosevelt. Representatives at the congress waxed enthusiastic about the need for collective security. The AYC itself continued to grow. Where it had claimed to represent 1.3 million young people at its 1936 meeting, by 1939 it claimed affiliation by groups with 4.7 million members.[43]

Youth groups were less frightened at working with the Communist party than politicians or labor leaders. As in other areas of work, however, the Party discovered that it could become a vital part of a larger coalition by dropping its revolutionary rhetoric and accepting liberal policy goals.

17

The Negroes

FOR their first decade the American Communists, preoccupied with their factional struggles, did not pay much attention to Negroes or their problems. The Workers party program in 1924 mentioned that "the Negro workers of this country are exploited and oppressed more ruthlessly than any other group." Four years later the Party formulated twelve demands that would end oppression of Negroes. The demands boiled down to an "abolition of the whole system of race discrimination. Full racial, political and social equality for the Negro race." Its militantly egalitarian rhetoric notwithstanding, the Communist party found it difficult to gain access to Negro workers. The American Negro Labor Congress was created to serve as a Party auxiliary in 1925, but it failed to make a dent among its potential clients. James Ford later confessed that during its five-year existence, the congress "was almost completely isolated from the basic masses of the Negro people." A more telling indication of the Communists' straits was their inability to recruit Negro members. On the eve of the Depression, Jack Stachel reported that no more than 200 blacks had Party cards.[1]

Toward the end of the decade, the Comintern stepped in. At its sixth Congress in 1928, the American Communists accepted a new doctrine defining Southern Negroes as an oppressed group deserving the right to secede from America and create a separate black nation. The Comintern's final resolution, published in New York in February 1929, ordered the Party to "come out openly and unreservedly for the right of Negroes to national self-determination in the southern states, where the Negroes form a majority of the population." Earl Browder even boasted that the new line was imported: "We could not have arrived at our program only upon the basis of our own American experience."[2]

The theory had not been discussed in America. Its most vocal advocate was Harry Haywood, a young American Negro who was studying at the Lenin School. Other Americans in Moscow, both black and white, were vehemently opposed on the grounds that the doctrine smacked of Jim Crowism or that Negroes only wanted equality. Haywood himself was barely known in the Party. Born to former slaves in Omaha, Nebraska, in 1898, he joined his older brother, Otto Hall, in the Communist party in 1925. Just one year later he was selected to study in Russia and spent the next four years abroad. The theory he championed traced its pedigree to Joseph Stalin's work advocating the right of self-determination for the oppressed minorities of the Tsarist empire. They had to be free to choose whether they wished to be part of Russia, even after the Bolshevik revolution. As the Soviet expert on the national question, Stalin was the obvious instigator in applying his theory to America.[3]

The new Comintern line did not immediately catch on in America. Otto Huiswood, one of the Party's leading Negro functionaries, attacked the idea that there was no difference between "the National-colonial character of the Negro question in Africa and the West Indies and the racial character of this question in the United States." American Negroes were not a nation. The solution to their problems was "race equality as well as political and social equality." Huiswood discreetly made no mention of self-determination. Another Communist admitted in March 1930 that the American Party had yet to discuss the issue of self-determination and was "proceeding very slowly in approaching our Negro work from such an angle."[4]

Meanwhile, the Comintern was divided about the implications of the theory. When Max Bedacht and Will Weinstone discussed their draft thesis with the Comintern's Political Secretariat in March 1930, "the Negro question" was a prominent portion of the agenda. The Secretariat had before it a draft letter to the American Party prepared by one of its subcommittees, authored by Haywood and N. Nasanov, a Young Communist International functionary and former YCI "rep" in America, demanding "that self-determination must be turned from propaganda slogan into political action aim." Otto Kuusinen argued that emphasizing the "struggle for self-determination [as opposed to the] concrete fight against discrimination against Negroes is a flight from realities to abstractions." The consensus of the Comintern leaders was: "Self-determination slogan is agitation slogan, while aim of immediate action is the concrete fight against Jim Crowism and other discriminatory actions of the bourgeois state." Bedacht and Weinstone cabled their colleagues that they did not have to advocate the actual separation of the "Black Belt" from the United States:

POLITSECRETARIAT CONSIDERS THAT AT PRESENT TIME THERE IS NO REASON TO THINK STATE SEPARATION OF NEGROES HAS BECOME IMMEDIATE QUESTION IN USA AND THEREFORE AT PRESENT NOT EXPEDIENT FROM VIEWPOINT OF MOBILIZING NEGRO MASSES IN STRUGGLE AGAINST IMPERIALISM TO EMPHASIZE THIS POINT TOO MUCH (STATE SEPARATION). SUCH PLACING OF QUESTION OF COURSE DOES NOT CONFLICT AT ALL WITH CONCEPTION OF COMMUNIST PARTY ON FULL RIGHT OF POPULATION TO SELFDETERMINATION.[5]

The news from Moscow came too late to change the revised draft thesis, which declared that "our Party fully recognizes the right of the Negro masses to self-determination to the point of separation." Luckily, the draft program had still one more revision to go. The final version got it right. Communists "openly and unreservedly fight for the right of Negroes for national self-determination in the South." At the same time, Party leaders also took to heart the Comintern's advice that they need do no more than talk and agitate about self-determination. Reporting on the Seventh Party Convention, Browder dutifully criticized the rightist deviation that denied "the validity of the slogan of self-determination" and the leftist mistake "that the slogan must be immediately transformed from a propaganda slogan into a slogan of action."[6]

The Comintern was not, however, finished with the self-determination issue, offering another resolution in August 1930. In certain key respects, this resolution totally reversed the 1929 document and the March 1930 instructions. The struggle for equal rights applied to all Negroes but was no longer to be the "central slogan." In the South, "the main Communist slogan must be: The Right of Self-Determination of the Negroes in the Black Belt." Communists were instructed in all concrete struggles "to concentrate the attention of the Negro masses not so much on the general demands of mere equality, but much more on some of the revolutionary basic demands arising from the concrete situation." The resolution also added two other basic demands: "confiscation of the landed property of the white landowners and capitalists for the benefit of the Negro farmers" (italicized in the resolution), and the creation of one governmental unit from the separate states of the Black Belt. Nor were these demands only window dressing: "It is also incorrect to say that the Communists are only to carry on propaganda or agitation for the right of self-determination, but not to develop any activity to bring this about." Partial demands had to be linked "with the revolutionary fundamental slogans brought up by the question of power." The resolution noted: "Even if the situation does not yet warrant the raising of the question of uprising, one should not limit oneself at present to propaganda for the demand, 'Right to Self-Determination,' but should organize mass actions, such as demonstrations, strikes, tax boycott movements, etc." While supporting the *right* of self-determination, Communists were not required to call for actual separation. "If the proletariat has come into power in the United States," the Comintern fantasized, "the Communist Negroes will not come out for but *against* separation of the Negro Republic from federation with the United States."[7]

Despite accepting the theory of self-determination, Communists never got many benefits from it. The Party could never make this Comintern creation useful in recruiting or inspiring successful activities. It became, Earl Browder admitted, "a Sunday ritual" regularly quoted in literature and resolutions but hardly ever discussed at the grass roots level. B. D. Amis confessed the Party's failure to popularize the slogan among Negroes. The theory was anathema to the largest and most influential civil rights organizations such as the NAACP, which denounced it as a subtle form of segregation. Even many Negro Communists were appalled by its implications.[8]

Self-determination might have had theoretical and ideological significance, but as a practical matter it was all but irrelevant. In its stead, the Party focused on the problem of discrimination and racial insensitivity within its own ranks. The Comintern's 1928 resolution on "the Negro question" sharply reminded the CPUSA that "white chauvinism" was "even reflected in various forms in the Party itself" and had to "be fought with the utmost energy." The 1930 Comintern resolution demanded that white Communists struggle against "Negrophobia" and enjoined them to take the lead in combatting racists. They had to "boldly jump at the throat of the 100 percent bandits who strike a Negro in the face." Browder warned that "white workers express white chauvinist ideas without even being conscious of it" because "we no longer smell this stink in the slave market that still hangs around our clothes."[9]

Within the Party, numerous incidents demonstrated that Communists had not cleansed themselves of prejudice. One sure sign of white chauvinism, according to the New York district bureau, was the "small attendance of white comrades at interracial affairs, dances, etc." There was a general indifference to Negro work. The worst offenders were the

Party's foreign-language clubs and their members. A restaurant owned by a Chicago Lithuanian organization refused to serve Negro delegates to an unemployed conference because doing so would be bad for business. A Russian cooperative restaurant in Gary, Indiana, refused to hire Negroes. When one Negro man was finally taken on, he was promptly fired. The Jewish Workers Club placed one member, the wife of a tailor shop owner, on probation for trying to prevent Negro workers from attending a Party meeting at her house by directing them elsewhere when they arrived early.[10]

B. D. Amis, analyzing a sharp disparity between the Party's organizational growth and its influence in the Negro community, was convinced that it had not done better because of white chauvinism. That "vitriolic capitalist venom," he declared, had infected some Party members and caused Negro workers to doubt the Communists' sincerity. He criticized the typical Party effort to rectify things as feeble. It was "not enough," he said, "to pass resolutions of protest a week later" or import a Negro Communist to chastise the guilty comrades. A "tenacious, systematic and consistent fight against this Yankee arrogance" was required. Fortuitously, a "chauvinist" was at hand, ready to be an example.[11]

August Yokinen was a janitor in the Finnish Workers Club in Harlem and belonged to the Communist party. Sometime in December 1930, three Negroes appeared at a club dance. Instead of being welcomed, they were rudely shunted off to a corner and even threatened with expulsion. Party members who were present did not intercede. The Harlem Party "immediately undertook a complete and thorough investigation," and the Finnish comrades, "all except Comrade Yokinen," repented and admitted their mistake in not ejecting the Negro-baiters from the dance. Yokinen compounded his error by arguing "that if the Negroes come into the club and into the pool room, they would soon be coming into the bathroom, and that he for one, did not wish to bathe with Negroes."[12]

The Communist party brought August Yokinen to trial before a "worker's court" in Harlem on March 1, 1931. Fifteen hundred people, including 211 delegates from 113 "mass and fraternal organizations," packed the hall. The trial, Israel Amter proudly noted, followed the legal procedures of the Soviet Union. A jury of seven whites and seven Negroes was selected. With a sure touch for theater, the Party selected Clarence Hathaway to prosecute and assigned Richard Moore, a leading Negro Communist, to defend Yokinen. Neither side presented any witnesses. Hathaway demanded Yokinen's expulsion from the Party, accusing him of "acting as a phonograph for the capitalists," aiding their offensive against the workers, increasing the danger of race riots, and threatening the future of American communism. Moore placed the blame for his client's guilt on "this vile, corrupt, oppressive system" and, while agreeing that Yokinen "must be condemned," suggested as a mitigating circumstance his inability to read English and thus "get the benefit from all our resolutions and documents" denouncing white chauvinism. Yokinen himself spoke in Finnish and confessed to being "under the influence of white chauvinistic ideology." He pleaded for mercy and pledged to fight white chauvinism in the future. The jurors expelled him but recommended that he participate in struggles against white chauvinism if he wished to reapply to the Party. Yokinen accepted the verdict. The court then broke into the *Internationale* and dispersed. Yokinen's travail was not yet complete, however. Representatives of the Immigration Department had attended the trial and made a stenographic record. He was quickly arrested and deported to Finland the next year.[13]

The Party was so happy with the Yokinen trial that a spate of others followed. By early 1933 Browder had to tell the Sixteenth Plenum that the "large mass production of white chauvinism trials" had led to a sacrifice of quality for quantity. "We have begun to develop," he joked, "a certain 'Model T' white chauvinist trial" in which "the cylinders don't hit, you know, the fenders drop off, the workmanship on the thing is the most inexpert and sloppy work." The Party leader pleaded for "quality" trials that would be better able to convert workers.[14]

The anti-chauvinism campaign confused many Party members. As more and more cases were exposed, some Communists grew concerned that the publicity was hampering the recruitment of Negroes by fostering the impression that the Party was a hotbed of fascism. Other Communists insisted that every manifestation of chauvinism had to be rooted out before the Party attempted to engage in mass work; they turned to judging their colleagues with a vengeance. The Central Committee condemned both of these "opportunist" attitudes. The overall impression, though, was positive. The Party's Thirteenth Plenum in September 1931 proudly reported that, with regard to work among Negroes, the Yokinen trial had marked the Party's turn from agitation and propaganda to mass activity. Bill Gebert boasted a few months later that one-quarter of Chicago's 2,000 Communists were Negro. "The prerequisite for successful work among the Negro masses," he reported, was a determined struggle against white chauvinism. Browder admitted surprise that the trial had received extensive national publicity and had become "sensational news for all America" and said that he saw "a big wave of sympathy and approval" emanating from workers of both races. He even credited the Yokinen trial with enabling the Party to seize the initiative in the Scottsboro case later that year: the latter had been "seized upon by the entire Party without hesitation largely as a result of the educational and agitational effects of the Yokinen case. I think we can say that without the Yokinen case, the Scottsboro case would never have been heard of."[15]

Show trials were not the only way to struggle against white chauvinism. The Central Committee demanded that "in all of the mass activities of the Party Negro work must be brought into the foreground." The most obvious way was to make Negroes visible within the Communist party itself. Until 1929, no Negro had ever served as a full member of the Central Committee. By 1932 no Central Committee was complete without a few. Communist electoral tickets were suddenly peppered with names of blacks. The most arresting symbol appeared in 1932. Clarence Hathaway dramatically proposed to the Communist nominating convention "an action *never before taken* by any national political party." He put forward James Ford as William Foster's running mate in the Presidential campaign. Ford's selection, Hathaway emphasized, was "a further step in convincing the masses of the revolutionary sincerity of the Communist Party."[16]

His nomination catapulted the soft-spoken Ford into the limelight. For the next decade he was the Party's foremost Negro leader. His sudden prominence was as much a product of default as his own qualities. The Party's Negro veterans were a small band, and several had been contaminated by their reluctance to accept the self-determination line. Cyril Briggs had been denounced in a 1930 draft thesis for succumbing to hatred of "all whites without distinction of class." B. D. Amis had been unable to breathe life into the Party's newest auxiliary for Negroes, the League of Struggle for Negro Rights. Harry Haywood was briefly considered as a Vice Presidential candidate but was handicapped by his youth and an ideological rigidity that, Browder later complained, was all too common among graduates of the Lenin School.[17]

Ford, on the other hand, was safe. Born in 1893 in Pratt City, Alabama, a suburb of Birmingham, he had worked his way through Fisk University. After World War I, he moved north to Chicago and found a job with the post office. Active in a union, he was recruited into the Communist party via the American Negro Labor Congress in 1926. At that time, there was only a handful of Negroes in the Party. Ford had one advantage they lacked, a trade union background, which got him appointed to the American delegation to the Profintern congress in 1928. Once in Moscow he was named to the Profintern's Executive Committee and stayed nine months. He organized a meeting of the International Trade Union Committee of Negro Workers for the Profintern in Hamburg in 1930 and then returned home for good in 1931. He had not publicly disagreed with the Comintern's new line in 1928. For the better part of the three years following the announcement, he had been abroad. As was the case with Browder, his voluntary exile had removed him from the sniping and backbiting within the American Party. "Tall, solidly built, a rather handsome, distinguished-looking man," Ford could be relied on to make a good impression while reflecting and defending Party policy without protest.[18]

Despite all their efforts to prove their bona fides to Negroes, the Communists had little to show for results. Browder did boast in 1930 at the Party's convention that more than 1,000 new Negro members had been recruited. Yet a year later he complained that "we still have something less than 1,000 Negro members in our Party." One-half were in Chicago. Only two other districts—Philadelphia and Pittsburgh—had as many as 100 Negro members, although the Alabama region, which had not reported, would have boosted the number to three. The most embarrassing statistic in the membership report came from New York. The entire city counted only seventy-four Negro Communists. The Party's auxiliary for work on Negro problems was also in dire straits. The American Negro Labor Congress, founded in the 1920s, had limped into the new decade barely alive. It did not have a single organizer in the entire South. When its convention met in September 1930, Herbert Newton reported the ANLC's "shortcomings and failure in organizational work." Prospects for recovery were so grim that the ANLC was scrapped and replaced by a new auxiliary, the League of Struggle for Negro Rights (LSNR).[19]

The new organization was no less dominated by the Party than the old one. The manifesto, written by Harry Haywood, included all three revolutionary demands for the South: state unity of the Black Belt, self-determination, and confiscation of white landowners' property. Among the 113 delegates were such Party luminaries as Earl Browder, William Foster, Robert Minor, Bill Dunne, Clarence Hathaway, and Sam Darcy. Only 71 Negro delegates attended. The LSNR proclaimed that "only the overthrow of capitalism and the establishment of a workers' state can guarantee mankind from becoming cannon-fodder in imperalist massacres." No sooner had the LSNR been created than conflicts arose over its role. Browder admitted that many of "the leading Negro comrades" opposed the league's formation because they feared that it would relieve the Communist party of the responsibility for work on Negro problems. The Comintern fired off a directive in late January 1931 that criticized tendencies to consider the LSNR "as a substitute for the Party or revolutionary unions." The Central Committee quickly criticized "some comrades" who had "tended in practice to transfer the leading role of the Party in the struggle for Negro rights to the LSNR, to look upon the LSNR as a substitute for the Party on the Negro field and to relegate all work among Negroes to Negro comrades and to the LSNR."[20]

The LSNR, however, was so greatly identified as a Communist organization that it could only attract the already converted. As with the TUUL and the Unemployed Councils, it suffered from an absence of qualified cadres. Browder complained in August 1931 that the LSNR was still "largely loose local groupings with perhaps six or seven notable local and neighborhood exceptions." The league's newspaper, *The Liberator*, suspended publication early in 1932. Nothing had changed by 1933. After admitting that numerous opportunities had been created by the Scottsboro case, Browder wistfully asked: "Is it not possible that the LSNR can be successfully brought forward as the answer to the problem of organizing the broad Negro liberation movement?" Yet, B. D. Amis sadly admitted in 1935 that the newspaper and the league were "weak organizations, with little mass base and mass influence among the Negro people."[21]

The TUUL did not fare much better among Negroes. The Profintern criticized its activities among black workers, calling it "the weakest phase of our movement. We have little or no organization contact with the Negro masses, even in those industries where they have actively participated in the strikes led by the revolutionary unions." Only the Unemployed Councils enjoyed even a modest success in the Negro community. Their struggles against evictions in Chicago and Harlem earned respect, if not membership, from Negroes. The Chicago Unemployed Councils had an active program, with hundreds of workers joining to foil efforts to displace tenants who were unable to pay their rent. In one incident on August 3, 1931, 500 people had finished returning furniture to the house of a Negro widow when a convoy of police suddenly began firing point-blank into the crowd. Three Negroes were killed. All week long, mass protest meetings of 5,000–8,000 people were held and 1,500 police patrolled the South Side with riot guns and tear-gas bombs. The bodies of Abe Gray, a Communist, and Jim O'Neil, a member of an Unemployed Council, lay in state underneath a large portrait of Lenin. A funeral procession, claimed to be 60,000 strong, was led by workers carrying Communist party banners and was cheered on by 50,000 onlookers, blocking all traffic. John Williamson exultantly called it "the largest demonstration in the history of the Communist Party in Chicago." Within days, 2,500 applications for the Unemployed Councils and 500 for the Party were filled out. Chicago, however, was a shining exception.[22]

When the Communist party did begin to make inroads in the Negro community, it was in the South. Atlanta police arrested six organizers in the spring of 1930 and charged them with "inciting to insurrection." The Communist party, a pamphlet on the case proclaimed, "proudly pleads guilty" to "the charge of arming to defeat and to overthrow the rule of the capitalist class." Another Atlanta arrest, that of Negro Angelo Herndon, attracted more attention. Born near Cincinnati in 1913, Herndon joined the Communist party in 1930 after participation in the Birmingham Unemployed Councils. He was sent to Atlanta in 1931, where he organized a biracial unemployed demonstration at the county courthouse. Days later he was arrested, held incommunicado for almost two weeks, finally charged with "inciting to insurrection," and sentenced to twenty years on a Georgia chain gang. "The most telling blow against me," Herndon later stated in his autobiography, was the prosecution's use of the Communist position on "setting up a nigger Soviet Republic in the Black Belt." For several years, "Free Angelo Herndon" was as ubiquitous a slogan at Party rallies as "Free the Scottsboro Boys." Herndon was eventually freed by a court decision overturning the insurrection law and briefly served on the Party's Central Committee before being expelled from the Party during World War II for Negro nationalism.[23]

The Party's biggest prize from the episode was one of Herndon's defense attorneys. Benjamin Davis, the son of a prominent Atlanta Negro leader, had been educated at Amherst and Harvard Law School. During the trial he joined the Communist party. His talents were far too valuable to waste in Georgia; shortly afterward, he was brought to New York to edit the ailing *Liberator*. Soon Davis was on his way to more important posts, eventually being elected to the New York City Council and elevated to the Politburo, replacing Ford as the most powerful Negro in the Party.

Hard as it was to work in even the South's larger cities, the Communists set out to organize black sharecroppers in rural Alabama. As usual, the initial impulse came from the Comintern. In 1930 its Political Secretariat instructed the Americans to concentrate their rural organizing "upon the demands of the Negro tenants and share-croppers of the South." Henry Puro soon called for the creation of leagues of tenant farmers and sharecroppers, especially in the South. An opportunity quickly arose. Desperate tenant farmers from Tallapoosa County, Alabama, sent pleading letters to the Party's *Southern Worker* asking for help, and Mack Coad, a Negro steelworker and Communist from Birmingham, was dispatched to Camp Hill.[24]

In mid-July 1931, police raided a secret meeting of local sharecroppers organized by Coad. They soon killed one of the fledgling union's leaders, Ralph Gray. Coad managed to escape to Atlanta. Another Negro was killed, several were wounded, several dozen were arrested, and four disappeared. The Party's Central Committee called on Southern Negroes to form a "self-defense corps" to protect themselves, and it insisted that the Camp Hill battle was a vivid illustration that Negro rights in the South could only be vindicated by the right of self-determination.[25]

Police intimidation lowered membership in the Sharecroppers' Union from 800 to 500 by the spring of 1932. Nevertheless, the Communist party persisted in its dogged efforts to organize. Coad was replaced as Party organizer by Al Murphy, a Negro born in Georgia who had joined the Party in 1930 in Birmingham. Murphy was constantly underground, and the union functioned in secret: "The croppers would walk distances of six to seven miles" to vacant houses to listen to speeches. Eventually small gatherings of the union's fifty locals met. Some were even able to win minor concessions from a few landlords, with pay being raised slightly and sharecroppers on one plantation winning the right to sell their own cotton. The union sensibly shied away from any direct confrontation with the owners, distributing their demands on handbills "placed in mail boxes, sometimes on porches, some in cars in town."[26]

The uneasy calm did not last long. Backed by other union members, Cliff James—a black farmer in Reeltown, Alabama, a union leader, and a Communist—defied a police attempt to seize his livestock for payment of a debt. The lawmen opened fire, and the sharecroppers responded. Four deputies were wounded: at least seven blacks were killed. More disappeared. *The Daily Worker* reported that "the roads to the hills are crowded with Negro women babies in their arms fleeing the landlord terror." Murphy, who was in Birmingham when the violence took place, tried to get back to Reeltown with several other organizers. They were stopped by a mob, and only by convincing it that they were relatives of some of the victims were they able to avoid a lynching. Five croppers were later convicted of assault with intent to murder and given sentences of five to fifteen years.[27]

To the Communist party, the Sharecroppers' Union demonstrated a new spirit of resistance to capitalism. One of the Party's experts on Negro issues proclaimed that "Tallapoosa has shown that every struggle by the Negro peasantry even for the most elementary economic and social demands strikes sparks just as certainly as when flint hits steel." Al Murphy

334

suggested that the major flaw in the Party's work was its inattentiveness to the slogan of the right of self-determination: "In the South itself we shall never be able to mobilize the Negroes for the struggle to fight for their rights . . . until we popularize this slogan." If Southern Negroes only knew about and understood what it meant, "we would mobilize additional hundreds of Negro masses in the struggles." In the meantime, Murphy lamented, "we have not been able to organize one single white farmer" into the union despite its 2,000–3,000 members. The Sharecroppers' Union grew steadily through 1933 and 1934, reaching 10,000 members, including some whites, before being absorbed by the CIO. A leading Negro Communist finally admitted in 1935 that the sharecroppers' struggle had not been so revolutionary: it had only given the landowners a "momentary alarm." Nonetheless, the union's activities had at the time fortified the Communists' belief that no area of the United States was immune from the outbreak of revolutionary militancy.[28]

Another challenge to Alabama justice provided the Party greater opportunities in the Negro community. Nine black youngsters were arrested and charged with raping two white women on a freight train near Scottsboro, Alabama, in 1931. The Communists were quick to offer assistance. A *Southern Worker* writer noticed an early story about the case in a Chattanooga paper, traveled to Scottsboro for the arraignment, returned appalled at the lynch-mob atmosphere and the defendants' incompetent attorney, and notified *The Daily Worker*. Lowell Wakefield, an International Labor Defense organizer, sat through the first day of the trial on April 6 and quickly wired his superiors that another Sacco-Vanzetti case was in the offing. By early April the Scottsboro case was front-page news. The Central Committee labeled it a "legal lynching." The League of Struggle for Negro Rights revived long enough to send a protest on behalf of its largely mythical "tens of thousands membership." The ILD dispatched one of its attorneys to visit the convicted boys, and soon *The Daily Worker* happily informed its readers that "all nine young workers welcomed the aid of the International Labor Defense."[29]

The NAACP belatedly sought to capture control of the defense, provoking a lengthy tug of war with the ILD. The Communists accused the NAACP of cooperating with "Southern boss lynchers." In contrast to the legal emphasis of the NAACP, the Party believed that only a massive pressure campaign could win the defendants' freedom. Once they had obtained control of the case, the Communists supplemented the legal wrangles with a variety of slogans to dramatize larger issues. These ranged from "Demand Immediate Release of the Nine Innocent Boys" and calls for a new trial with a half-black jury to "Equal Rights for Negroes" and "Right of Self-Determination for the Negro People in the Black Belt." By the end of 1931, the NAACP had withdrawn from the case, leaving the Communists in complete control of what one Party editorial called "the most important case that has ever appeared on behalf of the suffering Negro people since the Dred Scott case." The very day that the NAACP bowed out, the Party's Negro Department, meeting in New York, formulated instructions to the ILD attorneys now in charge of defending the Scottsboro Boys.[30]

The Communists were convinced that legal maneuvers alone could never save the Scottsboro Boys' lives. The Central Committee issued a directive which stressed that the "chief immediate objective" was to mobilize "great numbers of non-Party elements" to pressure the authorities. Robert Minor demanded that "every meeting of the Buro of Districts and Sections without exception must receive at least an information report on the execution of the campaign."[31]

The Party quickly learned how effective an issue it had. For the first time, Communist speakers were given platforms in Negro churches. Black newspapers began urging support of the ILD and the LSNR. Walter White, head of the NAACP, charged that so many Scottsboro mothers were touring the country that some of them had to be frauds. There were innumerable Scottsboro parades to protest the injustice. A typical one in Harlem was broken up by police. The marchers had been denied a permit but set off anyway, led by none other than August Yokinen. Suddenly, Negro policemen "rushed out and began murderously clubbing and mauling the Negro and white workers." The protesters "heroically defended their banners" and managed to hold an open-air meeting. Four arrests were made. In July 1932, "tens of thousands" were reported to have demonstrated around the country. No Party gathering, march, or event was complete without placards demanding that the Scottsboro Boys be freed. No Party auxiliary could hold a meeting or issue a set of demands without denouncing Alabama justice.[32]

Several united front conferences enabled the Party, for the first time, to attract Negroes from outside its auxiliaries. Two hundred and eighty-five delegates attended a Chicago meeting, including representatives from eighteen Negro churches and sixteen clubs and lodges. An All-Southern United Front Scottsboro Defense Conference in Chattanooga, Tennessee, drew 200 delegates despite harassment and attacks by black ministers and the NAACP. Intellectuals around the world rallied to the cause. In Germany a committee boasting the names of Albert Einstein, Thomas Mann, and Lion Feuchtwanger called for freedom for the Scottsboro Boys. The National Committee for Defense of Political Prisoners, led by Theodore Dreiser, was formed to help in this case.[33]

The Communists were overjoyed by the response. The campaign, Earl Browder boasted, "has on the whole been a magnificent success for the Party" despite "the weakness with which we have carried out the popularization . . . of the slogan of self-determination." The Party's Thirteenth Plenum proudly claimed: "The Scottsboro case was seized upon by the entire movement, without hesitation, as a rallying point for this struggle, with brilliant success in rousing hundreds of thousands of Negro and white workers to active protest and struggle."[34]

Demonstrations, however, were ephemeral. If the Communists wanted to accomplish anything lasting, they knew it was necessary to sink organizational roots. The directives issued by the Central Committee urged the building of ILD units and local LSNR groups that could form a basis for continuing work "under the direction of our Party fractions." Robert Minor criticized the Party's early efforts: "The organizational work is not being done." Merely visiting non-Communist groups and appealing for support were insufficient and smacked of a "united front from the top," since the Party's access to these groups then depended on the latter's leaders. "The united front in this case," Minor lectured, "as in all others, must be primarily and at all costs a united front from the bottom." Ironically, the Communists' very success proved worrisome. To have attracted so many people, particularly nonworkers, implied that impermissible and opportunistic compromises with reformism must have taken place. Harry Haywood protested in early 1932 that "in nearly all districts of the Party, the correct line was sacrificed in an attempt to establish a 'united front from the top.'" Haywood was especially disturbed by the presence of Masonic lodges and "friendly Negro preachers" and by the prominence of black churches at the Southern Scottsboro meeting. Instead of pursuing the favors of these groups, the Party needed to build its own auxiliaries, work to defeat Negro reformists, and link immediate demands on the Scottsboro case to revolutionary demands, "especially the demand for the right of self-determination."[35]

The Party only grudgingly accepted cooperation with large non-Communist groups on the Scottsboro case. Harry Haywood denounced *The Daily Worker* in 1931 for printing a statement by William Pickens, the NAACP's field organizer, that supported a united front under the leadership of the ILD and LSNR. After the Comintern's limited united front overture in 1933, the ILD, badly in debt, accepted an NAACP offer to meet the expenses of Scottsboro defendant Haywood Patterson's appeal and all future trials. The Politburo asked whether the ILD had forgotten that the "main battles" to save the Scottsboro Boys had to be directed "in the first place against this corrupt group of leaders" in the NAACP. Accepting the NAACP's money was a "right opportunist error." When the offer of help came, it should have been met with "such a straightforward and clear proposal of mass struggle and of mobilization of the masses against the capitalist frame-up courts and the Jim Crow legal system as would have compelled these misleaders, if they accepted it, to take a position that would have amounted to a public repudiation of their past (and present and future) actions in support of the lynch courts and the ruling class Jim Crow system of national oppression." Negro comrades were rebuked for forgetting that the united front was a device "to destroy the influence of the reformist leaders."[36]

The Party did try to expand the Scottsboro campaign, forming a National Scottsboro Action Committee that included Roger Baldwin, J. B. Matthews, Adam Clayton Powell, Heywood Broun, A. J. Muste, and even an Episcopalian bishop. Its first major activity was a march on Washington. Numbering between three and five thousand, two-thirds Negro, the marchers paraded down Pennsylvania Avenue in May 1933, alternating between chanted demands to free the Scottsboro Boys and the singing of the *Internationale*. Delegations met with the House Speaker and the Vice President on Capitol Hill. Ruby Bates, one of the alleged rape victims, told the House leader that she had perjured herself at the first trial. Both politicians agreed only to refer bills presented by the delegations to appropriate committees; the Speaker reminded his guests that Congress had no authority to intervene in the case. A combined delegation called at the White House, where they met with President Roosevelt's secretary, Louis Howe, but were rebuffed when they asked to see FDR himself.[37]

The ILD fought relentlessly and courageously to win a legal victory. Roger Baldwin of the ACLU provided one endorsement: "You have done a job that no other agency could do or would do, not only in arousing world-wide opinion and protest but in the selection of counsel for skillful handling of the moves in the court." The Party, however, was not content to judge its performance in so reformist a vein. It actually welcomed Patterson's conviction as a salutary lesson about capitalist society. The verdict, the Politburo stated, had destroyed "legalistic illusions of a possible turn in favor of 'justice' within the Party." Another Communist identified the chief error of the Scottsboro campaign as the "failure better to politicize the struggle, to raise it to higher levels by bringing in the basic revolutionary demands." The Party had failed "to carry on mass actions, raising each succeeding one to a higher level, in conjunction with the court proceedings" and had failed to expose the ILD's own lawyer, Samuel Leibowitz, as a "politician and a careerist."[38]

The ILD jeopardized its control of the Scottsboro case in 1934. Hearing that Victoria Price, one of the alleged victims, was willing to change her story, three ILD representatives brought her a bribe. All three were arrested by Alabama authorities in October. Samuel Leibowitz angrily demanded the removal of all Communists from the defense, broke with the ILD, and managed to patch together an American Scottsboro Committee to support him. The defendants swung from one group to the other in as bewildering a fashion as they had once hopped from the NAACP to the ILD and back again. Despite all their efforts, however, the anti-Communists could not eliminate the ILD from the case, and the two sides agreed to a division of labor. After the Seventh Congress, the Party was willing to cede its leading role in the fight. Robert Minor approached the NAACP and Norman Thomas to suggest a new united front. In December 1935 the Scottsboro Defense Committee was formed to take over supervision of the case. With one representative each from the ILD, NAACP, ACLU, League for Industrial Democracy, and Methodist Federation for Social Service, the committee marked the end of the Party's control over the Scottsboro defense.[39]

The Communists' rigidity proved costly to their hopes that lasting organizational results would come from the case. Midway through 1932, two of the Party's Southern leaders admitted that after three years "our organizational results have been unbelievably small." Browder confessed that in New York the Party had "almost nothing" among Negroes. "In Harlem, the Party is isolated from the Negro workers," added the New York district organizer. A Party plenum in the fall of 1932 charged that in spite of some successes, "fundamentally the Party's work among the Negroes remains in the same groove." Nor did things get better. Only ninety Negroes in all of Harlem belonged to the Party shortly after the 1933 Open Letter was issued. By March 1934 there were only 240.[40]

There were racial tensions within the Harlem Party as well. A majority of the Harlem Section membership was white. Personal relations with black members were bitter and divisive. So many white Communists were charged with racism and chauvinism that one Negro organizer felt that it almost seemed "the duty of a Negro worker in the Party was to accuse a white worker of white chauvinism" and noted that "the situation within the Party in Harlem was rotten." The Party's condition was embarrasing enough that early in 1934 the leadership designated Harlem a national concentration point and assigned James Ford as section organizer. He moved quickly to rearrange the Party's leadership, replacing old-timers like Cyril Briggs and Richard Moore with newer faces such as Ben Davis and Abner Berry. To buttress them, the Party assigned several of its most talented Negro organizers to Harlem.[41]

Ironically, black nationalism, which Communists rhetorically supported in the South, caused problems elsewhere in the country. In Harlem the more virulent nationalists demanded the firing of white workers and spouted anti-Semitic language at Jewish merchants. "Don't Buy Where You Can't Work" campaigns were popular among many unemployed Negroes. At the Party's 1934 convention, the threat of "petty-bourgeois nationalism" was a constant theme. Browder insisted that "in this fight against Negro nationalism, it is especially the Negro Communists who have to be the most active and alert." Harry Haywood denounced "Negro comrades in Harlem" who had "brought forth the petty-bourgeois nationalist line of replacement of white workers by Negroes." Soon after the convention, Ford attacked Cyril Briggs and Richard Moore for playing into the hands of black nationalists and white segregationists. William Nowell, a Negro functionary in Detroit, and Manning Johnson, from Buffalo, were both reprimanded for petty-bourgeois nationalist sins.[42]

The most prominent Communist turned black nationalist was George Padmore. Born Malcolm Nurse in the West Indies, he had joined the Communist party in 1927. He accompanied William Foster to Russia in 1929 and was soon appointed head of the Profintern's Negro Bureau. Active at the 1930 Hamburg Conference of Negro Workers, Padmore was selected to replace James Ford as editor of *The Negro Worker* when the latter returned to America. For the next three years he ran its operations from Vienna. Late in 1933 he resigned from the Party, charging that in its need to placate Britain and France now that Hitler had come to power, the Comintern had sacrificed its anti-imperialist work. Harry Haywood devoted some time during his Eighth Convention speech to a denunciation of Padmore for falling into the "swamp of counter-revolutionary petty-bourgeois nationalism." James Ford later contended that Padmore's false charges against Russia, associations with spies, and support for Liberia, a "vassal state of American imperialism," had led to his removal from the International Trade Union Committee of Negro Workers and his subsequent resignation from the Party. Padmore settled in London, where his writings made him one of the leading world spokesmen for Pan-Africanism and influenced and educated a generation of young African nationalists. Following Ghana's independence in 1957, Kwame Nkrumah, one of Padmore's protégés, invited him to Accra to serve as his adviser.[43]

Black nationalism remained a potent force in Harlem. By the end of 1934, however, the "Don't Buy Where You Can't Work" campaign had collapsed, amid charges of racketeering on the part of its leaders. The Communists' new Harlem leadership had in the meantime emphasized interracial picketing of department stores to force the hiring of Negroes without the firing of white employees. Although resented by the nationalists, the Party's tactics made a favorable impression on the Harlem community. The Communists were able to demonstrate that they could mobilize some whites to fight with Negroes. The Party could and did point to its white chauvinism trials, high-ranking Negro cadres, and efforts on behalf of the Scottsboro Boys and Angelo Herndon as proof of its dedication to Negro causes and the value of an alliance with the Party.

Prior to the Seventh Comintern Congress, the Party in Harlem was able to build some modestly successful united fronts with different segments of the community. Its most improbable ally, and perhaps the oddest the American Communists ever embraced, was Father Divine, a charismatic Negro preacher. Following an invitation, Divine's followers marched in a New York demonstration sponsored by the American League Against War and Fascism in August 1934, carrying banners proclaiming that "Father Divine Is God." They were back for May Day in 1935 and at subsequent Party affairs. James Ford and Robert Minor, in turn, spoke at the International Righteousness Government Convention of the Father Divine Peace Movement. Not all Communists found this coalition to their liking. After the first march, a *Daily Worker* editorial admitted that "some of our comrades were startled and confused" but cautioned them to draw the preacher's followers into the united front, not argue about his divinity. James Ford wrote of a conversation with a Negro woman who had explained that "you Communists" had been sent by God. He urged respect for the religious sensibilities of the masses: "Should we argue with such a woman about this statement when we are trying to make a united front on Scottsboro? Of course not: it would be stupid." The Communists remained enamored of this unlikely united front for another year before Father Divine's continuing anti-union statements forced the Party to exclude him from the 1936 May Day parade.[44]

One sign of the Party's new respectability in Harlem was the community's response to the Harlem riot of 1935. On the afternoon of March 19, a security guard at the Kress Department Store on 125th Street apprehended a teenage shoplifter. Enraged onlookers became convinced that he was being beaten and began a demonstration inside the store. As rumors spread that the boy had been seriously injured, an angry crowd gathered outside. By 6:00 P.M., members of a Communist-led youth group, the Young Liberators, had set up a picket line. Police moved in, broke it up, and arrested several speakers. A Young Liberator leaflet had meanwhile been circulated, telling of a brutal beating administered to the shoplifter by the police. False reports of his death soon spread. By early evening a mob of 3,000 people was rampaging through the streets, breaking windows and looting stores. Before the violence ended, 500 uniformed police and hundreds of plainclothesmen had been mobilized, four blacks were dead or fatally injured, and property damage was estimated at $350,000.[45]

City officials quickly laid the blame for the riot on the Communists. Mayor LaGuardia attributed the events to the instigators who had circulated inflammatory handbills. The district attorney charged that "Communists distributed literature and took an active part in the riot," while the chief of police singled out the Young Liberators. A grand jury indicted seven people, including some Young Liberators, and the police raided Harlem Party headquarters, seizing equipment and literature. The charges, however, backfired. James Ford insisted that the Party had worked to stop the trouble once it started and that Communists had circulated through Harlem urging residents not to engage in a race riot. More importantly, however, community leaders agreed with the Party that economic distress and hardship were the root cause of the violence. The Reverend Adam Clayton Powell took the lead in forming an Emergency Citizens Committee of prominent Harlem figures, including Ford, which condemned "red-baiting" and laid responsibility on segregation and discrimination. The mayor set up a commission to investigate conditions. Party members came to its hearings well-prepared to refute many of the allegations about their role in the riot. They also succeeded in using this forum to denounce living conditions in Harlem. "Negro people are treated like dogs in New York," Ford charged, and he presented devastating statistics on unemployment, housing, relief, and health conditions.[46]

At the same time, Communists fought to win a place in the campaign to defend Ethiopia. The League of Nations stood by helplessly as Mussolini's legions invaded Ethiopia in October 1935, after several months of border skirmishes; seven months later they seized Addis Abbaba and drove Haile Selassie into exile. Black nationalists tried to portray the issue as a conflict between the white and black races. They were not seeking white assistance and were partial to the idea of punishing Italian merchants in Harlem for their countrymen's sins by boycotts. Revelations that even after the invasion the Soviet Union had continued to ship oil and other strategic material to Italy led George Padmore to assail the Soviet Union for selling out Africa. The NAACP and *The Am-sterdam News* joined the chorus, arguing that Communists were putting Soviet interests ahead of Negro interests.[47]

Only one Negro Communist of repute, Herman Mackawain, was upset enough to resign from the Party. Most blacks were more impressed by the Communists' enthusiastic participation in rallies on behalf of Ethiopia. Communists were among the organizers of a Provisional Committee for the Defense of Ethiopia. Within it they worked to persuade black-nationalist followers of Marcus Garvey, a Back-to-Africa advocate, not to direct their hostility toward Italian-Americans and they mobilized Italian sympathizers to participate in marches on behalf of Ethiopia. On August 3, 1935, all segments of Harlem united for a gigantic march and rally. *The Daily Worker* counted 40,000 marchers and 60,000 cheering onlookers; the capitalist press halved the count. The largely black marchers included prominent contingents of Italians and Communists urging aide to Ethiopia. In addition to a variety of Harlem ministers, civic leaders, and Garveyites, speakers from the American League Against War and Fascism and Robert Minor addressed the throng.[48]

One very formidable obstacle stood between the Party and full acceptance in the Negro community, however. Almost from the day it had been promulgated by the Comintern, the self-determination doctrine had been an albatross isolating the Party from virtually every Negro organization. The Communists continued to insist on the right of self-determination in the Black Belt, but slowly inched away from the policy in fact. At the 1934 convention, the doctrine was still central to the Party program. James Ford and James Allen, in their 1935 book *The Negro in a Soviet America,* explained that "the real test of freedom for the Negro people in the Black Belt lies in their right to self-determination" and then gravely considered how the timing of the Negro national revolution and the proletarian revolution would determine whether the Communists would support or oppose the actual separation of the Black Belt.[49]

At first glance the Seventh Congress seemed to make no discernible difference in Party policy. Georgi Dimitroff made no mention of self-determination. He did hint that the doctrine should not be allowed to stand in the way of the Party's new tasks; the Farmer-Labor party which the Communists were to help build should "[fight] for the equal status of the Negroes." Browder, reporting to the American Party on his return home, charged that opponents of self-determination were "advocating the forcible unification of the Negroes, which means their segregation as a subject, oppressed nationality." By the November 1935 plenum, however, Browder had assimilated the hint from the Seventh Congress. He announced that the Party would not press the issue of self-determination upon the National Negro Congress. This did not mean that the Party was abandoning the doctrine, but "it is clear that the Negro masses are not yet ready to carry through the revolution which would make possible the right to self-determination." The Party consequently would join with other Negroes to fight Jim Crowism while continuing to propagandize on self-determination. The Party's Ninth Convention pushed self-determination further into the background. Its resolutions spoke about the struggle against discrimination and lynchings and emphasized civil rights, but were silent about self-determination. Harry Haywood was so upset that he spoke to the convention about self-determination being at the heart of the Party's line on Negroes. During the 1936 Presidential campaign, James Ford avoided the topic while emphasizing the struggle for equal rights. He also charged that self-determination "prevented the development of a broad movement. The masses did not understand this full program."[50]

One of the more revealing signs that self-determination was doomed was the deteriorating political fortunes of Harry Haywood. More than any other Negro Communist, he was identified with the doctrine. From his days as a very junior student at the Lenin School, he had ridden it to the Politburo and the leadership of the League of Struggle for Negro Rights. Haywood's problems first surfaced in 1934. Unable to get along with James Ford in Harlem, he lost his post as leader of the LSNR to Abner Berry and was assigned to Chicago late in the year as Southside regional organizer and chairman of the Cook County Party Committee. He lacked experience and ability as an organizer, and his tenure in Chicago was marked by conflicts and confrontations. By the fall of 1935 Haywood was in such disfavor that he was not part of the large contingent of American Communists attending the Seventh Congress. Although he was the only Politburo member in the Abraham Lincoln Battalion, he had little authority and wound up with a posting as an adjutant political commissar. His departure from Spain in the fall of 1937, amid charges of cowardice and disputes with superiors, did nothing to reverse the decline in Haywood's fortunes. He was dropped from the Politburo in 1938 and sent to Baltimore to supervise work on Negro problems. After one year he was removed from that position, ending his days as a Party functionary. Although he briefly resurfaced after Earl Browder's overthrow brought self-determination back into vogue, Haywood never again won the confidence of Party leaders.[51]

Downgrading the importance of self-determination did not mean totally abandoning it. The Party only shelved the issue; it refused to repudiate the idea. A young white Southern Communist, for example, rede-fined Negroes as "an oppressed national minority" in a controversial article in *The Communist* in 1938 but still paid formal tribute to the right to self-determination. Even that alteration was rejected as too weak. *The Communist* published a refutation that reminded Party members to "con-tinuously bear in mind our full program on the Negro question—land and the right to self-determination for the Negro national majority of the Black Belt." That same year, James Allen repeated that demanding equal rights only partially met Negroes' needs: "In the South, and therefore in the North too, the Negroes can only be assured true equality by winning the demand of the right of self-determination, the most important of all democratic rights." Allen admitted, however, that in practice the Com-munists had surrendered the doctrine; they did "not pose agreement with their ultimate program as a condition for their participation in any united front of democratic forces." Although this was hardly a magnanimous concession by the Party—no other sizable independent Negro group would have cooperated with the Communists otherwise—it demonstrat-ed once again how practical and accommodating the Party could be in pursuit of whatever aim the Soviet Union and Comintern deemed appropriate.[52]

Once the Communists surrendered the chimera that they could at-tract the black masses into auxiliaries with thinly disguised Party pro-grams, they made rapid progress in forging an alliance with non-Com-munists. From its inception the LSNR had been in trouble. In January 1935 Browder ordered Communists to "shift the scene of our attention to the existing mass organizations among Negroes, no matter what." James Ford complained that the LSNR had fallen "into the same sectarian method of work as the American Negro Labor Congress" and suffered from the same organizational woes. He ordered functioning local branches to transfer their allegiance to the National Negro Congress. Small and weak branches "should be liquidated. The national organiza-tion has ceased to exist." With its own ineffectual, sectarian group out of the way, the Party could devote all of its energies to one of the most successful of its Popular Fronts, the National Negro Congress.[53]

The NNC grew out of a May 1935 Conference on the Status of the Negro Under the New Deal, held at Howard University. The ostensible organizers of the affair were Howard's Social Science Division, chaired by Ralph Bunche, and the Joint Committee on National Recovery, a coali-tion of Negro organizations aimed at guaranteeing equality in New Deal programs and led by John P. Davis. James Ford had been proposing the idea of a national meeting of Negroes ever since January 1934. He explained to a group of Negro Communists that Davis had become interested in the plan after the January 1935 Unemployment Congress. Subsequently, Ford reported: "We had meetings with John P. Davis before this conference and we worked out together with him how the idea of a National Negro Congress should be projected." Davis, a graduate of Harvard Law School, publicly denied Party associations at the time but years later testified before the Civil Service Commission that from 1935 to 1942 he "considered himself 'agreeable to carry out a Communist program' and as a CP member." After the May gathering, an organizing committee which represented "every shade of political and religious opinion" among blacks, and which included Ford, issued a call for a National Negro Congress.[54]

The goals of the NNC were straightforward and not very radical. The congress proclaimed its desire to mobilize American Negroes to fight for decent wages, educational opportunities, unemployment insurance with no discrimination, adequate relief, and aid to Negro farmers, sharecroppers, tenants, and Ethiopia; and to combat lynching, police brutality, war, and fascism. At a meeting of the Party's Negro cadres in October 1935, Ford had mentioned still another goal that the Party envisaged for the NNC, albeit one that could not be publicly avowed. He defended the plan to invite as broad a sample of black organizations as possible, including churches and fraternal groups, and explained that "then we can go into these organizations and get rank and file delegates over the heads of the leaders."[55]

By the time the NNC met in February 1936, the injunctions of the Seventh Congress had made such crude resorts to a united front from below unfashionable. The Party, moreover, had a prominent and respected role in the proceedings. Ben Davis was secretary of the New York Sponsoring Committee. The Harlem Party, although remaining in the background, did much of the organizing work in New York for the NNC. When the hundreds of delegates gathered at the National Guard Armory in Chicago, the Party's presence could not be missed. Ford was a major speaker, and prominent Communists were among the delegates. In addition to Ford, B. D. Amis served on the eleven-member committee that drafted plans for a permanent National Negro Congress, and ten of the seventy-five members of the NNC Executive Committee were Party members. About the only disappointing note for the Communists, in fact, came when National Guard officers prevented Earl Browder from entering the building to address the delegates.[56]

There had never been such a broad coalition of Negro groups gathered in one place before. More than 800 delegates from 550 organizations claiming to represent 33 million members were present. The opening session drew 5,000 people. The delegates ranged from representatives of church groups and fraternities to Roy Wilkins of the NAACP and Lester Granger of the Urban League, from Republicans and Garveyites to Communists. A. Phillip Randolph, a prominent Socialist and leader of the Brotherhood of Sleeping Car Porters was elected president. Most of the delegates were not Communists but, like Randolph, they were prepared to cooperate with them, particularly since the Party made no revolutionary demands. Accepting the presidency, Randolph urged the delegates to build a united front and a Farmer-Labor party, both Communist tactics. "The National Negro Congress," he stated, "has Communists in it. It has Republicans in it. It makes no apology for this." Delighted, the Party hailed Randolph as "an outstanding Negro Socialist in America."[57]

The Communists had not always regarded him so highly. For many years he had battled with them in the labor and socialist movements. Despite this background, Randolph was prepared to cooperate with the Party in 1936. Like Randolph, it now favored a Farmer-Labor party, and the NNC represented an opportunity to bring the entire spectrum of Negro groups—from the conservative churches to the Communists, from business organizations to labor unions—into one body that would press for the advancement of the race. At the same time, the leadership of the NNC enhanced Randolph's own stature. By the end of 1938 he was hailed in *The Daily Worker* as a contributor to the ILD's "neediest cases." So long as the Party's goals remained ecumenical and it traveled along the same path as his, Randolph was content to cooperate.[58]

Communists and their allies also dominated Harlem cultural life during the Popular Front. The WPA arts projects, ranging from the Writers' Project to the Theatre Project, were heavily influenced by Party members. Prominent Harlem entertainers performed at Party events and for Party auxiliaries. No one symbolized the Party's attraction for Negro intellectuals better than Paul Robeson. Robeson, who had been an All-American football player at Rutgers University, where he had also been elected to Phi Beta Kappa, was a world-renowned singer and actor, and one of the best-known and most acclaimed Negroes in America. During the Third Period, the Party had not been impressed: "Robeson Kowtows to Imperialism," one headline had read. In the midst of self-imposed exile from American racism, Robeson first visited Russia in 1934, attracted by claims about its treatment of minority nationalities. He was seduced. Upon arriving there, he proclaimed, "This is home to me," and was so impressed that he enrolled his son in a Russian school for two years. Not even the execution of "counterrevolutionaries" dimmed his enthusiasm. "I can only say that anybody who lifts his hand against [Russia] ought to be shot." From his return to America in 1939 onward, Robeson was a staple in Party causes and as an entertainer for sympathetic organizations.[59]

His sympathy for Russia and support for Communist-backed causes to the contrary, Robeson never actually joined the Party. In this respect, he was no different from most Negroes. Neither the Party's respectability in the Negro community nor the inauguration of the Popular Front could substantially improve its Negro composition. It got more Negro members, but only because it got more members. From 240 in March 1934, a bare 4 percent of the New York District, Negro membership grew to 1,039, or 6.5 percent, in 1936. Nearly all the members—850—were in Harlem, which had been split into three sections to accommodate its new size. There, Negroes now made up nearly half the Party membership compared to only one-fifth in 1933. Nationally, the percentage of Negroes hardly changed between the Eighth Convention in 1934 and mid-1936, going from 9.1 percent of the Party to 9.5 percent, or 3,895, at the latter date. Even that figure was attained only because 1,300 Negroes were recruited between January and April of 1936. Fred Brown boasted: "Through the activities around the Negro Congress our comrades were able to entrench themselves in many Negro mass organizations and recruited very influential Negro workers into our ranks." Overall, however, the figures were disappointing and alarming, leading to "the conclusion that no real efforts have been made by the whole Party to connect such struggles [Ethiopia, Scottsboro, Herndon, NNC] with mass recruiting of Negro workers."[60]

Things did not get much better. Between 1936 and 1937 there was actually a slight decline in Negro membership. A recruitment drive between September 1937 and February 1938 brought in 2,890 Negroes, more than were in the Party before it began and bringing their total up to nearly 5,000. At the 1938 Party convention, it was announced that 6,900 Negroes belonged to the Communist movement, making them 9.2 percent of the Party. In New York, however, Negroes made up just 6 percent of the Party, and in Harlem they were only 30 percent, or about 650. Membership fluctuation among Negroes was the heaviest of any group; the Party lost more Negroes than anyone else. In comparison with what it hoped to achieve, the Communist party came up well short among American blacks.[61]

18

The Intellectual
Merry-Go-Round

THE POPULAR FRONT, so unifying a tactic among other groups, proved disruptive to Party efforts among American intellectuals. Not that the Party failed to make headway among intellectuals. But, the Party's activities generated an organized anti-Communist movement. Moreover, just at the moment when proletarian culture seemed to be thriving, it had to be abandoned. Bourgeois culture and its creators suddenly became respectable as the Communist party searched for allies in the struggle against fascism. Not all the intellectuals who had been attracted to Communism by its rejection of bourgeois culture and support for revolution were enamored of the new glorification of America and its values that characterized the Democratic Front. Many were unable to go along.

Communist-dominated or sponsored cultural activities were thriving before the Comintern's adoption of the Popular Front. The Pierre Degeyter Clubs, named for the composer of the *Internationale*, enlisted such members as Charles Seeger and Aaron Copland. The clubs arranged an American tour for Hans Eisler, chairman of the International Music Bureau, "an international union of revolutionary musicians" and himself "the foremost revolutionary composer" in the world. Leopold Stokowski spoke at a Lenin memorial meeting, wrote an ode to Lenin, and had the *Internationale* sung at his Young People's Concert.[1]

The revolutionary theater hit its stride as well. The Workers Laboratory Theatre, an organ of the Workers' International Relief, specialized in mobile agitprop plays, often performing in New York subways. The League of Workers' Theatre was set up "to spread the idea of the class struggle, to participate actively in the class struggle by raising funds for campaigns and for the revolutionary press, and by recruiting workers into the revolutionary unions and mass organizations, and especially to arouse the workers for the defense of the Soviet Union against the coming imperialist attack." By 1934 the league claimed to have more than 300 affiliated workers' theaters. The Theatre Union, a united front venture started in 1933, produced such successful revolutionary plays as *Peace on Earth* and *Stevedore*, while the Group Theatre put on the most acclaimed proletarian drama of the decade, Party-member Clifford Odets's *Waiting for Lefty*.[2]

After struggling for several years, the John Reed Clubs also experienced a surge by 1934. Young, enthusiastic writers, many unknown, were attracted by the opportunity to get their works published in such little club magazines as *Left Front, Left Review, Leftward, Cauldron, Blast, Dynamo, Anvil,* and *Hammer.* John Reed Clubs sprang up in such unlikely centers of revolutionary culture as Oklahoma City and Davenport, Iowa. Reviewing one of the new magazines, a writer in *The Daily Worker* was cheered by the wide geographical scope of the new activity: "It is not confined to a few metropolitan areas. For the first time a really national literature, free from sophisticated importations, is being given form by the many regional revolutionary magazines." Forty delegates representing 1,200 members attended the clubs' second national conference, held in Chicago in late September 1934, and were assured of their key role by Alexander Trachtenberg, head of International Publishers.[3]

Communist critics congratulated one another about the new maturity of their cultural activities. Granville Hicks pronounced 1934 "a good year, an exceptionally good year" for both proletarian literature and the revolutionary movement among writers. "New writers have appeared. Sympathizers have drawn closer to the movement. Accepted revolutionary writers have surpassed themselves." Isidor Schneider proclaimed: "The exciting thing is that proletarian culture is now adult; it has passed its childhood of revolutionary 'baby talk.'" The circulation of *The New Masses*, only 6,000 as a monthly, jumped to 24,000 per week in early 1935. It outsold *The New Republic* and was within 9,000 of *The Nation;* its newsstand sales were higher than those of both its liberal competitors combined.[4]

Not all portents were so favorable. The Degeyter Clubs were small, the revolutionary theaters were financially precarious, and proletarian literature did not sell. One author lamented that "few of our novels and other literary books reached beyond a thousand copies. We may aim 'to speak to millions' but so far we have hardly begun the job." And some Communist intellectuals spoke out on the need for central discipline. To Max Eastman's charge that they marched in lockstep with the Kremlin, Joshua Kunitz proudly admitted: "Yes we are artists in uniform. We are Leninists, Communists, Bolsheviks."[5]

Things were, however, about to change. At the 1934 John Reed Clubs meeting, Alexander Trachtenberg insisted that writers be left alone to write, freed from demands that they spend their time organizing:

> The purpose of the John Reed Clubs is to win writers and artists to the revolution. The duty of political leaders is to help them carry out this purpose. The party in no way wishes to interfere with the free exercise of talents, or to absorb talented people in other work, and any cultural organization which fails to observe this is taking the wrong line.

The John Reed Clubs, however, had not been chosen to share this new, relaxed attitude toward culture. In a Party fraction meeting at the conference, Trachtenberg announced the clubs' forthcoming abolition and the formation of an American Writers' Congress limited to well-known literary figures. Richard Wright, who attended the meeting, was shocked and vainly protested, asking what would become of the eager literary neophytes who had flocked to the clubs and regarded them as a haven. "There was no answer." Orrick Johns, a Party member since 1932, informed readers of *The New Masses* a few weeks after the conference that the shortcomings of the clubs had necessitated a congress of anti-fascist writers so that "a basis will be found for a higher type of writers' organization."[6]

Despite their desire to expand their appeal and influence, the Communists dominated the planning and execution of the American Writers' Congress. The congress resembled an auxiliary of the Third Period far more than a Popular Front organization. The original call was signed by sixty-four people. Party members and their close collaborators dominated the list, including Granville Hicks, Joseph Freeman, Mike Gold, Richard Wright, Joshua Kunitz, Malcolm Cowley, Lincoln Steffens, and John Howard Lawson. A bevy of proletarian writers filled up the list, along with such Party notables as Earl Browder, Clarence Hathaway, Mossaiye

Olgin, and Alexander Trachtenberg. The document called on writers "who have achieved some standing in their respective fields; who have clearly indicated their sympathy to the revolutionary cause; who do not need to be convinced of the decay of capitalism, of the inevitability of revolution" to organize to "fight against imperialist war and fascism, defend the Soviet Union against capitalist aggression; for the development and strengthening of the revolutionary labor movement; against white chauvinism."[7]

Communists carefully controlled the gathering, which opened on April 26, 1935. The preplanning committee—Trachtenberg, Henry Hart, Cowley, Michael Blankfort, Edwin Seaver, and Orrick Johns—was largely Communist. Twelve of sixteen members of the presiding committee were Party members. A Party caucus, enlarged by a few dependable non-Communists, held a small meeting on the evening of April 27 while other delegates attended regularly scheduled panels and "a host of ideas were consolidated." The next day the group's suggestion that a League of American Writers be formed was presented to the congress by Mike Gold, Orrick Johns, John Lawson, and Jack Conroy and was approved, along with a list of nominees for positions. Waldo Frank, a non-Communist whose ties to the Party went back to the 1932 Professional Groups for Foster and Ford, was selected as chairman. At least ten of the seventeen members of the Executive Committee were Communists, as was a significant proportion of the National Council.[8]

Party leaders had considered but rejected the idea of inviting such prominent non-Communists as Sidney Hook, Lewis Corey, Charles Beard, Louis Adamic, Louis Hacker, Ben Stolberg, and Clifton Fadiman. In spite of their absence and the Party's domination of the event, John Chamberlain discerned a new mood among the Communists; in an "agreeable surprise" there were no more denunciations of other radicals as "scabby rats" and an ebbing of "the terrorist spirit on the literary left."[9]

On the opening evening, Malcolm Cowley praised Soviet culture and denounced the brutality of American society. A marine worker, Hays Jones, invited writers "to come to the proletariat, the only live thing in capitalist society" and warned them that their only choice was "the uniform of the proletariat" or "the straight-jacket of fascism." If they opted for the latter, "we will bury them with the dead and throw the dirt over them." Waldo Frank told the congress that "Communism must come and must be fought for." Mike Gold talked of a Soviet America. When Kenneth Burke had the temerity to suggest that "the people" was a more effective revolutionary symbol for Communists than "the workers," he

352

was subjected to a barrage. One participant warned that Burke's chosen word was "historically associated with demagoguery of the most vicious sort." Another pointed out that Hitler used similar language. Joseph Freeman insisted on the central role of the proletariat in transforming capitalist society. Even though Burke gave a spirited defense of his views, he was chosen to the League of American Writers' Executive Committee. Soon afterward, Burke praised the Communists whose "vitality and organizational ability" had made the congress possible. Although not a Communist, he believed that "those who approach the issues of today from the standpoint of cultural survival must have sympathy at least with communism as a historical direction." [10]

Burke's escape from purgatory may have been due to Party leader Earl Browder. Appearing on the program the first evening, Browder affirmed the importance of cultural work: "The first demand of the Party upon its writer-members is that they shall be good writers, constantly better writers, for only so can they really serve the Party. We do not want to take good writers and make bad strike leaders out of them." Besides reassuring established writers that the new organization would not require them to sacrifice literary work for political action, Browder also hastened to deny that the Party sought to put artists in uniform: the "method of our work in this field cannot be one of Party resolutions giving judgments upon artistic, aesthetic questions. There is no fixed 'Party line' by which works of art can be automatically separated into sheep and goats." So long as they accepted the Party's political line, it seemed, intellectuals would be given some leeway in cultural affairs. [11]

The League of American Writers was designed as an organization for established figures. Several months after the congress, Isidor Schneider reported that the new group's membership was only 125, far fewer than the 400 who had been delegates. "Applications for membership flow in," he wrote, "but the standard is kept high, membership is granted only to creative writers whose published work entitles them to a professional status." The league did manage to enlist a number of prominent writers of whom little more was demanded than the use of their names once the Popular Front was inaugurated. Thomas Mann, John Steinbeck, Ernest Hemingway, Theodore Dreiser, James Farrell, Archibald MacLeish, Lewis Mumford, Van Wyck Brooks, Lillian Hellman, William Carlos Williams, Nelson Algren, William Saroyan, Nathanael West, Clifton Fadiman, and Dale Carnegie were just a few of the men and women of letters who participated in league affairs over the next few years. Most, however, did little more than send greetings to a meeting or sign an occasional petition. The league held public lectures to raise money and made abortive efforts to set up a lecture bureau and launch a magazine. One regional organization was set up, a Western Writers' Conference in San Francisco in November 1936. But no attempt was made to create the local groups that had given the John Reed Clubs their life until 1937.[12]

The League of American Writers was not even able to produce a glittering array of names to endorse the Communist ticket in 1936. Although a Committee of Professional Groups for Browder and Ford was patched together for the occasion, its forty-seven members were a pale imitation of its distinguished 1932 predecessor. A few renowned non-Communists like Kenneth Burke, S. J. Perelman, Aaron Copland, and Waldo Frank were included, but to fill out the 1936 roster required enlisting such Party members as Ben Gold and Louise Thompson to go along with fellow Communists like Freeman, Gold, Hicks, Anna Rochester, and William Gropper. Only ten veterans of 1932 signed up. Aside from the initial announcement of its formation, the committee received little publicity in the Party press.[13]

The writers had met before the Seventh Congress spelled out more clearly the new Comintern goals. Their congress, therefore, had featured the Party in a prominent role. By the time the American Artists Congress got together in mid-February 1936, it was less obvious who had organized it. The call eschewed revolutionary rhetoric and lacked the names of Communist politicians. This Congress met "for the express purpose of combatting the reactionary forces in the world which are threatening the destruction of culture by Fascism and war." With Lewis Mumford presiding, 400 artists and critics—including Stuart Davis, Rockwell Kent, Margaret Bourke-White, Art Young, and Meyer Schapiro—lauded the Soviet Union and discussed the relationship between art and capitalist society.[14]

By the time the Second American Writers' Congress met in June 1937, the openly pro-Communist tone of the 1935 meeting had disappeared. The call, dominated by the theme of combatting fascism, lacked the revolutionary language of its predecessor. Absent from the list of signers this time were not only the names of Party politicians like Browder and Hathaway but also the most prominent Party intellectuals—Gold, Freeman, and Hicks. The latter was so upset that he complained to the league's executive secretary that Communists had been shoved into the background. Other signers included Van Wyck Brooks, James Weldon Johnson, Claude McKay, and Carl Van Doren. Few of the officers or members of the Executive Council were open Communists. Most of the papers and talks focused on the fate of culture under fascism and the need to defend the Spanish Republic.[15]

The most conspicuous participant in the congress was the Party's newest literary hero, Ernest Hemingway. Back from Spain where he had cheered on the Lincoln Battalion and gloried in the heroism of the Popular Front resistance to fascism, Hemingway spoke to the opening session, denouncing fascism as "a lie told by bullies. A writer who will not lie cannot live or work under fascism." Archibald MacLeish, a future Librarian of Congress, presided at the first session and defended cooperation with Communists: "The man who refuses to defend his convictions for fear he may defend them in the wrong company, has no convictions. . . . Even if the danger of rape exists the tender spirit need not necessarily submit.[16]

The Party did not go so far as to let the League of American Writers drift along unsupervised. Its executive director, Francis Folsom, was a Party stalwart. And its president, Donald Ogden Stewart, elected in 1937, was a secret Party member. Stewart had an unlikely background for his role. Educated at Exeter and Yale, he had realized his fondest dream in 1916 when elected to Skull and Bones, the exclusive Yale Club. Following several unsuccessful flings in the business world, Stewart had two parodies accepted by *Vanity Fair* and was launched on a successful career as a writer of light satire and musical comedy for Broadway and the screen. Not only was he a regular among the Algonquin wits, but he also hobnobbed with such rich socialites as Jock Whitney and James Forrestal. He was so lacking in sympathy for the oppressed and the underdog that he crossed a Screen Writers Guild picket line in 1934 to sit with his good friend, studio executive and union-hater Irving Thalberg, at an awards ceremony.

Writing a play with a minor Communist character in 1935, Stewart needed to learn how such an odd fellow would talk, asked a bookseller for some Party literature, and was given some of British Communist John Strachey's writings. The playwright began to pay attention to politics for the first time in his life. As his horrified friends and relatives watched, Donald Ogden Stewart became a mainstay of a dozen Party auxiliaries. The one-time playboy not only was active in the Screen Writers Guild he had once scorned but lent his support to striking agricultural workers. He became president of the Hollywood Anti-Nazi League and the League Of American Writers. Along the way to becoming one of the ornaments of the Popular Front, he also acquired a new wife, Ella Winter, the widow of Lincoln Steffens and herself a long-time Party supporter. Sometime in 1936 Stewart apparently joined the Communist party, but it made little material difference in his life: "I saw no reason," he reported, "to stop dancing or enjoying the fun and play in life." Communism was another elite club. "Unconsciously, I suppose, I wanted to tap these 'workers' for Skull and Bones."[17]

Under his stewardship, league membership jumped from 220 to 610 by 1938 and stood at 750 in 1938. Seventy-two writers signed the call for the third congress in 1939. Agreement was so widespread that there was "no need to spend [the league's] energies arguing the connection between politics and literature." Instead, most discussion focused on craft problems. So respectable had the League of American Writers become that when Van Wyck Brooks offered President Roosevelt honorary membership inasmuch as "your writings constitute a unique contribution to the body of American letters," Roosevelt responded with "hearty appreciation" in accepting the invitation.[18]

In this glow of good feeling, some old intellectual enemies were forgiven past sins. Upton Sinclair had been excoriated just a few years before as a prime example of American social-fascism. *The Daily Worker* serialized his new novel, *Little Steel,* and Earl Browder announced that he and Sinclair were in "fundamental agreement." Taxed by the anti-Communist journalist Eugene Lyons for cooperating with the Party, Sinclair patiently explained that the Communists had finally come around to his position and now "support and cooperate with the democratic peoples."[19]

The Party's gains, however, were more than offset by defections and organized attacks. During the Popular Front years, an articulate, determined band of enemies gathered to contest the Party for the allegiance of American intellectuals. New recruits joined the small group of defectors from the Professional Groups for Foster and Ford and those appalled by the 1934 Madison Square Garden riot.

The inability of the League of American Writers to make much progress in 1935 and 1936 only made the activities of the New York John Reed Club even more embarrassing. Stronger and more intellectually vigorous than its counterparts, the club refused to go meekly out of existence in early 1935. Not only did it continue to sponsor cultural events and symposia on its own, but *Partisan Review*, its journal, begun in early 1935, had become the most prominent little magazine in the left-wing movement. Among the original editors were Joseph Freeman, Sender Garlin, Jack Conroy, Joshua Kunitz, Louis Lozowick, and Philip Rahv. Mike Gold helped secure funding. Joe Freeman and Granville Hicks contributed to the first issue. Concerned largely with cultural and aesthetic questions, *Partisan Review* was less explicitly political than *The New Masses.* It also took issue with Marxist critics like Granville Hicks and proletarian literature which "distorts and vulgarizes the complexity of human nature." Works of literature could not be evaluated simply in terms of their political content and stance. Hicks, for example, did not care what an author chose to write about: "It is the author's attitude that counts, not his theme."[20]

Partisan Review's two most influential editors were soon making other Party critics nervous. William Phillips, a one-time graduate student and teacher at New York University, had become active in the John Reed Club early in the 1930s. Although he never joined the Communist party, he quickly moved close to its positions, even writing book reviews for *The Communist* under the name of Wallace Phelps. Philip Rahv, born in the Ukraine, had worked in advertising after high school. He joined the John Reed Club in the early 1930s and also became a Party member. Late in 1934, Hicks questioned whether there was any need for such little magazines. Neither Phillips nor Rahv played a prominent role in the proceedings of the Writers' Congress. A plan to make *Partisan Review* the official organ of the League of American Writers fell through on the grounds that the journal was too leftist. Trachtenberg tried several times to shut it down. Mike Gold denounced the magazine for its lack of charity to politically sound authors. Cut off from its original political base and facing insurmountable financial problems, *Partisan Review* suspended publication late in 1936.[21]

By far the harshest critic of the Communist party's cultural stance was James Farrell. The author of the *Studs Lonigan* trilogy was a fervent Marxist who had no patience with literary or political trimming. At the first Writers' Congress he denounced "that species of over-politicalized and ideologically schematized criticism which had been too dishearteningly frequent in the literary sections of revolutionary journals." As the congress drew to a close, Farrell embarrassed its Party directors by calling on the delegates to conclude the ostensibly nonpartisan gathering by singing the *Internationale*. The following year he produced a withering blast at virtually every Communist critic, accusing Mike Gold, Granville Hicks, Isidor Schneider, and Joseph Freeman of a host of sins ranging from inconsistency to mechanistic and infantile Marxism.[22]

For some radical intellectuals, the Communist party's increasingly moderate policies were as disconcerting as its cultural and literary judgments. More and more of them began to look to the figure of Leon Trotsky. In opposition to Stalin's doctrine of socialism in one country, he had continued to stand for worldwide revolutionary militancy. However, for years after his defeat in Russia's inner-party politics, neither his luminous intellect nor his eloquent pen nor his extensive revolutionary experience could attract many Americans, intellectual or not, to his banner. The Trotskyists were a tiny sect. A handful of distinguished intellectuals had previously dabbled around the fringes of the Trotskyists or been allied with them, including Max Eastman, Sidney Hook, and Felix Morrow. But it took Stalin's full assault on Trotsky to rally larger numbers of American intellectuals to his defense.

Faith in the Soviet Union was a far more potent bond of allegiance to Communism for many intellectuals than any other tie. When the purge trials began, their faith was put to the test. Accused of forming a terrorist bloc with Trotsky to assassinate Soviet leaders, Grigori Zinoviev and Lev Kamenev were convicted and executed in August 1936. Karl Radek and Grigori Pyatakov were the leading defendants early in 1937 during another trial, charged with holding secret meetings with Trotsky and plotting with the Nazis. Not long after Pyatakov's execution, it was announced that Marshall Tukhachevsky and virtually the entire general staff of the Red Army had been executed for working for the Nazis. One year later, in March 1938, three members of Lenin's Politboro (Nikolai Bukharin, Alexei Rykov, and Nikolai Krestinsky), one fabled Bolshevik and ex-Trotskyist (Christian Rakovsky), the recently deposed head of the secret police and architect of earlier trials (Genrikh Yagoda), and a handful of Stalin's former lieutenants stood in the dock, accused of crimes ranging from espionage, sabotage, and plotting the return of capitalism and dismemberment of the Soviet Union to killing the famed novelist Maxim Gorki. The public trials were only a tiny part of the terror. Uncooperative Communists like Sergo Ordzhonikdje conveniently died under mysterious circumstances. The Comintern was particularly hard-hit. Ossip Piatnitsky and Bela Kun disappeared. Refusing to honor a recall to Moscow in 1938, Willi Munzenberg was expelled from the movement he had so creatively served. Italians and Yugoslavs in Moscow were eliminated by the hundreds. So many Polish Communist leaders were executed that the Polish party was disbanded.[23]

If the confessions of his alleged co-conspirators were to be believed, Leon Trotsky had orchestrated the most extensive and diabolical plot in all of history. He had somehow united left-wing Zinovievites, right-wing Bukharinites, and disgruntled Stalinites with his own followers and then plotted with both Nazi Germany and Imperial Japan to overthrow the Soviet regime and install capitalism. Trotsky moved from Turkey to France to Norway in search of a haven. Everywhere he went, nervous governments, urged on by local Communist parties, encouraged him to leave or expelled him. He finally landed in Mexico early in 1937 and bent all his resources to defending himself and exposing the Moscow trials as a monstrous frame-up, calling into question the legitimacy of the Soviet regime and the ideological justification of the Popular Front.

American Communists seized on reports of the trials from such non-Communists as American Ambassador Joseph Davies and Walter Duranty of *The New York Times* to buttress their claims that justice was being done. Early in 1937, Browder told one Party audience that the guilt of all the defendants in the trials to date was so clearly established that any further discussion was useless. Trotskyism worked "with the deadliness of cholera germs," and Trotsky himself was "the advance agent of fascism and war throughout the world." An editorial applauded the execution of Tukhachevsky and his fellow officers as "a crushing blow to the advance Fascist guard of the capitalist encirclement of the Soviet Union." One *Daily Worker* Moscow correspondent nominated Nikolai Yezhov, the director of the purge, for the Nobel Peace Prize. Local Party units passed resolutions denouncing the Trotskyist-Bukharinite "traitors" and demanded "full Socialist justice." As the furor mounted, such friends of the Soviet Union as Corliss Lamont described the trials as "transitory phenomena." Although Lamont said he personally abhorred violence, executions, or "any sort of bloodshed," those guilty of treason "deserved the utmost severity." Lamont professed puzzlement that so much was being made about the trials, observing, no doubt accurately, that "the Soviet people are not talking as much about these trials as some people in America."[24]

The stream of personal abuse directed at Trotsky brought back memories of the Third Period. Ella Winter likened him to the assassin of Lincoln. Mike Gold felt Trotsky was "the most horrible Judas of all history." The Trotskyists, Earl Browder warned, were doing work which "equals or exceeds in its destructiveness the open reactionary forces and their newspapers." And, the Party newspaper published in full a long speech by Stalin under the ominous headline: "The Measures for Liquidation of Trotskyites and Other Double-Dealers." Stalin denounced the offenders as "a gang without principle, without ideas, of wreckers, diversionists, intelligence service agents, spies, murderers, a gang of sworn enemies of the working class, working in the pay of the intelligence services of foreign states."[25]

Trotsky's travails brought him support in America that his politics never had. A committee to secure him asylum, formed in 1936, included Norman Thomas, James Farrell, Edmund Wilson, Bertram Wolfe, Joseph Wood Krutch, John Chamberlain, Louis Hacker, and Diego Rivera. It was succeeded by an American Committee for the Defense of Leon Trotsky. A Commission of Inquiry, chaired by John Dewey, heard Trotsky's defense against Stalin's charges. Dewey, Ben Stolberg, Suzanne LaFollette, Carleton Beals, Mauritz Hallgren, Otto Ruehle, and Alfred Rosmer visited Mexico in the spring of 1937 to take Trotsky's testimony and afford him a forum for defending himself. That September the Dewey Commission gave its verdict: not guilty. The commission earned more than its share of abuse. The resignations of Beals, Hallgren, Lewis Gannett, and Freda Kirchwey were each hailed as dramatic evidence that the commission was not independent at all but a sounding board for Trotskyist propaganda. Those who dared to remain were attacked constantly. Mike Gold sneered at "Trotsky-bred intellectuals." He denied worrying about their apostasy: "I must confess I was never alarmed, I believe evacuation of the bowels is necessary to a healthy body." Dewey himself was castigated as a liar, a tool of reaction, and a doddering fool.[26]

Any suggestion that Trotsky deserved a hearing was vehemently rejected. William Foster called Trotsky's request for a forum a "sham," asking why he did not return to Moscow to face a Russian court. Sixty prominent American intellectuals signed an open letter to liberals warning that the American Committee for the Defense of Leon Trotsky had no interest in securing justice but was an instrument to attack and defame the Soviet Union. Most of the names were familiar signatures on Party petitions, including Newton Arvin, Heywood Broun, Theodore Dreiser, Louis Fischer, Lillian Hellman, Granville Hicks, Corliss Lamont, Henry Roth, and Mary Van Kleeck. The signatures soon grew to eighty-eight— "the most distinguished list of names ever gathered on a single document in America in support of the Soviet Union," Browder boasted in *Pravda*. One hundred and fifty artists, writers, actors, and academics signed a statement that the verdicts in the Bukharin trial had been established beyond doubt and had to be supported by American progressives in the interests of American democracy.[27]

Fellow travelers, no matter how distinguished, were not expected to confine their cooperation to domestic issues. The Party exacted a price for a place in the intellectual Popular Front. When *The New Republic* suggested that the Trotsky-Stalin dispute was an internal Russian matter which should not be allowed to disrupt unity among progressives in America, Alexander Bittelman responded that "those who fight reaction and war in the United States" had "at the same time to fight the Trotsky-fascists." Waldo Frank learned that lesson. His credentials as a devoted fellow traveler went back to the 1932 Professional Groups for Foster and Ford. He had been chosen to head the League of American Writers in 1935. During the 1936 Presidential campaign he traveled around the country with Browder. Early in 1937, however, he wrote the Party leader that he found the Moscow trials "difficult to reconcile with reason." When he made his complaint public, Frank was considerably more restrained. He wrote that, while he personally felt Trotsky's charge of a frame-up to be unreasonable, many sincere people believed it, in part because the evidence against Trotsky had been supplied by "self-confessed liars, traitors, assassins." Speaking as "a friend of the Communists" and ally of the Soviet Union, Frank appealed for a court of inquiry to investigate the charges against Trotsky. He took care to criticize the "partisanship" of the Dewey Commission and suggested as one possibility that the Second and Third Internationals undertake a joint investigation.[28]

Frank's caution won him no plaudits. Browder accused Frank of a "miserable libel," speaking "nonsense," and mouthing the insults of "black reaction." In an embarrassing piece of timing, the Second Writers' Congress was due to open in June. Frank, as the first chairman, might have been expected to preside or play a prominent role. In fact, he was not in attendance. Browder devoted most of his speech to denouncing Frank and his ally Reinhold Niebuhr. Communists, the Party leader explained, did not want to regiment writers. However, just as he, Browder, would justifiably be criticized for writing a bad novel, so writers had to expect attacks for poor political judgments. Without reference to Frank's literary merits, Browder thereupon expelled him from the Popular Front: "When the democratic front is fighting the open enemy before us, it shall not be attacked from the rear by those who pretend to be part of it."[29]

Even the most innocuous of acts could call one's loyalties into question. Farrar and Rinehart published Joseph Freeman's autobiography, *An American Testament*, to glowing reviews in 1936. Preparing to leave on a promotional tour, Freeman was summoned by Browder and informed that his book had been condemned by the Comintern for its less than totally negative treatment of Trotsky. Rather than have a public confrontation, Browder asked Freeman to suppress his own book. Like a good soldier, Freeman promptly canceled his speaking tour, asked Party organs to stop mentioning the book, and succeeded in restricting its sales. Freeman incurred further Soviet displeasure as editor of *The New Masses;* his correspondent in Russia, Joshua Kunitz, was not sufficiently enthusiastic in his reporting of the first of the Moscow trials and was denied a visa to cover the Pyatakov-Radek trial. A long essay that Freeman wrote on left-wing literary critics was suppressed. Heartsick about the purge trials, Freeman drifted further and further from the Party. In 1939 Philip Dengel, once a Comintern representative in America, flayed Freeman publicly for his failure to "rouse hatred for the vile Trotskyite enemies of the working class" in his autobiography and added a condemnation of

The Daily Worker for its early praise of so flawed a work. Freeman quietly dropped out of the Party he had served so loyally and long. A few years later he produced an autobiographical novel, *Never Call Retreat*, announcing his disillusionment with Marxism.[30]

Dissident writers quickly learned that their political sins were paid for in literary currency. John Dos Passos, long the great hope of revolutionary literature, broke with the Party during the Spanish Civil War after an old friend was executed, presumably by the Soviet secret police. The individual novels in his *U.S.A.* trilogy had won Communist applause when first published. Suddenly, Mike Gold had second thoughts. Before, he explained, he had "ignored the merde" in Dos Passos' work. Now he clearly saw that it had always been there and that Dos Passos had "sunk back into it, as into a native element." His future novels found little favor with major reviewers or the Party. James Farrell had been engaged in a running battle with Hicks, Gold, Freeman, and other Party critics for several years. So long as the dispute remained primarily literary, his fiction remained in favor. As late as mid-1936, Hicks praised the author of *Studs Lonigan* as one whose "work has been noticeably quickened and invigorated by contact with the revolutionary movement." By 1937, however, Farrell had openly aligned himself with the defense of Leon Trotsky. Not only did he face condemnation in the Party press, but *The New Republic*, whose literary editor was Malcolm Cowley, attacked Farrell's work and even printed a joint letter from twenty-six heretofore unknown people calling Farrell a "palpable fraud."[31]

On the other hand, joining the Popular Front could enhance a writer's reputation with the Communists and earn him their literary plaudits. For years Archibald MacLeish had been insulted in the Party press. Mike Gold linked him to "the fascist unconscious" in 1933. The following year a *New Masses* reviewer called the poet "a dirty Nazi" and "a Nazi, at least a kind of ur-Nazi, whether he wants to be or not." In 1935 this repellent figure wrote a play, *Panic*, which attacked fascism. *The New Masses* sponsored a performance. By 1936 MacLeish's new poems were "among the most beautiful and effective in revolutionary literature." The following year he was chosen to preside at the opening session of the Second Writers' Congress.[32]

Not all intellectuals left the Party or the Popular Front quietly or with little public fuss. At the Second Writers' Congress, several participants declared their support for Trotsky at the session on criticism. More disconcertingly, *Partisan Review* resumed publication in November 1937 after a year's hiatus, under the control of Dwight MacDonald, Mary McCarthy, William Phillips, Philip Rahv, and Fred Dupee. The first two had been among the "Trotskyist" disrupters at the Second Writers' Congress; Phillips had been very close to the Communists, and Rahv and Dupee, once Party members, had recently been expelled. *The New Masses* was livid: the good name of an honorable magazine had been stolen "with slight regard for what that name once stood for." Once loyal to Communism, its two primary editors, Rahv and Phillips, had now "attacked the Communist Party, the people's front, the League of American Writers and the Soviet Union." In their defense, Rahv and Phillips insisted that *Partisan Review* had always had a higher calling than serving the Party; from the beginning it had been distinguished from *The New Masses* by "our struggle to free revolutionary literature from domination by the immediate strategy of a political party."[33]

Partisan Review quickly became the center of a radical, anti-Communist intellectual community. While the Communists and their Popular Front allies could corral hundreds of signatures on letters and petitions defending the Soviet Union, their liberal and radical opponents could now marshal shorter but more distinguished lists to condemn both Nazism and Communism. A Committee for Cultural Freedom was organized in early 1939 to combat totalitarianism in all its guises and its American defenders. More than 140 well-known intellectuals and cultural figures signed the committee's manifesto, including John Dewey, Sidney Hook, Sherwood Anderson, V. F. Calverton, George Counts, Max Eastman, Ira Gershwin, John Haynes Holmes, Jerome Kern, Sinclair Lewis, Thomas Mann, John Dos Passos, James Rorty, Norman Thomas, and Oswald Garrison Villard. Many of them had once been sympathetic to the Party.[34]

All these troubles angered and depressed Mike Gold. He had little patience with defectors from the Party. Brooding about Dos Passos' newfound hostility to the Party, Gold mused that "intellectuals are the most unstable and untrustworthy group in modern society, one is forced to believe. Dos Passos has been, during a period of ten years, a nihilist, an anarchist, a half-baked Communist, an escapist and a lot of other strange things." Intellectuals, Gold concluded a few weeks later, were too susceptible to fascism. By the fall of 1937, with the Trotskyist virus active among American intellectuals, Gold decided that the word "intellectual" itself should be expunged from the English language and replaced by "white collar worker." The old term connoted a "wise guy" who thought he knew a lot. Gold had to admit, however, that the combination of the Popular Front era and the defections of many young intellectuals had cost the Party much of the old élan characteristic of the early 1930s. A "young and exceedingly talented proletarian poet" told Gold how shocked he was upon returning to New York in 1937 after a year's absence: "The whole left-wing cultural movement has been shot from under our feet." Nothing had been spared, the returnee lamented:

> Our theatres have folded up. All our literary magazines have folded up. The post-depression group of writers have gotten tired, and have settled down to office jobs. The youngest generation of writers that came after them isn't going leftward at all. It's a new opportunist generation and it makes me sick. They write one short story and begin at once scheming for a crack at Hollywood and the big money.

Gold sadly agreed.[35]

The Party did not suffer from any lack of intellectual allies during the Popular Front. The League of American Writers and League of American Artists enlisted scores of prominent intellectuals. Hundreds offered their endorsement of Stalin's murder of his Old Bolshevik comrades. Influential journals of opinion like *The New Republic* and *The Nation* either did the same or suggested silence for fear of endangering the Popular Front. Party-sponsored causes, ranging from support for Loyalist Spain to support for the New Deal, brought money and publicity from the cultural world. While the Party's strength and reach were not to be underestimated, it clearly had lost its role as cultural pacesetter. The Communists' very respectability made them less attractive to those intellectuals who regarded Marxism as a revolution in culture as well as politics. Watching the Party trim its cultural sails to prevailing political winds was a revelation that they could not ignore. Long before the Nazi-Soviet Pact made the Party anathema to a large portion of American liberals, it had a dedicated band of intellectual opponents.

Cultural activity in the Party could never be autonomous. It had to serve some political purpose. Every intellectual effort had to fit into or advance the immediate political line. Since the mortality rate of political lines was so high, the mortality rate of cultural material and intellectuals was equally high. Those who had joined the Party in the 1920s and early 1930s, inspired by the dream of creating or midwifing a new revolutionary culture, had to adjust themselves to the requirements of a Popular Front culture after 1935. No sudden literary or aesthetic revelation accounted for the change. The real intellectual authority within the Communist party always rested not with intellectuals, but with the politicians and their intellectual pundits. Sooner or later, most Communist intellectuals learned that lesson.

19

A More Popular

Party

FOR YEARS the Comintern had demanded concrete organizational results to measure Party success. Only more live, signed-up members could demonstrate that the American Communists were on the right track. By that criterion, the Third Period had been a major disappointment. In 1935, prior to the Seventh Comintern Congress, there were more than 30,000 Party members. In percentage terms, the increase was dramatic. Yet, after six years of economic depression, there were still fewer Communists than there had been in 1919. The Party had been unable to grow by even a pitiful 25,000 members during the worst economic crisis in American history. Measured against that depressing statistic, the Popular Front years represented prosperity.[1]

Party spokesmen and publications provided at least three different sets of figures dealing with membership, corresponding to three distinct acts expected of every Communist. The most common figure for computing Party membership was based on recruitment. The first step in becoming a Communist was to sign a Party card and pay a modest initiation fee—10¢ for the unemployed and 50¢ for the employed. Recruitment figures always gave the largest possible Party membership. A second figure was derived from Party registration. In January of every year—and after 1937, in mid-year as well—all members were required to appear at unit meetings to receive their new Party books. Registrants were always fewer than the number officially listed on paper because the units usually never were able to draw all the recruits to the January meetings. In 1937, for example, New York, with probably the best record in the Party, registered only 70 percent of its members. The other 30 percent had disappeared, been lost, or failed to show up. J. Peters laid much of the blame on the units. They "had no records of members, they don't know who is transferring in, who is transferred out; who is recruited, who has dropped out, why, etc., etc." A third set of figures, traditionally the lowest, gave the number of dues-payers. Prior to 1936, dues were payable weekly. The Ninth Convention put them on a monthly basis. Members two months in arrears were no longer in good standing; after four months of nonpayment they were dropped from the rolls. The actual number of paid-up Communists never matched the registration; in December 1937, for instance, only 40,000 of the 62,000 members paid their assessment. Early in 1937, with a recruited membership of more than 45,000 and 37,000 registered, only about 32,000 paid their dues.[2]

When the Communists gathered for their Ninth Convention in the spring of 1936, they claimed 41,000 members. Between then and mid-1937 there was stagnation. In June 1937, the Central Committee unhappily noted only a "little over 40,000," called the situation "particularly alarming" and "intolerable," and demanded that all Party organizations immediately initiate discussions to step up recruiting. The campaign coincided with the Party's embrace of Roosevelt and the New Deal and led to a big explosion in membership. In the first eight months of 1937, 14,448 signed Party cards; during the last four months, 18,050 people joined. By December 1937 there were 62,000 members. In January 1937, 37,000 Communists had registered; a year later the count was more than 55,000. The new Democratic Front policy did nothing to slow membership. Earl Browder happily reported that the Party had reached 75,000 in February 1938. At the end of the year he claimed 82,000.[3]

Speaking to the Party's Tenth Convention in May 1938, Browder boldly predicted that the combined membership of the Party and the Young Communist League would go over 100,000 by the end of June. Even that was only the beginning: "The first hundred thousand," he told the excited convention, "is the hardest. The second hundred thousand should come in easy." The first hundred thousand, however, proved difficult enough. Not until 1939 did Party leaders boast that it had been achieved. In fact, Browder later admitted that the Party "never reached a hundred thousand." That magical number was achieved only by adding YCL membership.[4]

Unfortunately for the American Communists, what they perceived as the beginning of their journey to a mass membership was actually their high-water mark. Within a few months of the Party's approaching 100,000 members, the Nazi-Soviet Pact sent it into a decline from which it never fully recovered. The renewal of the Popular Front during World War II was not enough to rebuild Communist fortunes to their 1939 levels. Even before the pact, however, there were a few disturbing signs of a slowdown in Party growth. Membership doubled from 1936 to 1938 as the Party's newfound political moderation enabled it to draw in sympathizers and fellow travelers who had long hesitated to embrace Communism fully. By 1939 all those Party allies who were going to had taken the plunge. The available reservoir of sympathizers were drying up, and growth slowed.[5]

The Party was also able to grow because it managed to keep more of its recruits than ever before. Between 1930 and 1934, 60,000 people joined the Communist party. Yet, starting the decade with 7,000 members, the Party counted only some 26,000 in the latter year. More than 41,000 people had passed through its ranks. For every seven members who joined in 1930, two stayed and five left. That dismal record began to improve by 1934. During the Popular Front era, further improvements took place. In 1936 some 25,000 people signed Party cards, and membership should have stood at some 56,000 in January 1937. Actually it was 37,700, a loss of 18,300 members or a turnover rate of 72 percent. The following year more than 30,000 were recruited and 14,000 were lost, leaving a net membership of 54,000 and a turnover rate of just 46 percent.[6]

Most Communists who left the Party did so voluntarily. The Central Control Commission, renamed the National Control Commission in 1938 and composed "of the most exemplary Party members," was charged with discipline in cases "concerning violations of Party unity, discipline or ethics, or concerning lack of class vigilance and Communist firmness in facing the class enemy or concerning spies, swindlers, double dealers and other agents of the class enemy." Reporting to the Tenth Convention in 1938, the commission noted that expulsions had been drastically reduced. After averaging 343 a year from 1933 to 1935, expulsions had only averaged 188 over the next two years in a larger Party. The most serious problems in 1937 had arisen in Nebraska, where 16 percent of the tiny Party contingent had to be cut loose. In larger districts like New York, less than one-half of 1 percent of Party members were expelled.[7]

The Party tried to make it easier to be a Communist. Organizational Secretary Fred Brown told the Ninth Convention that Party meetings should end with singing, excursions, or picnics so that people would see Communists as "not strange people, but 'regular fellows,' part and parcel of the American masses." A twenty-three point list of hints on "How to Recruit" advised Communists to "attend dances and other affairs where you know the people you desire to recruit will be present. Mingle with them socially; show them that Communists are friendly beings." One lovelorn Party member wrote *The Daily Worker* asking if cadres could have a personal life. Alexander Bittelman thought it an excellent idea: "Such comradeship and love greatly increase [the cadres'] effectiveness and value to the movement by removing sources of difficulty that might damage their activity." Similarly, Brown saw organizational value in having new recruits retain old relationships. "The Party must make clear, again and again, that good Communists do not underestimate their family ties or their circles of friends. One of the good qualities of a Communist is his keeping close to his dear ones and to his friends, bringing them closer to the revolutionary movement and into the Party. It is much easier to convince relatives and close friends than outsiders."[8]

Not all close friends and relatives were wanted. Prior to the Tenth Convention, Party units debated and discussed a new draft constitution. One article provided that: "No Party member shall have personal or political relationship with confirmed Trotskyites, Lovestoneites, or other known enemies of the Party and of the working class." Some comrades objected, but Roy Hudson warned them that personal relationships were "merely a Trotskyite cloak of camouflage for drawing unsuspecting Party members into political relationships. Is it not clear that this is nothing more than a trip to catch, weaken, demobilize and eventually destroy the usefulness of good working class elements?" For those who thought they could separate the personal from the political, Hudson pointed to the danger that continuing a friendship with "organized agents of international fascism" could create. One's fellow workers would grow suspicious. Logically enough, Hudson also demanded greater "vigilance and political alertness" among those Communists who had objected to the ban.[9]

The Party's political turn to moderation was matched by organizational reforms designed to ease the burdens of membership. Being a Party member became less onerous after 1935. Where once Party leaders demanded "every night to Party work," they suddenly discovered the virtues of well-rounded Communists. Fred Brown remarked, "There is nothing in our program or constitution which states that a member of our Party must give all of his or her time (day and night) to Party work. All that the Party demands is that every member shall participate in some activity on the basis of his ability." Charles Krumbein reminded functionaries that those now being attracted to Communism were stable family men: "They have their social life, which we do not want to disconnect them from." The Party now expected less of its new recruits. "Joining the Party," Krumbein stated, "does not mean that a worker immediately shakes off his past and becomes a Bolshevik." The Ninth Convention issued a directive on organization that ordered: "It shall be the task of the units to make of every worker who joins the Party a full-fledged, active Communist rather than to expect him to be such before joining the Party." As part of a sweeping reorganization, the convention instituted monthly rather than weekly dues and even approved of semi-monthly unit meetings.[10]

While the Party insisted on retaining its shop units, the Central Committee decided at a November 1935 plenum that "the Party was to make experiments in the direction of adapting its organizational form and structure to the situation in each locality." The Ninth Convention followed up by calling for the combination of "Leninist principles of organization and the best traditions of the American political structure." Industrial units were to be composed of Communists in a given local or international union or in the same industry. Unlike party union fractions, which involved themselves solely with union matters, the industrial units were concerned with the whole gamut of issues appropriate to any other Party body. By January 1938, 10,500 people belonged to 582 units, more than the 7,500 in 550 shop units. Almost immediately, however, problems cropped up. The industrial units inevitably tended to focus narrowly on union issues. They separated Communist workers from nonproletarian Communists. A report to the Tenth Convention complained that "professional units have sprung up and developed without control, separating the professional in our ranks from the proletarian elements." While retaining the industrial units, the convention urged a close, one-by-one review of them to decide whether each should be continued. Larger ones were to be split up by territory and others transformed into shop units.[11]

Organizationally, however, the Party's bow to the new political situation was the abolition of the street nuclei, or units, and their replacement by branches. The street units had rarely coincided with political subdivisions; the Communists had long scorned the Socialists' electoral alignment as another species of reformism. Once they too had decided that traditional politics required their major attention, the Communists had the disadvantage of their organizational structure not allowing easy coordination during election campaigns. The November 1935 plenum took the first step, deciding to enlarge the street units and base them on existing political subdivisions. The Ninth Convention formally changed their name to "branches" and suggested fifty members as an optimal figure. The larger units were expected to improve Party life. Potential recruits would be more impressed by vibrant, substantial Party branches than by small, semi-clandestine street units. Each branch would be able to engage in more activities. Increasing the units' size would also better the probability that each branch would have several comrades capable of leadership. The Party even sanctioned experiments with other forms of organization. A few women's day units were created. Composed of housewives, many with children, these units met on weekday mornings at convenient neighborhood centers such as theaters. The new watch-word was flexibility.[12]

The branches immediately prospered. In New York they were based on assembly district lines. Max Steinberg explained the benefits of the new setup: "The people in the neighborhoods will recognize us as a political party because we correspond to their conception of a Party." By early 1938, 33,000 of the Party's 51,000 registered members were assigned to branches. They were given the task of "penetration of all existing neighborhood organizations." Their members were expected to root themselves in their communities and lead political struggles over the most mundane as well as the most cosmic issues. The Party's 1938 convention heard a glowing report on their effectiveness.[13]

Higher Party units were not exempt from the new focus on territorial forms of organization. Israel Amter explained in 1936 that "the sections up until recently were organized almost on arbitrary lines, without regard to the political or electoral units that they contain." The fact that such arbitrary lines reflected the Comintern and Party's previous indifference to American politics or political tradition was left unsaid. New York's Communists hastened to set up county committees in the Bronx and Brooklyn, the better to participate in borough politics. Most of the old multi-state districts were split up into separate state organizations so that the Communist party more nearly resembled traditional parties. The state organizations were headed by state secretaries, nomenclature less jarring to American ears than "district organizer."[14]

The Party reorganization was not entirely successful. Industrial units proved troublesome, and shop units continued to stagnate. Nor were the branches a panacea for the problems that had vexed the street units. They may have linked Communists with community life, but Party meetings remained dull. When Mike Gold wrote a column complaining that nothing had changed at the lower levels and "dull unit meetings" were the heaviest cross the Party bore, he was inundated with letters of agreement. Many of the hoped-for-improvements did not materialize. Leadership at the lower levels often got worse, not better. Because the organizational shake-up coincided with the Party's increased activity in the CIO and other non-Communist organizations, preoccupied Party leaders lacked the time to supervise the reorganization as carefully as they wanted. Many units drifted aimlessly. Members did yeoman service in all kinds of organizations but were uninvolved in their branches and "under the direct guidance of the leading committee." Branches were denuded of their most capable forces, who were being absorbed into non-Party work and not replaced. Charles Krumbein complained that Party leaders were devoting so "much of their attention to the growing mass movements, they are at the same time neglecting Party organizational problems." Ironically, the Party's growing success had not alleviated its internal problems but exacerbated them. In the sectarian old days, Party life was dreary and dull precisely because it was so inwardly focused. In its new incarnation the Party attracted many more recruits, but the best of them threw themselves into the mass movements with which the Party worked. The internal life of the Communist party did not significantly change. The new problems, however, had to be welcome ones. They were the consequences of success, not failure. Once upon a time the Party had had a troop of cadres with no soldiers to lead.[15]

To cope with the shortage of cadres, the number and variety of Party schools grew. The National Training School adopted a full-time six-month curriculum late in 1935. Districts were warned that only well-prepared comrades should be sent; the school was not designed as either a vacation for burned-out Communists or an introduction to Party life. Enrollment was approximately sixty people per term. In addition to this training for future Party leaders, there were newly established regional schools in the Midwest. A special ten-week program for twenty-four promising Negro comrades was organized in 1937. A Southern Regional School had to meet in Philadelphia but drew its students from all over the South. The districts scrambled to meet the demand for trained Marxist-Leninist pedagogues. The New York District organized summer schools to train Communist teachers. Ohio and California tried evening and weekend classes to train gifted Communists to assume leadership in lower Party units. Thirty professionals volunteered to pay their own way in the summer of 1938 to visit smaller cities and towns to teach classes. Workers' Schools, which provided evening classes for Communists and non-Communists alike, existed in most big cities.[16]

One hundred thousand members alone could not make the Party a major influence in American life. However, those who persist in denigrating or downplaying Communist influence on the basis of its membership lists fail to understand its full impact. Party leaders were not reticent about boasting that their membership figures grossly underestimated Communist influence. Earl Browder spoke, undoubtedly with some exaggeration, of the multitudes who took their political cues from the Communists: "What we think, what we say and especially what we do, have an influence a hundredfold, five hundredfold, beyond our membership. Large strata of the population guide themselves by what they see our Party doing." William Foster struck a more sinister note, suggesting that not all the Party strength was visible to unfriendly eyes: "The Communist Party's influence in all the progressive movements of the day, including those under the non-Communist official leadership, far exceeds what it appears on the surface and cannot be measured simply by the numerical strength of our Party." Reporting to the National Committee just days before the Nazi-Soviet pact, Browder claimed that "millions of people consider and are influenced by our decision."[17]

Not all the Communist boasts can be accepted without qualifications. Many of the membership claims of auxiliaries were wildly inflated. In some cases the numbers were largely meaningless. The American League Against War and Fascism—with its name changed to the American League for Peace and Democracy to accommodate the Party's new positions on collective security and the Popular Front—claimed millions of adherents in 1937 by virtue of their membership in organizations affiliated to the league. But, according to Browder, the league's active membership was only 8,000–9,000. Only 10 percent of these were Communists. Less than a thousand Communists, then, dominated a modest-sized organization that had an impressive paper membership. Such an overstatement was not unknown in other groups. Moreover, memberships in many auxiliaries overlapped. Many of the American League's affiliates were themselves Party auxiliaries, so numerous people were counted twice when the Communists toted up all those whom they influenced. Still, Party fronts, or auxiliaries, flourished as never before.[18]

In bygone days the Communist party had not been bashful about advertising its control over its auxiliaries. The new line professed puzzlement that anyone could mistake the auxiliaries for Party organizations.

The first organization to adopt the new tactic was the American League for Peace and Democracy. In November 1937, Browder announced that the Party was withdrawing from the league. As the only political party affiliated with the league, it stood out and had become "the subject of all the attacks of our enemies who try thereby to label the American League as a Communist organization." Reverend Harry Ward, its leader, conceded that Communists had once been prominent in his organization but denied to the Dies Committee that they had ever "given a communistic slant to the program or policies of the league." He dated the league's full independence to his own elevation to leadership in 1934.[19]

The International Labor Defense, founded by the Party, was the American affiliate of the International Red Aid as late as 1932. Two of its four national officers, Anna Damon and William Patterson, were open Communists. A third, Robert F. Dunn, ostensibly the non-Communist head of the Labor Research Association, was a secret Party member. Yet, the only non-Communist officer, Vito Marcantonio, asserted that before accepting a place in the ILD, he had "ascertained that it was definitely not connected with the Communist Party." Anna Damon professed ignorance about the ILD's past and denied that it had any connection with or was subservient to the Communist party. The International Workers' Order found it harder to disguise its past. Still, it tried. Max Bedacht, its general secretary, told an incredulous Dies Committee that the Communist party had nothing to do, either directly or indirectly, with the founding of the fraternal body and did not interfere or concern itself with its operation.[20]

One of the most notable aspects of the Popular Front was the ability of a few Communists to dominate organizations filled with non-Communists. There were never more than 100,000 American Communists at any one time, yet labor unions, youth groups, peace organizations, civil rights bodies, and a host of miscellaneous clubs, gatherings, and assemblies faithfully followed the Party's direction. In part, of course, this success was due to the presence of sympathizers or fellow travelers in all these groups, people who believed in the Party or willingly cooperated with it for the sake of policies they believed in. But it was also a consequence of the Communists' energy.

Man may not be, as Aristotle claimed, a political animal—but professional revolutionaries are. In this respect they have an enormous advantage over ordinary people, who are only partially or not at all interested in politics. A minority that works at politics twenty-four hours a day, seven days a week, can compensate for its numbers by its energy and activity. It gets out its members at meetings, volunteers for jobs and responsibilities, steps into the breach whenever an opening occurs, and ensures that its acolytes fill it. Political power has never flowed only from numbers but has been always dependent on activity. Well-organized minorities have more than compensated for lack of numbers by their constant attention to detail and business. One man working ten hours a day may be more than the equivalent of ten men working one hour a day, because that one man will be given or seize responsibility and will accumulate knowledge enabling him to wield authority within the organization. Communists are not the only ones who have benefited from this political law, but they used it to better advantage than almost any other group during the Popular Front.

No political organization can long run without money. The American Communist party was blessed with thousands of devoted members who volunteered their services without expectation of immediate recompense. Its hordes of functionaries willingly worked long hours for minimal pay. Still, supporting hundreds of Party workers, financing a daily newspaper and scores of foreign-language papers, and running a variety of campaigns did not come cheap. Compounding the normal vicissitudes of raising money was the fact that the Party's natural constituency was hardly wealthy.

Party finances have always been one of the murkier corners of Communist history. The national organization's income in 1931 was $88,434. It rose to $135,033 in the election year of 1932 and fell to $97,806 in 1933. The advent of the Popular Front filled the Party treasury as well as the membership rolls. Party income soared to around $360,000 in 1936, fell back to $258,000 in 1937, and fell again to $192,000 in 1938. The decline did not signify financial hardship but a reduction after a national political campaign and a change in the dues structure that resulted in a larger percentage going to local and state Parties. These figures, however, understate enormously the Party's income. *The Daily Worker* was financed separately. Sales and advertisements were far from sufficient to keep it afloat. In 1938 alone, the New York State Party organization gave $85,000 to the newspaper's campaign. Its substantial yearly deficit was always met by a special fund drive among Communists and their sympathizers. The districts also raised and spent their own money. In some cases the sums were substantial. The National Office took in about $40,000 in dues in 1931, $33,000 in 1932, $25,000 in 1933, $69,000 in 1936, $77,000 in 1937, and $65,000 in 1938. Most dues, however, remained at lower Party levels. In the early 1930s, more than half the dues were transferred to the National Office; the Ninth Convention allocated 25 percent to the branch, 20 percent to the section, 20 percent to the district, and 35 percent to the National Office. Between 1936 and 1938, then, total Party income from dues alone was in the vicinity of $200,000 a year.[21]

Even that figure does not begin to encompass the Party's income. The New York Communists' budget in 1938 was roughly $160,000. When special, separate accounts such as *The Daily Worker* drive, literature payments, and payments to the National Office were added in, the state party had raised $427,000. Dies Committee accountants who examined subpoenaed bank records testified that between March 1937 and March 1939, William Browder, the Party's state treasurer, had deposited $1,302,173 in two checking accounts and a savings account. And William Weiner, the Communist party's financial secretary, testified that as late as 1939 some of the Party's business was done on a cash basis and could not be documented. The Dies Committee audited forty-three bank accounts held by the Party, its subsidiaries, publishing houses, and auxiliaries. Most went back two to three years, but the account of *The Daily Worker's* parent corporation was apparently examined back to 1932 or 1933. The accountants unfortunately did not provide details, but the total deposits in those forty-three accounts were $10,164,730.91. Clearly the Communist party, its affiliates, and its auxiliaries raised and spent very large sums of money in the 1930s.[22]

Where did the money come from? Dues provided a proportion of Party income but, being quite modest, could not account for most of it. In 1936 the Ninth Convention set them at 10¢ a month for incomes up to $10 a week, 50¢ a month for those making $11–25 a week, and $1.00 for those earning $26–40 a week. For each $10 a week over $40, an extra 50¢ was added. Since the average weekly manufacturing wage in America was only $23.82 in 1937, most Party members were probably paying no more than $6 a year in dues. Many Communists, moreover, were still unemployed, were housewives, or made less than $10 a week and so paid only 10¢ a month, or $1.20 a year. Total 1937 dues came to about $220,000. Membership during the year ranged from around 40,000 to 62,000, which means that the average member contributed a relatively small amount. That year, dues income accounted for less than one-third of the National Office's income.[23]

Two other sources of money were listed on Party balance sheets as "Donations—Organizations" and "Donations—Individuals." The former, totaling $68,000 in 1937, represented the National Office's share of money raised in districts at mass meetings. When Earl Browder spoke at Madison Square Garden, for example, the New York Party and the National Office split the proceeds. Individual donations of close to $60,000 were obtained the same year. Some of it came from the estates of workers, often foreign-born, who left all or part of their life's accumulations to the Party. Most, however, came from a small corps of wealthy Americans. Starting in 1934, Browder began to cultivate contributors. By the end of the decade, about one hundred people annually gave between $100 and $5,000 to the Party. For instance, A. A. Heller, born in Russia, earned millions in America as founder of an oxygen business that was later sold to Union Carbide. A long-time Socialist, he transferred his loyalties to the Communist party in the early 1920s. He was granted a concession in Russia during the New Economic Policy period, introduced the acetylene welding business to his old homeland, and made more money. Heller invested large chunks of it in the revolutionary movement. Between 1924 and 1939 he sank more than $110,000 into International Publishers alone, which never showed a penny of profit.[24]

Other sources of money were more obscure. Some income may have found its way to the Party from the profits of small businesses capitalized by Communist funds. Elizabeth Bentley, a self-confessed Soviet spy, recounted how the Party set up the United States Service and Shipping Corporation to move freight and passengers between America and Russia. According to her account, the Party also provided $15,000 of the initial financing. The Cafe Society nightclub in New York opened in Greenwich Village in 1938. Started, according to one of its originators, "to raise money for the Communist Party," it also launched a number of show-business careers, including those of Billie Holliday, Lena Horne, Josh White, and Zero Mostel. House of Representatives investigations into tax-exempt foundations heard allegations that American foundations had financed many Communist activities; supporting evidence, however, was scant.[25]

During the 1920s the Comintern supplied large blocs of cash to the financially strapped Americans. Years later Earl Browder admitted that between 1930 and 1935 the Comintern provided about 10 percent of the Party's funds, a subsidy he managed to eliminate a year after becoming general secretary. Nat Honig, one-time editor of *Labor Unity*, told the Subversive Activities Control Board that his TUUL publication had received a Comintern subsidy between 1930 and 1934 that kept it afloat. Louis Budenz charged that throughout the decade "the party was openly subsidized by the Soviet government through the Runag News Agency." Secret funds, he alleged, were continually funneled into Party coffers. Hede Massing, once Gerhart Eisler's wife and herself a self-confessed Soviet spy in America, recounted meeting a disappointed Browder who had thought that she was delivering money to him after a European trip.

She also told of paying large sums of Comintern money to J. Peters in return for false passports for use by her apparatus. The substantial colony of American Communists in Moscow on Comintern business, ranging from students at the Lenin School to American representatives at the Profintern and Comintern, were subsidized by the Russians. Hundreds of Americans employed in the United States by Amtorg, the Soviet government's trading corporation, were either Communists or sympathizers who, it was alleged, had to kick back part of their salary to the Party in return for their sinecures.[26]

Where did all the money go? Party leaders were not paid munificent salaries. Browder received $40 a week in 1938; most top leaders were paid in the same range. The general secretary also made about $4,000 in 1938 from writing and lectures. That same year the National Office paid out $31,600 in wages. One of the Party's largest expenses was subsidies designed to help weak, struggling districts get established. As late as 1936, every district but New York and Connecticut received some minimal payment, with the largest, $3,858, going to Alabama. In 1938, $39,108 was returned to the districts. There were also subsidies to such Party auxiliaries as the YCL, WESL, LSNR, Unemployed Councils, and Mooney Congress, and to the Party press. Between 1936 and 1938 some $50,000 was expended on industrial struggles, much of it to support Party organizers like Bill Gebert, who was working to aid the CIO. Party meetings and travel expenses consumed more money. By the end of the decade, America was also a net exporter of funds to aid Communism. Between 1936 and 1938, roughly $35,000 a year was sent to foreign Parties in financial need, such as the beleaguered German and Spanish Communists, and parties in Cuba, Mexico, and the Philippines.[27]

Dr. D. H. Dubrowsky, a charter member of the Communist party, testified to even more staggering transfers of money. He held a series of appointments representing agencies of the Soviet government, principally the Russian Red Cross, in the United States. Appalled by Stalin's ruthlessness, he severed his ties to the Russians in 1935. Dubrowsky told the Dies Committee that the Soviets raised millions of dollars a year in America through film concessions, estate and insurance claims, advertising requirements for firms doing business with Amtorg, and other "swindles"—more than enough money, he suggested, to finance Communist propaganda activities. Dubrowsky claimed that the American Communists had directly benefited from this largesse in the 1920s and implied that the practice had continued into the 1930s.[28]

The Communists' monetary resources enabled them to support functionaries, create auxiliaries, and provide a full cultural life for their members and sympathizers. At all levels "an army of at least three to four thousand active leading people" somehow lived off this income. When pressed, the Party could quickly raise large amounts of cash. New York State, for example, took in $180,000 in just forty-five days in 1937. More than a million dollars in cash plus hundreds of thousands more in merchandise and material was allegedly gathered by Party-led organizations to aid Spain. Earl Browder later claimed that on top of all its other resources, the Party had indirect control of another $150,000 a year from people willing to make contributions to groups it favored. All of these financial assets gave the Communists the tools to organize day after day for cause after cause, dwarfing their competitors on the American left.[29]

Social Background

For the most part, the Party improved its social composition during the Popular Front days. From a Party of the unemployed in the Third Period, the Communists made great strides as the nation recovered from the Depression. As late as 1934, Browder had to report that about two-thirds of his party was out of work. By 1936 a majority was employed. At the Tenth Convention, 63 percent of the 75,000 members were employed. As a corollary, the proportion of trade unionists in the Party also improved, although the biggest jump came not with the rise of the CIO but with the strike upsurge of 1934; in the latter half of the decade the Party failed to increase appreciably its percentage of union members. Only about one-fifth of the Communists belonged to unions in 1934. The next year the figure rose to 36 percent and then to 40 percent in 1936. It hovered in that area for the rest of the decade. In 1938 it was necessary to add the unemployed members of the Workers' Alliance to get "50% of the membership active in trade unions and unemployed organizations."[30]

Not all of the Party's new recruits were proletarians. For the first time in its history, American Communism proved significantly attractive to white-collar workers and professionals. Jack Stachel analyzed more than 16,000 people who signed Party cards in 1937–1938. The largest single group was professionals, followed by office workers. More had white-collar occupations than were in heavy industry. Most of the CIO's white-collar unions, small as they were, were Communist-dominated. The American Federation of Teachers, particularly in New York, was another source of Party strength. Bella Dodd later estimated that as many as 1,000 teachers were Party members. The Newspaper Guild had a relatively large Party minority. A small but significant number of doctors were associated with the Party. A Communist movement among social workers made some headway. A band of Communist psychologists, mostly from New York, were instrumental in starting the Psychologists' League. The National Lawyers Guild included a substantial number of Communist attorneys. The Party's growing attraction to these groups had its costs. Such involvements diluted its proletarian base. Also, one functionary confessed, it was in New York that these Communists were concentrated; there "the Party has made real headway in recruiting thousands of professionals and white collar workers."[31]

In one sense, the Party was no longer a New York organization. The most startling difference between the Communist movements of the Third Period and the Popular Front was the Party's newfound geographical breadth. Once vast stretches of American real estate were barren of Communists. During the latter part of the decade, such deserts blossomed. Remote outposts like Oklahoma and Florida developed thriving Communist parties. In mid-1937, twelve of the Party's thirty-five state organizations claimed more than a thousand members; only three had fewer than a hundred (see Table 1).

Despite the Communists' greater geographical balance, the weight of the New York Party became even greater as the Popular Front developed. New York Communists, virtually all of whom resided within the five boroughs of New York City, made up 22 percent of the Party in 1934, 38 percent in 1936, 44 percent in 1937, and 40 percent in 1938. Far back in second place came California, with 6,000 members in 1938. One New York section alone, the second, located between Lexington and Seventh Avenues and running from Union Square to 55th Street, started in September 1937 with 1,500 members. Few state organizations were as large.[32]

New York's predominance had both benefits and costs. The Communists' concentration gave them inordinate power in New York political life. Both Democrats and Republicans courted the Communist vote and vied for the support of the American Labor party, in which Communist influence was strong. Many thousands of Communists supported a plethora of cultural organizations, which further cemented individual loyalty to the movement. They created a radical community which gave the Party a visibility it lacked in many other places. Since New York was America's financial, cultural, intellectual, and media center, the Party's presence and influence reverberated around the nation. On the other

TABLE 19.1

Party Membership, 1936–1938

District	Regis-tration, 1/1/36	Regis-tration, 1/1/37	Membership on Record, 6/30/37	1938
1. New England	750	993	1,283	2,000[a]
2. New York	11,805	16,306	19,838	30,000[b]
3. Eastern Pennsylvania, Delaware	1,450	1,530	2,164	—
4. Kansas (Estab. 3/1/37)		106	162	—
5. Western Pennsylvania	986	1,204	1,577	5,000[c]
6. Ohio	1,992	1,730	2,221	3,500[d]
7. Lower Michigan	1,277	960	1,466	2,600[e]
8. Illinois	2,705	2,714	3,490	6,000[f]
9. Minnesota	988	859	1,106	2,100[a]
10. Nebraska	97	28	48	—
11. North Dakota	124	71	132	—
12. Washington, Oregon, Idaho	1,130	1,137	1,714	2,115[g]
13. California, Nevada, Arizona	2,510	3,391	5,313	6,000[a]
14. New Jersey	646	783	1,044	—
15. Connecticut	562	626	747	—
16. North and South Carolina	176	247	275	—
17. Alabama, Georgia, Mississippi	425	250	327	900[h]
18. Wisconsin	638	913	1,057	—
19. Colorado, Wyoming, New Mexico	333	216	296	—
20. Texas	174	242	409	500+[i]
21. Missouri, Arkansas	372	280	522	—
22. West Virginia	173	157	208	—
23. Kentucky	29	142	167	—
24. Louisiana	80	107	123	—
25. Florida	228	236	304	572[j]
26. South Dakota	216	153	181	—
27. Upper Michigan	540	366	395	—
28. Indiana	294	224	325	—
29. Virginia	—	86	111	—
30. Montana	—	70	106	—
31. Oklahoma	29	114	259	500+[i]
32. Iowa	—	132	157	—
33. Tennessee	—	61	99	—
34. Maryland, Washington, D.C.	—	364	504	859[i]
35. Utah	—	79	88	—
TOTAL	30,836	36,877	48,223	

SOURCE: Figures for the first three columns are from "National Membership Report, January 1–June 30, 1937" (mimeographed), Draper Papers, Box 1, Folder 43. Figures in the fourth column are derived as follows:

[a] *Daily Worker*, May 31, 1938, p. 7.

[b] Max Steinberg, "Rooting the Party Among the Masses in New York," *Communist*, September 1938, pp. 829–838.

[c] This figure is for Pennsylvania as a whole and thus includes Districts 3 and 5. *Daily Worker*, July 19, 1938, p. 4.

[d] *Daily Worker*, September 14, 1938, p. 3.

[e] This figure is for all of Michigan, comprising Districts 7 and 27. *Daily Worker*, May 31, 1938, p. 7.

[f] Morris Childs, "Building the Democratic Front in Illinois," *Communist*, September 1938, p. 816.

[g] *Party Organizer*, March 1938, pp. 22–23.

[h] This figure is for Alabama alone. *Daily Worker*, May 27, 1938, p. 5.

[i] "Report on Organization," 1938, in *Investigation of Un-American Propaganda Activities*, Vol. 14, pp. 8714–8718.

[j] "Proceeding of Second State Convention, Florida Communist Party, May 1938," ibid., Executive Hearings, Vol. 2, p. 501.

hand, New York was not a random slice of America, and the New York Party reflected its peculiarities. New York Communists were more likely to be foreign-born. In 1938, 53 percent of New York Communists had been born abroad, though two years earlier the national Party had become 50 percent native-born. Despite the presence of Harlem, the New York Party had a small percentage of blacks—only 6 percent in 1938. Fewer New York Communists worked in basic industries; more were employed in light industry and held white-collar or professional jobs. New Yorkers were more likely than their Communist counterparts in other states to be employed and to belong to a trade union. And, although the Party did not provide any statistics, they were much more likely to be Jewish.[33]

No transformation was more symbolic than the development of a native-born majority in the Party. The foreign-born component had been shrinking ever since 1929. By 1935, 40 percent of the members were American-born. New recruits were overwhelmingly natives: the immigrants had fallen to 52.2 percent in January 1936. Sometime that summer, the number dropped below 50 percent and Fred Brown exulted: "Today for the first time the majority of our Party members are native-born workers." The proportion continued to climb. During the big recruiting drive of 1937–1938, 65 percent of the new members were American-born. The Party pushed its American-born workers to the fore. For too long it had felt the onus of being an alien force in American politics; it now yearned to demonstrate its appeal to older strains in American life. Charles Krumbein urged "bringing forward, promoting and developing American elements." He assured the Party that the foreign-born "look to American workers for leadership." At the Tenth Convention in 1938, 80 percent of the delegates were native-born. The Central Committee had been 38.5 percent native-born in 1934; two years later it was 52.2 percent. Never again would it have a majority of immigrants.[34]

The Party did not neglect the foreign-born in its rush to Americanize itself. In fact, the new line encouraged a fresh approach to the whole question of ethnicity in America. In another one of the many ironies that marked the history of American Communism during the Popular Front, the Party finally began to cultivate the groups from among whom it had been born. Communism had first developed within the foreign-language federations of the Socialist party. The American Communists had been overwhelmingly foreign-born. For years, American Communists lectured themselves and heard lectures from the Comintern on the need to Americanize. All of the lectures had an impact. The Party turned its back on "language work." The most capable of the Communists still working among their ethnic comrades were transferred into general Party work by 1930. Ambitious cadres sought escape from a Party backwater populated by aging Communists who were even further removed from the American mainstream than their English-speaking comrades. In the early 1930s the language federations were frequently denounced for white chauvinism and reluctance to participate in the class struggle. With the drying up of immigration in the mid-1920s, Communist leaders expected that assimilation would soon destroy the distinctive cultures and languages that marked language work. Nationality groups, they thought, "were fast disappearing as significant factors in American political life." At the very moment that the Fish Committee was attacking it as an alien force, the Communist party was studiously trying to forget its alien roots.[35]

All that was changed by the Popular Front. Millions of Americans, it turned out, had remained proud of their ethnic origins and committed to ancient traditions. The Party's about-face began in 1937 and was confirmed at the 1938 convention, not without rhetorical bows to the wisdom of the Comintern. Communist writers admitted that it had taken Georgi Dimitroff to awaken them to the importance of cultivating national groups. Inspired by Dimitroff's proclamation that he was proud to be a Bulgarian, Israel Amter summed up the injunctions of the 1938 convention: "It is necessary that our comrades be not only *good Communists,* but *good Germans, good Jews, good Irishmen.*" Irene Browder lamented the "crude and vulgar attacks upon their religion" and the militant atheism that had alienated many ethnic Americans from the Party. A "Report on National Groups" to the Tenth Convention detailed the Party's problems. Only the Jewish Bureau, with 4,000, had more than 1,000 members. Trailing it with between 500 and 800 members each were the German, Italian, Hungarian, Ukrainian, Lithuanian, Russian, Finnish, and Greek Bureaus. Only 400 belonged to the Polish group, with 300 in the Slovak, Croat, and Armenian ones. The Czechs, Rumanians, Bulgarians, Serbs, Scandinavians, and Chinese trailed far behind. Most of the national bureaus suffered from high membership fluctuation, weak leadership, and inadequate finances. Virtually all the bureaus published newspapers, but most were marginal operations. Only a handful had been successful in initiating united front activities.[36]

By all odds the most successful was the Jewish Bureau. Not only was it numerically the largest, it also engaged in many more activities than any other. It published several newspapers and magazines; led the 38,000-strong Jewish section of the International Workers' Order; ran children's schools that enrolled 8,000 students; sponsored fifty workers' choruses; directed the ICOR, an auxiliary to support colonization of Jews in Birobidzhan, Russia; and directed Proletpen, a writers' organization. The bureau had also taken the lead in setting up such united fronts as the Jewish People's Committee and the IKUF (World Alliance of Jewish Culture), a Yiddish cultural organization. The Jewish Communists had made a remarkable recovery from their self-inflicted wounds in 1929 when the *Freiheit*'s endorsement of Arab attacks on Jewish settlers in Palestine had turned the Communists into pariahs in the Jewish community. The Popular Front policy had enabled Jewish Communists to parade as the staunchest opponents of Nazism. The Party toned down the vociferous assimilationism and atheism that had marked the Third Period. During that era Party leaders, especially if they were Jewish, had taken pains to express contempt for Jewish tradition. After 1935, Jewish holidays, given a secular content, found their way into the curriculum of the IWO's schools. When Israel Amter ran for public office, *Freiheit* emphasized his Jewish ties. The New York State Jewish Bureau published *Jewish Life* to appeal to the second generation, who were more comfortable with English. Even Jack Stachel, heretofore not known for his devotion to his origins, announced that "a good Communist can also be a good Jew loyal to his people."[37]

No one symbolized the new emphasis on Jewish culture better than Moissaye Olgin, editor of *Freiheit*. Born in 1878, Olgin had first joined the revolutionary movement in 1900 while studying at the University of Kiev. He was drafted into the army as punishment for his activities, and after his discharge he resumed his career as a full-time activist for the Jewish Bund. By the time he left for America in 1915, Olgin had become one of the Bund's best-known pamphleteers. In New York he wrote for *The Jewish Daily Forward* and received a doctoral degree from Columbia University. His Socialist loyalties inclined him against the Russian Revolution; he was so vociferously anti-Bolshevik that he embarrassed even Abe Cahan, *The Forward*'s bitterly anti-Communist editor. A 1920 visit to his homeland softened his attitude. A year later he left the Socialist party and joined with the Communists. Although he served on the Central Committee for a number of years, Olgin never became a power within the Party, handicapped by his reluctance to surrender his interest in Jewish affairs. His reputation in the CPUSA rested on his authorship of *Why Communism?* and the authoritative denunciation of Trotskyism he penned in 1935.[38]

Olgin's professional training and interest in matters Jewish made him an ideal advocate of the new line. He enthusiastically endorsed the new emphasis on Jewish culture. Furthermore, he confessed to a New York State Party convention in 1938, the Party had erred in its attitude toward Jewish nationalism: "We fought Zionism which was correct" but "we forgot also that the craving, the desire for nationhood is not in itself reactionary." Olgin lived just long enough to witness the Nazi-Soviet Pact. He applauded it on the grounds that it brought two million more Jews under Soviet rule and guaranteed that "a change to the better is imminent" for the Jews of central Europe. Before he could see just how much their lives had improved, Olgin was dead.[39]

The Tenth Convention targeted Germans, Jews, Italians, Poles, South Slavs, and the Spanish-speaking for Communist attention in its push to increase Party influence among ethnic Americans. No better way to reach them existed than the International Workers' Order, founded in 1930 by Communists departing from the Workmen's Circle, a Socialist-controlled Jewish fraternal society. The IWO's leaders had made no secret of their sympathies. Enlisting as "part of the battle-front of the working-class," the organization announced in 1930 that "we therefore endorse the Communist Party." The IWO quickly became a haven for Communist functionaries. Its first general secretary, Rubin Saltzman, was a veteran leader of the Party's Jewish Federation. Max Bedacht's appointment as its head in 1932 coincided with a determined effort to broaden the IWO's reach beyond its largely Jewish constituency. During much of Bedacht's tenure, William Weiner, the Party's financial secretary, was the IWO's president. Rebecca Grecht, Bedacht's assistant, had served as a district organizer. Emmanuel Levin, national education director, had headed the Workers Ex-Servicemen's League. Anthony Gerlach, Croatian language secretary, was a TUUL and Party veteran. And so on.[40]

The IWO contributed in many ways to the Party. It advertised heavily in Party newspapers. Its officers appealed for contributions to the Party and its causes. It provided employment for loyal Communists. None of these benefits would have been possible without the explosive growth in the IWO's membership. Chartered with fewer than 5,000 members, it reached 35,000 by 1933. Thereafter, few fraternal benefit societies in America could match its record. From 62,153 members in 1934 it went to 97,468 in 1935, 116,407 in 1936, and 141,364 in 1938. At the IWO's 1939 convention, Bedacht claimed 150,000 dues-payers and confidently predicted that the organization would double in size very shortly. That dream was dashed by the Nazi-Soviet Pact, but even with 150,000 members the IWO's resources were considerable. By the end of 1937 a reserve fund of $1,243,512 had been accumulated, and dues and premium payments brought in roughly $110,000 a month in 1939.[41]

Although the IWO had English-speaking branches, it was overwhelmingly an organization of the foreign-born. Amter estimated that

135,000 of its 150,000 members were ethnic Americans. The single largest component was always Jewish, but a majority of the members belonged to other orders. In 1935, for example, two-thirds of the membership came from Hungarian, Slovak, Ukrainian, Italian, and Serbo-Croat units. For many foreign-born Americans too timid or frightened to join the Communist party, membership in the IWO enabled them to participate in the "progressive" movement without suffering any serious consequences. Others joined to take advantage of the inexpensive term insurance often unavailable elsewhere to workers. Most members were not Communists. While the IWO had 116,407 adherents in 1936, only 20.7 percent of the nation's roughly 41,000 Communists belonged, meaning that a bare 7.3 percent were Communists. The Party therefore eagerly looked to the IWO as a recruiting ground. Jack Stachel told a Central Committee meeting that in Butler, Pennsylvania, where once only one Communist had lived, fifteen more had been recruited from the IWO. "The difference between one and fifteen," he told his comrades, "not only in one town but in many Butlers all over the country, will give you an idea of how many Party members can be recruited from the I.W.O." IWO lodges played a significant role in garnering support for the Steel Workers Organizing Committee in Pennsylvania and Ohio. The lodges formed a significant percentage of the American League Against War and Fascism's affiliates—25 percent in New York alone. Few of the Party's auxiliaries served it as well.[42]

The exact reach of the Party's writ during the People's Front era was significant. Besides its own avowed membership, secret members occupied positions of influence in a variety of groups. Many non-Communists willingly accepted Party guidance, while others had no qualms about cooperating with Communists on particular issues. The Communists had always used discipline and energy to exercise disproportionate organizational influence. What had changed from the early 1930s was that the views their auxiliaries and members now espoused no longer branded the Communists as strays from American politics.

20

The Nazi-Soviet Pact

Y THE SUMMER of 1939, American Communists had come a long way from those days when they talked largely to themselves. Few liberal organizations were without a significant Communist presence. Politicians in states all over the country vied for Communist support, albeit quietly. Hundreds of prominent intellectuals, performers, and artists applauded the Soviet Union's every action. Well-known Communists held leading posts in the trade union movement.

The Nazi-Soviet nonaggression pact presented Communists around the world with the most agonizing crisis thus far in their history. There had been shifts in the line before, some of them drastic. But most Parties had not been mass organizations when they took place but small, rather isolated and ineffectual sects. The American Communists had virtually nothing to lose by following orders to change course in 1929; the Party itself was small and had few allies in political life, the labor movement, or mass organizations. For the first time in its history, the Communist party in 1939 had something substantial to lose. What was even more unsettling was that the Communists and their allies were being forced to endorse not just any change of line but an alliance with Nazism, after years of boasting that there were no more determined and resolute foes of fascism than the Soviet Union and the Comintern.

Throughout 1938 and 1939, rumors that Russia and Germany might patch up their political differences circulated in the West. At the Eighteenth Party Congress in March 1939, Stalin warned that he would not "allow our country to be drawn into conflicts by war-mongers who are accustomed to have others pull the chestnuts out of the fire for them." Maxim Litvinov, the Soviet foreign minister, a Jew, and a symbol of Russia's commitment to collective security, resigned his post early in May. On July 22 came an announcement that Russian-German trade talks had been resumed; an agreement was signed on August 19. Three days later came news that Foreign Minister Ribbentrop was flying to Moscow to ink a nonaggression pact. Signed on August 23, the pact cleared the way for the German invasion of Poland on September 1, provided sanction for the Soviet entry into eastern Poland on September 17, and enabled the Russians to gobble up Estonia, Latvia, and Lithuania and invade Finland. Soviet Foreign Minster Molotov bluntly explained that "it is our duty to think of the interests of the Soviet people, the interests of the Union of Soviet Socialist Republics." Although convinced that Soviet interests coincided with those of other peoples in the world, Molotov derided "some short-sighted people even in our own country who, carried away by over-simplified anti-fascist propaganda" recoiled from such an arrangement.[1]

Shocked, stunned, unprepared, and uncoached, the American Communists groped at first for lifelines to preserve their ties to progressive groups and to the Popular Front, clinging desperately to hopes that the pact would have as limited an impact as earlier commercial agreements with fascist states. As each lifeline was sliced by Soviet actions, Communists searched for a new course that would take them out of choppy waters. It came, as usual, from abroad. With Comintern help the Party found its bearings.

Prior to the pact, suggestions of a Communist-Nazi agreement were denounced as plots to drive a wedge between America and Russia. Earl Browder sneered at the reports: "There is as much chance of Russo-German agreement as of Earl Browder being elected President of the Chamber of Commerce." A front-page editorial in the *Freiheit* blasted the *Jewish Daily Forward* for "chewing the dirty lie of an 'agreement' with Hitler when the facts have always shown that this is a lie." Four hundred American intellectuals signed an open letter to denounce the newly formed Committee for Cultural Freedom, which opposed all totalitarian movements. By implying that Russia and Germany shared anything in common, the anti-Communist committee members were "sowing suspicion between the Soviet Union and other nations interested in maintaining peace."[2]

Publicly, the American Communists took the news of the Soviet-German agreements in stride. Harry Gannes, *The Daily Worker*'s foreign affairs editor, thought the trade agreement of August 19 would "immensely help the forces of world peace" by compelling England and France to conclude a treaty with the Soviet Union. The Party's first official reaction was that the non-aggression pact would help guarantee peace, discourage another Munich over Poland, weaken Germany, and divide the Axis powers. In short, it represented no departure at all from previous Soviet policy. Another editorial announced that "the Soviet Union has made one of the most valuable contributions to the peace of the United States and the world." Clarence Hathaway told Brooklyn Communists that the Soviet Union "did more to smash the axis within a period of 12 hours than Chamberlain has done in a period of 12 months." Returning from vacation, Browder held a press conference on August 23. Badgering reporters threw old *Daily Worker* quotations at him; the Party leader called their charges that the pact represented a Soviet change of policy "nonsense."[3]

Browder's confidence to the contrary, the Party had no idea what the pact meant. Browder told the press that he had "exactly the same information that you gentlemen have." The Politburo met briefly on August 24 but reached no decisions. Still feeling his way, Browder delivered a speech on September 1 to a mass Party meeting in Chicago Stadium celebrating American Communism's twentieth birthday. Rather than try to explain the nuances of the pact and their implications, he safely read long quotations from Molotov's speech to the Supreme Soviet, a sure sign that Party leaders did not want to rush to judgment. Lacking any other guidance, the Party for the time being stayed in a holding pattern, pretending that the Soviet agreement with Germany accomplished just as much as, if not more than, what a collective security pact would have done. The Americans misread what the Comintern wanted very badly. Ironically, their incorrect line helped tide the Party over a rough period, staving off an immediate and shocking crisis while giving it time to prepare to embrace a German-Soviet alliance.[4]

The Communists continued to urge support for Poland, hostility to aggressors, support for President Roosevelt, and the Democratic Front. Immediately after the Nazi invasion, a *Daily Worker* editorial noted decisively: "There can be no question that the people of the United States will give every possible support to the heroic and beleaguered Polish people." One of the slogans issued by Browder in a report to the Party's National Committee on September 3 was "Full moral, diplomatic and economic help for the Polish people and those who help Poland defend its national independence." In a similar fashion, the Party denied that the pact meant the Soviet Union had abandoned Poland. Just before the Nazi invasion, the *Daily Worker* "Questions and Answers" column dealt with whether Russia would aid Poland in the event of war. While hedging the response, the writer concluded that "the Soviet Union's policy is to assist every nation that becomes a victim of aggression and fights for its independence." Three days later, in the same feature, readers could learn that: "No serious person would ask whether the Soviet Union would enter into an agreement with fascist Germany to help attack a third Party. The Soviet Union will join no one to attack anyone."[5]

There was no question in Communist minds that Germany was an aggressor and that there was a fundamental distinction between the Nazis and the Western powers. The Party continued to press for repeal of the "fake 'Neutrality Act' " and denounced isolationists who wanted to prevent placing "America's mighty influence on the side of peace, against the aggressor." One editorial insisted that it was not in America's interest to "shut off its trade with Poland, England, France, Canada and Australia," and another called for an "embargo [of] all shipments to Germany and Japan for the defeat of fascist aggression." As late as September 11, a frantic front-page editorial entitled "All Aid to the Heroic Polish People!" called for more Anglo-French assistance to the beleaguered Poles who were fighting "to save their independence from Nazi barbarism." Browder summed up the Party's attitude in his report to the National Committee on September 2: he was delighted that the "majority opinion in this country is now crystallized definitely against 'neutrality' and 'appeasement' toward the Axis Powers."[6]

The Party continued to look to Franklin Roosevelt for leadership of the Democratic Front. One editorial applauded Roosevelt's demand for repeal of the Neutrality Act, and another praised his determination to stay out of the war. Browder's report to the National Committee charged that congressional Tories were out to get the President and fully supported his reelection: "Most important of all, however, is the sweep of the movement to draft Roosevelt for a third term, which has embraced and united all sections of the working class." Browder also noted that "our Party has the supremely important task of insuring the unity of the democratic front." On September 11, Foster and Browder, in the name of the Communist party, sent the President a letter pledging support for his policies: "At this moment the hope of firm national unity lies in rallying all Americans in support of this policy, and in support of the President who has best expressed the hearts and minds of the people." The Communist party still believed it was possible to preserve the basic outlines of the Popular Front.[7]

That illusion did not last long. The Popular Front in Europe and America had been made possible by the changed needs of Soviet foreign policy. Fear of Nazi Germany, not a sudden surge of concern for the fate of local Parties, had prompted the about-face in Comintern tactics in 1934 and 1935. Because the Soviet Union had wanted to include America among its potential allies in a system of collective security to halt fascist aggression, American Communists had received permission to embrace the New Deal and President Roosevelt. What had been done with the blessings of the Soviet Union, however, could also be undone. Just as Soviet relations with Germany dictated one kind of Comintern policy early in the decade and another in its latter half, so a third stage required Communist parties to alter radically their every position in 1939.

Sometime around September 10 to 12, Browder later recalled, he got a short wave radio message from Moscow which contained the startling information that the war was an imperialist conflict, not a contest between fascism and democracy. "We never on our own brought forward that formulation and we wouldn't have," he insisted.[8] Browder was slated to give a major address at Madison Square Garden on September 11. There was apparently not enough time to recast totally his speech, which included one pregnant line: "Britain is playing the same game with Poland in 1939 which she played with Belgium in 1914." To bring the change of line to the Party faithful, *The Daily Worker* resorted to the awkward device of interviewing Browder. Harry Gannes asked him to elaborate on that cryptic remark in his speech. Browder's answer could not have been more stunning and might have caused some Communists to wonder why he had not been clearer in his prepared remarks:

These things have finally made clear beyond all possibility of doubt that what we have to deal with is an imperialist war in which the rulers of both sides are equally guilty; it is not a war waged for the destruction of fascism, but is carried on to extend and perpetuate imperialist control over the world. The character of this war in no principle [sic] respect can be said to differ from that of the late World War. This war has nothing to offer the masses of any participating country except death and destruction, further miseries and burdens.[9]

Within a few days the Political Committee convened to reevaluate a host of positions. For several years the Party had denounced the neutrality legislation enacted early in 1937 that prohibited American shipment of goods to combatants, no matter whom the aggressor. Of all the supporters of President Roosevelt's call for revision of the legislation's embargo provisions, none had been more fervent than the Communist party. In May 1939, Browder had urged "every mass pressure upon Congress to repeal the Neutrality Act, or fundamentally modify it to penalize the aggressor and aid the victim of aggression." For two weeks the Party had pleaded for aid to Poland. Since the war was now defined as imperialist, should the Party abandon its support for repeal, on the grounds that it might drag America into the conflict on behalf of Anglo-French imperialism? For several years the Party had dropped its demand for socialism, content to support the New Deal as part of the Democratic Front. Should the Party abandon its cautious ways and raise the possibility of transforming the imperialist war into a civil war that would put socialism once again on the American agenda? Finally, since 1937 the American Communists had been among the most fervent admirers of Franklin Roosevelt. Should they now sever their ties to the administration and seek out new friends who shared their hostility to the Allies and to the idea of American aid to them? None of the answers was as obvious as they would become a week later when the Soviet Union joined Germany in carving up Poland. The American Communists were temporarily on their own, required to adapt a specific program to the general policy enunciated from abroad. For years Party leaders had scurried off to Moscow when a policy provoked disagreement or confusion. Moscow was now temporarily inaccessible. William Foster called this period "the most important occasion the Party had ever lived through as a united party."[10]

For Browder's enemy on the Political Committee, the first opportunity to rebound from a long train of humiliations and defeats seemed at hand. Of all Browder's rivals for Party leadership from the early 1930s, only William Foster was left. Reinforced by Alex Bittelman, he had ineffectually protested about the Democratic Front and other ideological heresies for several years. Foster now sensed Browder's potential vulnerability.

The Political Committee meeting began on September 14, 1939, with a report by Bittelman. He had been a charter Communist, emerging from the Jewish Federation in the early 1920s to become a key Party leader in Foster's faction. Never much involved in mass work, Bittelman specialized in interpreting the twists and turns of the Comintern and the Soviet Party. He had been one of the arch-factionalists of the 1920s and had been removed from the American scene by the Comintern in 1929. Kept in Russia while others trooped home to reconstitute the Party after Lovestone's removal, he had been appointed vice chairman of the Far Eastern Secretariat. Early in 1930 Bittelman was sent to India as a Comintern representative and was expelled by the British. In poor health, he was allowed to return home. On his arrival he discovered his old comrades less than enthusiastic about welcoming him back into the leadership. After brief service with the Anti-Imperialist League, he moved to southern California, where he occasionally aided the district Party. In the summer of 1934, Bittelman returned to New York to work in the Agitprop Department. He was soon given greater responsibility, supervising the "Questions and Answers" column in *The Daily Worker* and then in January 1936 writing a monthly "Review of the Month" to lead off every issue of *The Communist*.[11]

As befitted an idealogue who had chafed under the compromises required by the Democratic Front, Bittelman wanted to return to a harder line. He speculated that the character of the war being waged by Germany could change, leading to a Soviet-German alliance against Britain, France, and America. Or, he suggested, the war could still be turned against Russia, transforming an "ordinary imperialist war" into "an imperialist counterrevolutionary class war." Because the situation remained fluid and the outlook unclear, Bittelman urged "mental readiness for quick, for rapid changes in the world situation again, which may necessitate again a new tactic for the CP to pursue." He also suggested dropping the Party's call for peace, since Communists might soon have to urge not peace but the transformation of imperialist war into civil war. Bittelman harnessed much of his enthusiasm for a call to abandon the Democratic Front. The Party had to oppose a third term for Roosevelt, discard the slogan "Social and National Security for America" adopted in late 1938, add a demand for socialism to its list of slogans, and, he even mused, think about an alliance with Senator William Borah, the Republican isolationist. Bittelman floundered around on what position to take on revision of the Neutrality Act, lamely opposing both Roosevelt's suggested changes and maintenance of the act.[12]

William Foster was more cautious: he wanted to retain the peace slogan but also add a call for socialism and favor retention of the Neutrality Act, while avoiding an open break with the Roosevelt administration at the present time. Foster was clearly entranced with the dream that a realignment of class forces in Germany was in the offing, which "would mean beginning of that delayed phenomenon of 1908 and 1919, which is the sweeping away of imperialist forces in Europe and, of course, it would go beyond Europe." Browder might have expected Bittelman and Foster to revert to habit; he was, he later recalled, surprised to discover that for the first time Gene Dennis adopted an independent position.

Dennis, agreeing with Foster that the Party should oppose revision or repeal of the Neutrality Act, also urged pussyfooting on the third-term issue: Communists "should not raise very strongly the question of the third term, if brought forward in unions should not fight against it, but should not take the initiative." He advocated a safe slogan, "Defense of the Soviet Union," but warned that differences still remained between democratic and fascist countries.[13]

No one at the meeting was as exposed as Earl Browder. Policies he had pursued were under attack. The painstaking work of half a decade was in danger of being lost. His enemies on the once-pliant Political Committee, sniffing blood, had dared to launch an attack; shockingly, they had been joined by one of his close advisers. Browder's immediate reaction was to fuzz the differences within the committee and find a way to avoid having to eat old words. "First of all," he noted, "I think it is clear that the main line of [Bittelman's] report is absolutely sound, unassailable, the only possible conclusions that can be drawn." That said, he insisted on standing on the old Party line as much as possible. He labeled a slogan that advocated socialism as "a fundamental error of strategy" and reiterated that the Party "must be for repeal of Neutrality act at this session of Congress." He conceded, however, that the Communists should not be "just simply for repeal of Neutrality Act in the same way that we were before" and opposed "hooking on" to Senator Borah at the expense of the New Deal.[14]

The meeting concluded with a sharp exchange between Bittelman and Browder. The former wanted the Party to be for neither revision of the act nor neutrality, but for rallying the masses against imperialist war. To vote for repeal, no matter for what reasons, would be construed as supporting Britain and France. Browder felt that not taking a stand for or against neutrality would involve impossible contradictions: "It will lead us into sectarian position, into divorcing broadest masses of the country." In the same fashion, Bittelman urged support for Borah's position "as the main spokesman of desires of overwhelming mass of American people not to be drawn into war" and because Borah "has more support among the masses than we have." Browder retorted that a lineup of Hearst, Norman Thomas, the Trotskyites, the Communist party, and Republican isolationists versus the New Deal would be impossible. Bittelman responded that the alternative was for the Party to align itself with J. P. Morgan. With that, a decision was reached to continue the discussion two days later to give time for Foster, Browder, Stachel, Green, Dennis, and Bittelman to discuss the issues further and seek an agreement.[15]

The subcommittee of six was evidently unable to reach a consensus.

When the Political Committee resumed its deliberations on September 16, a few minor issues were disposed of: Bittelman agreed that the call for socialism should be a separate slogan—not included along with such staples as jobs, security, and democracy—and he accepted the peace slogan. But he remained adamant that the Party had to dissociate itself from the New Deal. In a not-so-veiled warning to Browder, he attacked Browder's refusal to break immediately with the Roosevelt administration: "We cannot afford the head of the Party to swim along in haziness, not even for a day." Foster added a plea to begin preparing to transform the imperialist war into a civil war. While conceding that the Party might have to break with the President, Browder was not ready to do so just yet: "I am not ready to agree that this is the probable perspective even though I must register its possibility."[16]

Browder, however, had changed his mind about the neutrality legislation. Convinced now that it was no longer of major consequence, he indicated his willingness to support Bittelman's first position, that the Party neither oppose nor endorse revision. Jack Stachel spoke up to endorse Browder's suggestion. Bittelman too, however, had changed his mind. Backed by Foster and Dennis, he demanded that the Party oppose any effort to change the Neutrality Act. The confused Party leaders had now come full circle. Browder had accepted Bittelman's initial proposal, which Bittelman now adamantly opposed. The unhappy Party leader indicated how disturbed he was at the workings of the Political Committee and then called for a brief adjournment. When its members returned, they took a consultative vote. Six were in favor of Browder's original call for repeal of the Neutrality Act—Browder himself, Krumbein, Green, Stachel, Roy Hudson, and Henry Winston. Foster, Bittelman, and Dennis were opposed. Stachel then proposed abstention on the issue. Bittelman agreed to accept that position for the sake of Party unity; after considerable jockeying, so did Foster. Browder still felt that repeal was the best policy, but since it was a minor issue he too supported abstention. Dennis was the last holdout, insisting he was opposed on principle to anything but retaining the Neutrality Act. After still another adjournment to the evening, Dennis finally acceded and the Political Committee unanimously agreed that in the upcoming special congressional session on the Neutrality Act, "we favor neither revision nor repeal nor retention."[17]

The Political Committee also appointed Browder, Bittelman, and Dennis to draft a statement on the issues discussed. To balance the two anti-Browder voices, the Party leader was authorized to write the first draft and the entire committee had to approve the final document. The text, published in *The Daily Worker* on September 19, was entitled "Keep

America Out of the Imperialist War." It started out in ringing, unequivocal terms:

> The war that has broken out in Europe is the Second Imperialist War. The ruling capitalist and landlord classes of all the belligerent countries are equally guilty for this war.
>
> This war, therefore, cannot be supported by the workers. It is not a war against fascism, not a war to protect small nations from aggression, not a war that workers can or should support. It is a war between rival imperialisms for world domination. The workers must be against this war.

After a spirited attack on Britain and France, a denunciation of the Polish government as "fascist in character," and an unqualified endorsement of the Soviet invasion of Poland as a defense of "the cause of world peace," the Party insisted that America stay out of the conflict. The Neutrality Act issue was dismissed as "no longer an important or decisive issue." While retaining the call for "jobs, security, democracy and peace," the statement suggested briefly that the working class would soon begin to advance toward socialism. President Roosevelt was mentioned but once, in a favorable vein. Much more of the document was given over to denunciations of "hidden enemies of peace" ranging from pro-German appeasers to pro-Allied interventionists, with special vitriol reserved for such "Judas creatures" as the social democrats, Trotskyites, and Lovestoneites.[18]

Left to their own devices, the American Communists had been unable and unwilling to change specific policies. "Keep America Out of the Imperialist War" was at best a holding operation. It took another message from Moscow to push the Party off dead center. Late in September 1939, the Comintern sent a 600-word coded message to Browder via shortwave radio and followed it up with another communiqué early in October. The first message warned that the old slogan of "Democracy Against Fascism" was no longer valid. The consequences, it added, were not limited to Europe: "Thereby is undermined the 'democratic front.' USA will not be an exception." The Americans "must cease to trail in wake of FDR, adopt independent position on all fundamental questions." The second cable elaborated: "New situation changes our relationship to FDR, always understanding main enemy is camp of imperialist bourgeoisie. But much depends on FDR." While the Comintern was convinced that Roosevelt and the American bourgeoisie wanted to help Britain and France, it was leaving open to its American section the option of precisely how and when to adjust its policies. The Comintern message was more decisive about the nature of the war. Hitler was barely mentioned and then in a way to suggest that he was doing the Communists' work: "Hitler without knowing it leads to shattering bourgeoisie." The main Communist fire had to be directed against Britain and France to expose their "'anti-fascist' demagogy." The conflict in Europe was "no longer simply fight against fascism, but against capitalism as a whole."[19]

Browder may have been slow to break with the New Deal, but he now knew better than most Communists what the Comintern now wanted. He was not about to persist in a quixotic campaign to retain old ties in the face of such a clear signal. On October 13 the Political Committee unanimously adopted a resolution on "America and the International Situation." In addition to repeating much of what had appeared in both Comintern cables, the resolution announced the Party's break with bourgeois democrats and "the Roosevelt government." It also pronounced the death of the Democratic and Popular Fronts:

> In view of the political changes and realignments taking place within the country, bourgeois democrats are gravitating towards and being drawn into the imperialist camp, and not only the old division between the Republican and Democratic parties but also that between the New Deal and anti–New Deal camps, is losing its former significance.

Even the united front was subordinated to the war issue. While there were anti-war elements "in and around both parties, especially the Democratic Party" with whom temporary political agreements could be made, no cooperation was possible with social democrats or other pro-war elements since "these issues dominate all other considerations." With this manifesto, the American Communists had finally gotten their theories straight. Nearly eight weeks after the news of the Nazi-Soviet Pact had shocked Communists around the world, the Party had embraced the view that there was no difference between the democracies and Nazi Germany in war.[20]

Although the Comintern had warned the Party that the new world situation required breaking with the administration, the Communists hesitated about attacking Roosevelt head on. On October 22 William Foster denounced American foreign policy but blamed Under-Secretary of State Sumner Welles, repeating a tactic the Party had used when it liked the President but disliked his policies. The first critical *Daily Worker* editorial did not come until October 28, following Browder's indictment on passport charges. Until early December, the Party remained somewhat reserved. Even Browder, stung by his indictment, claimed only that Roosevelt was receiving overtures from Wall Street and economic royalists and that he "reciprocates their advances." FDR really became an object of abuse after he had expressed "profound shock" and disapproval of the Soviet invasion of Finland in late November. An editorial accused him of egging on the reactionary Finnish government. For good measure, Roosevelt was also charged with provoking Japanese aggression in the Far East against Russia. Another front-page editorial identified Roosevelt with an emerging anti-Soviet bloc: "The Administration has become a leading world sponsor of the imperialist puppets operating their provocative conspiracy at the borders of the Soviet Union." The newspaper even began a campaign to prove that the U.S. government and, specifically, then Assistant Secretary of the Navy Franklin Roosevelt had begun to plot a Finnish attack on Russia as early as 1919. "U.S. State Department Files Give Secret of F.D.R.'s Drive to Use Finland as War Base" went one headline; "Roosevelt's Anti-USSR Moves in Arctic Began with 1919 Intervention" read another.[21]

Every one of the slurs cast at the President in the past was resuscitated. Browder insisted that the two major parties were no different: "Tweedledum and Tweedledee are back again in their original act, somewhat more tawdry and shopworn, but the same old team." Foster announced that FDR had "become the political leader of the warmongers and his accepted task is to lead the country as far and as fast into the war as the financial oligarchs deem necessary." Browder charged that "Roosevelt's course is essentially for America the same direction which Hitler gave for Germany in 1933," while Gene Dennis resurrected another old formula to explain that FDR was "not a lesser evil than Willkie, is not a barrier to, or a guarantee against, the establishment of fascism."[22]

It was the President's announcement in September 1940 of the lend-lease agreement with Britain, however, that inspired the most rabid remarks comparing him with the Nazis. Browder, speaking to a campaign rally in Los Angeles by a recording since he was forbidden by a court from leaving New York following his conviction on the passport charge, shrilly concluded that the President had made himself "an unlimited military dictator," bypassing Congress, the "Hitler Reichstag." Browder compared FDR to Louis Napoleon and, more ominously, charged him with "flagrant adoption of the techniques of Adolf Hitler." Browder muttered that Roosevelt, in his cakewalk over the corpse of the Constitution, had joined with banker Thomas Lamont to engineer a "coup d'état" to deprive a genuine conservative, Senator Robert Taft, of the Republican nomination for President and give it to Wendell Willkie, a "pro-war big business renegade Democrat" who acquiesced in "the joining of the United States into the British Empire." An editorial in *The Communist* explained that the Party was concentrating its criticism on FDR because he had succeeded in deceiving the masses about his actions. While he and other liberals *"pretend to be* the leaders of the masses," they were "actually betraying the masses." Foster succinctly summed up the Communist position with his customary hyperbole: "Undoubtedly, in the years to come, when the folly and criminality of the present war become so clear that all can see it, the war policy of the Roosevelt administration will stand out as perhaps the greatest crime ever committed against the American people by its government and the ruling class."[23]

For several years Communists had praised Roosevelt and his programs. How could they have cooperated with him? Was the past a mistake? Browder, for one, did not think so. He insisted that "it is not we who have changed but rather the Roosevelt Administration." Other Party leaders denied that the New Deal alliance had produced very much of value. Gene Dennis, for example, charged that the administration's honeyed words and occasional actions on behalf of world peace had not stopped "the Roosevelt Government throughout the whole New Deal period, from steering an imperialistic path; from helping strangle Ethiopia, Austria, Spain and Czechoslovakia," from aiding Japanese aggression, from pursuing imperialistic interests in Latin America, from "encouraging and abetting the Chamberlains and Daladiers" in their plots "to provoke and precipitate an anti-Soviet war." Only for a brief time did the New Deal follow "a policy in the interests of the less reactionary elements of the bourgeoisie, which at times coincided to a limited degree with certain immediate interests of the masses."[24]

William Foster went even further. Recalling that the Communist party had charged the early New Deal with fascist tendencies, he said the President had made "very limited concessions to the rising labor and democratic movement" during the "Second New Deal" period. Foster accused Roosevelt of "compromise, retreat, of gradual abandonment of the progressive features of the New Deal, of eventual surrender" from 1937 to 1939, the exact period when the Party had embraced him. Foster summed up the New Deal's achievements then as a Soil Conservation Act, a "modest" housing act, "small improvements" in Social Security, a "watered-down" Wages and Hours Bill, a new Food and Drug Act, and "revamped" railroad pension and unemployed bills. Nothing was done on an anti-lynching bill, a youth act, a national health bill, or anti-monopoly legislation while military expenditures went up and the WPA was cut. The Communist party, it seemed, had supported the New Deal more from hope of what it might do than for any of its accomplishments. The collaboration had been a failure.[25]

The 1930s ended for the Communists as they had opened. Georgi Dimitroff gave the signal to return to the concepts of yesteryear that he had been so instrumental in abolishing in 1935. The imperialist war was linked to a growing, acute crisis of capitalist society; the social democrats were denounced in tones not heard in years ("the leading circles of the Second International are fulfilling the most filthy and criminal role in the blood-dripping slaughter machine of the war"); and Communists were ordered to launch a campaign in which they had once specialized ("working class unity can and must be achieved *from* below" and "apart from and against the leadership of these parties").[26]

American Communists needed little urging to adopt similar views and language. Browder announced that "America itself, despite the political backwardness as yet of our working class, is technically, objectively, the country which is the most ripe, the most prepared, for a quick transition to socialism, for which it lacks only the understanding and the will of the masses to that goal." Foster announced that "liberals and social-democrats are the best political war leaders for capitalism," while V. J. Jerome insisted that social democracy "must be destroyed by the proletariat."[27]

Communist spokesmen minimized the differences between bourgeois democracy and fascism and even suggested that the former was the greater enemy. Browder explained that there had taken place the "rapid disappearance of the differences between the so-called democratic and fascist capitalist states which become indistinguishable insofar as their dictatorial character is concerned." The fascist states had one important virtue, however, which the democracies lacked: "The so-called democracies become even more hostile to the Soviet Union than the fascist states." William Foster was not unhappy at the thought of a Nazi victory, since "the British Empire is the very cornerstone of the world capitalist system, the main enemy of everything progressive, and its serious weakening or overthrow by Hitler, or by the world revolutionary forces, would shake the very foundations of the entire capitalist system." Gil Green sagely discerned that "the only remaining point of difference between the internal regimes of Germany and France" was that the latter had several bourgeois political parties while the former had but one: "This is the sum and substance of French bourgeois democracy today. A fraud and mockery."[28]

The Communists, in accordance with Dimitroff's instructions, did not strictly identify their opponents with fascism but made it clear that they would make no agreements with them. The Political Committee announced in October: "*United fronts are impossible with those tendencies and groups in the labor movement which follow the treacherous policy of Social-Democracy, support the imperialist war, seek to drag America into it, incite against the Soviet Union and hamper the struggle of the working class against imperialism, capitalism and intensified capitalist reaction and exploitation.''* Not all united fronts were ruled out, however. Gene Dennis explained that they were acceptable if "built *primarily from below*, on a class struggle basis." The chief task of the labor movement in the upcoming elections, he wrote in 1940, was "to forge working class unity and a united people's front from below against the imperialist war, reaction and capitalist exploitation."[29]

While political and labor leaders who refused to oppose the "imperialist war" or supported the Roosevelt administration's policies were persona non grata, the Party was willing to flirt with those who opposed the war on very different grounds than those enunciated by the Comintern. In October 1939, the Political Committee endorsed *"temporary* political understandings" with groups that reflected, "even though distortedly," certain "anti-war and anti-monopoly attitudes of farmers and middle classes." In editorials and news stories, *The Daily Worker* began to praise isolationist senators who opposed revision of the Neutrality Act. In one eight-day period, front-page headlines included "Sen. LaFollette Hits Imperialist War Aims of Allies"; "Nye Says Embargo Repeal Will Prolong Bitter War"; "Taking Sides Leads to War, Sen. Frazier Says"; "Sen. Clark Indicts Allies for Turning Down Peace"; and "Sen. Johnson Raps War Hysteria Repeal Drive."[30]

American Communism had increased its membership, won the sympathy and respect of thousands of others, and become a key force in scores of organizations on the basis of its call for a popular front against fascism. The Party's about-face was not made without severe costs. Membership declined. Carefully cultivated relationships were severed. New enemies were made. The Party's store of trust and good will was severely depleted. It would take many years for the full accounting to be made because the Soviet-American alliance during World War II, and the Party's consequent patriotism, helped push this one-and-a-half-year unpleasant interlude from mind. But the bonds broken in 1939 and 1940 were never completely healed.

Few Party functionaries resigned, although many were confused, upset, or bewildered by the events. Browder airily noted during a late September 1939 speech in Philadelphia that there had been only "about a dozen" resignations. The most prominent was that of Granville Hicks, who announced his decision in *The New Republic* early in October. Several of the defectors—including Nat Honig, one-time editor of *Labor Unity* and representative to the Profintern, and Manning Johnson, a district organizer in Buffalo and national Negro organizer for the TUUL—later surfaced as friendly witnesses for the government against their old comrades. Melech Epstein, an editor of the *Freiheit,* organized a small group of Jewish defectors. Overall membership dropped precipitously. In one year, Roy Hudson revealed, 15 percent of the Party had quit; actually the decline was probably far greater.[31]

Late in October 1939, Mike Gold admitted "a trend of a sort" for sympathizers to defect, but he denied any "demoralization among fellow-travellers of Communism." In fact, one after another, prominent intellectuals and political figures who had long cooperated with the Party or defended the Soviet Union announced their disgust and despair. Not everyone was disillusioned at the same moment. For some it was the pact itself that precluded further cooperation with Communists, for others the American Party's tortured justification of the dismemberment of Poland, and for some the invasion of Finland. Some defectors no longer wanted anything to do with Communists, while others only felt that Popular Front organizations had now outlived their usefulness. Some continued for months to work within the old organizations, hoping to preserve them and change their policies.[32]

Vincent Sheean apologized for the pact, then wrote in *The New Republic* that the Soviet Union, which he had defended in the notorious Open Letter of August, represented the "most horrifying and bloodthirsty terrorism of modern times." Louis Fischer announced that he had been giving the Soviet Union the benefit of every doubt for too long; it could be excused no longer. After the invasion of Finland, Ralph Bates proclaimed: "I am getting off the train." Dr. John Haynes Holmes confessed that "we liberals" were "disgracefully wrong" on Russia. "The masquerade," Heywood Broun admitted, "is over." Roger Baldwin and James Waterman Wise resigned from the American League for Peace and Democracy. Lewis Mumford and Stuart Davis quit the American Artists Congress. Among the hardest hit was the League of American Writers. Its executive director confessed that by 1940, 100 of its 800 members had formally resigned. Although he brightly reported new recruits, most of the prominent names associated with the league—including Thomas Mann, Van Wyck Brooks, Archibald MacLeish, and Matthew Josephson—had departed. Malcolm Cowley charged that so many officers had quit the league that it could no longer print a letterhead.[33]

Cowley's response was instructive. He had never gone so far as to become a Party member, but he maintained an abiding faith in the Soviet Union. Responding to criticism of his gushing reporting of the national Hunger March, he assured his liberal readers in early 1933 that if 3,000 Russian capitalists marched on the Kremlin "they would be efficiently suppressed (not executed, the day of mass executions has passed in Russia)." Workers in Russia would not, of course, march "because the Soviets are their own government." Cowley wrote for *The Daily Worker*, adorned Party auxiliaries, and defended and supported Party policies from his perch as literary editor of *The New Republic*. Despite his professed disgust with the pact and American Communists' acquiescence, Cowley continued to disparage Stalin's enemies. After a futile effort to prevent the League of American Writers from condemning the war as imperialist, he resigned in August 1940, charging that the league now stood in the same camp as Father Coughlin, Henry Ford, and *The Chicago Tribune*.[34]

Other party auxiliaries were devastated. After losing a fight to gain control of the National Lawyers Guild in May 1940, anti-Communist liberals—including Attorney-General Robert Jackson, Jerome Frank, Thurman Arnold, Abe Fortas, Adolph Berle, and Morris Ernst—resigned *en masse*, leaving the guild an ineffectual shell. Liberals Melvyn Douglas and Philip Dunne, enraged when the Motion Picture Democratic Committee endorsed a pro-neutrality, anti-Roosevelt resolution in October, led a drive to endorse the administration's foreign policy and repudiate the Communist party. Failing, they and other New Dealers resigned. The American League for Peace and Democracy, designed to combat fascism, solved its embarrassing predicament by dissolving itself in February 1940.[35]

Still other Popular Front organizations lost their most prominent non-Communist leaders. Late in 1939, David Lasser angrily charged that control of the Workers' Alliance "had passed into the hands of representatives of one political group" and its policies had been harnessed "behind the national and international program of this political group." He resigned in June 1940 and formed a new unemployed organization, the American Security Union, which banned Communists and fascists from membership and soon surpassed the dwindling Workers' Alliance. Lasser's Communist cohort, Herbert Benjamin, had been withdrawn by the Party earlier in 1940 in a futile attempt to avoid a split. Benjamin briefly served in the IWO before going to St. Louis as a district organizer.[36]

The National Negro Congress had spent most of its energies on traditional civil rights issues and economic struggles. At its 1940 convention, its Communist members denounced President Roosevelt and substituted support for Soviet foreign policy. A. Philip Randolph denounced servility to the program of any white organization, the Communist party included, and resigned the presidency. His successor, Max Yergan, was much closer to the Party. Although the NNC lingered on for some years, it never regained its prestige or membership.[37]

Joseph Lash was appalled by the Nazi-Soviet Pact and the invasion of Finland; the American Student Union overwhelmingly approved of both. Once on the verge of joining the Party, Lash was expelled from the organization "by a much bigger majority than any of us thought possible." He went on to set up a rival International Student Service to combat Party influence among students.[38]

The Party's alliances in state politics came under strain. In Washington, Howard Costigan quietly quit the Party early in 1940; later in the year he endorsed Roosevelt for reelection. Defections wracked the Old-Age Pension Union. Seven Commonwealth Federation state legislators condemned the Russian invasion of Finland; they were denounced by the Washington Commonwealth Federation, and those who were Communists were ousted from the Party. Communists and fellow travelers retained control of the WCF under the leadership of Hugh DeLacy. A Phi Beta Kappa graduate of the University of Washington, DeLacy had done a short stint at sea before returning to his alma mater as a teaching assistant and joining the Communist party. In 1937 he was elected to the Seattle City Council and chosen president of the WCF. In 1940, his "not voting" was the only dissent from a unanimous Democratic convention endorsement of Franklin Roosevelt for reelection. He also lost his bid for reelection to the council.[39]

The California Popular Front fell into tatters after the pact. Culbert Olson remained loyal to Roosevelt and turned on the Party. The Yorty and Tenney Committees began their probes of Communism. Lieutenant Governor Ellis Patterson headed an anti-FDR slate in the 1940 primary elections that closely followed the Communist party's views on domestic and foreign policy. It finished a poor fourth. Minnesota Communists were more fortunate in their choice of allies. Both former governor Benson and ex-congressman Bernard swung from support of collective security to support of total neutrality. The strong Farmer-Labor tradition of isolationism in foreign affairs muted somewhat the pro-Roosevelt sentiment in the state. Communists even rediscovered the virtues of Senators Shipstead and Lundeen. The Benson forces finally won control of the Farmer-Labor party in 1940, but it was a hollow victory. Farmer-Labor candidates for statewide office suffered overwhelming defeats.[40]

The pact also fractured the American Labor party leaders' tolerance of Communists. Prior to August 1939, only the noisy but small Social-Democratic Federation had publicly raised the Communist issue. Early in

October the ALP state Executive Committee, dominated by the Rose-Hillman-Dubinsky leadership, passed a resolution supporting the President's foreign policy and condemning the Soviet invasion of Poland. Even Vito Marcantonio briefly continued to support the concept of collective security after the Party had returned to isolationism, voting for the Cash and Carry Bill allowing arms sales to Britain. By the summer of 1940 Marcantonio had regained his bearings, casting the only negative vote on bills to expand the U.S. navy and air force. The ALP became a battleground between the union leaders and the Communists and their Popular Front allies. Mike Quill was denied the ALP's renomination to the New York City Council for adopting the Communists' views on foreign policy. From 1939 until 1943, when they despaired of ever being rid of Communists, Alex Rose and David Dubinsky battled them in the ALP. Then, angered by Sidney Hillman's decision to work with Communists, they formed the Liberal party, formally barring Party members.[41]

Severe as the Party's losses were, particularly among its auxiliaries, its main body remained intact. Tens of thousands of Communists stayed faithful, no matter what they thought of the pact and its consequences. Recruited in the People's Front era, these members accepted the reversal of doctrine with few murmurs. Amid this orgy of denouncing immediate past allies and embracing recent enemies—some of whom had been allies before their hostility to collective security soured the relationship—the Party was able to continue cheering John L. Lewis. The CIO leader made a stirring anti-war speech at the organization's 1939 convention and engineered adoption of a legislative program that called for attention to domestic matters and studiously avoided words of encouragement for the Allies. The Party called the CIO's legislative program "a remarkable document" which "breaks through the babble and hubbub of the war hysteria and gives a clear-cut lead to the American people in these crucial days." It was much easier to proclaim fidelity to Lewis as justification for opposing American foreign policy than to present the Comintern's case.[42]

The Party encouraged greater union militancy and, fortified by increasingly overt government involvement in labor-management relations, did not weep when bitter strikes disrupted plants engaged in war production. The number of strikes led by Communist unionists was small. While there was a barrage of charges that the strikes were intended to disrupt war production, in virtually all instances there were good and sufficient trade union reasons for striking. Wyndham Mortimer led 3,700 UAW workers on strike at Vultee Aircraft in Los Angeles in November 1940. Harold Christoffel, a close Party ally if not a member, led a bitter two-and-a-half-month UAW strike at the Allis-Chalmers plant in Milwaukee in early 1941. That May, Elmer Freitag, the Communist president of the UAW local, Lew Michener, the union's regional director and a Communist, and Mortimer led a strike at North American Aviation in Los Angeles that was disavowed by the UAW and broken by 2,500 federal troops who seized the plant on the basis of an executive order signed by the President. These strikes helped to fuel the anti-Communist feelings in the country. Congressmen threatened to outlaw defense strikes, and the chairman of the House Judiciary Committee suggested legislation to send strikers "to the electric chair."[43]

The Party also nurtured the hope that with the aid of Lewis it would be able to build a third political party with a genuine trade union base. As the New Year dawned in 1940, the Communists resurrected the dream of a farmer-labor party in which they would play a key role. Gene Dennis announced that "a burning need of the hour is the creation of a broad, united people's front movement and party, an anti-imperialist party of peace which could be depended upon to keep America out of the imperialist war." The Party's National Committee, meeting in mid-February 1940, called for labor and its allies "to crystallize a new political instrument—a mass farmer-labor party "to compete in the 1940 elections on a platform of "Keep America Out of the Imperialist War!," "Put America Back to Work; Curb the Monopolies; Jobs, Security for All!," "Higher Wages, Shorter Hours—An American Standard of Living for All!" and "Protect and Extend Civil Liberties!" In addition to the CIO and Labor's Non-Partisan League, the farmer-labor movement would hopefully attract groups like the Farmers Union, American Youth Congress, and National Negro Congress, all of which had adopted anti-war stands.[44]

The dream died with John L. Lewis's refusal to commit himself to a third party. A frustrated William Foster conceded that the CIO leader had taken "the most advanced stand by any union leader" but grumbled that Lewis's simple isolationism was one of his "grave weaknesses." Finally, late in October 1940, Lewis stunned the country by making a nationwide radio broadcast endorsing Republican Wendell Willkie as the only alternative to war and dictatorship and announcing that he would resign his presidency of the CIO if the President were reelected. Lewis, Browder concluded, was "a giant," but his decision "flies in the face of truth and common-sense. . . . It is incredible." Other CIO leaders were far less comforting than Lewis. Sidney Hillman enthusiastically supported FDR; shortly after, he was selected as labor's chief representative on the National Defense Advisory Commission. Gene Dennis was soon denouncing Hillman as an "inimitable class collaborationist," while Foster charged him with being a "renegade" and opportunist trying to hide his radical past. Lewis's replacement as CIO leader, Phil Murray, was much more friendly to Roosevelt.[45]

Even before Lewis endorsed the Republican candidate and while they were still hoping for a third party, the Communists announced plans to run their own ticket in the 1940 election. At its February meeting, the National Committee announced that a separate Communist Presidential ticket would be in the field "to clarify the issues, to popularize its socialist aims" and achieve other goals related to building "a broad anti-imperialist peace front." Once more Browder and Ford went out to do battle, although the Party leader was forbidden by a court order in September from leaving Manhattan while his conviction was under appeal. Communist efforts to get on the ballot met violent resistance in some states, with canvassers arrested, beaten up by mobs, and harassed. In some states, people who signed petitions to put the Party on the ballot were threatened and faced with prosecution, loss of jobs, and public exposure. In New York, the Party's stronghold, the Communists had lost their line on the ballot by failing to get 50,000 votes in the 1938 gubernatorial election, when they supported Herbert Lehman. Although the Party submitted 43,000 signatures, over 30,000 more than required to get on the ballot by petition, the American Legion launched a campaign that culminated in the required number of signatures in four counties being declared invalid. The Party was left off the ballot; in fourteen other states it met a similar fate after legal challenges. Browder and Ford appeared on the ballot in only twenty-two states.[46]

During the campaign, Gene Dennis railed at labor leaders and other progressives who preferred Roosevelt to Willkie for falling under the "reactionary influence of the disastrous Social-Democratic theory of the 'lesser evil,'" the same theory that "helped pave the way for fascism in Germany and France." Browder bemoaned the fact that Roosevelt had helped Willkie steal the Republican nomination from "Senator Robert A. Taft, that old-fashioned conservative Republican who voted against the Conscription Law!" If only Taft had run, Browder sighed—leaving little doubt who would have been the lesser evil in that case—"Can anyone doubt that the result would have been such a Republican landslide that it would have wrecked the Democratic Party for all time? " And, reporting to the National Committee after the election, the Party leader discerned that the masses had voted for FDR "with obvious reluctance, with suspicion and only because Willkie was committed to identical policies and was obviously dishonest in his last-minute peace demagogy." Browder had no doubt that a Republican, even one so conservative as Taft—who was opposed to conscription, military appropriations, and lend lease—would have swept the country. The Party had come a long way from those days in 1936 when it insisted that Alf Landon had to be defeated at all costs, even if it meant the election of Franklin Roosevelt. The Party had come all the way, in fact, to yearning for an honest conservative isolationist whom it clearly did regard as a lesser evil than Franklin Delano Roosevelt.[47]

Despite all its handicaps, the Party made a respectable showing. A Party candidate in the San Francisco municipal elections received an all-time high of 30,000 votes. The Communist vote in Youngstown, Ohio, increased threefold. A Party member in Detroit polled a record vote, and the mayoral candidate in Boston did the same. The Party did show a decline in the New York council races, from 74,115 first-place votes in 1937 to 48,027 in 1939. All of those votes, however, were write-ins, since the Communist candidates had been ruled off the ballot on a technicality. Most remarkably, Pete Cacchione got 24,132 votes in Brooklyn, less than 6,000 below his 1937 total. The Presidential election returns in 1940 were similarly skewed. Browder and Ford's anemic vote of 48,548, off 30,000, would have been considerably more impressive if they had been permitted to run in New York and Ohio, where they had received 41,000 votes four years earlier. In ten large states where they remained on the ballot, Browder and Ford actually increased their vote by 41 percent. If they could have done the same in New York and Ohio, their total vote would have been about 104,000, almost exactly what William Foster had polled in 1932, the last time the Party had actually urged a vote for a Communist Presidential candidate.[48]

If the Communists felt betrayed that Roosevelt had remained loyal to the policies he—and they—had been advocating, they were indignant that he seemed to have given approval to a legal assault upon the Party and its leaders. The Dies Committee had conveniently scheduled testimony from Party leaders shortly after the pact was signed. The Communists had not yet broken with the Roosevelt administration. In contrast to their defiant revolutionary rhetoric to the Fish Committee, they were positively restrained. Browder took pains to deny that the American Party was organizationally affiliated to the Comintern; that it had ever turned over dues to Moscow or submitted regular reports, minutes, or documents there; and that it currently had regular delegates assigned to Moscow. The tone was even sometimes jocular. Browder, when asked how the Soviet Union could be a democracy if there were only 3.5 million Communists in a country of 170 million people, answered with a non sequitur: "The best way to answer that question is to ask how many members there are of the Democratic Party in the United States." To which a Republican committee member responded: "Too many." William Foster was also far more discreet than he had been in 1930. He no longer considered the statutes of the Comintern very important and denied that they were even followed by the CPUSA: they were "more or less in abeyance" and "are honored more in the breach than in the observance." He loyally spoke up for the independence of his Party: "Nothing that has ever been said at any Comintern or discussion about the American situation has been said without consultation with the American delegates and for the most part was written by them." Foster gamely repudiated his affirmation to the Fish Committee that Communists regarded the red flag as their own and even hedged when Dies asked: "Do you regard it as a paramount duty of a Communist to defend the Soviet Union?" He answered lamely: "It depends on what you mean by defend."[49]

Not all exchanges between Communists and members of the Dies Committee were so cordial. Browder introduced a new ploy when pressed about whether he had ever traveled to Russia on a false passport—he took the Fifth Amendment, declining to answer on the grounds of self-incrimination. By the time the committee got around to questioning lower-level Party bureaucrats, there was no pretense to politeness. James Dolsen, a charter member of the Party with long overseas experience in Moscow and China, knew nothing of the Fifth Amendment. He simply refused to identify other Communists and was cited for contempt. Phil Frankfeld, district organizer in Boston, never even got to testify. Demanding to present a petition signed by 10,000 citizens of Massachusetts, he quickly got into a shouting match with Chairman Dies, who swiftly held him in contempt and ordered him removed.[50]

Party leaders faced a battery of charges. Old cases were pulled out of government files and indictments obtained for past indiscretions. Browder had blurted out that he had once used a false passport before taking refuge in the Fifth Amendment. Arrested late in October 1939, he was sentenced to four years in prison. William Weiner and Harry Gannes were also indicted on passport charges in December. That same month William Schneiderman, the Party's leader in California, went on trial as the government attempted to denaturalize him for his Party membership. Sam Darcy was arrested in September for perjury on a California charge dating back to 1934.[51]

In 1940 Congress passed the Voorhis Act, which required organizations subject to foreign control to register with the attorney general and provide detailed information about their officers, meeting places, contributors, activities, and propaganda. Direct or indirect affiliation with an "international political organization," or policies arrived "at the suggestion of, or in collaboration with" such an organization, were deemed sufficient evidence of foreign control. Reporting favorably on the bill, the House Judiciary Committee noted that "there is no question but what the Communist Party will be required to register by reason of this definition of foreign control, inasmuch as it is affiliated with the Comintern." The drafters were, however, thwarted. At an emergency convention called in November 1940, the Party disaffiliated from the Comintern and amended its constitution to reflect its new formal independence.[52]

The consequences of the Nazi-Soviet Pact did not drive the Communist party back to the isolation of the Third Period. Its losses, although severe, still left the Party with most of its membership, footholds in numerous organizations, and many friends and allies. The membership, however, would never again reach the level attained in the summer of 1939. The auxiliaries and coalitions of the 1940s and 1950s would never be as broad or numerous. The Party's friends and allies would never be as influential. Its enemies would be much more numerous. The Nazi-Soviet Pact ended the most successful era in American Communist life, clearly demonstrating that loyalty to the Soviet Union took precedence over any and every other consideration for the entire Party. No one could escape the conclusion that the Communists' domestic policy was hostage to Soviet foreign policy.

21

The Party's Over

SOONER OR LATER, Communist parties begin to repeat themselves. The rhetoric and tactics of an earlier era reappear, and Party lines are far less interesting the second time around. Between 1939 and 1941, American Communists sacrificed the Popular Front for a Third Period line. The Nazi invasion of Russia in June 1941 revived the Popular Front. The Party swiftly changed directions. It agitated for American involvement in the war and once more gave its enthusiastic support to Franklin Roosevelt. After the Japanese attacked Pearl Harbor, there were no Americans more patriotic than the Communists. They adopted a no-strike policy and shelved their calls for socialism in the interests of national unity.[1]

The Communists remained largely cut off from Moscow during the war. Whatever guidance they received from the Comintern could arrive only indirectly. The most startling piece of news to assimilate arrived in June 1943 when the Comintern dissolved itself. Five months later the Allied leaders, Roosevelt, Churchill, and Stalin, met in Teheran and pledged continued cooperation after the war.

Earl Browder interpreted these signals as a grant of independence to the Communist party. In January 1944 he proposed that the Party be replaced by a Communist Political Association, which would work within the two-party system to support progressive candidates committed to peaceful cooperation between America and Russia. Earl Browder foresaw an era of class peace in postwar America. William Foster opposed parts of Browder's plan in a Political Committee meeting but found little support. Even though the Comintern had been dissolved, Browder took the precaution of sending copies of Foster's protest and minutes of the relevant meetings to Georgi Dimitroff. He received in return a radio message with advice to Foster to remain quiet. A jubilant and united conclave dissolved the Communist party and formed the Communist Political Association on May 20, 1944. Less than one year later, Jacques Duclos, a leading French Communist, harshly denounced Browder's "Teheran policy" and the dissolution of the Party in *Cahiers du Communisme*. Open criticism of another Communist party was unusual enough. Duclos, however, freely quoted from the material Browder had sent to Moscow, a clear sign that his attack had been sponsored at the highest levels.[2]

At a series of emergency meetings, Browder resisted pleas from his colleagues in the Party leadership that he acknowledge his errors. He stubbornly refused to back down and become a zombie, "a dead person who has been raised up by some magical process and walks around under the control of another will." His associates, however, had long memories. They remembered what had happened to the last Party leader to defy Stalin. None of them wanted to suffer the political fate of Lovestone's allies. Gene Dennis and Gil Green attacked Browder. Robert Minor confessed his love for the Party leader but dissociated himself "because there are and can be no friendships that pollute the political honesty of comrades." Only Browder opposed a resolution offered by Dennis accepting Duclos' criticisms.[3]

All that remained was to find a new leadership and tidy up the debris. Foster, Dennis, and John Williamson were elected as the Secretariat on June 18, with Robert Thompson, a Foster protégé, added later. An emergency Party convention met in late July, rejected "Browderism," and reconstituted the Communist party. The man once hailed as the greatest Marxist-Leninist in America was expelled from the Communist party in February 1946. Dennis was named general secretary in July 1946.[4]

Why did Browder persist in his defiance? Like so many of his comrades in the leadership, he had lived through the brutal 1929 episode that had demonstrated what would happen if a Party leader defied the Comintern. For long years Browder had never given any hint that he was either stupid or foolhardy. He had gone along, albeit somewhat reluctantly, in 1939 when the turn-around demanded of him had been far more drastic and surely even less palatable. Why did he not do so in 1945? Browder himself had told the Political Board that he refused to

411

subordinate his mind to others. He certainly held little respect for his colleagues, particularly Foster, and undoubtedly chafed at the thought of being forced to abase himself before them.

Moreover, Browder still had hope that he would be vindicated in Moscow. In 1939 he had successfully avoided an immediate break with the Popular Front, over the opposition of Foster and Dennis, until an unequivocal signal for a break came from Dimitroff. In 1945 he may have been waiting for a similarly clear portent. The Duclos article was ambiguous enough—given both its factual errors and confusions and its stated purpose of merely informing French Communists of developments in America—that Browder could speculate that it was based on a misunderstanding or represented only one view in a divided Soviet leadership. At the emergency convention, he suggested to the delegates that they did not have the last word and that the issues which divided him from them would "be finally decided and closed only by an international consensus of opinion of Marxists of all lands." The following year Browder received a visa to visit Moscow, where he met with both S. Lozovsky and V. Molotov. Although the visit won him no credit among American Communists, he was still considered friendly enough to the Soviet Union to be offered a position as American representative of the Soviet publishing house, which he accepted. For several more years he continued to hope for some message from Moscow recalling him to prominence. It never came. As the Cold War became more frigid late in the 1940s and purge trials in Eastern Europe linked his name and theories to the behavior of disgraced Communists, he gradually drifted out of the Communist orbit.[5]

A remarkably large number of the Party's most prominent leaders of the 1930s did not remain in its ranks. Sam Darcy was expelled in 1944 for opposing Browder's plan to dissolve the CPUSA. Although Darcy was praised by Duclos in 1945 and subsequently held discussions with Dennis and Foster, he never rejoined the Party. He became a successful furniture merchant in Philadelphia. Browder's immediate predecessor as Party leader, Max Bedacht, was expelled in 1948 for accusing the leadership of surrendering to bourgeois nationalism in its ethnic work. He became a New Jersey chicken farmer (and was quietly readmitted into the Party a few years before his death in 1972). Clarence Hathaway was expelled for drunkenness in 1940. He too was readmitted, and even served as the New York Party leader in the late 1950s. Alex Bittelman was expelled in 1959 for expressing "Browderist" views. Roy Hudson quit in the late 1940s. Bill Dunne was expelled in 1946 along with Harrison George, charged with forming a leftist faction in the Party. Herbert Benjamin quietly quit in the early 1950s. Harry Haywood was expelled for "ultra-leftism" in 1959. Henry Puro was dropped out of the Party in 1943. Among the other leading Party cadres of the thirties who either left or were expelled were Albert Weisbord, John Steuben, Fred Beal, John Pace, Pat Chambers, Angelo Herndon, Joe Zack, Charles Taylor, Rob Hall, Nat Ross, George Charney, Louis Budenz, George Powers, John Santo, Howard Costigan, George Padmore, Steve Nelson, and John Gates. Labor leaders ranging from Lee Pressman to Mike Quill repudiated their ties to the Party.

Still other Communists left the United States. Fred Brown returned to Italy after World War II, while Bill Gebert fled to Poland. J. Peters accepted deportation to Hungary. John Williamson was deported to England after serving a jail sentence for violating the Smith Act. Some Party leaders stayed the course. William Foster, Robert Minor, Jack Johnstone, Gene Dennis, Pete Cacchione, Jack Stachel, and James Ford died still members. Will Weinstone, Gil Green, Si Gerson, Gus Hall, Lem Harris, and others remain Communists today.

The movement they still serve is a shadow of what it once was. Seven thousand people were in the Party in 1930; 60,000 more filled out application cards between 1930 and 1934. Recruits poured in even faster thereafter—19,200 in 1935, 25,000 in 1936, 33,600 in 1937, and an estimated 75,000 in 1938 and 1939. Somewhere between 200,000 and 250,000 people were Communists—many of them for less than a year—during the 1930s.[6] During the Popular Front, moreover, formal Party membership was not as important as it had once been. Thousands of Americans took their lead from the Communist party without affiliating with it. Secret Party members held positions of influence in numerous non-Communist organizations. Browder sourly complained to a Party plenum in June 1936 that too many mass leaders were hiding their Party identity. "How shall we dissipate the Red Scare from among the Reds?" he asked. "Some of these comrades hide as a shameful secret their Communist opinion and affiliations; they hysterically beg the Party to keep as far away from their work as possible."[7]

During the Third Period, the Party's auxiliaries remained small because they so faithfully echoed extreme Communist positions. When the auxiliaries reflected the Party's pro–New Deal politics, their leaders hesitated to expose themselves unnecessarily to the government or enemies by openly proclaiming Party membership. This covert behavior helped spawn wild charges linking genuine New Dealers or labor leaders with Communists masquerading as such. In turn, these indiscriminate charges protected actual Communists. A kind of Gresham's law operated: the more non-Communists who were branded Communists—whether from

413

malice, confusion, or error—the greater the tendency to discount anyone named as a Communist.[8]

In later years the Republican party accused the New Deal of perpetuating "twenty years of treason." The Communists, however, had little love for the New Deal or Franklin Roosevelt until 1937. The keynote of the Democratic Front was that the Communists went over to the New Deal; the New Deal did not go over to the Communists. Anything which kept the Party from snuggling up to Roosevelt was lopped off or put in cold storage. Anything which was identified with the New Deal was approved and supported, even if it had once been anathema. This gave the Communist party new opportunities, but at a price: it had to accept tacit limitations on its program and propaganda.

From October 1937 until September 1939, when the Nazi-Soviet Pact upset the Party's carefully crafted applecart, there was no greater ostensible loyalty to the New Deal than among the American Communists. Not accidentally, both ends of this era of good feelings were marked by foreign-policy decisions—the Quarantine Speech of October 1937 and the outbreak of World War II in September 1939. During this period, the Communists applauded Roosevelt's actions, criticizing him only to the extent that he failed to fight enough for his own policies. Their full embrace of the New Deal, however, came long after its reforming impulse had petered out. Franklin Roosevelt suffered his first and most severe congressional setback in 1937 with the failure of his scheme to pack the Supreme Court. Although the Court suddenly began to find Constitutional justifications for New Deal measures, the Congress then became more resistant. In the 1938 elections, Republicans made major gains. The Dies Committee, set up to probe Un-American Propaganda Activities, swiftly began a crusade to link Democrats with Communism. New Dealers had all they could do to prevent a rollback of progressive legislation; extending the legislation was almost impossible. The American Communists jumped on the New Deal bandwagon as it slowed down. They did not start it up, nor were they riders during its heyday.

When it suited their purposes the Communists could shift from the most belligerent hostility to the most abject wooing of former enemies, making up in intensity what they lacked in consistency. Every change of line required a new set of friends and enemies. The same politician castigated as an American Hitler in 1932 might be applauded as a progressive statesman in 1937. The labor leader denounced as a betrayer in 1934 could become a militant tribune in 1937. Most of the men the Communists reviled during the Third Period lived long enough to be wooed with the kindest phrases during the Democratic Front, and some of them managed to be reviled, wooed, and reviled again. The moral seems to be that no one who was attacked by the Communists, no matter how savagely, needed give up the hope of becoming their favorite at some future time.

There were some flies in this ointment, however. For one thing, such gyrations damaged the Party's credibility. Once burned by a change in line, some people refused to get near the fire ever again. Moreover, the history of American Communism has shown that if a member remained in the Party for more than five years, he would have to swallow a new line with new tactics, friends, and enemies. To remain Communists, the tens of thousands who poured into the ranks during the Popular Front were expected to acquiesce to a different sectarian line. Further, if they had joined because of a particular Communist policy, they had to transfer their loyalty from the policy to the Party itself. Those who took issue with this left. The remaining members were Communists irrespective of what the Party stood for.

The Party's lurches were not in response to any internal changes in American society or the Party itself, but reflected the pull of an external force. If the needs of Russian policy dictated a revolutionary or sectarian Comintern policy, the American Communists swung over to the left. When those needs changed, they swung back to a more reformist or opportunistic line. Within the limits of their knowledge, American Communists always strove to provide what the Comintern wanted, no more, no less. The Party could encourage strikes or discourage them, talk in ultrarevolutionary or ultrareformist language, furiously denounce other left-wingers or assiduously court right-wingers with equal facility; it all depended on what was required by Moscow. To pretend otherwise is to misunderstand and distort the history of American Communism and to miss the essential clue about its nature.

In the last analysis, one thing gave every Communist party its specific character among radical movements—its special relationship to the Soviet Union. When the American Communists' enemies began to call them "Stalinists" to suggest their slavish adherence to the Russian dictator, Browder in 1934 proudly appropriated the term: "We are indeed Stalinists, and we hope to become ever more worthy of such a glorious name." The Communists, he admitted in 1938, judged potential allies and enemies by how they evaluated Stalin. Any enemy of Stalin's was an enemy of theirs. "Anyone who is politically literate, who reads the current literature, who is informed about world affairs, and yet at the same time gives a negative reaction to Stalin—that person is moving towards, or is under the influence of, fascist ideologies."[9]

There was nothing unique or peculiar about Communists as people.

They came out of all environments, had all sorts of motives for becoming members, and differed greatly in their commitment to the cause. But once a person entered the Party, and especially once in the leadership, only unconditional and unwavering loyalty to the dictates of Soviet policy, both foreign and domestic, enabled one to stay. Whoever refused to give such loyalty had to, sooner rather than later, get out. Whoever stayed long enough had to make this one motive uppermost and decisive because, from time to time, he had to sacrifice everything else for it. While Party policy might have been applied in America, it was being made abroad, not to suit the needs of American Communists but to satisfy the needs of the Soviet Union. There was one rationale that sanctioned such behavior. Believing that the Soviet Union embodied the socialist dream and that its defense against capitalist and imperialist nations intent on destroying it was of the first priority, Communists willingly sacrificed other interests on Russia's behalf. Speaking at the Seventh Congress, the Italian Communist Palmiro Togliatti publicly boasted that one of the Soviet Union's strategic assets was that in the capitalist world "millions of people are ready to fight for the defense of the Soviet Union with all their strength."[10]

If there was ever a period congenial to the growth of American Communism, it was the Depression decade. No great schisms shook the Party. Government repression was far less systematic or efficient than before or later. The American economic, political, and social system underwent upheavals. Hostility toward the Soviet Union was nowhere near as intense as it had been in the 1920s or would become during the Cold War. And yet, the Party failed. The Communist party still survives and will continue to do so, but only as an historical relic, its aging members recalling those glorious years when they erroneously thought the future was theirs.

NOTES

Chapter 1

1. *Manifesto and Program, Constitution, Report to the Communist International* (Chicago: Communist Party of America, 1919), p. 1.

2. V. I. Lenin, "The Terms of Admission into the Communist International," in Lenin, *Collected Works*, Vol. 31 (Moscow: Foreign Languages Publishing House, 1960), p. 208; "Statutes of the Communist International Adopted at the Second Comintern Congress," in Jane Degras, *The Communist International 1919–1943 Documents*, Vol. 1 (London: Oxford University Press, 1956), p. 163.

3. The definitive account of these early years is Theodore Draper's *The Roots of American Communism* (New York: Viking Press, 1957).

4. Jack Stachel, "Organizational Report to the Sixth Convention of the Communist Party of the U.S.A.," *Communist*, April 1929, pp. 179–189, and May 1929, pp. 234–249. "Open Letter of the E.C.C.I. to the Convention of the Workers (Communist) Party of America," in *On the Road to Bolshevization* (New York: Workers Library Publishers, 1929), p. 23.

5. Jay Lovestone, "More Communist Strongholds," in *The Party Organization* (Chicago: Daily Worker Publishing Company, 1925), p. 4.

6. Organizational definitions and charts can be found in *The Party Organization*, pp. 20–21, 41–44.

7. "Constitution of the Workers (Communist) Party of America," in Lovestone, *The Party Organization*, pp. 38–39.

8. Lenin, *Collected Works*, Vol. 1, p. 57.

9. The Comintern cable stated: "Categorically insist upon Lovestone's Central Executive Committee membership." Theodore Draper, *American Communism and Soviet Russia* (New York: Viking Press, 1960), p. 144.

10. Max Bedacht, "The Sixth Convention of Our Party," *Communist*, March 1929, p. 102. I have more fully explored this controversy in Harvey Klehr, "Leninism and Lovestoneism," *Studies in Comparative Communism*, Vol. 7, Spring–Summer 1974, pp. 3–20.

11. Joseph Stalin, "Speech Delivered in the American Commission of the Presidium of the E.C.C.I., May 26, 1929," in Stalin, *Speeches on the American Communist Party* (San Francisco: Proletarian Publishers, n.d.), p. 11.

12. Joseph Stalin, "Speech Delivered in the Presidium of the E.C.C.I. on the American Question, May 14, 1929," in ibid., pp. 30–31.

13. Earl Browder, *Report to the Eighth Convention Communist Party* (New York: Workers

Library Publishers, 1934), p. 81; *Daily Worker*, March 30, 1930, p. 4; "How the Polcom is Splitting the Party," mimeographed, Theodore Draper Papers, Emory University, Box 1, Folder 2. The ouster of J. O. Bentall, a member of the Central Control Commission, from the Party was reported in an October 14, 1929, *Daily Worker* announcement. An October 27 *Daily Worker* report indicated widespread chaos in the Los Angeles area as expulsions took place.

14. *Program of the Communist International* (New York: Workers Library Publishers, n.d.), pp. 85–88.

15. *Investigation of Communist Propaganda: Hearings Before a Special Committee to Investigate Communist Activities in the United States*, Part 1, Vol. 4 (1930), p. 384.

16. "Theses and Resolutions: The International Situation and the Tasks of the Communist International," *International Press Correspondence*, November 23, 1928, pp. 1567–1568.

17. *The World Situation and Economic Struggle: Theses of the Tenth Plenum E.C.C.I.* (London: CPGB, 1929), p. 3; *XIth Plenum of the Executive Committee of the Communist International: Theses, Resolutions and Decisions* (New York: Workers Library Publishers, 1931), p. 7; Otto Kuusinen, *Prepare for Power: The International Situation and the Tasks of the Sections of the Comintern* (New York: Workers Library Publishers, 1932), pp. 29, 118, 125; *Capitalist Stabilization Has Ended* (New York: Workers Library Publishers, 1932), p. 14.

18. Joseph Stalin, *Works*, Vol. 6 (Moscow: Foreign Languages Publishing House, 1955), pp. 294–295. See Theodore Draper, "The Ghost of Social Fascism," *Commentary*, February 1969, pp. 29–42, for a review of the development of the concept of social-fascism.

19. S. Gusev, *The Next Step in Britain, America and Ireland* (New York: Workers Library Publishers, 1929), p. 9.

20. V. Molotov, "Concluding Speech at the XVIth Party Congress of the CPUSSR," *International Press Correspondence*, July 25, 1930, p. 657.

21. V. I. Lenin, *Left-Wing Communism: An Infantile Disorder* (New York: International Publishers, 1940), p. 70; "Extracts from the Theses on Tactics Adopted by the Fifth Comintern Congress," in Degras, *Communist International*, Vol. 2, pp. 151–152; *Protokoll: 10th Plenum des Exekutivkomitees der Kommunistichen International*, July 3–19, 1929 (Hamburg-Berlin: Verlag C. Hoym, 1929), p. 77.

22. *Daily Worker*, October 19, 1929, p. 1.

23. *Daily Worker*, October 26, 1929, p. 2; October 28, p. 1; October 29, p. 1. The Political Bureau later criticized the Party for not realizing the importance of the crash and noted that "the Party press especially reflects this underestimation"; *Daily Worker*, January 10, 1930, Section 2, pp. 1–2.

24. *Daily Worker*, January 10, 1930, Section 2, p. 2; December 11, 1929, p. 4. *Political Committee Minutes*, November 13, 1929, Draper Papers, Box 1, Folder 10.

25. Lozovsky's proposals are in *Political Committee Minutes*, February 20, 1928.

26. *The Trade Union Unity League: Its Program, Structure, Methods and History* (New York: Trade Union Unity League, 1930), p. 21; A. Lozovsky, "Results and Prospects of the United Front," *Communist International*, March 15, 1928, p. 146.

27. William Foster, "Right Tendencies at the Trade Union Unity Congress," *Communist*, July 1929, p. 371.

28. *Daily Worker*, October 30, 1929, p. 1; January 10, 1930, p. 7; February 18, p. 4. Max Bedacht, "American Democracy on the Way to Fascism," *Communist*, October 1930, pp. 877–878.

29. *Daily Worker*, October 17, 1929, p. 3.

30. The original Secretariat document (not published) is in Draper Papers, Box 1, Folder 23; a copy of the Party's draft is available in Draper Papers, Box 1, Folder 27.

31. *Daily Worker*, April 17, 1930, p. 4; April 21, p. 6. The original cables, given by Earl Browder to Theodore Draper, are in Draper Papers, Box 1, Folder 23, in a file marked "Max [Bedacht] & Will [Weinstone] 1930 Cables." *Thesis and Resolutions for the Seventh National Convention of the Communist Party of the U.S.A., by Central Committee Plenum*, March 21–April 4, 1930. pp. 11–12.

32. *Daily Worker*, April 5, 1930, p. 5; March 18, p. 2; January 7, 1932, p. 4. A. B. Magil, "Toward Social Fascism—The Rejuvenation of the Socialist Party," *Communist*, April 1930, p. 316.

33. *Daily Worker*, July 24, 1930, p. 1; April 19, p. 1. Alexander Bittelman, "August 1, 1931," *Communist*, July 1931, p. 589. "The Tasks of the Communist Party, U.S.A.," *Commu-*

nist, April 1932, p. 313. William Z. Foster, *Toward Soviet America* (New York: Coward-McCann, 1932), p. 225.

34. Draper, *American Communism and Soviet Russia,* pp. 398–403.

35. Milorad Drachkovitch and Branko Lazitch, eds., *The Comintern: Historical Highlights* (New York: Praeger, 1966), pp. 49–51, 383–384; *Political Committee Minutes,* November 13, 1929, Draper Papers, Box 1, Folder 10; *Daily Worker,* November 12, 1929, p. 4; September 11, 1930, p. 4.

36. It was the capitalist *New York Times* which first named the members on July 10, 1929, p. 30. Years later, Foster published the names in his *History of the Communist Party of the United States* (New York: International Publishers, 1952), p. 274. Max Bedacht interview with Theodore Draper, June 18, 1954, Draper Papers, Box 3, Folder 13.

37. Bedacht interview with Draper. Max Bedacht, *The Memoirs of Your Father: On the Path of My Life,* unpublished autobiography, Tamiment Library, New York University. Bedacht's California years are discussed in Ralph Shaffer, "Formation of the California Communist Labor Party," *Pacific Historical Review,* February 1967, p. 70; and "Communism in California, 1919–1924: 'Orders from Moscow' or Independent Western Radicalism," *Science and Society,* Winter 1970, p. 423.

38. Joseph North, *Robert Minor: Artist and Crusader* (New York: International Publishers, 1956); Draper, *American Communism and Soviet Russia,* pp. 405–406, 416–417, 423–425.

39. Draper, *American Communism and Soviet Russia,* p. 252; Solon DeLeon, *The American Labor Who's Who* (New York: Hanford Press, 1925), p. 245.

40. William Z. Foster's *From Bryan to Stalin* (New York: International Publishers, 1937) and *Pages from a Worker's Life* (New York: International Publishers, 1939) provide biographical information. Arthur Zipser's *Workingclass Hero: The Life of William Z. Foster* (New York: International Publishers, 1981) is an uninformative Party-line biography.

41. Draper, *American Communism and Soviet Russia,* pp. 143–152; Stalin, *Speeches,* p. 28; Alexander Bittelman interview with Theodore Draper, January 20, 1969, Draper Papers, Box 3, Folder 18; Bedacht interview with Draper.

42. For Browder's background, I have relied on letters he wrote to Theodore Draper, January 24 and February 29, 1956, in Draper Papers, Box 2, Folder 13. See also James Ryan, "The Making of a Native Marxist: The Early Career of Earl Browder," *Review of Politics,* July 1977, pp. 332–362.

43. Earl Browder, unpublished autobiography, Chapter 5, pp. 37–40, in Earl Browder Papers, Syracuse University.

44. Browder, unpublished autobiography, pp. 9, 18–19; Browder interview, Columbia Oral History Project, pp. 172–174.

45. James Cannon, *The First Ten Years of American Communism* (New York: Pathfinder Press, 1962), p. 213. See also Alexander Bittelman, unpublished autobiography, Tamiment Library, New York University, p. 514; and *Daily Worker,* February 11, 1929, p. 3; February 25, p. 1; February 27, p. 4.

46. *Daily Worker,* August 20, 1929, p. 1. Herbert Benjamin interview with Theodore Draper, October 29–30, 1970, Draper Papers, Box 2, Folder 42. Benjamin recalled Bedacht using the "Uriah Heep" phrase.

47. Bittelman interview with Draper; Earl Browder interview with Theodore Draper, September 29, 1953, in Draper Papers, Box 2, Folder 3; Browder interview, Columbia Oral History Project, pp. 225–226; *Daily Worker,* October 15, 1929, p. 1. The new Secretariat was not mentioned at the time in the Communist press. It was reported in the Trotskyist *Militant,* November 1, 1929, p. 7. The Trotskyists still had excellent sources within the Party. Curiously, however, the statement of ownership of the *Communist* (April 1930, p. 290) did list Bedacht, Minor, and Browder as comprising the Secretariat.

48. *Daily Worker,* August 9, 1930, p. 1; April 15, p. 6. Earl Browder "Preparing for the Seventh Party Convention," *Communist,* May 1930, pp. 439–444. See *Daily Worker,* June 23, 1930, pp. 1, 3; June 25, p. 4; and June 26, p. 6, for excerpts from Bedacht's speech. A short excerpt from Browder's speech was finally published in *Daily Worker,* August 15, 1930, p. 4. Browder did write summary articles for the Party press. See *Daily Worker,* July 9, 1930, p. 3; and Earl Browder, "The Bolshevization of the Communist Party," *Communist,* August 1930, pp. 684–692.

49. Browder, Columbia Oral History Project, p. 223. At the Seventh Convention, "G. Williams" had delivered the indictment of the Party. *Daily Worker,* September 11, 1930, p.

4. Bedacht's new job is noted in *Daily Worker*, November 19, 1930, p. 1. Foster revealed the Secretariat's composition in his *History of the Communist Party of the United States*, p. 292. Weinstone's return from Russia was mentioned in *Daily Worker*, July 8, 1931, p. 1.

50. For information on Puro, see Auvo Kostiainen, *The Forging of Finnish-American Communism, 1917-1924* (Turku, Finland: Turun Yliopisto, 1978), p. 223. For Gebert, see *Daily Worker*, June 7, 1929, p. 3; April 4, 1930, p. 1. For Alpi, see George Charney, *A Long Journey*, (Chicago: Quadrangle Books, 1968), p. 51. For information on Peters, see *Daily Worker*, May 24, 1929, p. 2. Whittaker Chambers' *Witness* (New York: Random House, 1952) and Allen Weinstein's *Perjury: The Hiss-Chambers Case* (New York: Alfred Knopf, 1978) both discuss Peters' underground career in detail.

51. Sam Darcy interview with Theodore Draper, April 30–May 1, 1957, Draper Papers, Box 3, Folder 53. Interview with Sam Darcy, Daniel Bell Papers, Box 10, Closed Section, Tamiment Library, New York University.

52. *Daily Worker*, October 17, 1929, p. 1; Draper Papers, Box 3, Folder 106.

Chapter 2

1. Fred Beal, *Proletarian Journey* (New York: Hillman-Curl, 1937), pp. 27–135. For a description of the Southern textile industry, see Tom Tippett, *When Southern Labor Stirs* (New York: Jonathan Cape & Harrison Smith, 1931), pp. 23–26. A good account of the strike is Theodore Draper, "Gastonia Revisited," *Social Research*, Spring 1971, pp. 3–29.

2. Vera Buch Weisbord, *A Radical Life* (Bloomington: Indiana University Press, 1977), pp. 173, 182–183, 186–187, 207–208. Soon after, Albert Weisbord conceded that white workers did not have to establish social relations with blacks or intermarry, a position that subjected him to charges of white chauvinism. See Albert Weisbord, "My Expulsion from the Communist Party," *Class Struggle*, December 1, 1929, p. 9.

3. Tippett, *When Southern Labor Stirs*, p. 96; Weisbord, *A Radical Life*, pp. 216–289.

4. Weisbord, *A Radical Life*, pp. 270–271. Beal later testified that Leon Josephson, the Communist party's legal representative at the trial, was unhappy with his testimony, desiring a more militant stand. See *Hearings Regarding Leon Josephson and Samuel Liptzen*, House Committee on Un-American Activities, 80th Congress, 1st Session, p. 54. Beal's trial conduct was criticized by the Party's Political Committee. See the Minutes, November 14, 1929, p. 5, in Draper Papers, Box 1, Folder 10. To expunge Beal from the historical record, Foster rewrote history and credited Bill Dunne with leading the strike; see William Z. Foster, *From Bryan to Stalin* (New York: International Publishers, 1937), p. 235. Tippett, *When Southern Labor Stirs*, pp. 118–130. *Labor Unity*, June 8, 1929, p. 5. *Daily Worker*, February 27, 1930, p. 4; June 10, p. 4; June 20, p. 4.

5. Weisbord, *A Radical Life*, pp. 292–300. Weisbord disbanded his group in 1937 and became an A.F. of L. organizer. He died in 1977.

6. William Dunne, *Gastonia, Citadel of the Class Struggle in the New South* (New York: Workers Library Publishers, 1929), pp. 22, 50. *Daily Worker*, October 22, 1929, p. 1; October 17, p. 3.

7. *Daily Worker*, December 5, 1929, p. 4.

8. *Daily Worker*, February 13, 1930, p. 4; February 21, p. 4.

9. These instructions are found in B. Vassilev, "How the CI Formulates at Present the Problem of Organization," mimeographed, in Draper Papers, Box 1, Folder 21, pp. 1–2, 16.

10. *Daily Worker*, December 16, 1929, pp. 1, 3; December 24, p. 4. The *New York Times*, December 15, 1929, pp. 1, 3, claimed only 500 demonstrators.

11. A. B. Magil and Joseph North, *Steve Katovis: Life and Death of a Worker* (New York: International Publishers, 1930). *Daily Worker*, January 27, 1930, pp. 1, 3; January 29, pp. 1, 3; February 21, p. 4. *Party Organizer*, March 1930, p. 13.

12. *Daily Worker*, January 28, 1930, p. 1; January 29, p. 1; February 10, p. 4; February 17, p. 1; March 6, pp. 1–2.

13. This account is based on reports in the *Daily Worker*, March 7, 1930, pp. 1–2; and the *New York Times*, March 7, 1930, pp. 1, 2; and Sam Darcy, unpublished autobiography, pp. 509–516, in Mr. Darcy's possession.

14. *Daily Worker*, March 7, 1930, p. 1; March 14, p. 1; March 21, p. 1. Will Weinstone,

"March 6th in the U.S.A.," *International Press Correspondence*, March 20, 1930, p. 257. *Daily Worker*, April 1, 1930, p. 1.

15. *Daily Worker*, April 25, 1930, p. 4; May 19, p. 4. Earl Browder, "Faith in the Masses—Organization of the Masses," *Communist*, July 1931, p. 603.

16. Dimitri Manuilsky, "The World Economic Crisis and the Revolutionary Wave," *International Press Correspondence*, May 8, 1930, pp. 408–409. Sam Darcy interview with Theodore Draper, May 14, 1957; Herbert Benjamin interview with Draper, October 19, 1970. Both in Draper Papers, Box 3, Folder 53; Box 2, Folder 42.

17. Letter from the Anglo-American Secretariat to the CPUSA, February 15, 1930, Draper Papers, Box 1, Folder 19. Draft thesis for Seventh Party Convention, Draper Papers, Box 1, Folder 27. Radiogram from William Weinstone (referred to as Randolph) February 27, 1930, in Browder Papers, Syracuse University, Series 1-86.

18. *Daily Worker*, April 21, 1930, p. 6; cables from Max Bedacht and William Weinstone, March 16, 1930, March 23, 1930, in Draper Papers, Box 1, Folder 19.

19. *Struggles Ahead!* (New York: Communist Party of the U.S.A., 1930), pp. 16–17.

20. *Daily Worker*, July 25, 1930, p. 4; July 26, p. 6.

21. *Daily Worker*, July 25, 1930, p. 6.

22. Dimitri Manuilsky, "Discussions on the Report of Comrade Molotov," *International Press Correspondence*, August 7, 1930, p. 734; *Daily Worker*, December 30, 1930, p. 4.

23. *Investigation of Communist Propaganda: Hearings Before a Special Committee to Investigate Communist Activities in the United States*, House of Representatives, 71st Congress, 2nd Session (Washington, D.C.: U.S. Government Printing Office, 1930), Part 1, Vol. 4, pp. 358–359, 380, 384.

24. Ibid., Part 1, Vol. 2, pp. 13, 19–20; Part 3, Vol. 3, p. 36; Part 3, Vol. 4, p. 469. House Report No. 2290, 71st Congress, 3d Sess., pp. 63–65.

25. *Struggles Ahead!*, p. 20; *Labor Unity*, September 14, 1929, pp. 2, 4; Minutes of the TUUL Convention, August 31–September 2, 1929, FBI File 61-714-817.

26. *The Trade Union Unity League: Its Program, Structure, Methods and History* (New York: Trade Union Unity League, 1930), pp. 11–13, 22; Dimitri Manuilsky, "The World Economic Crisis and the Revolutionary Wave," *International Press Correspondence*, May 8, 1930, p. 409; *Struggles Ahead!*, pp. 20–21.

27. William Z. Foster, "Right Tendencies at the Trade Union Unity Congress," *Communist*, July 1929, p. 371.

28. Sam Darcy, "The Declining American Federation of Labor," *International Press Correspondence*, August 28, 1930, p. 835; William Z. Foster, "The Organization of the Unemployed," *Labor Unity*, April 27, 1929, p. 5.

29. S. Mingulin, "The Crisis in the United States and the Problems of the Communist Party," *Communist*, June 1930, p. 512; *Daily Worker*, August 30, 1929, p. 6; *R.I.L.U. Magazine*, February 1932, p. 245. None of this has prevented Philip Foner from claiming that "the TUUL was not viewed by its founders as a 'dual union' but simply a means of advancing the program of organizing the unorganized and battling for those already organized until the progressive forces once again gained influence in the A.F. of L.," in "Lenin and the American Working Class Movement," *New World Review*, Winter 1970, p. 130n.

30. *Labor Unity*, February 22, 1930, p. 3; "Resolutions of the Political Secretariat of the ECCI on the Situation and Tasks of the CPUSA," Draper Papers, Box 1, Folder 22.

31. *Labor Unity*, April 12, 1930, p. 4; May 3, p. 1; June 25, p. 1; December 6, p. 2; December 13, p. 2. S. Lozovsky, "The World Crisis, Economic Struggles and the Tasks of the Revolutionary Trade Union Movement," *International Press Correspondence*, September 11, 1930, p. 923. *Daily Worker*, September 25, 1930, p. 4. The original suggestion of 50,000 TUUL members came in a radiogram dated March 18, 1930 signed by Lozovsky, Weinstone (referred to as Randolph), and Bedacht (Draper Papers, Box 1, Folder 23). As of June 1930 the TUUL fell 43,000 short.

32. *Labor Unity*, January 4, 1930, p. 1. *Daily Worker*, April 30, 1930, p. 4; July 3, p. 4; July 30, p. 1; August 20, p. 4; September 25, p. 4. Earl Browder, "Putting the XIth Plenum Decisions into Life," *Communist*, August 1931, p. 686. John Watt and William Boyce, president and vice president, were replaced by Freeman Thompson and Frank Borich in June. The NMU had also had the temerity to change its name to the Mine, Oil and Smelter Workers Industrial Union, but the Party ordered the old name restored.

33. Jack Stachel, "Coming Struggles and Lessons in Strike Strategy," *Communist*,

March 1931, p. 208. *Daily Worker,* October 10, 1930, p. 4; September 16, p. 4. *Labor Unity,* February 1, 1930, p. 1.

34. *Labor Unity,* March 29, 1930, p. 2. *Daily Worker,* March 27, 1930, p. 4; October 17, 1929, p. 3; January 22, 1931, p. 4. March 18, 1930 cablegram, in Draper Papers, Box 1, Folder 23.

35. John Williamson, "Some Burning Problems of Organization," *Communist,* June 1930, pp. 522–523; Earl Browder, *Report of Polburo to CC, 13th Plenum,* August 21–23, 1931, p. 10, in Draper Papers, Box 1, Folder 31; *Labor Unity,* January 1932, p. 10.

36. *Labor Unity,* May 1, 1930, p. 8; July 16, p. 8; December 13, p. 2.

37. *Resolution of the Political Secretariat of the ECCI on the Situations and Tasks of the CPUSA,* Draper Papers.

38. Since Foster spent most of 1930 in jail for the March 6 demonstration, John Schmies had been in charge of the TUUL. *Daily Worker,* December 13, 1930, p. 2; February 28, 1931, p. 4. *Labor Unity,* May 23, 1931, pp. 6–7; April 4, p. 6.

39. *Daily Worker,* February 13, 1931, p. 4; March 24, 1932, p. 4. *Labor Unity,* February 28, 1931, pp. 1, 3; May 1932, pp. 24–25. Jack Stachel, "Some Lessons of the Lawrence Strike," *Communist,* May 1931, p. 34.

40. Nat Kaplan, "Notes on Strike Strategy in Lawrence," *Party Organizer,* January 1932, p. 11. *Daily Worker,* October 27, 1931, p. 1; November 7, p. 1.

41. William Weinstone, "The United Front Tactics in the Lawrence Strike," *Communist,* January 1932, pp. 9–16; "Lessons of the Strike Struggles in the U.S.A.," *Communist,* May 1932, p. 410; *Labor Unity,* June 1932, p. 6. John Ballam still made the claim several years later that the NTWU had led both Lawrence strikes. See John Ballam, *70,000 Silk Workers Strike for Bread and Unity* (New York: Labor Unity Publishers, 1934), p. 7.

42. *Labor Unity,* January 1932, pp. 19–20; July, pp. 7–8. I have been unable to discover what happened to Berkman. Isaac Don Levine ("The Mystery of Mrs. Earl Browder," *Plain Talk,* December 1948, pp. 19–22) charged that both Berkman and her immigration file had vanished and that Earl Browder's wife had entered the United States as Raissa Berkman, using Edith Berkman's passport, although she had not been known by that name in her native Russia.

43. *Labor Unity,* April 4, 1931, p. 3; April 18, p. 1; April 11, p. 7. See also *The West Virginia Miners Union 1931* (Huntington, W. Va.: Appalachian Movement Press, 1972). The quotation referred to the West Virginia strike: a similar comment was made about the Pennsylvania conflict.

44. Frank Borich, "How the Present Miners Strike Was Prepared," *Party Organizer,* August 1931, pp. 2–4; "Developing Leaders," *Party Orgainizer,* August 1931, p. 25. See also *War in the Coal Fields* (Huntington, W.Va.: Appalachian Movement Press, 1972). *Labor Unity,* June 13, 1931, pp. 2, 3.

45. "Motions on Mining Situation, Politburo, July 5, 1931," in Robert Minor Papers, Box 13, Columbia University. *Labor Unity,* June 27, 1931, p. 7; August 22, p. 1. S. Willner, "Some Lessons of the Last Miner's Strike," *Communist,* January 1932, p. 43. The Ewart story is related in Harry Haywood, *Black Bolshevik: Autobiography of an Afro-American Communist* (Chicago: Liberator Press, 1978), pp. 371–372.

46. *Daily Worker,* August 3, 1931, p. 4; Willner, "Some Lessons," p. 31; "Lessons of the Strike Struggles," p. 404; Foster, *Pages from a Worker's Life* (New York: International Publishers, 1939), p. 182.

47. This discussion of Harlan owes much to Theodore Draper's "The Communists and the Miners," *Dissent,* Spring 1972, pp. 371–392. Letter of September 18, 1931, from Clara Holden to Secretariat in Draper Papers, Box 1, Folder 34; letter dated October 28, 1931 to the Secretariat from James Allen. Letter of October 28, 1931, from Earl Browder to James Allen; letter of November 3, 1931, from Harry Wicks to Clara Holden. This folder contains a series of letters on the Harlan strike, many ostensibly written by James Allen, which Draper obtained from the widow of Harry Wicks. James Allen was editor of the *Southern Worker.* Internal evidence from at least one of the letters (dated March 19, 1932, and signed by Allen) indicates, however, that the writer was Wicks. This letter contains an account of "Allen's" party history. The writer recalls his role in the International Typographers Union strike in 1921 and organizing work on the Pacific Coast against World War I. The letter also mentions his service on the Politburo and the Central Committee prior to 1929. All these facts fit Harry Wicks but not Jim Allen. Draper ("The Communists and the Miners") identi-

fies "Allen" as Jim Allen but does not mention this letter. To complicate matters even more, Jim Allen was the Party name of Sol Auerbach, a former instructor at the University of Pennsylvania. It is, of course, possible that Jim Allen–Auerbach adopted Wicks's pseudonym when he became editor of the *Southern Worker*. Or, he may well have written some of the "Allen" letters on Harlan.

48. Letter of November 5, 1931 from Tom Johnson to Harry Jackson, Clara Holden, Jim Allen, and Dan Slinger; Letter of November 22, 1932, unsigned; letter of March 19, 1932, from Jim Allen (Harry Wicks); letter of January 2, 1931 to "Dear Comrade"; Frank Borich, report to the Politburo, January 28, 1932, in Draper Papers, Box 1, Folder 34. Jack Stachel, "Lessons of Two Recent Strikes," *Communist*, June 1932, pp. 530–532; Minutes of Meeting of District Buro 17, March 13, 1932, in Draper Papers, Box 1, Folder 34.

49. See *Harlan Miners Speak* (New York: DaCapo Press, 1970), pp. 67–68, 77.

50. Dreiser was arrested after detectives placed toothpicks against the door of his room, into which he and a young woman had retired. When they were still standing in the morning he was charged with adultery. See Draper, "The Communists and the Miners," p. 388*n*. A recent pamphlet includes several articles and reports from *Labor Defender*, the ILD organ, on the strike and terror tactics: *Harlan and Bell Kentucky 1931–2: The National Miner's Union* (Huntington, W.Va.: Appalachian Movement Press, 1972). See also Malcolm Cowley, "Kentucky Coal Town," *New Republic*, March 2, 1932, p. 67; and Joseph Lash, "Students in Kentucky," *New Republic*, April 20, 1932, p. 269.

51. *Labor Unity*, May 1932, p. 16; October, p. 15; October 1933, pp. 13–14. *Daily Worker*, October 25, 1933, p. 1; December 21, pp. 1–2.

Chapter 3

1. Earl Browder, *Out of a Job* (New York: Workers Library Publishers, 1930), pp. 3, 8, 9, 22.

2. *Daily Worker*, December 9, 1929, p. 4. Albert Prago, *The Organization of the Unemployed and the Role of Radicals 1929–1935* (unpublished doctoral dissertation, Union Graduate School, 1976), pp. 55–56. Prago has claimed that the councils were modeled on those depicted in Sergei Malyshev's *Unemployed Councils in St. Petersburg in 1906* (New York: Workers Library Publishers, 1931), a book that was published in translation by the Party. *Daily Worker*, January 25, 1930, p. 1.

3. *Labor Unity*, February 8, 1930, p. 8; February 22, p. 3. *Daily Worker*, December 20, 1929, p. 1.

4. *Daily Worker*, March 29, 1930, pp. 1, 5; March 30, pp. 1, 3.

5. *Daily Worker*, April 28, 1930, p. 4; May 19, p. 1. Devine was deported in 1931 after pleading guilty to obtaining an American passport in 1930 by falsely swearing he was a citizen. *New York Times*, May 28, 1931, p. 16. Weekly Org. Letter No. 27, issued by Central Office, Communist Party of the United States, May 19, 1930, p. 3, in Draper Papers, Box 1, Folder 26. *Daily Worker*, July 7, 1930, pp. 1, 3; July 9, pp. 1, 3; July 17, p. 4; July 18, p. 4.

6. Clarence Hathaway, "An Examination of Our Failure to Organize the Unemployed," *Communist*, September 1930, pp. 788–789; *Daily Worker*, September 10, 1930, p. 4.

7. *Daily Worker*, August 29, 1930, p. 1; Earl Browder, "Next Tasks of the Communist Party of the USA," *Communist*, November–December 1930, p. 973.

8. *Resolution of the Political Secretariat of the ECCI on the Situation and Tasks of the CPUSA*, Draper Papers, Box 1, Folder 22, pp. 2, 4–6.

9. The description of events both inside and outside of City Hall is drawn from the *New York Times*, October 17, 1930, pp. 1, 3, and October 18, p. 1; and from the *Daily Worker*, October 17, 1930. p. 1, and October 20, p. 1. The *Times* cleaned up the mayor's language, reporting him as shouting, "You dirty whelp, that little remark prompts me to come down and thrash the life out of you."

10. *Daily Worker*, December 17, 1930, pp. 1, 3; Browder, "Next Tasks," p. 973; "Comintern Documents," *Communist*, May 1931, pp. 402–403. The directive, from the Political Secretariat, was dated January 31, 1931.

11. Alfred Wagenknecht, "The Struggle Against Unemployment in the U.S.A.," *International Press Correspondence*, March 26, 1931, pp. 340–341; *Daily Worker*, February 6, 1931,

p. 1. See also Mark Naison, *The Communist Party in Harlem 1928–1936* (unpublished doctoral dissertation, Columbia University, 1976), pp. 73–76; Vern Smith, "Types and Activities of the Unemployed Councils in the U.S.A.," *International Press Correspondence*, February 19, 1931, pp. 143–144; and Paulene Rogers, "Women and Unemployment in the U.S.A.," *International Press Correspondence*, February 28, 1931, pp. 194–195.

12. *Daily Worker*, November 19, 1930, p. 1; February 11, 1931, p. 1; February 13, p. 3. *New York Times*, February 11, 1931, p. 3.

13. *Congressional Record*, House of Representatives, February 11, 1931, pp. 4628–4644.

14. Ossip Piatnitsky, *Urgent Questions of the Day* (London: Modern Books, Ltd., 1931), pp. 5–6.

15. Ibid., p. 15. *Daily Worker*, April 9, 1930, p. 2. Louis Gibarti to Secretariat, CPUSA, March 22, 1930, in Draper Papers, Box 1, Folder 23. *Daily Worker*, April 3, 1931, p. 4; April 13, p. 4.

16. Piatnitsky, *Urgent Questions*, pp. 18–22.

17. *Daily Worker*, May 4, 1931, p. 4; Earl Browder, "To the Masses—To the Shops! Organize the Masses," *Communist*, October 1931, pp. 802–803.

18. "Resolution of the Prague Conference on the Question of Unemployment," *Communist*, December 1931, pp. 1006–1014. *Daily Worker*, October 8, 1931, p. 4; August 29, Section 2, p. 2.

19. *Daily Worker*, September 28, 1931, p. 4; July 13, 1932, p. 1. The government tried, but failed, to deport Mills in the summer of 1932.

20. The biographical information on Benjamin comes from interviews held with him by Theodore Draper on October 29–30, 1970, and letters to Draper from Herbert Benjamin, November 17, 1970, and November 22, 1970, in Draper Papers, Box 2, Folder 42.

21. *Daily Worker*, November 26, 1931, p. 1; November 28, p. 1; December 4, p. 1. *New York Times*, December 3, 1931, p. 8; December 7, pp. 1, 3.

22. *New York Times*, December 8, 1931, pp. 1, 6; *Daily Worker*, December 8, pp. 1, 3.

23. *New York Times*, December 9, 1931, p. 2.

24. *Party Organizer*, August 1932, p. 12; *Labor Unity*, July 1932, p. 15; Nydia Barker, "Uniting the Struggle of Employed and Unemployed: Briggs Hunger March," *Party Organizer*, January 1932, pp. 3–7; *Daily Worker*, February 8, 1932, p. 2.

25. *Daily Worker*, March 9, 1932, pp. 1, 3; March 19, pp. 1, 3; March 23, p. 4. Maurice Sugar, "Bullets—Not Food for Ford Workers," *Nation*, March 23, 1932, pp. 333–335.

26. Oakley Johnson, "After the Dearborn Massacre," *New Republic*, March 30, 1932, pp. 172–174; Robert Cruden, *The End of the Ford Myth* (New York: International Pamphlets, 1932), pp. 11–15. Foster had spoken in Detroit the night before the march but had then left town.

27. Cruden, *The Ford Myth*, p. 15.

28. A Comintern letter, dated April 10, 1930, urged the formation of self-defense detachments able to protect demonstrations and, if the police attacked, "to attack the police from behind or from the side." This echoed an earlier cable from Bedacht and Weinstone calling for the creation of "defense groups." (The letter and cable are in Draper Papers, Box 1, Folder 19.) Known first as the Workers' Defense Corps, the organization spent most of its time "training in defensive and fighting tactics." *Daily Worker*, June 7, 1930, p. 3; May 8, p. 1; May 16, p. 2; February 3, 1931, p. 4.

29. *Veterans—Close Ranks! Fight for the Bonus* (New York: Workers Library Publishers, 1931), pp. 13, 25. *Daily Worker*, May 26, 1932, p. 3; July 26, p. 4; August 2, p. 1.

30. Roger Daniels, *The Bonus March* (Westport, Conn.: Greenwood Press, 1971), pp. 76–99. W. W. Waters, as told to William White, *B.E.F.* (New York: John Day, 1933), pp. 4–17. *Daily Worker*, June 6, 1932, p. 1.

31. *Daily Worker*, June 1, 1932, p. 1. *New York Times*, June 3, 1932, p. 2; June 8, p. 19; June 9, pp. 1, 19. *B.E.F.*, p. 94.

32. *Daily Worker*, June 8, 1932, pp. 1, 3.

33. See Pace's testimony in *Communist Tactics Among Veterans Groups*, House Committee on Un-American Activities, 82nd Congress, 1st Session, July 13, 1951, pp. 1942, 1951, where he estimated that there were 100 Communists in the BEF. Pace also testified before the Special Committee on Un-American Activities, *Investigation of Un-American Propaganda Activities*, House of Representatives, 75th Congress, 3rd Session, Vol. 3, pp. 2268–2287. He had left the Party in 1935. Jack Douglas, in *Veterans on the March* (New York: Workers

Library Publishers, 1934), p. 164, gives 400–500 as the estimate of the squatters, while the *Daily Worker*, June 21, 1932, p. 1, claimed 5,000.

34. Hoover and MacArthur are quoted in Daniels, *The Bonus March*, pp. 174–175; *Daily Worker*, July 5, 1932, p. 4.

35. Earl Browder interview with Theodore Draper, June 23, 1955, Draper Papers, Box 2, Folder 5. Browder's recollection is confirmed in Joseph Zack's and John Pace's testimony, *Communist Tactics Among Veterans' Groups*, pp. 1942, 1945. The Comintern criticism is found in *The Next Step in Britain, America and Ireland* (New York: Workers Library Publishers, 1932), pp. 21, 72.

36. "Lessons of the Bonus March," *Communist*, September 1933, pp. 792–793, 794, 802.

37. *Daily Worker*, May 13, 1932, p. 4; May 18, p. 4.

38. B. K. Gebert, "How the St. Louis Unemployed Victory Was Won," *Communist*, September 1932, pp. 786–791; A. Allen, "Unemployed Work—Our Weak Point," *Communist*, August 1932, pp. 683, 684.

39. *New Leader*, January 9, 1932, p. 2. See also Ernest Patterson, "The Jobless Help Themselves," *New Republic*, September 28, 1932, pp. 168–170; Irving Bernstein, *The Lean Years* (Baltimore: Penguin Books, 1966), p. 432; and S. Willner, "Organizational Problems in Our Unemployment Work," *Communist*, March 1932, pp. 218–219.

40. "The Sharpening Capitalist Offensive, the Rising Tide of Mass Struggles and the Next Tasks of the Party," *Communist*, October 1932, p. 807. Even the liberal *New Republic* had published an article by Nathaniel Weyl, "The Khaki Shirts—American Fascists," September 21, 1932, pp. 144–145. W. W. Waters, leader of the Bonus March, had organized the group.

41. "The United Front Policy and the Fight Against Sectarianism," *Communist*, December 1932, p. 1061; John Williamson, "The United Front—A Tactic of Struggle, Not Peace," *Communist*, p. 1091.

42. *Daily Worker*, November 17, 1932, Part 2, p. 3. A. Verblin, "The United Front in Chicago," *Communist*, December 1932, p. 1102. Verblin's real name was Albert Goldman, and he was expelled in 1933. He went on to become a prominent Trotskyist. *Daily Worker*, June 15, 1933, p. 4; "The United Front Policy," p. 1062.

43. *New Leader*, March 4, 1933, p. 7; *Daily Worker*, December 2, 1932, p. 1. Nathaniel Weyl, in "Organizing Hunger," *New Republic*, December 14, 1932, p. 118, stated that the Unemployed Councils had 300,000 members. *Daily Worker*, November 17, 1932, Part 2, p. 1.

44. *Daily Worker*, September 30, 1932, p. 3; January 17, 1933, p. 4; October 24, 1932, p. 3; FBI File 61-6699-399.

45. *Daily Worker*, December 17, 1932, p. 4; December 2, p. 1. Israel Amter, in "National Hunger March and the Next Steps," *Party Organizer*, January 1933, p. 2, estimated that only 30 percent were Communists.

46. Malcolm Cowley, "King Mob and John Law," *New Republic*, December 21, 1932, p. 155; *Daily Worker*, December 5, 1932, p. 3.

47. *Daily Worker*, December 6, 1933, p. 3; December 9, p. 4. Cowley, "King Mob," p. 154. Herbert Benjamin to Theodore Draper, November 26, 1971 in Draper Papers. An FBI report, File 61-6699-379, contains the longest version of Benjamin's speech to the marchers that I have found. What had caused the Government to back down? Almost the entire Politburo of the Communist party was in Washington secretly. Browder remembered a division of opinion between those welcoming a clash and those hoping for an accommodation. He credited Congressman Fiorello LaGuardia with initiating negotiations that led to permission to march to the seat of Congress but send small delegations into the buildings to see the authorities. LaGuardia told the House that he had met with Benjamin on December 6 but did not indicate any personal role in arranging a compromise. The "Little Flower" did denounce the police for holding the hunger marchers captive even though they had broken no law. Years later, Benjamin could not recall meeting with LaGuardia but disclaimed knowledge of what his Communist superiors might have been doing. Earl Browder, Columbia Oral History Project; *Congressional Record*, House of Representatives, December 7, 1932, pp. 134–135; Herbert Benjamin to Theodore Draper, November 26, 1971, in Draper Papers.

48. *New York Times*, December 7, 1932, p. 3. The police counted 2,699 marchers, consisting of 2,199 white males, 154 white females, 52 black females, and 294 black males. FBI File 60-6699-399.

49. *Daily Worker*, December 7, 1932, p. 4; Israel Amter, "The Revolutionary Upsurge and the Struggles of the Unemployed," *Communist*, February 1933, pp. 115, 121.

50. *Daily Worker*, December 8, 1932, p. 1. Reynolds had been arrested at the 1922 Bridgman convention and was a veteran Party organizer. FBI File 61-6699-415 (copy of the Official Bulletin of the National Hunger March, issued December 5, 1932). The hunger march committee was made up of Carl Winter, Tony Minerich, Ben Caruthers, Lawrence McCuiston, Ann Burlak, Emmanuel Levin, Roy Hudson, Charles Gwynn, and two obscure figures whose last names were Morton and Davis.

Chapter 4

1. *Daily Worker*, July 15, 1930, p. 4.

2. Earl Browder, "A 'Fellow Traveler' Looks at Imperialism," *Communist*, June 1930, p. 568; *Daily Worker*, January 8, 1930, p. 4. The book was *The Twilight of Empire*.

3. *New Masses*, September 1930, p. 4; *Daily Worker*, September 18, 1930, p. 4.

4. Daniel Aaron, *Writers on the Left* (New York: Avon Books, 1965), pp. 102–104; *Worker*, July 21, 1957, p. 7.

5. Aaron, *Writers on the Left*, pp. 86–90; Joseph Freeman, *An American Testament* (New York: Farrar & Rhinehart, 1936).

6. *New Masses*, September 11, 1934, pp. 21–22; December 1930, p. 4.

7. *New Masses*, September 1930, pp. 4–5; September 1929, p. 22.

8. Joseph Freeman, "Social Trends in American Literature," *Communist*, July 1930, p. 651.

9. *New Masses*, December 1930, p. 4; January, p. 21; February, p. 20. Shemitz was married to Whittaker Chambers.

10. *New Masses*, May 1930, p. 2; January, p. 21.

11. Among the guests at the conference were the novelist Josephine Herbst and her husband John Herrmann, who was reputedly an important figure in the Ware Group, which recruited government officials to turn over documents. See Alan Weinstein, *Perjury* (New York: Alfred Knopf, 1978), pp. 137–141. The report on the conference is in *New Masses*, February 1931, pp. 6–8. Gold and Magil were put on the Presidium and Potamkin made a member of the Control Commission. For a blistering account of the congress, see Max Eastman, *Artists in Uniform* (New York: Alfred Knopf, 1934).

12. *New Masses*, June 1931, p. 13; July, p. 22; August, pp. 11–13, 21.

13. *New Masses*, July 1931, p. 13; April 1932, p. 28. *Daily Worker*, June 15, 1931, p. 2; July 18, p. 4.

14. *Daily Worker*, March 19, 1930, p. 2; March 26, p. 1. The full list was printed in the *New York Times*, May 19, 1930, p. 19. *New Masses*, June 1930, p. 9.

15. *New Masses*, March 1931, p. 5; August 1930, p. 23. *Daily Worker*, October 11, 1930, p. 4; May 20, 1931, p. 3. There was also a California branch of the committee whose secretary was Orrick Johns. *New Republic*, October 26, 1932. *Daily Worker*, November 3, 1930, p. 1; May 9, 1931, p. 6. Dreiser's letter requesting Party membership, dated July 20, 1945, is in *Masses and Mainstream*, December 1955, pp. 23–25. A. B. Magil, executive secretary of the Workers' Cultural Federation, fretted, however, that Dreiser had to adopt dialectical materialism to resolve his literary problems. *Daily Worker*, August 28, 1931, p. 4.

16. *New Masses*, February 1932, p. 31; *Daily Worker*, February 1, 1932, p. 4. Dunne continued his attack on Gold on February 2 and 3. The first article implied that Gold was not a Party member at the time.

17. The discussion in this and the preceding paragraphs is based on *The First National Conference of the John Reed Clubs*, May 29, 1932, mimeographed copy of minutes, in Draper Papers, Box 4, Folder 82. The officers also included Louis Lozowick, international secretary; and Joe Freeman, Conrad Komorowski, Eugene Gordon, Mendelson, Jan Wittenbauer, Harry Carlisle, and Nalterstadt, members of the Executive Committee. Listed in pencil as being members of the committee are William Gropper and Whittacker [sic] Chambers. The latter's presence at Chicago has been in dispute, with Alan Weinstein suggesting he was not there (in *Perjury*, pp. 382–383). However, Chambers is listed as a member of the Resolutions Committee in the Minutes, p. 18.

18. Aaron, *Writers on the Left*, pp. 335–340; *Daily Worker*, January 12, 1929, p. 4; William Foster, "Calverton's Fascism," *Communist*, February 1931, pp. 107-111. See also A. Landy, "Cultural Compulsives or Calverton's New Caricature of Marxism," *Communist*, October 1931, pp. 851–864; November, pp. 941–959.

19. *New Masses*, September 1932, p. 20. As late as March 1933, however, Gold was still signing an appeal with Eastman and other writers in support of the National Student League. *New Republic*, March 15, 1933, p. 133. *New Masses*, January 1933, pp. 24–26. Ramsey and Calmer's article was eighteen pages long. From their quotations, it does appear that Calverton was guilty at least of gross carelessness in using sources. V. F. Calverton, *Modern Monthly*, April 1933, pp. 150–151; Sidney Hook, "The Modern Quarterly, the Modern Monthly," in Joseph Conlin, ed., *The American Radical Press 1880-1960* (Westport, Conn.: Greenwood Press, 1974), p. 603. Ramsey's real name was Hyman Rosen; he had been Calverton's protégé. He soon became Browder's speechwriter.

20. Edmund Wilson to Allen Tate, May 28, 1930, in Elena Wilson, ed., *Edmund Wilson: Letters on Literature and Politics 1912-1972* (New York: Farrar, Straus & Giroux, 1977), pp. 196–197; Edmond Wilson, "An Appeal to Progressives," *New Republic*, January 14, 1931, pp. 234–238.

21. See George Soule, "Hard-Boiled Radicalism," *New Republic*, January 21, 1931, p. 265; Upton Sinclair and Norman Thomas letters to editor, *New Republic*, February 11, 1931, pp. 351, 354; Matthew Josephson, "The Road of Indignation," *New Republic*, February 18, 1931, p. 15; *Modern Quarterly*, Summer 1932, p. 11.

22. *Daily Worker*, January 29, 1931, p. 4; January 30, p. 4; July 18, p. 6. *The First National Conference of the John Reed Clubs*, p. 24.

23. Wilson, *Edmund Wilson*, pp. 223–224; *The Van Wyck Brooks–Lewis Mumford Letters* (New York: Dutton, 1970), p. 82; Sidney Hook interview with Theodore Draper, May 17, 1957, Draper Papers, Box 4, Folder 110.

24. Granville Hicks, *Part of the Truth: An Autobiography* (New York: Harcourt Brace & World, 1965); Granville Hicks interview with Theodore Draper, January 28–30, 1957, Draper Papers, Box 3, Folder 108; Louis Adamic, *My America* (New York: Harper & Brothers, 1938), p. 91; David Ramsey interview with Theodore Draper, March 27, 1957, Draper Papers, Box 4, Folder 80.

25. Granville Hicks interview with Draper. The list of contributors and their topics included: Sidney Hook (A Preface on Marxism [later dropped]), Lewis Corey (Social and Economic Scene), Clifton Fadiman (Novel), Newton Arvin [later Morris Schappes] (Poetry), Bernard Smith (Criticism), Granville Hicks (Magazines), Sidney Hook (Philosophy), Corliss Lamont [later Felix Morrow] (Religion), Merle Curti (Historiography [later dropped]), Hyman Rosen [David Ramsey] (Science), Howard Doughty (University Education), Frederick Schuman (Newspapers), Meyer Schapiro (Fine Arts), Elliot Cohen (Sports), Hyman Rosen (Music), Harry Allan Potamkin [later Matthew Josephson] (Movies), John Dos Passos (Theatre), James Rorty (Radio), Lionel Trilling (Cultural Minorities), and Herbert Solow (Intellectuals).

26. *Daily Worker*, May 17, 1932, p. 2; June 21, p. 1; June 3, p. 3. Matthew Josephson, *Infidel in the Temple: A Memoir of the Nineteen-Thirties* (New York: Alfred Knopf, 1967), pp. 125, 150, 153; Mrs. Lewis Corey interview with Theodore Draper, Draper Papers, Box 3, Folder 44.

27. James Rorty interview with Theodore Draper, February 9, 1954, Draper Papers, Box 4, Folder 88; "How Shall I Vote," *Forum*, November 1932, p. 258: *Culture and the Crisis* (New York: Workers Library Publishers, 1932), pp. 3, 22, 23, 28. Years later Browder tried to label the pamphlet an "ultra-left manifesto" written by Corey and Hook, which he had unsuccessfully tried to moderate. See Columbia Oral History Project, pp. 251, 254.

28. *Daily Worker*, September 30, 1932, p. 3; October 12, p. 4. By the end of the campaign the Socialists had garnered a more impressive roster, including Paul Douglas, Morris Cohen, John Dewey, Reinhold Niebuhr, Oswald Garrison Villard, W. E. B. Dubois, Joseph Krutch, Edna St. Vincent Millay, Robert Lovett, F. P. Adams, George Gershwin, and Elmer Davis. See David Shannon, *The Socialist Party of America* (Chicago: Quadrangle Books, 1967), p. 222.

29. *Daily Worker*, October 14, 1932, p. 1; "Summary of Secretary's Report, League of Professional Groups, November 21, 1932," Draper Papers, Box 3, Folder 44; Rorty interview with Draper, February 9, 1954. *Daily Worker*, November 1, 1932, p. 1; November 3. p.

1. Patterson endorsers included Cowley, Wilson, Rorty, Hook, Robert Cantwell, and Donald Henderson.

30. "Program of the League of Professional Groups" (1933). Mrs. Esther Corey permitted Theodore Draper to make notes of this document. Draper Papers, Box 3, Folder 44.

31. The Rorty interview with Draper states that David Ramsey obtained the pamphlet and then refused to return it, claiming it had been lost. A committee eventually rewrote it. Lewis Corey to James Rorty, February 21, 1933; James Rorty letter to members of the Executive Board, May 4, 1933; Minutes of the Executive Board, April 19, 1933, Lewis Corey Papers, Box 9, Columbia University.

32. Rorty interview with Draper; "Program Committee Memorandum" by James Rorty (undated); James Rorty to Lewis Corey, June 16, 1933, Lewis Corey Papers, Box 9.

33. The signers were J. Edward Bromberg of the Group Theatre, Dr. Edwin Berry Burgum of New York University, Winifred Chappell of the Methodist Federation for Social Action, Malcolm Cowley, Kyle Crichton, an editor of *Scribner's* magazine, novelists Guy Endore and Josephine Herbst, and Meyer Schapiro. *Daily Worker,* November 6, 1933, p. 2.

34. *Daily Worker,* December 14, 1932, p. 4. V. J. Jerome, "Unmasking an American Revisionist of Marxism," *Communist,* January 1933, p. 82. Earl Browder, "The Revisionism of Sidney Hook," *Communist,* February 1933, pp. 133–146; March, pp. 285–300.

35. Harrison's letter of resignation from the *New Masses* is in the February 1933 issue, p. 24. *Daily Worker,* January 23, 1933, p. 2.

36. For a full list of proletarian novels see Walter Rideout, *The Radical Novel in the United States, 1900–1954* (Cambridge, Mass.: Harvard University Press, 1956), pp. 295–298. Granville Hicks provided a Communist assessment in *New Masses,* January 1, 1935, p. 36. Kunitz's full list was: Kenneth Burke, Robert Cantwell, Jack Conroy, Edward Dahlberg, John Dos Passos, James Farrell, Kenneth Fearing, Joe Freeman, Mike Gold, Horace Gregory, Josephine Herbst, John Herrmann, Granville Hicks, Langston Hughes, Orrick Johns, Melvin Levy, Grace Lumpkin, Albert Maltz, Sam Ornitz, Paul Peters, Isidor Schneider, Alfred Kreymborg, Max Bodenheim, George Sklar, the Siftons, Edwin Seaver, Mary Heaton Vorse, Charles R. Walker, John Wexley, Ella Winter, Sol Funaroff, Alfred Hayes, Fred Miller, Edwin Rolfe, and Allan Calmer. *New Masses,* May 8, 1934, p. 25; May 1933, p. 20. *Daily Worker,* May 14, 1934, p. 5; June 24, p. 1. *New Masses,* October 23, 1934, p. 15.

Chapter 5

1. Earl Browder, "Faith in the Masses—Organization of the Masses," *Communist,* July 1931, pp. 601, 603; *Daily Worker,* May 5, 1932, p. 4; "The Sharpening Capitalist Offensive, the Rising Tide of Mass Struggles and the Next Tasks of the Party," *Communist,* October 1932, p. 902.

2. Earl Browder, "'Fewer High-Falutin' Phrases, More Simple Every-Day Deeds—Lenin," *Communist,* January 1931, p. 9; Clarence Hathaway, "For a Complete Mobilization of the Party for Real Mass Work in the Election Campaign," *Communist,* May 1932, p. 426.

3. Ossip Piatnitsky, *Urgent Questions of the Day* (London: Modern Books, Ltd., 1931), pp. 6–7; *XIth Plenum of the E.C.C.I.* (New York: Workers Library Publishers, 1931), p. 17.

4. Browder, "Fewer High-Falutin' Phrases," p. 8.

5. *Daily Worker,* January 20, 1932, p. 2; May 5, p. 1; Earl Browder told an Extraordinary Party Congress in 1933 that "we have had difficulties in our Party leadership last year. These difficulties were already largely solved and removed." See *Communism in the United States* (New York: International Publishers, 1935), p. 159. *Daily Worker,* March 2, 1934, p. 2; October 3, 1932, p. 1; January 19, 1934, p. 1. Joseph North, *William Z. Foster* (New York: International Publishers, 1956), p. 35.

6. *Daily Worker,* September 26, 1932, p. 1; October 17, p. 1; October 14, p. 1; November 25, p. 1; August 5, 1933, p. 6. Joseph North, "The Communist Party Convention," *New Masses,* April 17, 1934, p. 8. *Daily Worker,* July 9, 1935, p. 7, began the myth that Browder had been chosen general secretary in 1930.

7. *Daily Worker,* April 2, 1932, p. 1; May 31, p. 1; April 15, 1933, p. 1; July 12, p. 4; January 26, 1934, p. 6.

8. *Daily Worker*, April 25, 1932, p. 3; July 12, p. 1. The Party's official campaign song managed to incorporate most of the demands in a musical form (italics show the chorus):

> All workers and farmers, vote red, vote red!
> It's class against class we'll remember
> To strike at the bosses who take our bread
> We'll vote Foster and Ford in November.
>
> *Come all you workers Negro and white (let's unite)*
> *The bosses candidates we will fight (we will fight)*
> *From coast to coast we will fight as one*
> *Till worker-farmer rule has won.*
>
> We stand for workers' and farmers' relief
> For an end to all starvation
> We stand for the Negro's equal rights
> Against all exploitation.
>
> The Communist Party will be our guide
> Against the wars of the ruling classes
> The Soviet Union we'll always defend
> We'll protect the Chinese masses.

9. *Daily Worker*, November 10, 1932, p. 1. The nationwide figures are from *Statistical Abstract of the United States, 1953* (Washington: U. S. Government Printing Office, 1953, p. 321. Other figures are from *Daily Worker*, November 10, 1932, p. 1, and November 12, p. 1; and *New York Times*, April 4, 1933, p. 1. Earl Browder, "The End of Relative Capitalist Stabilization and the Tasks of our Party," *Communist*, March 1933, p. 245.

10. Ben Field, "The First Red Mayor," *New Masses*, September 1933, p. 22–23.

11. *Daily Worker*, April 28, 1932, Section 2, p. 2; June 10, p. 3; January 23, 1934, p. 3.

12. *U.S.A.* v. *Dennis et al.* (1949), Vol. 15, p. 11552. Browder interview, Columbia Oral History Project, p. 317; *Daily Worker*, June 25, 1932, p. 3; May 28, p. 8. "Literature Division CC to all Party Editors," June 7, 1932, Draper Papers, Box 3, Folder 85. Philip Jaffe interview with Harvey Klehr, August 2, 1979, noted that Browder told him the book had actually been written by Joel Shubin, a Comintern representative then in the United States. Shubin was later the husband of Anna Louise Strong.

13. William Z. Foster, *Toward Soviet America* (New York: Coward-McCann, 1932), pp. 271–317. Similar apocalyptic visions were presented in M. J. Olgin, *Why Communism?* (New York: Workers Library Publishers, 1933), a popular pamphlet reprinted in 1935.

14. North, "The Communist Party Convention," p. 8. *Daily Worker*, November 30, 1933, p. 6; December 1, p. 6.

15. The figures are from Earl Browder, *Report to the 8th Convention* (New York: Workers Library Publishers, 1934), p. 81. Slightly different figures are given in various other places, but Browder's seem to be the ones used most often. Ossip Piatnitsky, *The Work of the Communist Parties of France and Germany and the Tasks of the Communists in the Trade Union Movement* (New York: Workers Library Publishers, 1933), p. 72. "Party Growth Fluctuation, Chart B," Earl Browder Papers, Syracuse University, Series 2-36.

16. Ossip Piatnitsky, "Speech of Comrade Piatnitsky," *International Press Correspondence*, July 6, 1931, p. 680; Earl Browder, "To the Masses—To the Shops! Organize the Masses," *Communist*, October 1931, p. 805.

17. J. Tsirul, "How the Self-Criticism Campaign and the Checking-up of the Fulfillment of the Decisions are Carried Out in the Communist Party of America," *Communist International*, August 15, 1932, p. 516; *Party Organizer*, September–October 1932, p. 3. Browder claimed later that by 1929 only 1,000 charter members of the Party were still Communists. Earl Browder, "Some Remarks on the Twentieth Anniversary of the C.P.U.S.A.," *Communist*, September 1939, p. 798. *Party Organizer*, March 1931, p. 14.

18. *Party Organizer*, April 1934, p. 16. *Daily Worker*, May 16, 1930, p. 4; November 19, 1929, p. 4; July 14, 1931, p. 4. S. Gusev, "At a New Stage: Main Tasks of the Anglo-American Sections of the C.I.," *International Press Correspondence*, November 3, 1932, pp. 1059–1060; Earl Browder interview with William Goldsmith and Daniel Bell, July 26, 1955, Taminent Library.

19. Earl Browder, "Report of the Political Committee to the Twelfth Central Committee Plenum, C.P.U.S.A., November 22, 1930," *Communist*, January 1931, p. 28; *Daily Worker*, May 24, 1932, p. 1.

20. *Daily Worker*, August 29, 1932, p. 4; August 30, p. 4; November 9, p. 1; November 10, pp. 1, 4; March 8, 1933, p. 5.

21. *Daily Worker*, March 13, 1933, p. 1; March 15, p. 1; March 17, p. 1; March 20, p. 3.

22. *Daily Worker*, July 8, 1933, p. 5. Reprinted in Earl Browder, *What Is the New Deal?* (New York: Workers Library Publishers, 1933).

23. *Daily Worker*, October 21, 1933, p. 3; November 25, p. 6.

24. Earl Browder, "Why an Open Letter to Our Party Membership," *Communist*, August 1933, pp. 707, 713; *An Open Letter to All Members of the Communist Party* (New York: Central Committee, Communist Party U.S.A., 1933), p. 11.

25. Gil Green, "The Open Letter and Tasks of the Y.C.L.," *Communist*, August 1933; John Schmies, "The Open Letter and Our Tasks in the Detroit District," *Communist*, August 1933. *Party Organizer*, August–September 1933.

Chapter 6

1. See Theodore Draper, "The Ghost of Social Fascism," *Commentary*, February 1969, pp 35–37.

2. *Capitalist Stabilization Has Ended: Thesis and Resolutions of the Twelfth Plenum of the Executive Committee of the Communist International* (New York: Workers Library Publishers, 1932), pp. 12–13.

3. Otto Kuusinen, *Prepare for Power: The International Situation and the Tasks of the Sections of the Comintern* (New York: Workers Library Publishers, 1932), pp. 87–88, 106; "Tactics of the United Front," *Communist*, October 1932, p. 943. This article was reprinted from the July 13 issue of *Bolshevik*.

4. The text of the Comintern appeal is in *Daily Worker*, March 18, 1933, p. 1. *Theses and Decisions: Thirteenth Plenum of the E.C.C.I.* (New York: Workers Library Publishers, 1934), pp. 7, 16.

5. *Daily Worker*, January 17, 1933, p. 4; February 15, p. 4.

6. *Daily Worker*, January 31, 1933, p. 4; February 3, p. 1; February 4, p. 2. Theodore Draper interview with James Rorty, Draper Papers, Box 4, Folder 88.

7. *Daily Worker*, March 30, 1933, p. 1; April 3, p. 1; April 11, p. 2.

8. *Daily Worker*, May 22, 1933, p. 2; June 3, p. 3.

9. Earl Browder, "Why an Open Letter," *Communist*, August 1933, pp. 752–753; Clarence Hathaway, "A Warning Against Opportunist Distortions of the United Front Tactic," *Communist*, June 1933, p. 534.

10. *Daily Worker*, April 24, 1933, p. 1; May 4, p. 1; April 3, p. 1. Clarence Hathaway, "Maneuvers to Sabotage a United Front of Struggle," *Communist*, May 1933, p. 428, reported that the Socialist National Executive Committee vote was 6 to 5.

11. *Daily Worker*, May 18, 1933, p. 1.

12. *Daily Worker*, April 7, 1933, p. 4; April 29, p. 2. J. B. Matthews, *Odyssey of a Fellow Traveler* (New York: privately published, 1938). *New York World Telegram*, April 29, 1933, p. 11. *Daily Worker*, May 17, 1933, p. 1; May 30, p. 2.

13. *Daily Worker*, May 10 1933, pp. 1–2; May 12, p. 2. Richard Frost, *The Mooney Case* (Stanford, Calif.: Stanford University Press, 1968), p. 444.

14. *Daily Worker*, May 30, 1933, p. 2. Hathaway, "A Warning," p. 527. *Daily Worker*, May 3, 1933, p. 2. Earl Browder, *Communism in the United States* (New York: International Publishers, 1935), p. 125. *Daily Worker*, May 10, 1933, pp. 1, 4; August 5, p. 3. The real director of the committee was Alfred Wagenknecht. Muste was removed from his position when his organization fell from Communist grace. *Daily Worker*, May 16, 1934, p. 3.

15. *Daily Worker*, April 8, 1933, p. 3; April 26, p. 1; October 20, p. 3; November 30, p. 3; December 9, p. 3. Israel Amter, "Low Ebb of Unemployed Work Contrary to Open Letter Lure," *Party Organizer*, November 1933, p. 31.

16. *Daily Worker*, May 13, 1933, p. 5; May 14, p. 3; May 16, p. 1; May 17, p. 1; May 19, p. 1; June 7, p. 2, Karl Borders, "Statement on National Convention of Unemployed Work-

ers League in Chicago, May 13-15, 1933," *Socialist Party Papers* (Glen Rock, N.J.: Microfilming Corporation of America, 1975), Reel 27.

17. V. I. Lenin, *On Party Construction* (Moscow: Foreign Languages Publishing House, 1956), pp. 640–641. Lenin, *Works*, 4th ed., Vol. 21 (Moscow: Foreign Languages Publishing House, 1952), p. 30. Clarence Hathaway, "On the Use of 'Transmission Belts' in Our Struggle for the Masses," *Communist*, May 1931, pp. 412, 413. *Daily Worker*, June 7, 1930, p. 3; October 11, p. 4. "Assignment of Party Tasks," *Party Organizer*, February 1931, p. 9.

18. Hathaway, "On the Use of 'Transmission Belts,'" pp. 412–413; *Party Organizer*, December 1931, p. 27; J. Peters, *The Communist Party: A Manual on Organization* (New York: Workers Library Publishers, 1935), pp. 101–102.

19. Earl Browder, "Report of Political Committee to the 12th CC Plenum," *Communist*, January 1931, pp. 29–30.

20. Israel Amter, "Low Ebb of Unemployed Work," p. 31; Max Bedacht letter for Secretariat, September 29, 1930, Draper Papers, Box 1, Folder 15; George Papcun, "Lack of Democracy in the Trade Unions' Aristocratic Attitude to the Masses," *Party Organizer*, September–October 1931, p. 25.

21. *Daily Worker*, May 13, 1932, p. 4. Organization Bulletin of the New York District, March 26, 1931, quoted by Hathaway, "On the Use of 'Transmission Belts,'" p. 409. See also letter to Communist Fraction of the International Labor Defense from Communist Fraction of the Executive Committee of the International Red Aid, January 26, 1930, Draper Papers, Box 1, Folder 17. In this letter, the IRA criticized the ILD for its tendency "to transfer automatically the Communist Party slogans into the ILD." Bedacht letter for Secretariat.

22. C. Roselle, "How to Stabilize Finances in the Districts," *Party Organizer*, June 1931, p. 9; *Daily Worker*, June 6, 1933, p. 2; Browder, "Why an Open Letter," p. 742.

23. *XIth Plenum of the E.C.C.I.* (New York: Workers Library Publishers, 1931), p. 20; *Capitalist Stabilization Has Ended*, p. 39. Ironically it was the Japanese invasion of Manchuria, not European imperialism, that had suddenly alarmed the Russians.

24. Walter Stoecker, "The Friends of the Soviet Union and the Anti-War Congress," *International Press Correspondence*, September 15, 1932, p. 869; *The World Congress Against War* (New York: American Committee for Struggle Against War, 1932), p. 4; Babette Gross, *Willi Munzenberg: A Political Biography* (Ann Arbor: Michigan University Press, 1974), pp. 222–227.

25. "Manifesto of the Amsterdam World Conference Against Imperialist War," *International Press Correspondence*, September 15, 1932, pp. 866–868. See also George, "After the World Congress Against War. What Next?" *International Press Correspondence*, September 8, 1932, p. 847. A report in the *Daily Worker*, September 17, 1932, p. 4, claimed that ten Trotskyist disrupters opposed the manifesto.

26. J. Berlioz, "A Congress of the United Anti-Fascist Front," *International Press Correspondence*, June 16, 1933, p. 573; "Manifesto of the European Workers' Anti-Fascist Congress," ibid., pp. 574–575; A. Korolski, "The European Anti-Fascist Congress," *International Press Correspondence*, June 23, 1933, pp. 611–612; "Amalgamation of the World Committee Against Imperialist War with the European Workers' Anti-Fascist Union," *International Press Correspondence*, September 8, 1933, pp. 856–857.

27. *Daily Worker*, August 17, 1932, p. 2; November 9, p. 2. The American delegates and the organizations they represented were: Henry Alsberg (International Committee for Political Prisoners), Sherwood Anderson, Joseph Brodsky (International Workers' Order), N. Buchwald (John Reed Club of New York), Stella Buchwald, Joseph Cohen (National Student League), H. W. L. Dana (Friends of the Soviet Union), Leon Dennenberg (John Reed Club of New York), Lillian Furness (Education Workers' League), Joseph Gardner (Workers Ex-Servicemen's League), Elizabeth Gilman (Fellowship of Reconciliation), Dr. Israel Goldstein, Minna Harkavy (John Reed Club of New York), Karl Herrmann (Pen and Hammer Club), Vivienne Hochman (Bureau of Educational Experiment), Sonia Karozz (Lithuanian Working Women's Alliance), Lola Lloyd (Women's Peace Society), J. C. McFarland (Marine Workers Industrial Union), Clara Meltzer (New York Unemployed Council), Scott Nearing, J. G. Roth (Friends of the Soviet Union), I. Schendi (Hindustan Gardar party), Margaret Schlauch, John Scott (Metal Workers Industrial Union), William Simons (Anti-Imperialist League), Samuel Stember (Workers Ex-Servicemen's League), Bernhard Stern (John Reed Clubs), Maurice Sugar (John Reed Club of Detroit), Bella Taub (Office Workers Union),

Charlotte Todes (John Reed Club of New York), Lloyd Westlake (Friends of the Soviet Union). *World Congress Against War*, pp. 26–27. Only thirty-one delegates are listed. Dreiser presumably was the other one.

28. Matthews, *Odyssey of a Fellow Traveler*, pp. 71, 73; letter of American Committee for Struggle Against War, June 3, 1933, in *Socialist Party Papers*, Reel 26; "Minutes of Meeting for Organizing the U.S. Congress Against War, June 14, 1933," in ibid.

29. "Minutes of the Meeting of the NEC, Held in Reading, Pa., July 24, 1933," in ibid. See also Harry Laidler, Julius Gerber, and Edward Levinson to J. B. Matthews, July 6, 1933; and Laidler, Gerber, and Levinson to Clarence Senior, July 11, 1933, in ibid.; *Daily Worker*, July 17, 1933, p. 4.

30. Hillquit tried to have the National Executive Committee rescind its decision to participate. See Morris Hillquit to Clarence Senior, July 28, 1933, in *Socialist Party Papers*, Reel 26. Also see Algernon Lee, Jack Altman, and Bela Low to Members NEC, July 22, 1933, in ibid., where several New York Socialist Party leaders demanded that the Socialists withdraw. Browder, *Communism in the United States*, p. 53. For a list of the affiliated organizations, see "Call to the United States Congress Against War," *Struggle Against War*, August 1933, p. 1.

31. *Daily Worker*, July 17, 1933, p. 4; Edward Levinson to Clarence Senior, July 31, 1933; Levinson to Senior, August 1, 1933, August 5, 1933, in *Socialist Party Papers*, Reel 26; *Daily Worker*, July 31, 1933, p. 1.

32. An Earl Browder interview with Theodore Draper, June 23, 1955, Draper Papers, Box 2, Folder 5, contains the remarkable claim that the Party accepted J. B. Matthews as league chairman to avoid a struggle with non-Communists.

33. *Daily Worker*, September 30, 1933, p. 1; October 2, p. 1.

34. *Daily Worker*, October 3, 1933, p. 1; Matthews, *Odyssey of a Fellow Traveler*, p. 77.

35. *Daily Worker*, October 3, 1933, p. 6; October 23, p. 6. In the final draft, "consistent peace policy" was whittled down to "a positive and vigorous peace policy."

36. Earl Browder, "Situation in the United States of America," *Communist International*, January 15, 1934, p. 78; *Daily Worker*, October 21, 1933, p. 4.

37. Sam Darcy interview with Harvey Klehr, August 22, 1979. Hynes Exhibit No. 3 in *Hearings*, Special Committee to Investigate Communist Activities in the U.S., House of Representatives, 71st Congress, 2d Session, 1930, vol. 4, pp. 420, 428, 431; *Daily Worker*, January 22, 1930, p. 1; February 5, p. 4. Browder wrote Roger Baldwin on January 27, 1930, accepting responsibility for the anti-Chernov activities. Browder Papers, Syracuse University, Series 1-1; *Daily Worker*, March 27, 1930, p. 1. James Cannon, *The History of American Trotskyism* (New York: Pathfinder Press, 1972), p. 70.

38. Clarence Hathaway, "For a Complete Mobilization of the Party for Real Mass Work in the Election Campaign," *Communist*, May 1932, p. 427; Earl Browder, "The End of Relative Capitalist Stabilization and the Tasks of our Party," *Communist*, March 1933, p. 233. This speech was made in January.

39. *Daily Worker*, February 13, 1934, p. 6; February 4, p. 1.

40. *New York Times*, February 15, 1934, pp. 1, 3; *Daily Worker*, February 15, pp. 1–2. The *Times* gave the lower estimate of the crowd.

41. *Daily Worker*, February 15, 1934, pp. 1, 2, 6; February 16, p. 1; February 17, p. 2. *New York Times*, February 16, p. 4. Melech Epstein, *The Jew and Communism* (New York: Trade Union Sponsoring Committee, 1959), p. 289.

42. *Daily Worker*, February 17, 1934, pp. 1, 2; February 24, p. 3 (Hathaway's description); *New York Times*, February 17, pp. 1, 3. The Socialists ended the *Internationale* with "the International Party shall be the human race"; the Communists substituted the word "Soviet" for "Party." Neither Woll nor LaGuardia appeared at the meeting.

43. "To John Dos Passos," *New Masses*, March 6, 1934, p. 9.

44. Earl Browder, "The Role of the Socialist Party Leaders in the Struggle Against War and Fascism," *Communist*, April 1934, pp. 330–335. The League for Industrial Democracy, a Socialist auxiliary, disaffiliated at this time also; *Labor Action*, October 1, 1934, p. 6.

45. The full statement is in Browder, "The Role of the Socialist Party Leaders," pp. 331–333. *Workers Age*, October 15, 1934; *Daily Worker*, October 1, 1934, p. 1.

46. Earl Browder interviews with Theodore Draper, June 23, 1953; September 29, 1953, Draper Papers, Box 2, Folder 3. In the former interview Browder also suggested that Hathaway had genuinely been a peacemaker who was treated brutally by Socialists opposed to a

united front. David Ramsey interview with Theodore Draper, January 15, 1957, Draper Papers, Box 4, Folder 80. There has been some dispute about whether Eisler was, in fact, a Comintern "rep." Browder insisted that Eisler was "just a stray German who wasn't wanted by his own Party and who was looking for a haven to make himself useful" (Columbia Oral History Project, p. 452). Far more persuasive, however, is the fact that Eisler, known here as Edwards, spoke at Party plenums, supervised *The Daily Worker*, and otherwise exercised the sort of authority that no Party would casually hand to a political refugee. See E. Edwards, "For an Intensive Struggle Against Right Opportunism," *Communist*, November 1933, pp. 1096–1107; U.S. Senate, Committee on the Judiciary, *Strategy and Tactics of World Communism*, Part 17, 84th Congress, 2nd Session, pp. 1596–1597; and Alexander Bittelman interview with Theodore Draper, Draper Papers, Box 3, Folder 18. "Forward in Struggle Against Hunger, Fascism & War!: Report of Comrade Earl Browder to the 18th Plenary Meeting of the Central Committee, C.P.U.S.A., January 16, 1934," *Communist*, February 1934, p. 145.

47. *Daily Worker*, February 23, 1934, p. 1; Louis Waldman, *Labor Lawyer* (New York: E.P. Dutton, 1941), pp. 258–274; Shannon, *The Socialist Party of America* (Chicago: Quadrangle Books, 1967, pp. 239–242.

Chapter 7

1. *Trade Union Unity League* (New York: Trade Union Unity League, 1930), p. 17; *Struggles Ahead!* (New York: Communist Party of the U.S.A., 1930), pp. 20–25; Jack Stachel, "Struggle for Elementary Needs—The Main Link in Winning the Masses," *Communist*, January 1933, p. 32; *Labor Unity*, May 23, 1931, p. 6.

2. *Labor Unity*, June 1932, pp. 7–9. Also see *RILU Magazine*, February 1932, pp. 246–247. Earl Browder, in "Place the Party on a War Footing," *Communist*, July 1932, pp. 601–602, explained that once revolutionary work was no longer possible in reformist unions, "we unhesitatingly establish these red unions."

3. *Capitalist Stabilization Has Ended: Thesis and Resolutions of the Twelfth Plenum of the Executive Committee of the Communist International* (New York: Workers Library Publishers, 1932), pp. 14, 15, 28, 33, 35.

4. Stachel, "Struggle for Elementary Needs," p. 32. Browder complained that too many TUUL unions had been formed from the top: "First you get a national office and a set of national officers and supplies of paper and all of the appliances of a union and then you go out and try to find some members." *Daily Worker*, March 25, 1932, p. 4; March 26, p. 4. Earl Browder, "The End of Relative Capitalist Stabilization and the Tasks of Our Party," *Communist*, March 1933, p. 239.

5. *Labor Unity*, January 1933, pp. 12–15; Stachel, "Struggle for Elementary Needs," pp. 23, 27.

6. Earl Browder, "Why an Open Letter," *Communist*, August 1933, pp. 718–719. The SMWIU did win a strike in Warren, Ohio, the first union triumph in steel since World War I, but stagnated for the next year. See *Daily Worker*, September 6, 1932, p. 4; September 6, 1933, p. 4. Stachel, "Struggle for Elementary Needs," p. 25. The TUUL's membership did grow between 1931 and 1932, but much of the growth was apparently in New York's Needle Trades Workers Industrial Union. Earl Browder, in "The Bolshevization of the Communist Party," *Communist*, August 1930, p. 693, gives a figure of 10,000 members. The *Daily Worker*, March 25, 1931, p. 4, notes that the TUUL continued to lose members into March. *Daily Worker*, February 23, 1932, p. 3, gave 17,000 members to the New York District.

7. *Daily Worker*, September 23, 1933, p. 4; August 15, 1932, p. 1; August 2, p. 4; August 3, p. 4. Union leaders included Frank Borich of the NMU, Ann Burlak and John Ballam of the NTWU, John Meldon and James Matles of the SMWIU, Sam Nessin of the Building Trades Workers, Ben Gold and Irving Potash of the NTWIU, Jay Rubin and Mike Obermeir of the Food Workers, Fred Biedenkapp of the Shoe and Leather Workers Industrial Union, Phil Raymond of the Auto Workers, and Roy Hudson of the Marine Workers, to say nothing of Foster, Schmies, and Stachel in the national office. Stachel, "Some Lessons of Recent Strike Struggles," *Communist*, August 1933, pp. 788–789.

8. *Labor Unity*, July 1932, p. 15; March 1933, pp. 21–24, February 1934, p. 15. Stachel, "Some Lessons," pp. 786, 788.

9. Browder, "Why an Open Letter," p. 719; Stachel, "Some Lessons," p. 200; *Labor Unity*, March 1933, p. 5; *Daily Worker*, February 13, 1933, p. 3. See *Daily Worker*, February 10, 1934, p. 4, for Stachel's demand for an explanation of how the Party had lost the initiative in the auto factories. Jack Stachel, "Lessons of the Economic Struggles and the Work in the Trade Unions," *Communist*, March 1934, p. 286. *Daily Worker*, April 7, 1934, p. 4.

10. *Daily Worker*, April 3, 1933, p. 1; June 3, p. 3; October 16, 1934, p. 3. By the end of 1933 the TUUL had also created such new unions as the National Furniture Workers Industrial Union, Packinghouse Workers Industrial Union, Fishermen and Cannery Workers Industrial Union, and National Lumber Workers Industrial Union.

11. Earl Browder, "Situation in the U.S.A.," *Communist International*, January 15, 1934, p. 78; *Daily Worker*, August 29, 1933, p. 3.

12. *Daily Worker*, July 8, 1933, p. 5; June 9, p. 1; July 20, p. 4. "Report of the Central Committee to the 8th Convention," Draper Papers, Box 1, Folder 42.

13. "The Rising Strike Movement," *Communist*, June 1933, p. 523. *Daily Worker*, August 26, 1933, p. 5; March 20, 1934, p. 3.

14. Stachel, "Some Lessons," p. 785; *Daily Worker*, July 14, 1933, p. 1.

15. Kutnick, in "The Revolutionary Trade Union Movement," *Communist International*, September 20, 1934, pp. 598–604, gives the 25,000 figure. Foster later claimed 40,000 in the *Daily Worker*, March 16, 1935, p. 5. *Daily Worker*, November 24, 1933, p. 3. John Meldon, "Swinging to the Offensive Against the N.R.A. in the Steel Mills," *Communist*, October 1933, p. 982. Browder, "Why an Open Letter," pp. 718–719.

16. *Daily Worker*, March 28, 1934, pp. 4–5; March 31, p. 4.

17. Earl Browder, "New Developments and New Tasks in the USA," *Communist*, February 1935, pp. 103–104.

18. John Williamson, "The Lessons of the Toledo Strike," *Communist*, July 1934, pp. 644, 646.

19. *Daily Worker*, August 4, 1934, p. 5. Bill Dunne was not filled with filial pride over the leadership of the strike by his four brothers, all of whom had become Trotskyists. "The four Marx brothers would have done a better job for the strikers," he sneered. *Daily Worker*, June 4, 1934, p. 3.

20. Sam Darcy, "The Great West Coast Maritime Strike," *Communist*, July 1934, pp. 660, 665. Sam Darcy interview with Daniel Bell, Bell Papers, Box 10, Closed Section, Tamiment Library. Al Richmond, *A Long View from the Left* (Boston: Houghton Mifflin, 1973), p. 216. David Mabon, *The West Coast Waterfront and Sympathy Strike of 1934* (unpublished doctoral dissertation, University of California, Berkeley, 1966), p. 28; Earl Browder, "The Struggle for the United Front," *Communist*, October 1934, p. 953; Jack Stachel, "Our Trade Union Policy," *Communist*, November 1934, p. 1101.

21. *New Masses*, July 23, 1935, p. 12; Charles Larrowe, *Harry Bridges: The Rise and Fall of Radical Labor in the U.S.* (New York: Lawrence Hill, 1972), pp. 226–245. *Bridges v. Wixon* 326U5157.

22. *Congressional Record*, Vol. 86, p. 9031; Larrowe, *Harry Bridges*, pp. 222, 299–312; Stachel, "On Trade Union Policy," *Communist*, November 1934, pp. 1104–1105.

23. *Western Worker*, May 21, 1934, pp. 1, 4; May 28, p. 1; June 4, p. 5.

24. *Daily Worker*, July 17, 1934, p. 2; Mabon, *The West Coast Waterfront*, pp. 153–154; Ella Winter, *And Not to Yield* (New York: Harcourt, Brace, 1963), pp. 203, 204.

25. *Western Worker*, July 2, 1934, p. 1; Browder, "Struggle for the United Front," pp. 951–952; Darcy, "The Great West Coast Maritime Strike," p. 682; *Daily Worker*, September 15, 1934, p. 4.

26. Darcy, "The Great West Coast Maritime Strike," p. 679; Sam Darcy interview with Theodore Draper, May 14, 1957, Draper Papers, Box 3, Folder 53; Browder, "The Struggle for the United Front," p. 952. Browder accused George Morris, editor of the Party's *Western Worker*, of writing as though "these mistakes out there were destined to become the dominating line of the Party nationally in its trade union work." Sam Darcy, "The San Francisco Bay Area General Strike," *Communist*, October 1934, p. 990.

27. *Labor Unity*, October 1933, pp. 14–15. This article gives the number of strikers as 65,000. John Ballam, *70,000 Silk Workers Strike for Bread and Unity* (New York: Labor Unity

Publishers, 1934), pp. 58, 62. See also *Labor Unity*, February 1934, p. 22. Jack Stachel, "Lessons of the Economic Struggles," *Communist*, March 1934, p. 286.

28. *New Republic*, September 26, 1934, p. 170; Robert Brooks, *The United Textile Workers of America* (unpublished doctoral dissertation, Yale University, 1935).

29. Browder, "The Struggle for the United Front," p. 832; Earl Browder interview with Daniel Bell, February 1956, Bell Papers, Box 18, Closed section. Carl Reeve, "Lessons of the Great National Textile Strike," *Communist*, November 1934, p. 1120; Jack Stachel, "Our Trade Union Policy," *Communist*, November 1934, p. 1105; Clarence Hathaway, *Communists in the Textile Strike* (New York: Central Committee, CPUSA, 1934); *Daily Worker*, September 25, 1934, p. 1.

30. *Labor Unity*, June 1934, p. 26; Jack Stachel, "Some Lessons," p. 786.

31. *Theses and Decisions: 13th Plenum of the ECCI* (New York: Workers Library Publishers, 1934), p. 15; *Daily Worker*, January 31, 1934, pp. 4–5; "The Eighth Convention of Our Party," *Communist*, May 1934, p. 447.

32. *Daily Worker*, December 28, 1933, p. 6. *Labor Unity*, January 1934, pp. 6–8; June, p. 27.

33. *Labor Unity*, February 1935, p. 4.

34. Theodore Draper, *American Communism and Soviet Russia* (New York: Viking Press, 1960), p. 293; Bridgman Convention Documents; *Investigation of Un-American Propaganda Activities*, Special Committee on Un-American Activities, House of Representatives, 76th Congress, 1st Session, 1939, Vol. 9, pp. 5431–5487.

35. Joseph Zack, "The Line Is Correct—To Realize It Organizationally Is the Central Problem," *Communist*, April 1934, p. 358. For further criticism by Zack and attacks on him, see also Joseph Zack, "How to Apply the Open Letter," *Communist*, February 1934, pp. 208–217; and Gertrude Haeseler, "How Not to Apply the Open Letter," *Communist*, March 1934, pp. 261–270. Jack Stachel, "Some Problems in Our Trade Union Work," *Communist*, June 1934, p. 526; *Investigation of Un-American Propaganda Activities*, Vol. 9, pp. 5434–5437.

36. *Daily Worker*, September 15, 1934, pp. 4–5; Institute of Marxism-Leninism, Central Committee of the CPSU, *Outline History of the Communist International* (Moscow: Progress Publishers, 1971), pp. 359, 363. The source of this information is listed as the Central Party Archives; Ossip Piatnitsky, "Problems of the International Trade Union Movement," *Communist International*, November 20, 1934, pp. 767–768.

37. Jack Stachel, "Our Trade Union Policy," *Communist*, November 1934, pp. 1103–1104. John Schmies had been brought back into TUUL headquarters in June 1934 to preside over its last gasps. See *Daily Worker*, June 4, 1934, p. 4.

38. Earl Browder, "For Working Class Unity! For a Workers' and Farmers' Labor Party!", *Communist*, September 1935, p. 795. Browder was in Moscow for that December Presidium. *Labor Unity*, February 1935, p. 4. William Frey interview with William Goldsmith, November 10, 1955, Bell Papers, Box 6, Closed Section.

39. *Daily Worker*, March 11, 1935, pp. 1–2; March 18, p. 1.

Chapter 8

1. "U.S. Agriculture and Tasks of the Communist Party, U.S.A.: A Draft Program Proposed by the Agriculture Committee of the C.E.C. for General Discussion," *Communist*, February 1930, pp. 104–105; Harrison George, "Causes and Meaning of the Farmers' Strike and Our Tasks as Communists," *Communist*, October 1932, pp. 926, 928; Earl Browder, " 'Fewer High Falutin' Phrases, More Simple Every-Day Deeds'—Lenin: Report of the Political Committee to the Twelfth Central Committee Plenum, CPUSA, November 22, 1930," *Communist*, January 1931, pp. 17–18; "Resolution on the Farmers' Movement" (adopted at Extraordinary Conference of Communist Party, U.S.A., held in New York City, July 7–10, 1933), in *The Communist Position on the Farmers' Movement* (New York: Workers Library Publishers, 1933), p. 6.

2. *The Fourth National Convention of the Workers (Communist) Party of America* (New York: Daily Worker Publishing, 1925), pp. 40–41; *Daily Worker*, June 16, 1930, p. 4. Bio-

graphical information on Knutson comes from Solon DeLeon, *American Labor Who's Who* (New York: Hanford Press, 1925), pp. 127–128, and Theodore Draper, *American Communism and Soviet Russia* (New York: Viking Press, 1960), pp. 178–179. Knutson's Party career is well chronicled in Lowell Dyson, "The Red Peasant International in America," *Journal of American History*, March 1972, pp. 958–973.

3. "U.S. Agriculture," *Communist*, February 1930, p. 105; April, p. 374. "Resolution of the Political Secretariat of the ECCI on the Situation and Tasks of the CPUSA," mimeographed, Draper Papers, Box 1, Folder 1, p. 8. *United Farmer*, May 1930, p. 1. The change in name seems analogous to the shift from the Trade Union Educational League to the Trade Union Unity League. In 1931 the UFL was called "non-Party but under Party guidance," in *Communist*, April 1931, p. 349.

4. *New York Times*, January 27, 1931, p. 2; January 31, pp. 1–2. *United Farmer*, January 1931, p. 1. Lowell Dyson interviewed Knutson, who identified himself as F. Brown; see Dyson, "Red Peasant International," p. 972. *Daily Worker*, January 15, 1931, p. 4; December 11, 1932, p. 4.

5. Quoted in Allen Weinstein, *Perjury: The Hiss-Chambers Case* (New York: Alfred Knopf, 1978), p. 109. Chambers' story was published as *Can You Hear Their Voices?* (New York: International Publishers, 1932).

6. Mike Karni, *Yhteishyvä—Or, For the Common Good: Finnish Radicalism in the Western Great Lakes Region, 1900-1940* (unpublished doctoral dissertation, University of Minnesota, 1975); *United Farmer*, October 1930, p. 1; Auvo Kostainen, *The Forging of Finnish-American Communism, 1917-1924: A Study in Ethnic Radicalism* (Turku, Finland: Turun Yliopisto, 1978), pp, 35, 136–137, 155, 223.

7. *Daily Worker*, September 17, 1931, p. 4; *Producers News*, December 11, 1931, p. 2; *Daily Worker*, May 19, 1932, p. 4.

8. *Daily Worker*, January 29, 1932, p. 4.

9. See Charles Vindex, "Radical Rule in Montana," *Montana*, January 1968, for a discussion of Charles Taylor. Here and there in the upper Midwest, one found towns like Plentywood. Belden, North Dakota, for example, was a small Finnish settlement where one-third of the population belonged to the UFL, earning it a reputation as "the communist center" in the state. Federal Writers' Project, *North Dakota: A Guide to the Northern Prairie State* (New York: Oxford Press, 1950), p. 209.

10. The most complete account of Milo Reno and the FHA is John Shover's *Cornbelt Rebellion* (Champagne: University of Illinois Press, 1965). *Producers News*, August 12, 1932, p. 2; August 19, p. 2. Bert was later reprimanded by Harrison George, in "Causes and Meaning of the Farmers Strike and Our Tasks as Communists," *Communist*, October 1932, pp. 928–930.

11. Ella Reeve Bloor, *We Are Many* (New York: International Publishers, 1940), p. 234. Lement Harris, in *Harold Ware (1890–1935) Agricultural Pioneer, USA and USSR* (New York: American Institute of Marxist Studies, 1978), p. 61, claims that Ware got in touch with his mother first.

12. Harris, *Harold Ware*, pp. 30, 59; George Anstrom, *The American Farmer* (New York: International Publishers, 1932), pp. 30–32. The attack on Ware, although he is not identified by name, is in George, "Causes and Meaning of the Farmers Strike," pp. 920, 922–923.

13. *Farmers' National Weekly*, April 26, 1935, p. 2; Shover, *Cornbelt Rebellion*, p. 68; Rob Hall interview with Theodore Draper, Draper Papers, Box 3, Folder 102.

14. Sam Darcy interview with Harvey Klehr, August 22, 1979. George was listed in the *Daily Worker*, October 4, 1930, p. 4, as chairman of the Party's agrarian commission.

15. Harris, *Harold Ware*, p. 62. Among the other Party members leading delegations were Fred Chase and Lew Bentzley. Chase was a Party leader in New Hampshire. When he died in 1933, granite cutters erected a hammer and sickle on his gravestone. His wife, Ella Chase, was for many years afterward a Party leader in the same state until she became a Maoist in the 1960s. A number of the Chase brood were Communists. Son Homer served in the Lincoln Battalion and later as CPUSA chairman in Georgia. In the early 1960s he was expelled as a left-winger. See *Farmers' National Weekly*, October 8, 1933, for Chase's obituary. Mildred Tunis, "Ella Chase Nelson," *Dartmouth College Library Bulletin*, 1968, pp. 59–66. On Lew Bentzley see Ella Bloor, "Unity of Farmers and Workers," *Party Organizer*, August–September 1933, p. 86. The FNRC platform can be found in *Farmers' National*

436

Weekly, February 10, 1933, p. 8. In 1979 Harris claimed 300 delegates. See Harris, *Harold Ware*, p. 62. Harris stated that the delegates represented 30 million Americans, in Farmers' National Relief Conference, *A Manuscript of Notes taken at the Conference* (Westport, Conn.: Greenwood Press, 1976), pp. 1, 11A.

16. *Farmers' National Weekly*, March 3, 1933, p. 1; John Shover, "The Communist Party and the Midwest Farm Crisis of 1933," *Journal of American History*, September 1964, pp. 254–255; Lief Dahl, "Nebraska Farmers in Action," *New Republic*, January 18, 1933, p. 265; Shover, *Cornbelt Rebellion*, p. 71. Lux denied belonging to the Party, but a Politburo memorandum identified him as a member. Lowell Dyson, *Red Harvest* (Lincoln: University of Nebraska Press, 1982), p. 110.

17. Bloor, *We Are Many*, pp. 240–241.

18. *Farmers' National Weekly*, July 10, 1933, p. 1; June 23, p. 5. Shover, "The Communist Party," pp. 261–262. *Farmers' National Weekly*, May 19, 1933, p. 1; February 10, p. 1; March 3, pp. 5, 8.

19. *Producers News*, March 17, 1933, p. 2. The delegation had noted that "we confidently look to you for action"; *Daily Worker*, February 18, 1933, p. 3. "Resolution on the Farmers' Movement, " pp. 8, 14, 20. Henry Puro, "The Tasks of the Party in the Work Among the Farmers," in *The Communist Position on the Farmers' Movement*, pp. 22–38.

20. "Resolution on the Farmers' Movement," p. 19. See also John Barnett's "On the Draft Program of the United Farmers' League," *Communist*, November 1933, pp. 1145–1146, where he warned of the danger of the FNCA replacing the UFL. *Farmers' National Weekly*, August 12, 1933, p. 5.

21. *Farmers' National Weekly*, October 28, 1933, p. 1. *Farmers Unite Their Fight: Report, Discussions and Resolutions of the Farmers National Conference Held in Chicago November 15–18, 1933* (Philadelphia: Farmers National Committee of Action, 1934). George Anstrom, "Class Composition of the Farmers' Second National Conference Chicago 1933," *Communist*, January 1934, p. 52. John Wiita to Harvey Klehr, March 18, 1979. Lem Harris blithely noted: "With the farm activity launched and rolling Ware found it possible to respond to the urging of the Communist Party to start the organization of farm workers" (*Harold Ware*, p. 66). Harris never mentioned the inner-party disputes over agriculture. See Weinstein, *Perjury*, pp. 14n, 132–137, for Ware's Washington activities.

22. Henry Puro, "The Farmers Are Getting Ready for Revolutionary Struggles," *Communist*, June 1934, p. 575. *Producers News*, July 12, 1934, p. 2; September 27, p. 3; March 29, 1935, p. 2; July 19, p. 2; July 26, p. 1; August 2, p. 2; August 9, p. 2; September 13, p. 1 (where the *News* became the organ of the Montana Holiday Association); November 8, p. 2. Charles Taylor interview with Lowell Dyson, Columbia University Oral History Project.

23. Although Henry Puro, in "My Experience in Work Among American Farmers During the 1930s Agrarian Crisis," Immigrant History Research Center, University of Minnesota, 1977, pp. 8–9, suggests that Tiala was a new recruit, fresh blood, he was actually a veteran Communist, having been a charter Party member and a long-time organizer. See Kostainen, *The Forging of Finnish-American Communism*, pp. 76, 82. *Farmers' National Weekly*, June 29, 1934, p. 7; July 20, p. 2; May 4, p. 2; May 18, p. 8.

24. *Farmers' National Weekly*, March 2, 1934, p. 1; June 22, p. 1; September 14, p. 2; October 26, p. 4.

25. Earl Browder, "The Struggle for the United Front," *Communist*, October 1934, p. 932. Earl Browder, "Report to the Central Committee Meeting of the CPUSA, January 15–18, 1935," *Communist*, March 1935, p. 213. *Farmers' National Weekly*, September 21, 1934, pp. 1–2; November 2, p. 1; November 9, p. 1; December 7, p. 1; Shover, *Cornbelt Rebellion*, pp. 168–172.

26. John Barnett, "Unity of the Farming Masses—A Paramount Issue," *Communist*, February 1935, p. 177; Louise Scott, "Some Problems of Party Work in the Countryside," *Communist*, May 1935, p. 435. In March, Puro and Tiala resigned their UFL posts. *Farmers' National Weekly*, April 5, 1935, p. 8. The new UFL president was Julius Walstad of South Dakota. Harry Correll of Oregon became national secretary, and headquarters were shifted from Chicago to Minneapolis.

27. *Farmers Emergency Relief Conference Proceedings* (Philadelphia: Farmers National Committee of Action, March 1935), pp. 41–45, 52. *Farmers' National Weekly*, April 26, 1935, pp. 1–2; May 3, p. 1; May 10, p. 3.

28. Clarence Hathaway, "Let Us Penetrate Deeper into the Rural Areas," *Communist*, July 1935, pp. 642, 652–658; *Farmers' National Weekly*, December 13, 1935, p. 5. The North Dakota UFL had joined the Holiday group in December 1934.

29. Henry Puro, "Some Experiences of My Work at Upper Michigan as Communist Party District Secretary," Immigrant History Research Center, University of Minnesota, 1977, pp. 1–8.

30. *Farmers' National Weekly*, July 10, 1936, p. 1; August 21, p. 1. Shover, *Cornbelt Rebellion*, p. 208.

31. John Barnett, "The United Farmers League Convention," *Communist*, August 1934, pp. 810–811; Shover, *Cornbelt Rebellion*, p. 177n; Jack Stachel, "Organizational Problems of the Party," *Communist*, July 1935, pp. 625–626; *Daily Worker*, January 2, 1935, p. 4.

32. Resolution of the Political Secretariat of the ECCI," p. 7. "U.S. Agriculture," pp. 373–374. "Resolution on the Farmers' Movement," pp. 2–3.

33. Stuart Jamieson, *Labor Unionism in American Agriculture* (Washington, D.C.: Department of Labor, U.S. Government Printing Office, 1945), pp. 9–69.

34. *Labor Unity*, June 29, 1929, p. 4; July 6, pp. 2, 4. Peggy Dennis, in *Autobiography of an American Communist* (Westport, Conn.: Lawrence Hill, 1977), p. 44, gives the number of strikers in January as 10,000, while contemporary Party accounts gave it variously as 4,000 and 8,000. *Labor Unity*, January 18, 1930, p. 1; February 1, p. 1. Dennis also implies that the TUUL organizers instigated the strike. So does *Labor Unity*, January 11, 1930, p. 1, but the version I have relied on is a summary article on the strike in *Labor Unity*, March 15, 1931, p. 6, and *Daily Worker*, June 27, 1930, p. 4.

35. *Labor Unity*, May 1, 1930, p. 8; February 1, p. 1. *Daily Worker*, May 23, 1930, p. 4; June 17, p. 1; June 27, p. 4. Dennis, *Autobiography*, pp. 51–57. Sam Darcy, then head of the ILD, opposed Waldron's request to go to Russia but was overruled by Browder. Sam Darcy interview with Theodore Draper, May 14–15, 1957, Draper Papers, Box 3, Folder 53. Darcy also claimed that when he arrived in California to serve as district organizer he checked Dennis's claim to have evaded arrest and a warrant and found it untrue. Darcy's animus against Dennis seems to have colored his memory. While the strikes themselves were failures, Dennis was wanted. See *Daily Worker*, May 28, 1930, p. 1.

36. David Selvin, in *Sky Full of Storm: A Brief History of California Labor* (Berkeley: Center for Labor Research and Education, University of California Press, 1966), p. 62, claims the TUUL led both strikes. Carey McWilliams, in his influential *Factories in the Fields* (Boston: Little, Brown, 1939), pp. 83, 213, does the same. Jamieson, in *Labor Unionism*, claims the TUUL gained control of the January strike and calls the AWIU "potent." Dennis, in *Autobiography*, p. 46, claims the TUUL led a successful February strike. Russell Stevens, "The Heroic Struggle of the Imperial Valley Workers in the U.S.A.," *International Press Correspondence*, January 22, 1931, pp. 61–62. Frank Spector, "First Anniversary of the Imperial Valley Struggle," *International Press Correspondence*, May 28, 1931, pp. 521–522. Spector, one of those convicted, was critical of the Party's handling of the case. Stevens confirmed the charge that both strikes were spontaneous and that both were lost. Jamieson, *Labor Unionism*, pp. 84–85; Harrison George, "Causes and Meaning of the Farmers' Strike," *Communist*, October 1932, p. 921.

37. *Western Worker*, October 31, 1932, p. 4; George, "Causes and Meaning," p. 921.

38. Jamieson, *Labor Unionism*, p. 85, and Selvin, *Sky Full of Storm*, p. 62, both credit the AWIU. For an admission of its absence see *Western Worker*, August 15, 1932, p. 2. Sam Darcy, "Agricultural Strikes," *Party Organizer*, August–September 1933, p. 83.

39. *Western Worker*, June 8, 1933, p. 1; June 12, p. 1; July 3, p. 2; July 10, p. 1; July 17, p. 1; August 7, p. 3.

40. *Western Worker*, August 21, 1933, p. 1; August 28, p. 1. Sam Darcy interview with Harvey Klehr, August 23, 1979.

41. *Western Worker*, October 2, 1933, p. 1; October 9, p 1; October 16, p. 1; October 23, pp. 1–2; October 30, p. 3; November 6, p. 4. Joe Evans, "15,000 Cotton Pickers on Strike," *Labor Unity*, December 1933, pp. 8–9.

42. *Western Worker*, November 20, 1933, p. 4; December 11, p. 1; April 9, 1934, p. 2.

43. *Western Worker*, January 15, 1934, p. 1; January 22, p. 1; January 29, p. 1; February 19, p. 2; February 5, p. 1; February 12, p. 6; March 19, p. 1; May 14, p. 1.

44. *Western Worker*, May 7, 1934, p. 1; September 3, p. 1; February 21, 1935, p. 1.

45. Jerold Auerbach, *Labor and Liberty: The LaFollette Committee and the New Deal* (New York: Bobbs-Merrill, 1966), pp. 186–196.

46. *Western Worker*, June 13, 1935, p. 1; July 22, p. 1. Stachel, "Organizational Problems of the Party," p. 626.

Chapter 9

1. Earl Browder, *What Is Communism?* (New York: Vanguard Press, 1936), p. 209. The Communist International credited the Party with over 24,000 at its Eighth Convention (*Communist International*, July 20, 1934, p. 554), while the figure was reported as 24,500 in "The Eighth Convention of Our Party," *Communist*, May 1934, p. 428. Earl Browder, "Forward in Struggle Against Hunger, Fascism, and War," *Communist*, February 1934, p. 172.

2. The fluctuation was greatest at the beginning of this period and lessened somewhat toward its end. *Party Organizer*, May–June 1934, p. 12. In 1930, for every seven members who joined, two stayed and five left. Ossip Piatnitsky, "Speech of Comrade Piatnitsky," *International Press Correspondence*, July 6, 1931, p. 680. By the end of 1933 the Party managed to keep half of its new recruits. Earl Browder, "The Open Letter," *Communist*, October 1933, p. 971. "Correct Registration of Party Members," *International Press Correspondence*, June 16, 1932, p. 564.

3. *Party Organizer*, May–June 1933, p. 10.

4. *Party Organizer*, June 1931, p. 1; *Daily Worker*, October 4, 1930, p. 5; *Party Organizer*, May 1931, p. 24; *Daily Worker*, September 9, 1930, p. 4; *Party Organizer*, March–April 1933, pp. 22–23.

5. *Daily Worker*, June 6, 1932, p. 4; *Party Organizer*, June 1931, pp. 1–2. *Daily Worker*, December 7, 1929, p. 4; October 1, 1932, p. 3.

6. *Party Organizer*, September–October 1932, pp. 3–4; January 1933, p. 22.

7. *Daily Worker*, May 15, 1931, p. 4; March 30, 1932, p. 4. *Party Organizer*, March 1934, pp. 2–3; September–October 1931, p. 25.

8. *Daily Worker*, May 25, 1932, p. 4; *Party Organizer*, May 1931, pp. 4–5; S. Gusev, "At a New State: Main Tasks of the Anglo-American Sections of the Communist International," *International Press Correspondence*, November 3, 1932, p. 1060.

9. *Daily Worker*, February 7, 1930, p. 4; *New Masses*, April 17, 1934, p. 7.

10. J. Peters, *The Communist Party: A Manual on Organization* (New York: Workers Library Publishers, 1935), pp. 26–27.

11. *Party Organizer*, November 1935, p. 17.

12. *Party Organizer*, August–September 1930, p. 11; *Daily Worker*, August 4, 1930, p. 4; Earl Browder, "To the Masses," *Communist*, October 1931, p. 807; A. Markoff, "The Training of New Cadres and Our School System," *Communist*, August 1932, p. 733; *Daily Worker*, November 21, 1933, p. 4. See "Report on the National Training School, January to March 1934," Daniel Bell Papers, Box 2, Closed Section, for a revealing report on the problems of one typical school.

13. *Daily Worker*, March 21, 1930, p. 1. Eisman soon moved permanently to the Soviet Union. See Kenneth Kann, *Joe Rapaport: The Life of a Jewish Radical* (Philadelphia: Temple University Press, 1981), pp. 203–204. *Daily Worker*, July 8, 1930, p. 1. *Kjar v. Doak*, 61 F. 2d566 (1932). A report by the American Council for Nationality Services, "Deportation for Membership in the Communist Party," Immigrant History Research Center, University of Minnesota, cited eleven circuit court cases involving obscure Party members who were ordered deported.

14. "Thesis on the Conditions of Admission to the Communist International," in *Theses, Resolutions and Manifestos of the First Four Congresses of the Third International* (London: Inks Press, 1980), p. 93; "Resolution of the Political Secretariat of the ECCI on the Situation and Tasks of the CPUSA," Draper Papers, Box 1, Folder 1. *Capitalist Stabilization Has Ended: Thesis and Resolutions of the Twelfth Plenum of the Executive Committee of the Communist International* (New York: Workers Library Publishers, 1932), p. 20.

15. *The Struggle Against Imperialist War and the Tasks of the Communist International* (New York: Workers Library Publishers, 1932), p. 18; Dimitri Manuilsky, *The Communist*

Party and the Crisis of Capitalism (Moscow: Co-Operative Publishing Society, 1931), p. 89; Ossip Piatnitsky, *The Communist Parties in the Fight for the Masses* (New York: Workers Library Publishers, 1934), p. 83; *Capitalist Stabilization Has Ended*, p. 20; *Theses and Decisions, Thirteenth Plenum of the ECCI* (New York: Workers Library Publishers, 1934), p. 16; Otto Kuusinen, *Fascism, the Danger of War and the Tasks of the Communist Parties* (New York: Workers Library Publishers, 1934), p. 65.

16. B. Vassiliev, "How the Communist International Formulates at Present the Problem of Organization," Draper Papers, Box 1, Folder 21, pp. 12–28.

17. Theodore Draper, *The Roots of American Communism* (New York: Viking Press, 1957), p. 390. *Daily Worker*, October 17, 1929, p. 3; February 23, 1934, p. 6.

18. Alan Weinstein, "Perjury, Take Three," *New Republic*, April 29, 1978, p. 21, quoting from a memo by Alden Whitman of an interview with Gil Green. Whittaker Chambers insisted that Bedacht had first recruited him for the underground, a charge Bedacht vigorously denied. Elizabeth Bentley implicated Browder as a willing participant in underground activities. Chambers, *Witness* (New York: Random House, 1952), pp. 275–280. Max Bedacht, *On the Path of My Life*, unpublished memoir in Tamiment Library. Elizabeth Bentley, *Out of Bondage* (New York: Devin-Adair Company, 1951), pp. 185–186.

The phrase "special work" was well known. The one-time editor of *Soviet Russia Today*, Liston Oak, testified in 1947 about his years in the Party. He told HUAC that Herbert Goldfrank and Cyril Lambkin, both active in Friends of the Soviet Union, had been part of a group including George Mink that transferred industrial information and patents to the Soviet trade agency Amtorg. "And it was generally understood among this group," he explained, "that they were all doing what was in the party called special work." *Hearings Regarding Leon Josephson and Samuel Liptzin*, Committee on Un-American Activities, 80th Congress, 1st Session, p. 7. Goldfrank had headed Friends of the Soviet Union in 1934. By 1938 he was the Party's administrative secretary in Ohio. In 1944 and 1945 he served on the *New Masses* editorial board, after which his name disappears. There is some evidence that he broke with the Party. *Daily Worker*, February 6, 1934, p. 8; *Party Organizer*, January 1938, p. 6. Cyril Lambkin was an old-timer. Born in Lithuania, he had joined the Party in 1919. A law-school graduate, arrested at the Bridgman convention in 1922, Lambkin briefly worked for the ILD before hooking up with Amtorg. He was living in Russia as late as 1964. Bridgman documents in my possession; Jacob Spolansky, *The Communist Trail in America* (New York: Macmillan, 1951), pp. 27, 30, 44–45, 146–147.

George Mink was born in Russia. A Philadelphia cab driver rumored to be related to S. Lozovksy, he became a leader in the Marine Workers Industrial Union. Arrested for attempted rape in Copenhagen in 1935, Mink was jailed for eighteen months after police discovered espionage paraphernalia in his room. He was linked to political assassinations in Germany and Spain before vanishing in the late 1930s. Ben Gitlow, *I Confess* (New York: E. P. Dutton, 1940), pp. 454, 460; David Dallin, *Soviet Espionage* (New Haven, Conn.: Yale University Press, 1955), pp. 408–410; Jan Valtin, *Out of the Night* (New York: Alliance Book Corporation, 1941), p. 363; *Investigation of Un-American Propaganda Activities*, Special Committee on Un-American Activities, House of Representatives, 76th Congress, 1st Session, 1939, Vol. 11, pp. 6548–6552.

19. Chambers, *Witness*, p. 204; *Hearings Regarding Communist Espionage in the U.S. Government*, House Committee on Un-American Activities, 80th Congress, 2nd Session, Part 1, pp. 1267–1290; U.S. Department of Justice, Immigration and Naturalization Service, File A-3404243, New York (2–617–478), Appeal 15, pp. 6–8, 14A. At immigration hearings prior to his deportation from the United States in 1949, one witness, a former Communist named Andrew Smith, provided authorities with a letter Peters had given him upon his journey to live in Russia in 1932. The letter was signed with Peters' title, "Acting Representative, Communist Party of the United States of America, ECCI." Four former Communists recalled Peters' presence at the Lenin School in 1931 and 1932. Five identified the picture on a passport issued to an Isador Boorstein, used in those years, as that of Peters. Remaining mute, Peters was deported from the United States. Still another ex-Communist, John Lautner, testified that Peters had once admitted to him that he had run the Party's underground in Washington during the 1930s. *Brownell v. Communist Party*, Hearings Before the Subversive Activities Control Board, 1951, p. 9559. See Weinstein, "Perjury, Take Three," p. 18, for a summary of the evidence on Peters.

Herbert Benjamin recalled speaking to forty Communist government employees at an underground convention run by Peters in Washington in 1938. Herbert Benjamin interview with Theodore Draper, Draper Papers, Box 2, Folder 42. Paul Crouch testified that Peters had paid for printing equipment stored in the rear of a Chapel Hill, North Carolina, bookshop in the late 1930s. The owners both took the Fifth Amendment. *Communist Underground Printing Facilities and Illegal Propaganda,* U.S. Senate, Judiciary Committee, 83rd Congress, 1st Session, pp. 4–26.

20. Louis Fraina had a short and unhappy tenure as a Comintern representative in Mexico in 1922. In later years Alex Bittelman performed a similar mission in India, Joe Zack in Venezuela, James Allen in the Philippines, and Harry Wicks in Australia. When Stalin wanted to remove Lovestone and his allies from power in 1929, the Comintern had offered to ship Ben Gitlow to Latin America and Bertram Wolfe to Korea as Communist International reps. A bevy of Americans had visited China in one capacity or another. Earl Browder had headed the Pan-Pacific Trade Union Secretariat in the late 1920s. Several lower-ranking Communists, including Harrison George and Marion Emerson, worked with him. Charles Krumbein and his wife, Margaret Undjus Cowl, were in contact with a secret Comintern organization in China in 1931. Gene Dennis worked in Shanghai on a Comintern assignment in 1934; an army intelligence report later linked him to the Sorge spy ring. Steve Nelson finished his studies at the Lenin School in 1933; on his way home he was delegated to carry money and instructions to the beleaguered Chinese Communists. On Krumbein, see his FBI File 100-17433; Peggy Dennis, *Autobiography of an American Communist* (Westport, Conn.: Lawrence Hill, 1977), pp. 80–85; Steve Nelson, James Barrett, Rob Ruck, *Steve Nelson, American Radical* (Pittsburgh, Pa.: University of Pittsburgh Press, 1981), pp. 140–150.

21. For descriptions of the methods used in obtaining false passports, see Herbert Solow, "Stalin's American Passport Mill," *American Mercury,* July 1939, pp. 302–309. Solow's investigation was prompted by the arrest in Moscow in 1937 of "Robinson" and "Rubens," two Soviet agents with false American passports. There was speculation that they were going to be used in a purge trial. Rubens, known in America under the name Ewald, was a Lett who ran the false passport business in America. His American-born wife, Ruth Boerger, contacted the American embassy before her arrest, precipitating a storm over Soviet mistreatment of an American citizen. After a meeting with an American diplomat, Mrs. "Rubens" asked that the United States cease its efforts in her behalf. The Robinson-Rubens case figured peripherally in the Alger Hiss case; one of the pieces of information Hiss turned over to Whittaker Chambers dealt with the affair. The Russians wanted to discover how far the government would go in its representations on her behalf. See Weinstein, *Perjury: The Hiss-Chambers Case* (New York: Alfred Knopf, 1978), pp. 245–247. Two years later, in 1939, three New Yorkers, one a member of the Party and two others who were fellow travelers, were convicted of participating in a ring that manufactured false passports.

Max Bedacht did not receive a passport in his own name until 1933, yet he made several trips to Russia before that. *Investigation of Un-American Propaganda Activities,* Vol. 7, p. 5852. An anonymous letter was sent to Browder from someone obviously in the government warning that one hundred Communists might be indicted. "Letter to Earl Browder from a Friend," postmarked July 23, 1939, Draper Papers, Box 23. The State Department's case included Jack Stachel, Harry Gannes, Marcel Scherer, Martin Young, Hans Eisler, Leon Josephson, William Weiner, William Browder, George Mink, Margaret Browder, Charles Krumbein, Joe Zack, William Foster, Harry Hynes, John Steuben and Alex Bittelman. World Tourists, a travel agency specializing in trips to the Soviet Union and run by Jacob Golos, a member of the Party's Control Commission, handled these fraudulent travel arrangements. Golos had his records seized in 1939 and pled guilty in 1940 to being an unregistered Soviet agent. See *The Scope of Soviet Activity in the United States,* Appendix 1, Part 23A, U.S. Senate, Judiciary Committee, 1957, for testimony and data by government officials detailing the extent of passport fraud. On Krumbein, see ibid., p. A83, FBI Files 100-17433-19, 100-17433-x1.

22. FBI File 61-6670-83. A good summary of Dozenberg's activities is in Theodore Draper, *American Communism and Soviet Russia* (New York: Viking Press, 1960), pp. 209–214. Further evidence that Party leaders were at least dimly aware of strange goings-on is that Albert Feirabend, a Lettish-American whom Dozenberg had recruited for Soviet military intelligence, was arrested in 1933 after returning from Europe with a false passport and

$28,700 in cash. Also found in his possession was a small white ribbon with a note that he was trustworthy and to be accorded all help in his mission. It was signed by Max Bedacht for the Secretariat. Bedacht admitted he signed such notes but could not remember this case or what it was for. See his testimony in *Hearings Regarding Communist Espionage*, p. 3547. On Poyntz, her FBI File 100-206603 details the bureau's fruitless efforts to learn her fate.

23. *Party Organizer*, January 1932, p. 13; November–December 1932. Earl Browder, "Why an Open Letter," *Communist*, August 1933, pp. 716–717. Earl Browder, *Report to the Eighth Convention Communist Party* (New York: Workers Library Publishers, 1934), p. 87; *Party Organizer*, August–September 1933, p. 28. Jack Stachel, "Organizational Problems of the Party," *Communist*, July 1935, pp. 626–627; *Daily Worker*, April 9, 1934, p. 1.

24. *Party Organizer*, February 1932, p. 3; Jack Stachel, "Recent Developments in the Trade Union Movement," *Communist*, December 1933, p. 1168; *Party Organizer*, August–September 1933, p. 25; *Daily Worker*, January 22, 1931, p. 4; Browder, "Why an Open Letter," p. 717; "Organizational Status of the Party," Earl Browder Papers, Syracuse University, Series 2-36. This document was apparently prepared for the Eighth Convention. Jack Stachel, "Organizational Problems," pp. 625–626, 635.

25. Browder, "To the Masses—To the Shops! Organize the Masses," *Communist*, October 1931, p. 794; "Report on Party Registration, November 1931," Draper Papers, Box 1, Folder 29.

26. F. Brown, "Our Work Among the Foreign-Born Workers," *Communist*, July 1934, p. 702. *Daily Worker*, May 13, 1931, p. 4; January 17, 1930, p. 4; February 7, p. 4. "Report on Party Registration." The number of Jews in the Party was certainly higher, since many who called themselves Russians were probably Jewish and several thousand did not report their nationality.

27. I have discussed these data more fully in Harvey Klehr, *Communist Cadre* (Stanford, Calif.: Hoover Institution Press, 1978), pp. 37–52, 106.

28. *Daily Worker*, January 15, 1931, p. 4; January 27, 1932, p. 4. *Party Organizer*, August–September 1933, p. 62. Stachel, "Organizational Problems," p. 627. *Daily Worker*, January 18, 1930, p. 3.

29. Clarence Hathaway, "On the Use of Transmission Belts in Our Struggle for the Masses," *Communist*, May 1931, p. 417; C. Smith, "The Problem of Cadres," *Communist*, February 1932, pp. 113–114; *Party Organizer*, May–June 1933, pp. 7–8; *Daily Worker*, September 29, 1934, p. 4; Stachel, "Organizational Problems," p. 635. San Francisco had 3,000 members in August 1934, or 13.6 percent of a party of 22,000. Earl Browder, "The Struggle for the United Front," *Communist*, October 1934, p. 965.

30. *Daily Worker*, April 3, 1930, p. 4; June 5, p. 4; March 12, 1931, p. 4. *Party Organizer*, May–June 1934, p. 16. The tenth split into four districts, "with still too much territory in all these districts." *Western Worker*, August 1, 1932, p. 2.

31. S. Gusev, "The End of Capitalist Stabilization," *Communist International*, October 15, 1932, p. 681; Earl Browder interview with Theodore Draper, June 28, 1955, Draper Papers, Box 2, Folder 6.

32. Earl Browder, "New Steps in the United Front," *Communist*, November 1935, p. 1010; Browder, *Report to the Eighth Convention*, pp. 81, 98.

33. Max Bedacht, "The I.W.O.—Workers' Fraternalism," *Communist*, June 1938, p. 541; Earl Browder, "Where Our Party Stood at the Seventh Convention and Where It Stands Now," Draper Papers, Box 13, Folder 13; *Daily Worker*, September 13, 1934, p. 6.

Chapter 10

1. Daniel Brower, *The New Jacobins: The French Communist Party and The Popular Front* (Ithaca, N.Y.: Cornell University Press, 1968), pp. 32–67; Celie and Albert Vassart, "The Moscow Origin of the French 'Popular Front,'" in Milorad Drachkovitch and Branko Lazitch, *The Comintern: Historical Highlights* (New York: Frederick Praeger, 1966), pp. 234–252. Vassart was the French Party's representative in Moscow at the time and drafted the unity pact.

2. Institute of Marxism–Leninism, Central Committee of the C.P.S.U., *Outline History*

of the Communist International (Moscow: Progress Publishers, 1971), pp. 351, 355, 359; Franz Borkenau, *European Communism* (New York: Harpers, 1933), p. 123.

3. Boris Nicolaevsky, *Power and the Soviet Elite* (New York: Frederick Praeger, 1965), pp. 30–32, 86–88; Roy Medvedev, *Let History Judge* (New York: Vintage Books, 1973), pp. 155–156.

4. Georgi Dimitroff, *Working–Class Unity—Bulwark Against Fascism* (New York: Workers Library Publishers, 1935), pp. 10, 11, 17–21; Wilhelm Pieck, *Freedom, Peace and Bread* (New York: Workers Library Publishers, 1935), pp. 10–11, 33–34, 38–41.

5. Ossip Piatnitsky, "Problems of the International Trade Union Movement," *Communist International*, November 20, 1934, pp. 759, 764.

6. Dimitroff, *Working–Class Unity*, pp. 32, 36, 38; Georgi Dimitroff, *The United Front Against Fascism and War* (New York: Workers Library Publishers, 1935), pp. 50, 53–57.

7. Pieck, *Freedom, Peace and Bread*, pp. 12, 17; *VII Congress of the Communist International: Abridged Stenographic Report of Proceedings* (Moscow: Foreign Languages Publishing House, 1939), p. 120.

8. Pieck, *Freedom, Peace and Bread*, pp. 44, 51–61.

9. Dimitroff, *Working–Class Unity*, p. 38.

10. Earl Browder, "The United Front—The Key to Our New Tactical Orientation," *Communist*, December 1935, pp. 1075–1076.

11. *Daily Worker*, March 13, 1934, p. 5.

12. *Daily Worker*, May 26, 1934, p. 5; August 25, p. 1; September 29, p. 5; October 18, pp. 1–2. Alex Bittelman, "Developments in the United Front," *Communist*, December 1934, pp. 1201–1213.

13. Socialist membership went from 20,951 in 1934 to 19,121 in 1935. *Report to the National Convention*, May 23–26, 1936, in Socialist Party of America Papers (Glen Rock, N.J.: Microfilming Corporation of America, 1975), Reel 77. Communist membership was roughly 26,000 in 1934 and 30,000 the following year. Earl Browder, *What Is Communism?* (New York: Vanguard Press, 1936), p. 209. *Daily Worker*, November 7, 1935, pp. 1–3.

14. *Daily Worker*, March 5, 1935, p. 1; November 1, p. 8; December 30, p. 1; December 14, Section 2, pp. 1–4.

15. James Cannon, *The History of American Trotskyism* (New York: Pathfinder Press, 1972), p. 182.

16. *Daily Worker*, December 3, 1934, p. 2; December 22, p. 7; January 22, 1935, p. 2.

17. *The Autobiography of Upton Sinclair* (New York: Harcourt, Brace, 1962); Upton Sinclair, *I, Governor of California and How I Ended Poverty: A True Story of the Future* (Los Angeles: privately printed, 1933).

18. *Western Worker*, January 29, 1934, p. 6. Sam Darcy, unpublished autobiography, p. 416. Sam Darcy interview with William Goldsmith, Tamiment Library, p. 9. Sam Darcy interview with Harvey Klehr, August 1979. *Western Worker*, April 9, 1934, p. 6; April 23, p. 6; April 30, p. 6; June 4, p. 6; July 24, p. 1; August 20, p. 1; August 23, p. 6.

19. Arthur Schlesinger, Jr., *The Politics of Upheaval: 1935–1936* (Boston: Houghton Mifflin, 1966), pp. 114–117. *Western Worker*, September 3, 1934, pp. 1, 6; October 1, p. 1.

20. *Daily Worker*, August 30, 1934, p. 6; *Western Worker*, October 18, 1934, p. 1.

21. *Daily Worker*, November 10, 1934, p. 1.

22. Robert Minor, "The 'EPIC' Mass Movement in California," *Communist*, December 1934, pp. 1214, 1218, 1230–1233.

23. Sam Darcy interview with Theodore Draper, May 14–15, 1957, Draper Papers, Box 3, Folder 53. Darcy, unpublished autobiography, p. 422.

24. *Daily Worker*, November 8, 1934, p. 1; Earl Browder, "New Developments and New Tasks in the U.S.A.," *Communist*, February 1935, pp. 101–103, 113–116.

25. *Outline History*, p. 362; Earl Browder interviews with Theodore Draper, June 23, 1955, October 10, 1955, Draper Papers, Box 2, Folders 5, 8. See *The Way Out: A Program For American Labor* (New York: Workers Library Publishers, 1934), p. 27, for the Party's praise of the Declaration of Independence. Browder recalled years later that he and Maurice Thorez had met prior to the ECCI session and agreed to coordinate their plans, since both faced opposition from the same sources. Browder identified his opponents as Chemadonov of the YCI, German Communists, and Martynov, a Comintern functionary.

26. *Daily Worker*, February 16, 1935, p. 7; January 19, p. 3. "On the Main Immediate Tasks of the C.P.U.S.A.," *Communist*, February 1935, p. 126.

27. *Daily Worker,* January 10, 1935, p. 5; Browder, "New Developments," pp. 114–115; "On the Main Tasks," p. 125.

28. *Daily Worker,* January 10, 1935, p. 5; January 21, pp. 1–2; February 16, p. 7. Earl Browder, "For Working-Class Unity! For a Workers' and Farmers' Labor Party!," *Communist,* September 1935, p. 791.

29. *Daily Worker,* October 1, 1934, p. 3; October 15, p. 6; October 25, p. 4; July 28, p. 6; January 25, 1935, p. 8; December 1, 1934, p. 5; August 24, p. 6; December 1, p. 5.

30. Joseph Stalin and H. G. Wells, *Marxism v. Liberalism: An Interview* (New York: New Century Publishers, 1937), p. 6.

31. *Daily Worker,* October 10, 1934, p. 6. The text was on pp. 1–2. See *Daily Worker,* January 1, 1935, p. 5, for the complete text.

32. *Daily Worker,* January 19, 1935, p. 8; January 26, p. 8; February 1, p. 2.

33. *Daily Worker,* July 5, 1935, p. 5; Alexander Bittelman, "Approaching the Seventh World Congress of the Communist International," *Communist,* June 1935, p. 523; F. Brown, "Toward the Study of Fasczation in the United States," ibid., p. 567.

34. *Daily Worker,* July 31, 1935, p. 8; July 30, p. 8.

35. *VII Congress of the Communist International,* pp. 150–152, 361.

36. I have put together this account from several versions Darcy has given over the years that differ only in small but unimportant details. They include his unpublished autobiography, pp. 230–234; Sam Darcy interview with Harvey Klehr, March 24, 1979; Sam Darcy interview with William Goldsmith, Bell Papers, Box 10, Closed Section, pp. 9–11; Sam Darcy interview with Theodore Draper, May 14–15, 1957, Draper Papers, Box 3, Folder 53.

37. Earl Browder to Theodore Draper, October 13, 1957, Draper Papers, Box 2, Folder 13. In an interview with Draper on October 10, 1955, Browder recalled Dimitroff's reference: "I can remember my reaction to it very well as considering it a very welcome development." Shortly after the 1936 election, Browder wrote that "the warning was directed against such people as the leaders of the Socialist Party and their policies." Earl Browder, "The Elections and the People's Front," *Communist,* January 1937, p. 18.

38. *Daily Worker,* September 19, 1935, p. 2; September 26, p. 7; November 5, p. 7; December 6, p. 12.

39. "The Farmer-Labor Party and the Struggle Against Reaction," *Communist,* December 1935, p. 1188.

40. *Foreign Relations of the United States: The Soviet Union 1933–1939* (Washington, D.C.: U.S. Government Printing Office, 1952), pp. 28–29; Donald Bishop, *The Roosevelt-Litvinov Agreements: The American View* (Syracuse, N.Y.: Syracuse University Press, 1965); Robert Browder, *The Origins of Soviet-American Diplomacy* (Princeton, N.J.: Princeton University Press, 1953), p. 150; *Daily Worker,* November 21, 1933, p. 6.

41. Beatrice Farnsworth, *William C. Bullitt and the Soviet Union* (Bloomington: Indiana University Press, 1967), contains an account of Bullitt's early life and behavior in Russia.

42. *Foreign Relations of the U.S.,* pp. 132–134, 220–223; Peggy Dennis, *Autobiography of an American Communist* (Westport, Conn.: Lawrence Hill, 1977), p. 86. The Dennis's son grew up a Soviet citizen.

43. *Foreign Relations of the United States,* pp. 221–222, 244–254, 262–264. The YCI's main resolution, published in the *Daily Worker,* December 18, 1935, p. 8, referred to America only briefly.

44. *Outline History of the Communist International,* p. 403. Curiously, Browder later insisted that Eisler was "just a stray German who wasn't wanted by his own Party and who was looking for a haven to make himself useful." According to Browder, by pretending to be a Comintern "rep," Eisler got more respect from gullible Communists than he deserved. See Browder interview, Columbia Oral History Project, p. 452, and Earl Browder, "Addendum to the Memorandum 'Relations Between the Comintern and the American Party,'" in Draper Papers, Box 2, Folder 8. On the other hand, before leaving Europe Eisler told his sister that he was going to America for the Comintern. See *Hearings on Gerhart Eisler,* House Committee on Un-American Activities, 80th Congress, February 6, 1947. Frank Meyer later testified that "it was common, sort of semi-public information" that Eisler was a Comintern rep. *Brownell* v. *Communist Party,* Hearings Before the Subversive Activities Control Board, p. 5592. Alexander Bittelman recalled that he, as a Party leader, always assumed that Eisler

represented the Comintern. Alexander Bittelman interview with Theodore Draper, Draper Papers, Box 3, Folder 18.

On Eisler's activities here, see Browder, Columbia Oral History Project, pp. 270–271; and E. Edwards, "For an Intensive Struggle Against Right Opportunism," *Communist*, November 1933, pp. 1096–1107. See U.S. Senate, Committee on the Judiciary, *Strategy and Tactics of World Communism*, Part 17, 89th Congress, 2nd Session, pp. 1596–1597, for the testimony of ex-*Daily Worker* editor James Glaser (Casey); and *Brownell* v. *Communist Party*, pp. 1498–1509, for Zack's account of Eisler's role in his troubles. Browder also later blamed Eisler for fomenting the Madison Square Garden riot of 1934; Earl Browder interview with Theodore Draper, June 23, 1955. Draper Papers, Box 2, Folder 5. During World War II, Eisler returned to New York as a refugee and quietly worked for the Party. Denounced as an important Soviet link to the CPUSA, he fled the country in 1949 while under indictment and settled in East Germany.

45. *Daily Worker*, June 30, 1938, pp. 1–4; *Investigation of Un-American Propaganda Activities*, Special Committee on Un-American Activities, House of Representatives, 76th Congress, 1st Session, 1939, Vol. 9, pp. 5334, 5337, 5345, 5417.

46. Earl Browder, "The Communists in the People's Front," *Communist*, July 1937, p. 599; Politburo Minutes, March 23, 1939, Draper Papers, Box 1, Folder 60; William Foster, "Political Leadership and Party Building," *Communist*, July 1937, p. 633; William Foster, "The Congress of the Communist Party of France," *Communist*, February 1938, p. 121. Harry Pollitt, in "The Ninth Congress of the C.P. of France—Its International Importance," *International Press Correspondence*, January 8, 1938, p. 18, noted that the actions of the French had "a very great importance for Communist Parties all over the world, but we think for Britain and America especially."

Chapter 11

1. Earl Browder, "The United Front—The Key to Our New Tactical Orientation," *Communist*, December 1935, p. 1093; Georgi Dimitroff, "The Threat of Fascism in the United States," *Communist*, October 1935, p. 908.

2. *Daily Worker*, January 1, 1936, p. 8; January 28, p. 2; February 1, pp. 1, 2; February 2, p. 5; March 15, p. 5. Browder later claimed that he already knew a Farmer-Labor party was not viable and was merely trying to jostle the Party leadership, forcing it to confront the alternatives. There is no independent evidence to support this assertion. See Earl Browder interview with Theodore Draper, June 2, 1953, Draper Papers, Box 2, Folder 3.

3. *Daily Worker*, March 16, 1934, p. 4; August 27, p. 3; February 16, 1935, p. 7. Earl Browder interview with Theodore Draper, June 23, 1955, Draper Papers, Box 2, Folder 5. Browder was not precise about the date of his conversation with Olson. In this interview he remembered that Olson told him he had just learned he had stomach cancer and was dying, which would put it in early 1936. In another interview on October 10, 1956, Browder dated the meeting as being just prior to Olson's late December 1935 appointment of Elmer Benson to the U.S. Senate. Browder was in Minneapolis on October 18 to talk about "The Farmer-Labor Party and the United Front Against War and Fascism." See *United Action*, October 1935; and George Mayer, *The Political Career of Floyd B. Olson* (Minneapolis: University of Minnesota Press, 1951), pp. 295–296.

4. Foster, "Fascist Tendencies in the United States," *Communist*, October 1935, p. 901. Browder, "The United Front," p. 1093. *Daily Worker*, April 3, 1936, p. 8; January 1, p. 8; February 9, p. 5.

5. David Bennett, *Demagogues in the Depression: American Radicals and the Union Party, 1932–1936* (New Brunswick, N.J.: Rutgers University Press, 1969), pp. 113–144, 147–184; Charles Tull, *Father Coughlin and the New Deal* (Syracuse, N.Y.: Syracuse University Press, 1965).

6. F. Brown, "Toward the Study of Fascization in the United States," *Communist*, June 1935, p. 567. *Daily Worker*, January 26, 1935, p. 7; November 5, p. 7. Alexander Bittelman, *The Townsend Plan: What It Is and What It Isn't* (New York: Workers Library Publishers,

1936), pp. 21–22; *Daily Worker,* January 19, 1936, p. 2; Alexander Bittelman, *How to Win Social Justice: Can Coughlin and Lemke Do It?* (New York: Workers Library Publishers, 1936), pp. 15, 17, 20, 21.

7. Browder interviews with Draper, June 2, 1953, June 23, 1955; Sam Darcy interview with Theodore Draper, May 15, 1957. Draper Papers, Box 3, Folder 53. Alexander Bittelman, in his unpublished autobiography, claimed that he first became convinced that the Party should endorse Roosevelt in March or April of 1936 and was able, over Browder's and Foster's protests, to convince the Politburo. When it was decided to aid Roosevelt, the policy was to be not to directly endorse him for fear of a backlash. Alexander Bittelman, unpublished autobiography, Tamiment Library; Alexander Bittelman interview with Theodore Draper, January 20, 1969, Draper Papers, Box 3, Folder 19. Bittelman's own writings from the period are filled, however, with calls for a Farmer-Labor party, charges that Roosevelt was moving to the right, and complaints about labor support of FDR. Not only is there contrary evidence of how the Party's tactics in 1936 were determined, but Bittelman's own writings belie his ex post facto claim that he was a Roosevelt enthusiast. See Bittelman, *The Townsend Plan,* p. 45, and Alexander Bittelman, "Review of the Month," *Communist,* February 1936, p. 102; April, pp. 298, 302; June, p. 489.

8. The *Daily Worker* announced on March 22, 1936, p. 5, that Browder's column was being discontinued for the present "due to unavoidable circumstances." The details are taken from Browder's interviews with Draper, June 2, 1953, and June 23, 1955; from a letter to Draper, October 13, 1957, in Draper Papers, Box 2, Folder 13; and from Darcy's interview with Draper, May 15, 1957. There are several small disagreements between the two accounts, but they are in accord on the major questions. There is a disagreement about whether Gene Dennis was present at the meeting. Browder told Draper that Dennis was already in Moscow when he and Foster arrived. Dennis's wife, Peggy, has written that she and her husband came back to America from their Comintern service in late January 1936. *Autobiography of an American Communist* (Westport, Conn.: Lawrence Hill, 1977), pp. 86–88. According to the *Daily Worker,* Dennis was district organizer in Wisconsin in mid-March. *Daily Worker,* March 16, 1936, p. 2. Did he return to Moscow just for this meeting? It seems unlikely that Dennis, not yet a national Party leader, would have been chosen to go. Darcy denied that Dennis was present. Sam Darcy to Harvey Klehr, June 22, 1980.

9. *Daily Worker,* April 27, 1936, p. 8; May 16, p. 8. *New Masses,* April 21, 1936, pp. 11–12.

10. Alexander Bittelman, "Review of the Month," *Communist,* June 1936, p. 484; *Sunday Worker,* May 24, 1936, pp. 9–10.

11. Browder interview with Draper, June 23, 1955. *Daily Worker,* May 8, 1936, p. 1; June 4, p. 2; June 1, p. 1. J. B. S. Hardman felt that the convention, under Communist inspiration, was about to launch a third-party movement until he protested and offered a resolution that had the effect of putting off any Farmer-Labor party indefinitely. J. B. S. Hardman interview with Theodore Draper, October 30, 1953, Draper Papers, Box 3, Folder 104. Browder, on the other hand, remembered telling Hardman that the Farmer-Labor movement could stay united only on the basis of support for Roosevelt. Browder interview with Draper, June 23, 1955.

12. *New Masses,* July 7, 1936, p. 9; *Daily Worker,* June 29, 1936, p. 2. Foster somewhat spoiled the decidedly nonrevolutionary atmosphere with a speech declaring: "I say our party will stand at the head of the government, and the government will be a soviet government."

13. Earl Browder, *The People's Front* (New York: International Publishers, 1936), p. 24.

14. *Daily Worker,* June 16, 1936, pp. 5–6. Also reprinted in *Resolutions of the Ninth Convention of the Communist Party* (New York: Workers Library Publishers, 1936).

15. *Daily Worker,* June 15, 1936, p. 5; Earl Browder, *Talks to Americans* (New York: Workers Library Publishers, 1936), p. 5; Earl Browder, *Democracy or Fascism* (New York: Workers Library Publishers, 1936), pp. 12, 17; *Sunday Worker,* September 27, 1936, p. 5; *Daily Worker,* August 8, 1936, p. 5.

16. *Daily Worker,* September 1, 1936, p. 5; September 8, p. 5. Earl Browder, "The Party of Lenin and the People's Front," *Communist,* February 1936, p. 129. Earl Browder, "Results of the Elections," *Communist,* January 1937, p. 25.

17. Arthur Schlesinger, Jr., *The Politics of Upheaval: 1935–1936* (Boston: Houghton Mifflin, 1966), pp. 518, 519, 553.

18. A competing Chicago newspaper, sensing an opportunity to embarrass the *Tribune*, offered a $5,000 contribution to charity if the story could be verified. The *New Masses* called it "A Safe $5000 Offer." *New Masses*, September 22, 1936, p. 20. According to an acquaintance, Day was the brother of *Catholic Worker* activist Dorothy Day. He broadcast from Germany during the last year of World War II and was imprisoned by the Americans for nine months as a suspected Nazi collaborator before being released. See *New York Times*, December 4, 1980, p. 30; December 24, 1946, p. 9. Earl Browder, *Hearst's Secret Documents in Full* (New York: Workers Library Publishers, 1936), p. 3.

19. Alexander Bittelman, "Review of the Month," *Communist*, June 1936, pp. 491–492.

20. Alexander Bittelman, "Review of the Month," *Communist*, June 1936, pp. 491–492; Browder, *Democracy or Fascism*, p. 14. *Daily Worker*, July 7, 1936, p. 3. *New York Times*, October 22, 1936, p. 12. *Daily Worker*, October 23, 1936, p. 1; October 26, p. 5.

21. George Charney, *A Long Journey* (Chicago: Quadrangle Books, 1968), p. 75; *New York Times*, August 30, 1936, p. 13; James Casey, *The Crisis in the Communist Party* (New York: Three Arrows Press, 1937). Casey's real name was James Glaser.

22. *Congressional Quarterly's Guide to U.S. Elections* (Washington, D.C.: Congressional Quarterly, 1975), pp. 290, 304, 783; *Daily Worker*, December 14, 1936, pp. 3–6.

23. Israel Amter, "The Elections in New York," *Communist*, December 1936, pp. 1150–1151; *Daily Worker*, December 14, 1936, pp. 3–6.

24. *Daily Worker*, July 14, 1936, p. 1; August 27, p. 1; September 12, p. 7; October 9, pp. 7–8. Browder was jailed for twenty-five hours. His case was then dismissed.

25. Earl Browder, "The Results of the Elections on the People's Front," *Communist*, January 1937, p. 23.

26. Ibid., pp. 23–29.

27. Ibid.

28. *Daily Worker*, January 7, 1937, p. 1; January 27, p. 6; April 21, p. 1; May 4, p. 1; May 17, p. 6. Alexander Bittelman, "Review of the Month," *Communist*, March 1937, p. 202.

29. Alexander Bittelman, "Review of the Month," *Communist*, April 1937, p. 295; Clarence Hathaway, "The People vs. the Supreme Court," *Communist*, April 1937, p. 311.

30. Earl Browder, "The Communists in the People's Front," *Communist*, July 1937, pp. 594–603.

31. Ibid.

32. Ibid.

33. "Building the Party in the Struggle for Proletarian Unity and the People's Front," *Communist*, August 1937, p. 737.

34. William Foster, "Political Leadership and Party Building," *Communist*, July 1937, p. 640; Alexander Bittelman, "Review of the Month," *Communist*, September 1937, p. 780; Browder, "Communists in the People's Front," p. 602.

35. Quoted in Adam Ulam, *Expansion and Coexistence: The History of Soviet Foreign Policy 1917–1967* (New York: Frederick Praeger, 1965), p. 228.

36. M. Ercoli, *The Fight for Peace* (New York: Workers Library Publishers, 1935), pp. 16, 56, 60–61, 91; *Resolutions: Seventh Congress of the Communist International* (New York: Workers Library Publishers, 1935), pp. 45–48.

37. Kermit McKenzie, in *Comintern and World Revolution 1928–1943* (New York: Columbia University Press, 1964), p. 156, implies that the congress gave its imprimatur to all such wars. But see Ercoli, *Fight for Peace*, p. 90. Early in May 1936, Dimitroff did concede that Communists might abstain on parliamentary votes on purely defensive measures, like building frontier fortifications, and even support actions like building gas shelters to protect civilians. Early in 1937, French Communists voted with their Popular Front partners to increase the army and air force and boost military spending. See Georgi Dimitroff, "The United Front of Struggle for Peace," *International Press Correspondence*, May 16, 1936, p. 613; and J. Berlioz, "The Defense of French Democracy," *International Press Correspondence*, February 13, 1937, p. 186.

38. *Daily Worker*, November 30, 1935, p. 7; March 28, 1933, p. 1. *Party Organizer*, April 1936, p. 4.

39. Alexander Bittelman, "Review of the Month," *Communist*, February 1936, pp. 110, 113; June, p. 494.

40. Bittelman, "Review," June 1936, p. 495; Browder interviews with Draper, June 23, 1955, and October 10, 1955. In the first interview Browder dated the slogan as having been

coined in 1934. It was prominently featured in the Party press in March 1936. See *Daily Worker*, March 25, 1936, p. 8; March 26, p. 1. Browder claimed that he was attacked in the Comintern for his concession to isolationism. Alexander Bittelman, "Review of the Month," *Communist*, February 1937, p. 106; Harrison George, "The War Threat and the World Peace Congress," *Communist*, August 1936, p. 693.

41. The most extensive discussion of the liberal views of Roosevelt's foreign policy is in the oft-times quirky but detailed James J. Martin, *American Liberalism and World Politics, 1931-1941* (New York: Devin-Adair, 1964), 2 vol. See Vol. 2, pp. 863–871, for reaction to the Chicago speech.

42. *Daily Worker*, October 6, 1937, p. 1; Earl Browder, "For a Common Front Against the War-Makers," *Communist*, November 1937, p. 1043.

43. Earl Browder, "Twenty Years of Soviet Power," *Communist*, November 1937, p. 993; Alexander Bittelman, "Review of the Month," ibid., pp. 979–980; Earl Browder, "The People's Front Moves Forward," *Communist*, December 1937, p. 1086.

Chapter 12

1. Clarence Hathaway, "The 1938 Elections and Our Tasks," *Communist*, March 1938, p. 216; Gene Dennis, "Some Questions Concerning the Democratic Front," *Communist*, June 1938, p. 535. Browder had stopped off in Spain on the way back from Moscow to visit the Americans who were fighting in the International Brigades and gotten a severe case of flu; Earl Browder, *Report to the 10th Convention of the CPUSA* (New York: Workers Library Publishers), p. 88. Browder's article appeared in *Pravda*, April 18, 1938, and was reprinted in the *Daily Worker*, April 19, 1938, p. 6.

2. "Lenin and Collective Security," *Communist*, January 1938, p. 20; Margaret Cowl, "Woman's Place in the People's Front," ibid. pp. 46–53; James W. Ford and George E. Blake, "Building the People's Front in Harlem," *Communist*, February, 1938, pp. 158–168; Jerry Coleman, "Farmers Advance in the Movement for the People's Front," ibid., pp. 169–176; Alexander Bittelman, "Review of the Month", *Communist*, March 1938, p. 205; James Ford, "Rally the Negro Masses for the Democratic Front," ibid., pp. 266–271; V. J. Jerome, "Charting the Course of the People's Front," *Communist*, April 1938, pp. 339–350; William Foster, "World Fascism and War," ibid., pp. 332, 333.

3. Alexander Bittelman, "A Historic View of the Struggle for Democracy," *Communist*, August 1938, p. 711; Dennis, "Some Questions," p. 535; Hathaway, "The 1938 Elections," p. 216.

4. "Draft Convention Resolutions," *Communist*, April 1938, p. 355.

5. *Daily Worker*, May 11, 1938, pp. 5–6.

6. Bittelman, "A Historic View," p. 720. Earl Browder, in "Greeting to the Soviet Union," *Communist*, November 1938, p. 979, employed a curious amalgam, referring to a "democratic people's front." Shortly after the Nazi-Soviet Pact was signed, Georgi Dimitroff sent a secret message to Browder noting that the new world situation "undermined the 'democratic front.' " Phillip Jaffe Papers, Emory University. R. Page Arnot, in "The Struggle to Establish a Democratic Peace Front in England," *Communist International*, June 1938, p. 541, suggested that a "wide democratic front of peace in Britain" should include Labor, Liberals, and even some Tories in opposition to the Chamberlain government, but this was apparently an isolated case. The Cuban Communists also used the concept.

7. *Daily Worker*, September 20, 1937, p. 9; Browder, *Report to the 10th Convention*, p. 88; *Daily Worker*, September 7, 1938, p. 3.

8. *Daily Worker*, November 15, 1938, p. 6; Browder, *Report to the 10th Convention*, pp. 90–94; James Ford, "Forging the Negro People's Sector of the Democratic Front," *Communist*, July 1938, p. 616.

9. Gene Dennis and Gil Green, "Notes on the Defense of American Democracy," *Communist*, May 1938, p. 418; Earl Browder, "The Results of the Elections and the People's Front," *Communist*, January 1937, pp. 47–49.

10. Dennis, "Some Questions," p. 534; *Daily Worker*, September 20, 1937, p. 9.

11. Alexander Bittelman, "Some Problems Before the Tenth Convention of the Com-

munist Party," *Communist*, July 1938, p. 628; William Foster, "Political Leadership and Party Building," *Communist*, July 1937, p. 641.

12. Jack Stachel, "Build the Party for Peace, Democracy and Socialism," *Communist*, March 1938, p. 237. *Daily Worker*, May 20, 1938, p. 3; June 7, p. 7.

13. Berger attended a congress of the American League Against War and Fascism in 1934. *Daily Worker*, October 1, 1934, p. 1. After visiting Russia, she wrote that "until we saw Russia some of us believed that no good could come of dictatorship. . . . Now that we have seen Russia we know that there are dictatorships and dictatorships." *New Masses*, November 5, 1935, p. 18. Not everyone was enamored of Dennis's accomplishments in Wisconsin. Sam Darcy charged he did little. The LaFollettes stayed aloof from the Party. Sam Darcy interview with Harvey Klehr, March 24, 1979.

14. Earl Browder interviews with Theodore Draper, June 23, 1955, and October 10, 1955, Draper Papers, Box 2, Folders 5, 8.

15. In an interview with Draper, October 10, 1955, Browder recalled that early in 1939, after the fall of the Spanish Republic, Foster suggested that the deteriorating world situation required a new Party leadership.

16. Political Committee Minutes, March 23, 1939, Draper Papers Box 1, Folder 60; Institute of Marxism-Leninism, Central Committee of the C.P.S.U., *Outline History of the Communist International* (Moscow: Progress Publishers, 1971), p. 422. The Secretariat, however, supported the American Party's efforts "to draw into the Popular Front the left elements of the Democratic Party." Browder himself mistakenly denied that the Farmer-Labor policy had even been discussed at this meeting. Browder interview with Draper, October 10, 1955. Browder claimed that during this visit the major issue was his formulation of the idea of a "sit-down strike of capital." The 1937 recession had not yet hit, however, and the phrase was not an issue until November. It was discussed in Moscow in January 1938.

17. William Foster, "Political Leadership and Party Building," *Communist*, July 1937, pp. 633, 636, 642, 644. Foster did manage to swallow the People's Front despite his past. He produced a *Communist* article that desperately rummaged in American history for evidence that "the People's Front is not an artificial importation from Moscow. It has a long and legitimate American parentage." Foster dug up examples of coalitions among farmers, workers, and the middle class ranging from the William Jennings Bryan campaign of the 1890s to the Farmer-Labor movement of the early 1920s and the LaFollette campaign of 1924. He neglected to mention that the Communists had opposed the latter two and were saved from a perfect record only because they had not yet come into existence in 1896. Foster even repudiated his own Presidential campaign of 1932, noting that "in the election campaigns of 1932 and 1936 we see the same class forces of workers, petty bourgeoisie and farmers" in a People's Front behind Roosevelt. William Foster, "American Origins of the People's Front," *Communist*, December 1937, p. 1105.

18. William Foster, "The Congress of the Communist Party of France," *Communist*, February 1938, p. 121. The *Sunday Worker*, January 30, 1938, p. 11, indicates Foster's presence in Moscow. Dennis's wife discusses the visit in Peggy Dennis, *Autobiography of an American Communist* (Westport, Conn.: Lawrence Hill, 1977), pp. 120–121. Browder mentions the trip in the *Daily Worker*, February 22, 1938, p. 6.

19. The least trustworthy account is that issued by the Soviet Union. The official Soviet version makes it sound as if the Comintern awarded victory to William Foster. While approving the concept of a Democratic Front against fascism, the ECCI also supposedly attacked "tailism" and "Browder's one-sided appraisal of the policy of the Roosevelt Government." Georgi Dimitroff is quoted as agreeing with limited support for Roosevelt but noting it was "wrong to create an apology of Roosevelt." Since the Party's policy after January 1938 was, if anything, more enthusiastic about and less critical of the President, the only way to square this account with reality is to assume that Browder flouted Comintern instructions and that the entire leadership, including his avowed enemies, not only failed to protest but happily concurred. Such a scenario is so improbable that it hardly merits serious discussion. *Outline History*, p. 422.

A second version of the meetings comes from Peggy Dennis. In her account the two Party leaders spoke only for themselves and not for the Politburo, whose middle ground had been shaped by Gene Dennis before he left for Moscow in 1937. At one extreme stood Browder: he "too often and too uncritically attributed to Roosevelt and the top labor leadership the leading role in the people's coalitions." At the other extreme was Foster, who "shrugged off as inconsequential the new kind of vanguard role we were exercising inside the mainstream." Supposedly accepting Gene Dennis's view that Communists should not surrender leadership in progressive coalitions or cease criticism of FDR, while they should meanwhile take care not to jeopardize cooperation, the Comintern decided to send him home as a "balance" in the national leadership. His wife's account of his role in Moscow in January 1938 suffers from a belated effort to distance Dennis from Browder, whose later disgrace required good Communists to search for occasions when they had first opposed his dangerous revisionism. Dennis, *Autobiography of an American Communist*, pp. 122–125.

Still a third version has been told by Browder, who recalled only Bittelman, Darcy, and Foster being unhappy about his position. The Comintern, Browder reported, had endorsed him and harshly criticized Foster. Browder's memory served him correctly. See Browder interview with Draper, October 10, 1955.

20. Political Committee Minutes, March 23, 1939, pp. 1–3, 8–9, in Draper Papers, Box 1, Folder 60.

21. In 1934 the *Daily Worker* had not thought Dunne's testimony in error, reprinting it verbatim through a full week. See, for example, *Daily Worker*, May 31, 1934, p. 4. See also Earl Browder interview with Theodore Draper, October 12, 1955, Draper Papers, Box 2, Folder 9; William Dunne FBI File 61–130; *Investigation of Un-American Propaganda Activities in the United States*, Special Committee on Un-American Activities, House of Representatives, 76th Congress, 1st Session, 1939, Vol. 7, p. 4395. The *Daily Worker*, September 27, 1946, p. 4, when announcing Dunne's expulsion from the Party, claimed that "in 1934, because of personal conduct unbecoming a member of our Party, and because of his complete irresponsibility, he was removed from leadership. During the last eight–ten years, Dunne had no assignment."

22. Darcy's story is taken from portions of his unpublished autobiography. The quotation is found on p. 528.

23. Rexford Tugwell, *The Democratic Roosevelt* (Garden City, N.Y.: Doubleday, 1957), pp. 444–446; Basil Rauch, *The History of the New Deal 1933–1938* (New York: Creative Age Press, 1944), pp. 294–298.

24. Eugen Varga, "A New Economic Crisis in the U.S.A.," *International Press Correspondence*, December 18, 1937, p. 1374.

25. Earl Browder, "The People's Front Moves Forward," *Communist*, December 1937, pp. 1088–1089. An expurgated account was republished as Earl Browder, "The Economic and Political Situation in the USA," *International Press Correspondence*, December 24, 1937, p. 1385.

26. The details of the argument in the Comintern are from Browder interview with Draper, October 10, 1955; Eugen Varga, "Economy and Economic Policy in the Second Half of 1937," *International Press Correspondence*, March 11, 1938, p. 203; and Browder, *Report to the 10th Convention*, p. 43.

27. On the International Brigades, see Verle Johnston, *Legions of Babel: The International Brigades in the Spanish Civil War* (University Park: Pennsylvania State University Press, 1967). There are descriptions of the Americans in Cecil Eby, *Between the Bullet and the Lie* (New York: Holt, Rinehart & Winston, 1969), and Robert Rosenstone, *Crusade of the Left: The Lincoln Battalion in the Spanish Civil War* (New York: Pegasus, 1969). There is no definitive list of Americans who fought in Spain. Edwin Rolfe, the battalion's historian, gives a figure of 2,800 in *The Lincoln Battalion* (New York: Haskell House, 1974), p. 9. Robert Rosenstone calculates that 3,000 joined (*Crusade of the Left*, p. 98). A more recent account of the battalion claims there were 3,300 Americans in Spain. Joe Brandt (ed.), *Black Americans in the Spanish People's War Against Fascism 1936–1939* (New York: no date or publisher), p. 4. Other useful works are Hugh Lovin, *The American Communist Party and the Spanish Civil War, 1936–1939* (unpublished doctoral dissertation, University of Washington, 1963), and Albert Prago, "Jews in the International Brigades," *Jewish Currents*, February 1979, pp. 15–21; March 1979, pp. 6–9, 24–27. Earl Browder, in "The Communists in the People's Front," *Communist*, July 1937, p. 613, gives the 60 percent figure. He was actually referring only to those in the Abraham Lincoln Battalion, but there is no reason to think that the percentages in other units would have varied.

28. Steve Nelson, *The Volunteers* (New York: Masses and Mainstream, 1953); Sandor Voros, *American Commissar* (Philadelphia: Chilton Company, 1961); John Gates, *The Story of an American Communist* (New York: Thomas Nelson and Sons, 1958). Rosenstone, in

Crusade of the Left, pp. 373–375, estimates that at least four of the eight were punished for desertion or rape. Eby, in *Between the Bullet and the Lie*, pp. 270–272, gives the higher figure. Philip Jaffe, in *The Rise and Fall of American Communism* (New York: Horizon Press, 1975), pp. 175–178, insists that Browder told him that he had learned that Merriman and Doran, two of the battalion's leaders, had been executed on orders from André Marty. This story seems highly fanciful, since the two vanished during a helter-skelter retreat.

29. Browder, *Report to the 10th Convention*, pp. 11–12; *Daily Worker*, May 14, 1939, p. 2.

30. *Sunday Worker*, March 26, 1939, p. 1. *Daily Worker*, May 27, 1938, p. 6; July 13, 1937, p. 2. *Sunday Worker Magazine*, June 26, 1938, p. 1. *Daily Worker*, May 14, 1938, p. 1.

31. *Daily Worker*, November 30, 1938, p. 3; February 6, 1939, p. 6. Earl Browder, *Social and National Security* (New York: Workers Library Publishers, 1938), pp. 19, 38–40.

32. Carl Reeve, "Lovestoneism—Twin of Fascist-Trotskyism," *Communist*, August 1938, pp. 736, 741; Earl Browder, "Lessons of the Moscow Trials," *Communist*, April 1938, p. 313; Roy Hudson, "The Charter of Party Democracy," *Communist*, August 1938, pp. 709–710.

33. *Daily Worker*, January 16, 1938, p. 6. Alexander Bittelman, "Review of the Month," *Communist*, July 1938, pp. 579, 581. *Daily Worker*, January 6, 1939, p. 6; January 7, p. 5.

34. *Daily Worker*, March 25, 1930, p. 1; February 25, p. 1; April 28, 1934, p. 7; June 15, 1935, p. 7. For a full view of the attitude toward religion, see Bennett Stevens (Dr. Bernhard Stern), *The Church and the Workers* (New York: International Publishers, 1932).

35. *Outline History*, p. 414. *Sunday Worker*, June 22, 1938, p. 8. *Daily Worker*, March 17, 1938, p. 5; May 9, pp. 1, 4; May 30, p. 6; May 12, p. 6. Browder, *Report to the 10th Convention*, p. 54.

36. *Daily Worker*, May 31, 1938, p. 5; May 27, pp. 1, 5, 7; May 28, p. 1. *New York Times*, May 27, 1938, p. 3.

Chapter 13

1. Theodore Draper, *American Communism and Soviet Russia* (New York: Viking Press, 1960), p. 296. *Daily Worker*, April 8, 1931, p. 1; July 18, 1933, p. 1; January 5, p. 3; April 13, 1935, p. 5; June 15, p. 8; July 1, p. 8; September 3, p. 6; September 16, p. 8; October 13, 1934, p. 8. William Foster, "Fascist Tendencies in the United States," *Communist*, October 1935, p. 897. Earl Browder, "Recent Political Developments and Some Problems of the United Front," *Communist*, July 1935, pp. 611–612.

2. Melvyn Dubofsky and Warren VanTine, *John L. Lewis: A Biography* (New York: Quadrangle Books, 1977), pp. 85, 100, 128; Len DeCaux, *Labor Radical* (Boston: Beacon Press, 1970), p. 208.

3. Irving Bernstein, *The Turbulent Years: A History of the American Worker 1933–1941* (Boston: Houghton Mifflin, 1970), pp. 386–402.

4. William Foster, *History of the CPUSA* (New York: International Publishers, 1952), p. 304; "Memo to F. Brown from Weinstock," Draper Papers, Box 1, Folder 41; Morris Childs, "Our Tasks in the Light of Changed Conditions," *Communist*, April 1935, pp. 304–305; *Daily Worker*, June 27, 1936, p. 5; Morris Childs, "Forging Unity Against Reaction in Illinois," *Communist*, August 1936, p. 769; *Sunday Worker*, March 15, 1936, Section 2, p. 5; Earl Browder, "For Working Class Unity! For a Workers' and Farmers' Labor Party!," *Communist* September 1935, p. 794. At the congress, Georgi Dimitroff proclaimed support for "the re-establishment of trade-union unity in each country." *Working Clr Unity—Bulwark Against Fascism* (New York: Workers Library Publishers, 1935), p. 63.

5. Earl Browder interview with William Goldsmith, February 1, 1956, Bell Papers, Box 8, Closed Section; Jack Stachel, "The 55th Convention of the A.F. of L.," *Communist*, November 1935, p. 1028. Stachel was referring to an amendment adopted at the convention barring Communist-led unions from state and city labor federations.

6. *Daily Worker*, November 12, 1935, p. 8; November 11, p. 1; Earl Browder interview with Theodore Draper, June 23, 1955, Draper Papers, Box 2, Folder 5.

7. *Daily Worker*, November 25, 1935, p. 8; November 26, p. 8; November 28, p. 5.

8. *Daily Worker*, February 12, 1936, pp. 1–2; November 26, pp. 1, 6. Political Committee Minutes, March 23, 1939, Draper Papers, Box 1, Folder 60.

9. *Daily Worker*, October 16, 1935, pp. 1, 8.

10. Gorman's girlfriend and future wife, Mary Bell, was also a Party member. Earl Browder interview with Daniel Bell, February 1956, Bell Papers, Box 18, Closed Section; *Testimony of Paul Crouch*, House Committee on Un-American Activities, 81st Congress, pp. 210–211; *Labor Fact Book III* (New York: International Publishers, 1936), pp. 152–153; Jack Stachel, "The 55th Convention," pp. 1020, 1031. Once they had fully embraced Lewis, the Communists did not hesitate to abandon Gorman. When Sidney Hillman elbowed him aside in the TWOC, the CPUSA made no protest. *Daily Worker*, December 15, 1938, p. 1.

11. Quoted in Bernstein, *The Turbulent Years*, p. 783.

12. *Daily Worker*, October 28, 1935, pp. 1, 6; Browder interview with Goldsmith, February 1, 1956; Browder interview with Draper, June 23, 1955. John Brophy, in his *A Miner's Life* (Madison: University of Wisconsin Press, 1964) and in an interview with William Goldsmith, was less than candid about his ties to the Party. He delicately pretended that he was unaware of who his allies were in the 1920s and never mentioned his meeting with Browder in the 1930s. Minutes of Party meetings from the 1920s demonstrate conclusively just how closely he was involved. See Party minutes presented to the Dies Committee by Ben Gitlow in *Investigation of Un-American Propaganda Activities*, Special Committee on Un-American Activities, House of Representatives, 76th Congress, 1st Session, 1939, Vol. 7, pp. 4724–4727.

13. William Weinstone, "Labor Radical: An Insider's Story of the CIO," *Political Affairs*, May 1971, p. 42; Brophy, *A Miner's Life*, p. 258; DeCaux, *Labor Radical*, pp. ix, 177, 220–221.

14. Lee Pressman, Oral History Interview, Columbia University; "Testimony" in House Committee on Un-American Activities, *Hearings Regarding Communism in the United States Government*, 88th Congress, 2nd Session, p. 2893.

15. *Daily Worker*, November 29, 1935, p. 6; Foster, *History of the CPUSA*, p. 349; *Investigation of Un-American Propaganda*, Vol. 1, p. 237; "Memorandum," John Frey Papers, Library of Congress, which lists the Party members; John Willamson, *Dangerous Scot* (New York: International Publishers, 1969), p. 125.

16. See Powers' testimony in *Investigation of Un-American Propaganda Activities*, Vol. 12, pp. 7421–7451. Additional details are in Vol. 17, pp. 10357–10358. Also see *Steel Labor*, October 1973, for Powers' obituary and George Powers, *Cradle of Steel Unionism: Monongahela Valley, Pa.* (East Chicago, Ind.: Figueroa Printers, 1972).

17. Biographical details about Hall come from an FBI Press Release, July 5, 1951, and Peggy Dennis, *Autobiography of an American Communist* (Westport, Conn.: Lawrence Hill, 1977), pp. 236–239. The Dies Committee heard testimony from the adjutant of the National Guard unit sent into Warren, an ex-speaker of the Ohio House of Representatives, that Hall had been identified by three other men. *Investigation of Un-American Propaganda Activities*, Vol. 3, pp. 2095–2116. The LaFollette Committee heard from the assistant prosecutor, who was less enthusiastic about the case against Hall. U.S. Senate, Subcommittee of the Committee on Education and Labor, *Hearings Pursuant to Sen. Res. 266, Violations of Free Speech and Rights of Labor*, Vol. 31, pp. 12809, 12988.

18. Jacob Spolansky, *The Communist Trail in America* (New York: Macmillan, 1951), pp. 59–61; *Party Organizer*, September 1936, pp. 13, 15; *Daily Worker*, October 26, 1936, p. 1; Clint Golden interview, October 26, 1955, Bell Papers; Foster, *History of the CPUSA*, p. 349.

19. See Sidney Fine, *Sit-Down* (Ann Arbor: University of Michigan Press, 1969), for an account of the strike. William Weinstone, "Labor Radical—An Insider's Story of the CIO," *Political Affairs*, May 1971, p. 45; Roger Keeran, *The Communist Party and the Auto Workers Unions* (Bloomington: Indiana University Press, 1980), pp. 150, 154, 167; Earl Latham, *The Communist Controversy in Washington: From the New Deal to McCarthy* (Cambridge, Mass.: Harvard University Press, 1966), pp. 109–110; Foster, *History of the CPUSA*, p. 352.

20. Keeran, *The Communist Party and the Auto Workers Unions*, pp. 160–161; Fine, *Sit-Down*, p. 221.

21. *Investigation of Un-American Propaganda Activities*, Vol. 4, pp. 3072–3080; *Daily Worker*, March 21, 1934, p. 5; Julius Emspak, Oral History Interview, Columbia University; Louis Budenz, *Men Without Faces: The Communist Conspiracy in the U.S.A.* (New York: Harper & Brothers, 1948), p. 57. See "The Yaleman and the Communist," *Fortune*, November 1943, pp. 146–148, 212–221, which discusses the cooperative labor-management relations between Sentner and future Senator Stuart Symington, then an executive with the

Emerson Electronic Manufacturing Company; Max Kampleman, *The Communist Party vs. the CIO: A Study in Power Politics* (New York: Frederick Praeger, 1957), pp. 127–128; and Sander Voros, *American Commissar* (Philadelphia: Chilton Books, 1961), p. 187.

22. *Party Organizer*, August 1933, p. 25; March 1935, p. 23. "Control Tasks Adopted at Enlarged District Committee Meeting, March 8, 1936," reprinted in *Investigation of Un-American Propaganda Activities*, Appendix, Part V, p. 1698. This appendix, devoted to the TWU, reprints a wealth of Party material. *Party Organizer*, August 1937, p. 40.

23. *Investigation of Un-American Propaganda Activities*, Vol. 13, pp. 7879, 7802–7952; Vol. 2, pp. 1044, 1069, 1077. Kampleman, *The Communist Party vs. the CIO*, pp. 149, 155. For a good journalistic account of Quill, see L. H. Whittemore, *The Man Who Ran the Subways: The Story of Mike Quill* (New York: Holt, Rinehart & Winston, 1968).

24. *Daily Worker*, June 11, 1934, p. 1; *A Communist in a Workers' Paradise*, House Committee on Un-American Activities, 81st Congress, 1st Session, March 1, 4, 5, 1963. For an account of Santo's "redefection," see William Rusher, *Special Counsel: An Inside Report on the Senate Investigations into Communism* (New Rochelle, N.Y.: Arlington House, 1968), pp. 159–182.

25. *Subversive Control of the United Public Workers of America*, U.S. Senate, Committee on the Judiciary, 82nd Congress, 1st Session, 1952, pp. 17, 48–56, 58, 82–83; Kampleman, *The Communist Party vs. the CIO*, p. 193n.

26. Daniel Leab, *A Union of Individuals: The Formation of the American Newspaper Guild: 1933-1936* (New York: Columbia University Press, 1970), p. 222; Lewis Merrill interview with Theodore Draper, Draper Papers, Box 4, Folder 37; DeCaux, *Labor Radical*, p. 299; Kampleman, *The Communist Party vs. the CIO*, p. 172. Herbert Fuchs named Nelson as a member of his Party unit, composed of employees of the federal government. *Hearings on Investigation of Communist Infiltration of Government*, House Un-American Activities Committee, 84th Congress, 1st Session, pp. 2966—2967.

27. This information is derived from the FBI files on Marcel Scherer, 100-107137-97, p. 16, and 100-107137-45; and from *Investigation of Un-American Propaganda Activities: Report on the C.I.O. Political Action Committee*, Special Committee on Un-American Activities, House of Representatives, 78th Congress, 2d Session, p. 85.

28. Foster, *History of the CPUSA*, p. 354; Walter Galenson, *The CIO Challenge to the AFL* (Cambridge, Mass.: Harvard University Press, 1960), p. 390: *Daily Worker*, June 8, 1933, p. 4. For a detailed account of Party maneuvering in the Furniture Workers, see the testimony of Arthur McDowell, *Subversive Influences in Certain Labor Organizations*, U.S. Senate, Judiciary Committee, 83rd Congress, 1st and 2nd Sessions. Vernon Jensen, *Non-Ferrous Metal Industry Unionism 1932-1954* (Ithaca, N.Y.: Cornell University Press, 1954), p. 53; Reid Robinson interview with Theodore Draper, Draper Papers, Box 4, Folder 84. Eckert, who broke with the Party, testified before the CIO. See *Report of the Committee to Investigate Charges against the International Union of Mine, Mill and Smelter Workers*, cited in Kampleman, *The Communist Party vs. the CIO*, pp. 175-177.

29. Appearing before the Dies Committee in 1939, March denied he was a Communist. So did Henry Johnson. *Investigation of Un-American Propaganda Activities*, Executive Hearings, Vol. 1, pp. 317, 343. For the identification of March, see *Sunday Worker*, June 27, 1948, p. 11. Also see Galenson, *The CIO Challenge*, pp. 366, 374; Kampleman, *The Communist Party vs. the CIO*, p. 68; and Donald Henderson, "The Rural Masses and the Work of Our Party," *Communist*, September 1935, pp. 866–880.

30. Rathborne denied Party membership to the Dies Committee. See *Investigation of Un-American Propaganda Activities*, Vol. 13, p. 8123. For the accusations see ibid., Vol. 1, p. 609; and Kampleman, *The Communist Party vs. the CIO*, pp. 195–196. For earlier Party attacks on Rathborne's red-baiting, see *Daily Worker*, January 4, 1935, p. 4. On the NMU see *Investigation of Un-American Propaganda Activities*, Vol. 11, pp. 6458, 6477, 6589; 6611; Murray Kempton, *Part of Our Time: Some Ruins and Monuments of the Thirties* (New York: Delta Books, 1967), pp. 86–104; and Helen Lawrenson, *Whistling Girl* (New York: Doubleday, 1978). Foster later admitted that a majority of the NMU board members were Communists. Foster, *History of The CPUSA*, p. 353.

31. See *Investigation of Un-American Propaganda Activities*, Vol. 7, pp. 4578, 4711, where Ben Gitlow presented minutes of Political Committee meetings that apparently confirmed Hapgood's one-time affiliation; Kampleman, *The Communist Party vs. the CIO*, p. 96; and *Investigation of Un-American Propaganda Activities*, Vol. 14, pp. 8616, 8620, 8629, 8637.

Balint denied he was a Communist; ibid., p. 8637. Cheyfitz, returning from a year's work in Russia in 1935, attacked Fred Beal, of Gastonia fame, who had denounced living conditions there. "The only way to be loyal to the cause of labor," he announced, "is to be loyal to the Soviet regime." *Daily Worker,* July 9, 1935, p. 8.

32. *Proceedings of the First Constitutional Convention of the Congress of Industrial Organizations,* Draper Papers, Box 3, Folder 39; Fred Brown, "The Importance of the Present Recruiting Drive for the Future of Our Party," *Communist,* October 1937, p. 917; Earl Browder, "The Communists in the People's Front," *Communist,* July 1937, p. 609.

33. *Sunday Worker,* September 5, 1937, p. 7; Bernstein, *The Turbulent Years,* pp. 116–125; William Iverson, *The Communists and the Schools* (New York: Harcourt, Brace, 1959), pp. 104–106; Bella Dodd, *School of Darkness* (New York: P. J. Kennedy & Sons, 1954), p. 105.

34. Galenson, *The CIO Challenge,* pp. 32, 389.

35. *Daily Worker,* June 27, 1936, p. 5; John Williamson, "Party Mobilization in Ohio," *Communist,* March 1937, p. 256; *Party Organizer,* August 1937, p. 10; William Foster, "Political Leadership and Party Building," *Communist,* July 1937, p. 635.

36. Saul Alinsky, *John L. Lewis: An Unauthorized Biography* (New York: Vintage Books, 1970), p. 154.

37. *Party Organizer,* June 1938, pp. 3, 5; Jack Stachel, "Build the Party for Peace, Democracy & Socialism," *Communist,* March 1938, pp. 224–226; Robert Alperin, *Organization in the Communist Party, USA 1931–1938* (unpublished doctoral dissertation, Northwestern University, 1959), p. 53; Robinson interview with Draper; Merrill interview with Draper; *Investigation of Un-American Propaganda Activities,* Vol. 13, p. 7950; Kempton, *Part of Our Time,* p. 98.

38. Earl Browder interview with Daniel Bell, July 26, 1955, Bell Papers, Box 8, Closed Section.

39. Earl Browder interview with Theodore Draper, June 23, 1955; DeCaux, *Labor Radical,* p. 318; *Hearings Regarding Communism in the United States Government,* p. 2888; Merrill interview with Draper; Earl Browder interview with Daniel Bell and William Goldsmith, January 10, 1956, Bell Papers, Box 8, Closed Section.

40. Earl Browder, "Twenty Years of Soviet Power," *Communist,* November 1937, p. 993; Alexander Bittelman, "Review of the Month," *Communist,* December 1937, p. 1068; *New Masses,* September 20, 1938, p. 5.

41. Jack Hardy, *The Clothing Workers* (New York: International Publishers, 1935), p. 199; *Daily Worker,* November 20, 1935, p. 3.

42. *Daily Worker,* November 29, 1935, pp. 4–6; Bill Gebert, "The U.M.W.A. Convention," *Communist,* March 1936, p. 218; Bill Gebert, "The Coal Miners in Convention," *Communist,* March 1938, p. 279.

43. Earl Browder, "The United Front, the Key to Our New Tactical Orientation," *Communist,* December 1935, p. 1113; Gebert, "The U.M.W.A. Convention," p. 215; Gebert, "The Coal Miners," p. 279; *Daily Worker,* February 3, 1938, p. 6; Bert Cochran, *Labor and Communism: The Conflict That Shaped American Unions* (Princeton, N.J.: Princeton University Press, 1977), p. 145.

44. *Daily Worker,* February 5, 1938, p. 6.

45. Earl Browder interview with Theodore Draper, October 12, 1955, Draper Papers, Box 2, Folder 9. Leab, *A Union of Individuals,* pp. 267, 268. The standard biographies of Broun are curiously myopic about his relations with the Communists. Dale Kramer, in *Heywood Broun: A Biographical Portrait* (New York: Wyn Books, 1949), is silent about the Party. Richard O'Connor, in *Heywood Broun: A Biography* (New York: G. P. Putnam's Sons, 1975), p. 186, inaccurately claims that Broun and Morris Ernst "did their utmost to combat the Communist inroads." Ernst, an anti-Communist, minimizes his close friend's flirtation with the Party in *The Best Is Yet* (New York: Harper & Brothers, 1945). It is true that Broun broke with the Party after the Nazi-Soviet Pact. For a discussion of the Party's ties to Garland Ashcraft, treasurer of the ANG and briefly a Party member, see Voros, *American Commisar,* pp. 568–583. Voros was a close adviser to Ashcraft. Jack Stachel, "Build the Party," *Communist,* March 1938, p. 233; *Daily Worker,* March 21, 1938, p. 4.

46. *Resolutions of the Ninth Convention of the Communist Party* (New York: Workers Library Publishers, 1936), p. 63; Merrill interview with Draper; *Daily Worker,* May 21, 1938,

p. 4. Whether the formal abolition of fractions meant their actual disappearance is not altogether certain. Party documents seized by the Dies Committee in raids around the country included instructions to Party fractions in such disparate organizations as the League of Women Shoppers and the International Workers' Order. *Investigation of Un-American Propaganda Activities*, Vol. 7, p. 4931; Vol. 12, p. 7667.

47. William Dunne, *The Struggle Against Opportunism in the Labor Movement: For a Socialist United States* (New York: New York Communications Committee, 1947), p. 32; William Foster, "Twenty Years of Communist Trade Union Policy," *Communist*, September 1939, p. 814.

48. *New York Times*, March 25, 1937, p. 1; March 26, p. 1; March 27, p. 1; April 3, p. 1. For accounts of the UAW battles from widely different perspectives, see Irving Howe and B. J. Widick, *The UAW and Walter Reuther* (New York: Random House, 1949), and Keeran, *The Communist Party and the Auto Workers Unions*.

49. *Daily Worker*, March 27, 1937, pp. 1, 4; April 6, p. 5. Browder interview with Draper, June 23, 1955. Earl Browder, "The Communists in the People's Front," *Communist*, July 1937, pp. 609–610. Keeran, in *The Communist Party and the Auto Workers Unions*, pp. 188–189, believes Browder was attacking a few rank and filers. Information pertaining to the Politburo meetings (see subsequent discussion) demonstrates conclusively that it was Weinstone who was being raked over the coals.

50. William Foster, "Political Leadership and Party Building," *Communist*, July 1937, p. 644.

51. *Daily Worker*, July 9, 1937, p. 4; July 22, p. 5. *Investigation of Un-American Propaganda Activities*, Vol. 4, p. 2692. Gebert denied he had made any such offer to Martin. *Daily Worker*, January 10, 1939, p. 6; September 16, 1937, p. 1.

52. *Daily Worker*, September 4, 1937, p. 4; Browder interview with Draper, June 23, 1955; Cochran, *Labor and Communism*, p. 138. Reuther himself may have briefly belonged to the Communist party. Nat Ganley, a top UAW Communist, maintained years later, while still in the Party, that he had collected dues from Reuther. See Martin Glaberman, "A Note on Walter Reuther," *Radical America*, Vol. 7, November–December 1973, pp. 113–117.

53. Politburo Minutes, December 23, 1937, January 28, 1938. Draper Papers, Box 1, Folders 47, 51.

54. The Politburo Minutes of December 23, 1937, include the statement that "our relationship is established now with F." See Clayton Fountain, *Union Guy* (New York: Viking Press, 1949), pp. 84–85, for a description of the change of line. See also Victor Reuther, *The Brothers Reuther and the Story of the UAW* (Boston: Houghton Mifflin, 1976), pp. 189–190; and *Daily Worker*, May 10, 1938, pp. 5–6.

55. Browder interview with Draper, June 23, 1955. Browder put the confrontation in Moscow somewhat vaguely in 1937. From other dates, the discussion appears more likely to have taken place in early 1938. As of 1980, Weinstone headed the Party's Historical Commission. Politburo Minutes, March 23, 1939, Draper Papers, Box 1, Folder 60.

56. *Congressional Record*, Vol. 83, Part 7, pp. 7573–7644; Part 9, pp. 1116–1118. The best general account of the Dies Committee is in Walter Goodman's *The Committee* (New York: Farrar, Straus & Giroux, 1968).

57. Among the CIO leaders whom Frey accused of being members of the Communist party were Morris Muster of the Furniture Workers; George Woolf of the Fish and Cannery Workers; Harold Prichett of the Wood Workers; Donald Henderson of the Cannery, Agricultural and Packing Workers; Lewis Merrill of the Office Workers; Ben Gold of the Fur Workers; Marcel Scherer of the Federation of Architects and Engineers; Mike Quill of the Transport Workers; Joe Curran of the National Maritime Union; Mervyn Rathborne of the Communications Workers; Abram Flaxer of the State, Country and Municipal Workers; James Matles of the UE; and Francis Gorman of the Textile Workers. Joseph Zack added to that list Heywood Broun of the Newspaper Guild and Powers Hapgood of the Shoe Workers. *Investigation of Un-American Propaganda Activities*, Vol. 1, pp. 91–277, Vol. 9, pp. 5462, 5465, 5467. Browder charged that Frey had been "delighted" to deal with James Matles's TUUL union when it had briefly sought succor in the A.F. of L. *Daily Worker*, September 7, 1938, p. 3.

58. Richard Boyer and Herbert Morris, *Labor's Untold Story* (New York: United Electrical, Radio and Machine Workers, 1972), p. 324; Joe Kamp, *Join the C.I.O. and Help Build a*

Soviet America (New York: Constitutional Education League, 1937); *Daily Worker,* January 14, 1938, p. 6; Benjamin Stolberg, *The Story of the CIO* (New York: Viking Press, 1938), pp. 48–49.

59. *Daily Worker,* February 5, 1938, p. 6; March 16, p. 5; September 6, 1937, p. 5.

60. Dubofsky and VanTine, *John L. Lewis,* p. 322; Galenson, *The CIO Challenge,* p. 111; Wyndham Mortimer, *Organize* (Boston: Beacon Press, 1971), pp. 162–165.

Chapter 14

1. Albert Acena, *The Washington Commonwealth Federation: Reform Politics and the Popular Front* (unpublished doctoral dissertation, University of Washington, 1975), p. 280. Except where otherwise noted, I have relied on Acena's account of the WCF.

2. The Seattle Unemployed Citizens League (UCL), founded in mid-1931 by Socialists, emphasized self-help projects and barter. The city quickly began to cooperate with it in providing relief. The Technocracy movement had been around since the early 1920s. The brainchild of Howard Scott, who was once on the fringes of the IWW, it combined ideas of Thorstein Veblen with a vision of a technological utopia, with goods priced according to the amount of energy needed to make them, thus ensuring a proper balance between consumption and production. Although Technocracy enjoyed a brief vogue around the nation, it caught on only in Seattle, where it attracted large numbers of middle-class citizens. See Arthur Schlesinger, Jr., *The Crisis of the Old Order 1919-1933* (Boston: Houghton Mifflin, 1964), pp. 461–464; Acena, *The WCF,* pp. 12–17. The Communists strongly attacked Technocracy. See V. J. Jerome, "Technocracy—A Reactionary Utopia," *Communist,* February 1933, pp. 171–187, where it was linked to social-fascism and denounced as a sham.

3. Noral had been the United Farmers League representative in Moscow and was a penitent Lovestoneite. On Raport, see Fish Committee, *Investigation of Communist Propaganda,* 1930, Part V, Vol. 2, p. 113. Acena, *The WCF,* p. 21–24, 71–75. "Organizational Status of the Party," Browder Papers, Syracuse University Series 2-36. *Voice of Action,* December 28, 1934, p. 3; February 1, 1935, p. 2.

4. *Voice of Action,* November 1, 1935, p. 2; December 13, p. 3. Alexander Bittelman, "Review of the Month," *Communist,* April 1936, p. 299. One ex–Party member and delegate reported that Raport was in a nearby room during the meeting coordinating the activities of Party members. Eugene Dennet testimony, *Investigation of Communist Activities in the Seattle, Washington Area,* House Un-American Activities Committee, 84th Congress, p. 401. On Dobbins, see Acena, *The WCF,* p. 114. For Eby, see Jane Sanders, *Cold War on Campus: Academic Freedom at the University of Washington, 1946-1954* (Seattle: University of Washington Press, 1979), pp. 68–70. Eby was investigated by the university in 1949 but not dismissed from his position. He had dropped out of the Party in 1946. See also Eby's testimony in *Second Report: Un-American Activities in Washington State,* Report of the Joint Legislative Fact-finding Committee on Un-American Activities, 1948, pp. 199–203. While testifying to his own membership, Eby refused to discuss others.

5. *Investigation of Communist Activities in the Pacific Northwest Area,* Part 1, House Un-American Activities Committee, 83rd Congress, 2d Session, p. 5978. Costigan told the Canwell Committee he had joined in early 1937 but told the Subversive Activities Control Board that he had done so in the fall of 1936 and the Un-American Activities Committee that he had signed up in December 1936. In all cases he was quite vague; *First Report: Un-American Activities in Washington State,* Report of the Joint Legislative Fact-Finding Committee on Un-American Activities, 1948, p. 359. *Pacific Northwest Hearings,* House Un-American Activities Committee, p. 5977. Raport told Albert Acena that he had been approached by Costigan; Acena, *The WCF,* p. 137n. Morris Raport, "The Washington State Elections," *Communist,* February 1937, pp. 178–179.

6. Eugene Dennet, president of the Inland Boatmen's Union, testified that he was a Party member between 1931 and 1934, from 1935 to 1943, and from 1945 to 1947, when he was finally expelled as a Trotskyist; *Pacific Northwest Hearings,* House Un-American Activities Committee, Part IV, pp. 6288, 6446, 6450. Acena, *The WCF,* pp. 146, 192–193, 253; *First Report,* pp. 72–78, 82, 194, 415–423.

7. Acena, *The WCF*, pp. 144–145, 147n.; *First Report*, pp. 63–68, 83. Pennock committed suicide while on trial under the Smith Act in 1953.

8. *Pacific Northwest Hearings*, Part 1, pp. 5980–5981; *First Report*, p. 84. One editor, Terry Pettus, admitted he had secretly joined the Party in 1938. Interview with Albert Acena, June 30, 1966, University of Washington Library.

9. Morris Raport, "The Commonwealth Federation Moves On," *Communist*, April 1937, p. 370; Morris Raport, "The Democratic Front and the Northwest Elections," *Communist*, January 1939, p. 73; *First Report*, pp. 85–92, 102, 194, 235–238, 415–420, 426, 435–437. Three of the legislators—Kathryn Fogg, Ellsworth Mills, and H. C. Armstrong—admitted that they had been Party members during their tenure. While there were some quibbles about several of the names, there was no doubt in the witnesses' minds that former state Senators Ernest Olson, N. P. Atkinson, and Thomas Rabbitt, as well as Representatives Emma Taylor, William Pennock, and George Henley, had been Communists.

10. Raport, "The Democratic Front," p. 69; Morris Raport, "The Communist Party in the State of Washington and the 1940 Elections," *Communist*, August 1939, p. 734.

11. Morris Raport, "The Commonwealth Federation," p. 372; Acena, *The WCF*, pp. 251–254; *Washington New Dealer*, November 30, 1939, p. 1; *First Report*, pp. 88, 104, 361–365, 415–420, 425.

12. The 1936 and 1937 figures are from "National Membership Report: January 1–June 30, 1937. Issued by the Organization Department," Draper Papers, Box 1, Folder 43. The 2,115 figure comes from *Party Organizer*, March 1938, pp. 22–23. The King County figure is from Louis Sass, "Party Building in the Northwest," *Communist*, December 1938, pp. 1134–1135. The 5,016 figure comes from Raport, "The Communist Party and the 1940 Elections," p. 734. Raport, "The Democratic Front," p. 74.

13. Terry Pettus interview with Albert Acena, June 30, 1966; *First Report*, pp. 96–101.

14. *United Action*, September 16, 1935, p. 2; August 15, pp. 2, 5.

15. *United Action*, August 15, 1935, pp. 4–5.

16. Ibid.

17. In 1931, 500 of the 800 Communists in the state were Finns. *Daily Worker*, May 13, 1931, p. 4. Registration figures are from "National Membership Report," Draper Papers, Box 1, Folder 43. Nat Ross interview with Theodore Draper, June 17, 1969, Draper Papers, Box 4, Folder 89. Ross remained in Minnesota until December 1938. From early 1939 until September 1943 he was in Moscow with his wife, who was stationed there as a *Daily Worker* correspondent. He returned to Minnesota for another stint as district organizer in 1943. Ross dropped out of active work in 1952, left the Party for good in 1956, and developed a very successful direct-mail business.

18. Earl Browder interview with Theodore Draper, June 23, 1955, Draper Papers, Box 2, Folder 5; *United Action*, December 13, 1935, p. 8.

19. *United Action*, December 31, 1935, pp. 1, 2.

20. *United Action*, January 31, 1936, p. 4; John Haynes, *Liberals, Communists, and the Popular Front in Minnesota: The Struggle to Control* (unpublished doctoral dissertation, University of Minnesota, 1978), pp. 24, 37, 65n; *United Action*, April 10, 1936, p. 2; *Investigation of Un-American Propaganda Activities*, Special Committee on Un-American Activities, House of Representatives, 75th Congress, 3rd Session, 1938, Vol. 2, p. 1372. Bittelman claimed that Communists had been in the FLA for a long time despite the bar. See Alexander Bittelman, "Review of the Month," *Communist*, April 1936, p. 300.

21. *United Action*, May 1, 1936, p. 4; Nat Ross interview with Theodore Draper, March 29, 1939, Draper Papers, Box 4, Folder 89; Clarence Hathaway, "Problems in Our Farmer-Labor Party Activities," *Communist*, May 1936, pp. 432–433.

22. Earl Browder, "The Results of the Elections and the People's Front," *Communist*, January 1937, p. 30.

23. Olson hired Lillian Schwartz to serve in the lieutenant governor's office. His aide, Abe Harris, employed Ruth Shaw, wife of Party functionary Eric Bert, as his secretary. Ross interview with Draper, June 17, 1969. Haynes, *Liberals, Communists*, pp. 38, 40; Harvey Klehr interview with Carl Ross, October 30, 1980; *Investigation of Un-American Propaganda Activities*, Vol. 2, p. 1409. Unlike Rutchick, Harris broke his alliance with the Party after the Nazi-Soviet Pact. On Benson see *Sunday Worker*, August 18, 1937, p. 1; and Sam Darcy interview with Theodore Draper, May 15, 1957, Draper Papers, Box 3, Folder 53. The only

biography of Benson is a potboiler by James Shields, *Mr. Progressive: A Biography of Elmer A. Benson* (Minneapolis: T. S. Demson & Company, 1971).

24. Ross interview with Klehr.

25. Haynes, *Liberals, Communists*, pp. 53–54; Gene Dennis, "The Socialist Party Convention," *Communist*, May 1937, p. 411.

26. Farrell Dobbs, *Teamster Politics* (New York: Monad Press, 1975); Millard Gieske, *Minnesota Farmer-Laborism: The Third-Party Alternative* (Minneapolis: University of Minnesota Press, 1979), p. 246; Haynes, *Liberals, Communists*, pp. 45–47.

27. Haynes, *Liberals, Communists*, pp. 42–43; Browder interview with Draper, June 23, 1955; Clarence Hathaway, "The Minnesota Farmer-Labor Victory," *Communist*, December 1936, p. 1121; Nat Ross, "The People's Mandate in Minnesota," *Communist*, June 1937, pp. 541–543; Gieske, *Minnesota Farmer-Laborism*, pp. 241–243.

28. Gieske, *Minnesota Farmer-Laborism*, pp. 255, 260; Haynes, *Liberals, Communists*, p. 72; Hyman Berman, "Political Antisemitism in Minnesota During the Great Depression," *Jewish Social Studies*, Summer–Fall 1976, pp. 247–264.

29. Martin Young to Central Committee, November 5, 1936, Browder Papers, Syracuse University, Reel 2, Series 1-84. Young had been the Central Committee representative to the district. *Daily Worker*, May 31, 1938, p. 7; Ross interview with Draper.

30. Darcy interview with Draper; Sam Darcy, unpublished autobiography, p. 528.

31. Haynes, *Liberals, Communists*, pp. 77–90.

32. Kenneth Waltzer, *The American Labor Party: Third Party Politics in New Deal–Cold War New York, 1936–1954* (unpublished doctoral dissertation, Harvard University, 1977), pp. 91, 224; *Daily Worker*, December 2, 1936, p. 6.

33. Alexander Bittelman, "Review of the Month," *Communist*, May 1936, pp. 393–397; August 1936, pp. 680–682. *Daily Worker*, August 8, 1936, p. 3. Israel Amter, "The Elections in New York," *Communist*, December 1936, p. 1152.

34. Israel Amter, "The Coming Municipal Elections," *Communist*, July 1937, p. 654. Earl Browder, "To the Masses—To the Shops," *Communist*, October 1931, p. 780. *Daily Worker*, August 6, 1934, p. 1; March 31, p. 8; June 14, p. 1; July 4, p. 2; July 30, p. 1; August 27, 1937, p. 6; October 1, p. 3; October 6, pp. 2, 6. Israel Amter, "The Farmer-Labor Party Movement in the Municipal Elections," *Communist*, October 1937, p. 929.

35. Charles Krumbein, "Lessons of the New York Elections," *Communist*, January 1938, pp. 31–33; *New Masses*, January 18, 1938, p. 5; *Daily Worker*, June 4, 1938, p. 6. Under the proportional voting system, voters ranked their choices from first to last. The candidate finishing last was eliminated, and his supporters' second-place votes were then allocated to candidates still in the running. This process continued until the full number of councilmen were elected.

36. Charles Krumbein, "Lessons," p. 34; *New Masses*, September 7, 1937, pp. 15, 31; *I. F. Stone's Weekly*, October 18, 1954, p. 2.

37. *Daily Worker*, December 22, 1937, p. 1.

38. Earl Browder, "The People's Front Moves Forward," *Communist*, December 1937, p. 1095. Krumbein, "Lessons," p. 29. *Daily Worker*, April 19, 1938, p. 6; June 5, p. 1. Earl Browder, *Social and National Security* (New York: Workers Library Publishers, 1938), p. 19.

39. *Daily Worker*, July 14, 1938, p. 4; October 4, p. 3. Israel Amter, "The Democratic Front Moves Ahead in New York," *Communist*, October 1938, p. 917. *New Leader*, July 16, 1938, p. 8.

40. *Daily Worker*, November 5, 1938, p. 1; November 10, pp. 1, 5. Earl Browder, "Report to the National Convention," September 2, 1939, p. 48, Draper Papers, Box 1, Folder 62. *Daily Worker*, December 9, 1938, p. 4.

41. *New Leader*, June 11, 1938, p. 8; August 6, p. 2; May 13, 1939, p. 7. The Party had lost its official status on the ballot in 1936 when Robert Minor failed to get 50,000 votes for governor. Thereafter, its members were encouraged to enroll in the ALP. See Warren Moscow, *Politics in the Empire State* (New York: Alfred Knopf, 1948), pp. 102–119.

42. Healey told a California investigating committee in 1940 that he had previously been registered as a Communist. See Jack Tenney, *Red Fascism* (Los Angeles: Federal Printing Company, 1947), pp. 157, 158. For Connelly's denial and an identification of him as a Party member in 1938, see ibid., pp. 243 and 368 respectively. While he might not have been a Communist at this time, in 1942, he was by the late 1940s when he was indicted under the Smith Act. See Al Richmond, *A Long View from the Left* (Boston: Houghton

Mifflin, 1973), pp. 332–333. On Michener, see Roger Keeran, *The Communist Party and the Auto Workers Unions* (Bloomington: Indiana University Press, 1980), p. 212. On Hollywood, see Larry Ceplair and Steven Englund, *The Inquisition in Hollywood* (Garden City: Anchor Press, 1980), pp. 117–124. On the Workers' Alliance, see Robert Burke, *Olson's New Deal for California* (Berkeley: University of California Press, 1953), p. 83. For Party membership see "National Membership Report, January 1–June 30, 1957," Draper Papers, Box 1, Folder 43; and *Daily Worker*, May 31, 1938, p. 7. These figures include Arizona and Nevada. Schneiderman later estimated that there were 8,000–9,000 CP and YCL members in 1938–1939. Steve Murdock, "California Communists—Their Years of Power," *Science and Society*, Winter 1970, p. 482.

43. William Schneiderman, "The Election Struggle in California," *Communist*, October 1938, pp. 922, 926; William Schneiderman, "The Democratic Front in California," *Communist*, July 1938, pp. 663, 665; Murdock, "California Communists," p. 481; Richmond, *A Long View from the Left*, p. 272.

44. Burke, *Olson's New Deal*, p. 24; *Investigation of Un-American Propaganda Activities*, Vol. 3, pp. 2034–2038. Olson's activities included speeches to the American League for Peace and Democracy and the International Workers' Order. For a partial transcript of Whitney's speech, see Tenney, *Red Fascism*, p. 408. Al Richmond, *Native Daughter: The Story of Anita Whitney* (San Francisco: Anita Whitney 75th Anniversary Committee, 1942). On Browder's comments, see "Report of E.B. 8/26/38—State Executive Committee Meeting," in *Communist Party Documents*, a book of photocopied documents collected by Theodore Draper, in Draper Papers. *Sunday Worker*, December 11, 1938, p. 4.

45. On Patterson, see *Investigation of Un-American Propaganda Activities*, Vol. 3, pp. 938, 2034, 2036–2037; Burke, *Olson's New Deal*, pp. 22, 46, 143; *Fourth Report; Un-American Activities in California 1948: Communist Front Organizations* (Sacramento: Report of the Joint Fact-finding Committee to 1948 Regular California Legislature, 1948), p. 215. On McWilliams, see Tenney, *Red Fascism*, p. 366; and *Investigation of Un-American Propaganda Activities*, Vol. 17, pp. 10331–10349. In his autobiography, *The Education of Carey McWilliams* (New York: Simon & Schuster, 1979), he was quite reticent about his connections with the Party, saying only that his work with the labor movement between 1935 and 1939 "pushed me beyond the liberalism of the period in the direction of the native American radicalism with which I could readily identify" (p. 85). On the Young Democrats, see David Saposs, *Communism in American Politics* (Washington, D.C.: Public Affairs Press, 1960), p. 44. One witness identified Hawkins as a Party member. *Investigation of Un-American Propaganda Activities*, Vol. 3, p. 931. Hawkins was allied with Communists in such Popular Front auxiliaries as the National Negro Congress and was a supporter of the *People's Daily World* and American Youth for Democracy, among others. See Tenney, *Red Fascism*, pp. 288, 295, 297, 437, 525. Hawkins became nationally known as a sponsor of the Humphrey-Hawkins Full Employment bill in the 1970s. Earl Browder, "Mastery of Theory and Methods of Work," *Communist*, January 1939, p. 17.

46. The famed King-Connor-Ramsay case involved three men connected with the Marine Firemen's Union (King led it), who had been convicted of killing an anti-union chief engineer on the Point Lobos steamer. For a biased view of the case see Tenney, *Red Fascism*, pp. 398–414. On the SRA, see Edward Barrett, *The Tenney Committee: Legislative Investigation of Subversive Activities in California* (Ithaca, N.Y.: Cornell University Press, 1951), pp. 1–3.

47. Arthur Kent named Yorty in *Investigation on Un-American Propaganda Activities*, Vol. 3, p. 2084; Paul Cline, "The Los Angeles Mayoralty Recall Election," *Communist*, November, 1938, p. 1022; Burke, *Olson's New Deal*, p. 131. See *Investigation of Un-American Propaganda Activities*, Vol. 3, p. 2048, for the naming of Tenney.

48. Nat Ross boasted in 1934 that whites, many formerly in the Klan, were joining the Party. *Daily Worker*, February 9, 1934, p. 4. Another writer insisted that the Party had rooted itself in Birmingham steel mills, Carolina textile areas, and Alabama plantations. *Daily Worker*, October 5, 1934, p. 4. Mostly this was wishful thinking. *Daily Worker*, July 28, 1934, p. 4; September 26, p. 4.

49. *Testimony of Paul Crouch*, House Committee on Un-American Activities, 81st Congress, 1st Session, 1949, p. 218; *Communist Activities Among Aliens and National Groups*, Hearings Before the Subcommittee on Immigration and Naturalization, Committee on the Judiciary, U.S. Senate, 81st Congress, 1st Session, Part I, 1950. The picture of Crouch in a

Red Army uniform is in the *Daily Worker*, May, 1928, p. 3. Cedric Belfrage, in *The American Inquisition 1945-1960* (Indianapolis, Ind.: Bobbs-Merrill, 1973), provides a vicious vignette of Crouch.

50. *Southern Worker*, December 1934, p. 1; January 1935, p. 1. The *Daily Worker* erroneously jumped to the conclusion that these Socialists, who included Howard Kester, James Dombrowski, and Claude Williams, spoke for their state organizations; the latter denied any agreement. *Daily Worker*, December 7, 1934, p. 1; December 31, p. 6; November 16, p. 2; June 4, 1935, p. 4. Nat Ross, "The Next Steps in Alabama and the Lower South," *Communist*, October 1935, p. 974. *Southern Worker*, June 1935, pp. 1, 4.

51. *Southern Worker*, September 1937, pp. 5-7.

52. *DeJonge* v. *Oregon*, 299 U.S. 353 (1936); *Daily Worker*, January 6, 1937, p. 6; *Herndon* v. *Lowry*, 301 U.S. 242.

53. *Party Organizer*, August 1937, pp. 28–31; *Daily Worker*, September 27, 1937, p. 5. "National Membership Report," Draper Papers; *Daily Worker*, May 27, 1938, p. 5; "Report on Organization, 1938," in *Investigation of Un-American Propaganda Activities*, Vol, 14, pp. 8714–8718; *Southern Worker*, September 1937, p. 5.

54. The FBI file on the Southern Negro Youth Congress, 100-6548, contains reports on the group's activities, including information from telephone and microphone taps installed in its offices beginning in November 1943. Ed Strong joined the Party in the mid-1930s. By the 1950s he was a member of the Central Committee. He died at the age of 43; see his obituary in the *Daily Worker*, April 11, 1957. Louis Burnham joined the Party in the early 1930s and also rose to the National Committee; he died in 1960. James Jackson, who is married to Esther Cooper, had been a Communist since 1933. Indicted under the Smith Act, he was never convicted. Today he serves as the Party's national education director.

James Ford, "The Negro People in the People's Front!", *Communist*, August 1937, p. 732; James Ford, "Rally the Negro Masses for the Democratic Front!", *Communist*, March 1938, p. 269. Exhilarated by the new line, Francis Franklin, a young white Southerner, suggested that Communists direct Southern patriotism against Northern finance capital to attract whites to the Party. He pointed out that ever since Reconstruction, when "great numbers of carpet baggers" looted the South, the region had been exploited by the North. Franklin's heresy was too dramatic, however. He drew a rebuke from Harry Haywood for playing "into the hands of reaction" by presenting a negative view, however qualified, of Reconstruction. Francis Franklin, "For a Free, Happy and Prosperous South," *Communist*, January 1938, p. 67; Theodore Bassett, "The 'White' South and the People's Front," *Communist*, April 1938, p. 371. Harry Haywood, in *Black Bolshevik* (Chicago: Liberator Press, 1978), p. 492, explains that he wrote the latter article but it was published under Bassett's name.

55. Thomas Kreuger, *And Promises to Keep: The Southern Conference for Human Welfare, 1938-1948* (Nashville, Tenn.: Vanderbilt University Press, 1967), pp. 3–39.

56. Rob Hall, "The Southern Conference for Human Welfare," *Communist*, January 1939, pp. 60, 65. Nell Irvin Painter, *The Narrative of Hosea Hudson: His Life as a Negro Communist in the South* (Cambridge, Mass.: Harvard University Press, 1979), p. 291. Earl Browder to William Goldsmith, August 14, 1955, Browder Papers, Syracuse University, Reel 1–31. Browder insisted he did not know whether Gelders was a Communist or not.

57. *Southern Worker*, November 1936, p. 7; *Party Organizer*, November 1937, p. 14; Painter, *Hosea Hudson*, p. 256; Kreuger, *And Promises to Keep*, pp. 41, 77.

58. Kreuger, *And Promises to Keep*, pp. 79, 87–88. FBI File 65-62553-20 includes a memo reporting that Lee admitted Party membership from 1938 to 1949 in an interview with the bureau. Although nominally a Socialist, Claude Williams was actually a secret member of the Communist party. In August 1938 he inadvertently lost a handwritten letter to the Central Committee. Unfortunately for him, his friends in the Southern Tenant Farmers Union found it. In the letter, Williams asked for $500 to capture the STFU: "A situation has now arisen which offers an extraordinary opportunity to move into the most important organization in the agricultural south. H. L. Mitchell, who has always opposed the Party, is away on leave. J. R. Butler, who is friendly to our line, is in charge." Butler, one of those who discovered the letter, proved not to be quite that friendly. Williams was tried and expelled from the union. See H. L. Mitchell, *Mean Things Happening in This Land* (Montclair, N.J.: Allancheld, Osmun & Company, 1979), pp. 153–163. The full text of the letter can be found in *Investigation of Un-American Propaganda Activities*, Executive Hearings, Vol. 7, pp.

3048–3050. On Dobbs, see *Communism in New Orleans*, House Committee on Un-American Activities, 85th Congress, 1st Session, p. 165. The vice-chairman of the League of Young Southerners—it was originally called the Council of Young Southerners—was Junius Scales, a prominent North Carolina Communist. Kreuger, *And Promises to Keep*, p. 50.

59. Kreuger, *And Promises to Keep*, pp. 37–38; *Investigation of Un-American Activities*, Vol. 7, pp. 4765-4767; Paul Crouch, "The Southern Conference for Human Welfare: Anatomy of a Communist Front," *Plain Talk*, 1949, pp. 7–13. Crouch also claimed that he, Rob Hall, and Joseph Gelders, using Party finances, had organized the conference. See *Southern Conference Educational Fund, Inc. Hearings*, Judiciary Committee, U.S. Senate, 83rd Congress, 2nd Session, 1954, pp. 4, 15. *Report on Southern Conference For Human Welfare*, Committee on Un-American Activities, House of Representatives, 80th Congress, 1st Session, 1947, p. 17.

60. Morris Childs, "Building the Democratic Front in Illinois," *Communist*, September 1938, p. 812; John Williamson, "An Analysis of the Ohio Elections—What Next?," *Communist*, January 1939, p. 80; Gene Dennis, "The Wisconsin Elections," *Communist*, December 1936, p. 1127.

61. Earl Browder, "To the People Will Belong the Victory," *Communist*, February 1940, pp. 118–119. Browder specifically identified Governor Frank Murphy of Michigan as one who in 1938 "had long intimate conferences with Communists as to how best to conduct his campaign for governor."

62. Browder, *Social and National Security*, p. 24; Browder, "Mastery of Theory and Methods," p. 21; "Report of E. B. 8/26/38," Draper Papers.

63. Clarence Hathaway, "The Minnesota Farmer Labor Victory," *Communist*, December 1936, p. 1124.

Chapter 15

1. *New York Times*, April 10, 1933; April 23, Part IV, p. 6.

2. *New York Times*, May 20, 1933, p. 11; May 22, p. 3; May 25, p. 3. Mr. Dooley pithily explained: "How in the world can we expect an aggressive, fighting force of delegates when these delegates are filled with good old Army mulligan?"

3. *New York Times*, May 10, 1933, p. 8; May 11, p. 4; May 13, p. 5; May 14, p. 10; May 15, p. 3; May 17, p. 10; May 20, p. 11. Roger Daniels, *The Bonus March* (Westport, Conn.: Greenwood Press, 1971), pp. 230–231.

4. *Daily Worker*, October 21, 1933, p. 3; February 21, 1934, p. 3. Herbert Benjamin, "The Unemployment Movement in the U.S.A.," *Communist*, June 1935, p. 529.

5. *Capitalist Stabilization Has Ended: Thesis and Resolutions of the Twelfth Plenum of the Executive Committee of the Communist International* (New York: Workers Library Publishers, 1932), pp. 26–27; *Daily Worker*, January 20, 1934, p. 6.

6. *Daily Worker*, October 21, 1933, p. 3; August 5, p. 4; April 25, 1934, p. 3. *Unemployment, Old Age and Social Insurance: Hearings Before a Subcommittee of the Committee on Labor*, House of Representatives, 74th Congress, 1st Session, pp. 41–50, 285. Late in 1936, A. F. of L. officials persuaded the Federal Trade Commission to order Weinstock's committe to drop the A. F. of L. from its title and publication on the grounds that this inclusion was deceptive advertising. The text of the FTC ruling can be found in *Investigation of Un-American Propaganda Activities in the United States*, Vol. 13. pp. 7696–7702.

7. William Foster, "The Crisis in the Socialist Party," *Communist*, November 1936, p. 1044; *Daily Worker*, December 31, 1934, p. 1; *The Way Out: A Program for American Labor* (New York: Workers Library Publishers, 1934), pp. 23–24.

8. Earl Browder later claimed that Clarence Hathaway, an old Minnesota acquaintance, had visited Lundeen and won his support. Benjamin, however, claimed he had taken the initiative with Lundeen. The *Daily Worker* at the time had Benjamin giving the bill to the congressman and did not mention Hathaway. *Daily Worker*, January 16, 1934, p. 2. Earl Browder interview with Theodore Draper, October 10, 1955, Draper Papers, Box 2, Folder 8; Herbert Benjamin interview with Draper, October 30, 1970, Draper Papers, Box 2, Folder 42; *Daily Worker*, January 5, 1935, p. 1; February 3, 1934, p. 1; October 8, 1930, p. 4;

February 7, 1934, pp. 3, 6. Lundeen told the *Daily Worker* (February 6, 1934, pp. 1, 2) that he would vote for another version of unemployment insurance if he had to.

9. *Daily Worker*, February 5, 1934, pp. 1, 2; February 8, p. 1; February 7, p. 1; February 6, pp. 1–2.

10. *Daily Worker*, October 20, 1934, p. 4; November 17, p. 4; November 24, p. 4; January 19, 1935, p. 4; December 29, 1934, p. 5; January 7, 1935, pp. 1, 2.

11. *Daily Worker*, January 7, 1935, pp. 1, 2. Earl Browder, *Unemployment Insurance: The Burning Issue of the Day* (New York: Workers Library Publishers, 1935).

12. Edwin Wiite, *The Development of the Social Security Act* (Madison: University of Wisconsin Press, 1962); *Unemployment, Old Age and Social Insurance*, p. 689; Earl Browder, "Report to the Central Committee Meeting of the CPUSA, January 15–18, 1935," *Communist*, March 1935, p. 196; *Daily Worker*, February 1, 1935, p. 1. Wagner himself was pilloried as a "Tammany hack" specializing in "strike-breaking legislation." *Daily Worker*, July 21, 1935, p. 7.

13. Herbert Benjamin to Theodore Draper, December 5, 1971, Draper Papers, Box 2, Folder 42; *Unemployment, Old Age and Social Insurance*, pp. iii–v, 708. Greenfield's organization had a fascinating history. Controlled by the Party, it ran its own candidates for office in 1933, earning a rebuke for playing down revolutionary demands. *Daily Worker*, December 27, 1933, p. 4. Its Illinois counterpart was just as interesting. It was founded in early 1933 by Harry LaBeau, an ex-Socialist and Wobbly who worked as a real estate salesman in Chicago. He had joined the Party in 1932 and hit upon the idea of enlisting small home-owners threatened with foreclosure. Despite constant criticism by the Party's district leadership, the Small Home Owners Federation "led by Party members" continued to drift in the "worst opportunist legalistic nature." Instead of focusing on the class struggle, LaBeau emphasized legal action. He was expelled early in 1934. *Daily Worker*, March 5, 1934, p. 6. Had he been able to remain in the Party for another year, he and his organization would have received plaudits.

14. Benjamin interview with Draper, October 30, 1970; Benjamin letter to Draper, December 5, 1971. The *Daily Worker*, August 5, 1933, p. 4, first indicated that a group to enlist the cooperation of professionals was being formed. In a February 1934 article, Van Kleeck referred to it as a Professional Workers Association. The IPA was formally organized in April 1934. See Lorenz Finison, "Radical Professionals in the Great Depression, An Historical Note: The Interprofessional Association," *Radical History Review*, Vol. 4, 1977, p. 133. The Executive Board included Elmer Rice, Charles Seeger, Percival Goodman, Jacob Fisher, Joseph Gillman, K. Lonberg-Holm, Louis Hacker, Max Lerner, Maxwell Hyde, and Kyle Crichton. Benjamin letter to Draper, December 5, 1971.

15. *Unemployment, Old Age and Social Insurance*, pp. 73, 74, 129, 145, 203, 466, 688–698.

16. Browder interview with Draper, October 10, 1955; *Congressional Record*, April 11, 1934, pp. 3458–3459, 5857, 6069–6070; Witte, *The Development of the Social Security Act*, p. 99. The House vote on the Lundeen Amendment was by division, not roll call, so no list exists of who voted for it. Other progressives voting no on Wagner-Lewis were Usher Burdick and William Lemke of North Dakota and Paul Kvale of Minnesota. Most progressives voted for the bill.

17. *Daily Worker*, January 19, 1935, p. 1; Clarence Hathaway, "The Minnesota Farmer-Labor Victory," *Communist*, December 1936, p. 1118; Ben Gitlow, *The Whole of Their Lives* (New York: Charles Scribner's Sons, 1948), p. 361; *Daily Worker*, April 19, 1938, p. 6.

18. *Daily Worker*, February 4, 1938, p. 1, includes the full list of the House progressives. Joi nson was apparently not one of the thirty-four who actually met with the President early in 1938. See *Daily Worker*, February 8, 1938, pp. 1, 4. For a discussion of Maverick that is positive but laments his refusal to move to socialism, see Alexander Bittelman's article in the *Daily Worker*, July 24, 1937, p. 6. On the Wisconsin group see *New Masses*, February 9, 1937, pp. 7–8; and *Daily Worker*, September 22, 1937, p. 1. On Teigan, see *Daily Worker*, April 6, 1937, p. 3.

19. Nat Ross interview with Theodore Draper, Draper Papers, Box 4, Folder 89. Barbara Stuhler, in "The Man Who Voted Nay," *Minnesota History*, Fall 1972, p. 83, says that it was an Eveleth attorney who asked Barnard to run. Browder interview with Draper, October 10, 1955.

20. John Haynes, *Liberals, Communists, and the Popular Front in Minnesota*, (unpub-

lished doctoral dissertation, University of Minnesota, 1978), pp. 65–66; *Communist Activities in the Chicago Area*, House Committee on Un-American Activities, 82nd Congress, 2nd Session, pp. 3683–3699; Ross interview with Draper.

21. *Investigation of Un-American Propaganda Activities*, Executive Hearings, Vol. 2, p. 935. The same witness who named Havenner, John Leech, also named Congressman Lee Geyer, a California Democrat elected in 1938, as a Party member. *New Masses*, November 23, 1937, pp. 3–5; *Daily Worker*, June 23, 1937, p. 1; *First Report: Un-American Activities in Washington State* (Report of the Joint Legislative Fact-finding Committee on Un-American Activities, 1948), pp. 34–36, 165; *Investigation of Communist Activities in the Seattle Washington Area*, Part III, House Committee on Un-American Activities, 84th Congress, 1st Session, p. 597.

22. Peggy Dennis, *Autobiography of an American Communist* (Westport, Conn.: Lawrence Hill, 1977), p. 128. Dennis is in error, since Marcantonio was not in the House from 1936–1938. By the time he returned, Bernard was no longer there. *Daily Worker*, April 9, 1938, pp. 1, 4; January 10, p. 5. See Scott's contribution in *New Masses*, February 22, 1938, p. 3.

23. There are two biographies of Marcantonio. Alan Schaffer's *Vito Marcantonio: Radical in Congress* (Syracuse, N.Y.: Syracuse University Press, 1966) is a solid, excellent account. Salvatore LaGumina's *Vito Marcantonio: The People's Politician* (Dubuque, Iowa: Kendall-Hunt, 1969) is politically unsophisticated and much weaker. Among other things, LaGumina calls the People's Front "a leftwing organization" (p. 39). The best discussion of Marcantonio is in Kenneth Waltzer's *The American Labor Party: Third Party Politics in New Deal-Cold War New York, 1936–1954* (unpublished doctoral dissertation, Harvard University, 1977), pp. 182–215. Unless otherwise indicated, all the information on Marcantonio is derived from these three works. On the Party bill, see *Relief and Work Standards* (New York: National Joint Action Committee for Genuine Social Insurance, 1936). *New York Times*, April 3, 1936, p. 19. Information on Victor Baron can be found in Al Richmond, *A Long View from the Left* (Boston: Houghton Mifflin, 1973), p. 276. See also Harrison George's brief eulogy, "Close Ranks: Forward!" *Communist*, April 1936, p. 346.

24. The quotation from Browder, from the minutes of a private Party meeting, is found in Schaffer, *Vito Marcantonio*, p. 52. George Charney, *A Long Journey* (Chicago: Quadrangle Books, 1968), p. 106. Marcantonio had other problems in 1936. Some Italians were upset by his ever-so-gentle criticisms of Mussolini. In 1938 he numbered among his campaign workers a young ventriloquist named Paul Winchell who performed with a Tammany hack dummy called Jerry Mahoney.

25. The attempted recruitment of Marcantonio, based on an interview with George Charney, is in Waltzer, *The American Labor Party*, p. 546n. Browder claimed the Party preferred Marcantonio to remain an independent and that he "was the strongman in Congress, leading a large bloc of legislators." This was wishful thinking. Browder interview with Draper, October 10, 1955.

26. *Daily Worker*, December 4, 1933, p. 2; July 9, 1934, p. 3; October 25, p. 2; November 26, p. 6; December 29, p. 5.

27. *Daily Worker*, March 4, 1935, p. 1; March 5, pp. 1, 2. Herbert Benjamin interview with Theodore Draper, October 29, 1970; Draper Papers, Box 2, Folder 42. Amter had been taken out of unemployed work after the January 1935 congress and assigned to New York as district organizer. *Daily Worker*, April 9, 1935, p. 5. David Lasser addressed an angry letter to the *Daily Worker*, disputing its reporting. He charged that Benjamin had not been the only speaker to be warmly received and that the applause for Benjamin had come after his admission that the Unemployment Councils had made serious errors in the past. Moreover, while the convention had authorized unity negotiations, it had not done any more. It was not remarkable that Lasser would take offense at the implication that his organization had been stolen from beneath him. What was startling was that Clarence Hathaway printed his letter, accepted his corrections, and urged comrades who sent reports to the *Daily Worker* in the future "to be scrupulously accurate as to facts." *Daily Worker*, March 9, 1935, p. 2; March 7, p. 2.

28. *Daily Worker*, April 10, 1936, p. 1; April 12, pp. 1, 2. Two of the vice presidents, Angelo Herndon and Sam Wiseman, were Communists.

29. The text of Johnson's statement is found in *Investigation of Un-American Propaganda Activities*, Executive Hearings, Vol. 6, pp. 3069–3070. There are several letters from Johnson

to Herbert Benjamin dated March and April 1936 detailing Johnson's efforts to break various state NUL leaders away from the Musteites. Herbert Benjamin file, Draper Papers, Box 15. A letter of March 9, 1936, indicates that Lasser feared Johnson's switch was not as recent as he had implied and was part of a Party plot to capture the Workers' Alliance.

30. Benjamin interview with Draper, October 30, 1970; Louis Budenz, *This Is My Story* (New York: McGraw-Hill, 1947), pp. 126–127. Budenz claims that he recruited Johnson after joining the Party. *Daily Worker*, April 10, 1936, p. 1; February 15, 1933, p. 4; Polburo Minutes, October 2, 1936, Benjamin File, Draper Papers.

31. Herbert Benjamin, "Six Months of Unemployed Unity," *Communist*, November 1936, p. 1060; *Daily Worker*, January 9, 1935, p. 1; *Unemployment, Old Age and Social Insurance*, p. 203; Benjamin, "The Unemployment Movement," p. 545; "Report of the National Executive Board, Workers Alliance of America, to the Second National Convention," Benjamin File; Browder interview with Draper, October 10, 1955; Polburo Minutes, October 2, 1936, Benjamin File.

32. *Investigation and Study of the Works Progress Administration*, Hearings Before the Subcommittee of the Committee on Appropriations, House of Representatives, 76th Congress, 1st Session, pp. 37, 94, 95. Lasser used the 75 percent figure. The WPA administrator, Colonel F. C. Harrington, estimated that no more than 5 percent of the WPA's 2.8 million workers belonged to the Workers' Alliance (p. 22). Benjamin, "Six Months of Unemployed Unity," p. 1066; Herbert Benjamin, "After a Decade of Mass Unemployment," *Communist*, March 1940, pp. 264–265.

33. *Daily Worker*, April 2, 1936, p. 1; April 21, 1937, p. 1.

34. *Daily Worker*, June 25, 1937, p. 5; June 26, p. 6.

35. Herbert Benjamin, "Extending the Unity of the Unemployed," *Communist*, August 1937, p. 769. *Daily Worker*, July 28, 1937, p. 7; August 23, p. 1; August 24, p. 1; August 25, p. 1.

36. *Daily Worker*, July 23, 1937, p. 5; August 21, pp. 1, 4; August 25, p. 1; The exchange of letters among Hopkins, David Lasser, and Senator Schwellenbach on the issue are in *Daily Worker*, August 27, 1937, p. 5.

37. *Daily Worker*, August 26, 1937, p. 4. Herbert Benjamin, "Unemployment—An Old Struggle Under New Conditions," *Communist*, May 1938, pp. 425–427.

38. Browder interview with Draper, October 10, 1955. Benjamin remembered taking Browder to see Williams sometime after 1936, but he was not present during their conversation. Several of Browder's details, including the date—he put it in the spring of 1935—are clearly inaccurate. Benjamin interview with Draper, October 30, 1970; Herbert Benjamin to Theodore Draper, November 22, 1970, Draper Papers, Box 2, Folder 42.

39. See Niles' obituary, *New York Times*, September 29, 1952, p. 23. For Baker see *Daily Worker*, June 22, 1937, p. 4; and *New York Times*, September 20, 1967, p. 47. Kenneth Rexroth, in *An Autobiographical Novel* (Santa Barbara, Calif: Ross-Erickson, 1978), p. 278, claims to have known one unnamed high-ranking Hopkins aide in Seattle in the 1920s who worked on a Wobbly newspaper. Earl Browder interview with Theodore Draper, June 23, 1955, Draper Papers, Box 2, Folder 5.

40. These biographical details can be found in *Nomination of Aubrey W. Williams*, U.S. Senate, Committee on Agriculture and Forestry, 79th Congress, 1st Session; the Williams' quotes to the WPA are on pp. 138, 232. Benjamin to Draper, November 22, 1970. The WPA letter can be found in *Investigation and Study of the WPA*, p. 145. It was dated September 3, 1936.

41. Joseph Kamp, *The Fifth Column in Washington* (New Haven, Conn.: Constitution Educational League, 1940), p. 29; *Congressional Record*, March 26, 1940, p. 3445; *Nomination of Aubrey Williams*, p. 138.

42. *Nomination of Aubrey Williams*, pp. 47, 52, 233. Williams' papers at the Franklin D. Roosevelt Library at Hyde Park include a separate file on Communism; it is still closed to researchers, but archivists have assured me that it deals only with an investigation of Communism in California WPA projects. The roll-call vote on Williams' nomination is in *New York Times*, March 24, 1945, p. 15. For his obituary, see *New York Times*, March 3, 1965, p. 33.

43. *Investigation and Study of the WPA*, pp. 1109–1111. Charney, in *A Long Journey*, pp. 97–98, maintains that Duty's dissatisfaction was caused by her diminishing importance as the alliance withered with economic improvement. By 1940, twelve of the eighteen board

members were Communists. David Lasser, "An Answer to the NAC Statement of June 21 and Facts Regarding Communist Domination of the Workers' Alliance," Benjamin File.

44. Selden Rodman, "Lasser and the Workers' Alliance," *Nation*, September 10, 1938, pp. 242–244. Benjamin once suggested that Lasser was an ex-Lovestoneite. See *Daily Worker*, March 7, 1935, p. 2; December 9, 1937, p. 5. *Investigation and Study of the WPA*, pp. 67, 110, 257.

45. Frances Fox Piven and Richard Cloward, *Poor People's Movements: Why They Succeed, How They Fail* (New York: Vintage Books, 1979), pp. 90–91.

Chapter 16

1. *Communist International*, July 20, 1934, p. 554; J. Tsirul, "How the Self-Criticizing Campaign and the Checking-Up of the Fulfillment of the Decisions Are Carried on in the Communist Party of America," *Communist International*, August 15, 1932, p. 516; Jack Stachel, "Organizational Problems of the Party," *Communist*, July 1935, p. 627; "The Winning of the Working Class Youth Is the Task of the Entire Party," *Communist*, May 1934, pp. 477–488.

2. *Daily Worker*, October 11, 1930, p. 6. *The Boy Scouts Is an Organization for Capitalist Wars!* (New York: Young Pioneers of America, 1930). *Daily Worker*, February 16, 1931, p. 4; January 18, 1934, p. 5. The junior Communists even had their own journal, *New Pioneer*, edited by Helen Kay. She graduated to become the first secretary of the League of Women Shoppers, a Party auxiliary, and then an editor of the Party-led State, County, and Municipal Workers. She was an uncooperative witness before Senator Joseph McCarthy's Government Operations Committee; by then her name was Helen Kay Goldfrank. See *First Report: Un-American Activities in California 1943* (Sacramento: Report of the Joint Fact-finding Committee to 1943 Regular California Legislature, 1943), p. 100; *State Department Information Program*, U.S. Senate Government Operations Committee, 83rd Congress, 1st Session, p. 90.

3. *Report of the Fifth National Convention of the Young Communist League of U.S.A.* (New York: Young Communist League, 1929), p. 8; *Young Worker*, March 27, 1934, p. 2A; Gil Green, "The Open Letter and Tasks of the Y.C.L.," *Communist*, August 1933, p. 818.

4. Biographical details are drawn from Green's testimony in *U.S.A.* v. *Dennis et al.* (1949) and from an FBI press release, dated July 5, 1951 in my possession. On Harvey, see John Williamson, *Dangerous Scot* (New York: International Publishers, 1969), p. 66, Harry Haywood, *Black Bolshevik* (Chicago: Liberator Press, 1978), pp. 132–133. On Steuben, see Earl Browder, "Report to the Political Committee," *Communist*, January 1931, p. 21. Steuben was a Party organizer in Ohio and later became an organizer in the SWOC. During the early 1950s he edited a Party-linked magazine, *March of Labor*, before breaking with the Communists on his deathbed over the 1956 Hungarian Revolution. See Len DeCaux, *Labor Radical* (Boston: Beacon Press, 1970), pp. 529–531; *Daily Worker*, June 24, 1932, p. 4; Max Weiss, "Plenum of American YCL," *International Press Correspondence*, June 30, 1932, p. 600.

5. John Marks, "The Problems of the American Revolutionary Youth Movement," *Communist*, April 1933, p. 398. Earl Browder, *Report to the 8th Convention* (New York: Workers Library Publishers, 1934), p. 53; "The Results of the National Registration, July–August 1929 of the Y.C.L. of the U.S.A.," in *Hearings*, Fish Committee, Part 6, pp. 804–805. *Daily Worker*, January 29, 1932, p. 4; May 16, 1934, p. 3; April 22, 1935, p. 3. *Young Worker*, July 3, 1934, p. 9. Henry Winston, "The Young Communist League Prepares for Growth," *Communist*, April 1939, p. 324.

6. *Report of the Fifth National Convention of the YCL*, p. 12; Weiss, "Plenum of American YCL," p. 600; Gil Green, "The Open Letter," p. 818.

7. *Party Organizer*, September–October 1931, p. 32; *An Open Letter to All Members of the Communist Party* (New York: Central Committee, CPUSA, 1933), p. 21; Browder, *Report to the 8th Convention*, p. 53; *The Way Out* (New York: Workers Library Publishers, 1934), p. 91; Otto Kuusinen, *The Youth Movement and the Fight Against Fascism: Speech Delivered at the Seventh World Congress of the Communist International* (Moscow: Cooperative Publishing Society of Foreign Workers in the U.S.S.R., 1935), p. 31.

8. Marks, "The Problems of the American Revolutionary Youth Movement" p. 398; *Party Organizer*, April 1931, p. 7; *Daily Worker*, August 30, 1933, p. 6.

9. A Russian named Bob Mazat was in America in the early 1920s, to be followed by N. Nasanov, who later played a role in formulating the theory of self-determination in the Black Belt. The most mysterious such envoy was yet another Russian, known here only as Max. He apparently arrived in 1928 and remained at least ten years. James Wechsler recalled his brooding presence at important YCL meetings: "I learned quickly that one did not ask about it [his name] or about him. He was just there." And, "when we faced any ideological quandry, he laid down the law." Max traveled around the country, dabbled in other Party work, and thoroughly enjoyed his American interlude, so much so that leaders of the YCL felt he had become an American. He probably returned to Russia in 1938. Haywood, *Black Bolshevik*, p. 134; James Wechsler, *The Age of Suspicion* (New York: Random House, 1953), p. 95. For other references to the mysterious Max, see the testimony of Stanley Hancock, *Communist Activities in the State of California*, Part 1, House Un-American Activities Committee, 83rd Congress, 2nd Session, 1954, pp. 4548–4549, and the testimony of Frank Meyer in *Brownell v. the CPUSA*, pp. 5529, 5589. See also a memo written by Max to Browder in the late 1930s complaining that his advice was no longer being sought or followed; Browder Papers, Series 1-43. Both Carl Ross and Sam Darcy have identified Max to me as a YCI representative. *Program for American Youth* (New York: Youth Publishers, 1934), p. 14. *Daily Worker*, June 24, 1932, p. 4.

10. Kuusinen, *The Youth Movement*, p. 18; Gil Green, *Young Communists and the Unity of the Youth* (New York: Youth Publishers, 1935), p. 19.

11. S. Willis Rudy, *The College of the City of New York: A History 1847–1947* (New York: City College Press, 1949), pp. 412–413. Weiss became a leading YCL and CP functionary. One of the ten suspended was Max Gordon, who also enjoyed a long career in the Party before, like Weiss, quitting in 1958. Among those galvanized into political action by the affair was John Gates. See Gates, *The Story of an American Communist* (New York: Thomas Nelson and Sons, 1958), p. 18, and Theodore Draper, "City College's Rebel Generation," *New Masses*, November 22, 1934, p. 14.

12. *Student Review*, December 1931, p. 2. For the link between the Weiss case and the founding of the NYSL, see *Building a Militant Student Movement: Program and Constitution of the National Student League* (New York: no date or publisher), p. 8; *Daily Worker*, March 30, 1932, p. 3; *Student Review*, December 1934, p. 8; and February 1934, p. 16; Browder, *Report to the 8th Convention*, pp. 41–42; and *Daily Worker*, June 20, 1934, p. 4.

13. *Student Review*, March 1932, pp. 5–6; October, p. 15.

14. Rob Hall, president of the Columbia Social Problems Club and a member of the NSL's first National Executive Committee, was soon engaged in Party agrarian work with Hal Ware and Lem Harris. After a sojourn as a Party leader in Alabama in the 1940s, he became the *Daily Worker*'s Washington correspondent. Joseph Cohen, another member of the first NEC from Brooklyn College, became the NSL's executive secretary in 1934. Under his Party name of Joe Clark, he later became a YCL organizer before embarking on a career as a *Daily Worker* foreign correspondent. Another Brooklyn College alumnus, Theodore Draper, moved from the editorship of the NSL's *Student Review* to the *Daily Worker* and *New Masses*. One of his assistant editors, Joseph Starobin, had been expelled from CCNY in 1931 as a participant in the *Frontiers* controversy. He had joined the YCL in 1930 while still a student at DeWitt Clinton High School and later served as editor of the *Young Communist Review*. Like Clark, Starobin became a Party journalist and foreign editor for the *Daily Worker*. Adam Lapin, an editor of the *Student Review*, became a *Daily Worker* correspondent in Washington and then associate editor of the *People's World*, the Party's West Coast organ. Other New Yorkers took on various Party assignments. Clyde Johnson served as the NSL's Southern organizer before taking a leading role in the Sharecroppers' Union. Nathaniel Weyl left the League for Industrial Democracy and joined both the NSL and the Communist party in the winter of 1932–1933. Hired by the Agriculture Department, he became a member of the Ware Group. Hall became a newspaper executive in upstate New York after his break in 1956. Clark is now associated with the democratic socialist *Dissent*. Draper became the foremost historian of American Communism. Starobin wrote an outstanding history of the Party. Weyl, a critic and author, testified before a congressional committee. Information about them is scattered throughout a wide variety of books, articles, and congressional and court testimony. On Lapin, see Al Richmond, *A Long View from the Left*

Boston: Houghton Mifflin, 1973), p. 289. On Johnson, see *Student Review*, February 1934.

15. *Daily Worker*, March 26, 1932, p. 3; March 28, p. 1; March 29, pp. 1, 3. See also *Student Review*, May 1932, and James Wechsler, *Revolt on the Campus* (New York: Covici-Friede, 1935), pp. 100–105.

16. *Daily Worker*, April 5, 1932, p. 3.

17. *Daily Worker*, April 4, 1932, p. 3; April 7, p. 1. *Student Review*, May 1932, pp. 12–14. Wechsler, *Revolt on the Campus*, pp. 117–119. Twenty years later, Senator Joseph McCarthy used Harris's troubles to insist he was unfit to serve in a high position with the Voice of America.

18. *Daily Worker*, April 9, 1932, p. 4.

19. *Daily Worker*, August 4, 1931, p. 4. *Student Review*, Summer Issue, 1932, p. 14; April 1933, p. 8. *Daily Worker*, May 15, 1933, p. 1. Departmental Chairman Rexford Tugwell, preparing to join the Roosevelt administration, offered Henderson a terminal one-year assistantship in Russia; he spurned the offer.

20. *Daily Worker*, May 16, 1933, p. 1; May 25, p. 2; June 5, 1934, p. 3.

21. Oakley Johnson, "The Early Socialist Party of Michigan: An Assignment in Autobiography," *Centennial Review*, No. 2, 1966, pp. 147–162; *Daily Worker*, October 29, 1932, p. 4. For Johnson's admission of Party membership in 1934—he says nothing of earlier years—see Oakley Johnson, "Monthly Review," in Joseph Conlin, *The American Radical Press* (Westport, Conn.: Greenwood Press, 1974), p. 473.

22. *Daily Worker*, October 5, 1932, p. 1; October 28, p. 2; October 29, p. 4; November 3, p. 1. Oakley Johnson, "Campus Battles for Freedom in the Thirties," *Centennial Review*, No. 3, 1970, pp. 341–361. Rudy, *The College of the City of New York*, pp. 415–417; *Sunday Worker*, November 7, 1937, p. 11. *Magazine*.

23. *Student Review*, October 1932, p. 11; February 1933, pp. 12–15. *Daily Worker*, January 17, 1933, p. 4.

24. *Daily Worker*, June 1, 1933, p. 1; June 2, p. 2; June 14, p. 1. *Student Review*, December 1933, pp. 7–9. Rudy, *The College of the City of New York*, pp. 418–419.

25. *New Masses*, October 23, 1934, p. 6; November 27, pp. 13–14. Rudy, *The College of the City of New York*, pp. 421–433.

26. The letter and the SLID's response are in *Student Review*, December 1933, and February 1934, p. 16. *Daily Worker*, December 28, 1933, pp. 1–2.

27. Wechsler, *Revolt on the Campus*, pp. 171–174; *Daily Worker*, April 14, 1934, p. 1.

28. *Daily Worker*, March 30, 1932, p. 1. *Student Review*, February 1933, p. 5; February 1934, pp. 5–6. *Daily Worker*, December 28, 1933, p. 1. *Student Review*, December 1933, p. 21. *Investigation of Un-American Propaganda Activities*, Special Committee on Un-American Activities, House of Representatives, 76th Congress, 1st Session, 1939, Vol. 11, pp. 7074–7075 (Testimony of Joseph Lash).

29. Green, *Young Communists and the Unity of Youth*, p. 8. *Daily Worker*, December 30, 1935, pp. 1, 2; December 31, p. 1; February 14, p. 2. Among the prominent members of the ASU were Irving Howe, Bruce Bliven, Jr., Katherine Meyer (Graham), and Robert Lane. Wechsler, *The Age of Suspicion*, p. 5. Strack, a member of Phi Beta Kappa and the national women's debating champion, had been expelled from the University of California for "communist agitation." She later became a leader in the California Party and was tried under the Smith Act. *Student Review*, December 1934, p. 3. Gerber spoke on behalf of the YCL at the convention and admitted his membership. *Daily Worker*, February 14, 1936, p. 5.

30. *New Masses*, January 10, 1939, p. 11.

31. George Rawick, *The New Deal and Youth: The Civilian Conservation Corps, the National Youth Administration, and the American Youth Congress* (unpublished doctoral dissertation, University of Wisconsin, 1957), pp. 304–306.

32. Rawick, *The New Deal and Youth*, pp. 309–315; *Daily Worker*, April 22, 1936, p. 5.

33. Rawick, *The New Deal and Youth*, pp. 321–328. The YCL'ers were Herbert Witt, Brinton Harris, Celeste Strack, and James Wechsler. *Daily Worker*, December 28, 1937, p. 1; December 29, p. 1; December 29, 1938, p. 5. The last quotation is cited in Hal Draper, "The Student Movement of the Thirties," in Rita Simon, ed., *As We Saw the Thirties* (Urbana: University of Illinois Press, 1967), p. 180.

34. *Daily Worker*, February 14, 1936, p. 2; *Student Review*, October 1935, p. 2; *Investigation of Un-American Propaganda Activities*; Executive Hearings Made Public, Vol. 6, 83rd Congress pp. 2780–2813; *Daily Worker*, October 19, 1937, p. 2; Joseph Lash, *Eleanor Roose-*

velt: A Friend's Memoir (Garden City, N.Y.: Doubleday, 1964), p. 72. Lash's attendance may have been the reason that an ex-YCL'er, Kenneth Goff, named Lash as a fellow Communist to the Dies Committee. See *Investigation of Un-American Propaganda Activities*, Vol. 9, pp. 5593–5594.

35. Rawick, *The New Deal and Youth*, pp. 284–289; Green, *Young Communists and the Unity of Youth*, p. 6.

36. *Daily Worker*, August 17, 1934, p. 1; *New Masses*, November 13, 1934, pp. 6–11.

37. *Daily Worker*, August 18, 1934, p. 1; August 20, p. 2.

38. Earl Browder, "The Struggle for the United Front," *Communist*, October 1934, p. 958; Kuusinen, *The Youth Movement*, p. 14n; *Youth Marches Toward Socialism* (New York: Workers Library Publishers, 1935), p. 40. Wilhelm Pieck also singled out the Americans and French for "great results in their work among the youth." Wilhelm Pieck, *Freedom, Peace and Bread* (New York: Workers Library Publishers, 1935), p. 101.

39. Wechsler, *The Age of Suspicion*, p. 71. *Hearings, State Department Information Program*, Part IV, Committee on Government Operations, U.S. Senate, 83rd Congress, 1st Session, p. 267. *Investigation of Un-American Propaganda*, Vol. 9, pp. 5593–5594; Vol. 11, p. 7056. Hinckley's wife was a member of the Party. See Rawick, *The New Deal and Youth*, p. 337n. Cadden's obituary in the *New York Times*, June 17, 1980, p. B10, calls him a former member of the Communist party. He had denied Party membership to the Dies Committee along with Hinckley.

40. *Daily Worker*, July 5, 1939, p. 5; "Testimony of Jack R. McMichael," *Hearings Before the House Committee on Un-American Activities*, 1953, p. 2696. See also Ralph Roy, *Communism and the Churches* (New York: Harcourt, Brace, 1960), pp. 312–316.

41. Green, *Young Communists and the Unity of Youth*, pp. 6–8; Max Weiss and Charles Wilson, "Problems of the United Front," *International of Youth*, 1935, p. 11.

42. Rawick, *The New Deal and Youth*, pp. 297–299, 322–330. Weiss and Wilson, "Problems of the United Front," p. 11. *Daily Worker*, July 7, 1936, pp. 1, 2; July 5, 1939, p. 5.

43. Joseph Lash, *Eleanor Roosevelt*, p. 5; *Daily Worker*, February 21, 1939, p. 3. For a full list of patrons, see FBI File 100-3587-23. *Daily Worker*, June 22, 1938, p. 2; August 2, p. 3; August 17, p. 1; August 20, p. 2. *Youth Demands a Peaceful World: Report of the Second World Youth Congress* (New York: World Youth Congress, 1938). *Daily Worker*, July 6, 1936, p. 1. Testimony of William Hinckley in *Investigation of Un-American Propaganda Activities*, Vol. 11, p. 7043.

Chapter 17

1. *Program and Constitution: Workers Party of America* (Chicago: Workers Party of America, 1924), p. 9; *The Platform of the Class Struggle* (New York: Workers Library Publishers, 1928), p. 52; James Ford, *The Negro and the Democratic Front* (New York: International Publishers, 1938), p. 82; Jack Stachel, "Organizational Report to the Sixth Convention," *Communist*, April 1929, p. 245. Earl Browder, in "The Bolshevization of the Communist Party," *Communist*, August 1930, p. 688, put the number at "hardly 50."

2. Theodore Draper, *American Communism and Soviet Russia* (New York: Viking Press, 1960), p. 350; "C. I. Resolution on Negro Question in U.S.," *Communist*, January 1930, p. 49. In 1932 the Black Belt was defined as a "continuous stretch of land, extending like a crescent moon from Southern Maryland to Arkansas, in which Negroes outnumber the whites." *Daily Worker*, November 11, 1932, p. 4; Earl Browder, "For National Liberation of the Negroes! War Against White Chauvinism!," *Communist*, April 1932, p. 297.

3. Harry Haywood, *Black Bolshevik* (Chicago: Liberator Press, 1978), pp. 5–175; Isaac Deutscher, *Stalin: A Political Biography* (New York: Vintage Books 1960), pp. 182–185.

4. Otto Huiswood, "World Aspects of the Negro Question," *Communist*, February 1930, pp. 133, 146; Jos. Prokopec, "Negroes as an Oppressed National Minority," *Communist*, March 1930, p. 239.

5. The original cables, dated March 16, 1930, March 23, 1930, and March 30, 1930, are in Draper Papers, Box 1, Folder 23. The contestants are identified only as "H" (Haywood), "N" (Nasanov), "S" (Safarov), "P" (Piatnitsky), "Man" (Manuilsky), and "Ku"

(Kuusinen). Harry Haywood confirmed their identities to me in a personal interview on October 25, 1979. The March 30 cable noted that Kuusinen claimed that the idea of separation had been eliminated from the Comintern draft "by a very authoritative Leninist." Haywood informed me that the person was Stalin.

6. *Thesis and Resolutions for the Seventh National Convention of the CPUSA, by Central Committee Plenum*, March 21-April 4, 1930, p. 61; *Struggles Ahead!* (New York: CPUSA, 1930), p. 26. Browder later admitted that the Comintern's discussion prompted the change. *Daily Worker*, April 21, 1930, p. 6; Browder, "The Bolshevization of the Communist Party," p. 689.

7. Haywood, *Black Bolshevik*, pp. 331–333; "Resolution of Communist International," October 1930, in *The Communist Position on the Negro Question* (no date or publisher), pp. 41–56.

8. Earl Browder interview, Columbia Oral History Project, p. 282; B. D. Amis, "How We Carried Out the Decision of the 1930 C. I. Resolution on the Negro Question in the U.S.," *Communist International*, May 5, 1935, p. 512; Wilson Record, *The Negro and the Communist Party* (Chapel Hill: University of North Carolina Press, 1951), p. 65.

9. "C. I. Resolution on Negro Question in U.S.," p. 52; *Daily Worker*, October 17, 1929, p. 4; "Resolution of Communist International," *Communist*, February 1931, p. 157; Earl Browder, "Wipe Out the Stench of the Slave Market," in *The Communist Position on the Negro Question*, p. 19.

10. *Daily Worker*, March 22, 1930, p. 4; February 19, 1931, p. 4; November 25, 1929, p. 4; July 18, 1930, p. 4; December 10, p. 4; January 16, p. 1.

11. *Daily Worker*, December 10, 1930, p. 4; Haywood, *Black Bolshevik*, pp. 352–353.

12. *New York Times*, March 2, 1931, p. 1; *Race Hatred on Trial* (New York: Workers Library Publishers, 1931), pp. 7–8. This pamphlet contains an expurgated account of the proceedings of Yokinen's trial. The exact date of the incident is never given, but an article in the *Daily Worker* on December 10, 1930, p. 4, refers to it. Israel Amter claimed in the *New York Times*, February 28, 1931, p. 22, that it had taken place six weeks earlier, which would have put it in January.

13. *New York Times*, February 28, 1931, p. 22; March 2, pp. 1–2. *Daily Worker*, February 24, 1931, p. 1; February 28, p. 1; March 3, p. 1; March 4, p. 1. *Race Hatred on Trial*, pp. 8–47.

14. Earl Browder, "The End of Relative Capitalist Stabilization and the Tasks of Our Party," *Communist*, March 1933, p. 242.

15. *Daily Worker*, March 23, 1931, p. 4; September 17, pp. 3–4; December 19, p. 4. Earl Browder, "For National Liberation of the Negroes," *Communist*, April 1932, p. 298. Earl Browder, "Report of the Political Bureau to the Central Committee, 13th Plenum," Draper Papers, Box 1, Folder 31.

16. *Daily Worker*, March 21, 1931, p. 4; Harvey Klehr, *Communist Cadre* (Stanford, Calif.: Hoover Institution Press, 1978), pp. 62–63; *The Communist Position on the Negro Question*, p. 29. A Foster-Ford Committee for Equal Negro Rights, led by William Jones, managing editor of the *Baltimore Afro-American*, enlisted such prominent Negroes as Kelley Miller, Countee Cullen, and George Murphy, Jr. *Daily Worker*, October 29, 1932, p. 1; November 4, p. 1.

17. "Draft Thesis for 7th Party Convention," Draper Papers, Box 1, Folder 25, The published thesis omitted Briggs' name, referring to "some comrades." *Struggles Ahead!*, p. 25; Haywood, *Black Bolshevik*, p. 380; Earl Browder interview with Theodore Draper, June 16, 1953, Draper Papers, Box 2, Folder 3.

18. *Daily Worker*, May 30, 1932, p. 1; September 24, 1936, p. 5. *Sunday Worker*, July 5, 1936, p. 1. George Charney, *A Long Journey* (Chicago: Quadrangle Books, 1968), p. 93.

19. Browder, "The Bolshevization of the Communist Party," p. 689. Earl Browder, "To the Masses—To the Shops! Organize the Masses!", *Communist*, October 1931, p. 803. Earl Browder, "Membership Report," 1931, Draper Papers, Box 1, Folder 29. *Daily Worker*, June 13, 1930, p. 3; June 25, p. 3. "Minutes of the Convention of the League of Struggle for Negro Rights Held in St. Louis, Missouri, November 15 and 16, 1930," FBI Files 100-148082. Years later, however, William Weinstone claimed a scant 100 Negro members in 1930. Very high turnover rates may have accounted for part of the discrepancy. Never very successful at retaining members, the Party had even more trouble in keeping Negroes. John Williamson admitted in 1931 that in Chicago "large numbers of Negro workers have been recruited but lost." Six hundred Negroes joined the Harlem Party after police killed two

Negro organizers, but only 10 percent remained members. William Weinstone, "An Important Chapter in the Party's History of Industrial Concentration," *Political Affairs*, September 1949, p. 79; John Williamson, "The Party Nucleus—A Factor in the Class Struggle," *Communist*, May 1931, p. 431; *Daily Worker*, October 11, 1931, p. 4.

20. Haywood, *Black Bolshevik*, p. 343; *Daily Worker*, December 11, 1930; p. 4; "Minutes of the Convention," FBI Files; Browder, "The End of Relative Capitalist Stabilization," p. 240; "Comintern Documents," *Communist*, May 1931, p. 408; *Daily Worker*, March 23, 1931, p. 4; *Party Organizer*, March 1931, p. 19.

21. Browder, "To the Masses," p. 803; *Daily Worker*, January 19, 1932, p. 5; Earl Browder, "Why an Open Letter to Our Party Membership," *Communist*, August 1933, p. 740; Amis, "How We Carried Out," p. 508.

22. *Labor Unity*, May 23, 1931, p. 7. The Needle Trades Workers Industrial Union, for example, was accused of acquiescing to differential pay scales for its black and white workers. *Labor Unity*, December 13, 1930, p. 2. Haywood, *Black Bolshevik*, p. 351. *Daily Worker*, August 4, 5, 6, 7, 8, 10, 1931, pp. 1–3; August 19, p. 4. The turnout and response were so successful that they overwhelmed the Party's section leadership.

23. *Death Penalty Demanded* (New York: Workers Library Publishers, 1930), p. 30. The Atlanta Six were never brought to trial. Charges were finally dropped in 1939. Charles Martin, *The Angelo Herndon Case and Southern Justice* (Baton Rouge: Louisiana State University Press, 1976), p. 212n; Angelo Herndon, *Let Me Live* (New York: Arno Press, 1969), p. 228.

24. "Resolution of the Political Secretariat of the ECCI," p. 9, Draper Papers Box 1, Folder 1; Henry Puro, "The Tasks of Our Party in Agrarian Work," *Communist*, February 1931, p. 148. *Southern Worker*, January 3, 1931, p. 4; April 4, p. 4. Haywood, *Black Bolshevik*, p. 398. Nell Irvin Painter, *The Narrative of Hosea Hudson: His Life as a Negro Communist* (Cambridge, Mass.: Harvard University Press, 1979), p. 84. The letters indicated that economic conditions were desperate. "The croppers are starving here," wrote one, pleading for help. Other farmers wrote: "I have not got a dollar"; and "I have seven children and a wife, and no job and my landlord said he could not let me have nothing else." *Southern Worker*, February 28, 1931, p. 1; July 25, p. 1.

25. *Daily Worker*, July 18, 1931, p. 1; July 20, pp. 1, 3. *Southern Worker*, July 25, 1931, pp. 1, 2; August 1, p. 4. *New Masses*, October 1932, p. 16. B. D. Amis, "Croppers in Southern United States Fight to Live," *International Press Correspondence*, August 20, 1931, p. 821. *New York Times*, July 18, 1931, p. 30; July 19, p. 6.

26. *Daily Worker*, July 20, 1931, p. 1; Haywood, *Black Bolshevik*, pp. 399–401; *Daily World*, July 27, 1978, p. 8. In his *Daily World* article, Murphy refers to Coad as Mack Cole. *Party Organizer*, January 1933, p. 14; *Daily Worker*, December 31, 1932, p. 6.

27. Painter, *Hosea Hudson*, pp. 147–148. *Daily Worker*, December 22, 1932, p. 1; December 23, p. 1; December 31, p. 6. *Southern Worker*, May 20, 1933, p. 2. One of those convicted, Ned Cobb, later told his story in Theodore Rosengarten's *All God's Dangers* (New York: Alfred Knopf, 1974).

28. *Daily Worker*, December 31, 1932, p. 6; James Allen, "Prologue to the Liberation of the Negro People," *Communist*, February 1933, p. 168; "Achievements and Tasks of the Sharecroppers' Union," in *The Communist Position on the Farmers' Movement* (New York: Workers Library Publishers, 1933), pp. 39, 41, 44, 45. Murphy's comments are from a speech he made to the Party's Extraordinary Conference in July 1933. *Daily Worker*, December 29, 1934, p. 3; Amis, "How We Carried Out," p. 498.

29. *Daily Worker*, April 20, 1932, p. 2. Dan Carter, *Scottsboro: A Tragedy of the American South* (New York: Oxford University Press, 1971), pp. 51–52. *Daily Worker*, April 10, 1931, pp. 1, 3; April 15, p. 1.

30. *Daily Worker*, April 15, 1931, p. 3; July 4, p. 6; May 5, p. 1. "Memo of Meeting of the Negro Department's Central Committee, January 4, 1932," Robert Minor Papers, Box 12, Columbia University. Present were Amis, Bedacht, Haywood, Wakefield, George Maurer, Hope, and Joseph Brodsky.

31. *Daily Worker*, July 4, 1931, p. 6; May 14, pp. 1, 4.

32. *Daily Worker*, April 22, 1931, p. 1; May 4, p. 1; November 22, 1932, p. 4. J. Louis Engdahl, head of the ILD, died of pneumonia in Moscow at the end of one tour with one of the Scottsboro Boys' mothers, Mrs. Wright. William Patterson replaced him as ILD leader. William Patterson, *The Man Who Cried Genocide* (New York: International Publishers, 1971),

pp. 126–127; Carter, *Scottsboro*, p. 143. *Daily Worker*, July 15, 1931, p. 4; July 17, p. 1; April 27, p. 1; April 28, p. 1; July 11, p. 1. *New York Times*, July 1, 1931, p. 9.

33. *Daily Worker*, May 27, 1931, p. 1; June 1, p. 1. Five delegates to the Chattanooga meeting, including Amis, Minor, and Haywood, were arrested leaving the hall and charged with loitering. *Daily Worker*, July 6, 1931, p. 1; May 20, p. 3.

34. *Daily Worker*, July 15, 1931, p. 4; September 17, p. 3.

35. *Daily Worker*, May 14, 1931, pp. 1, 4; January 19, 1932, p. 4. See also Harry Haywood, "The Scottsboro Decision," *Communist*, December 1932, pp. 1065–1075. Walter White, in "The Negro and the Communists," *Harper's*, December 1931, p. 71, admitted with some relief that if the Communists had been less rigid about the united front plea, "there is no way of estimating how deeply they might have penetrated into Negro life and consciousness."

36. Pickens had withdrawn his statement of support, provoking Haywood's outburst. *Daily Worker*, May 4, 1931, p. 3; April 27, p. 4; January 19, 1932, p. 4. "The Scottsboro Struggle and the Next Step: Resolution of the Political Bureau," *Communist*, June 1933, p. 575; Clarence Hathaway, "A Warning Against Opportunist Distortions of the United Front Tactics," ibid., p. 533.

37. *Daily Worker*, May 3, 1933, p. 2; May 4, p. 2; May 8, p. 1; May 9, p. 1; May 15, p. 2. *New York Times*, May 9, 1933, p. 38.

38. *Daily Worker*, June 28, 1933, p. 2; "The Scottsboro Struggle and the Next Steps," p. 579; Amis, "How We Carried Out," pp. 501–503.

39. Carter, *Scottsboro*, pp. 313–334.

40. *Daily Worker*, July 2, 1932, p. 6. *The Communist Position on the Negro Question*, p. 18. *Daily Worker*, May 11, 1932, p. 4; October 1, p. 3; June 15, 1936, p. 2. James Ford and Louis Sass, "Development of Work in the Harlem Section," *Communist*, April 1935, p. 232.

41. *Party Organizer*, May–June 1934, p. 62; *Daily Worker*, March 20, 1934, p. 4; Mark Naison, *The Communist Party in Harlem: 1928–1936* (unpublished doctoral dissertation, Columbia University, 1976), pp. 186–232, 260, 295–296.

42. Browder, *Report to the 8th Convention* (New York: Workers Library Publishers, 1934), pp. 51, 109. See *Daily Worker*, April 6, 1934, pp. 1, 3, where Nowell was called Noel. Nowell dropped out of the Party in 1936 and became a cooperative witness before the Dies Committee. See *Investigation of Un-American Propaganda Activities*, Special Committee on Un-American Activities, House of Representatives, 76th Congress, 1st Session, 1939, Vol. 11, pp. 6984–7007. Manning Johnson left the Party in 1939; he too later became a professional witness for the government. *The Way Out* (New York: Workers Library Publishers, 1934), pp. 41–42; *Daily Worker*, April 26, 1934, p. 2.

43. James Hooker, *Black Revolutionary: George Padmore's Path from Communism to Pan-Africanism* (New York: Frederick Praeger, 1967). *Daily Worker*, April 6, 1934, p. 3; August 2, p. 6.

44. *Daily Worker*, August 6, 1934, pp. 1, 2, 6; January 19, 1936, p. 4. James Ford, "The United Front in the Field of Negro Work," *Communist*, February 1935, p. 130. *Daily Worker*, July 6, 1936, p. 7. Earlier in the year, Ben Davis admitted that Divine's proposal for a federal law to regulate union dues—which, Divine claimed, were so high as to exclude Negroes from the labor movement—was wrong-headed but defended him as a progressive and urged Communists to work with him and change his mind. *Daily Worker*, February 11, 1936, p. 2.

45. *New York Times*, March 20, 1935, p. 1. *Daily Worker*, March 21, 1935, pp. 1, 2; March 29, p. 1.

46. *New York Times*, March 21, 1935, pp. 1, 3. *Daily Worker*, March 22, 1935, p. 1; March 23, p. 1. Naison, *The Communist Party in Harlem*, pp. 319, 324–325. James Ford, *Hunger and Terror in Harlem* (New York: Communist Party, 1935), p. 13.

47. See Padmore's article in *The Crisis*, May 1935, pp. 302, 315; and Naison, *The Communist Party in Harlem*, pp. 368–369.

48. *Daily Worker*, August 25, 1935, p. 2; March 25, p. 3; August 5, p. 1. *New York Times*, August 4, 1935, p. 28.

49. *The Way Out*, pp. 82, 96; James Ford and James Allen, *The Negro in a Soviet America* (New York: Workers Library Publishers, 1935), pp. 26–32.

50. Georgi Dimitroff, *Working-Class Unity* (New York: Workers Library Publishers, 1935), p. 42; Earl Browder, *New Steps in the United Front* (New York: Workers Library Publishers, 1935), pp. 22–23; Earl Browder, *Build the United People's Front* (New York:

Workers Library Publishers, 1936), p. 60; *Resolutions of the Ninth Convention of the Communist Party* (New York: Workers Library Publishers, 1936), p. 28; *Daily Worker,* June 27, 1936, p. 2; Haywood, *Black Bolshevik,* p. 465; James Ford, *The Negro and the Democratic Front* (New York: International Publishers, 1938), p. 83.

51. *Daily Worker,* March 23, 1935, p. 2. One of Haywood's conflicts in Chicago was with black novelist Richard Wright. See Patterson, *The Man Who Cried Genocide,* p. 149. Haywood is "Buddy Nealson" in Wright's autobiographical account in Richard Crossman, ed. *The God That Failed* (New York: Bantam Books, 1965). During the late 1950s Haywood was expelled as an ultra-leftist; as of 1980 he was a leader of the pro-Chinese group, the Communist Party (Marxist-Leninist), still committed to the self-determination doctrine he had helped formulate a half-century before. Haywood, *Black Bolshevik,* pp. 442–495; Harry Haywood interview with Harvey Klehr, October 25, 1979.

52. Francis Franklin, "For a Free, Happy and Prosperous South," *Communist,* January 1938, p. 60; Theodore Basset, "The 'White' South and the People's Front," *Communist,* April 1938, pp. 378–379. The latter was an article that Haywood wrote but was published under Basset's name. See Haywood, *Black Bolshevik,* p. 492; and James Allen, *Negro Liberation* (New York: International Publishers, 1938), pp. 29, 34.

53. Earl Browder, "Report to the Central Committee Meeting of the C.P.U.S.A., January 15–18, 1935," *Communist,* March 1935, p. 213; James Ford, "The National Negro Congress," *Communist,* June 1936, pp. 559–560.

54. The material on Davis is found in James Ford's FBI File, 100-14632-101, p. 14. James Ford, "The National Negro Congress," *Communist,* April 1936, p. 318; Ford, *The Negro and the Democratic Front,* p. 11; "Special Meeting of the Negro Commission of the C.E.C. and the Section Committee Harlem Section, October 19, 1935," in FBI File 61-6728-151. This FBI file deals with the National Negro Congress.

55. *Daily Worker,* January 25, 1936, p. 4; "Special Meeting," in FBI File 61-6728-151.

56. *Daily Worker,* January 26, 1936, p. 4. Naison, *The Communist Party in Harlem,* p. 408. *Daily Worker,* February 17, 1936, pp. 1, 2; February 18, p. 1. James Ford, "The National Negro Congress," *Communist,* June 1936, p. 561. Haywood, *Black Bolshevik,* p. 461.

57. *Daily Worker,* February 17, 1936, pp. 1, 2; Lawrence Wittner, "The National Negro Congress: A Reassessment," *American Quarterly,* Winter, 1970, pp. 884–886; *Resolutions of the National Negro Congress* (Chicago: 1936), p. 5; *Daily Worker,* February 16, 1936, pp. 1, 2.

58. A. Philip Randolph's biographer insisted that he "had no idea, soon after assuming the presidency of the National Negro Congress, that the Communists were contributing so heavily to its support and slowly dominating its internal machinery." Jervis Anderson, *A. Philip Randolph: A Biographical Portrait* (New York: Harcourt Brace Jovanovich, 1972), pp. 205, 234. *Daily Worker,* February 16, 1936, p. 1; December 16, 1938, p. 3.

59. Mark Naison, "Communism and Harlem Intellectuals in the Popular Front: Anti-Fascism and the Politics of Black Culture," *Journal of Ethnic Studies,* Spring 1981, pp. 8–15; *Daily Worker,* March 19, 1931, p. 2; Paul Robeson, *Here I Stand* (New York: Othello Associates, 1958), p. 44; *Daily Worker,* January 15, 1935, p. 6. See Charles Wright, *Robeson: Labor's Forgotten Champion* (Detroit: Balamp Publishing, 1975), for accounts of Robeson's labors on behalf of left-wing causes. His protestations of support for Russia destroyed his entertainment career. Speaking at a World Peace Conference in Paris in 1949, Robeson declared it "unthinkable for myself and the Negro people to go to war in the interests of those who have oppressed us for generations," especially against a country "which in one generation has raised our people to the full dignity of mankind." Returning home to a furor over his statement, Robeson refused to back down, proclaiming that he "loved the Soviet people more than those of any other nation." Slightly different versions of the quotation are given in *New York Times,* April 21, 1949, p. 2; and *Daily Worker,* April 20, 1949, p. 9. *New York Times,* June 20, 1949, p. 7.

60. Robeson, *Here I Stand,* pp. 46–47. Manning Johnson, an unreliable witness, accused him of being a Communist in *Hearings Regarding Communist Infiltration of Minority Groups,* Part I, House Committee on Un-American Activities, 81st Congress, 1st Session, p. 13. *Daily Worker,* June 15, 1936, p. 2; July 10, p. 5. *Party Organizer,* July–August 1936, p. 7.

61. *Party Organizer,* June 1938, p. 2; Jack Stachel, "Build the Party," *Communist,* March 1938, p. 223; *Daily Worker,* May 28, 1938, p. 5; Max Steinberg, "Rooting the Party Among the Masses in New York," *Communist,* September 1938, pp. 829, 838–839; *Party Organizer,* June 1938, pp. 15–16.

Chapter 18

1. See *Daily Worker*, March 22, 1934, p. 5, for an account of Copland's first recital of his own works. See *New Masses*, May 1, 1934, p. 1, for a prizewinning score by Copland of a revolutionary poem, "Into the Streets May First." *Hearings Regarding Hans Eisler*, House Un-American Activities Committee, 80th Congress, 1st Session, pp. 30–34; *Soviet Music*, March–April 1933, p. 126; *Daily Worker* March 1, 1935, p. 5. Eisler was the brother of Gerhart Eisler, a CI rep, and Ruth Fisher, who had once led the German Communist party. Forced to leave the United States in 1939 when his visa expired, Eisler desperately sought to gain readmission. Eleanor Roosevelt was persuaded to write to the State Department on his behalf. Even though the department's files indicated his Communist connections, Eisler was allowed to return in 1941 after denouncing Stalin. He earned his living writing scores for Hollywood. Subpoenaed in 1947, he denied being a Communist and refused to take responsibility for what use Communists had made of his work. He was allowed to leave the country voluntarily. A sympathetic portrait of Eisler is in Harold Clurman, *All People Are Famous* (New York: Harcourt Brace Jovanovich, 1974), pp. 127–135. On Stokowski, see *Daily Worker*, January 19, 1934, p. 2; January 27, p. 7; March 31, pp. 1, 7.

2. Morgan Himelstein, *Drama Was a Weapon: The Left-Wing Theatre in New York 1929–1941* (New Brunswick, N.J.: Rutgers University Press, 1963), p. 23. *Daily Worker*, January 23, 1934, p. 5; March 12, p. 7. On *Waiting for Lefty*, see Harold Clurman, *The Fervent Years* (New York: Hill and Wang, 1957).

3. *Daily Worker*, September 12, 1934, p. 5; July 12, p. 5. *New Masses*, October 30, 1934, pp. 25–26.

4. *New Masses*, January 1, 1935, pp. 34, 38. *Daily Worker*, February 8, 1934, p. 5; April 20, 1935, p. 7.

5. Himelstein, *Drama Was a Weapon*, p. 28. *Daily Worker*, December 30, 1935, p. 7; April 13, p. 7. *New Masses*, May 8, 1934, p. 25.

6. Richard Wright, in *American Hunger* (New York: Harper & Row, 1977), p. 89, reports that he complained that Chicago Communists had "demanded that writers be assigned the task of producing pamphlets for the use of trade unions." *New Masses*, October 30, 1934, p. 26. A. B. Magil, a leading Party cultural spokesman, has denied that any such faction meeting occurred. A. B. Magil to Harvey Klehr, May 1, 1980. Horace Gregory, a radical poet, denounced the decision in the *New Masses* and was rebuked by Edwin Seaver and Meridel LeSueur. *New Masses*, October 30, 1934, p. 26; February 12, 1935, pp. 20–21; February 19, pp. 21–22.

7. Such retrospective efforts to link the congress to the emerging Popular Front—as in Malcolm Cowley's *The Dream of the Golden Mountains: Remembering the 1930s* (New York: Viking Press, 1980), p. 270—severely underestimate the Party's domination of the event. See *New Masses*, January 22, 1935, p. 20, for the call. As another indication of the gathering's narrowness, eighteen of the sixty-four signers had endorsed the *Culture and the Crisis* pamphlet supporting Foster and Ford in 1932 (Fielding Burke, Erskine Caldwell, Robert Cantwell, Lester Cohen, Malcolm Cowley, Waldo Frank, Eugene Gordon, Horace Gregory, Granville Hicks, Langston Hughes, Orrick Johns, Louis Lozowick, Grace Lumpkin, Sam Ornitz, Isidor Schneider, Edwin Seaver, Lincoln Steffens, and Ella Winter). At least another twenty-two were Party members or long-time sympathizers publicly identified with Party causes.

8. Henry Hart (ed.), *American Writers' Congress* (New York: International Publishers, 1935), pp. 165, 175, 187–188. None of this prevented Browder from telling the writers that they were "overwhelmingly unaffiliated with our Party."

9. "Thirty Years Later: Memories of the First American Writers' Congress," *American Scholar*, Summer 1966, p. 500. *Saturday Review*, May 4, 1935, p. 11; May 11, pp. 3–4, 17–18.

10. *Daily Workers*, April 29, 1935, p. 3; Kenneth Burke, "The Writers' Congress," *Nation*, May 15, 1935, p. 571. For Burke's speech at the congress see Kenneth Burke, "Revolutionary Symbolism in America," in Hart, *American Writers' Congress*, pp. 87–94, 167–171. For a fictional portrayal of the incident see James Farrell, *Yet Other Waters* (New York: Viking Press, 1952), pp. 123–124. Before his talk, Burke had shown the speech to a Communist friend who assured him it was unexceptionable.

11. *Daily Worker*, April 29, 1935, p. 3.

12. *Publishers Weekly*, November 2, 1935, pp. 1656–1657, quoted in John Sessions,

"League of American Writers," unpublished manuscript in my possession. This paper, originally prepared for a volume on the Party role in auxiliaries, was made available by John Roche. Cowley, *The Dream of the Golden Mountains*, pp. 293–300.

13. *Daily Worker*, September 2, 1936, p. 2; Granville Hicks interview with Theodore Draper, Draper Papers, Box 3, Folder 108; Sessions, "League of American Writers."

14. *Daily Worker*, February 19, 1936, p. 7; *New Masses*, October 1, 1935, p. 33.

15. Sessions, "The League of American Writers," p. 46; Henry Hart (ed.), *The Writer in a Changing World* (New York: Equinox Cooperative Press, 1937).

16. Hart, *The Writer in a Changing World*, pp. 57–58, 69.

17. Folsom, a Rhodes scholar, who was formerly active in the Philadelphia unemployed movement and a Party member, took up his duties in 1937. Folsom had edited *The Hunger Fighter*. See *Daily Worker*, August 27, 1934, p. 7. Donald Ogden Stewart, *By a Stroke of Luck: An Autobiography* (London: Paddington Press, 1975), pp. 161, 211. 214–225. Larry Ceplair and Steven Englund, *The Inquisition in Hollywood: Politics in the Film Community 1930–1960* (New York: Anchor Press, 1980), p. 161.

18. FBI File on the League of American Writers, 100-7322-78, p. 71; *New Masses*, June 20, 1939, p. 22; President's Personal Files, 6418, FDR Library, Hyde Park, New York.

19. *Daily Worker*, August 13, 1938, p. 1; *New Masses*, March 8, 1938, p. 6.

20. Wallace Phelps and Philip Rahv, "Problems and Prospects in Revolutionary Literature," *Partisan Review*, June–July 1934, p. 2. PR's position was endorsed by a number of writers at the 1934 John Reed Clubs meeting. "National John Reed Clubs Conference," *Partisan Review*, November–December 1934, p. 60; *New Masses*, January 1, 1935, pp. 36–37.

21. James Gilbert, *Writers and Partisans: A History of Literary Radicalism in America* (New York: Wiley, 1968), pp. 110–113, 142. *New Masses*, October 19, 1937, p. 21; December 18, 1934, p. 23. Sessions, "League of American Writers," p. 38–A. The information on Trachtenberg came from Sessions' interviews with Horace Gregory, Malcolm Cowley, and James Farrell. See *New Masses*, February 18, 1936, p. 22; December 15, p. 27.

22. James Farrell, "The Short Story," in Hart, *American Writers' Congress*, pp. 103–104, 192; James Farrell, *A Note on Literary Criticism* (New York: Vanguard Press, 1936).

23. Two excellent accounts of the purges are Robert Conquest, *The Great Terror: Stalin's Purge of the Thirties* (New York: Macmillan, 1968), and Roy Medvedev, *Let History Judge: The Origins and Consequences of Stalinism* (New York: Vintage Books, 1973).

24. *Daily Worker*, February 6, 1937, p. 3; June 14, p. 7; March 8, 1938, p. 7; March 11, p. 2. Corliss Lamont, *The Story of Soviet Progress* (New York: Soviet Russia Today, 1938), p. 33. *Daily Worker*, June 30, 1939, p. 2.

25. *Daily Worker*, February 12, 1937, p. 2; Earl Browder, "The People's Front Moves Forward," *Communist*, December 1937, p. 1084; *Daily Worker*, March 30, 1937, pp. 4–5.

26. John Belton, *The Commission of Inquiry into Charges Made Against Leon Trotsky in the Great Purge Trials in Moscow* (unpublished master's thesis, Emory University, 1977); *Daily Worker*, April 3, 1937, p. 2; *Sunday Worker*, April 18, p. 2; Mauritz Hallgren, *Why I Resigned from the Trotsky Defense Committee* (New York: International Publishers, 1937); *New Masses*, December 7, 1937, p. 3; *Daily Worker*, December 14, 1937, p. 4.

27. William Foster, *Questions and Answers on the Piatakov-Radek Trial* (New York: Workers Library Publishers, 1937), pp. 71–72. The *Daily Worker*, February 9, 1937, lists only fifty-one names. Eugene Lyons, in *The Red Decade* (Indianapolis, Ind.: Bobbs Merrill, 1941), pp. 254–255, lists eighty-four. *Daily Worker*, April 9, 1937, pp. 1–2; April 28, 1938, p. 3.

28. Alexander Bittelman, "Review of the Month," *Communist*, March 1937, p. 208; Waldo Frank to Earl Browder, January 7, 1937, Browder Papers, Reel 1-26; Waldo Frank, "Communication," *New Republic*, May 12, 1937, pp. 19–20.

29. Earl Browder, "Communication," *New Republic*, May 20, 1937, p. 76; *Daily Worker*, June 5, 1937, pp. 1, 5. Frank had sent a letter of resignation as chairman on May 1, 1936, citing his busy schedule, and affirming his support for the LAW. I am indebted to Art Casciato for this information.

30. Daniel Aaron, *Writers on the Left* (New York: Harcourt, Brace & World, 1961), pp. 380–383. Sam Darcy sat on the Comintern committee that considered Freeman's book, along with Clement Gottwald and André Marty. Years later he recalled only that the book had been denied a review in the *Communist International* because it contained too much sex and too little politics. Sam Darcy interview with Theodore Draper, June 11–12, 1957, Draper

Papers, Box 3, Folder 53; P. Dengel, "Book Reviewing Is a Serious Matter," *Communist International*, August 1939, p. 947.

31. *Daily Worker*, February 26, 1938, p. 7. For Dos Passos' disillusionment with Communism, see Townsend Ludington, *John Dos Passos: A Twentieth Century Odyssey* (New York: E. P. Dutton, 1980). For a savage account of Dos Passos' fall from favor, see Herbert Solow, "Substitution at Left Tackle: Hemingway for Dos Passos," *Partisan Review*, April 1938, pp. 62–64. *New Masses*, June 23, 1936, p. 23. On Farrell see Alan Wald, *James T. Farrell: The Revolutionary Socialist Years* (New York: New York University Press, 1978), pp. 36–37. Sherwood Anderson had fallen out of favor even earlier, in 1934, for his praise of the Roosevelt Administration. That made it "really painful" for Mike Gold to read him. *Daily Worker*, January 9, 1934, p. 5.

32. Mike Gold, "Out of the Fascist Unconscious," *New Republic*, July 26, 1933, p. 295. *New Masses*, January 16, 1934, p. 26; March 12, 1935, p. 1; March 21, 1936, p. 21. MacLeish began to distance himself from the Party in 1939 but did not resign from the League of American Writers until he became Librarian of Congress. Consulted in 1940 when Sidney Hook urged President Roosevelt to resign his membership in the league, MacLeish insisted that many of the league's members were not sympathetic to the Party and denied that he was aware of any effort by the Party to influence him. President's Personal Files, 6418, FDR Library, Hyde Park, New York.

33. Hart, *The Writer in a Changing World*, pp. 225–228. *New Masses*, October 19, 1937, p. 2; September 14, pp. 9–10; October 19, p. 21. *Partisan Review*, December 1937, p. 3.

34. The list of signers can be found in Lyons, *The Red Decade*, p. 345.

35. *Daily Worker*, July 31, 1937, p. 7; August 16, p. 7; September 10, p. 7; September 2, p. 7.

Chapter 19

1. Earl Browder, *What is Communism?* (New York: Vanguard Press, 1936), p. 209.

2. *Party Organizer*, February 1937, pp. 8–9; December 1936, pp. 12–13. Unless otherwise specified, all membership figures given are based on recruitment. Politburo Minutes, January 6, 1938, Draper Papers, Box 1, Folder 49; "National Membership Report: January 1–June 30, 1937" issued by the Organization Department, Draper Papers, Box 1, Folder 43.

3. *Daily Worker*, June 25, 1936, p. 1; *Party Organizer*, July–August 1936, p. 7; "Building the Party in the Struggle for Proletarian Unity and the People's Front," *Communist*, August 1937, pp. 746–748; Politburo Minutes, January 6, 1938, January 28, 1938, Draper Papers, Box 1, Folder 51; Jack Stachel, "Build the Party for Peace, Democracy, and Socialism," *Communist*, March 1938, pp. 220–221; *Daily Worker*, February 22, 1938, p. 1; Earl Browder, *Social and National Security* (New York: Workers Library Publishers, 1938), p. 27.

4. Earl Browder, "Summation Speech at the Tenth National Convention," *Communist*, July 1938, p. 598. Hathaway gave 90,000 in the Party and 20,000 in the YCL. See *Daily Worker*, January 2, 1939, p. 6; January 13, p. 6. Earl Browder interview with Theodore Draper, October 10, 1955, Draper Papers, Box 2, Folder 8. Foster referred to "well over" 100,000 in the Party in "Twenty Years of Communist Trade Union Policy," *Communist*, September 1939, p. 814. Most YCL members were not Party members. Henry Winston reported that only 620 of New York's 10,000 YCL'ers also belonged to the adult organization in early 1939, in "The Young Communist League Prepares for Growth," *Communist*, April 1939, p. 325.

5. Between 1930 and 1935 the Party gained only about 4,000 members a year. Over the next four years the increases averaged 17,500 a year. In round figures, 11,000 were added to Party rolls in 1936, 19,000 in 1937, 22,000 in 1938, and 18,000 in 1939 (accepting Party claims of 100,000 members). The rate of growth, 36.6 percent in 1936, shot up to 46.3 percent in 1937, was an impressive 36.6 percent in 1938, but then tumbled to 21.9 percent (based on 100,000) in 1939.

6. "Report on Organization," May 1938, reprinted in *Investigation of Un-American Propaganda Activities*, Special Committee on Un-American Activities, House of Representa-

tives 77th Congress, 1st Session, 1941, Vol. 14, p. 8717. The same figures are given in *Party Organizer*, June 1938, p. 5.

7. *The Constitution and Bylaws of the Communist Party of the United States of America* (New York: Workers Library Publishers, 1938), pp. 18–19; "Report of Central Control Commission C.P.U.S.A. to the Tenth National Convention, End of May 1938," in *Investigation of Un-American Propaganda Activities*, Vol. 14, p. 8727. Most members were ousted for personal flaws or irresponsibility. Relatively few expulsions were for political unreliability.

8. *Daily Worker*, July 21, 1935, p. 5; *Party Organizer*, April 1938, p. 25; *Daily Worker*, September 14, 1935, p. 7; Fred Brown, "The Recruiting Drive," *Communist*, October 1937, pp. 920–921.

9. Roy Hudson, "The Charter of Party Democracy," *Communist*, August 1938, pp. 708–710. The word "confirmed" was added to the article at the convention.

10. *Daily Worker*, January 29, 1936, p. 6; July 8, p. 5; September 15, p. 5; *Resolutions of the Ninth Convention of the Communist Party* (New York: Workers Library Publishers, 1936), p. 61.

11. Israel Amter, "Organizational Changes in the New York District of the Party," *Communist*, May 1936, p. 465; *Resolutions of the Ninth Convention*, pp. 54–55. The resolutions complained that Party shop units, composed of all workers in a given factory, suffered from "general stagnation." "Report on Organization," pp. 8714–8720.

12. Amter, "Organizational Changes," pp. 471–472. See *Party Organizer*, May 1937, p. 16, and March 1938, p. 39, for descriptions of some of these units. More open and visible Party units were not required in the South or in company towns where secrecy was still necessary. *Resolutions of the Ninth Convention*, p. 60.

13. *Party Organizer*, January 1936, p. 13; "Report on Organization," pp. 8714, 8719; *Resolutions of the Ninth Convention*, p. 58.

14. Amter, "Organizational Changes," p. 466; *Resolutions of the Ninth Convention*, p. 59.

15. *Daily Worker*, November 27, 1937, p. 7; December 10, p. 7. Fred Brown, "The Importance of the Recruiting Drive," *Communist*, October 1937, p. 918. *Party Organizer*, May 1937, p. 2.

16. "Report on the Training of Cadres Between the Ninth and Tenth Conventions of the Party," in *Investigation of Un-American Propaganda Activities*, Vol. 14, pp. 8721–8725, 8745–8751.

17. Earl Browder, "The Communists in the People's Front," *Communist*, July 1937, p. 612; William Foster, "Political Leadership and Party Building," *Communist*, p. 638; Earl Browder, *Unity for Peace and Democracy* (New York: Workers Library Publishers, 1939), p. 24.

18. Browder, "The Communists in the People's Front," p. 614.

19. Browder, "The People's Front Moves Forward!," *Communist*, December 1937, p. 1098; *Investigation of Un-American Propaganda Activities*, Vol. 10, p. 6268.

20. *Daily Worker*, October 29, 1932, p. 4. Upon his death in 1977, Dunn was eulogized by Si Gerson as "part of us for virtually all his adult life." *Daily World*, February 8, 1977. Dunn was identified as a non-Communist by Marcantonio, in *Investigation of Un-American Propaganda Activities*, Vol. 10, pp. 5962–5963, 5970. The Labor Research Association was founded by Dunn, Grace Hutchins, Anna Rochester, Solon DeLeon, and Alexander Trachtenberg, all Communists. See ibid., pp. 5938–5939, for Damon's remark. Marcantonio assured the Dies Committee that the ILD would not hesitate to defend "any individual who has ever been deprived of his civil rights by the Communists or by the Soviet Republic." Three days after Marcantonio's testimony, Fred Beal, who had jumped bail and fled to Russia after his conviction for murder in Gastonia, North Carolina, testified that he had returned to America because of disillusionment with the Soviet regime. While he desperately sought to overturn his conviction for the Gastonia events, he got no help from either the Communist party or the supposedly non-partisan ILD. Ibid, p. 6145. For Bedacht, see ibid., p. 5831.

21. "Cash Statement for 1931–1933," Draper Papers, Box 1, Folder 38. 1936 and 1937 financial statements can be found in the *Daily Worker*, May 31, 1938, p. 1. The 1938 figures are from the *Daily Worker*, March 28, 1939, p. 5. Testimony of William Browder in *Investiga-*

tion of Un-American Propaganda Activities, Vol. 7, p. 4814; *Party Organizer*, December 1936, pp. 12–13.

22. *Investigation of Un-American Propaganda Activities*, Vol. 7, pp. 4783–4788, 4813, 4818, 4821, 4822, 4833, 4838–4848. William Weiner testified that Illinois' budget was $35,000 in 1938. If the Illinois Party had raised as much money for special funds as New York, it would have had an income of around $100,000.

23. *Party Organizer*, December 1936, pp. 12–13; *Historical Statistics of the United States*, Vol. 1 (Washington, D.C.: Department of Commerce, 1975), p. 169. The $220,000 figure was derived by assuming that the $77,000 in dues income received by the National Office was 35 percent of the total dues.

24. Earl Browder interview with Theodore Draper, October 12, 1955, Draper Papers, Box 2, Folder 9. One large estate which came to the Party was that of Bishop William Montgomery Brown, a defrocked minister and Communist stalwart. A small group of wealthy individuals either joined the Party or sympathized with it. Lem Harris was the son of an investment banker. Corliss Lamont was the scion of a Morgan partner. Anna Rochester, the great granddaughter of the founder of Rochester, New York, was the daughter of the treasurer of Western Union. For Heller see *Investigation of Un-American Propaganda Activities*, Vol. 7, pp. 4867–4883. Heller left the Party when his close friend Earl Browder was expelled in 1945.

25. Elizabeth Bentley, *Out of Bondage* (New York: Devin-Adair, 1951), pp. 124–127. John Hazard Reynolds, a member of the Social Register and ex–Wall Street broker, was installed as the corporation's head and Bentley herself given an office. Helen Lawrenson, *Whistling Girl* (Garden City, N.Y.: Doubleday, 1978), p. 86. Also see Louis Budenz, *Men Without Faces* (New York: Harper & Brothers, 1948), p. 109.

Ex-Communist Maurice Malkin told one group of credulous congressmen that Ludwig Martens, the first Soviet representative to America after the revolution, had ordered American Communists as far back as 1919 to infiltrate charitable organizations "in order to drain their treasuries" to finance Communist activities. Two years later the Reece Committee's counsel, René Wormser, charged that six foundations, including the prestigious John Simon Guggenheim Foundation, "had been successfully penetrated or used by Communists." Louis Budenz revealed the existence of a subcommission of the Party's cultural commission that was devoted entirely to penetrating and influencing foundations. If such a body ever existed, it had a dismal record. The slim reeds upon which the charges rested were a handful of grants to Communists, Party sympathizers, and fellow travelers. Doxey Wilkerson, a black Communist, had been employed by Gunnar Myrdal to do research for his Carnegie Foundation–sponsored study of American blacks. Aaron Copland, Langston Hughes, and Alvah Bessie had been among an infinitesmal handful of "undesirable" Guggenheim grantees. Hans Eisler, Gerhart's brother, had received a small stipend.

Only a handful of foundations had clear links to the Party. The Garland Fund had distributed large grants to numerous radical organizations during the 1920s. Robert Marshall, chief of the Recreation Division of the U.S. Forestry Service, died in 1939 leaving $1.5 million to be used to support groups advocating production for use. Among his foundation's trustees were his brother, George Marshall, an inveterate fellow traveler; Gardner Jackson; and former congressman Jerry O'Connell. Nearly one million dollars in grants were handed out in the foundation's first decade, including some $120,000 to the National Federation for Constitutional Liberties and its successor, the Civil Rights Congress; $64,000 to the National Negro Congress; $30,000 to the Southern Negro Youth Congress; $20,000 to Farm Research; and $130,000 to various affiliates of the Farmers Union, the Party's preferred Popular Front organization in agriculture. While such support kept a number of Party "fronts" afloat, there is no evidence that any of it went to the Party itself.

Hearings before the Select Committee to Investigate Tax-Exempt Foundations and Comparable Organizations, House of Representatives, 82nd Congress, 2nd Session, pp. 692, 717; Maurice Malkin, *Return to My Father's House* (New Rochelle, N.Y.: Arlington House, 1972); René Wormser, *Foundations: Their Power and Influence* (New York: Devin-Adair, 1958), p. 175. On the Garland Fund see Theodore Draper, *American Communism and Soviet Russia* (New York: Viking Press, 1960), p. 204. The details of the Marshall Foundation's structure and expenditures were revealed by an indignant Martin Dies in *Congressional Record*, 77th

Congress, Vol. 88, Part 6, pp. 7449–7455, and by Harold Velde in ibid., 82nd Congress, Vol. 97, Part 10, p. 13395. Lem Harris declined to answer a congressional committee that asked him his role in securing Marshall Foundation support for the Farmers Union. See *Hearings Regarding Communist Activities Among Farm Groups,* House Committee on Un-American Activities, 82nd Congress, 1st Session, pp. 1884–1923.

26. Benjamin Gitlow told the Dies Committee that there were contributions of $25,000 for the 1924 election campaign, $35,000 to start the *Daily Worker,* $35,000 for the 1928 campaign, and thousands, perhaps hundreds of thousands, more during the decade. See *Investigation of Un-American Propaganda Activities,* Vol. 7, pp. 4541–4557. For a more detailed discussion of Party finances in the 1920s, see Draper, *American Communism and Soviet Russia,* pp. 202–209. The 10 percent figure is given on p. 207. See also Earl Browder interview with Theodore Draper, September 29, 1953, Draper Papers, Box 2, Folder 3, and Earl Browder, "Addendum to the Memorandum on Relations Between the Comintern and the American Party," Draper Papers, Box 2, Folder 9. Some of that Comintern money may have also paid traveling expenses of Communists going abroad. Congressional and Justice Department investigations revealed that dozens of accounts with World Tourists—run by Jacob Golos, a high-ranking Communist—were actually paid by the Party. The expenses did not show up on Party balance sheets. See *Scope of Soviet Activities in the United States,* U.S. Senate, Committee on the Judiciary, 85th Congress, 1st Session, Appendix 1, Part 23-A, pp. 1207–1235; Honig's testimony is in *Brownell v. Communist Party,* Hearings Before the Subversive Activities Control Board, 1951, p. 4440. Budenz, *Men Without Faces,* pp. 23, 107–108; Hede Massing, *This Deception* (New York: Duell, Sloan & Pearce, 1951), pp. 143, 188. On kickbacks, see the testimony of Robert Pitcoff, a former Amtorg employee, in *Investigation of Un-American Propaganda Activities,* Vol. 9, pp. 5821–5822. Earl Browder was ineptly questioned by the Dies Committee about the possible infusion of foreign funds into the American Party. Asked if the Americans received any financial assistance from the Soviet Communist party or the Soviet government, he blandly answered, "No Sir." No one asked if the Comintern had provided any money. Ibid., Vol. 7, p. 4322.

27. *Investigation of Un-American Propaganda Activities,* Vol. 7, p. 4279. Some figures are from Party balance sheets cited in note 21; Browder interview with Draper, October 12, 1955. Otto Katz, a Czech-born Communist who also used the name Andre Simone, made several lucrative journeys to America to raise money for the German Communists. Katz, a protégé of Willi Munzenberg, boasted to acquaintances that "Columbus discovered America and I discovered Hollywood." Posing as a simple anti-Nazi, he raised large sums of money, first under Munzenberg's tutelage and then for the German Communists once his mentor had broken with the Comintern. An excellent sketch of Katz-Simone is in Theodore Draper, "The Man Who Wanted to Hang," *Reporter,* January 6, 1953, pp. 26–30. The Earl Browder Papers, Series 1, contain a letter dated April 13, 1939 to "Dear Comrade Earl Browder" signed by Franz Dahlem and Paul Merker for the German Party's Central Committee asking assistance in helping Comrade O. K. Simon "utilize his good relations to many prosperous American personalities" to raise money for the German Party's underground. Katz was hung after being convicted of spying for the Americans, British, and French in the service of Zionism during the Slansky trials in the early 1950s.

28. *Investigation of Un-American Propaganda Activities,* Vol. 8, pp. 5137–5171, 5206–5257.

29. *Party Organizer,* January 1936, p. 6. *Daily Worker,* May 17, 1938, p. 5; September 6, 1937, p. 2. The success of the Party's fund-raising for Spain is challenged by John Sessions in "American Communists and the Civil War in Spain," unpublished manuscript in my possession. Sessions notes that between May and August 1937 the North American Committee to Aid Spanish Democracy raised $90,258 but sent only $31,437 to Spain, consuming $47,781 in operating expenses. The Medical Bureau to Aid Spanish Democracy likewise spent more than 50 percent of its revenues on operating expenses. Ibid., p. 22; Browder interview with Draper, October 12, 1955.

30. *Party Organizer,* July–August, 1936, p. 8. Also see Earl Browder, *Report to the Eighth Convention* (New York: Workers Library Publishers, 1934), p. 87; Jack Stachel, "Build the Party for Peace, Democracy and Socialism," *Communist,* March 1938, p. 223; *Daily Worker,* May 28, 1938, p. 5; *Party Organizer,* June 1938, p. 3; *Party Organizer,* July–August 1936, p. 9; Jack Stachel, "Organizational Problems of the Party," *Communist,* July 1935, pp. 625–626.

31. Stachel, "Build the Party," pp. 223–225. Dodd testimony in "Report of Senate

Internal Security Subcommittee," reprinted in *U.S. News and World Report*, July 31, 1953, p. 78. Lorenz Finison, "Unemployment, Politics, and the History of Organized Psychology," *American Psychologist*, November 1976, pp. 747–755; May 1978, pp. 471–477. Percival Bailey, *Progressive Lawyers: A History of the National Lawyers Guild, 1936–1958* (unpublished doctoral dissertation, Rutgers University, 1979), p. 153. On the NLG, see also the testimony of Mortimer Riemer, its secretary and a Communist, in *Hearings, Investigation of Communist Infiltration of Government*, Part 2, House Committee on Un-American Activities, 84th Congress, 1st Session, pp. 3022–3042; *Party Organizer*, June 1938, p. 4.

32. I used a national figure of 75,000 for 1938 to accord with the 30,000 figure given for New York in Table 1. Jack Stachel, "Build the Party," p. 222; *Daily Worker*, September 25, 1937, p. 3.

33. Max Steinberg, "Rooting the Party Among the Masses in New York," *Communist*, September 1938, pp. 829–838.

34. *Political Affairs*, September 1949, pp. 7–9. *Party Organizer*, July–August 1936, p. 8. Fred Brown, "Building the Party in the Elections," *Communist*, October 1936, p. 966. Jack Stachel, "Build the Party," p. 224. *Daily Worker*, July 8, 1936, p. 5; May 28, 1938, p. 5. Harvey Klehr, *Communist Cadre* (Stanford, Calif.: Hoover Institution Press, 1978), p. 25.

35. Irene Browder, "The National Groups in the Fight for Democracy," *Communist*, September 1939, p. 866.

36. Israel Amter, "Work Among National Groups—A Central Communist Task," *Communist*, May 1939, p. 462. Georgi Dimitroff, *Working Class Unity—A Bulwark Against Fascism* (New York: Workers Library Publishers, 1935), p. 31; Irene Browder, "Problems of the National Groups in the United States," *Communist*, May 1939, p. 462; "Report on National Groups," Browder Papers, Reel 3, Series 2-2.

37. "Report on National Groups"; Melech Epstein, *The Jew and Communism; 1919-1941*, (New York: Trade Union Sponsoring Committee, 1959), pp. 319–341.

38. Epstein, *The Jew and Communism*, pp. 382–389; M. J. Olgin, *Trotskyism: Counter-Revolution in Disguise* (New York: Workers Library Publishers, 1935). Olgin's attack on Trotsky, whom he had once extravagantly praised, was entirely in keeping with his instinct for survival. Olgin had an unfortunate habit of befriending unreliable Communists but an unerring instinct for denouncing them when required. Among his closest Party allies in the 1920s had been J. B. S. Hardman and Ludwig Lore, both of whom he excoriated in time to save his own Party career.

39. Epstein, *The Jew and Communism*, pp. 302–303; M. J. Olgin, *Leader and Teacher* (New York: Workers Library Publishers, 1939), p. 15. Neither the Party nor Olgin was willing to support Zionism. The Communists' reaction to the Arab revolt of 1936, however, was far less offensive to Jews than it had been in 1929. There were no shrieking headlines. Communists denied that their brethren in Palestine supported the revolt. At Party-sponsored meetings, Hathaway, Browder, and Olgin appealed for "brotherhood between Arabs and Jews." The Party did not, however, relax its opposition to Zionism. Browder distinguished between pogroms in Germany and the "rising revolutionary movement of the oppressed people fighting for its national independence" in Palestine. He supported an end to Jewish immigration, and a unified struggle of Arab and Jewish workers against British imperialism leading to an independent Arab state with guarantees of Jewish national rights. By distinguishing between Zionist leaders and the Jewish community, the Communists were able to avoid a head-on collision with Jewish opinion. They would not go further, however. When a British commission recommended partition of Palestine, the Political Committee, spurred on by Alex Bitteman, rejected Melech Epstein's plea that a Party endorsement would immeasurably aid its efforts among Jews. Because of their position on Palestine, the ICOR and the IWO were barred from the World Jewish Congress. Earl Browder, *Zionism* (New York: Yidburo Publishers, 1936), pp. 5, 20–21; Epstein, *The Jew and Communism*, pp. 328–329.

40. William Goldsmith, *The Theory and Practice of the Communist Front* (unpublished doctoral dissertation, Columbia University, 1971), pp. 507–509; Epstein, *The Jew and Communism*, pp. 103, 147. In 1933 Max Bedacht learnedly discoursed in the *Daily Worker* on "The Place of the I.W.O. in the Revolutionary Movement." Earl Browder told the Eighth Convention that "we have made another important addition to the list of mass revolutionary organizations. This is the mutual benefit society, International Workers' Order." *Daily*

Worker, February 3, 1933, p. 4; Earl Browder, *Communism in the United States,* (New York: International Publishers, 1935), p. 74. The *Daily Worker,* May 7, 1939, p. 4, contains an extensive list of IWO officers. After World War II, Bedacht was succeeded by Samson Milgrom, better known as A. W. Mills, under which name he had directed Party unemployment work in the early 1930s. See his obituary in *Daily World,* September 7, 1977.

41. *Investigation of Un-American Propaganda Activities,* Vol. 10, pp. 5855–5856. Max Bedacht confirmed that from 1937 to February 1939, the IWO placed about $27,799 worth of ads in the *Daily Worker.* Max Bedacht, "The I.W.O.—Workers' Fraternalism," *Communist,* June 1938, p. 541; *Daily Worker,* March 7, 1939, p. 4; *Investigation of Un-American Propaganda Activities,* Vol. 10, pp. 5834, 5889. See Arthur Liebman, *Jews and the Left* (New York: John Wiley & Sons, 1979), pp. 310–325, for a discussion of the IWO's schools and summer camps.

42. Goldsmith, *The Theory and Practice of the Communist Front,* pp. 524, 528–529; *Party Organizer,* July–August 1936, p. 9; Stachel, "Build the Party," p. 234.

Chapter 20

1. In 1938, Walter Duranty of the *New York Times* noted in a dispatch that "Stalin has shot more Jews in two years of the purge than were killed in Germany." Some readers took this as evidence of a Soviet bid to Hitler. The line did not appear in Duranty's *Times* article on October 11, 1938, p. 11, but the *New Leader,* October 22, 1938, p. 1, noted that it had been included in the version sent out for syndication. Eugene Lyons mentioned that "insistent reports that Stalin is seeking a rapprochement with Adolph Hitler gain in credibility" in the *New Leader,* January 14, 1939, p. 8. An editorial in the same journal predicted that "if Hitler and Stalin within the next year or two declare their affection for each other and establish an alliance between Communism and Nazism it need surprise no one"; February 25, 1939, p. 8. Max Beloff, *The Foreign Policy of Soviet Russia, 1936–1941* Vol. 2; (London: Oxford University Press, 1948), pp. 255–278. Joseph Stalin, "Report on the Work of the Central Committee," *Communist International,* Special Number, 1939, p. 526. V. M. Molotov, *The Meaning of the Soviet-German Non-Aggression Pact* (New York: Workers Library Publishers, 1939), pp. 7, 8.

2. *Daily Worker,* July 6, 1939, p. 4; Epstein, *The Jew and Communism: 1919–1941* (New York: Trade Union Sponsoring Committee, 1959), p. 347; *Daily Worker,* August 14, 1939, pp. 1–2. The statement was initiated by a group of Communists and fellow travelers: Dashiel Hammett, Corliss Lamont, George Marshall, Vincent Sheean, Donald Ogden Stewart, Maxwell Stewart, Mary Van Kleeck, Dorothy Brewster, Walter Rautenstrauch, and Rebecca Timbres.

3. *Daily Worker,* August 22, 1939, pp. 1–2; August 23, p. 1; August 25, p. 1; August 27, p. 3; August 24, pp. 1, 6. A full transcript of the press conference is in Draper Papers, Box 13, Folder 49.

4. *Daily Worker,* August 24, 1939, p. 1; Earl Browder interview with Theodore Draper, October 12, 1955, Draper Papers, Box 2, Folder 9. "Political Committee Minutes," September 14, 1939, Philip Jaffe Papers, Emory University, Box 35, Folder 5; Browder's text of the Chicago speech is in Draper Papers, Box 13, Folder 52.

5. *Daily Worker,* September 2, 1939, p. 6; September 5, p. 1; September 1, p. 2; September 4, p. 6.

6. *Daily Worker,* September 1, 1939, p. 6; September 4, pp. 1, 6; September 5, p. 6; September 6, p. 6; September 11, p. 1. Earl Browder, "Report to the National Committee," September 2, 1939, p. 22, Draper Papers, Box 1, Folder 62.

7. *Daily Worker,* September 1, 1939, p. 6; September 2, p. 6. Browder, "Report to the National Committee," pp. 17, 37. *Daily Worker,* September 12, 1939, p. 1.

8. The quote is from Browder interview with Draper, October 12, 1955. Browder suggested the message was a "brief resume of an article of Dimitroff's by radio" and that it was published a week or so later in *Communist International.* Dimitroff's article there, however, did not appear until October 1939, so perhaps Browder was confusing this communication with a later one, received in later September. Melech Epstein, then editor of the

Freiheit, later wrote that the radio message had arrived on September 12 (*The Jew and Communism,* p. 353). It may have come earlier. On September 10, Milton Howard included a curious phrase in his article in the *Sunday Worker.* He seemed to blame both sides for the conflict and called it an "imperialist war." His hint, however, was balanced by continued editorial support for aid to Poland on both September 10 and 11. *Sunday Worker,* September 10, 1936, p. 6; Second Section, p. 1. *Daily Worker,* September 11, p. 1. Browder later suggested that Howard must have heard talk about the Moscow radio message around Party headquarters. Browder interview with Draper, October 12, 1955.

9. *Daily Worker,* September 13, 1939, pp. 1, 3. Aside from labeling the war imperialist, the Comintern message was not absolutely clear. Browder remembered that the cable was ambiguous. There was a "great deal of confusion in the thinking of everyone concerned," he recollected. When the Party leader met Granville Hicks for lunch on September 12, the *Daily Worker* had not yet published his curious interview with Gannes. Hicks, on the verge of quitting the Party in despair, poured out his doubts about the pact. Browder warned him subtly that worse was yet to come: "I have already faced doubts that haven't even occurred to you yet," he told the critic, "and I wonder what will happen when they do." Browder interview with Draper, October 12, 1955; Granville Hicks, *Part of the Truth* (New York: Harcourt, Brace, 1965), p. 182. Hicks mistakenly claims that the *Daily Worker* had already labeled the war imperialist.

10. *Sunday Worker,* May 14, 1939, p. 10; *Daily Worker,* May 12, 1939, pp. 1, 4; "Political Committee Minutes," September 14, 1939, p. 32.

11. Alexander Bittelman, unpublished autobiography, Tamiment Library; Alexander Bittelman interview with Theodore Draper, January 20, 1969, Draper Papers, Box 3, Folder 19; Earl Browder interview with Theodore Draper, January 20, 1969, Draper Papers, Box 2, Folder 10.

12. "Political Committee Minutes," September 14, 1939, pp. 1–28.

13. "Political Committee Minutes," September 14, 1939, 28–53; Browder interview with Draper, October 12, 1955.

14. "Political Committee Minutes," September 14, 1939, pp. 56–61.

15. Ibid., pp. 61–70.

16. "Political Committee Minutes," September 16, 1939, Jaffe Papers, Box 35, Folder 5, pp. 71–97.

17. Ibid., pp. 97–147.

18. *Daily Worker,* September 19, 1939, pp. 1.

19. On his last visit to Moscow, just after the Munich crisis, Browder had received instructions from Dimitroff to obtain a short-wave radio receiver and tune in on a specific frequency at specified times. This information is based on what Browder told Philip Jaffe, related in Jaffe's *The Rise and Fall of American Communism* (New York: Horizon Press, 1975), p. 40. Copies of the two messages are in the Jaffe Papers. It is unclear whether the first message received from the Comintern, around September 10, came the same way. Browder hinted that it did in his interview with Draper, October 12, 1955. All quotations are from the decoded messages.

20. *Daily Worker,* October 15, 1939, p. 2. "In the first days of the war," Gene Dennis recalled in May 1940, "we did not adequately understand the significance of the so-called neutrality position of the American bourgeoisie and the government, nor the changed role and the increasingly aggressive imperialist policies of the Roosevelt Administration," But, Dennis merely criticized "some comrades," without naming anyone, who took a while to understand the need to "resist and combat the imperialist war plans and policies of the Roosevelt Government in both the foreign and domestic arena." Gene Dennis, "The Bolshevization of the Communist Party of the United States in the Struggle Against the Imperialist War," *Communist,* May 1940, p. 407.

21. *Daily Worker,* October 22, 1939, p. 1; October 28, p. 6. Earl Browder, *The Second Imperialist War* (New York: Workers Library Publishers, 1940), p. 201–202. *Daily Worker,* December 2, 1939; p. 1; December 9, p. 1; December 1, p. 1. *Sunday Worker,* December 10, 1939, Second Section, p. 1. Eleanor Roosevelt enjoyed a short period of grace. When, however, she attacked Communists as "foreign agents," an editorial charged that "one whiff of gun powder can go to a person's head and render his (or her) views indistinguishable from those of Martin Dies, William Randolph Hearst and Coughlin." Even her defense

of the American Youth Congress and consumer groups at the time of the Dies Committee hearings only won her more suspicion: "Mrs. Roosevelt is playing a very sinister and crafty game." *Daily Worker,* November 24, 1939, p. 6; December 15, p. 6.

22. Earl Browder, "The Domestic Reactionary Counterpart of the War Policy of the Bourgeoisie," *Communist,* July 1940, p. 604; William Foster, "Seven Years of Roosevelt," *Communist,* March 1940, p. 246; Browder, "The Domestic Reactionary Counterpart," pp. 595–598; Gene Dennis, "Labor and the Elections," *Communist,* September 1940, p. 828.

23. Earl Browder, "The Most Peculiar Election Campaign in the History of the Republic," *Communist,* October 1940, pp. 885–887; "Editorials," *Communist,* January 1941, p. 9; William Foster, "Earl Browder and the Fight for Peace." *Communist,* June 1941, p. 497.

24. Browder, "The Most Peculiar Election Campaign," p. 885. Gene Dennis, "Roosevelt, the War, and the New Deal," *Communist,* January 1940, p. 24; Dennis, "Labor and the Elections," p. 828.

25. Foster, "Seven Years of Roosevelt," pp. 236–241, 243–244.

26. Georgi Dimitroff, "The War and the Workingclass of the Capitalist Countries," *Communist International,* October 1939, pp. 1107–1109.

27. Earl Browder, *The Second Imperialist War* (New York: International Publishers, 1940); p. 154; William Foster, "World Socialism and the War," *Communist,* June 1940, p. 500; Foster, "Seven Years of Roosevelt," p. 249; V. J. Jerome, *Social Democracy and the War* (New York: Workers Library Publishers, 1940), pp. 4, 36, 39, 47. As usual, some of the worst abuse was reserved for Norman Thomas. The Socialist leader had been agitating to keep America out of war for years; in 1938 he had helped form a committee with that name. Since the Communists were then at the height of their collective security campaign, he won no plaudits for his isolationism. Thomas strongly opposed American involvement in World War II; he was critical of British and French imperialism and convinced that entry into the war would only provoke a repeat of the repression and disillusionment of World War I. On the surface he would have seemed a natural ally for the Party on this issue. His sympathy for Finland and denunciation of Stalin for the pact were, however, major obstacles. Jerome warned that "scratch the reddish veneer of a Norman Thomas, and you will find the solid White Guard base." For Thomas's position on the war see Bernard Johnpoll, *Pacifist's Progress* (Chicago: Quadrangle Books, 1970), pp. 205–231.

28. Earl Browder, "On the Twenty-Second Anniversary of the Socialist Revolution," *Communist,* November 1939, pp. 1022–1023; Foster, "World Socialism and the War," p. 513; Gil Green, "Imperialist War and 'Democratic Demagogy,'" *Communist,* June 1940, pp. 528–529.

29. *Daily Worker,* October 15, 1939, p. 2; Dennis, "The Bolshevization of the Communist Party," p. 405; Dennis, "Roosevelt, the War and the New Deal," p. 36.

30. *Daily Worker,* October 15, 1939, p. 2; October 13, p. 1; October 14, p. 1; October 15, p. 1; October 17, p. 1; October 21, p. 1.

31. Al Richmond, *A Long View from the Left* (Boston: Houghton Mifflin, 1973), p. 283; Peggy Dennis, *Autobiography of an American Communist* (Westport, Conn.: Lawrence Hill, 1977), pp. 135–136; George Charney, *A Long Journey* (Chicago: Quadrangle Books, 1968), pp. 123–124; *Daily Worker,* October 1, 1939, p. 6. Hicks had joined the *New Masses* as literary editor in the fall of 1933. He became a Party member in 1935 "for it seemed ridiculous that anyone should be working with the Party as closely as I was without being a member." Hicks, *Part of the Truth,* pp. 128, 140–141. Granville Hicks interview with Theodore Draper, Draper Papers, Box 3, Folder 108. Hicks announced his resignation in a letter in the *New Republic,* October 4, 1939, pp. 244–245. Epstein, *The Jew and Communism,* pp. 362–366; Roy Hudson, "For a Greater Vote and a Stronger Party," *Communist,* August 1940, p. 709. Hudson claimed the decline had been stopped in May 1940. However, despite 10,000 new recruits in 1941 and a modest increase in membership in early 1942, the Party could claim only 50,000 members in April 1942. John Williamson, "Strengthen the War Effort by Building the Party," *Communist,* May 1942, pp. 326, 329. The April 1942 figure is found in Nathan Glazer, *The Social Basis of American Communism* (New York: Harcourt, Brace & World, 1961), p. 209n; Glazer had access to a private Party document. Either the hemorrhage in membership continued in 1941 or the loss in 1939–1940 was closer to half of the Party.

32. *Daily Worker,* October 30, 1939, p. 7.

33. Vincent Sheean, "Brumaire," *New Republic,* November 8, 1939, p. 7; Louis Fischer,

"An Inexcusable Treaty," *New Republic,* September 13, 1939, pp. 150–151; Eugene Lyons, *The Red Decade* (Indianapolis, Ind: Bobbs-Merrill, 1941), pp. 356–369; "Communications," *New Republic,* August 26, 1940, pp. 279–280.

34. "Letter," *New Republic,* January 18, 1933, p. 272; Malcolm Cowley, *The Dream of the Golden Mountains: Remembering the 1930s* (New York: Viking Press, 1980); Malcolm Cowley, *And I Worked at the Writer's Trade: Chapters of Literary History 1918-1978* (New York: Penguin Books, 1979), pp. 153–158; Malcolm Cowley "In Memorium," *New Republic,* August 12, 1940, pp. 219–220.

35. Percival Bailey, *Progressive Lawyers: A History of the National Lawyers Guild, 1936–1958* (unpublished doctoral dissertation, Rutgers University, 1979), pp. 250–251; Larry Ceplair and Steven Englund, *The Inquisition in Hollywood* (Garden City, N. Y.: Anchor Press, 1980), pp. 143–148. Some Party auxiliaries were barely affected by the turmoil. The International Workers' Order had grown by an average of 20,000 members a year for the previous five years. It had just introduced an attractive new membership option that did not require the purchase of insurance. While membership declined, the drop was not precipitous, from 161,363 to 155,237 in 1940. William Goldsmith, *The Theory and Practice of the Communist Front* (unpublished doctoral dissertation, Columbia University, 1971), pp. 545–546.

36. "Statement of National President David Lasser to the National Administrative Committee, December 12, 1939," in Benjamin File, Draper Papers, Box 15; Herbert Benjamin interview with Theodore Draper, October 29, 1930; Herbert Benjamin to Theodore Draper, November 22, 1970, Draper Papers, Box 2, Folder 42. Hired as a labor consultant by the WPA in 1941, Lasser soon became the victim of congressional anger. Despite pleas that he was an anti-Communist, the House adopted an amendment proposed by Representative Everett Dirksen forbidding any part of the WPA appropriation to be used to pay Lasser's salary. The same kind of bill of attainder had been used a year earlier to drive David Saposs, a radical but anti-Communist economist, from the National Labor Relations Board. One year later the tactic was used to force Robert Morss Lovett and two others from their government positions. Several sympathetic congressmen sheperded a repeal of the amendment through the House in 1942, and Lasser found a job with the War Production Board. *Congressional Record,* 77th Congress, 1st Session, pp. 2540, 5110–5113; *Washington Daily News,* July 14, 1941.

37. Jervis Anderson, *A. Philip Randolph: A Biographical Portrait* (New York: Harcourt, Brace & Jovanovich, 1972), pp. 235–238, includes Ralph Bunche's eyewitness report of the convention. On Yergan, once a YMCA executive in South Africa, see his testimony after he had broken with the Communists, in *Institute of Pacific Relations,* Part 13, Hearings Before the Senate Internal Security Subcommittee, 82nd Congress, 2nd Session, pp. 4596–4597. John Davis was replaced as executive secretary of the NNC in 1943 by Party member Edward Strong. FBI File 61-6728-284. On the later activities of the NNC, see FBI File 61-6728-235.

38. *Investigation of Un-American Propaganda Activities,* Executive Hearings Made Public, Vol. 6, p. 2801.

39. Albert Acena, *The Washington Commonwealth Federation* (unpublished doctoral dissertation, University of Washington, 1975), pp. 176, 306–389, 449. *First Report: Un-American Activities in Washington State,* Report of the Joint Legislative Fact-Finding Committee on Un-American Activities, 1948, p. 68. *Pacific Northwest Hearings,* House Un-American Activities Committee, 83rd Congress, 2nd Session, 1954, p. 5977. DeLacy was named as a fellow Communist by Costigan and several other ex–Party members. By 1944 DeLacy was once more a loyal New Dealer and won election to Congress for one term. After his reelection defeat, DeLacy moved to Ohio, where he was active in Henry Wallace's 1948 campaign and eventually wound up building homes in southern California.

40. John Haynes, *Liberals, Communists and the Popular Front in Minnesota* (unpublished doctoral dissertation, University of Minnesota, 1978), pp. 116–185.

41. *Daily Worker,* October 6, 1939, pp. 1, 4; *Sunday Worker,* October 15, Section 2, p. 2; Kenneth Waltzer, *The American Labor Party: Third Party Politics in New Deal–Cold War New York, 1936–1954* (unpublished doctoral dissertation, Harvard University, 1977), p. 228. Caught off guard once again by the Party's newfound enthusiasm for war after the German invasion of Russia, Marcantonio hesitated until the fall of 1941 before announcing his readiness to vote for war. After the brief honeymoon between the Communists and the rest

of the nation during World War II, Marcantonio became a prime target for anti-Communists. The collapse of the American Labor party, the dismal failure of Henry Wallace's Progressive party, and the Communists' growing sectarianism gradually destroyed his political base. Election laws were changed to prevent him from running in several primaries, and in 1950 the Democrats, Republicans, and Liberals agreed on a single candidate, thus ending his political career.

42. Saul Alinksy, *John L. Lewis: An Unauthorized Biography* (New York: Vintage Books, 1970), pp. 161–172. Philip Taft, *Organized Labor in American History* (New York: Harper & Row, 1964), pp. 530–536. *Daily Worker*, December 17, 1939, p. 4; October 11, p. 1; December 19, p. 6.

43. Bert Cochran, *Labor and Communism* (Princeton, N. J.: Princeton University Press, 1977), pp. 156–195. Freitag had registered to vote as a Communist in 1938. *Investigation of Un-American Propaganda Activities*, Vol. 14, p. 8564. Michener later admitted that he had been a Party member from 1938 to 1944. The Party demonstrated just how far it would go to avoid strikes when the interests of the Soviet Union required it. Once Hitler attacked Russia, whatever economic justifications had been used to sanction walkouts vanished. Mike Quill, for example, had been threatening for months to shut down New York's public transit system in July 1941 when the TWU contract with the city expired, unless the union won a closed shop. When the deadline passed with no progress, Quill backed down to avoid harming the war effort; in the interim, Russia had been attacked. L. H. Whittemore, *The Man Who Ran the Subways: The Story of Mike Quill* (New York: Holt, Rinehart & Winston, 1968), pp. 104–107.

44. Dennis, "Roosevelt, the War, and the New Deal," p. 36; "Resolutions Adopted by the National Committee of the Communist Party, U. S. A.," *Communist*, March 1940, pp. 215–216; Dennis, "The Bolshevization of the Communist Party," pp. 405–406.

45. William Foster, "The Trade Unions and the War," *Communist*, October 1940, pp. 893, 895–896; Earl Browder, *The Way Out* (New York: International Publishers, 1940), pp. 147–148; Gene Dennis, "Labor and the Elections," *Communist*, September 1940, p. 823; William Foster, "Organized Labor's Two Conventions," *Communist*, January 1941, p. 48.

46. "Resolutions Adopted by the National Committee," *Communist*, March 1940, p. 217; Maurice Isserman, *Peat Bog Soldiers: The American Communist Party During the Second World War, 1939–1945* (unpublished doctoral dissertation, University of Rochester, 1979), pp. 121–127.

47. Gene Dennis, "Labor and the Elections," *Communist*, September 1940, pp. 821, 826; Earl Browder, "The Most Peculiar Campaign," *Communist*, October 1940, pp. 886–887; Earl Browder, "The 1940 Elections and the Next Tasks," *Communist*, December 1940, p. 1078.

48. *Daily Worker*, November 22, 1939, p. 1; November 15, p. 1. Amter got 12,118 votes in Manhattan, Isadore Begun 9,731 in the Bronx, and Paul Crosbie 2,047 in Queens; *Guide to U. S. Elections* (Washington, D. C.: Congressional Quarterly, 1975), pp. 25, 304. The ten states were California, Connecticut, Iowa, Massachusetts, Michigan, Minnesota, New Jersey, Pennsylvania, Washington, and Wisconsin. The largest jump came in New Jersey, from 1,595 votes to 8,814. There were declines in Connecticut and Michigan.

49. *Investigation of Un-American Propaganda Activities*, Vol. 7, pp. 4310–4317, 4337–4338, 4341; Vol. 9, pp. 5334, 5337, 5417.

50. Ibid., Vol. 7, p. 4374; Vol. 12, pp. 7351–7353, 7608–7609.

51. Isserman, *Peat Bog Soldiers*, pp. 112–127. Born in Russia in 1905, Schneiderman had been brought to America around 1908. He worked his way through three years of school at UCLA but dropped out to pursue other activities. He had been a founder of the Young Workers League in 1922 and its first educational director. In the spring of 1939, the U. S. government attempted to cancel his citizenship on the grounds that it had been illegally procured. Schneiderman had become a naturalized citizen in 1927, five years after he had joined the YWL. He had never been arrested or involved in any act of violence; in his testimony he insisted on his attachment to the American Constitution and denied that the Communist party had ever advocated overthrow of the government by force or violence. Two lower courts nonetheless ordered him stripped of his citizenship. The Supreme Court agreed to hear Schneiderman's appeal; defeated Republican presidential candidate Wendell Willkie agreed to argue the Communist's case before the high court without fee.

By the time a divided Court handed down its decision in 1943, the Soviet Union and the United States were wartime allies. The majority decision, written by former Michigan governor Frank Murphy, ruled that denaturalizaton proceedings required the state to present a clear and compelling case that Schneiderman's own conduct had belied his oath of allegiance to the United States. Absent such clear evidence and concerned that any lesser standard might endanger the rights and security of millions of other naturalized Americans, the Court overturned the lower courts and allowed the Communist leader to retain his citizenship. In so doing, Justice Murphy, who had himself had extensive experience with Communists in Michigan, accepted their argument that they were just another American political party whose aims were to be achieved within the confines of the Constitution. Even the dictatorship of the proletariat, he divined, would not "necessarily mean the end of representative government or the federal system."

There was no evidence in documents placed in the record to indicate that the Party advocated denying civil rights to some Americans. Even if there had been references to the use of force and violence to change the government in some Communist documents, Murphy would not have regarded the evidence as conclusive. "We would deny our experience as men if we did not recognize that official party programs are unfortunately often opportunistic devices as much honored in the breach as in the observance," he noted, citing James Bryce's *The American Commonwealth* to suggest that the American Communist party behaved like typical American political organizations. Carol King, *The Schneiderman Case: United States Supreme Court Opinion* (New York: American Committee for Protection of Foreign-Born, 1943); *Schneiderman v. United States,* 320 U. S. 118.

52. *Statutes at Large,* 76th Congress, 3rd Session, Chapter 897, pp. 1201–1202. House of Representatives, 76th Congress, 3rd Session, Report No. 2582. *Daily Worker,* November 17, 1940, p. 1; November 25, p. 2. The old document was *The Constitution and By-Laws of the Communist Party of the United States of America* (New York: Workers Library Publishers, 1940). Among other changes, the hammer and sickle was eliminated as a Party emblem, no mention was made of a Party control commission, and membership was limited to citizens.

Chapter 21

1. A detailed account of the Party in the period is Maurice Isserman, *Which Side Were You On? The American Communist Party During the Second World War* (Middleton, Conn.: Wesleyan University Press, 1982).

2. The Duclos article was printed in a translation in the *Daily Worker,* May 24, 1945, pp. 7–9. For extensive discussions of the circumstances under which it was written and speculation about its provenance, see Philip Jaffe, *The Rise and Fall of American Communism,* (New York: Horizon Press, 1975), pp. 69–78; Joseph Starobin, *American Communism in Crisis,* (Cambridge, Mass.: Harvard University Press, 1972), pp. 78–83; and Maurice Isserman, *Peat-Bog Soldiers: The American Communist Party During the Second World War, 1929–1945* (unpublished doctoral dissertation, University of Rochester, 1979), pp, 458–463.

3. "Minutes, National Board, May 22, 1945"; "Minutes, National Board CPA, June 2, 1945," in Jaffe Papers. Minor was hardly the only Communist to scurry off Browder's ship before it capsized, although his about-face was accomplished more quickly than most. Israel Amter was not a member of the National Board. Informed in February 1944 of Foster and Darcy's attack on the "Teheran line" while vacationing in Florida, he had typed out an eight-page letter to Browder and the Political Committee pledging his undying loyalty to the prevailing line and asserting that he would have "added my voice and my vote" to its defense if he had been present. He then denounced Foster for factionalism, exulted that "Browder's leadership is uncontested in the Party," and suggested removing Foster as Party chairman. When the Party's National Committee met on June 18, 1945, to complete the formality of exorcising Browderism from the Party line, Amter complained that "a regular lynch atmosphere pervaded the meeting" of February 1944, which had rejected Foster's protests. Other Party leaders who had been singing Browder's praises for years could not wait to confess how hollow and shallow they had been, how easily they had suppressed reservations about his policies, and how deeply they resented his supposed dictatorship of the Party. Steve Nelson succinctly expressed the Party's dilemma and condition when he told his National Committee comrades that "if we had a Comintern now, this organization

would be in receivership." There was, however, no Comintern, and the bankrupts had to discover their own way out of insolvency. Israel Amter, "Memorandum to Comrade Browder for the Political Committee, 3/27/44," Browder Papers, Series 1-1; "Minutes, National Committee Meeting, June 18, 1945, June 19, 1945," in Jaffe Papers.

4. The details can be found in "Minutes, June 18–20, 1945," Jaffe Papers. Starobin, *American Communism in Crisis*, pp. 93–106. Browder's disgrace was so total that both his dentist and his insurance agent asked him to find replacements. See Browder Papers, Series 1-7, 1-32.

5. Starobin, *American Communism in Crisis*, p. 104; Jaffe, *The Rise and Fall of American Communism*, pp. 18, 27–38, 138–156.

6. These figures are derived as follows: The 1930 figure is given in J. Peters, "Problems of Party Growth," *Communist*, October 1934, p. 1005. The 1935 figure is derived from *Party Organizer*, April 1936, p. 6, which reports a monthly average recruitment of 1,600. The figure may be slightly high, since the same magazine in December 1935, p. 15, gave a figure of 13,500 for January–October and in February 1936, p. 5, gave 1,788 for December. This implies that nearly 4,000 people would have had to join in November. The 1936 figure is from *Party Organizer*, March–April 1937, p. 1. The 1937 figure is from Jack Stachel, "Build the Party," *Communist*, March 1938, p. 222. It is slightly higher than the figure given in *Party Organizer*, June 1938, p. 5. On the other hand, Politburo Minutes, Draper Papers, Box 1, Folder 43, gives 11,300 recruits for January through June 1937, and *Sunday Worker*, February 20, 1938, p. 3. claims that 22,000 joined between September and December. Adding July and August figures would push the total well above 35,000. Both 1938 and 1939 figures are less reliable. I estimated that 21,000 joined in the first half of the year on the basis of a report that 54,012 were registered in January 1938 and membership was about 75,000 by June; *Party Organizer*, June 1938, p. 5. The last seven months' recruits were estimated on the basis of 4,000 a month, about the same number for the first part of the year. The 1939 figure was estimated on the basis of a 50 percent turnover and a Party of 100,000.

7. Earl Browder, "The Communists in the People's Front," *Communist*, July 1937, p. 620.

8. The wildest charges were spread in Elizabeth Dilling's *The Red Network* (privately printed, 1934) and Joseph Kamp's *The Fifth Column in Washington* (New Haven, Conn.: Constitution Educational League, 1940). Inevitably, a certain proportion of the "red-baiters" had more important fish to fry than Communists. For them, the Communist conspiracy was only a cover for more nefarious plots against Western, Christian civilization. An expert on Communism from the American Legion sagely explained to the Dies Committee that Negro Communists "will readily admit that their interest in communism lies in white women." Representative Jacob Thorkelson of Montana, seeing a Jewish plot, warned his colleagues that the federal government was controlled by Communists following in the footsteps of one Heinrich Mordecai, alias Karl Marx, one Chaim Goldman, alias Lenin, and Benjamin Cohen, alias Bela Kun. He also reported that his sources had informed him "that this same Bela Kun is in Chicago at the present time, no doubt preparing for an American communistic revolution." Kun, who had already probably been executed on Stalin's orders, no doubt would have preferred to be in Chicago. *Investigation of Un-American Propaganda Activities*, Special Committee on Un-American Activities, House of Representatives, 71st Congress, 2nd Session, Vol 3, p. 1934; *Congressional Record*, Vol. 84, Part 13, pp. 2716–2717.

9. Earl Browder, *Report to the Tenth Convention* (New York: Workers Library Publishers, 1938), p. 85; Earl Browder, "Mastering Bolshevik Methods of Work," *Communist*, June 1938, pp. 507–508.

10. M. Ercoli (Togliatti), *The Fight for Peace* (New York: Workers Library Publishers, 1935), p. 20.

INDEX

Index